Third Edition

# MANAGING CHANGE

## A Strategic Approach to Organisational Dynamics

## BERNARD BURNES

An imprint of **Pearson Education**

Harlow, England · London · New York · Reading, Massachusetts · San Francisco · Toronto · Don Mills, Ontario · Sydney
Tokyo · Singapore · Hong Kong · Seoul · Taipei · Cape Town · Madrid · Mexico City · Amsterdam · Munich · Paris · Milan

**Pearson Education Limited**

Edinburgh Gate
Harlow
Essex CM20 2JE
England

and Associated Companies throughout the World

*Visit us on the World Wide Web at:*
*www.pearsoneduc.com*

_____

First edition published under the Pitman imprint 1992
Second edition published under the Pitman imprint 1996
**Third edition 2000**

ISBN 0 273 64166 2

*British Library Cataloguing-in-Publication Data*
A catalogue record for this book is available from the British Library

*Library of Congress Cataloging-in-Publication Data*
Burnes, Bernard, 1953-
    Managing change: a strategic approach to organisational dynamics / Bernard Burnes.--
3rd ed.
        p. cm.
    Includes bibliographical references and index.
    ISBN 0-273-64166-2
    1. Organizational change--Management.   I. Title
HD58.8.B882   2000
658.4'06--dc21                                                              00-036725

10  9  8  7  6  5  4  3  2  1
04  03  02  01  00

Typeset by 43
Printed and bound in Great Britain by T.J. International Ltd., Padstow, Cornwall.

To Sue, Duncan, Stuart and Hobbes

# Contents

# Acknowledgements

The third edition of this book, like the first and second, would not have been possible without the generous encouragement and assistance of a large number of people. Space does not permit me to name them all, but I am nevertheless extremely grateful to them, one and all. However, there are five members and ex-members of the Manchester School of Management for whose assistance, ideas and comments I would like to give special thanks: Ron Coram, Jens-Peter Reinhardt, Mohammad Salauroo, Thina Saltvedt and Penny West. I would also like to thank Professor David Buchanan of De Montfort University and Professor Dexter Dunphy of the Australian Graduate School of Management for their support and assistance. In addition, Pearson Education deserve many thanks for their encouragement and patience.

Lastly, and mostly, I am irredeemably indebted to my wife, Sue. Her painstaking reading and editing of draft after draft of this book have improved it beyond recognition. It is not too much to say that she deserves as much credit as I do for what is good about this book.

Nevertheless, despite all the help and assistance I have received, any faults or shortcomings in the final product are mine and mine alone.

# INTRODUCTION

There is nothing so practical as a good theory. (Kurt Lewin)[1]

All models are wrong, some models are useful. (George Box)[2]

The above two quotations could have been written especially to sum up the dilemma most people face when trying to come to terms with the literature on organisational change. What almost everyone would like is a clear and practical change theory which explains what changes organisations need to make and how they should make them. Unfortunately, what is available is a wide range of confusing and contradictory theories, approaches and recipes. Many of these are well thought out and grounded in both theory and practice; others, unfortunately, seem disconnected from either theory or reality. Also, though change theory requires an interdisciplinary perspective, each of the major approaches tends to view organisations from the disciplinary angle of their originators – whether it be psychology, sociology, economics, or whatever – which can result in an incomplete and biased picture. So, regardless of what their proponents may claim, we do not possess at present an approach to change that is theoretically holistic, universally applicable, and which can be practically applied. Nevertheless, we do know that, to paraphrase George Box, whilst all change theories are partial, some theories are useful. This means that for those wishing to understand or implement change, the prime task is not to seek out an all-embracing theory but to understand the strengths and weaknesses of each approach and the situations in which each can best be applied.

There can be few who now doubt the importance to an organisation of the ability to identify where it needs to be in the future, and how to accomplish the changes necessary to get there – although there is a great deal of dispute about how difficult or possible this is. However, though some might assume that managers do not need to understand organisation theory, strategy theory, change theory or any other theory in order to manage and change their organisations, this would be to underestimate the extent to which managers and others in organisations are influenced, assisted or potentially misled by theory. Increasingly, managers are exhorted to adopt the teachings of the latest management guru. Nevertheless, as Part 1 will demonstrate, and as Mintzberg and Quinn (1991: xii) observed:

---

[1] Quoted in Marrow (1969).
[2] Quoted in Norrie (1993).

One can, however, suffer not just from an absence of theories, but also from being dominated by them without realizing it. To paraphrase the words of John Maynard Keynes, most 'practical men' are the slaves of some defunct theorist. Whether we realize it or not, our behavior is guided by the systems of ideas that we have internalized over the years. Much can be learned by bringing these out into the open, examining them more carefully, and comparing them with alternative ways to view the world – including ones based on systematic study (that is, research).

These 'systems of ideas', or organisation theories as they are more commonly called, are crucial to change management in two respects. First, they provide models of how organisations should be structured and managed. Second, they provide guidelines for judging and prescribing the behaviour and effectiveness of individuals and groups in an organisation.

To understand why and how to change organisations, it is first necessary to understand their structures, management and behaviour. As Mintzberg and Quinn indicate, it is clear that in many organisations there is no clear understanding of these theories. It follows that choices with regard to the appropriateness of particular structures and practices, the way they are chosen and implemented, are founded on limited knowledge and perhaps false assumptions. Change cannot hope to be fully successful under these circumstances. On the contrary, a full understanding of these theories is necessary if informed choices are to be made when instigating and implementing change. For this reason, these will be examined critically in relation to each other, and also in comparison with how organisations actually operate, as averse to how theorists suppose them to. The aim is not to provide a 'hands-on' practical guide to organisational change – though readers should find that this book is useful in that respect as well. Rather the aim is to provide an understanding of the theories and approaches to change that are on offer, to indicate their usefulness and drawbacks, and to enable the reader to choose for her- or himself which 'models are useful' and when.

The central purpose of this book, therefore, is to aid this search for understanding both by describing and discussing the key approaches to and theories of organisational change, and also by setting these within the broader framework of the development, operation and behaviour of organisations and those who populate them. The intention is to allow those who study and carry out organisational change to make their own judgements about the benefits, applicability and usefulness of the approaches on offer. Therefore, the key themes underpinning the book are as follows:

- There is a need to understand the wider theoretical and historical context within which organisations operate and the pressures and options they face for change.
- Organisational change cannot be separated from organisation strategy, and vice versa.
- Organisations are not rational entities *per se*, though those who manage them strive to present their deliberations and decisions as being based on logic and rationality.

- There is a strong tendency to present the various approaches to change as being limited in number and mutually exclusive. However, in practice, the range of approaches is wide, and they can be and often are used either sequentially or in combination.

- The appropriateness of each of the available approaches is dependent upon the type of change being considered and the constraints under which the organisation operates, although these constraints and objectives can themselves be changed to make them more amenable to an organisation's preferred approach to change or style of management.

- Organisations and managers can and do exercise a wide degree of choice in what they change, when they change and how they change.

The book is organised into four parts.

**Part 1: The rise and fall of the rational organisation** provides a comprehensive review of organisation theory and behaviour. Chapter 1 deals with the development of organisations from the Industrial Revolution through to the early years of the twentieth century, when the first fully-fledged organisation theory, the Classical approach, first appeared. This is followed in Chapter 2 with reviews of the next two organisation theories to appear: the Human Relations approach and Contingency Theory. Chapter 3 examines and compares the three main and most influential contemporary approaches to structuring and managing organisations: the Culture–Excellence and organisational learning approaches, primarily developed in the West, and the Japanese approach. Chapter 4 introduces the postmodern perspective on organisations and, in particular, the importance and implications of culture, power and politics. Chapter 4, and Part 1, conclude that, by accident and design, organisation theories attempt to remove choice from organisations by specifying what they need to do in order to be successful. However, the review of postmodern organisation theory, and culture, power and politics, together with evidence from the earlier chapters, shows that managers do have a wider scope for shaping decisions than much of the organisation literature suggests. This theme of managerial choice is continued in Part 2.

**Part 2: Theoretical perspectives on strategy development and change management** comprises four chapters, examining the literature on strategic management and change management respectively. Chapters 5 and 6 examine the dominant approaches to strategy and the main tools and techniques available to organisations for its development and implementation. In particular, these two chapters draw attention to the differences between the Prescriptive and Analytical schools of strategy, and they highlight the importance of the relationship between organisational strategy and organisational change. Chapters 7 and 8 review, and go beyond, the two dominant approaches to organisational change: the Planned approach and the Emergent approach. These chapters show that neither approach is applicable to all change situations but that both can be used within the same organisations. Chapter 8 concludes by arguing that, though organisations face significant constraints on their freedom of choice, these constraints can be influenced and changed in order to allow organisations to choose the particular approach to strategy and change that best suits them.

**Part 3: Case studies in strategy development and change management** comprises three case study chapters. The ten studies they contain are all of real organisations, though in some cases their names and some of the details that would identify them have been changed to protect confidentiality. Nevertheless, the situations described are drawn from real life and show the opportunities, difficulties and constraints faced in developing strategy and implementing change.

**Part 4: Managing choice** comprises the concluding three chapters of the book. Chapter 12 combines the insights and perspectives from Parts 1 and 2 to analyse the ten case studies presented in Part 3. From this, the chapter identifies key lessons for the theory and practice of organisational change and paves the way for the Choice Management–Change Management model of organisational change presented in Chapter 13. This model, which comprises three interlinked processes – choice, trajectory and change – provides an understanding of how managers and organisations can and do exercise choice and manage change. Given the import- ance attached to the role of managers in developing strategy and managing change, Chapter 14 reviews what managers do and how they do it. In particular, the role of leadership and management development is examined. The chapter and the book conclude that if, as argued, managers have considerable choice over what to change and how to change it, then this lays a considerable responsibility on their shoulders. How organisations change and develop has enormous con- sequences, not just for their employees and owners but for society at large. In order to minimise social fragmentation and exclusion, and the destruction of the natural environment, managers need to act in the broader interests of all their stakeholders – employees, shareholders, themselves and the wider community.

## The third edition

Since the publication of the second edition of this book, I have received many helpful comments and suggestions for improving and developing this book both from my own students and colleagues at UMIST and from readers and users elsewhere. I am very grateful for these and have tried to utilise them in preparing this third edition. Whilst retaining a similar structure and approach to the second edition, the third edition has been expanded from 11 to 14 chapters, and substantially revised to incorporate the following:

- an entirely new section on organisational learning in Chapter 3;
- an entirely new section on postmodernism in Chapter 4;
- the expansion of Part 2 from two to four chapters to incorporate a much more detailed and rigorous review and analysis of the strategy and change literatures;

- a new chapter in Part 4 to facilitate the separation of the analysis of the case studies from the presentation and discussion of the Choice Management–Change Management model;
- the inclusion of two new case studies and the updating of existing ones.

In addition to the above specific changes, all the other chapters have been revisited, updated and revised. As in the first and second editions, unless apparent from the text, I have used the terms her and him interchangeably.

# Part 1

## THE RISE AND FALL OF THE RATIONAL ORGANISATION

# Chapter 1

# FROM TRIAL AND ERROR TO THE SCIENCE OF MANAGEMENT

## The rise of organisation theory

### Learning objectives

After studying this chapter, you should be able to:

1 understand the development of work organisation from the Industrial Revolution until the end of the nineteenth century;

2 approoiate the reasons for the antagonistic relations between labour and employers in the nineteenth century;

3 discuss the different roles played by technology and people in the development of the factory system;

4 describe the main features of the Classical approach;

5 understand why the Classical approach developed as it did in the USA, France and Germany;

6 discuss the differences and similarities between the work of Taylor, Fayol and Weber;

7 list the main advantages and disadvantages of the Classical approach to structuring organisations and designing jobs;

8 describe the key features of the Classical approach to organisational change.

## INTRODUCTION

In Britain and the rest of the industrial world today, it is almost impossible to imagine life without the plethora of organisations that comprise and make possible our everyday life. Yet organisations in their modern form – indeed, in almost any form – were virtually unknown before the Industrial Revolution, 200 years ago. In the intervening period, as Morgan (1986) remarked, we have developed into an 'organizational society'. However, not only have organisations, in their many shapes, sizes and manifestations, come to reach into every facet of our lives, but they have also acquired an equally diverse range of theories, nostrums and semi-sacrosanct beliefs about how they should be structured, managed and changed.

This chapter sets out to explore and discuss the origins of organisations, from the Industrial Revolution to the early years of the twentieth century, when the first detailed and comprehensive organisation theory emerged. The key themes of this chapter are as follows:

- Although industrialisation was primarily concerned with the move from a subsistence economy to a money-market economy, the main enabling mechanism for this was the creation of the factory system.

- The pattern and purpose of industrialisation varied from country to country. Whilst in Britain and the USA it was very much driven by individuals seeking profit maximisation, in mainland Europe a different approach can be seen. In Germany in particular, but also in France, industrialisation was largely state-sponsored, and aimed more to further the economic and military objectives of the state than to increase the profit-making capacity of individuals.

- The development of organisation theory was synonymous with the need by managers to legitimate and enhance their authority to initiate change.

The chapter begins by showing how the rapid expansion of national and international commercial activity created the conditions for the British Industrial Revolution, from which emerged the factory system, the precursor of all modern organisations. It is argued that the driving force behind this development was the merchant class. It will also be stressed that two key features of the early factory system were its *ad hoc*, trial-and-error nature, and the antagonistic relationship between owners and employees, or – to use the terminology of the times – masters and servants.

The chapter then goes on to show that British industrial practices, methods and technologies were 'exported' to other European countries and the USA, with similar results in terms of employer–employee relations. As the nineteenth century progressed, and organisations grew in number and size, trial and error increasingly gave way to more considered and consistent approaches to work organisation. This development was especially pronounced in the USA and continental Europe, as industrial leadership moved away from Britain and towards these areas.

What emerged, separately, were three different but complementary attempts by Frederick Taylor in the USA, Henri Fayol in France and Max Weber in Germany to replace the *ad hoc*, rule-of-thumb approach to organisations with a universally applicable blueprint or theory for how they should operate. These three approaches, each focusing on different organisational aspects, coalesced into what later became known as the Classical school of organisation theory. This approach to organisations is characterised by the horizontal and hierarchical division of labour, the minimisation of human skills and discretion, and the attempt to construe organisations as rational-scientific entities. It is argued that one of the key objectives of the Classical school, especially the Scientific Management component, was to legitimise the managerial right to plan and implement change by showing that it was the only group able to analyse the work situation scientifically and rationally, and to devise the most appropriate and efficient methods of operation.

The chapter concludes by arguing that the Classical approach, whilst being a significant advance on what went before, was badly flawed. In particular, its view of human nature and motivation was not only inaccurate, but also alienated workers from and made them resentful of the organisations that employed them. However, the precepts of the Classical school were not solely aimed at constraining workers' ability to make and block change; in addition, by laying down hard and fast rules of what was and was not best practice, they constrained management's freedom of action, thus alienating many managers as well as workers.

With hindsight, the attempt by Taylor, Fayol and Weber each in their own way to formulate a system of reciprocal obligations between managers and workers appears to be less a decisive break with the past and more an attempt to recast feudalism in a more scientific-rational framework. Certainly, in the late nineteenth century, French, German and American managers of European descent did share a recent and common feudal heritage which might make them well-disposed towards a system that substituted a code of joint obligation in place of management–worker conflict. Indeed, in Germany the rise of bureaucracy which Weber described was itself a direct product of the Prussian feudal tradition. However, though many managers undoubtedly did long for and believe in an – albeit mythical – age when workers readily did as they were told, this ignored the fact that most American immigrants left Europe to escape just such a system, whilst French workers took pride in the belief that their Revolution had ended feudal despotism. Only in Germany was it possible to say that the feudal tradition remained strong, though not unopposed.

## THE RISE OF COMMERCE AND THE BIRTH OF THE FACTORY

The pivotal event that shaped the world into the form we now see around us was the British Industrial Revolution, which began in the late eighteenth century. Before it, most societies were based on small-scale, self-sufficient agricultural production, with the vast majority of the population, some 80–90 per cent, living in the countryside. By the end of the nineteenth century, after the Industrial Revolution had run its course, the reverse became the case, in the leading industrialised countries at least, with most people living in urban centres and depending on industrial and commercial activities for their livelihood (Landes, 1969).

Britain was the pioneer industrial country; it was the model that other European nations and the USA sought to emulate in their attempts to transform traditional agrarian economies into urban societies based on science and technology (Kemp, 1979). The key development of the Industrial Revolution towards this process of societal transformation was the creation of the factory system. It was this that gave the impetus to and created the model for all that was to follow. As Weber (1928: 302) pointed out, the factory's distinguishing characteristic was '...in general ... not the implements of work applied but the concentration of owner-ship of workplace, means of work, source of power and raw materials in one and the same hand, that of the entrepreneur'. Or, to put it another way, it was the way the entrepreneur 'organised' the elements of production that distinguished it from what went before.

This tells us what changed, but it does not explain why or how in a few score years organisations came to dominate our lives. To answer this, it is necessary to appreciate the great surge of economic activity – especially the international trade in textile products – that arose in the seventeenth and eighteenth centuries. This trade gave an enormous impetus to textile production in Britain, which in turn had a knock-on effect in all other spheres of economic activity (Mathias, 1969).

Before and during the early part of the British Industrial Revolution, textile production was carried out as an agricultural by-occupation based on family units. However, as demand increased in the eighteenth century, some 'men and women [became] specialist spinners or weavers, thinking first of wool, treating work on the land as, at most, a by-occupation' (Ashton, 1948: 23). Allied to this, a new mechanism sprang up to link producer and consumer: the 'putting-out' system, whereby a large merchant would 'put out' work to a number of independent domestic producers.

The advantage to the merchant was threefold: it was cheap – there were few overheads; it was flexible – production could be easily expanded or contracted; and it avoided the difficulties involved in directly employing a workforce. However, as demand continued to increase in the late eighteenth century, this system became more complex and more costly, and eventually it became too cumbersome (Pollard, 1965). The chain of intermediaries linking producer to consumer became increasingly difficult for the large merchant to control. There were many problems with the putting-out mechanism: dishonesty (on both sides) was rife; deliveries were late; and quality often poor. Laws attempting to control producers could do nothing to rectify the fundamental weaknesses in the system. The incompatibility between the large and complex organisation of distribution and the multitude of tiny domestic workshop units, unsupervised and unsupervisable, was bound to set up tensions and drive merchants to seek new ways of production – ways whereby they could establish their own managerial control over the production process (Pollard, 1965).

There was also an incompatibility between different cultures. For the merchant, the expansion of markets was a chance to maximise profits in order to live in the grand style. For the rural domestic producer, involved in long hours of back-breaking work, it created the conditions for increased leisure. As Marglin (1976: 35) commented: '...wages rose and workers insisted on taking out a portion of their gains in the form of greater leisure. However sensible this may have been from their own point of view, it is no way for an enterprising capitalist to get ahead.'

Therefore, it was the merchant who began the move towards the factory system – not because the merchant had an innate desire to run factories or exercise direct control over labour, but in order to take full advantage of expanding market opportunities to reap ever greater rewards.

Nevertheless, there was no headlong rush to create a new economic order overnight. The earliest factories, if that is not too grand a word for them, were small, unpowered weaving or spinning sheds which used existing technology and methods. A few very large factories – such as Wedgwood's Etruria Works in Stoke-on-Trent – were established, but these were the rare exceptions. Indeed, in 1780, the investment in fixed equipment and stock in the textile industry, which was the leading edge of the Industrial Revolution, was only £10 per worker, and the average factory employed no more than 10 or 12 people. By 1830, when the textile industry had grown to employ 100,000 people and the average factory size was 137, the investment in fixed equipment and stock had only increased to £15 per worker, and 50 per cent of the workforce were still home-based (Hobsbawm, 1968; Pollard, 1965; Tillett, 1970). Given this situation, it is hardly surprising that capital investment was quickly recovered and that it was running expenses, mainly wages and raw materials, which formed the bulk of manufacturing costs. It is this, and the original motive for moving to the factory system in the first place (to have greater control over labour), which explains the prevailing attitude of employers towards labour in the nineteenth century.

## The relationship between employers and employees

British employers based their attitude towards employees on two basic propositions:

1 Labour is unreliable, lazy and will only work when tightly controlled and closely supervised.

2 The main controllable business cost is labour; therefore the key to increased profits is to make it cheaper, and/or increase its productivity, by getting employees to work harder, or for longer hours, for the same, or less, money.

In this respect, as contemporary writers such as Charles Babbage (1835) and Andrew Ure (1835) observed, workers' skill was seen as at best an inconvenience and at worst a threat, because it could be scarce, costly and allow workers a strong bargaining position.

As might be expected, employers' hostility was reciprocated by labour. Workers exhibited a strong dislike for, and reluctance to become part of, the factory system. As Pollard (1965) noted, this was for three main reasons:

1 It involved a wholesale change of culture and environment and the destruction of small, tightly knit communities in which they lived. Hard though the life of

13

cottage industry was, it had given workers a measure of independence and some control over what they did, when they did it and how.

2 The discipline of the factory was harsh and unremitting with men, women and small children all expected to work long hours, often seven days a week, in appalling conditions.

3 Given the lack of alternative organisational forms on which to establish factory life, employers often modelled them on workhouses or prisons. Indeed, to square the circle, some workhouses and prisons turned themselves into factories and their inmates into little more than slaves. Thus factories acquired the same stigma as was attached to prisons and workhouses.

Therefore, the antagonism that existed between owners and workers was based on a genuine clash of interests – one which has echoed through the industrial world ever since.

If this picture of the factory system in the nineteenth century seems bleak to us, it is nevertheless accurate, as is shown in the work of its proponents such as Charles Babbage and Andrew Ure, social reformers such as Seebohm Rowntree, political activists such as Frederick Engels and contemporary novelists such as Charles Dickens. Nor was this aspect of industrialisation restricted to Britain. Studies of other European countries and the USA have shown similar tensions, sometimes even more violent, between the old and the new methods of working, and between employers and employees (Bruland, 1989; Chapman and Chassagne, 1981; Mantoux, 1964; Pelling, 1960).

In defence of the factory owners, who must take responsibility for what emerged, it should be said that their own experience was limited and there were no textbooks to guide them. That they should 'copy' what models existed reflected both the common view of labour amongst the owning classes, and a lack of alternative organisational forms on which to base the emergent factory system. As other nations industrialised, notably Germany, France and the United States, they too adopted similar organisational forms and espoused similar attitudes towards labour. Partly this was because they were seeking to emulate Britain's success by copying her approach. It was also because these societies, like Great Britain, were riven by hierarchical and horizontal divisions which were inevitably reproduced in the workplace.

## Industrialisation and the organisation of work

The system of organising work that came to characterise industrial life in Britain and most of Continental Europe, and even the USA, by the end of the nineteenth century was based on the hierarchical and horizontal division of labour. Though this represented a significant break with the past in terms of how work had previously been organised, it was not out of step with the social stratification of European society nor with feudal traditions of obedience. The articulation and propagation of the principle of the division of labour owed much to the work of Adam Smith. In his book *The Wealth of Nations*, published in 1776, Smith used the now famous example of pin-making to illustrate what he saw as the advantages of the division of labour. He pointed out that a pin could be made entirely by one person doing everything, or by a number of people each specialising in one aspect of its production. For three reasons, he believed the latter was more efficient:

1 A worker who constantly performs one simple task will quickly acquire greater dexterity than one who performs a variety of tasks.
2 It avoids the loss of time necessitated by one person moving from one task to another.
3 The concentration of attention on one special task leads to the invention of machines which aid the productivity of labour and allow one person to do the work previously performed by many.

Smith's ideas were given flesh and form in Britain by pioneering factory owners such as Josiah Wedgwood, and Matthew Boulton and James Watt. At his Etruria pottery works, Wedgwood developed a production system that split the work process down into separate departments, each with its own specialist supervisor. Work was organised almost on a flow-line basis with the skill involved in each operation reduced to a minimum in order, in Wedgwood's own words, 'to make machines of men as cannot err' (quoted in Tillett, 1970: 37). Matthew Boulton and James Watt developed a similar approach at their Soho Works in Birmingham in the 1770s. They also kept detailed production records, a practice virtually unknown at the time (Roll, 1930). Wedgwood, Boulton, Watt and a few others were the architects of the factory system. By their organisation of work on and off the shopfloor, they created models which later managers would copy and adapt to their own needs and circumstances.

This approach to the organisation and control of work spread outwards from Britain. As Bruland (1989: 165) observed:

> There was a fairly direct international diffusion of these changes from Britain, the originating economy: British workers, in most parts of Europe, played a significant role in spreading the new work systems, in training local workers, and in the adaptation of the work force to the new rhythms of work.

As the nineteenth century progressed, this approach to work organisation became more developed and systematised. Charles Babbage (1835) developed a method of applying the division of labour principle to the detailed analysis of any job. He emphasised the need for and advantage of dividing tasks between and within mental and manual labour. He envisaged three 'classes' employed in the work process: the entrepreneur and his technical specialists who would design machines and plan the form of work organisation; operative engineers and managers who would be responsible for executing such plans and designs, based on only partial knowledge of the processes involved; and the mass of employees, needing only a low level of skill, who would undertake the actual work. Thus, in Babbage's (1835: vii) view:

> ... the master manufacturer, by dividing the work to be executed into different processes, each requiring different degrees of skill or force, can purchase exactly the precise quality of both which is necessary for each process...

Though coming from separate traditions, Smith's work was also in tune with the Prussian bureaucratic school, and undoubtedly the efficient organisation of German industry in the late nineteenth century owes much to a combination of the two approaches.

The pioneers of these developments in work organisation, whether in Britain, Germany or other European countries, tended to be strict disciplinarians who used their personal authority to impose the new working arrangements on a usually reluctant workforce (Chapman and Chassagne, 1981). Therefore, change tended to be managed by imposition and force rather than negotiation and agreement. Nor is it surprising that it should be so. In the main these were countries which had been, in the recent past, feudal economies dominated by warrior elites. In Germany, this was still the case. Even where, as in France, there had been a decisive break with the past, this seems merely to have reinforced rather than removed patterns of social rigidity and authoritarianism.

In such situations, resistance to or questioning of change was unlikely to be met by understanding or tolerance. Predictably, there was strong resistance, both active and passive, to the introduction of new working patterns and methods (Kriedte *et al*, 1981). Though this resistance could and did take the form of physical violence against factories and equipment, a more frequent manifestation was high labour turnover. One of the largest Manchester cotton spinning firms, McConnell and Kennedy, had an average turnover in the early nineteenth century of 100 per cent per year, a high but not uncommon rate (Fitton and Wadsworth, 1958; Pollard, 1965). A similar situation existed in other European countries. In Germany, for example, employers 'were generally satisfied if they achieved partial success in creating a stable core of skilled workers... Turnover was the most persistent labour problem confronting employers' (Lee, 1978: 460). This situation clearly gave those workers whose skills were most in demand a significant bargaining position, which allowed them to raise their wages and determine the pace of work. However, it also acted as a spur to employers to seek methods of reducing their reliance on skilled labour (Bruland, 1989). One of the main ways that entrepreneurs responded was through technological developments aimed at replacing or reducing employers' reliance on skilled labour.

A contemporary observer of the nineteenth century industrial scene, Andrew Ure (1836: viii–ix), drew special attention to the role that technology could play in this process:

> By developing machines ... which require only unskilled instead of skilled labour, the cost of labour can be reduced [and] the bargaining position of the worker reduced.

It becomes clear why workers not only opposed the advent of the factory system but also, even when it became established, continued to oppose strongly changes in work practices and the introduction of new equipment. Even in the present day, where change tends to be preceded by consultation and its beneficial effects are stressed, there is still a tendency for those concerned to feel apprehensive of, if not downright resistant towards, change (Smith *et al*, 1982). Therefore, in a harsher and more authoritarian age, where organisational and technological change was seen as a weapon in the battle for control of the workplace, it is not surprising that change management should be achieved by imposition and coercion, and occasion the response that it did.

Nevertheless, despite the increasing opposition of 'organised' labour, the work practices associated with the factory system gradually permeated every aspect of industrial and commercial life, albeit only on a piecemeal basis. Even by the end of the nineteenth century, there was no unified or accepted approach that managers could apply to organisations in their entirety, though in Germany the application of the Prussian bureaucratic model allied to the approach to industrial organisation of Adam Smith was proving influential. Yet the developing factory system could not shake off the legacy of its origins or ignore the continuing battle between labour and management over control, rewards and skill. As the following shows, this was as much the case in continental Europe and the USA as it was in Britain.

## Europe

The history of Europe since 1800, at least in economic terms, is essentially the history of industrialisation, of structural change through which industrial sectors grew and non-agricultural sectors came for the first time to dominate economic life. In general, for most of the nineteenth century, continental Europe lagged behind Britain in terms of industrial development. However, just as Britain was something of a patchwork quilt in terms of the pace of development of individual industries and regions, so too was the rest of Europe (Davis, 1989). As Pollard (1981) explained, European industrialisation developed from a few core regions. In Britain, southern Lancashire, the West Riding of Yorkshire, and that part of the West Midlands called the Black Country were the engines of growth. In northern Europe, the area between the Scheldt, the Meuse and the Rhine rivers had a special role to play, whilst to the east, Silesia, Bohemia and Moravia became leading centres of industrial progress. In the south, it was northern Italy and Catalonia that led the way.

Nevertheless, though mainland Europe did have its pockets of progress, industrialisation did not spread from these at the same rate nor in the same manner as it had in Britain. The most outstanding feature of British industrialisation was its self-generating or autonomous nature. Nowhere else could these conditions be exactly reproduced. To use an analogy, once the wheel has been invented, others cannot reinvent it. What they can do is adopt it and adapt it to their needs and circumstances.

Therefore, Britain became a model to be consciously followed. In the same way that Japan became a focus for study, discussion and emulation by Westerners in the 1980s, so Britain was similarly regarded in the early nineteenth century. Regular visits were made by foreign governments and private entrepreneurs to discover and copy British methods and technologies. In some instances, British investors, entrepreneurs and inventors were encouraged by the governments of France, Germany and other European states to help develop their economies – all with the aim of reproducing and overtaking Britain's industrial lead.

For some, especially Germany and France, the process of industrialisation was less a matter of material progress by organisations and individuals pursuing profit maximisation, and more concerned with the maintenance of their position in the world. Just as they sought to challenge Britain's military might, so they sought to emulate her industrial power. They could not and would not let Britain dominate the world without a struggle. Therefore, though the advent of industrial capitalism was in all countries characterised by the rise of a class of industrialists who aggressively sought to maximise their own wealth, the context in which this occurred varied from country to country.

In Britain and the USA, the context favoured individual entrepreneurs pursuing their own self-interest. In Germany, and to a lesser extent France, industrialisation was sponsored by the state and for the state. The prime motive was to build the economic and military might of the state rather than the wealth of the individual. Where these were compatible, the state was happy to maintain a watching brief. However, where free enterprise and competition were seen as counter-productive to the objectives of the state, it intervened to reduce competition either through the creation of cartels and monopolies, or by state ownership/funding, as was the case with much of the European railway system. In Denmark, on the other hand, the operation of the market was constrained not by the state but by the creation of co-operatives, which allowed small-scale farming and business, and the way of life they represented, to survive where in other countries such enterprises were overwhelmed by larger competitors.

Therefore, though other countries used Britain as a model and benchmark, the actual process of industrialisation in each depended upon the unique political, social and economic circumstances that prevailed there. In some cases these gave primacy to profit maximisation, in others the interests of the state held sway, whilst in further cases sectional interests successfully challenged the power of the market. Consequently, influential though the British example was, once the necessary technique, capital and enterprise were introduced abroad and any element of conscious emulation had worn off, the industrialisation assumed a different character (Kemp, 1979). The continental countries did not and could not simply duplicate British experience.

There were, however, some fundamental similarities. All European societies, to a lesser or greater extent, were structured on a hierarchical basis, with those in positions of power strongly influenced in their view of the rest of society by feudal traditions of subservience and obedience. This was as much the case in post-revolutionary France as in Britain, and even more so in Prussia and Russia. It follows that the organisational forms and labour relations that characterised the emerging factory system in Britain found fertile ground elsewhere in Europe (Cipolla, 1973).

Despite this, other countries did not copy Britain unthinkingly or on a wholesale basis. As latecomers, they could, especially with the encouragement of the state, leapfrog some of the stages of industrialisation, which was one of their principal advantages, but they could not close the gap between themselves and Britain overnight. Ashworth (1987) commented that even as late as 1850, apart from Belgium, Europe had little mechanised industry to speak of; however, 50 years later, Germany had overtaken Britain as the leading industrial nation, and other nations were also poised to do so. The reasons for this are many and complex, involving social and political as well as economic factors (Mathias and Davis, 1989). A brief look at industrial development in Germany, France and Scandinavia illustrates this.

### Germany

Within the space of a generation in the middle years of the nineteenth century, Germany was transformed from a collection of economically backward states forming a political patchwork in Central Europe into a unified empire, driven forward by a rapidly expanding, technologically driven industrial base (Kemp, 1979). Germany's progress was so rapid that, though it industrialised much later, by the end of the nineteenth century it had overtaken Britain as the world's premier industrial nation. This transformation, accompanied as it was by the deliberate resort to military force as an instrument of national policy, and an atmosphere of fierce nationalism, represented an event of major historical significance (Borchardt, 1973).

The two key factors that were primarily responsible for the nature and pace of German industrial development were the geographical and political conditions of the country, and the fact that German industrialisation was state-promoted rather than market-driven.

To look first at geography and politics: not until the late nineteenth century did Germany possess an integrated territory with an economic and administrative centre. Up to the nineteenth century, Germany was a collection of feudal fiefdoms which often warred with each other, rather than a unified nation. In 1789, 'Germany' comprised some 314 independent territories each with their own rulers, internal markets, customs barriers, currencies and trading monopolies. This internal fragmentation, as much as anything else, was probably the key obstacle to industrial progress. This did not change until the Congress of Vienna in 1815, which reduced the number of German states to 39. Each individual state then began to remove internal customs barriers and develop better communications systems, which opened the way for greater economic co-operation with other states.

However, unlike other countries, economic progress was neither driven nor accompanied by a democratisation of society. German society in the nineteenth century remained dominated by a feudal hierarchy. This was characterised by Prussian 'Junkerdom' with its military traditions and ambitions, and its autocratic behaviour. Unlike their counterparts in other countries, the German nobility were not diminished by industrial progress; rather they managed to seize the reins of commercial power to bolster their position. This was due, in many instances, to their retention of regional monopolies over trade, industry and the supply of labour.

This leads on to the second key feature of German industrialisation – the fact that it was state-promoted rather than free-market driven. The drive for industrialisation, especially in Prussia, which came to dominate the rest of Germany, was not primarily motivated by economic reasons. Rather industrialisation was seen as the process of building a strong and powerful state in which the old nobility continued to dominate. Therefore, for Germany, the fact that industrialisation was accompanied by the development of a strong military machine and the continued dominance of the Prussian Junkers was not an unfortunate coincidence, but its major objective.

Industrial progress in Britain exerted a strong influence on Germany. This was partly because it provided a model to emulate, but mainly because Germany saw industrial power and military power as two sides of the same coin. Unless Germany could catch up with and overtake Britain's industrial lead, Germany felt that it would be relegated to the status of a second-class state.

The transformation of Germany into an industrial superpower owed much to the role played by Prussia. From the early nineteenth century onwards, Prussia used its economic and military position as the most powerful German state to subdue the other German states and exclude possible rivals, especially Austria. The prime weapon in the Prussian arsenal was the creation of an all-German customs union (the *Zollverein*). Because of its size, Prussia could determine the rules for the *Zollverein* and, whenever and wherever it was extended, could ensure it was to Prussian advantage.

The customs union, because it opened up trade, also gave a boost to the development of better transportation and communication links, especially railway building (though the latter really took off once the Prussian military came to appreciate its strategic significance for the rapid transit of troops and materials). It seems very clear that, more than the emergence of any one industry, it was the creation of a single market and the boost to consumption that this brought about which was the key factor in Germany's economic progress in the nineteenth century (Kemp, 1979).

By 1834, practically all of Germany was included within the customs union and, though it did not come about until 1871, this provided the essential precondition for political unification. The fact that both political and economic unification were driven by and dominated by Prussia gave German industrialisation its unique character. The new German state that was established in 1871, for all its acceptance of universal suffrage and a national parliament, remained an autocracy ruled by the Hohenzollern dynasty, which still rested on the support of the traditional landed nobility of eastern Germany. It incorporated the bureaucratic and militarist traditions of the old Prussia and remained profoundly conservative.

Indeed, it was the adoption of the Prussian bureaucratic model by both state and industry, combined with close links between both, which gave German industry its unique character. Unlike Britain, where the majority of firms remained relatively small and business operated in an *ad hoc* fashion, with each company pursuing its own interests, in Germany large, bureaucratically structured organisations became the norm. In addition, the state did not hesitate to intervene directly, for example when it nationalised the railways, if it believed the private sector could not or would not serve the national interest.

Given that the state saw German industry as almost an extension of government, it is not surprising that it sought to bolster managerial authority and restrict workers' rights. This also very much reflected the Prussian autocratic tradition of expecting and enforcing obedience from those lower down the social order. Therefore, in most – though not all – enterprises, employers took the view that they had a right to treat their workers however they pleased. A German employer regarded himself as a patriarch, as the master in his own house in pre-industrial terms, with total responsibility for the whole social organism of his enterprise and generally well beyond this. This type of self-esteem made German employers particularly unyielding in any situation of conflict.

One consequence of this was that the industrial and political climate became increasingly radical after the political and economic unification of Germany in 1871, though to no great effect. This period also saw the rapid development of the German economy. In 1870, the leading British enterprises were much bigger than their largest German competitors; by 1900, this position had been reversed. In many cases this was the result of governmental and banking encouragement to move to vertical integration. Also, cartels and monopolies, frowned upon elsewhere, received official endorsement in Germany, which allowed more orderly growth and longer-term investment decisions than might otherwise have been the case.

By the end of the nineteenth century the German economy had outstripped its British counterpart, but had not succeeded in avoiding either the same debilitating conflict between employers and employees, or the rise of political groups and parties which challenged the nature and purpose of capitalism. However, the influence of the Prussian autocratic tradition, the development of a strong bureaucratic approach within both private and public sector organisations, and the close relationship between industry and state, meant that industrial and political resistance was met by a unified and implacable alliance between employers and government. Though prepared to use welfare provisions, sickness benefit, old age pensions, etc., to reduce social tensions, the state was not prepared to cede one iota of industrial or political authority.

### France

As in Germany, the process of industrialisation in France was driven by the desire to emulate Britain, rather than by any form of 'spontaneous combustion'.

However, despite having the advantage of much earlier state encouragement than Germany, France's industrial revolution was late in starting and did not reach maturity until towards the end of the nineteenth century (Dunham, 1955; Fohlen, 1973). The slow and late development of industry in France appears to have been caused by two key factors: political change and agrarian stagnation, both of which were inextricably linked with the French Revolution of 1789.

In the eighteenth century, little separated France and Britain in industrial terms. With much encouragement from the monarchy, French industry adopted British machines and equipment. British entrepreneurs and inventors were even persuaded to establish factories in France. During the last years before the French Revolution, the King paid great attention to the economy. A twin-track approach to industrial development was instituted. On the one hand, much state aid and encouragement were poured into industry; whilst on the other hand, there was the suppression of every obstacle to individual entrepreneurship, whether they be the privileges of the craft guilds or the ancient rights of the aristocracy.

Though these initiatives gave a significant boost to industrialisation, progress was halted, and even reversed, by the French Revolution in 1789 (Marczewski, 1963). To an extent this is surprising, given that those who dominated the Revolutionary Assemblies were men of property and substance, though drawn from the law and professions rather than the business world. They believed in upholding property rights, abolishing hereditary privilege and vested interests, and providing a favourable climate for entrepreneurship. They also introduced laws that placed employees in an inferior legal position to their employers and which prohibited them from combining for the purpose of bargaining. Never-theless, the benefits of these to entrepreneurs were outweighed by other consequences of the Revolution. Foremost amongst these was the loss of France's colonial empire, together with its isolation, by the British naval blockade, from key markets such as the United States. The result was not only that France lost crucial imports and exports, but also that it was cut off from the prime source of technical and organisational innovation, Britain.

It was not until the final defeat of Napoleon in 1815 that France was once again able to concentrate on developing its economy rather than fighting wars. As before, the state took a lead in encouraging economic development, notably through the development of roads, canals and later railways. It also sought to stimulate the domestic economy by introducing import controls. However, this seems only to have allowed industry to keep outdated methods and equipment and maintain higher prices longer than might have been the case if it had not operated in a protected market. Only after 1850, with the upsurge in economic activity across Europe and the coming to power of Napoleon III, does the French economy really seem to have taken off.

The other main factor which held back industrialisation was the backward state of agriculture. The peasantry were already developing as an important group even before the French Revolution. However, the price they exacted for supporting the Revolution, the ownership of the majority of agricultural land, made them a powerful but reactionary force to which all sections of the property-owning classes had to pay attention. The consequences of this for industrialisation were twofold. First, the agricultural sector, unlike its counterparts Britain and Germany, remained self-sufficient and inefficient for most of the nineteenth century. As such, it was incapable of generating either wealth for investing in industry or demand for manufactured goods produced by industry. Second, by depressing the rate of population growth, it prevented the mass population exodus from the countryside to the towns and thus starved industry of a ready supply of cheap labour. This situation was further exacerbated by the continuing opportunities for home work which, by supplementing agricultural incomes, extended the viability of rural life longer than might otherwise be the case.

Nevertheless, the continued existence of a large rural population, even up to the dawn of the twentieth century, was not just a product of land ownership and the presence of home work. It also owed a great deal to the presence of import barriers which allowed peasants to maintain, in comparison with their British counterparts, inefficient production methods, and reduced the need either to borrow money for new equipment or to sell plots that were too small to be viable.

Import barriers also produced a strong bond of self-interest between peasants and factory owners, both of whom saw free trade as a threat to their way of life. As one observer commented, 'Competition was always possible in France, it simply did not happen to be a preferred form of conduct' (Sheahan, 1969: 25).

For industrialists, the result was similar. The absence of foreign competition, allied to low levels of domestic demand, allowed the typical business to remain family-owned, and also relatively small. Finance for industrial expansion was raised from family members rather than financial institutions, which in turn restricted the size of the banking sector. Indeed, such was the shortage of domestically generated capital and risk-orientated entrepreneurs that the building of railways, so vital to the development of the French economy, could not have taken place without foreign capital and state support (Kemp, 1979).

Therefore, unlike Britain, industrialisation in France was never driven by, or resulted in, individual enterprise or profit maximisation. For the state, the objective was a strong France. For the peasant and small entrepreneur, the objective was to make a reasonable living in the context of the rural and urban cultures they supported and valued.

### Scandinavia

Having looked at how the three largest and most advanced European countries – Britain, Germany and France – industrialised, we shall now move on to examine how three of the smaller states – Sweden, Denmark and Norway – responded to the challenge of industrialisation. In 1800, the total population of these three countries was just over four million people: Sweden, 2.35 million; Denmark, 0.93 million; and Norway, 0.88 million. By 1910, it was still less than 11 million: Sweden, 5.5 million; Denmark, 2.8 million; and Norway, 2.4 million. The historical links between these countries were very close, and up to the First World

War they operated a monetary union. Although, owing to their sea-faring traditions, each had occupied a position of importance on the international stage, by the mid-nineteenth century the standing of all three countries had declined. In fact, Norway and Sweden had become two of the poorest countries in Europe, which was a prime reason for the large-scale emigration from these countries to the USA in the nineteenth century (Milward and Saul, 1973).

Despite growing pockets of industrial production, in the nineteenth century their domestic economies were weak, and all three countries depended heavily on exporting the products of their agricultural, mining and forestry industries to their more industrialised neighbours, especially Britain. That they were able to adapt their export efforts to the changing demands of the international economy bears witness to the entrepreneurial skills of these countries.

However, political, economic and social developments in these three countries in the nineteenth century, particularly in Denmark, laid the foundations for the creation of the 'Nordic model' of industrial relations which emerged in the 1930s. This arose from the so-called 'historic compromise' between capital and labour, which extended co-operation between employers and social democratic governments over national economic policy into the industrial relations field. At a national level, it was agreed that the efforts of social democratic governments to bring about economic growth would not challenge the capitalist nature of production. Trade unions accepted this approach in exchange for basic trade union rights. This paved the way for an end to lock-outs and other such tactics by employers, and the creation of government-backed approaches to industrial democracy and further extensions of workers' rights (Dolvik and Stokland, 1992; Ferner and Hyman, 1992; Kjellberg, 1992).

These developments happened at different times and at a different pace in each country. Denmark led the way in the late nineteenth century, and Norway and Sweden followed a decade later, though the 'Nordic model' did not really establish itself fully until the 1930s and 1940s. However, the close ties between these three countries meant that political and industrial developments in one affected the other two. Hence the phrase 'Nordic model' was coined to describe similarities between the tripartite approaches adopted by government, employers and trade unions in each country, and the fact that these were distinct from practices elsewhere in Europe (or the rest of the world for that matter). However, for the moment, we are more concerned with the process of industrialisation in the nineteenth century and how this paved the way for these later developments.

For **Sweden**, the nineteenth century brought a rapidly rising population, which was matched an by increasingly productive agricultural sector that not only fully met domestic needs, but also developed a strong export market in grain, especially to Britain. The productivity of agriculture reflected the growing flexibility and commercialisation of this sector, facilitated by a series of gradual and peaceful rural reforms.

The iron trade also occupied an important position in the Swedish economy for much of the nineteenth century. This was due in no small part to its ability to adopt technological innovations, mainly from Britain, and the ability of Swedish ironmasters to seek out new international markets. By the end of the century, this had led to fewer but larger units of production, and the industry began to reflect the structures and methods of the leading European producers.

Despite the growth of agriculture and iron production, the most spectacular element in the growth of the Swedish economy was the boom in timber exports (Jorberg, 1973). Up to the 1830s, Swedish exports were only a fraction of those of Norway. However, the increasing urbanisation of Britain, and growing demand for timber from France and Germany, transformed the pattern of demand and supply. By the 1860s, softwood accounted for 40 per cent of all Sweden's exports, a situation which lasted well into the 1880s.

With over 20 million hectares of productive forest, Sweden possessed the largest such area in Europe, after Russia. The growth in markets was matched by the introduction of new methods and techniques, especially the use of steam engines and fine-bladed saws at the mills. The transfer of land ownership from the state to the private sector, in the early nineteenth century, also aided the development of the timber industry by allowing entrepreneurs to obtain timber rights often at ridiculously low prices, sometimes for no more than a sack of flour. Such a situation attracted many ruthless entrepreneurs whose regard for reforestation and conservation was negligible.

This combination of high demand, cheap wood and ruthless entrepreneurs created the conditions for a very sharp boom in timber exports, at least in the short term. Although after 1875 the state reversed its policy and began to reacquire forests, the timber companies also began to buy farmland, with its attendant forest rights. Gradually, the industry came to be dominated by a few large companies, some of which were foreign-owned. However, this concentration of ownership did make it easier for the state to oblige producers to take a more responsible approach to conservation and reforestation.

Given the dominance of the forestry industry, which relied almost exclusively on waterways for transportation, it is not perhaps surprising that railways came late to Sweden – not until the 1850s. It is also not surprising, given this situation, that it was government push rather than demand pull which gave the impetus to the Swedish railway system. Remarkably, by 1914, Sweden had 25 km of railway per 1000 inhabitants, twice that of any other European country. It also had a thriving industry producing rolling stock and engines for both the domestic and export markets (Jorberg, 1973).

Nevertheless, in 1870, industry and handicrafts only employed 15 per cent of the population. There were no industrial centres to rival those of Britain, Germany and France. Even the iron districts were small separate communities. However, after 1870, there was a rapid expansion of the Swedish industrial base, so much so that in the 40 years up to 1914, the Swedish economy grew faster than any other in Europe. Even so, to put this picture into perspective, it should be noted that all the workers involved in Swedish engineering exports in 1912 totalled no more than those to be found in one large German railway works.

For a small country, dependent on its natural resources, Sweden's progress was significant. There were a number of reasons for this. First, changes in the eighteenth century had removed barriers to social mobility and created the conditions for the emergence of entrepreneurs. Second, these entrepreneurs showed an unrivalled ability to exploit Sweden's natural resources and take advantage of developing export markets. An additional factor was the high quality of the Swedish educational system. This provided an educated workforce able to adapt to changing industries, technologies and products. Therefore, though it would be wrong to underestimate the great asset of Sweden's natural resources, neither should one forget the contribution made by human capital. The combination of a less hierarchical society than elsewhere in Europe and a well-educated and skilled workforce clearly paved the way for the advent of the social democratic approach to society which became the hallmark of Sweden in the twentieth century.

On the other hand, it would be misleading to forget that, as elsewhere in Europe, industrialisation was a harsh process. Entrepreneurs could be very rapacious, and much of the technology and many of the methods they employed were imported from the more advanced nations, especially Britain. Consequently, though the Swedish government tended to be more keen to intervene than was the case in Britain, industrialisation was accompanied by the same sort of clashes between capital and labour, and the growing incompatibility between an agricultural economy based on self-sufficiency and a capitalist economy based on money.

By the end of the nineteenth century, Sweden had developed a small industrial base, by comparison with Britain, Germany and France, but one that was flexible and competitive. However, the organisation of labour and the technology deployed tended to be imported from the bigger industrial nations. It imported the poor labour relations that existed elsewhere as well.

Though Sweden's industrial base was modest by international standards, it was in advance of that of Denmark and Norway (Jorberg, 1973). For **Denmark**, as for Sweden, it was changes to agricultural production that gave a large boost to the economy in the nineteenth century.

Traditionally, Denmark had relied on the export of two commodities, grain and cattle (though, in the eighteenth and the first half of the nineteenth centuries, its economy also benefitted considerably from its colonial possessions in Asia and the West Indies, particularly in terms of sugar production and the slave trade). Trade in the former grew rapidly in the nineteenth century. However, much of the grain was produced on marginal land, which was no longer economically viable after the collapse of world grain prices in the 1870s. After the early 1880s, imports outstripped exports.

On the other hand, the keeping of livestock and dairy produce showed a remarkable growth throughout the century. By the end of the nineteenth century, Denmark had a thriving export trade in butter and beef. By 1913, Denmark exported 80 per cent of its butter production, mainly to Britain where it had 40 per cent of the market; in that year, only Holland and Argentina exported more live cattle than Denmark. The latter part of the nineteenth century and the early twentieth century also saw a twelvefold rise in the production and export of pork (Milward and Saul, 1973).

One hindrance to the export of pork was the incompatibility between the large scale of the export market and the numerous small producers. However, this was overcome in the 1880s with the establishment of the first co-operative bacon factory. By 1914, 53 per cent of pig breeders were supplying to co-operatives. The idea of co-operatives to buy, process and sell produce had grown up in the dairy industry, and was later taken up by egg producers as well as pig breeders. Similar organisations were also used to purchase bulk feedstuffs and fertilisers. The impetus behind the development of co-operatives was the smaller farmers' fear of being exploited by their larger colleagues, who could afford to purchase the latest technology exclusively for their own use (Jorberg, 1973).

Therefore, unlike most other European countries, Denmark found a method of making small-scale farming production compatible with large-scale international demand. Nor were these co-operatives purely economic and technical organisations. Though this was their primary purpose, they also had a social and political role, and were anti-landowner. The growth of co-operatives along with their attendant 'folk high schools' was crucial, not only in educating farmers, but also in uniting them as an effective political force. Indeed, the party of small farmers, in alliance with the social democrats, headed governments from 1909 to 1910 and from 1913 to 1920. Not only does this show the political influence and socialist leanings of the co-operative movement, but it explains the emergence of the 'Nordic model' in Denmark some 20 years earlier than in the other two Scandinavian countries. The development of co-operatives was also one of the main reasons why there was no reduction in the numbers employed in Danish agriculture in the nineteenth century.

Though in some ways Denmark had a relatively thriving economy, its industrial base was, even relative to its size, on a more modest scale than in Britain, France or Germany. As an example, by 1911, the Danish cotton industry employed only 3282 people, no more than one big mill in Britain. In total, there were only 108,000 workers employed in factories at this time.

In contrast, there was a tremendous growth in the service sector, not just in transport and communications, but also in financial and trading services. These latter tended to be concentrated in Copenhagen, where by 1910 half the country's population lived. By 1911, service activities accounted for 36 per cent of the occupied population, as averse to 32 per cent in Norway and 19 per cent in Sweden.

One of the remarkable features of Danish industrialisation in the nineteenth century was the degree to which it preserved rather than destroyed the peasant and craft traditions. In agriculture, this was mainly due to the rise of co-operatives for processing and selling produce. In industry, the need to cater mainly for a small and discerning home market, allied to a well-educated workforce, kept alive the craft tradition, and – for most of the nineteenth century – the guild system.

Even in 1914, 84 per cent of Danish workers were still in establishments employing five or less people. By contrast, in Sweden in 1912, only 24 per cent of workers were in establishments employing 10 or less people.

Therefore, if Denmark was less industrially advanced than some bigger European countries, it could however claim to have avoided the clash of cultures and the rise of industrial conflict that characterised the industrial revolution elsewhere in Europe.

Just as the process of industrialisation differed considerably between Sweden and Denmark, so was also the case with **Norway**. Like the other two countries, it was dependent on exports, but in Norway these were service-based rather than product-based. Shipping was its chief earner. In 1880, shipping accounted for 45 per cent of all exports.

Its links with Sweden and Denmark tended to be political rather than economic. Up to 1814, it was part of the Kingdom of Denmark, and in that year the King of Sweden also became the King of Norway. However, Denmark sided with France during the Napoleonic Wars and as a consequence of Napoleon's defeat lost the sovereignty of Norway to Sweden. Norway was given its own parliament and constitution, though its political and economic ties with Sweden were considerable until it achieved full independence in 1905.

Of the three Scandinavian countries, Norway was slowest to industrialise and, unlike the other two, this was neither preceded nor accompanied by the modernisation of agriculture. Nor was the stimulus to industrialisation generated internally. Rather, when industry really began to flourish, just before the First World War, it was brought about by an influx of foreign capital wishing to take advantage of Norway's potential for cheap hydro-electricity.

However, up to this point, Norway had made few steps towards becoming an industrial economy. In agriculture, Norway was held back by a combination of poor soils, difficult climate and extremely inefficient internal communications. Indeed, a marked feature of the Norwegian economy was the very poor contact and bad communications between various regions within the country, no doubt a consequence of the mountainous terrain, which meant that it was often easier to import goods from abroad rather than to move them from one part of Norway to another (Jorberg, 1973). This led to a dual economy: the increasingly prosperous urban areas which grew rich on the export of goods and services, and a subsistence agricultural economy in the countryside.

Accordingly, the towns prospered and the countryside stagnated with small peasant farmers tending to be the agricultural norm into the twentieth century. At the end of the nineteenth century, such was the low level of productivity of Norwegian agriculture that butter exports, worth 3.3 million Kr, were dwarfed by imports of grain and animal feedstuffs worth 83 million Kr. Norway had no other food exports of importance, except for fish (Milward and Saul, 1973).

On the other hand, Norway was mercifully free of the social rigidity of many other European countries where the nobility stood at the top of the social pyramid. Instead, uniquely, merchants and gentlemen farmers formed the top layers of society, serfdom was rare, and there was a lack of the social injustice that seemed inevitably to accompany industrialisation in the more advanced countries. This may account for the willingness of employers and trade unions, particularly in the metal industries, to favour co-operation over conflict from the early 1900s (Dolvik and Stokland, 1992; Kjellberg, 1992).

The staple industries of the Norwegian economy in the nineteenth century were fishing, timber and shipping, along with a shipbuilding industry that was a product of all three. In the early years of the century, it also exported iron, but this trade was virtually killed by British and Swedish competition after Danish trade protection was abolished in 1814. The main employers were shipping, where some 33,000 were employed in the merchant marine in 1860, and fishing, both of which had only weak links to the rest of the economy. There was also a small, fragmented, engineering industry which in 1850 only comprised 12 factories employing a total of 200 workers. From the 1840s there was a rapid growth in the textile sector. Even so, in 1860 this still only accounted for 3,000 workers out of a total of just under 20,000 industrial workers. The biggest industrial sector was forestry, employing almost one in three workers (Jorberg, 1973).

Therefore, because of its small population size, the lack of demand from the countryside, and the reliance of the towns on exports for their prosperity, Norway's industrial expansion was linked very closely to the export trades. When exports boomed, domestic demand increased; when exports fell, so did domestic demand. In addition, because its industrial sector was small, Norway found it difficult to generate capital domestically. As an example, in 1870, half of the mining industry was foreign-owned. However, with the development of closer economic links with Sweden in 1873, the market for Norwegian industry was expanded considerably.

Developing quite separately from the rest of the economy, the real growth industry of the nineteenth century was shipping. Shipping emerged during the eighteenth century as a subsidiary of the timber trade, but in the nineteenth century it developed entirely independently of Norway's own transport needs. Instead, it catered to the needs of other countries, especially Britain and Denmark and their colonies. It owed its existence to the country's shipbuilding tradition, the availability of local timber and the ready supply of cheap labour. From 1850, the industry grew rapidly, growing fivefold in the years up to 1880, by which time it was the third largest in the world, greater even than that of France and Germany. However, after 1900, the industry declined, owing to a fall in freight rates and to the advent of steam-powered vessels. The industry was very fragmented, which meant that raising capital was difficult. Though this was not a problem with the small, wooden ships which had been the backbone of the industry, it became one with the need for larger, steam-powered vessels which were much more expensive. Also, Norway lacked both the raw materials, iron and steel, and the skills to build steam ships. Indeed, in the immediate pre-war years, only 20 per cent of the industry's requirements were met from home production. Even so, in 1914, the Norwegian shipping industry was the fourth largest in the world behind Britain, the USA and Germany, though there were signs that it was in decline.

The advent of hydro-electric power at the end of the nineteenth century did, however, make a significant difference to Norway's industrial development. Once the technology had been established, no country in Europe was better placed to exploit it than Norway, with its plentiful supply of waterfalls. However, to turn this into a reality required both capital and a use for the resultant cheap electricity. Both of these were to come from abroad. By 1914, hydro-electric power, financed by foreign capital, was used to produce synthetic fertiliser and aluminium. The attraction for foreign investors was cheap power. Almost all of the output was sold abroad, much of it without further processing. These developments had a significant impact in terms of increasing Norway's foreign earnings. The result was that some 14 per cent of the industrial labour force was directly employed by foreign firms by 1909, with considerable numbers being indirectly employed. These workers tended to be concentrated in the more capital-intensive industries and larger workplaces. This led to a law being passed which limited foreign ownership of Norwegian industry.

In many respects, with the stagnation of timber and shipping, the advent of modern chemical and metal industries was highly desirable. In another respect, though, they also showed the weakness of Norwegian industrialisation. Both these industries were heavily dependent on foreign capital; both were capital- as averse to labour-intensive; and neither developed or needed a local supply or distribution network. Therefore, neither really impacted greatly, at least in the pre-war period, on the wider Norwegian economy. For this reason, in relation to its Scandinavian neighbours, Norway remained a relatively poor country, which certainly accounted for the large waves of emigration it experienced in the nineteenth and early twentieth centuries. In relation to political democracy and educational provision, though, particularly for women, it was in advance of most other European countries before 1914.

Considering these three Scandinavian countries as a whole, the picture of industrialisation by the early twentieth century was very mixed. Sweden was probably the most advanced, with Denmark not far behind but Norway trailing somewhat. However, because of population size, natural resources and history, none had developed an industrial base capable of competing with those of the leading European countries.

As elsewhere in Europe, all three tended to import methods and technologies from the more advanced countries, especially Britain. It would appear that the process of industrialisation, where it was reliant on foreign capital and methods, tended to reproduce the British experience of poor labour relations. However, particularly in Denmark, there were signs that different organisational forms allied to existing social structures and expectations, together with the growth of social democracy, held out the promise of avoiding the vicious employer–employee clashes experienced elsewhere.

Nevertheless, in Europe as a whole, for the most part, those who created and controlled the large business organisations that were becoming the norm still had to rely on their own experience and judgement, but with growing frustration over their inability to control and organise these bodies fully and effectively. There was also a realisation amongst some that, whilst change was inevitable, they lacked an effective and, as far as their employees were concerned, acceptable way of managing it. Therefore, by the end of the nineteenth century, there was a growing awareness of the need to develop an approach to organising work that was more systematic and less harsh and arbitrary than what had gone before. Although this was already, to an extent, taking place in Germany with the rise of bureaucracy, the USA was the country where the most conscious and consistent search was being pursued for a comprehensive theory of how to structure and run organisations.

## The USA

In the USA, for a number of reasons, the need for a workable, overall approach to organisational design and control, which legitimised the authority of managers to initiate change, was perhaps more acute than anywhere else. The USA had industrialised far more rapidly and on a larger scale than any other nation. Only in the 1860s, after the Civil War, did the USA begin to industrialise in earnest; but by 1914 it had become the premier industrial nation, with the highest per capita income in the world. In the period 1860 to 1914, employment in manufacturing rose from 1.3 million to 6.6 million, and the population as a whole rose from 31 million to 91 million (Habakkuk and Postan, 1965). The USA at this time was still very much influenced by Europe, and initially at least adopted similar approaches and methods in organising and running industry. However, the size of the typical American organisation quickly grew much larger than those in Europe. Whilst the average British and French business was still the small, family-owned firm, in the USA it was the monopoly, which dominated an entire industry, or the conglomerate, which had substantial holdings in several industries. As an example, in 1900 Dale Carnegie sold his steel company for the enormous sum of $419 million to a group of financiers. They merged it with other steel concerns to create a monopoly steel producer employing 200,000 workers and valued at $1.3 billion. This was at a time when the British steel industry, which had led the world, comprised 100 blast furnaces owned by 95 separate companies.

As might be imagined, the numbers of Americans employed in factories and offices grew rapidly – almost tripling between 1880 and 1910 (Levine, 1967; Zinn, 1980). The rocketing increase in demand for labour could not be met by the indigenous population alone and was fuelled by successive waves of immigration. Whilst solving one problem – the shortage of labour – this created others. The culture shock of industrial work, a foreign language, and problems of housing and social integration created enormous pressures in American society. Alongside this was the arbitrary and ruthless discipline of the factory system, where workers were treated as so much industrial cannon fodder. It was a time of rapid social, technological and organisational change: a time where entrepreneurs did not so much expect to manage change as to impose it, and those who could not or would not accept this situation were treated harshly. Consequently, most industries found themselves sitting on a pressure cooker which could, and frequently did, explode in unexpected and violent ways. If management–labour relations were poor in most European countries, they were far worse in the USA (Pelling, 1960).

The American approach to industrial development owed little to government aid or encouragement, and much to individual entrepreneurship. For this reason American entrepreneurs had much more in common with the free market approach to industrial expansion of their British counterparts than to the state-sponsored traditions of Germany or France. Therefore, the German approach to industrial organisation, bureaucracy, which might seem appropriate given the size of American companies, was not attractive. In any case, it tended to operate best in situations where growth and demand was stable or predictable, which in Germany the government tried to facilitate. However, American growth patterns were volatile and unpredictable.

Consequently, there was great pressure to find organisational arrangements that would allow employers to control and organise their employees in a manner that reduced conflict, was cost-effective, and was applicable to the American environment and philosophy. It was also becoming recognised that it was not sufficient just to develop a more systematic approach to the organisation of work; there was also a need to develop an approach to managing change, which would persuade workers to accept rather than reject or resist the introduction of new methods, techniques and technologies. Therefore, with the spirit of endeavour, determination and confidence that seemed so much a part of the American character at this time, managers and engineers set out to remedy this situation. Though similar developments were taking place in Europe, they lacked the intensity, commitment and scale of events in the USA. This is no doubt why one of the earliest and most enduring approaches to organisation theory emerged in the USA, and why the USA has continued to dominate the development of organisation theory.

## ORGANISATION THEORY: THE CLASSICAL APPROACH

As can be seen, at the end of the nineteenth century there was a clear need to replace the rule-of-thumb approach to organisational design and management with a more consistent and organisation-wide approach. This was not because of an academic interest in the functioning of organisations, though this was present, but in order to improve their performance, enhance their competitiveness and – an increasing concern at the time – to sustain and legitimate managerial authority. This was certainly the case in the USA, where explosive growth and a workforce suffering from culture shock had created dangerous social pressures which questioned the legitimacy of managerial power, and even the capitalist system itself. This was also true in Europe: although Europe industrialised earlier, it was not only having to come to grips with the increase in size and complexity of business life, but it was also facing considerable, and unexpected, competitive pressure from the United States.

Nevertheless, these difficulties could not quench the innate optimism of the age. It was a time, much more than now, when people dealt in certainties and universal truths. There was a feeling of confidence that any goal, whether it be taming nature or discerning the best way to run business, could be achieved by the twin power of scientific study and practical experience. All over the industrialised world, groups of managers and technical specialists were forming their own learned societies to exchange experiences, to discuss common problems, and to seek out in a scientific and rational fashion the solution to all organisational ills: to discover 'the one best way'.

Out of these endeavours emerged what was later termed the Classical approach to organisational design and management. It was an approach, as the name suggests, which drew heavily on what had gone before; taking from writers such as Adam Smith and practitioners such as Josiah Wedgwood and leavening their ideas with contemporary experience, views and experiments. This approach, reflecting the age in which it emerged, portrays organisations as machines, and those in them as mere parts which respond to the correct stimulus and whose actions are based on scientific principles. The emphasis was on achieving efficiency in internal functions; seeing organisations as closed and changeless entities unaffected by the outside world. Though this approach first originated in the early part of this century, its influence on managerial practices and assumptions is still strong today, but its credibility amongst academics has waned (Kelly, 1982a, b; Rose, 1988; Scott, 1987).

The Classical approach, or the Scientific-Rational approach as it is sometimes called, whilst not being homogeneous, is characterised by three common propositions:

- *Organisations are rational entities*: they are collectivities of individuals focused on the achievement of relatively specific goals through their organisation into highly formalised, differentiated and efficient structures.

- *The design of organisations is a science*: through experience, observation and experiment, it has been established that there is one best universal organisational form for all bodies. This is based on the hierarchical and horizontal division of labour and functions, whereby organisations are conceived of as machines which, once set in motion, inexorably and efficiently will pursue and achieve their pre-selected goals.

- *People are economic beings*: they are solely motivated by money. This instrumental orientation means that they will try to achieve the maximum reward for the minimum work, and will use whatever bargaining power their skills or knowledge allow to this end. Therefore, jobs must be designed and structured in such a way as to minimise an individual's skill and discretion, and to maximise management control.

The key figures in the development of the Classical approach were Frederick Taylor (1856–1915) and two of his main promoters, the pioneers of motion study,

Frank and Lillian Gilbreth (1868–1924 and 1878–1972 respectively) in the USA, Henri Fayol (1841–1925) in France and Max Weber (1864–1920) in Germany. All were writing in the first two decades of the twentieth century, though Weber's work was not generally available in English until the 1940s. Below is an outline of their work.

## Frederick Taylor's Scientific Management

Frederick Winslow Taylor was born into a prosperous Quaker-Puritan family in Germantown, Pennsylvania in 1856. Although he passed the entrance exam for Harvard Law School, instead of becoming a lawyer as his family wished, in 1874 he took a manual job in an engineering company and became a skilled pattern maker and machinist. In 1878, he joined the Midvale Steel Company as a labourer, but eventually rose to become its Chief Engineer. Having had enough of working for other people, in 1893 he set up his own consultancy (Sheldrake, 1996). Taylor was an accomplished and talented engineer, and became a leading authority on metal cutting and a successful inventor; however, it is for his contribution to work organisation that he is most famous (or infamous).

Taylor was a highly controversial figure during his lifetime and still remains so more than 80 years after his death. This was partly because his theory of management was a direct challenge to both workers and managers. However, a large part of the hostility he generated during his lifetime was due to his own character. Rose (1988: 23) stated that 'Taylor was a notorious neurotic – many would not hesitate to write crank; and there is even a case for upgrading the diagnosis to maniac.' He was certainly a zealot when it came to promoting his own ideas, and would brook no challenge to them, whether from workers or management. Not surprisingly, though he attracted devoted followers, he also engendered fierce dislike.

Through his experience as a shopfloor worker, manager and consultant, Taylor made a major contribution to the development of managerial theory and practice in the twentieth century (Locke, 1982; Rose, 1988). Yet, his original attempts to improve productivity (or, as he put it, to stamp out 'soldiering') were less than successful. Not only was his use of sacking, blacklisting and victimisation counter-productive, but also the bitterness which this provoked haunted him for the rest of his life. It was his failure to achieve change by, as Rose (1988: 37) termed it, 'managerial thuggery' that led him to seek an alternative method of change management which the workers, and management, would accept because they could see that it was rational and fair. Thereafter, his sole preoccupation became the pursuit and promotion of a scientific approach to management.

Drawing on his work at the Midvale Steel Company and the Bethlehem Steel Company, Taylor constructed a general ideology of efficiency. It was only in 1911, when a group of his supporters met to discuss how better to promote his work, that the term 'Scientific Management' was first used to describe his approach to work organisation (Sheldrake, 1996). Though initially sceptical, Taylor embraced the term and there can be little doubt that the publication, in the same year, of his *Principles of Scientific Management* laid the foundation stone for the development of organisation and management theory. Taylor's primary focus was on the design and analysis of individual tasks; this process inevitably led to changes in the overall structure of organisations. Such was the impact of his work that it created a blueprint for, and legitimated, the activities of managers and their support staff. In so doing, he helped to create the plethora of functions and departments which characterise many modern organisations.

Before Taylor, the average manager tended to operate in an idiosyncratic and arbitrary manner with little or no specialist support. Taylor saw this as being at the root of much industrial unrest and workers' mistrust of management. Though criticised for his anti-labour postures, Taylor was also highly critical of management behaviour, which may account for this group's initial lack of enthusiasm for his ideas (Scott, 1987). After Taylor, managers were left with a 'scientific' blueprint for analysing work and applying his 'one best way' principle to each job in order to gain 'a fair day's work for a fair day's pay'.

These last two phrases sum up Taylor's basic beliefs:

- It is possible and desirable to establish, through methodical study and the application of scientific principles, the one best way of carrying out any job. Once established, the way must be implemented totally and made to operate consistently.

- Human beings are predisposed to seek the maximum reward for the minimum effort, which Taylor referred to as 'soldiering'. To overcome this, managers must lay down in detail what each worker should do, step by step; ensure through close supervision that the instructions are adhered to; and, to give positive motivation, link pay to performance.

Taylor incorporated those beliefs into his precepts for Scientific Management, comprising three core elements: the systematic collection of knowledge about the work process by managers; the removal or reduction of workers' discretion and control over what they do; and the laying down of standard procedures and times for carrying out each job.

The starting point is the gathering of knowledge:

> **The managers assume ... the burden of gathering together all the traditional knowledge which in the past has been possessed by the workman and then of classifying, tabulating and reducing this knowledge to rules, laws and formulae...** (Taylor, 1911b: 36)

This lays the groundwork for the second stage: increased management control. As long as workers possess a monopoly of knowledge about the work process, increased control is impossible. But once the knowledge is also possessed by managers, it becomes possible not only to establish what workers actually do with their time, but also by 'reducing this knowledge to rules, laws and formulae', to decrease the knowledge that workers need to carry out a given task. It also, importantly, paves the way for the division of labour.

The last stage is that 'All possible brain work should be removed from the shop and centred in the planning ... department ...' (Taylor, 1911a: 98–9). The divorce of conception from execution removes control from the worker, who no longer has discretion as to how tasks are carried out.

> Perhaps the most prominent single element in modern scientific management is the task idea. The work of every workman is fully planned out by management ... and each man receives in most cases complete written instructions, describing in detail the task which he is to accomplish, as well as the means to be used in doing the work. This task specifies not only what is to be done but how it is to be done and the exact time allowed for doing it. (Taylor, 1911b: 39)

Allied to this last element was Taylor's approach to worker selection and motivation. Taylor carried out many experiments to identify and reward workers. He believed that organisations should only employ 'first class men' and they would only get the best results if they were paid by results. As he commented on his time as a consultant at the Bethlehem Steel Company (Taylor, 1911b: 55–6):

> When the writer left the steelworks, the Bethlehem pieceworkers were the finest body of picked labourers that he has ever seen together. They were practically all first class men, because in each case the task they were called upon to perform was such that only a first class man could do. The tasks were all purposely made so severe that not more than one out of five labourers (perhaps even a smaller percentage than this) could keep it up. It was clearly understood by each newcomer as he went to work that unless he was able to average at least $1.85 per day he would have to make way for another man who could do so.

The 'task idea' allied to Taylor's approach to selecting and paying workers completes the process of gaining control over workers by managers. The workers become 'human machines', told what to do, when to do it and how long to take. But, more than this, it allows new types of work organisation to be developed, and new work processes and equipment introduced; thus workers move from having a monopoly of knowledge and control over their work to a position where the knowledge they have of the work process is minimal, and their control vastly reduced. The result is not only a reduction in the skills required and the wages paid, but also the creation of jobs which are so narrow and tightly specified that the period needed to train someone to do them is greatly reduced. This removes the last bargaining counter of labour: scarcity of skill.

According to Taylor, this transforms not only workers' jobs but also managers' jobs:

> The man at the head of the business under scientific management is governed by rules and laws ... just as the workman is, and the standards which have been developed are equitable. (Taylor, 1911a: 189)

Taylor stated that the 'scientific' basis and equal applicability of his methods meant they were neutral between labour and management; therefore they legitimated managerial action to analyse and change work methods, because managers are merely applying science to determine the best method of work. He claimed that his approach benefited both the worker and the company. The worker was enabled and encouraged to work to his maximum performance and be rewarded accordingly, whilst the company benefited from higher output:

> It would seem so self-evident that maximum prosperity for the employer, coupled with maximum prosperity for the employee, ought to be the two leading objects of management, that even to state this fact should be unnecessary. And yet there is no question that, throughout the industrial world, a large part of the organization of employers, as well as employees, is for war rather than peace... (Taylor, 1911b: 9–10)

Though seen as something of an anti-trade unionist, which he probably was, as the above implies, he was also strongly critical of management. He believed that many of the problems organisations faced in implementing change were due to the arbitrary and inconsistent approach of managers. In fact, though trade unions were very suspicious of Scientific Management in general and Taylor in particular, managers seemed even more antagonistic. Indeed, after his death, Taylor's acolytes spent much time in the 1920s wooing the American unions with a considerable degree of success; they never achieved the same success with management (Rose, 1988). The main reason for this was that, though managers were anxious to find an approach which would curtail labour resistance to change and improve productivity, they were not prepared to subject themselves to a similar degree of discipline.

As Taylor's biographer, Copley (1923: 146) stated in relation to managerial resistance to Scientific Management at the Bethlehem Steel Company:

> Let us consider what Taylor was contending for. It was essentially this: that the government of the Bethlehem Steel Company cease to be capricious, arbitrary and despotic; that every man in the establishment, high and low, submit himself to law [i.e. that managers should obey the principles of Scientific Management].

Taylor believed passionately in the need to reform managerial authority: to base it on competence rather than the power to hire and fire. However, it is one thing to ask one's subordinates to change their ways and accept new rules and methods; it is another thing entirely for management to acknowledge that they too need to change, and change radically. No wonder that Taylor met managerial as well as worker resistance.

Nevertheless, even though managers resisted the full implementation of Taylorism, the new and rapidly expanding breed of industrial engineers, charged with developing and implementing new methods, techniques and technologies, found in Taylor and his contemporaries' work a blueprint for transforming the workplace and increasing their control and status. One consequence of this, brought about by the use of job cards and other forms of work recording and analysis systems, was a massive increase in the amount of paperwork that needed to be processed. Managers complained about the growth of 'industrial bureaucracy', but the benefits it brought by enabling average times and costs, etc., to be calculated easily outweighed the increase in clerical costs.

Nowhere was this demonstrated more dramatically than at Henry Ford's Highland Park plant – the home of the world's first mass-produced motor car, the Model T Ford. From 1909/10, when 18,664 Model Ts were sold, sales and production doubled year-on-year. However, every increase in production required a commensurate increase in the plant's workforce. In 1911/12, the plant produced 78,440 Model Ts with 6,867 employees. The next year production doubled and the number of employees doubled. Not surprisingly, Ford was desperate for ways of increasing employee productivity. The solution he adopted was to redesign the assembly operation around Scientific Management principles, and then couple this with the introduction of the moving assembly line. This allowed Ford once again to double production, but this time the workforce actually decreased (Lacey, 1986). So the 1910s saw the birth of the twin, and very much related, neologisms that both dominated and revolutionised industrial life for much of the twentieth century – Taylorism and Fordism.

Throughout the 1920s, the adoption of Scientific Management grew in America, though rarely in the full form laid down by Taylor. It was also introduced on a very limited basis into Europe, but met with much scepticism from managers and hostility from workers (Rose, 1988). Only in Russia did there seem any great enthusiasm for it. Indeed, Lenin saw Scientific Management combined with common ownership as the prime basis for Russian industrialisation: 'We must organize in Russia the study and teaching of the Taylor system and systematically try it out and adapt it to our own ends' (Lenin, 1918: 25). Taylor's work also attracted some interest in Japan. However, it was not until after the Second World War, through the auspices of the Marshall Plan for rebuilding Europe's war-torn economies, that Scientific Management was promoted and adopted on any significant scale outside America. Ironically, the contribution of American trade unions, through their role in the Marshall Plan, was crucial in promoting Scientific Management in European enterprises (Carew, 1987).

Taylor claimed that his system was innovative and unique, which indeed it was in terms of the way he synthesised and systematised a host of previously disparate practices and presented them as scientific and neutral (Aitken, 1960; Rose, 1988). Yet in reality, it can be seen that Taylor drew on many of the management practices and negative attitudes towards labour that were prevalent during the nineteenth century. He was also heavily indebted to many contemporaries and associates who helped develop the work study techniques necessary to implement Scientific Management, especially Henry Gantt and Carl Barth, who worked closely with him (Kempner, 1970; Sheldrake, 1996). Perhaps his greatest debt was to Frank and Lillian Gilbreth. As well as being the pioneers of motion study, they were the driving force in establishing the Society for the Promotion of Scientific Management, which was later renamed the Taylor Society, and did much to promote Taylor's work both before and after his death in 1915 (Rose, 1988; Sheldrake, 1996).

## The Gilbreths and motion study

Much of modern work study (a central element of the Classical approach) owes its origins to the methods and techniques of motion study developed in the first quarter of this century by Frank and Lillian Gilbreth (*see* Gilbreth and Gilbreth, 1914). Their work on motion study was initiated by Frank Gilbreth, who was a contemporary of Taylor's. In many respects their careers were similar. Taylor, turning his back on Harvard Law School, began his career on the shopfloor and later rose to eminence as a manager and management consultant. Frank Gilbreth, after passing the entrance exam for but declining to enter the Massachusetts Institute of Technology, rose from being a bricklayer to running his own construction and consultancy companies. He was also, along with his wife, a leading campaigner for Scientific Management.

Although the development and promotion of motion study was begun by her husband, there is no doubt that Lillian Moller Gilbreth was an equal partner. Despite contemporary prejudices against women and education, she obtained Bachelor's and Master's degrees in English. She was only denied a doctorate in psychology by the University of California because family commitments prevented her, after her thesis had been approved, from spending the post-thesis year on campus that the regulations required (Sheldrake, 1996; Thickett, 1970).

In justifying their work, Frank Gilbreth stated in his 1909 book on bricklaying that motion study:

> ...will cut down production costs and increase the efficiency and wages of the work-man... To be pre-eminently successful: (a) a mechanic must know his trade; (b) he must be quick motioned; and (c) he must use the fewest possible motions to accomplish the desired results. (Quoted in Sheldrake, 1996: 28)

The Gilbreths developed a number of procedures for breaking work down into its constituent components. Flow process charts were used which split human motion into five basic elements: operations, transportation, inspection, storage and delay. Arising out of this, they developed a method of minutely analysing tasks which broke handwork into 17 basic elements. Examples of these are as follows:

*Grasp*    Begins when hand or body member touches an object. Consists of gaining control of an object.

*Release*    Begins when hand or body member begins to relax control of object. Consists of letting go of an object.

*Plan*    Begins when hand or body members are idle or making random movements while worker decides on course of action. Consists of determining a course of action. Ends when course of action is determined.

The purpose of this microanalysis was not only to establish what was done, but also to discover if a better method of performing the task in question could be developed. In this respect, they did much original work in establishing the distinction between necessary and unnecessary movements. The latter were to be eliminated immediately and the former further analysed in more detail to see if they could be improved, combined or replaced by special equipment.

If this sounds remarkably similar to Adam Smith's observations on pin-making, mentioned earlier, this is no accident. The Classical approach is descended from Smith through the nineteenth century pioneers of work organisation. Though remarkable in the level of minute detail to which they reduced the motions individuals make when undertaking manual tasks, the Gilbreths were only, as they saw it, taking Smith's maxims to their logical conclusion. If in the process they give the impression of dealing more with machines than people, that too is no accident. Like others who propounded the Classical approach, they viewed organisations and workers very much as machines. The work study methods developed by the Gilbreths and their successors are still widely used today, not just in manufacturing industries, but in all areas of life from hospitals to computer programming (Grant, 1983).

The Gilbreths were also concerned that, having established the best way to carry out a task, this should not be undermined by selecting the wrong person to carry it out or by creating the wrong environment. Therefore, they set about analysing employee selection and establishing environmental criteria with the same determination they had applied to analysing work performance. However, in neither case could they achieve the same microanalysis that characterised their work study technique; what finally emerged were effectively opinions based on their own 'experience', rather than being the product of experiment and observation.

The Gilbreths, like Taylor, were devoted to one objective – to discover the best method of doing any job. The difference was that whereas Taylor was concerned with reducing the time taken to perform a task, the Gilbreths were more concerned with reducing the motions taken to accomplish the task. Though this differing emphasis did lead to some friction with Taylor (Nadworthy, 1957), they were, none the less, among his main promoters and saw their efforts as comple-mentary to, and aimed at enhancing, Scientific Management. The fact that work study is now often labelled 'time and motion' study perhaps shows this. Like Taylor, they saw themselves as creating a neutral system that benefited both labour and management. They felt that any increase in boredom or monotony brought about by their methods would be compensated for by workers' opportunities to earn more money.

While the Gilbreths and Taylor devoted their efforts to improving the produc-tivity of individual workers, there were others who took a wider but complementary perspective.

## Henri Fayol and the principles of organisation

Born in 1841 and educated at the *lycée* in Lyon and the National School of Mines in St Etienne, Fayol was promoting his ideas in France at the same time as Taylor was propounding his views on Scientific Management in the USA. He began his working life as a mining engineer in 1860 and, in 1888, was appointed Managing Director of an ailing mining company, which he quickly turned into a much-admired and financially strong enterprise. He retired as Managing Director in 1918, though he stayed on the Board until his death in 1925. In his 'retirement' he founded the Centre d'Etudes Administratives, whose role was to propagate Fayol's ideas through management education. He chaired weekly meetings of prominent industrialists, writers, government officials, philosophers and members of the military. This direct contact with opinion-formers and decision-makers is undoubtedly one of the main reasons why the Centre had such a profound influence on the practice and theory of management in both the public and private sectors in France.

Fayol did not draw his views on organisations solely from his own experience as a manager. His education at one of the *grandes écoles*, and his subsequent career as an executive of a large mining company, placed him among the elite of senior administrators in business, government and the armed forces. Therefore, though he spent his working life in the coal mining industry, his practical knowledge of business was informed by and fits within the intellectual and administrative traditions of French society.

His working life, in the late nineteenth and early twentieth centuries, coincided with a period of rapid industrialisation in France. It was a time when industrial unrest was rife, with frequent strikes by railway workers, miners and civil servants. As was the case in the USA, in this period of rapid growth and change, there was an unwritten consensus that French business and government needed a theory of management, no matter how basic (Cuthbert, 1970). Unlike Taylor and the Gilbreths, however, Fayol's focus was on efficiency at the organisational level rather than the task level: top down rather than bottom up (Fayol, 1949). Though this clearly reflects Fayol's own practical experience, it also shows the combined influence of the French intellectual tradition, with its preference for addressing philosophies rather than practicalities, and the administrative tradition, which sought to identify and lay down general rules and restrictions applicable to all situations.

Given his background, it is not surprising that Fayol was more concerned with general rather than departmental or supervisory management, and with overall organisational control as averse to the details of tasks. This does not, however, place him in opposition to Taylor. Rather the combination of Taylor's work at the task level and Fayol's at the organisational level make their views complementary rather than contradictory. In addition, both emphasised strongly the need for professionally educated managers who would 'follow the rule' rather than acting in an arbitrary or *ad hoc* fashion.

As the following shows, Fayol (like all the Classical school) was concerned with developing a universal approach to management that was applicable to any organisation:

> There is no one doctrine of administration for business and another for affairs of state; administrative doctrine is universal. Principles and general rules which hold good for business hold good for the state too, and the reverse applies. (Quoted in Cuthbert, 1970: 111)

Therefore, in business, public administration, or indeed any form of organisation, the same universal principles apply. According to Fayol, these are as follows (quoted in Mullins, 1989: 202–3):

1 *Division of work*. The object is to produce more and better work from the same effort, through the advantages of specialisation.

2 *Authority and responsibility*. Wherever authority is exercised, responsibility arises. The application of sanctions is needed to encourage useful actions and to discourage their opposite.

3 *Discipline*. This is essential for the efficient operation of the organisation. Discipline is in essence the outward mark of respect for agreements between the organisation and its members.

4 *Unity of command*. In any action, any employee should receive orders from one superior only; dual command is a perpetual source of conflicts.

5 *Unity of direction*. In order to co-ordinate and focus effort, there should be one leader and one plan for any group of activities with the same objective.

6 *Subordination of individual or group interests*. The interest of the organisation should take precedence over individual or group interests.

7 *Remuneration of personnel*. Methods of payment should be fair, encourage keenness by rewarding well-directed effort, but not lead to over-payment.

8 *Centralisation*. The degree of centralisation is a question of proportion and will vary in particular organisations.

9 *Scalar chain*. This is the chain of superiors from the ultimate authority to the lowest ranks. Respect for line authority must be reconciled with activities that require urgent action, and with the need to provide for some measure of initiative at all levels of authority.

10 *Order*. This includes material order and social order. The object of material order is avoidance of loss. There should be an appointed place for each thing, and each thing should be in its appointed place. Social order requires good organisation and good selection.

11 *Equity*. There needs to be fairness in dealing with employees throughout all levels of the scalar chain.

12 *Stability of tenure of personnel*. Generally, prosperous organisations have a stable managerial team.

13 *Initiative*. This represents a source of strength for the organisation and should be encouraged and developed.

14 *Esprit de corps*. This should be fostered, as harmony and unity among members of the organisation are a great strength in the organisation.

According to Fayol (1949), it is the prime responsibility of management to enact these principles. Consequently, in order to achieve this, he prescribed the main duties of management as follows:

- **Planning**: examining the future, deciding what needs to be done and developing a plan of action.
- **Organising**: bringing together the resources, human and material, and developing the structure to carry out the activities of the organisation.
- **Command**: ensuring that all employees perform their jobs well and in the best interests of the organisation.
- **Co-ordination**: verifying that the activities of the organisation work harmoniously together to achieve its goals.
- **Control**: establishing that plans, instructions and commands are correctly carried out.

Fayol was a gifted and highly successful businessman who attributed his success to the application of his principles rather than personal ability. Certainly, he was one of the pioneers of management theory, and many of his principles are still taught and practised today. However, part of the success of his work lay in the fact that he was writing for a receptive audience, and at a time when management practice and ideas were becoming international currency. Just as Taylor's system arose at the time when a need for a management theory had grown amongst the business community in the USA, so Fayol's was aimed at a similar demand in France, where the business community was developing rapidly but in an unplanned way.

Unlike Taylor, though, he attempted neither to denigrate trade unions openly nor to castigate managers. Nor did he share with Taylor a belief that the interests of managers and workers were necessarily the same or ultimately reconcilable. He did, however, believe that much industrial unrest could be eliminated by fairer, more consistent, and firmer management, particularly where this reduced the need for trade unions or their ability to organise. He also believed in the need to educate and train managers. His views were not seen as a direct attack on existing managers; rather, they were in harmony with the approach taken by managers in the larger private enterprises and those operating in government and the armed services. This is not surprising because, by and large, they and Fayol were educated in the *grandes écoles* and shared a common intellectual approach. In addition, Fayol did not generally try to impose his ideas directly on individual organisations. Instead, he preferred to influence managers indirectly through a process of education. In the light of the reaction in America to Taylor's attitude, many would consider this a wise move.

Though there were attempts in France to promote *'Fayolisme'* in opposition to Taylorism, Fayol rejected this, preferring to see them as complementary (Sheldrake, 1996). As Urwick (1949: 9–10) commented in the Introduction to the English version of Fayol's book on *General and Industrial Management*:

The work of Taylor and Fayol was, of course, essentially complementary. They both realized that the problem of personnel and its management at all levels is the key to industrial success. Both applied scientific method to this problem. That Taylor worked primarily at the operative level, from the bottom of the industrial hierarchy upwards, while Fayol concentrated on the managing director and worked downwards, was merely a reflection of their very different careers.

The USA and France were not the only countries where developments in management practice and thought were being studied and documented. In Germany, at this time, Max Weber was charting the growth and merits of bureaucracy.

## Max Weber on bureaucracy

Weber was born in 1864 into a well-to-do Prussian family. He pursued an academic career, obtaining a doctorate in 1889. In 1894, he was appointed Professor of Political Economy at the University of Freiburg, and in 1896 he accepted the Chair in Economics at Heidelberg. Unfortunately, in 1897, he suffered a mental break-down which plagued him for many years. He resigned from his university post and spent much of his time travelling in Europe and the USA. He also moved the focus of his academic studies from economics to sociology.

Weber was an ardent German nationalist, and, at the age of 50, he volunteered for military service in the First World War. Until his honourable discharge in 1915, he was responsible for establishing and running nine military hospitals. Despite this, he was a fierce and open critic of the Kaiser, whom he accused of being a dilettante hiding behind the divine right of kings. He believed that Germany's problems at home and abroad could only be solved if the monarchy were replaced with a constitutional democracy. After the war, he became a member of the Commission that drew up the Constitution for the Weimar Republic, and once again took up university teaching, this time in Munich. Unfortunately, when he died in 1920, most of his work was unpublished and his papers were in a state of chaos. It was not until the 1930s that his work began to be organised and published, and it was the 1940s before his work on bureaucracy was published in English (Sheldrake, 1996; Weber, 1948).

There is a considerable affinity between Weber's work on bureaucracy and Fayol's work on the principles of management. Both were concerned with the overall structuring of organisations, and the principles which guide senior managers in this task. Though a contemporary of Fayol and Taylor, it is unlikely that they were aware of his work on bureaucracy, though the reverse is possible (that he may have been aware of their work).

However, unlike Taylor and Fayol, Weber was never a practising manager. His observations on administrative structures and organisational effectiveness arose from his study of the development of Western civilisation. From this, Weber concluded that the rise of civilisation was a story of power and domination. He noted (Weber, 1948) that each social epoch was characterised by a different form of political rule, and that for a ruling elite to sustain its power and dominance, it was essential for them both to gain legitimacy and to develop an administrative apparatus to enforce and support their authority.

Weber (1947: 328) identified what he called 'three pure types of legitimate authority':

1 *Rational-legal*: resting on a belief in the 'legality' of patterns of normative rule, and the right of those elevated to authority under such rules to issue commands.

2 *Traditional*: resting on an established belief in the sanctity of immemorial traditions and the legitimacy of those exercising authority under them.

3 *Charismatic*: resting on devotion to the specific and exceptional sanctity, heroism or exemplary character of an individual person, and of the normative patterns or order revealed or ordained by them.

For Weber, legitimacy is central to almost all systems of authority. He argued that there are five concepts on which rational-legal authority is based. According to Albrow (1970: 43), these are as follows:

1 That a legal code can be established which can claim obedience from members of the organization.

2 That the law is a system of abstract rules which are applied in particular cases, and that administration looks after the interests of the organization within the limits of the law.

3 That the man exercising authority also obeys this impersonal law.

4 That only *qua* [in the capacity of] member does the member obey the law.

5 That obedience is due not to the person who holds authority but to the impersonal order which has granted him his position.

Weber argued that, in the context of the rational-legal authority structures which prevailed in Western societies in the early twentieth century, the bureaucratic approach to organisation was the most appropriate and efficient. Under bureaucracy, laws, rules, procedures and predefined routines are dominant and not subject to the vagaries and preferences of individuals. They give form to a clearly defined system of administration – whether it be public administration, such as a government department dealing with pensions and social security payments, or private administration, such as an insurance company – where the execution of routine, pre-programmed procedures is all-important. Weber considered this approach to be both appropriate, because it was the ideal tool for a centralised administration where the legitimacy of those in power was underpinned by the rule of law; and efficient, because the bureaucratic approach mechanises the process of administration in the same way that machines automate the production process in factories.

Weber frequently asserted that the development of bureaucracy eliminates human fallibility:

Its [bureaucracy's] specific nature, which is welcomed by capitalism, develops the more perfectly the more bureaucracy is 'dehumanised', the more completely it succeeds in eliminating from official business, love, hatred, and all purely personal, irrational and emotional elements which escape calculation. (Weber, 1948: 215–16)

Bureaucracy is characterised by the division of labour, a clear hierarchical authority structure, formal and unbiased selection procedures, employment decisions based on merit, career tracks for employees, detailed rules and regulations, impersonal relationships, and a distinct separation of members' organisational and personal lives. It must, however, be borne in mind that Weber's bureaucratic model (or 'ideal' organisation), though inspired by developments in Germany at the time, was a hypothetical rather than a factual description of how most organisations were structured. It was his view of the characteristics that organisations should exhibit in modern societies based on rationality and law. How Weber saw these organisational characteristics supporting and reproducing rational-legal authority is best seen by contrasting them with the traditional administrative forms based on patronage (*see* Table 1.1) (Weber, 1947 and 1948).

For Weber, therefore, bureaucracy provided a rational-legal form of organisation which distinguished itself from, and eradicated the faults and unfairness of, previous administrative forms by its mechanical adherence to set rules, procedures and patterns of authority. It removed the system of patronage and eliminated human variability, replacing it by the rule of law. In Weber's view, the principles of bureaucracy, especially the legitimation of authority and the subordination of all in the organisation to the same rules and procedures, were universally applicable to all organisations, big or small, public or private, industrial or commercial.

It can be seen that Weber's belief in the standardisation of, and obedience by all to, rules and procedures is the counterpart of the standardisation of production techniques advocated by Taylor and akin to the principles of administrative management prescribed by Fayol. Also, just as the work of Taylor and Fayol can be understood as representing a combination of their backgrounds and the state of the societies in which they lived, so is this the case with Weber. The Prussian bureaucratic tradition dominated both the public, and to a large extent, the private sectors in Germany. It was seen by the ruling elite as the ideal method for ensuring that the objectives of the state and the objectives of individual enterprises were adhered to. It also fitted in with the Prussian militaristic tradition of unquestioning obedience to superiors, which was a prevalent view in both public and private organisations. It must be remembered, of course, that the state and private enterprises in Germany were not primarily obsessed with profitability or individual aggrandisement. The key objective was to build Germany as the premier military and industrial power in Europe. Competition at the level of the individual or the individual enterprise was a concept that carried much less force in Germany, and even France, than in the USA or Britain. German industry and government were more concerned with ensuring that all sections of the country pulled in the same direction. Where competition threatened this, it was eliminated by the state, either by direct intervention, such as nationalisation of the railways, or by indirect intervention, through the formation of cartels and

**Table 1.1 Comparison of Weber's concept of rational-legal authority with traditional authority**

| Characteristics of rational-legal authority | Characteristics of traditional authority |
| --- | --- |
| Areas of jurisdiction are clearly specified: the regular activities required of personnel are allocated in a fixed way as official duties. | The allocation of labour is not defined, but depends on assignments made by the leader, which can be changed at any time. |
| The organisation of offices follows the principle of hierarchy: each lower office is controlled and supervised by a higher one. However, the scope of authority of superiors over subordinates is circumscribed, and lower offices enjoy a right of appeal. | Authority relations are diffuse, being based on personal loyalty, and are not ordered into clear hierarchies. |
| An intentionally established system of abstract rules governs official decisions and actions. These rules are relatively stable and exhaustive, and can be learned. Decisions are recorded in permanent files. | General rules of administration either do not exist or are vaguely stated, ill-defined, and subject to change at the whim of the leader. No attempt is made to keep permanent records of transactions. |
| The 'means of production or administration' (e.g. tools and equipment or rights and privileges) belong to the office, not the office-holder, and may not be appropriated. Personal property is clearly separated from official property, and working space from living quarters. | There is no separation of a ruler's personal household business from the larger 'public' business under their direction. |
| Officials are personally free, selected on the basis of technical qualifications, appointed to office (not elected), and recompensed by salary. | Officials are often selected from among those who are personally dependent on the leader, e.g. slaves, serfs, and relatives. Selection is governed by arbitrary criteria, and remuneration often takes the form of benefices – rights granted to individuals which, for instance, allow them access to the ruler's stores, or give them grants of land from which they can appropriate the fees or taxes. Benefices, like fiefs in feudalistic systems, may become hereditary and sometimes are bought and sold. |
| Employment by the organisation constitutes a career for officials. An official is a full-time employee and looks forward to a lifelong career in the agency. After a trial period, he or she gains tenure of position and is protected against arbitrary dismissal. | Officials serve at the pleasure of the leader, and so lack clear expectations about the future and security of tenure. |

monopolies. In carrying out this grand plan for German development, bureaucracy was found to be the ideal tool.

In Germany, the advent of the First World War highlighted the incompatibility between industrial bureaucracies based on the rule of law, and a government run on autocratic lines for militaristic ends. Weber argued that the rule of law applied not only to the operation of organisations but also, and more importantly, to the running of society. If society was not based on the rule of law, if democratically elected governments did not hold power, then the authority of those who ruled must be called into question. This was the basis of Weber's attacks on the Kaiser and the military during the First World War. He believed that, in the modern age, rational-legal authority, based on democratically elected governments and laws governing property rights, was the best and most effective way for society and organisations to be governed. For Weber, the rise of bureaucracy and the rise of liberal democracy went hand in hand.

As can be seen, bureaucracy did not need a Taylor or a Fayol to develop or promote it; it already existed, was accepted by management, and was prospering, in Germany and other advanced countries, especially in the public sector. What Weber did was to give it intellectual respectability by arguing that it was particularly suited to the needs of (what he saw as) the rational, secular and increasingly democratic societies that were becoming the norm in the Western world.

The appeal of bureaucracy, to governments and large organisations at least, can be seen in the way that bureaucracy is an ever-present and pervasive feature of modern life. However, it would be misleading to give the impression that its development in Germany, or elsewhere, was uncontentious. In Germany, in the early years of this century, it tended to be the purpose and consequences of bureaucracy rather than its principles that were attacked. At an overall political level, the growth of radical parties of the left reflected growing concerns over Germany's military aims and the state's concomitant close links with business, and in particular its perceived preference for aiding capital rather than labour. At the level of the individual enterprise, the growth of militant trade unions, often linked to the parties of the left, reflected the growing frustration of workers who resented the autocratic approach of management and its resistance to collective bargaining.

## CONCLUSIONS

It is not an inevitable fact of life that modern societies are characterised by organisations, of all shapes and sizes; this is the product of a particular combination of circumstances. The rise of capitalism in Britain and other European countries in the seventeenth and eighteenth centuries created new opportunities and new problems which could not be accommodated under the old order. The result was a move away from self-sufficient, autonomous, individual units to collective units of production controlled by an entrepreneur. It was entrepreneurs who, in pursuit of ever greater profits, created the factory system in Britain which became the basis of modern organisational life. The central features of the factory system were autocratic control, division of labour, and antagonistic relations between management and labour.

Though starting at different times and moving at their own pace, most European countries, followed by the USA, adopted and adapted the British approach to industrial organisation. However, as the nineteenth century progressed, the nature of industrialisation began to vary from country to country, reflecting the unique circumstances and needs of the host society. In Germany, the objectives of the state determined that large-scale public and private bureaucracies became the norm. In France, the state also played a role in shaping industrialisation, but in this case it was to perpetuate small-scale, inefficient business and agricultural operations. In both countries, individual pursuit of profit maximisation was less important than in either Britain or the USA. In Scandinavia, especially Denmark, the emergence of a more collective and less ruthless approach to industrialisation could be discerned.

Nevertheless, in the transition from a subsistence economy to a money economy, one clear image stands out above all else: the antagonism between employers and employees. The factory did not emerge because it was a more efficient means of production *per se*; it emerged because it offered entrepreneurs a more effective means of controlling labour. This meant that the factory was also a battleground, with employers seeking to impose new conditions and technologies, and workers – when they could – attempting to resist change.

As the nineteenth century progressed, managers became increasingly aware of the shortcomings of their *ad hoc* and inconsistent responses to new challenges and opportunities, and the counter-productive nature of resistance to change. The need for a more coherent approach to structuring and running organisations was required: one that legitimated managerial authority, especially to initiate change. This crystallised into the Classical approach.

Though writing in different countries and from different perspectives, the proponents of what later came to be known as the Classical approach all adopted a similar perspective towards what they saw as one of the main issues for modern societies: how to create organisations that efficiently and effectively pursue their objectives. Taylor, supported by the work of the Gilbreths and others, concentrated very much on the operational level, arguing for his 'scientific' method of analysing, designing and managing jobs. However, his insistence on the consistent and unbiased application of scientific principles, and the emphasis he placed on all members of an organisation obeying rules and procedures, were as much a challenge to managerial beliefs and behaviour as they were to the beliefs and behaviour of shopfloor workers. Fayol, in contrast, was concerned less with operational issues and more with the overall administration and control of organisations. Therefore, to an extent, his could be called a top-down approach, whilst Taylor was working from the bottom up. Weber sought to put organisations in a wider historical and societal context, bringing together both the detailed tasks to be carried out in organisations and the general principles governing them.

Though Taylor's approach required a radical change in managerial behaviour and a significant increase in organisational bureaucracy, the objective of his system was to improve the productivity and efficiency with which manual workers carried out the tasks ordained for them by management. Everything else was, as Taylor would have put it, the outcome of pursuing this objective to its logical conclusion. The need to provide managers with rules and systems for running the entire enterprise, and not just that part of it dealing with manual labour, was a means of achieving his objective rather than a prime aim. This is where the work of Fayol and Weber has proved so crucial: together with Taylor's work, it comprises a system for running an entire business in a coherent, standardised and consistent fashion.

Therefore, taken together, their views are, broadly, complementary, and reflect an approach to organisations and people based upon a number of basic assumptions:

- There is a 'one best way' for all organisations to be structured and operate.
- This approach is founded on the rule of law and legitimate managerial authority.
- Organisations are rational entities: collectivities consistently and effectively pursuing rational goals.
- People are motivated to work solely by financial reward.
- Human fallibility and emotions, at all levels in the organisation, should be eliminated because they threaten the consistent application of the rule of law and the efficient pursuit of goals.
- For this reason, the most appropriate form of job design is achieved through the use of the hierarchical and horizontal division of labour to create narrowly focused jobs encased in tight standardised procedures and rules, which remove discretion, dictate what job-holders do and how they do it, and which allow their work to be closely monitored and controlled by their direct superiors.

Seen in the context of the early twentieth century, when there appeared to be a substantial questioning of – and challenge to – managerial authority by workers, the Classical approach had many merits: not least in its attempt to replace arbitrary and capricious management with rules and procedures that apply equally to everyone in the organisation.

Similarly, it is important to see this work in terms of what went before. Weber explicitly drew on history to support his views; the historical debts of Taylor and Fayol, though not openly acknowledged in their work, are clearly there. From Smith, through Wedgwood, Boulton and Watt, Babbage and Ure can be traced key elements of the Classical approach: the division of labour, the distrust of human variability, the need for written rules, procedures and records, and the need for rational and consistent management and objectives. Parallel to these are key themes that run through other aspects of nineteenth century life: the search for the rational, scientific, universal principles that govern the natural world, the belief in the Protestant work ethic, the emergence of Social Darwinism, the greater democratisation of societies, and the gradual reduction of laws favouring one class or group over another.

All these strands coalesced – not always neatly – in the Classical approach, creating (in retrospect) the first real and consistent attempt at a theory, a set of guidelines, for constructing, managing and changing organisations. However, given that it grew out of and was designed to meet particular circumstances, so its appropriateness began to be questioned and criticised as these circumstances changed.

Taylor and his adherents have been criticised both for their lack of scientific rigour and for their one-dimensional view of human motivation (Burnes, 1989; Kelly, 1982a, b). Indeed, as Rose (1988) argued, Taylor portrayed human beings as 'greedy robots': indifferent to fatigue, boredom, loneliness and pain, driven solely by monetary incentive. For Taylor, material incentives are the only effective incentives to work. For this reason, he opposed everything else in the workplace which, in his opinion, undermined managers' attempts to introduce individual incentive systems, whether it be friendships, group loyalty, trade unions, or whatever. Taylor has also been attacked for over-emphasising the merits of the division of labour. The critics' argument is that the creation of jobs which have little intrinsic satisfaction leads to poor morale, low motivation and alienation. Indeed, such are the forces aligned against Scientific Management that it is difficult to find a facet of it that has not been attacked (Littler, 1978; Locke, 1982).

Fayol has been attacked on three fronts: first, that his principles are mere truisms; second, that they are based on questionable premises; and third, that the principles occur in pairs or clusters of contradictory statements (Massie, 1965; Simon, 1957). In addition, Fayol, like Taylor, can be construed as being against trade unions. Certainly, he believed in the pre-eminence of management and its right to make changes how and when it wanted, so long as these were based on his general principles. He also believed, unlike Taylor, that management and labour were fundamentally in conflict. Therefore, his recommendations were partly aimed at eliminating the conditions in which trade unions can flourish, in the interests of his overall aim of establishing the legitimacy of managers to manage.

Weber's arguments for bureaucracy have also received criticism. For instance, Udy (1959) questioned Weber's assertion that bureaucracies are necessarily rational, whilst Parsons (1947) suggested that Weber puts forward contradictory arguments for the basis of authority within bureaucracies. Robbins (1987) pointed out that bureaucracy is most frequently attacked for encouraging goal displacement:

- Rules become ends in themselves rather than means to the ends they were designed to achieve.
- Specialisation and differentiation create sub-units with different goals which then become primary to the sub-unit members. Not only does this lead to conflict between sub-units, but the accomplishment of sub-unit goals becomes more important than achieving the organisation's overall goals.

- Rules and regulations become interpreted as setting minimum standards of performance rather than identifying unacceptable behaviour. Staff can become apathetic and merely perform the bare minimum of work.
- The unthinking and rigid application of standardised rules and procedures can lead to their being applied in inappropriate situations, with dysfunctional consequences.

Robbins (1987) also pointed out that bureaucracy can alienate both employees and customers or clients. For the former, being treated as mere cogs in a machine leads to a sense of powerlessness and irrelevance. For the latter, being presented with a rigid and faceless organisation, which appears to serve its own ends rather than those of its customers or clients, can be frustrating and, when the provision of welfare services is involved, even heart-breaking. Mullins (1993) also pointed out that bureaucracy is often associated with secrecy and attempts to prevent legitimate public access to vital information on the performance of government and large organisations. Weber's work on bureaucracy has also received criticism because of his lack of attention to informal and social processes, in particular the way that individuals and groups can and do struggle to promote their own interests and goals above those of others in the organisation (Crozier, 1964).

It should also be noted that, though broadly complementary, the approaches of Taylor, Fayol and Weber were developed separately and with different objectives in mind. There are, consequently, tensions and inconsistencies between them. Fayol stresses the importance of *esprit de corps* and individual initiative. Taylor and Weber would find the former irrelevant and the latter dangerous. Likewise, the unchanging rigidity of bureaucracy, as portrayed by Weber, leaves little scope for the continuous search for improvement in methods and productivity advocated by Taylor and Fayol. Taylor's advocacy of functional supervision, which in effect meant a worker being responsible to different supervisors for different aspects of his/her job (some four or five supervisors in total), would have been viewed as a threat to discipline and good order by both Weber and Fayol, who were fierce advocates of unity of command – each worker should receive orders from one superior only.

One of the main criticisms of the Classical approach as a whole is that its view of people is negative. Bennis (1959: 263) called the Classical perspective one of 'organisations without people' because it is founded on the belief that people can be reduced to the level of cogs in a machine. It can also be argued that, in any case, it is impossible to remove the element of human variability from the running of organisations and that attempts to do so are counter-productive. Rather than making people work more efficiently in pursuit of organisational goals, it alienates them from their work and makes them resentful of it (Mayo, 1933). This is a point developed by Argyris (1964), who argued that the Classical approach restricts the psychological growth of individuals and causes feelings of failure, frustration and conflict. Instead, he believes that the organisational environment should provide a significant degree of individual responsibility and self-control; commitment to the goals of the organisation; productiveness and work; and an opportunity for individuals to apply their full abilities. These developed as central issues for the proponents of the Human Relations approach, which emerged in the 1930s as a reaction to the 'de-humanised' Classical approach. This, together with Contingency Theory – the third approach to organisations to emerge in the twentieth century – will be discussed in the next chapter.

## TEST YOUR LEARNING

### Short answer questions

1 What was Adam Smith's main contribution to the development of work organisation?
2 What was the putting-out system?
3 What was the main impetus for the move to the factory system?
4 What are the key tenets of Scientific Management?
5 According to Fayol, what are the prime functions of a manager?
6 What was Weber's main justification for advocating bureaucracy?
7 What are the implications for organisational change of the Classical approach?

### Essay questions

1 To what extent can the move to the factory system be seen as a clash of cultures as averse to a clash of economic systems?
2 Evaluate the case for seeing the work of Taylor, Fayol and Weber as forming a coherent school of thought.

## SUGGESTED FURTHER READING

1 Wilson, JF (1995). *British Business History*, 1720–1994. Manchester University Press: Manchester.
Despite its title, this book neither confines itself to British history nor examines business in a narrow sense. Amongst other things, John Wilson's book provides an excellent review of the development of management in Britain, Germany, Japan and the USA from the early days of the Industrial Revolution.

2 Pollard, S (1965). *The Genesis of Modern Management*. Pelican: Harmondsworth.
Though published over 30 years ago, Sydney Pollard's book still provides one of the best descriptions of the development of management, and the reaction of labour, in the eighteenth and nineteenth centuries.

3 Rose, M (1988). *Industrial Behaviour*. Penguin: Harmondsworth.
Michael Rose's book provides a well-researched and thorough account of the rise and development of Scientific Management.

4 Sheldrake, J (1996). *Management Theory: From Taylorism to Japanization*. International Thompson Business Press: London.
Michael Sheldrake gives an excellent summary of the lives and contributions of Taylor, Fayol and Weber.

# Chapter 2

# DEVELOPMENTS IN ORGANISATION THEORY

## From certainty to contingency

### Learning objectives

After studying this chapter, you should be able to:

1 understand the reasons for the emergence of the Human Relations approach;

2 identify the key features and key proponents of the Human Relations approach;

3 list the advantages and disadvantages of the Human Relations approach;

4 describe the differences between the Human Relations approach and the Classical approach to organisational design;

5 discuss the reasons for the emergence and popularity of Contingency Theory;

6 identify the key features and key proponents of Contingency Theory;

7 state the advantages and disadvantages of Contingency Theory;

8 appreciate how Contingency Theory seeks to incorporate both the Classical and Human Relations approaches;

9 recognise the implications for organisational change of the Human Relations approach and Contingency Theory.

## INTRODUCTION

The orthodoxy of the 1980s and 1990s, fostered by influential writers such as Tom Peters, Rosabeth Moss Kanter and Charles Handy, was that organisations had to become smaller and more focused in order to increase their competitiveness (Handy, 1989; Kanter, 1989; Peters, 1993). In support of this view, there have been many examples of companies divesting themselves of non-core activities. The move by BAT to split its insurance operations from its tobacco business and merge them with Zurich follows a similar logic. There have even been instances of conglomerates, such as Hanson Trust and Lonrho, dismembering themselves in their entirety.

Nevertheless, as it has been in the past, the trend in reality still seems to favour expansion, mainly through acquisitions and mergers, rather than contraction

(Burton *et al*, 1996). Indeed, the trend seems to be more pronounced than ever. On a single day in 1997, Western Europe saw some $130 billion of mergers and acquisitions, whereas the entire total for the previous year was only $250 billion. In America, Warner (1997: 3) commented that:

> To find a similar period of economic change and merger frenzy, you might need to go back all the way to the 1890s ... Out of it were born such companies as Standard Oil and American Tobacco, the very prototypes of the vertically integrated modern corporation.

Nor does the pace of change appear to be slackening. In the motor industry, the merger of Daimler-Benz and Chrysler in 1998 created the fifth largest vehicle company in the world, with a turnover of $130 billion. In the same year, the takeover of Rolls Royce by Volkswagen shows that Volkswagen's acquisitiveness has not diminished as it attempts to transform itself into a global company. General Motors, despite Tom Peters' (1989) frequent criticisms, still remains the world's biggest motor vehicle company, with a turnover of $178 billion, up over 40 per cent in the last ten years. In the financial field, the $160 billion merger of Citicorp and Travellers is just the largest example of a positive frenzy of merger activity. In the UK, the de-mutualisation of building societies and their takeover by larger financial institutions is another example of the same forces at work. The same can be seen in the rest of the European financial services industry where, in advance of the Euro, cross-border mergers were especially prevalent. The same 'urge to merge' seems present in all industries; the coming together of Guinness and GrandMet to form one of the world's largest food and drink companies is another example. Even the on–off merger of Glaxo and SmithKline Beecham, which finally materialised in 2000, shows the shape of things to come.

Though each merger or acquisition has its own rationale, the underlying motives appear to be a combination of the forces of globalisation, technological evolution and changes in government which are reshaping entire industries. Whether or not these changes will bring increased benefits to shareholders and customers is debatable (*The Economist*, 1998). However, what is clear is that those seeking to promote a trend towards smaller organisations will find little to encourage them in the private sector. The public sector, on the other hand, in the 1980s and early 1990s, appeared to offer more fertile ground for their ideas.

In the nineteenth century, the public sector in most advanced countries probably employed no more then a few tens of thousands and accounted for a relatively small percentage of GNP (gross national product). In the UK, for example, the public sector only employed around 16,000 civil servants in 1854. By the early 1990s, in the UK, it employed nearly five million people and accounted for nearly 40 per cent of GNP. Indeed, such is the size of the public sector that the National Health Service in Britain is Europe's largest employer, with almost one million staff and a turnover in excess of £40 billion (NHS Executive, 1999).

As with the private sector, the reasons for the growth of the public sector are many and varied. Probably the single biggest factor is the growth of welfare provision: health, pensions, unemployment benefits, etc. In most countries, these account for the largest proportion of government expenditure, although defence, education and support for industry are also big spenders.

Yet, from the early 1980s onwards, the growth in the size of the public sector began to be reversed. Beginning with the election of the first Thatcher government in the UK in 1979, there was a general attack on the size and purpose of government. This led to the privatisation and contracting-out of many functions. This tendency took hold in many European countries in the late 1980s, and, despite the election and re-election of a Democrat to the White House, found favour in the USA (Flynn, 1993; Osborne and Gaebler, 1992). However, the election of left(ish) governments in Europe seems to be reversing the trend towards downsizing and outsourcing the public sector. This is particularly the case in the UK, where the election of the Blair Government has seen the market mechanisms put in place by the previous Conservative governments being replaced with more collective mechanisms for controlling public services.

So, whilst there has been much talk and some evidence, in both the private and public sectors, of organisations becoming smaller and more focused, there is also a great deal of evidence to the contrary. It may be that the liking for smallness is a temporary fashion rather than a permanent trend; only time will tell. If, though, smallness does prove to be the shape of things to come, then the period dealt with in this chapter, the 1920s to 1960s, may well be looked back on as the golden age of organisational growth; when those who ran both public and private sector bodies became convinced of the need for and their ability to run ever larger organisations. This period also saw the further take-up and development of the Classical approach. In the public sector, and in large private sector concerns, bureaucracy was unquestionably seen as 'the one best way'. The other key element of the Classical approach, Scientific Management, was less well received. In the USA, the death of the irascible Taylor did much to overcome the early opposition to Scientific Management, especially among trade union leaders. However, despite its espousal by Lenin in Russia, it met with stiff resistance in Europe. In the 1930s, Scientific Management and a streamlined version, the Bedeaux system, were rejected by both unions and management in a large number of European countries (Carew, 1987; Rose, 1988).

Therefore, although the Classical school could claim some success, especially in the USA, there was much antagonism towards it. The growth of organisation size and complexity, and the lack of support for the Classical school (or at least the Tayloristic part of it), acted to spur both academics and practitioners to greater efforts to understand the activities of, and provide guidelines for, organisations. This could have led to the development and strengthening of the Classical approach, and clearly this did happen to an extent (see the work of Ralph Davis, 1928, on rational planning). However, as this chapter will show, what emerged were two new approaches to organisations: the Human Relations approach, which originated in the 1930s, and the Contingency approach, which was developed in the 1960s.

The first half of this chapter describes the Human Relations approach. This approach was a reaction against the mechanistic view of organisations and the pessimistic view of human nature put forward in the Classical approach. It attempted to reintroduce the human element into organisational life, and claim for itself the title of the 'one best way'. In particular, it contended that people have emotional as well as economic needs, and that organisations are co-operative systems which comprise informal structures and norms as well as formal ones. This left managers with something of a dilemma: which 'one best way' should they adopt, the Classical or Human Relations one?

As the second half of this chapter will show, it was in response to this dilemma that Contingency Theory developed in the 1960s. Contingency Theory began by questioning and rejecting the idea that there is a 'one best way' for *all* organisations. Instead, it argued for a 'one best way' for *each* organisation. It did not, therefore, reject the Classical approach and the Human Relations approach; instead it maintained that the structures and practices of an organisation are dependent (i.e. contingent) on the circumstances it faces. The main contingencies it proposed were environmental uncertainty and dependence, technology and organisation size. After discussing the merits and drawbacks of the Human Relations approach and Contingency Theory, the chapter concludes that neither appears to be the solution to all known organisational ills that their proponents claim. In particular, it is argued that both fail to reflect and explain the complexities of day-to-day organisational life.

## THE HUMAN RELATIONS APPROACH

Even while the Classical approach was still struggling to establish itself, the seeds of a new approach to organisational design were already being sown. The origins of what later became known as the Human Relations approach can be traced to studies on work fatigue carried out in Britain during the First World War and work in the USA, at the same time, on employee selection, which gave new insights into employee motivation (Burnes, 1989). This work was developed and extended in the 1920s by Myers (1934) in Britain and Mayo (1933) in the USA, providing new perspectives on organisational life. These studies gave substance to a growing suspicion that the Classical view of organisations as being peopled by human robots motivated by money was badly flawed. Indeed, in 1915, the United States Congress took a stand against the use of Taylor's techniques in their establishments – although Scientific Management was becoming more accepted in private industry and was beginning to cross national boundaries, not always successfully (Rose, 1988). Similarly, though the growth of bureaucracy was gathering pace, so too was people's antagonism towards faceless, machine-like organisations where employees and customers alike lost their individuality and became numbers.

In addition, as Davis and Canter (1955) argued, it is necessary to recognise that jobs and work organisation are social inventions put together to suit the specific needs and to reflect the culture, ideology and the governing concept or ethos of the time. Therefore, to understand the emergence of the Human Relations movement, it is necessary to be aware of the changes taking place in Western society prior to and just after the Second World War.

In the 1930s, in many countries, there was the emergence of a more collectivist ethos than had previously been the case. In the USA, this was brought about by the reaction to the Depression of the 1920s and 1930s. The election of F D Roosevelt and the advent of his 'New Deal' introduced a new element of collective provision and concern into a previously highly individualistic nation. It also heralded the advent of 'Big Government' in the USA. In Europe, this collectivist ethos led to greater social concern; collective provision was led by the Scandinavian countries, and reflected the election of social democratic governments and a general mood of co-operation rather than conflict in industry in these countries. Similar developments also became the cornerstone of the rebuilding of Western Germany after the end of the Second World War. The legacy of the collective effort needed to win the war was also evident in the UK with the construction of the Welfare State.

It was in the USA in the 1930s and 1940s that substantial evidence first emerged in print which challenged the Classical view of organisations and allowed the Human Relations approach to stand alongside, if not quite supersede, it. The main precepts of the Human Relations approach were almost diametrically opposed to those of the Classical approach. In particular, it argued the following points:

- *People are emotional rather than economic-rational beings.* Human needs are far more diverse and complex than the one-dimensional image that Taylor and his fellow travellers conceded. People's emotional and social needs can have more influence on their behaviour at work than financial incentives.

- *Organisations are co-operative, social systems rather than mechanical ones.* People seek to meet their emotional needs through the formation of informal but influential workplace social groups.

- *Organisations are composed of informal structures, rules and norms as well as formal practices and procedures.* These informal rules, patterns of behaviour and communication, norms and friendships are created by people to meet their own emotional needs. Because of this, they can have more influence on individual behaviour and performance, and ultimately on overall organisational performance, than the formal structure and control mechanisms laid down by management.

For these reasons, organisations can never be the predictable, well-oiled machines envisaged by the Classical approach. Therefore, in most respects, the Human Relations approach represents a distinct break from the ideas of the Classical school. However, in two important ways, similarities exist. The first is their shared belief in organisations as closed, changeless entities. Once organisations have structured themselves in accordance with the correct precepts, then, regardless of external or even internal developments, no further changes are necessary or desirable. This leads on to the second similarity: proponents of both believed they had discovered the 'one best way'; regardless of the type, nature or size of organisation, their precepts were the correct ones.

With that in mind, we can now begin to examine in detail the case for Human Relations. Despite the work of precursors, no one doubts that the Human Relations approach began in earnest with the famous Hawthorne Experiments.

## Elton Mayo (1880–1949) and the Hawthorne Experiments

Elton Mayo was born in Adelaide, Australia in 1880. He had a somewhat chequered career. He failed three times to qualify as a medical doctor, and eventually became a lecturer in logic, psychology and ethics at the University of Queensland in 1911. There he developed a strong interest in the political problems of industrial society, and a lifelong commitment to achieving social and industrial harmony. However, he was never very happy at Queensland and, in 1922, he emigrated to America. There, Mayo was fortunate in that his ideas on resolving industrial conflict attracted the attention of the Laura Spelman Rockefeller Memorial Foundation which funded his entire career at the Harvard Business School. In effect, this meant that Mayo could pursue his own research without let or hindrance from university authorities. This was a major factor in the single-mindedness and success with which he undertook his work.

Elton Mayo is considered by many as the founder and leading light of the Human Relations movement. On his retirement as Professor of Industrial Research at Harvard Business School in 1947, Mayo was one of the most celebrated social scientists of the age. In praise of his achievements, the business magazine *Fortune* wrote of him:

Scientist and practical clinician, Mayo speaks with a rare authority that has commanded attention in factories as well as Universities. His erudition extends through psychology, sociology, physiology, medicine and economics, and his experience comes from a lifelong first-hand study of industry. (Quoted in Smith, 1998: 222)

Much of his fame rested on the 'Hawthorne Experiments' carried out at Western Electric's Hawthorne Works in Chicago in the 1920s and 1930s. However, within 10 years of his departure from Harvard, his reputation was in tatters: his expertise as a researcher was seriously questioned, his work was criticised for being too 'managerialist' and, perhaps most importantly, his contribution to the Hawthorne Experiments was considered as no more than a public relations exercise for Western Electric (Rose, 1988; Sheldrake, 1996; Smith, 1998).

The Hawthorne Experiments, as Gillespie (1991: 1) commented:

...are still among the most frequently cited and most controversial experiments in the social sciences ... They are acclaimed as a landmark study in both sociology and psychology ... Surveys in the key developments in organization and management theory consistently note the seminal contribution of the experiments to their field.

Yet, for most of the 80 years since the Hawthorne Experiments were initiated, it has been difficult to identify Mayo's exact role (Smith, 1987). That the name of Elton Mayo is inextricably linked with the Hawthorne Experiments is undeniable. That Mayo publicised and was given credit for masterminding these is also undeniable. Until recently, though, key questions have remained unanswered: did Mayo design and implement the experiments himself? What was the role of his colleagues at Harvard? How frequently did he visit the Hawthorne Works? Now, with the availability of family records and other archival material, Smith (1998) claims to have answered Mayo's detractors and to have re-established him both as the key figure in the Hawthorne Experiments and as the dominant figure in the Human Relations movement. Nevertheless, given the vehemence of Mayo's critics (Rose, 1988), one suspects that the debate over the 'Mayo mystique' is not yet over.

Despite the difficulty in separating out the myth from the man, we should not let that undermine the significance of the Hawthorne work or what we know of Mayo and his colleagues' contribution, even if we cannot clearly identify who did what. The Hawthorne programme was originally devised by Western Electric's own industrial engineers in 1924. Western Electric was the manufacturing division of the American Telephone and Telegraph Company. The Hawthorne Works, which at the time employed some 30,000 people, was considered a prime example of the application of the mass production techniques and work organisation methods advocated by Frederick Taylor and Henry Ford. However, this was tempered by the company's personnel and welfare policies which provided pension, sickness and disability benefits, a share purchase plan, medical treatment, extensive recreational facilities and a system of worker representation. This example of 'welfare capitalism' had the twin aims of reducing worker dissatisfaction and resisting trade union influence (Sheldrake, 1996).

The first phase of the Hawthorne Experiments, which lasted on and off until 1927, was the Hawthorne Illumination Tests (HIT) which were designed to examine the effects of various levels of lighting on workers' productivity. The engineers established control and experimental groups: the latter were subject to different levels of illumination as they carried out their work whilst the lighting of the control group was left unchanged. At the outset this looked like a standard Scientific Management experiment in the mould of Taylor and the Gilbreths. What the engineers were expecting was a set of unambiguous results which would allow them to establish the 'one best' level of illumination. This did not happen and, instead, data began to emerge which challenged the very basis of Scientific Management.

The engineers had expected the performance of the experimental group to vary with increases and decreases in illumination and for an optimum level to be established, but as the illumination was varied, so output continued to increase. Indeed, output only decreased in the experimental group when the lighting became so dim that it was difficult to see. More puzzling still, output in the control group, where no changes were made, also increased.

In 1927 the company began the second phase of the Hawthorne Experiments. Building on the HIT work, the company wanted to establish the effects on productivity of increased rest periods, a shorter working day, a reduced working week, free refreshments, changes to payment systems, better and friendlier communication, and a relaxation in the customary discipline usually imposed by first line supervisors. The first group to be involved were six women in the Relay Assembly Test Room (RATR). As Gillespie (1991: 59) noted:

> [Their] privileged status and a modicum of control over work days brought about a strong identification with the test room among the workers ... With the introduction of refreshments during the morning rest period, the women's status soared higher still.

By 1929, productivity in the RATR group had increased by some 30 per cent. In the interim, the company also initiated a further series of experiments in which, from 1928 onwards, Elton Mayo and his colleagues were closely involved. In the years that followed, successive groups of workers were subjected to changes in hours, payment systems, rest periods, etc. The subsequent changes in output, and the reasons put forward for these, undermined many of the assumptions regarding organisations and human behaviour previously perceived as sacrosanct (Mayo, 1933; Roethlisberger and Dickson, 1938).

The experiments were monitored continuously; from this work, Mayo and his colleagues concluded that it was not the changes in working conditions that affected output, but the fact that those workers involved had been singled out for special attention. This acted to increase their morale and make them want to perform better. It was the very fact that they were being studied which produced the increased performance; this later became known as the 'Hawthorne Effect'. This accounted for the improved performance by the original HIT control group, even with no changes to the lighting in their area: they also felt 'special' because they were being studied. These findings led Mayo and his group to move the focus of their work away from the reaction of individual workers to changes in their working conditions. Instead, they began to investigate the role and behaviour of the 'informal' groups that workers themselves established, and the norms and attitudes of these groups.

As a result of this work, Mayo and his colleagues put forward two major propositions which came to form the core of the Human Relations approach. The first related to the importance of informal groups within the formal structure of organisations. The Western Electric studies demonstrated the need to see the work process as a collective, co-operative activity as averse to an individual, isolated one. The studies showed in particular the important effect that the informal, primary work group has on performance. These groups tend to develop their own norms, values and attitudes which enable them to exert strong social, peer group pressure on individuals within the group to conform to group norms, whether this be in relation to the pace of work or attitudes towards other groups and supervisors. Taylor, years before, had also noted the pressure that groups of workers could exert over their members to make them conform; however, he believed that this was abnormal behaviour which could be remedied by tight managerial control. What the Western Electric studies demonstrated was that far from being abnormal, such behaviour was perfectly normal.

The second proposition put forward by Mayo and his colleagues was that humans have a deep need for recognition, security and belonging. Rather than being purely economic beings, it was argued that the Hawthorne Experiments demonstrated that workers' performance and attitudes could be influenced more by their need for recognition and security, and also by the feeling of belonging engendered by informal groups. This latter point in particular reflected, in Mayo's view, a deep-seated desire by humans as social beings for intimacy, consistency and predictability. Where these social certainties were lacking, workers would deliberately seek to manufacture them by creating their own informal work groups. Therefore, rather than seeking to eradicate or undermine the workings of these informal groups, as Taylor had advocated, the Western Electric studies showed that management needed to gain the collaboration and co-operation of such groups if they were to get the best performance from workers.

It is generally agreed (Mullins, 1989; Rose, 1988) that the Western Electric studies had a dramatic effect on management and organisation theory. The studies ushered in an era where the Economic Man of the Classical approach was supplanted by Social Man. It was no longer possible for managers to ignore the effects of organisational structures and job design on work groups, employee attitudes and management–worker relations. The crucial issue became one of social relationships – Human Relations – in the workplace. In future, the focus of good management practice would shift to the importance of leadership and communication in order to win over employees. As the 1930s and 1940s progressed, other work began to emerge which both substantiated and broadened those findings.

## Chester Barnard (1886–1961) and co-operative systems

Chester Barnard was born in Malden, Massachusetts in 1886. On leaving school, he became a piano tuner, but later attended Harvard University where he studied economics. On leaving university, he went to work for the American Telephone and Telegraph Company, in whose subsidiary, Western Electric, the Hawthorne studies were carried out. He was initially employed as a statistician, but quickly rose to hold a number of senior executive positions including, by the age of 41, becoming President of the New Jersey Bell Telephone Company. He also established his credentials as a prolific writer and lecturer with strong links to a number of universities, including Harvard. On retiring in 1948, he became President of the Rockefeller Foundation.

Barnard is best known for his book *The Functions of the Executive* (1938) which has a comparable place in the Human Relations literature to that of Fayol's work in the literature of the Classical school. In this work, Barnard put forward the idea of organisations as co-operative systems. In so doing, this gave him a double claim to fame: not only did he draw attention to the co-operative nature of organisational life, but he was also one of the first to treat organisations as systems rather than machines. He was in frequent touch with Mayo and his colleagues at Harvard, and closely followed their work at Western Electric. Therefore, although *The Functions of the Executive* was a personal and idiosyncratic work, reflecting Barnard's own distinct views and opinions, it was far from being bereft of academic substance. Indeed, his book was the first systematic attempt in English (Weber's work on bureaucracy was still not translated into English at this time) to outline a theory of organisations as a whole. In this respect, Barnard can claim both to have made a substantial contribution to the Human Relations approach and to have laid the ground work for subsequent writers such as Selznick and Simon (Robbins, 1987; Scott, 1987).

Barnard had close links with Harvard Business School and, along with Elton Mayo, Talcott Parsons (who first translated Weber's work into English) and Joseph Schumpeter, was a member of the Harvard Pareto Circle. This group was established to discuss and promote the work of the Italian sociologist Vilfredo Pareto, whose writing placed great emphasis on social systems and social equilibrium (Sheldrake, 1996).

The influence of Pareto's social systems view can be seen in Barnard's depiction of organisations as co-operative systems. An organisation is a co-operative system, he argued, because without the willingness of its members to make contributions to and to pursue its goals, it cannot operate effectively. Like others who espoused the Human Relations approach, he believed co-operation could not be achieved solely by monetary incentives. Instead, he advocated a mixture of monetary and non-monetary inducements. Similarly, co-operation by itself would not be effective unless an organisation also possessed a common purpose: clear and realistic goals and objectives which the organisation's members could understand, relate to and pursue. Establishing this common purpose, in Barnard's opinion, had to be the responsibility of those at the top of the organisation, but achieving it required the co-operation of those at the bottom, and all levels in between. This leads to another of Barnard's assertions: the flow of authority is not from the top down but from the bottom up. He defined authority not as a property of management but as a response by subordinates to superiors. If subordinates did not respond willingly and appropriately, then no authority existed. In this example, as in many others, he both reflected the influence of and supported the findings of the Western Electric studies, which drew attention to the ability of workers through social groupings to facilitate or frustrate the will of management.

In order to avoid a negative response from workers, Barnard advocated systematic and purposeful communication. He saw communication, through both formal and informal structures, as being the key function of the executive. Indeed, he portrayed the organisation as a purposeful, co-ordinated system of communications linking all participants in a manner that not only encouraged the pursuit of the organisation's common purpose, but also legitimated the premises on which it was based. However, he argued that this does not happen automatically or accidentally; it is the product of effective leadership. This is why Barnard stressed the key role of the executive in leading the organisation by facilitating communication and motivating subordinates to high levels of performance; such developments could only come from the top. He also saw the executive as having a role in shaping and reinforcing the organisation's value systems or, as modern writers would put it, its culture.

Given the emphasis placed by Barnard on the setting and pursuit of clear objectives, and in his approach in general, there is a degree of overlap with the work of the Classical School. However, what significantly distinguishes him from them is his insistence on the non-rational, informal, interpersonal, and indeed moral basis of organisational life. His view of effective leadership also distinguishes him from the Classical school. Rather than seeing leadership as dependent on position, Barnard argued that successful leadership arose from the interplay between the individual leader, the followers and the context.

Above all, Barnard rejected the idea of material incentives being the only incentives to make people work purposefully. Indeed, he saw them as being 'weak incentives' which needed to be supported by other psychological and sociological motivators if organisations were to be successful in achieving their common purpose. In thus challenging the effectiveness of material incentives, he was to receive substantial support a few years later from a more academic source.

## Abraham Maslow's (1908–1970) hierarchy of needs

Abraham Maslow was born in Brooklyn, New York in 1908. He trained as a psychologist at the University of Wisconsin and, apart from a brief period working in the family business, spent his working life in academia. Maslow was one of the first to differentiate between and classify different types of human need. For Taylor and his adherents, there was only one form of need: material/monetary need. Mayo *et al* and Barnard took a different view; they drew a distinction between material and non-material needs, but made no distinction within these two categories. Maslow (1943) identified five distinct forms of human need which he placed in a hierarchical order. He argued that, beginning at the lowest level, a person had to satisfy substantially the needs at one level before they could move up the hierarchy and concentrate on 'higher order' needs.

In ascending order, the five levels in Maslow's hierarchy of needs are as follows:

- **Physiological needs**: hunger, thirst, sleep, etc.; only when these basic needs have been satisfied do other needs begin to emerge.
- **Safety needs**: the desire for security and protection against danger.
- **Social needs**: the need to belong, to gain love and affection; to be in the company of others, especially friends.
- **Esteem needs**: these reflect a person's desire to be respected – esteemed – for their achievements.

- **Self-actualisation needs**: self-actualisation is the need to achieve one's full potential. According to Maslow, this will vary from person to person and, indeed, may differ over time, as a person reaches a level of potential previously considered unattainable and so goes on to strive for new heights. For these reasons, self-actualisation is a continuously evolving process throughout a person's lifetime.

Maslow (1943: 383) recognised that there were weaknesses in his theory of needs: 'Since, in our society, basically-satisfied people are the exception, we do not know much about self-actualisation, either experimentally or clinically.' He accepted that the strength of the hierarchy might differ with individual circumstances – some people's aspirations may be so deadened by their experiences that they would be satisfied by having enough to eat. He also saw that cultural differences between societies could have an impact on the extent and order of needs. Nevertheless, he did believe that his theory was generally applicable and that where people's higher aspirations were thwarted or unmet, the result was likely to be frustration and de-motivation.

Though not designed specifically for organisational analysis, but rather in the context of life in general, it can be seen why Maslow's work was so readily accepted by proponents of the Human Relations approach. For them, it explained why in some situations Tayloristic incentives were effective, whilst in other situations, such as the Hawthorne Experiments, other factors proved more important.

Applying Maslow's hierarchy of needs to human behaviour in organisations, it can be seen that people will first of all be motivated by the desire to satisfy physiological needs through monetary rewards. However, once those have been substantially satisfied, workers will seek to satisfy – be motivated by – their safety needs, such as job security and welfare benefits. In a similar fashion, once safety needs are substantially met, these will fade into the background and social needs will come to the fore; people will want to be accepted as part of a group, to share common intents and aspirations with the group, to experience the bonds of friendship and loyalty. Clearly, these social needs played an important role in the Hawthorne Experiments, as did esteem needs. After social and esteem needs are substantially met, finally self-actualisation needs come to the fore. However, as mentioned above, the need for self-actualisation never wanes but tends to act as a continuing spur to further achievements.

Clearly, Maslow's work cannot be transferred fully into the organisational setting, given that the constraints on freedom of action imposed by most jobs do not allow individuals to approach, let alone attain, self-actualisation (Rose, 1988). Even very basic physiological needs are beyond the reach of many millions of people in the world. Nevertheless, in pointing to the negative effects of thwarting an individual's aspirations, and in distinguishing between types of intrinsic (non-material) and extrinsic (material) motivators, and arguing that, at any one time, it is the unmet needs which act as positive motivators, Maslow has had an enormous impact on job design and research (*see* Child, 1984; Smith *et al*, 1982). The influence of Maslow's theory of needs can be seen in the work of other exponents of Human Relations, especially Douglas McGregor.

## Douglas McGregor (1906–1964) and Theory X–Theory Y

Douglas McGregor was born in 1906. He received his doctorate in psychology from Harvard, and spent much of his working life at the Massachusetts Institute of Technology where, from 1954 until his death in 1964, he was the first Sloan Fellows Professor. McGregor is one of the most widely cited Human Relations writers. He developed his views from his personal experience and observations as an academic, consultant and university administrator rather than from empirical research.

In his book *The Human Side of Enterprise* (1960), McGregor argued that decisions taken by top managers on the best way to manage people were based on their assumptions about human nature. McGregor maintained that there are basically two commonly-held views of human nature: a negative view – Theory X; and a positive view – Theory Y. He believed that managers' behaviour towards their subordinates was based upon one or other of these views, both of which consist of a certain grouping of assumptions about human behaviour.

Theory X, which he believed dominated the literature and practice of management, consists of the following assumptions:

- The average person dislikes work and will avoid it wherever possible.
- Employees must be coerced, controlled or threatened with punishment if they are to perform as required.
- Most people try to avoid responsibility and will seek formal direction whenever possible.
- Workers place security above other factors relating to employment and will display little ambition.

Theory Y, on the other hand, comprises a group of assumptions that give a much more positive view of human nature:

- Most people can view work as being as natural as rest or play.
- Workers are capable of exercising self-direction and self-control.
- The average person will accept and even seek responsibility if they are committed to the objectives being pursued.
- Ingenuity, imagination, creativity and the ability to make good decisions are widely dispersed throughout the population and are not peculiar to managers.

Theory X and Theory Y are not statements about what people are actually like, but rather the general assumptions that managers, and the rest of us, hold about what people are like. The fact that such views may not have a base in reality is irrelevant if managers act as though they are true. Managers who adhere to Theory X will use a combination of stick and carrot methods to control their subordinates, and will construct organisations that restrict the individual's ability to exercise skill, discretion and control over their work. Those managers who adhere to Theory Y will adopt a more open and flexible style of management. They will create jobs that encourage workers to contribute towards organisational goals and allow them to exercise skill and responsibility, and where the emphasis will be on non-material incentives.

Obviously, Theory X is akin to the Classical view of human nature and organisational design, whereas Theory Y falls more in the Human Relations tradition. Though McGregor favoured Theory Y, he recognised that it could not be fully validated. Instead, he saw Theory Y as a challenge to the orthodoxy of Theory X and, as he put it (McGregor, 1960: 53), as an 'invitation to innovate'. He argued that there was nothing inevitable about which approach to adopt. The choice lies with managers; those who adhere to Theory X will create a situation where workers are only able and willing to pursue material needs (as Maslow observed). Such workers will be neither prepared nor in a position to contribute to the wider aims and objectives of the organisation that employs them. Managers who follow Theory Y precepts are likely to receive an entirely different response from their employees; workers will identify more clearly with the general interests of the organisation, and be more able and more willing to contribute to their achievement.

Though stressing the element of choice, McGregor, along with other Human Relations adherents, believed that changes in the nature of modern societies meant that organisations were moving, and should move, more in the direction of Theory Y.

## Warren Bennis (1925–) and the death of bureaucracy

By the 1950s and 1960s, the Human Relations approach and the values it espoused were in the ascendancy. One clear sign of this was the widely-held view in the 1960s that bureaucracy was dying and being replaced by more flexible, people-centred organisations which allowed and encouraged personal growth and development. One of the main exponents of this view is Warren Bennis.

Warren Bennis trained as an industrial psychologist and held a number of senior academic appointments, including Professor of Management at the University of Southern California. He is now best known for his work on leadership, and has acted as an adviser to four US presidents. In terms of the Human Relations movement, Bennis (1966) is credited with coining the phrase and making the case for 'the death of bureaucracy'. Bennis argued that every age develops an organisational form appropriate to its time. Bureaucracy was, in his view, appropriate for the first two-thirds of the twentieth century but not beyond that. He believed that bureaucracy emerged because its order, precision and impersonal nature was the correct antidote for the personal subjugation, cruelty, nepotism and capriciousness which passed for management during the Industrial Revolution.

Bureaucracy, he stated, emerged as a creative and wholesome response to the needs and values of the Victorian Age. Up to this point, there is little to distinguish

Bennis from Weber; however, he then went on to argue that the Victorian Age, and its needs, were dead and that new conditions were emerging to which bureaucracy was no longer suited. These conditions were as follows:

- **Rapid and unexpected change**: bureaucracy's strength lies in its ability to manage efficiently the routine and predictable; however, its pre-programmed rules and inflexibility make it unsuitable for the rapidly changing modern world.

- **Growth in size**: as organisations become larger, then bureaucratic structures become more complex and unwieldy, and less efficient.

- **Increasing diversity**: rapid growth, quick change and an increase in specialisation create the need for people with diverse and highly specialised skills; these specialists cannot easily or effectively be fitted within the standardised, pyramid structure of bureaucratic organisations.

- **Change in managerial behaviour**: the increasing adoption of the Human Relations approach by managers challenges the simplistic view of human nature put forward by the Classical school, which underpins bureaucracy. If coercion and threats administered in a depersonalised, mechanistic fashion are counter-productive as a way of controlling people in organisations, then the case for bureaucracy is severely diminished.

For Bennis and others such as Daniel Bell (1973), Alvin Toffler (1970) and E F Schumacher (1973), bureaucracy was rightly dying and being replaced by more diverse, flexible structures which could cope with the needs of the modern world.

## Job Design: operationalising Human Relations

Though intellectually strong, the Human Relations school remained operationally weak up to the 1950s and 1960s because, unlike the Classical school, it lacked a clear set of operational definitions and guidelines which allowed organisations to understand and implement it in the same way that they could with Scientific Management or bureaucracy. The advent of the Job Design movement in both the USA and Europe rectified this.

In the last 40 years, Job Design, or work humanisation as it has also been called, has become a powerful technique for rolling back the worst excesses of the Classical school, especially in the area of manual work, where Scientific Management and its clones have had such an impact. It was in America in the 1950s that Davis and Canter (1955), influenced by the work of the Human Relations school, questioned the Tayloristic basis of job design and work organisation. They suggested that it would be possible to design jobs which satisfied not only human needs but also organisational ones as well. They argued that increased job satisfaction and increased organisational performance went hand in hand. Since then many other writers, especially in Europe, have contributed to the development of Job Design theory (Davis *et al*, 1955; Guest, 1957; Hackman and Oldham, 1980; Likert, 1961; Trist *et al*, 1963; Warr, 1987).

Job Design is a direct attack on the precepts of the Classical approach. Whereas Taylorist tradition seeks to fit people to rigidly defined and controlled jobs, Job Design theorists argue that jobs can and should be fitted to human needs. The basic tenets of Job Design are relatively straightforward and follow on from the work of the proponents of the Human Relations approach, especially Maslow. It is argued that the Classical approach to jobs, with its emphasis on fragmenting jobs and reducing workers' autonomy and discretion, is counter-productive to both individual fulfilment and organisational performance. This is because boring, monotonous and meaningless jobs lead to poor mental health and feelings of dissatisfaction. In turn, this can result in lack of motivation, absenteeism, labour turnover and even industrial unrest (Arnold *et al*, 1998).

The solution to these problems follows from the analysis. If Tayloristic trends in job design are counter-productive, then they should be reversed and 'variety, task completeness and, above all, autonomy' should be built into jobs (Wall *et al*, 1984: 15). Such a move would promote workers' mental health and job satisfaction, bringing in turn increased motivation and performance. Just as Taylor believed his approach would benefit both workers and management, so too do the proponents of Job Design; the difference is that the benefit to the worker is personal fulfilment rather than increased wages, though in both systems the benefit to management is increased productivity (Friedman, 1961; Hackman and Lawler, 1971; Herzberg *et al*, 1959; Kelly, 1982a, b).

In practice, there are three main variants of Job Design:

- **Job enlargement**, which concentrates on increasing work variety by combining previously fragmented tasks together, or by rotating people between different types of work (Guest, 1957).

- **Job enrichment**, which concentrates on increasing workers' control over what they do by rearranging work so that some of the responsibilities previously borne by supervisors and support staff are given to individuals or, more often, semi-autonomous work groups (Herzberg, 1968).

- **Socio-technical systems theory**, which is a variant on Job Design involving a shift of focus from the individual job to the organisation as a whole. Socio-technical systems theory sees organisations as being composed of inter-dependent social and technical systems. The theory argues that there is little point in reorganising the social system in isolation from the technology being used, and that the level of performance achieved is dependent on the degree of fit between the two. This view sees technology as acting as a limitation on the scope for redesigning individual jobs (Davis, 1979; Dunphy and Griffiths, 1998; Trist *et al*, 1963). It follows, therefore, that Job Design must go hand-in-hand with technological change if it is to be successful.

Job Design emerged and attracted so much attention in the 1950s and 1960s for three main reasons:

1 The first flows from the work of Maslow (1943). As workers have become better educated and more affluent, their higher order needs such as self-actualisation have come to the fore. This means that in order to obtain the best performance from workers, jobs have to be designed to meet their psychological as well as their financial needs (Kelly, 1982b).

2 As markets have become more global, more competitive and more volatile, organisations need to be more responsive to the needs of their customers. This requires workers to be more flexible, possess a greater range of skills, and be able to work as part of a team rather than on an individual basis (Aglietta, 1979; Streeck, 1987).

3 Low unemployment in the 1950s, 1960s and 1970s led to high rates of labour turnover and absenteeism and endemic industrial unrest in industries and organisations with poor job design (Pruijt, 1997). This was certainly a major reason for Volvo's adoption of Job Design in the 1970s (*see* Chapter 10).

Since the 1950s, the USA and most European countries have initiated some form of officially sponsored 'Work Humanisation' programme. Not surprisingly, Norway and Sweden, with their traditions of industrial co-operation and demo-cracy, and what was West Germany, with its post-war commitment to industrial consensus and worker rights, have led the way in terms of financial and legal backing. Norway initiated the process with its Industrial Democracy Project (1962–1975). However, Sweden has probably been the most consistent, establishing the Work Environment Fund in 1972, with a budget of SEK 500 million per year, and creating the New Factories Programme at the same time. In 1976 it enacted the Co-determination Act, which ensures that trade unions have a right to be consulted on all major changes in working conditions. In 1977, the Swedish government created the Centre For Working Life (later the Institute For Work Life Research) to initiate and promote work humanisation. In the 1980s, it initiated the Swedish Development Programme (1982–1987), the Leadership, Organisation and Co-determination Programme (1985–1990), and the People, Data, Working Life Programme (1987–1992). Germany has seen a similarly consistent approach with the Humanisation of Working Life Programme (1974–1989) and the Work and Technology Programme (1989–). Germany also provided subsidies (around DM 100 million per year) to encourage the adoption of Job Design practices (Pruijt, 1997).

Some of the Job Design initiatives in these countries were inspired by Norwegian researchers such as Einar Thorsrud, who propagated the concept of semi-autonomous work groups. Others derived from the work on the socio-technical systems approach carried out by the Tavistock Institute in London (Auer and Riegler, 1990). In the UK, however, despite the presence of the Tavistock Institute and the establishment of the Work Research Unit in 1974, official backing has been noticeably lukewarm. Indeed, even the modest expenditure devoted to the Work Research Unit was cut back considerably in the 1980s, and the Unit has now been disbanded. Successive UK governments now seem to share the American view that 'Quality of Working Life' programmes are the purview of individual organisations rather than something to be promoted by government.

To a great degree, the popularity of Job Design seems to have fluctuated with employment levels. In the full-employment era of the 1950s and 1960s, governments and employers in the West seemed relatively receptive to it. However, with the recessions of the 1970s and 1980s, in most countries interest fell away. The exceptions were Sweden and Germany, both countries where unemployment remained relatively low in the 1970s and 1980s. Despite this, there can be little doubt that Job Design precepts have permeated Western society on a significant scale, and provide the main operational alternative to the Classical approach; however, as Pruijt (1997) noted, Tayloristic work practices have proved far more persistent than the proponents of Job Design had expected.

## The Human Relations approach: summary and criticisms

Though many tend to associate the Human Relations movement exclusively with the work of Mayo, the above shows that it is a much more diverse school of thought. Indeed, some have argued that to call it a school owes more to academic convenience than to reality (Rose, 1988). Nevertheless, there are continuing and overlapping themes in the work of the writers cited above which strongly bond them together. The first, and most obvious, is their almost total rejection of the Classical movement's mechanistic-rational approach towards people and organisation structures. As Dunphy and Griffiths (1998: 21) noted:

> In particular, they attacked the notion of employees as interchangeable parts, stressing that individual employees had different motivations; that the specialisation of labour and deskilling had created widespread alienation and demotivation; and that excessive supervision had crushed employee initiative.

The second and more fundamental feature is that whilst approaching the issues involved from different perspectives and emphasising separate aspects, they create an organisational model which possesses both coherence and plausibility.

The Human Relations model stresses three core elements:

- leadership and communication;
- intrinsic job motivation (as well as extrinsic rewards);
- organisation structures and practices which facilitate flexibility and involvement.

These elements are underpinned by two central propositions:

- *Organisations are complex social systems*, with both formal and informal social structures, and are not mechanical contrivances. Therefore, they cannot effectively be controlled by close supervision, rigid rules and purely economic incentives.

• *Human beings have emotional as well as economic needs*. Organisation and job structures need to be designed in such a way as to enable workers to meet both their material and non-material needs. Only in this way will workers perform efficiently and effectively in the best interests of the organisation.

It is not difficult to see why the Human Relations approach proved popular. In a period when many people were becoming increasingly worried about the growth of impersonal bureaucracies, it provided an attractive alternative. It is an approach which stresses that human beings are not mere cogs in a machine but that they have emotional needs: humans want to 'belong', achieve recognition, and develop and fulfil their potential. As mentioned earlier, the Depression of the 1930s and the Second World War and its aftermath created, in the USA and Europe, a greater sense of collectivism and community than had hitherto been the case; another reason why the Human Relations doctrine found such a ready audience. Also, implicitly, it offers an approach to change management that has a surprisingly modern ring to it. The stress on organisations having clear objectives, effective communication systems and proactive leadership, coupled with the need to obtain the willing co-operation of employees, are central to many modern approaches to change management.

Despite its attractiveness and plausibility, a substantial and often vitriolic body of opinion came to be ranged against the Human Relations approach in the 1950s and 1960s (Rose, 1988). Economists rejected the argument that non-material incentives have a potentially stronger motivating influence than material incentives. The emphasis placed by the proponents of Human Relations on people's need for 'togetherness' and 'belonging' was seen by some as a denial of individualism. Others thought that it belittled workers and portrayed them as irrational beings who, given the chance, would cling to management as a baby clings to its mother. It was also attacked from both a management and a trade union viewpoint. Some of the former felt that its supposedly powerful manipulative techniques were either useless or inoperable; whilst representatives of the latter saw Human Relations as a vehicle for manipulating labour, and undermining – or attempting to eliminate – trade unions. Sociologists criticised it for attempting a sociological analysis of organisations without taking into account the larger society within which each organisation exists (Kerr and Fisher, 1957; Landsberger, 1958; Rose, 1988; Whyte, 1960).

Many of the criticisms were clearly directed at the work of Mayo and his colleagues, including inconsistencies between them. Landsberger (1958), for example, was one of the first to point out the difference between Mayo's (1933) interpretations of the Hawthorne Experiments and those of his colleagues, Roethlisberger and Dickson (1938), though Smith (1998) disputes this and many of the other criticisms of Mayo. However, by no means were all the criticisms levelled at Mayo and his colleagues. Maslow's work, a key theoretical cornerstone of the Human Relations approach, was found to lack empirical substance when researchers attempted to validate it, and certainly later theories of motivation seem to adopt a different approach (Arnold *et al*, 1998; Hall and Nougaim, 1968; Lawler and Suttle, 1972; Sheldrake, 1996). Similarly, Bennis's views were attacked. The Aston Studies in the 1960s (Pugh *et al*, 1969a, b) showed that bureaucracy was growing rather than declining. Also, Miewald (1970) argued that Bennis did not understand the nature of bureaucracy; in his view, far from being rigid, it could and did adapt to changing and dynamic environments. Kelly (1982b) also attacked the proposition that increased job satisfaction leads to increased performance.

There is one further criticism of the Human Relations approach, one which it shares with the Classical approach: it claims for itself the title of the 'one best way'. Yet, the question was posed, how can any approach claim that there is only one method of structuring and managing organisations, and that it holds good for all organisations and for all time? Indeed, the seed of this criticism can be found in Bennis's (1966) work, where he argued that organisations in the last third of the twentieth century would experience rapid and unexpected change, continue to increase in size – with the problems of complexity which this brings, and become more diverse and specialised. Clearly, whilst not explicitly advocating it, Bennis was making the case for an approach to organisations which recognised not only that they face different situations but also that these are not stable over time. Similarly, Trist *et al*'s (1963) argument regarding the need to fit social systems to technical ones can also be seen as making a case for a situationalist approach to job design. Indeed, the most telling argument against the 'one best way' approach is that presented by Davis and Canter (1955), mentioned earlier. If jobs and work organisation are social inventions designed to meet the needs of societies and organisations at particular points in time, then there can never be a one best way for all organisations and for all times. What is needed, instead, is an approach that links approaches to work design to the particular context to which they are best suited. In the 1960s and 1970s, such an approach emerged.

## THE CONTINGENCY THEORY APPROACH

Contingency Theory emerged in the 1960s out of a number of now classic studies of organisation structure and management (*see* Child, 1984; Mullins, 1989; Scott, 1987). Since the 1970s, it has proved – as a theory at least – to be more influential than either the Classical or Human Relations approach. In essence, Contingency Theory is a rejection of the 'one best way' approach previously sought by managers and propounded by academics. In its place is substituted the view that the structure and operation of an organisation is dependent ('contingent') on the situational variables it faces – the main ones being environment, technology and size (Burnes, 1989). It follows from this that no two organisations will face exactly the same contingencies; therefore, as their situations are different, so too should their structures and operations be different. Consequently the 'one best way' for *all* organisations is replaced by the 'one best way' for *each* organisation.

As Scott (1987: 23) pointed out, one of the clear distinctions between Contingency Theory and its predecessors is as follows:

> The previous definitions tend to view the organisation as a closed system, separate from its environment and comprising a set of stable and easily identified participants. However, organisations are not closed systems, sealed off from their environments but are open to and dependent on flows of personnel and resources from outside.

As Robbins (1987) noted, there is wide agreement that the systems approach offers important insights into the working of an organisation. Systems theory is not new: it has been used in the natural and physical sciences for years. However, its application to business organisation only really emerged in the 1960s. The systems approach views the organisation both as a whole, and as part of a larger environment. The idea is that any part of an organisation's activities affects all other parts. Organisations, rather than being closed (as previous theories assumed), are viewed as open systems operating within a wider environment and having multiple channels of interaction (Mullins, 1993). Therefore, organisations are not in complete control of their own fate; they can be, and often are, affected by the environment in which they operate, and this can and does vary from organisation to organisation.

One of the earliest writers to lay the groundwork for Contingency Theorists was Herbert Simon. Writing in the 1940s (Simon, 1957), he criticised existing approaches as providing managers with nothing more than proverbs or lists of 'good practice' based on scant ideas, many of which contradicted each other. He argued that organisation theory needed to go beyond superficial and over-simplified precepts, and instead study the conditions under which competing principles could be applied.

Nevertheless, it was not until the 1960s that a considered approach emerged, which broke with the Classical and Human Relations movements' attempts to establish a universal approach suitable to all organisations. The former had concentrated on the formal structure and technical requirements of organisations, and had attempted to establish sets of general principles. The latter, the Human Relations movement, focused on the informal aspects of organisations and the psychological and social needs of their employees. As with the Classical approach, this produced lists of good practice and desired objectives, but it lacked precise guidance on how these should be applied.

Contingency Theorists adopted a different perspective, based on the premise that organisations are open systems whose internal operation and effectiveness is dependent upon the particular situational variables they face at any one time, and that these vary from organisation to organisation. This is consistent with evidence that not all organisations – or even all successful ones – have the same structure, and that even within organisations, different structural forms can be observed (Mintzberg, 1979). Though many situational variables, such as the age of the organisation and its history, have been put forward as influential in determining structure, it is generally agreed that the three most important contingencies are as follows:

- **Environmental uncertainty and dependence**. It is argued that the management of any organisation is undertaken in circumstances of uncertainty and dependence, both of which change over time. Uncertainty arises because of our inability ever to understand and control events fully, especially the actions of others, whether outside or inside an organisation. Because of this, forecasting is an inexact and hazardous enterprise. Similarly, the dependence of management upon the goodwill and support of others, whether they be internal or external groupings, makes an organisation vulnerable, and may in some circumstances even threaten its very existence. Levels of uncertainty and dependence will vary, but can never be totally eliminated, and must therefore be taken into account – treated as a contingency – when designing organisational structures and procedures (Burns and Stalker, 1961; Child, 1984; Lawrence and Lorsch, 1967; Pugh, 1984; Robbins, 1987; Thompson, 1967).

- **Technology**. The argument for technology being a key variable follows similar lines to that of environment. Organisations creating and providing different products and services use different technologies. Indeed, even those producing similar products may use differing techniques. Given that these technologies can vary from the large and expensive, such as a car assembly line, to the relatively small and cheap, such as a personal computer, the form of organisation necessary to ensure their efficient operation will also vary. If so, there is a need to treat technology as a contingent variable when structuring organisations. However, there are distinct variants of the case for technology, which reflect the different definitions of technology that theorists and researchers have employed. The two best-developed approaches are found in Woodward's (1965, 1970) studies of 'operations technology' and Perrow's (1967, 1970) analysis of 'materials technology'. The former refer to the equipping and sequencing of activities in an organisation's work flow, whilst the latter refer to the characteristics of the physical and informational materials used. Woodward's work tends to relate more to manufacturing organisations, whereas Perrow's is more generally applicable (Hickson *et al*, 1969; Thompson, 1967; Zwerman, 1970).

- **Size**. Some would argue that this is not just *a* key variable but *the* key variable. The case for size being a significant variable when designing organisations has a long antecedence within organisation theory, being first cited by Weber in the early part of this century when making the case for bureaucracy (Weber, 1947). The basic case is quite straightforward. It is argued that the structure and practices necessary for the efficient and effective operations of small organisations are not suitable for larger ones. For small organisations, centralised and personalised forms of control are claimed to be appropriate, but as organisations grow in size, more decentralised and impersonal structures and practices become more relevant (Blau, 1970; Mullins, 1989; Pugh *et al*, 1969a, b; Scott, 1987).

The main figures in developing and establishing Contingency Theory were academics in Britain and the USA, among whom the pioneers were Burns and Stalker.

## Tom Burns and George Macpherson Stalker: the importance of environment

The first major study to establish a relationship between organisations' environment and their structure was carried out by Burns and Stalker (1961) in Britain. They examined 20 firms in a variety of industries in order to assess how their structures responded to the environment in which they operated. Their findings were to have a major impact on organisation theory, and provide concrete evidence for rejecting a universal, 'one best way' approach to organisational structure and practice. They identified five different types of environment, based upon the level of uncertainty that was present, ranging from 'stable' to 'least predictable'. They also identified two basic or ideal forms of structure: 'Mechanistic' and 'Organic'. Their data showed that Mechanistic structures were more effective in stable environments, whilst Organic ones were better suited to less stable, less predictable environments.

The Mechanistic structure, which is akin to the Classical approach, has the following characteristics:

- the specialisation of tasks;
- closely defined duties, responsibilities and technical methods;
- a clear hierarchical structure with insistence on loyalty to the organisation and obedience to superiors.

In contrast, the Organic form, which has some resemblance to the Human Relations approach, is characterised as follows:

- much greater flexibility;
- adjustment and continual redefinition of tasks;
- a network structure of control, authority and communication;
- lateral consultation based on information and advice rather than instructions and decisions;
- commitment to the work group and its tasks;
- importance and prestige being determined by an individual's contribution to the tasks of their work group rather than their position in the hierarchy.

As can be seen, Burns and Stalker neither reject nor accept what went before. Instead, they argued that both the Classical approach and the Human Relations approach can be appropriate, but that this depends on the nature of the environment in which the organisation is operating. In this respect, they not only built on the past rather than rejecting it, but also restored some responsibility to managers. Instead of being called on to adopt blindly the orthodoxy with regard to structure, managers would in future have to assess their organisation and its needs, and then adopt the structure and practices suitable to its situation (Child, 1984; Mullins, 1989; Scott, 1987).

## Paul Lawrence and Jay Lorsch: the case for environment continued

Burns and Stalker's findings on the relationship between organisational environment and structure were examined and developed by a number of researchers in Europe and the USA. One of the most significant pieces of work was that carried out by Lawrence and Lorsch (1967) in the USA. Their work went beyond that of Burns and Stalker, in that they were interested not only in the relationship between environment and a company's overall structure, but also how individual departments within companies responded to, and organised themselves to cope with, aspects of the external environment that were of particular significance to them. They undertook a study of six firms in the plastics industry, followed by a further study of two firms in the container industry and two in the consumer foods industry. The structure of each of the firms was analysed in terms of its degree of 'differentiation' and 'integration'.

Differentiation refers to the degree to which managers and staff in their own functional departments see themselves as separate and have distinct practices, procedures and structures from others in the organisation. Integration refers to the level and form of collaboration that is necessary between departments in order to achieve their individual objectives within the environment in which the firm operates. Therefore, differentiation is the degree to which departments are distinct from each other, whilst integration refers to the degree to which they have common structures, procedures, practices and objectives at the operational level. Generally, the greater the interdependence among departments, the more integration is needed to co-ordinate their efforts in the best interests of the organisation as a whole; however, this may not always be easy to achieve. In a rapidly changing environment, the conditions faced by individual departments may differ greatly, and a high degree of differentiation may be necessary. In such a situation, the need for integration is also likely to be great, but the diversity and volatility of the environment are likely to make this difficult to achieve (Cummings and Huse, 1989).

In their study of the plastics industry, Lawrence and Lorsch (1967) found clear differentiation between key departments such as research, production and sales. Research departments were more concerned with long-term issues and were under pressure to produce new ideas and innovations. These departments, in Burns and Stalker's terminology, tended to adopt an Organic form of structure. Production departments on the other hand were, for obvious reasons, concerned with short-term performance targets relating to output, costs, quality and delivery. Such departments tended to operate in a fairly stable environment and had Mechanistic structures. Sales departments tended to fall in between research and production in terms of environment and structure. They operated in a moderately stable environment and were concerned more with getting production to meet deliveries than with long-term issues.

Whilst highlighting the degree of differentiation between key departments, the study also found that the degree of integration was critical to a firm's overall performance. Indeed, the two most successful firms in their sample were not only amongst the most highly differentiated, but also had the highest degree of integration. These findings were confirmed by their studies of the container and consumer foods industries, which showed that differentiation and integration in successful companies varies with the demands of the environment in which they operate. The more diverse and dynamic the environment, the more the successful organisation will be differentiated and highly integrated. In a more stable environment, the pressure for differentiation is less, but the need for integration remains. Therefore, Lawrence and Lorsch found that the most effective organisa-tions had an appropriate fit between the design and co-ordination of departments and the amount of environmental uncertainty they faced. However, the most successful firms were the ones which, whilst operating in an environment that required a high level of differentiation, also managed to achieve a high level of integration.

Clearly, in a situation where departments have dissimilar structures, practices and procedures, achieving integration is not easy or conflict-free. Indeed, in such situations, organisational politics can be rife. Lawrence and Lorsch found that the effective firms avoided such a situation by openly confronting conflict, and by working problems through in the context of the overall needs of the organisation. In addition, in firms which dealt successfully with conflict, the success of those responsible for achieving integration was based mainly on their knowledge and competence rather than their formal position. This was because their colleagues in the different departments respected and responded to their perceived understand-ing of the issues involved. It follows that to achieve high levels of integration and differentiation, an organisation cannot rely solely on the formal managerial hierarchy. This must be supplemented with liaison positions, task forces and teams, and other integrating mechanisms.

As with Burns and Stalker, Lawrence and Lorsch did not reject the Classical and Human Relations approaches *per se*, but instead saw them as alternative options, depending on the environment in which an organisation operates. In looking at the internal operations of organisations in this way, Lawrence and Lorsch raised the issue of dependence as well as uncertainty. This was a subject that James Thompson tackled in greater depth.

## James Thompson: environmental uncertainty and dependence

Thompson's (1967) influential work took the environmental perspective forward in three important ways. The first was to argue that although organisations are not rational entities, they strive to be so because it is in the interests of those who design and manage the organisation that its work be carried out as effectively and efficiently as possible. In order to achieve this, organisations attempt to insulate their productive core from the uncertainty of the environment. However, it is not possible to seal off all, or perhaps even any, parts of an organisation, given that it must be open to and interact with its environment if it is to secure resources and sell its products. This leads on to Thompson's second major contribution: different levels of an organisation may exhibit, and need, different structures and operate on a more rational or less rational basis. Thompson's third contribution was to recognise that organisational effectiveness was contingent not only on the level of external environmental uncertainty, but also on the degree of internal dependence present. This echoes Lawrence and Lorsch's argument for integration and differentiation; however, Thompson made this point much more explicitly and related it to different structural forms. He formulated a three-type classification in relation to internal dependence:

- **Pooled interdependence**: where each part of an organisation operates in a relatively autonomous manner, but by fulfilling their individual purposes they enable the organisation as a whole to function effectively.

- **Sequential interdependence**: where the outputs from one part of an organisation constitute the inputs for other parts of the system.

- **Reciprocal interdependence**: where overall effectiveness requires direct interaction between an organisation's separate parts.

Thompson went on to argue that the type of interdependence could be related to the degree of complexity present: simple organisations rely on pooled interdependence; more complex organisations demonstrate both pooled and sequential interdependence; and in the most complex organisations, all three forms of interdependence may be present. Thompson envisaged that each form of interdependence would require distinct methods for co-ordinating activities. Pooled interdependence would be characterised by standardisation through the use of rules and procedures. Sequential interdependence would require the use of detailed plans and written agreements, whilst reciprocal interdependence would achieve co-ordination by means of personal contact and informal agreements between members of those parts of the organisation involved.

Therefore, in a nutshell, Thompson's main arguments are as follows:

- Different sections of an organisation will be characterised by varying levels of complexity, rationality and formalisation, depending on the extent to which managers can shield them from the level of uncertainty present in the environment.

- The higher both the overall level of uncertainty and that faced by each area of an organisation, the greater will be the dependence of one area on another.

- As this interdependence increases, co-ordination through standardised procedures and planning mechanisms will become less effective and the need for more personal contact and informal interaction will grow.

- The more that co-ordination is achieved through mutual reciprocity in this manner, the less rational will be the operation of the organisation.

Thompson's work is of seminal importance in the development of organisation theory, not only because of the case he made for linking external uncertainty to internal dependence, but also, as a number of writers have observed (*see* Robbins, 1987; Scott, 1987), because of the attention he drew to the fact that technology can influence organisation structures as well as environmental factors. Thompson's contribution in this respect lay in creating a classification scheme for technology, and arguing that technology determines the selection of the specific structural arrangements for reducing the effect of uncertainty on the various functions of an organisation. The issue of technology and structure had been raised earlier in a major study by Joan Woodward published in 1965.

## Joan Woodward: the case for technology

In the 1960s, Joan Woodward carried out a major study of 100 UK manufacturing firms in south-east Essex, in order to establish the validity of the claims made by advocates of the Classical approach that the adoption of a bureaucratic-mechanistic structure was essential for organisational success (Woodward, 1965, 1970). After much work, Woodward concluded that no such correlation existed; what she found, however, was that the more successful companies adopted an organisational form that varied according to their main production technology. By technology, Woodward meant not only the machinery being used, but also the way it was organised, operated and integrated into a distinct production process. From her sample, she identified three distinct types of production technology, ranging from least to most complex:

- **Small batch (or unit) production**: where customers' requirements were for one-off or small-volume specialist products.

- **Large batch (or mass) production**: where standardised products were made in large numbers to meet a forecast demand.

- **Process production**: where production was in a continuous flow such as an oil refinery.

When the firms were grouped in this manner, a pattern emerged which showed that though they apparently differed considerably in terms of their organisational structure, many of the variations for the more successful firms could be explained by reference to the technology employed. Among firms engaged in small batch production, the most appropriate structure appeared to be one with relatively few hierarchical levels and wide middle management spans of control. Woodward noted that technology became more complex as firms moved from small batch to large batch and finally process production. In turn, structures became taller and more narrowly based, with smaller middle management and larger chief executive spans of control. Within each category of technology, the best-performing companies were those closest to the median in the type of structure adopted. Therefore, Woodward's work clearly established a link between technology, structure and success which ran counter to the notion that there was a 'one best way' for all organisations.

Though qualified by later studies (*see* Child, 1984; Handy, 1986; Smith *et al*, 1982), Woodward's research remains a milestone in the development of Contingency Theory. In particular, she demonstrated the need to take into account technological variables in designing organisations, especially in relation to spans of control. Nevertheless, a major drawback of her work was the difficulty of applying it to non-manufacturing companies. This was remedied by the work of Charles Perrow.

## Charles Perrow: the case for technology continued

In the USA, Charles Perrow (1967, 1970) extended Joan Woodward's work on technology and organisation structure by drawing attention to two major dimensions of technology:

- the extent to which the work being carried out is variable or predictable;
- the extent to which the technology can be analysed and categorised.

The first, *variability*, refers to the incidence of exceptional or unpredictable occurrences, and the extent to which these problems are familiar and can be easily dealt with, or are unique and difficult to solve. For example, an oil refinery should experience few non-routine occurrences, whilst an advertising agency will encounter many unpredictable and exceptional occurrences. The second major dimension, *analysis and categorisation*, refers to the extent to which the individual task functions can be broken down and tightly specified, and also whether problems can be solved by recourse to recognised, routine procedures or if non-routine procedures have to be invoked. Bringing these two major dimensions of technology together, Perrow constructed a technology continuum ranging from routine to non-routine. With the latter, there are a large number of exceptional occurrences requiring difficult and varied problem-solving techniques to overcome them. Routine technology, on the other hand, throws up few problems, which can be dealt with by recourse to standard, simple techniques.

Perrow argued that by classifying organisations according to their technology and predictability (routine to non-routine) of work tasks, it is then possible to identify the most effective form of structure in any given situation or for any activity. Perrow's routine–non-routine continuum can be equated with Burns and Stalker's mechanistic and organic dimensions for organisation structures. In routine situations, where few problems arise and those that do are easily dealt with, a mechanistic structure is more effective because of the stable and predictable nature of the situation. However, in a dynamic and unpredictable situation, a more flexible, organic form of structure will be more effective in dealing with the non-routine and difficult problems that occur. By formulating his work in this manner (i.e. by combining technology and predictability) it became possible to apply it to non-manufacturing situations. Therefore, Perrow's work both reinforced and extended Woodward's case for recognising technology as a key situational variable to be taken into account when designing organisations. Nevertheless, whilst Perrow was developing his ideas, a further group of researchers were making the case for yet another 'key' contingency – size.

## The Aston Group: the case for size

Though there are many proponents of the case for organisational size being a key contingency (*see* Child, 1984; Robbins, 1987), perhaps the earliest and most ardent were a group of British researchers based at the University of Aston in Birmingham (who became known as the Aston Group). In the 1960s, they carried out a series of studies to examine and identify the relationship between different forms of organisational structures and their determinants (*see* Pugh *et al*, 1969a, b). The Aston Group began in the early 1960s by examining a sample of 87 companies, and, as the work developed, further samples were added to their eventually very impressive database. In analysing their results, the Aston Group found that size was the most powerful predictor of specialisation, use of procedures and reliance on paperwork. In effect, what they found was that the larger the organisation, the more likely it was to adopt (and need) a mechanistic (bureaucratic) structure. The reverse was also found: the smaller the organisation, the more likely it was to adopt (and need) an organic (flexible) structure.

This was clearly a major finding. Not only did it support (at least in terms of larger organisations) Weber's earlier work on bureaucracy, but it also struck a blow against those, such as Bennis, who saw bureaucracy as dysfunctional and dying. The work of the Aston Group, along with that of others such as Blau and Schoenherr (1971), who also argued that size is the most important condition affecting the structure of organisations, gave bureaucracy if not a new lease of life then, at least, a new lease of respectability. Bureaucracy, according to the Aston results, was both efficient and effective, at least for larger organisations; and, given the tendency for the average size of private-sector companies and public bodies to increase throughout the twentieth century, its applicability would grow.

There are two explanations for the relationship between size and bureaucracy, both of which have similar implications for organisational efficiency and effect-iveness. The first argues that increased size offers greater opportunities for specialisation – the Adam Smith argument, in effect. This will manifest itself in terms of greater structural differentiation and a high degree of uniformity amongst sub-units. In the first instance, this will make managerial co-ordination more difficult, especially with the emergence of functional autonomy. To counter this, senior managers will move to impose a system of impersonal controls through the use of formal procedures, standardised reporting and control systems, the written recording of information, etc. The second argument reaches similar conclusions, by pointing out that the difficulty of directing ever larger numbers of staff makes it highly inefficient to continue to use a personalised, centralised style of management. Instead a more decentralised system, using impersonal control mechanisms, has to be adopted. The introduction of such a system inevitably leads to the expansion of the administrative core (the bureaucracy) in organisations (Child, 1984).

As with all the Contingency theorists, those who argued for size as the key situational variable were not attempting to reinvent the 'one best way' approach for *all* organisations. Rather they were rejecting it in favour of an approach that saw organisational performance as dependent upon the appropriateness of the organisation's structure for its size. Therefore, like all the Contingency theorists, the Aston school adopted an approach which stressed that there is a 'one best way' for *each* organisation.

## Contingency Theory: summary and criticisms

The Contingency approach can be considered much more a cohesive school of thought than either the Classical or Human Relations approaches. It has three unifying themes:

- Organisations are open systems.
- Structure, and therefore performance, is dependent upon the particular circumstances, situational variables, faced by each organisation.
- There is no 'one best way' for all organisations.

The attractions of Contingency Theory are obvious. First, it was in tune with the times in which it emerged – the 1960s and 1970s. This was a period of rapid economic and technological change, with a tendency towards much larger organisations, and a significant increase in domestic and international competition. In this situation, Contingency Theory offered a plausible explanation of not only why these events were causing problems for organisations, but also how to resolve them (Burnes, 1989). Second, on the surface at least, it was simpler to understand and apply than the Human Relations approach. Finally, whilst rejecting the Classical approach, it was, in the main, a rational approach, based on matching known structural options to identifiable contingencies – size, technology and environment.

The approach to change management offered by Contingency Theory was, it follows, similar to that of the Classical school. In a rational fashion, managers should collect and analyse data on the situational variables the organisation faces and match these to the appropriate structural option. The theory then implies that for employees, faced with a plan for change based on such a 'scientific' approach, the only rational course of action is to accept the validity of the situation and co-operate with managers to achieve the required structural changes. However, it is at this point – the attempt to apply Contingency Theory rationally and mechanically – that problems and drawbacks emerge which give rise to a number of major criticisms of this approach, the main ones being as follows:

- Difficulty arises in relating structure to performance. A number of writers have pointed out that there is no agreed definition of 'good performance', and it therefore becomes difficult to show that linking structure to situational variables brings the benefits claimed (Hendry, 1979, 1980; Mansfield, 1984; Terry, 1976). Indeed, there are a wide range of factors other than structure which can influence performance, not least of which is luck. Davis and Star (1993) showed that seven of the twelve most profitable firms in the world are pharmaceutical companies, and that three of these are producers of anti-ulcer drugs. They conclude that the profitability of the pharmaceutical sector is attributable less to the nature of these organisations than to governments' over-generosity – clearly a case of an industry that is in the right place at the right time.

- Despite the length of time that Contingency Theory has been in circulation, there is still no agreed or unchallenged definition of the three key situational variables – environment, technology and size. The literature gives a wide and conflicting range of definitions of these, making it difficult not only to establish a link between them and structure, but also to apply the theory (Dastmalchian, 1984; Mullins, 1989; Pugh and Hickson, 1976; Robbins, 1987; Warner, 1984; Wood, 1979).

- Whilst, as argued above, a relationship has been established between size and structure, it has proved difficult to show that this relationship has an appreciable impact on performance. Some researchers have suggested that the link between size and structure relates to preferred systems of control, which may have more to do with the political and cultural nature of organisations than any attempt to improve performance (Allaire and Firsirotu, 1984; Child, 1984; Mansfield, 1984; Pugh and Hickson, 1976; Salaman, 1979).

- In examining the link between structure and contingencies, researchers use the organisation's formal organisational structure for comparison purposes. Yet, as the Hawthorne Experiments showed, the actual operation of an organisation may depend more on the informal structures created by workers than the formal ones laid down by management. This was a point made by Woodward (1965) in her study of technology and structure. She noted that organisation charts failed to show important relationships which, taken together, can have a significant impact on performance (Argyris, 1973; Burawoy, 1979; Selznick, 1948).

- Structure and associated practices and policies may be strongly influenced by external forces (Mullins, 1993). In the UK, privatised utilities are subject to regulation and face restrictions that have a significant influence on how they are structured and operate. Similarly, in the UK, financial service organisations are required to establish 'Chinese walls' between different parts of their business to avoid market-sensitive information being passed from one area to another.

- Rather than managers being the virtual prisoners of organisational contingencies when making decisions regarding structure, the reverse may be the case. Managers may have a significant degree of choice and influence over not only structure but also the situational variables. Whether this is called 'strategic choice' (Child, 1972), 'organisational choice' (Trist *et al*, 1963) or 'design space' (Bessant, 1983), the meaning is the same: those senior managers responsible for such decisions can exercise a high degree of freedom in selecting and influencing the technology to be used, the environment in which they operate and even the size of the organisation. Indeed, one of the architects of the technology-structure hypothesis, Charles Perrow, later claimed that technology is chosen and designed to maintain and reinforce existing structures and power relations within organisations rather than the reverse (Perrow, 1983). Other writers made the case for size and environment being manipulated in similar ways (Abell, 1975; Clegg, 1984; Hendry, 1979; Leifer and Huber, 1977; Lorsch, 1970).

- It is assumed that organisations pursue clear-cut, well-thought-out, stable and compatible objectives that can be fitted into a Contingency perspective. However, researchers and practising managers argue that this is not the case – in fact, even two of the proponents of Contingency Theory, Lawrence and Lorsch (1967), highlighted the presence and danger of conflicting objectives. In reality, objectives are often unclear, and organisations may pursue a number of conflicting goals at the same time. Clearly, the objectives of an organisation will impact on its situation and its structure. If these objectives are arbitrary, conflicting or open to managerial whim, it becomes difficult to apply a Contingency approach (Abodaher, 1986; Edwardes, 1983; Hamel and Prahalad, 1989; Mintzberg, 1987; Sloan, 1986).

- The last criticism is that Contingency Theory is too mechanistic and deterministic, and ignores the complexity of organisational life. As argued by the Human Relations school, organisations are by no means the rational entities many would like to believe (a point also made by Thompson (1967) in his support of Contingency Theory). There is a need to see organisations as social systems, with all the cultural and political issues which this raises. In this view, structure is the product of power struggles between individuals and groups within the organisation, each arguing and fighting for their own perspective and position (Allaire and Firsirotu, 1984; Buchanan, 1984; Hickson and Butler, 1982; Morgan, 1986; Pfeffer, 1981; Robbins, 1987; Salaman, 1979).

Therefore, despite its attractiveness, Contingency Theory, like the Classical and Human Relations approaches, fails to provide a convincing explanation for the way in which organisations do and should operate.

## CONCLUSIONS

For organisations, if not for academics, the key purpose of any organisation theory or approach is to help them analyse and rectify the weaknesses and problems of their current situation, and to assist them in bringing about the changes necessary to achieve their future objectives. Over the past 100 years, the design and management of organisations has moved from an *ad hoc* process based on – at best – guesswork, to one that is highly complex and informed by a host of practical and theoretical considerations. To the uninitiated, it might appear that this has made running organisations an easier and more certain process; yet a close examination of most organisations will reveal that this is far from being the case. Not only are organisations, in general, larger and more complex than in the past, but also the practical and theoretical reference points on which managers can draw are diverse and give conflicting and confusing signals.

Not surprisingly in such a situation, many managers look for simple, foolproof solutions: often ones which, as Douglas McGregor noted, appeal to their own basic orientation – whether that be Theory X or Theory Y. This is one of the reasons why the Classical approach, with its deep roots in the Industrial Revolution and its straightforward mechanical approach to organisations and their members, has proved so enduring – despite strong evidence of its lack of suitability in many situations. This search for simple, often quick-fix, solutions to the problems of organisational life has been manifested in many ways in the last decade, not least the emergence of a series of 'panaceas' such as new technology, human resources management, Total Quality Management, culture change, etc. This is not to deny the benefits these can bring but, taken on their own, at best they encourage a fragmented approach, and at worst they create an atmosphere of resignation within organisations as one 'flavour of the month' is succeeded by yet another, and none is given the time necessary to prove itself. Clearly, in such situations, without an overall, long-term plan, the result of these various 'solutions' is to make the situation worse rather than better (Burnes, 1991; Burnes and Weekes, 1989).

Organisations clearly need to reject a short-term piecemeal approach, and instead see themselves in their totality and adopt a consistent and long-term approach. But which approach should they choose? We have seen in this and the previous chapter that well-thought-out and well-supported cases exist for a number of different approaches, but each has its drawbacks and critics. It may well be that each is capable of assisting organisations to analyse and understand the strengths and weaknesses of their present situation. However, whether they can provide more effective organisational arrangements for the future is more debatable. Similarly, it is not obvious how organisations should actually achieve the process of transformation.

The Human Relations movement offers pertinent advice with regard to having clear objectives, good communication and leadership, but is less forthcoming on how change objectives should be set, and the concomitant changes planned and implemented. Contingency Theory though does give a procedure for setting objectives. It stresses the need to identify and analyse the situational variables an organisation faces in order to choose the most appropriate structure. However, it is also silent on the issues of planning and implementation, other than to imply that rational workers will accept rational propositions for change. In addition, even if organisations do manage to implement the recommendations of the Human Relations or Contingency advocates, it is not clear what degree of benefit they would derive from this, given the criticisms of these approaches.

In short, neither of the approaches discussed in this chapter appears to be the solution to all known organisational ills that their proponents seem to claim. They fail to reflect and explain the complexities of day-to-day organisational life that we all experience. In particular, the issue of organisational culture (Allaire and Firsirotu, 1984) gets short shrift; yet, over the last two decades, its importance as both a promoter of and a barrier to organisational competitiveness has become apparent. Nor do they appear to take account of national differences and preferences, or for that matter pay regard to many of the wider societal factors which now impact on our lives, such as the need to show greater social responsibility, whether it be in the area of 'green' issues or equal opportunities. Yet, it is clear that enormous changes are already taking place in the world, and others may be necessary if some of the worst predictions for the future are to be avoided. The next chapter describes three new perspectives on organisational life which, as the old approaches are perceived as inadequate, have become increasingly influential.

## TEST YOUR LEARNING

### Short answer questions

1 What were the main findings of the Hawthorne Experiments?

2 Describe Maslow's hierarchy of needs.

3 Briefly discuss Theory X and Theory Y.

4 State Bennis' reasons for declaring the 'Death of Bureaucracy'.

5 Define the term 'contingency' as used by Burns and Stalker.

6 What are the respective attributes of Mechanistic and Organic structures?

7 How did Perrow define technology?

8 According to the Aston Group, size is the key contingency; state their case for this assertion.

9 For each of the following, briefly state its implications for organisational change: (a) Human Relations and (b) Contingency Theory.

### Essay questions

1 In what ways can the Human Relations approach be said to be superior to the Classical approach?

2 In what manner can Contingency Theory be said to incorporate both the Classical and Human Relations approaches?

## SUGGESTED FURTHER READING

1 Rose, M (1988). *Industrial Behaviour*. Penguin: Harmondsworth.
  Michael Rose gives an invaluable account of the development of the Human Relations movement and provides an interesting review of the work of Joan Woodward and the Aston Group.

2 Sheldrake, J (1996). *Management Theory: From Taylorism to Japanization*. International Thompson Business Press: London.
  Michael Sheldrake also provides an excellent review of the lives and work of the key figures in the Human Relations movement.

3 Hendry, C (1979). Contingency Theory in practice, I. *Personnel Review*, 8(4), 39–44.
  Hendry, C (1980). Contingency Theory in practice, II. *Personnel Review*, 9(1), 5–11.
  Wood, S (1979). A reappraisal of the contingency approach to organization. *Journal of Management Studies*, 16, 334–54.
  Taken together, these three articles provide an excellent review of Contingency Theory.

# Chapter 3

# IN SEARCH OF NEW PARADIGMS

**Learning objectives**

After studying this chapter, you should be able to:

1 understand the reasons for the emergence of new organisational paradigms in the 1980s and 1990s;

2 describe the key features of the Culture–Excellence approach;

3 list the core advantages and disadvantages of the Culture–Excellence approach;

4 describe the core elements of the Japanese approach to management;

5 understand the key advantages and disadvantages of the Japanese approach;

6 discuss the main features of organisational learning;

7 appreciate the main advantages and disadvantages of organisational learning;

8 compare the similarities and differences between Culture–Excellence, organisational learning and Japanese management;

9 appreciate the implications for organisational change of these three paradigms.

## INTRODUCTION

Although he did not invent the word, it was the American philosopher of science Thomas Kuhn (1962) who, in his book *The Structure of Scientific Revolutions*, gave a new importance to the notion of 'paradigms'. He defined a paradigm as a universally recognised scientific achievement that over a period of time provides model problems and solutions to a community of practitioners. Kuhn was interested in how new ideas and frameworks for carrying out scientific work (i.e. paradigms) supplant old ones in the physical sciences. However, from the late 1960s onwards, a growing body of social scientists have adopted the Kuhnian approach to their own disciplines with great enthusiasm. In the intervening period, as Burrell (1997) noted, new, varying, competing and controversial definitions of the term have been put forward. As far as its applicability to organisations is concerned, a paradigm can be defined as a way of looking at and interpreting the world; a framework of basic assumptions, theories and models that are commonly and strongly accepted and shared within a particular field of activity at a particular point in time (Collins, 1998; Mink, 1992; Reed, 1992). However, as situations change and people's perceptions change, existing paradigms lose their relevance and new ones emerge. As Handy (1986: 389) noted:

> When Copernicus suggested that the earth was not at the centre of the universe he was, though he knew it not, a paradigm revolutionary. But it was the minds of men that changed, not the motions of the planets, and the way in which they now viewed that same universe had a profound effect on their beliefs, values and behaviour.

In the previous two chapters we have discussed the paradigms that, in the West at least, have emerged and become common currency in the field of management and organisation theory. Though these paradigms have their adherents as well as critics, increasingly managers have experienced real difficulties in achieving competitive success when applying them in today's turbulent, complex and diverse business world. In consequence, especially over the last two decades, both academics and practitioners have been searching for new recipes for organisational success.

It was in the USA that the search for new paradigms first became apparent. It was the rise of Japanese industrial and economic might which forced American businesses to question what they did and how they did it, as Morgan (1986: 111) observed:

> During the 1960s the confidence and impact of American management and industry seemed supreme. Gradually, but with increasing force, through the 1970s the performance of Japanese automobile, electronic, and other manufacturing industries began to change all this. Japan began to take command of international markets...

The productivity gap between Japanese and American companies was starkly highlighted in a *Harvard Business Review* article by Johnson and Ouchi (1974). The authors claimed that Japanese workers, assembling the same product using the same technology, were some 15 per cent more productive than their American counterparts.

> For an American audience this was a shocking statement, confirming the worst fears of a decline in the USA's competitive edge over the rest of the world. Since the Second World War American manufacturers had grown accustomed to out-producing and out-performing every foreign competitor. The era of the Cold War had led Americans to believe that the only danger to their general security sprang from communism and specifically the Soviet Union. The notion that their comprehensively vanquished enemies and strategic clients, the Japanese, might be poised to overhaul them technically and even economically was unpalatable, even unbelievable. (Sheldrake, 1996: 185)

It was not only the USA that took fright; in the 1970s and 1980s, all over the Western world, businesses and governments too woke up to the Japanese challenge. Even West Germany, which prided itself on producing well-engineered and high-quality products such as BMW and Mercedes cars, found that the Japanese were producing cars such as the Lexus which were not only half the price, but also better-engineered and of far superior quality (Williams *et al*, 1991).

Nor was it just the Japanese challenge that frightened the West. The 1970s also saw the return of unemployment and inflation, both assumed to have been eliminated, and the occurrence of the two 'oil shocks' which highlighted most Western nations' precarious reliance on imported energy. Therefore, old certainties were being challenged and new orthodoxies began to arise. Rather like Copernicus, Japan made the West see the world, and its place in it, from a new perspective.

Organisations have become increasingly aware that in the last 20 years or so, the world has turned on its axis. The days of the mass production of standardised products appear to be over; the key words for the future are variety, flexibility and customisation. As Perez (1983) and Freeman (1988) argued, a new techno-economic rationale is emerging. This new rationale has three main features:

- A shift towards information-intensive rather than energy- or materials-intensive products.

- A change from dedicated mass production systems towards more flexible systems that can accommodate a wider range of products, smaller batches and more frequent design changes – 'economies of scale' are being replaced by 'economies of scope'.

- A move towards the greater integration of processes and systems within companies and between suppliers and customers, which permits a more rapid response to market and customer requirements.

These developments have been given a variety of names. In the 1970s, Daniel Bell (1973) heralded 'The Coming of Post-Industrial Society'. In the 1980s, other writers spoke of the 'post-Fordist' or 'post-Taylorist' era (Whitaker, 1992). Increasingly, in the 1990s, the term 'postmodernism' was used to describe the changes taking place in the world in general and organisations in particular (Hassard, 1993). These terms, and particularly the debate around postmodernism, will be discussed in Chapter 4. However, for now, what we need to recognise is that it is not necessarily that the nature of organisations themselves has changed fundamentally, though significant changes in size, technology and complexity have certainly taken place. It is rather that, like those who listened to Copernicus, we are seeing their role in the established order from a different perspective and beginning to see new possibilities and new challenges.

It is the emergence of these new possibilities and challenges that is driving Western organisations to undertake a fundamental reassessment of their objectives and operations, rather than a mere change in fashion or managerial whim – though this is obviously present as well (Huczynski, 1993; Kennedy, 1994). In effect, what we can see from the beginning of the 1980s is the emergence of a paradigm shift, or, to be more accurate, the search for new, more appropriate paradigms. It seems as if the changes taking place in the business environment are so enormous and rapid that existing paradigms, whatever their past merits, are breaking down and new ones are emerging.

In this chapter, we examine the three proto-paradigms that came to dominate Western managerial thinking and writing in the 1980s and 1990s: the Culture–Excellence approach, the Japanese Management approach and the Organisational Learning approach. The first is very much an attempt to counter Japanese competitiveness by drawing on and re-shaping the American and British traditions of individualism and free market liberalism. It emerged in the early 1980s, and its principal exponents (Tom Peters and Robert Waterman, 1982; Rosabeth Moss Kanter, 1989; and Charles Handy, 1989) have attempted both to predict and to promote the ways in which successful (excellent) companies will and should operate in the future.

The Japanese Management paradigm is a very different animal. It has been developed in Japan over the last 50 years, and not only is it being extensively practised there, but, at least until recently, its success was not disputed. Because of the success of the Japanese economy and Japanese companies since the 1960s, the Japanese approach has attracted much interest in the West – a classic case of 'if you can't beat them, join them'. This is especially the case in the UK, where Japanese inward investment (by household names such as Honda, Nissan and Toyota) has generated a great deal of debate regarding the impact and merits of 'Japanisation' (Ackroyd et al, 1988; Dale and Cooper, 1992; Hannam, 1993; Turnbull, 1986; Whitehill, 1991). This is also the case in the USA, where Japan and Japanese methods are seen, in turn, as either a threat or a lifeline to American industrial pre-eminence (Kanter et al, 1992; Pascale and Athos, 1982; Peters, 1993; Schonberger, 1982).

The third approach, organisational learning, came to the fore in the early 1990s. Leading management thinkers, in particular Chris Argyris (1992), have been interested in organisational learning for over 40 years. However, it is only in the last decade that the concept has become popularised as an engine for organisational competitiveness through the work of Senge (1990) in the USA and Pedler, Boydell and Burgoyne (1989) in the UK. One of the key benefits claimed for organisational learning is that it is a universal approach which draws on and is consistent with both Western and Japanese organisational traditions (Hedlund and Nonaka, 1993; Probst and Buchel, 1997).

Though the Culture–Excellence and Japanese approaches have some similarities, for example the resemblance between the Japanese passion for quality and the Culture–Excellence school's fervent advocacy of the pursuit of excellence, the two also have significant differences, as will be shown. Whilst the Japanese approach has clearly influenced the Culture–Excellence thinkers, there is little indication that the reverse has been the case. The two may be competing approaches in the West, but certainly not in Japan. Nevertheless, both are dynamic and developing paradigms, with some common elements, and consequently, a merging or a blending of the two in the West is not beyond all possibilities. However, the organisational learning approach, though it draws on both Western and Japanese organisational traditions, is by no means an attempt to fuse or merge the Culture–Excellence and Japanese approaches. Instead, it represents yet another attempt to provide Western countries, particularly the USA, with an approach to managing organisations that will allow them in the twenty-first century to enjoy the sort of dominance they enjoyed for much of the twentieth century.

Nevertheless, it will be argued in the conclusion to this chapter that, although these three proto-paradigms offer new possibilities, they also raise familiar controversies, not least regarding the role and treatment of people. Therefore, as the following discussion of the three approaches will show, whilst attempting to become new paradigms, they still have to answer old questions.

## THE CULTURE–EXCELLENCE APPROACH

Though predominantly a North American perspective, the Culture–Excellence approach has also found its adherents in Europe. Therefore, the examination of this approach will draw on the work of key writers from both sides of the Atlantic, namely Tom Peters and Robert Waterman, Rosabeth Moss Kanter and Charles Handy. The writers are all practising and internationally recognised management consultants, though Handy and Kanter are distinguished academics as well. Consequently, though their work is attempting to predict and promote the way firms will or should operate in the future, it is firmly based on what they believe the best companies are doing now or planning to do in the future.

These three perspectives form the spearhead of the movement that is simultaneously charting and creating the new organisational forms that have begun to appear. Their work – though both complementary and distinct – is of profound influence in shaping our understanding of what the future holds in the field of management. This work will now be examined in detail, starting with the American perspectives of Peters and Waterman, and Kanter, and concluding with Handy's British perspective.

### Tom Peters and Robert Waterman's search for excellence

Tom Peters has been, arguably, the most influential management consultant of the 1980s and 1990s. His books sell in millions, his seminars fill auditoriums, and his newspaper column is syndicated across the world. He is also said to be one of the highest-paid management consultants in the world, reputedly charging some US$25,000 per seminar back in 1987 (Huczynski, 1993). He catapulted to international fame when he co-authored, along with Robert Waterman, *In Search of Excellence: Lessons from America's Best-Run Companies* (Peters and Waterman, 1982), which is the best-selling management book of all time. It is difficult to overestimate the impact this book has had. At a time when Western economies were on the rocks and Japanese companies appeared to be sweeping all before them, *In Search of Excellence* seemed to offer a way, perhaps the only way, for Western companies to regain their competitiveness (Crainer, 1995).

The origins of the book lie in a major study of the determinants of organisational excellence, which Peters and Waterman carried out when working for the management consultants McKinsey and Company. They used the now-famous McKinsey Seven S Framework (strategy, structure, systems, staff, style, shared values, and skills), which they had developed jointly with Richard Pascale and Anthony Athos, to study 62 of America's most successful companies. They concluded that it was the four 'soft' Ss (staff, style, shared values and skills) which held the key to business success. In stressing the 'soft' Ss, Peters and Waterman challenged the rational theories of management described in previous chapters. They argue that the rational approach is flawed because it leads to the following:

- **Wrong-headed analysis** – situation or information analysis that is considered too complex and unwieldy to be useful. This is analysis that strives to be precise about the inherently unknowable.

- **Paralysis through analysis** – the application of the rational model to such an extent that action stops and planning runs riot.

- **Irrational rationality** – where rational management techniques identify the 'right' answer irrespective of its applicability to the situation in question.

In the light of these criticisms, Peters and Waterman argue that the analytical tools that characterise the rational approach should only be used as an aid to, rather than a substitute for, human judgement. They believe that it is the freedom given to managers and employees to challenge the orthodox and to experiment with different solutions which distinguishes the excellent companies from the also-rans. In place of the rational approach, Peters and Waterman argue that there are eight key attributes that organisations need to demonstrate if they are to achieve excellence:

1 a bias for action

2 close to the customer

3 autonomy and entrepreneurship

4 productivity through people

5 hands-on, value-driven

6 stick to the knitting

7 simple form, lean staff

8 simultaneous loose–tight properties

These are discussed in more detail below.

### 1 A bias for action

One of the main identifiable attributes of excellent companies is their bias for action. Even though they may be analytical in approach, they also favour methods that encourage rapid and appropriate response. One of the methods devised for achieving quick action is what Peters and Waterman term 'chunking'. Chunking is an approach whereby a problem that arises in the organisation is first made manageable (i.e. broken into 'chunks') and then tackled by a small group of staff brought together specifically for that purpose. The main reason for the use of such groups, variously called project teams, task forces or quality circles, is to facilitate organisational fluidity and to encourage action. Key characteristics of these groups are as follows:

- They usually comprise no more than ten members.
- They are voluntarily constituted.
- The life of the group is usually between three and six months.
- The reporting level and seniority of the membership is appropriate to the importance of the problem to be dealt with.
- The documentation of the group's proceedings is scant and very informal.
- These groups take on a limited set of objectives, which are usually determined, monitored, evaluated and reviewed by themselves.

Chunking is merely one example of the bias for action that exists in excellent companies and reflects their willingness to innovate and experiment. These companies' philosophy for action is simple: 'Do it, fix it, try it.' Therefore, excellent companies are characterised by small, *ad hoc* teams applied to solving designated problems which have first been reduced to manageable proportions. Achieving smallness is the key, even though the subject or task may be large. Smallness induces manageability and a sense of understanding, and allows a feeling of ownership.

### 2 Close to the customer

Excellent companies really do get close to the customer, while others merely talk about it. The customer dictates product, quantity, quality and service. The best organisations are alleged to go to extreme lengths to achieve quality, service and reliability. There is no part of the business that is closed to customers. In fact, many of the excellent companies claim to get their best ideas for new products from listening intently and regularly to their customers. The excellent companies are more 'driven by their direct orientation to the customers rather than by technology or by a desire to be the low-cost producer. They seem to focus more on the revenue-generation side of their services' (Peters and Waterman, 1982: 197).

### 3 Autonomy and entrepreneurship

Perhaps the most important element of excellent companies is their 'ability to be big and yet to act small at the same time. A concomitant essential apparently is that they encourage the entrepreneurial spirit among their people, because they push autonomy markedly far down the line' (Peters and Waterman, 1982: 201). Product champions are allowed to come forward, grow and flourish. Such a champion is not a blue-sky dreamer, or an intellectual giant. The champion might even be an ideal thief. But above all, the champion is the pragmatist; the one who latches on to someone else's idea, and doggedly brings something concrete and tangible out of it.

In fostering such attitudes, the excellent companies have what they label 'championing systems', consisting of the following:

- **The Product Champion** – a zealot or fanatic who believes in a product.
- **A Successful Executing Champion** – one who has been through the process of championing a product before.
- **The Godfather** – typically, an ageing leader who provides the role model for champions.

The essence of this system is to foster, promote and sustain the budding entrepreneur. It is claimed that the three elements of the championing system are essential to its operation and credibility.

Another key part of this system is that, in some companies, product champions tend to be allocated their own 'suboptional divisions'. These are similar to small, independent businesses and comprise independent new venture teams, run by champions with the full and total support of senior management. The suboptional division is independent in that it is responsible for its own accounting, personnel activities, quality assurance and support for its product in the field. To encourage entrepreneurship further, teams, groups and divisions are highly encouraged by the companies' reward structures to compete amongst themselves for new projects.

Autonomy and entrepreneurship are also encouraged by the type of no-holds-barred communications procedures adopted by excellent companies. These exhibit the following characteristics:

- *Communication is informal* – even though there are lots of meetings going on at any one time, most meetings are informal and comprise staff from different disciplines gathering to talk about and solve problems.

- *The communication system is given both physical and material support* – blackboards, flip-charts and small tables that foster informal small group discussions are everywhere. The aim is to encourage people to talk about the organisation: what needs changing; what is going on; and how to improve things around the place. There are also people, variously described as dreamers, heretics, gadflies, mavericks, or geniuses, whose sole purpose is to spur the system to innovate. Their job is to institutionalise innovation by initiating and encouraging experimentation. They can also call on staff in other divisions of the organisation to assist them in this process, as well as having financial resources at their disposal.

- *Communication is intensive* – given the freedom, the encouragement and the support (financial, moral and physical) in the organisations, it is no wonder that the level of communication between and amongst workers is not only informal and spontaneous but also intense. This is borne out by the common occurrence of meetings without agendas and minutes. Also, when presentations are made in these meetings, questioning of the proposal is unabashed and discussion is free and open. Those present are expected to be fully involved in such meetings and there are no 'sacred cows' that cannot be questioned.

This intense communication system also acts as a remarkably tight control system, in that people are always checking on each other to see how each is faring. This arises out of a genuine desire to keep abreast of developments in the organisation rather than any untoward motive. One result of this is that teams are more prudent in their financial expenditure on projects. Another is that the sea of inquisitors act as 'idea generators', thereby ensuring that teams are not dependent entirely on their own devices to innovate and solve problems. This usually also ensures that all options are considered before a final decision is made. The concomitant result of this fostering of creativity is that senior management is more tolerant of failure; knowing full well that champions have to make many tries, and consequently suffer some failures, in the process of creating successful innovations.

### 4 Productivity through people

A cherished principle of the excellent companies is that they treat their workers with respect and dignity; they refer to them as partners. This is because people, rather than systems or machines, are seen as the primary source of quality and productivity gains. Therefore, there is 'tough-minded respect for the individual and the willingness to train him, to set reasonable and clear expectations for him, and to grant him practical autonomy to step out and contribute directly to his job' (Peters and Waterman, 1982: 239). There is a closeness and family feeling in such companies; indeed many of the 'partners' see the organisation as an extended family. The slogans of such companies tend to reflect this view of people: 'respect the individual', 'make people winners', 'let them stand out', 'treat people as adults'.

### 5 Hands-on, value-driven

Excellent companies are value-driven; they are clear about what they stand for and take the process of value-shaping seriously. There is an implicit belief that everyone in the organisation, from the top to the bottom, should be driven by the values of the organisation; hence the great effort, time and money spent to inspire people by and inculcate them with these values:

> . . . these values are almost always stated in qualitative, rather than quantitative, terms. When financial objectives are mentioned, they are almost always ambitious but never precise. Furthermore, financial and strategic objectives are never stated alone. They are always discussed in the context of the other things the company expects to do well. The idea that profit is a natural by-product of doing something well, and not an end in itself, is almost always universal. (Peters and Waterman, 1982: 284)

Implanting these values is a primary responsibility of the individual members of the management team. They set the tone by leading from the front. Coherence and homogeneity must, however, first be created among senior management by regular meetings (both formal and informal). The outcome of this is that management speak with one voice. They are passionate in preaching the organisation's values. They unleash excitement, not in their offices, but mainly on the shopfloor where the workers are. Inculcating these values, however, is a laborious process and persistence is vital in achieving the desired goal.

### 6 Stick to the knitting

Acquisition or internal diversification for its own sake is not one of the characteristics of excellent companies. They must stick to the knitting – do what they know best. But when they do acquire, they do it in an experimental fashion; by first 'dipping a toe in the waters'. If the water does not feel good, they get out fast. Acquisitions are always in fields related to their core activities and they never acquire any business that they do not know how to run. As a general rule, they 'move out mainly through internally generated diversification, one manageable step at a time' (Peters and Waterman, 1982: 279).

### 7 Simple form, lean staff

A guiding principle in excellent companies is to keep things simple and small. Structurally, the most common form is the 'product division'. This form, which is rarely changed, provides the essential touchstone that everybody understands and from which the complexities of day-to-day life can be approached. Since the use of teams, groups and task forces for specific projects is a common stock-in-trade of these companies, most changes in structure are made at the edges, such as by allocating one or two people to an *ad hoc* team. By adopting this approach, the basic structure is left in place, while all other things revolve and change around it. This gives these organisations great flexibility but still enables them to keep their structures simple, divisionalised and autonomous.

Such simple structures only require a small, lean staff at the corporate and middle management levels. This results in there being fewer administrators and more doers: '...it is not uncommon to find a corporate staff of fewer than 100 people running a multi-billion-dollar enterprise' (Peters and Waterman, 1982: 15). Therefore, in excellent companies, flat structures, with few layers, and slimmed-down bureaucracies – which together allow flexibility and rapid communication – are the order of the day.

### 8 Simultaneous loose–tight properties

This is the 'firm and free' principle. On the one hand, it allows the excellent companies to control everything tightly, whilst on the other hand allowing and indeed encouraging individual innovation, autonomy and entrepreneurship. These properties are jointly achieved through the organisation's culture – its shared values and beliefs. By sharing the same values, self-control and self-respect result in each person becoming their own, and everyone else's, supervisor. The individual members of the organisation know they have the freedom, and are encouraged, to experiment and innovate. However, they also know that their actions will be scrutinised and judged, with the utmost attention paid to the impact they have on product quality, targets and, above all, the customer. The focus is on building and expanding the frontiers of the business. The ultimate goal is to be the best company, and in the final analysis, this is the benchmark against which the discipline and flexibility of the individual will be measured.

Therefore, Peters and Waterman maintain that the main attributes of excellent companies are flat, anti-hierarchical structures; innovation and entrepreneurship; small corporate and middle management staffs; reward systems based on contribution rather than position or length of service; brain power rather than muscle power; and strong, flexible cultures.

Peters and Waterman's vision of the organisation of the future, based on their study of leading American companies, has proved extremely influential, not only in the business world but in academia as well. This is not to say (as will be shown later) that they are without their critics; however, there is little doubt that they laid the groundwork, especially in highlighting the important role played by culture, for other leading thinkers whose work draws on and gels with theirs.

Their vision of the future has not stood still. Peters has formed his own consultancy, The Tom Peters Group, and has used this as a vehicle for developing and implementing the Culture–Excellence approach. Though not fundamentally changing his view of the need for excellent organisations, in *Thriving on Chaos* (Peters, 1989) he argues that, as yet, none exist in the USA. In *Liberation Management* (Peters, 1993), he places more emphasis on the need to break organisations into smaller, more independent, more flexible units. Only by doing this, he argues, will managers be 'liberated', and thus able to achieve their – and their organisation's – full potential. In this book, Peters maintains that the age of the large corporations such as IBM and General Motors is over. He sees such companies as outmoded and uncompetitive dinosaurs, which are doomed to extinction unless they change rapidly and irreversibly. Peters argues that only rapid structural change can create the conditions for entrepreneurial cultures to emerge which both liberate managers and empower workers. Indeed, this book is nothing short of an out-and-out attack on the very existence of corporate America.

*The Circle of Innovation: You Can't Shrink Your Way to Greatness* (Peters, 1997a) is perhaps his most iconoclastic book. Even the format of the book is different from what has gone before. Indeed, its use of a multitude of different images, font types and font sizes and, in some cases, almost surreal page layouts, makes it more like a pop video than a traditional book. The message could not be clearer: just as this book is innovative in its format, so organisations must be innovative if they are to survive. His attack on present and past organisational practices, stability and any sense of permanence is keener and more vitriolic than ever. Professionalism, rules, balance, propriety, logic and consensus are all outmoded concepts, he argues.

Peters (1997a: 76) quotes Dee Hock, founder of the Visa Network, who said: 'The problem is never how to get new, innovative thoughts into your mind, but how to get the old ones out.' For Peters, organisational forgetting is far more important than organisational learning. Future success, he argues, is not related to what an organisation has done in the past, nor what is bringing it success now, but how innovative they will be in identifying new products, services and markets. He makes a strong, almost messianic, plea for organisations to centre themselves on innovation. Peters argues that innovation demands obsession, tension, being provocative, and having no market peers looking over your shoulder. As firms achieve parity in terms of quality and costs, he believes that only a constant commitment to being different, to continuous innovation, will allow companies to differentiate themselves from their competitors. Just as quality was seen as everyone's job in the 1980s, so Peters maintains that innovation must also become everyone's job now. In terms of structure, organisations must adopt a network or even a virtual structure, where small groups and even individuals have the freedom to self-manage themselves, to make connections and break connections as they see fit. Indeed, the subtitle of this book could well be 'Anarchy Rules!'

Whereas in *In Search of Excellence*, he and Robert Waterman put forward their eight attributes of excellence, this book is structured around his 15 points on The Circle of Innovation, which are as follows:

- Distance is dead.
- Destruction is cool.
- You can't live without an eraser.
- We are all Michelangelos.
- Welcome to the white-collar revolution.
- All values come from the professional services.
- The intermediary is doomed.
- The system is the solution.
- Create waves of lust.
- Tommy Hilfiger knows.
- Become a connoisseur of talent.
- It's a woman's world.
- Little things are the only things.
- Love all, serve all.
- We're here to live life out loud.

Trying to follow Peters' train of thought through his various books is like trying to catch mist – just when you think you have got it, it slips through your hands. Indeed, Peters (1997a: xv) takes pride in his inconsistency: '"They" call me inconsistent. I consider that a badge of honor.' Originally he saw the pursuit of 'excellence' as the only way to save corporate America from annihilation by its Japanese competitors (and thus maintaining the USA as the premier industrial nation). Then, in *Liberation Management*, Peters (1993) argued that corporate America needed to be destroyed in order for America to survive. The message from *The Circle of Innovation* is that, with the business world in a permanent state of chaos, the only way for any organisation to survive is by constantly reinventing itself through a ceaseless process of innovation and change.

Nevertheless, though he offers some new tools and techniques, and the tone of his work has become more strident and zealot-like over the years, in essence he is still promoting the concepts first developed in *In Search of Excellence*. The market is not simply the final arbiter of success, but the only arbiter. Meeting the ever-increasing appetite for instant gratification is the only way to survive. Innovation, i.e. autonomy and entrepreneurship, is now the prime attribute of excellence and the only guarantee of success. Peters' (1997a: 493) view of how organisations should be run is, perhaps, best summed up by a quotation he cites from the racing driver Mario Andretti: 'If things seem under control, you're just not going fast enough.'

## Rosabeth Moss Kanter's post-entrepreneurial model

Kanter is one of America's leading management thinkers. As well as being a professor at the Harvard Business School and a former editor of the *Harvard Business Review*, she is also a leading and influential management consultant with her own company, Goodmeasure Inc., reputedly charging some $17,000 per hour for her services in 1987 (Huczynski, 1993). Her early work concerned Utopian communities, such as the Shakers, but she then went on to study business organisations. Kanter first came to prominence with her (1977) book, *Men and Women of the Corporation*. This was an intensive examination of corporate America, which she saw as bureaucratic, unimaginative and uninspiring. In her next book, *The Change Masters* (Kanter, 1983), she offered her personal recipe for overcoming what she saw as the malaise and lack of competitiveness of the USA. The book painted corporate America as being in transition; it recognised that the corporatism of the past no longer worked, but was not sure where the future lay. Kanter (1983) argued that it lay in American and not Japanese ideas, and particularly in unleashing individual dynamism through empowerment and greater employee involvement.

Though her earlier books were clearly in tune with Peters and Waterman's work, it is Kanter's (1989) *When Giants Learn To Dance: Mastering the Challenges of Strategy, Management, and Careers in the 1990s* that most complements and develops their work by attempting to define what organisations need to be like in the future if they are to be successful. Kanter calls for a revolution in business management to create what she terms post-entrepreneurial organisations. She uses this term:

> ...because it takes entrepreneurship a step further, applying entrepreneurial principles to the traditional corporation, creating a marriage between entrepreneurial creativity and corporate discipline, cooperation, and teamwork. (Kanter, 1989: 9–10)

Kanter believes that:

> If the new game of business is indeed like Alice-in-Wonderland croquet, then winning it requires faster action, more creative manoeuvring, more flexibility, and closer partnerships with employees and customers than was typical in the traditional corporate bureaucracy. It requires more agile, limber management that pursues opportunity without being bogged down by cumbersome structures or weighty procedures that impede action. Corporate giants, in short, must learn how to dance. (Kanter, 1989: 20)

She argues that today's corporate elephants need to learn to dance as nimbly and speedily as mice if they are to survive in our increasingly competitive and rapidly changing world. Companies must constantly be alert and on their guard, and keep abreast of their competitors' intentions. By evaluating the response of modern organisations to the demands placed upon them, Kanter produced her post-entrepreneurial model of how the organisation of the future should operate. She sees post-entrepreneurial organisations as pursuing three main strategies:

1 Restructuring to find synergies.
2 Opening boundaries to form strategic alliances.
3 Creating new ventures from within: encouraging innovation and entrepreneurship.

These are detailed below.

### 1 Restructuring to find synergies

Synergy occurs where the whole adds up to more than the sum of its constituent parts. In an age where resources are scarce, one of the priorities of organisations is to make every part of the business add value to the whole. The essence of this approach is to identify and concentrate on the core business areas and to remove all obstacles and impediments to their efficient and effective operation. Therefore, all non-core activities are eliminated, and authority is devolved to the appropriate levels of the business: those in the front line. In practice this means selling off a company's non-core activities and ensuring that what remains, especially at the corporate and middle management levels, is lean and efficient. Nevertheless, it is not sufficient merely to have a strategy of reducing the size of the organisational bureaucracy. Companies must also ensure that the essential tasks that these people previously carried out are still undertaken. This can be accomplished in a number of ways, such as the use of computers to carry out monitoring and information-gathering; devolving greater responsibility and power down to individual business units; and contracting out services and tasks previously carried out in-house.

The result is to create flatter, more responsive and less complex organisations which have a greater degree of focus than in the past. However, Kanter argues that such radical changes need to be well planned, and executed with care and in a way which ensures that employee motivation is increased, not eliminated.

## 2 Opening their boundaries to form strategic alliances

With the slimming-down of the organisation and the contracting-out of some of its functions, there arises the need to pool resources with other organisations; to band together to exploit opportunities and to share ideas and information. These alliances take three forms: service alliances, opportunistic alliances and stakeholder alliances. The first, a service alliance, is where two or more organisations form a cross-company consortium to undertake a special project with a limited lifespan. Such alliances are usually considered when the resources of the various partners are insufficient to allow them to undertake the project by themselves. For this reason, and not surprisingly, many such alliances involve research and development (R&D) projects. The collaboration between Ford and General Motors on research into the development of new materials for making cars is an example of this. This approach allows organisations to mobilise resources, often on a large scale, whilst limiting their exposure and protecting their independence. It is the limited purpose of the consortium that makes it possible even for competitors to join together for their mutual benefit.

The second form, an opportunistic alliance, comprises a joint venture whose aim is to take advantage of a particular opportunity that has arisen: '...the two principal advantages behind this kind of alliance are competence-enhancing ones: technology transfer or market access or both' (Kanter, 1989: 126). An example of such an alliance is the link-up between the Rover Group and Honda Motors; the former gained access to Japanese know-how, whilst the latter gained greater access to the European market. However, as Kanter (1989: 126) pointed out, such alliances are not always equally beneficial: '...once one of the partners has gained experience with the competence of the other, the alliance is vulnerable to dissolution – the opportunity can now be pursued without the partner.'

The third form, a stakeholder alliance, unlike the previous two, is seen as a continuing, almost permanent partnership between an organisation and its key stakeholders, generally considered to be its employees, customers and suppliers. There is a growing awareness among employees, trade unions and management of the need to see each other as partners in the same enterprise rather than rivals. A similar case is made for treating customers and suppliers as partners too. The main reason for the organisation to exist is to serve its customers; therefore, there is a need to keep close to them, not only to be aware of their present concerns and future needs, but also to gain ideas regarding potential joint product development. In the same way, the organisation relies on its suppliers, who will in any case want to get closer to them as their customers. Stakeholder alliances have gained a growing band of adherents in Britain in recent years, especially, though not exclusively, amongst Japanese companies such as Nissan Motors (Partnership Sourcing Ltd, 1991a; Wickens, 1987). As Kanter points out, major innovations in technology and organisational systems require longer-term investments. Companies can only enter into such investments if they are secure in the knowledge that their key stakeholders are themselves committed to the same aims and approach.

The result of these alliances is that structures and positions within organisations will change, sometimes quite dramatically. This is especially the case amongst senior and line managers, but even previously protected groups – such as R&D specialists – will also see their roles and responsibilities change. They will have to work more closely not only with colleagues internally, but also with external groupings.

### 3 Creating new ventures from within – encouraging innovation and entrepreneurship

Traditional organisations face a difficult balancing act between gaining the full benefits from existing mainstream business, and, at the same time, creating new activities that will become the mainstream business of the future. Kanter argues that there is a feeling in many traditional companies that opportunities are being missed owing to their inability to give staff the flexibility to pursue new ideas and develop new products. The job of creating new products or ventures used to be the sole domain of the strategic planners or the R&D departments. However, in the post-entrepreneurial organisation, this will no longer be the case; innovation will move from these specialised domains to the centre stage. As the case studies in Part 3 will show, some organisations are deliberately forming new, independent units or entirely restructuring themselves to nurture innovation and entrepreneurship. New cultures are being created which encourage and aid innovation, and old barriers and restrictions are being eradicated. As a result of such changes, the innovative potential of employees is being and will be tapped, and a proliferation of new ideas, products and ways of working is emerging.

## The consequences of the post-entrepreneurial model

There is no doubt that the post-entrepreneurial model carries profound implications for both organisations and their employees. However, Kanter, unlike Peters and Waterman, does not see these new developments as being an unalloyed blessing, especially in the case of employees. In particular, she draws attention to three areas where the changes will have a major impact on employees: reward systems; career paths and job security; and lifestyle.

### Reward systems

Employers and employees will increasingly come to look for new and more appropriate ways of rewarding and being rewarded. Indeed, with the advent of performance-related pay, in both the private and public sectors, there is already a gradual change from determining pay on the basis of a person's position and seniority to basing it on their contribution to the organisation. These changes are being driven by four main concerns:

1 *Cost* – the concern is that the present system is too expensive for companies that must conserve resources to be competitive.

2 *Equity* – organisations are concerned to ensure that employees are fairly rewarded for their efforts.

3 *Productivity* – organisations want to adopt reward systems that motivate high performance from employees.

4 *Entrepreneurial pressure* – companies are aware that the present system does not always adequately reward entrepreneurs for their efforts.

These concerns are being approached through the application of three different, though not necessarily mutually exclusive, payment methods. The first is profit-sharing, whereby the pay of the employee is pegged to a company's performance. This means that salaries are not fixed but instead are related, by the use of a predetermined formula, to the profit of the organisation over a given period of time, usually the previous financial year. The second method is the use of individual performance bonuses, which are paid on top of basic salary and are related to a predetermined performance target. This method has the advantage of enabling individuals to establish a direct correlation between their personal effort and the bonus payment they receive. Though this method is not new, the sums involved are – sometimes as much as twice basic salary. The last is the venture returns method, which represents perhaps the most radical break with the past. This is a scheme whereby entrepreneurs and inventors within an organisation are given the opportunity to earn returns based on the performance, in the market place, of the particular products or services for which they are responsible. Through this mechanism, the entrepreneur or inventor remains within the corporate fold but is paid on a similar basis to the owner of a small, independent business. The advantage is that they get the personal satisfaction and reward of running their 'own' business, whilst the larger organisation benefits from having highly motivated and innovative people in charge of part of its operations.

The picture created by new reward systems is not, of course, totally rosy. Where there are winners, there may also be losers; not everyone will have the opportunity or drive to be an entrepreneur, or will be in a position that lends itself to some form of bonus system. Also, many people who currently benefit from reward systems based on seniority and position may find they lose out. Older workers, established in organisations and well down their chosen career path, could be particularly adversely affected by such changes. In addition, such payment systems may be divisive and create conflict. Kanter stresses the need for teamwork, yet a situation where some members of the team are receiving high bonuses is bound to create tensions which undermine co-operation and collaboration. It may be that profit-sharing schemes, which encompass everyone in the organisation, overcome this threat to teamworking, but if everyone receives the same share of the profits irrespective of their individual contribution, the motivating effect is likely to be diminished. The result of these various approaches to pay could be minimal in terms of motivation, or could even be demotivating and indeed drive out the most experienced people in the organisation.

### Careers and job security

As organisations become slimmer and more tasks are contracted out, organisation structures will become flatter as entire layers of hierarchy are dispensed with. The resultant effect may well be the demise of traditional forms of career path. Kanter argues that the idea of staying with one organisation and climbing the corporate career ladder is being replaced by hopping from job to job, not necessarily in the same organisation. Therefore, instead of people relying on organisations to give shape to their career, in future the onus will be on individuals to map out and pursue their own chosen route.

This change will also affect skill development in organisations. It will no longer be sufficient just to be skilled in a particular job or specialism, because these will certainly change over time or even entirely disappear. In future, individuals may find that the concept of job security is replaced by 'employability security' – the ability to adapt and enhance one's skills so as to be able to perform well in different types of jobs and organisations. Careers, therefore, will be shaped by professional and entrepreneurial principles: the ability to develop and market one's own skills and ideas, rather than by the sequence of jobs provided by one company. People will join organisations or accept particular jobs not, as in the past, because of job security or career progression, but in order to develop their skills, add to their knowledge and enhance their future employability.

Kanter argues that:

> ...what people are increasingly working to acquire is the capital of their own individual reputation instead of the organisational capital that comes from learning one system well and meeting its idiosyncratic requirements. For many managers, it might be more important, for example, to acquire or demonstrate a talent that a future employer or financial investor might value than to get to know the right people several layers above in the corporation where they currently work. (Kanter, 1989: 324)

Having painted this picture, it must also be acknowledged that there are contradictions and dilemmas that need to be resolved. What is being created are organisations and cultures that facilitate innovation and entrepreneurship, and change and flexibility. These will be organisations where employability and loyalty are transient concepts and what matters, almost exclusively, is the individual's present performance rather than their past or potential future contribution. The two main dilemmas from the organisational perspective are, therefore, how to reconcile the above with their stated objective of treating employees as long-term partners, and how to motivate employees to work in the organisation's interest rather than their own interest. This is an especially pointed dilemma in the case of the champions and entrepreneurs on whom it is argued the future of organisations depends. This is because it is this group of highly marketable individuals who are most likely to see their careers in terms of many different jobs and organisations.

### Workers' lifestyle

The future type of organisation is likely to be one where people will be given greater freedom to innovate and experiment, where there will be strong financial rewards for increased performance levels and where people will be given greater control over their area of the business. There is little doubt that in such situations people will be expected, and indeed wish, to work longer hours and centre what social life they have around their work. Nevertheless, where there are benefits, there may also be disbenefits:

> The workplace as a centre for social life and the workmate as a candidate for marriage mate is, on one level, a convenience for overloaded people who have absorbing work that leaves little time to pursue a personal life outside. It is also an inevitable consequence of the new workforce demographics. But on another level, the idea is profoundly disturbing. What about the large number of people whose personal lives are not contained within the corridors of the corporation? What about the people with family commitments outside the workplace? (Kanter, 1989: 285)

We already know the adverse cost that such work patterns can have on people's physical and mental health and on their family life. In the case of the latter, one might expect to see an increase in our already high divorce rate. Indeed, Kanter believes unmarried or divorced executives are already thought to be preferred to their married counterparts by some companies because it is assumed they can focus more on their job given their lack of home life. Therefore, the line between motivation and exploitation may be a narrow one, and crossing it may benefit neither the individual nor the organisation.

Much of Kanter's work supports the view of Peters and Waterman in terms of the need for and direction of organisational change. Certainly, on the issues of innovation and entrepreneurship, culture and flexibility, and structure and jobs, there is much common ground. To an extent we might expect this, given that they are both writing from an American perspective, and basing their views on the experience and plans of leading American companies. Where they differ, however, is that Kanter takes a much more critical view of these developments. In particular, she draws attention to the contradiction that lies at the heart of the post-entrepreneurial model: are people – their skills, motivation and loyalty – central to the success of the organisation of the future, or are they just another commodity to be obtained and dispensed with as circumstances and their performance require?

Like Peters, Kanter has developed her earlier work but in a broader context. In *The Challenge of Organizational Change*, she and her co-authors (Kanter *et al*, 1992: 382–3) turn their attention to the issue of managing change, and propose 'Ten Commandments for Executing Change':

1 Analyze the organization and its need for change.

2 Create a shared vision and a common direction.

3 Separate from the past.

4 Create a sense of urgency.

5 Support a strong leader role.

6 Line up political sponsorship.

7 Craft an implementation plan.

8 Develop enabling structures.

9 Communicate, involve people and be honest.

10 Reinforce and institutionalize change.

Looking at approaches to change, Kanter *et al* (1992) distinguished between 'Bold Strokes' and 'Long Marches'. The former relate to major strategic decisions or economic initiatives. These, they argue, can have a clear and rapid impact on an organisation, but they rarely lead to any long-term change in habits or culture. The Long March approach, on the other hand, favours relatively small-scale and operationally focused initiatives which are slow to implement and whose full benefits are achieved in the long term rather than the short term. However, the Long March approach can impact on culture over time. Bold Strokes are initiatives taken by a few senior managers, sometimes only one; they do not rely on the support of the rest of the organisation for their success. The Long March approach, however, does. Without the involvement and commitment of the majority of the workforce, such initiatives cannot succeed.

Kanter *et al* argue that these can be complementary, rather than alternative, approaches to change, though in practice companies appear to favour one or the other. Nevertheless, companies may need both the Bold Stroke and the Long March if they are to succeed in transforming themselves.

Kanter's, unlike Peters', works go far beyond the confines of the individual business enterprise to look at the workings of society as a whole. She has co-authored a book, *Creating the Future*, with Michael Dukakis, the former Governor of Massachusetts (Dukakis and Kanter, 1988) and worked on his failed campaign for the US Presidency. The influence of Dukakis and successive Democrat administrations in Massachusetts can be seen in Kanter's more recent book *World Class: Thriving Locally in the Global Economy* (Kanter, 1997). Here she argues that if local communities and regions are to achieve economic security, they must see themselves as competing bodies in a mercilessly competitive global economy. Kanter paints a picture of the global economy as one where free enterprise reigns supreme and where goods, and many services, can be supplied from anywhere in the world. She points out that in the 1980s and 1990s, both blue- and white-collar American jobs were exported to whichever part of the world offered the lowest labour costs. Though supporting this example of the working of the free-enterprise system as being ultimately to everyone's benefit, Kanter argues that if local communities and regions are to survive and prosper in such a fierce climate, they must learn how to defend themselves. In particular, she argues for an interventionist local state which forms alliances with local private enterprises and manipulates the local economy. By creating a business-friendly taxation system and by the selective use of public expenditure for education and infrastructure projects, it can aim to attract and retain employers, especially large corporations.

In *Innovation: Breakthrough Thinking at 3M, DuPont, GE, Pfizer, and Rubbermaid* (Kanter *et al*, 1997), Kanter returns to the internal world of the organisation and the tried and tested ground of the Culture–Excellence approach. The core arguments of the book are neatly summed up on the dust-jacket, which states that inside you will discover:

- Why it is impossible to approach innovation from a business school mentality.
- Why investigations of any cost or size will fail if tied too tightly to current marketplace needs.
- Why managers must learn to operate more intuitively.
- Why cross-functional teams are more productive than any other organizational configuration.
- How fostering a competitive internal environment results in a healthy, creative tension and hungry, entrepreneurial employees.

These points are fleshed out by drawing upon the practices of the companies in the book's title and the editors' own, anecdotal, experiences. In a book whose Foreword is written by Tom Peters, it is not perhaps surprising that many of the arguments mirror those of Peters' own book on innovation (Peters, 1997a). Indeed, the key thrust of the book is succinctly summed up in a phrase from Tom Peters' (1997b) Foreword: 'Tomorrow's victories will go to the masters of innovation! Period!' It speaks volumes for the credibility which the Culture–Excellence approach has achieved in the business world that, after nearly two decades, its two leading American proponents are still in agreement about what it takes to achieve success.

In the next (and last) section on Culture–Excellence, we will examine the emergence of new organisational forms from the perspective of a leading British theorist: Charles Handy.

## Charles Handy's emerging future organisations

Charles Handy is one of Britain's leading management thinkers. Indeed, in a 1997 European league table of global management gurus, he was placed third; all the others in the top ten were American (Rogers, 1997). Handy was educated at Oxford University and the Sloan School of Management at the Massachusetts Institute of Technology. He has been an oil executive, an economist and a professor at the London Business School. He has also acted as a consultant to a wide range of organisations in business, government, the voluntary sector, education and health.

Handy's first book, *Understanding Organizations*, which was published in 1976, has become a standard text on management courses and is now in its fourth edition (Handy, 1993). However, the book that brought him to public prominence and where he first began to articulate his views about the future direction of organisations was *The Future of Work* (Handy, 1984). As with Kanter and Peters, his work was inspired by the rise of Japan and the apparent decline of the West. In particular, he was concerned with the high level of unemployment in the UK at that time. Handy argued that if organisations were to survive and meaningful jobs were to be created for all those who wished to work, then both organisations and individuals would have to change the way they perceived jobs and careers. However, it was in his book *The Age of Unreason* (1989) that Handy fully articulated his views on the requirements for organisational success. He argues that profound changes are taking place in organisational life:

> The world of work is changing because the organisations of work are changing their ways. At the same time, however, the organisations are having to adapt to a changing world of work. It's a chicken and egg situation. One thing, at least, is clear: organisations in both private and public sectors face a tougher world – one in which they are judged more harshly than before on their effectiveness and in which there are fewer protective hedges behind which to shelter. (Handy, 1989: 70)

He asserts that British companies are fast moving away from the labour-intensive organisations of yesteryear. In future, new knowledge-based structures, run by a few smart people at their core who will control a host of equally smart computerised machines, will be the order of the day. Already, he notes, leading British organisations are increasingly becoming entities that receive their added value from the knowledge and the creativity they put in, rather than from the application of muscle power. He contends that fewer, better-motivated people, helped by clever machines, can create much more added value than large groups of unthinking, demotivated ones ever could.

Like Peters and Kanter, Handy believes that the emerging future organisations will be smaller, more flexible and less hierarchical. Similarly, he also believes that the new organisations will need to treat people as assets to be developed and motivated, rather than just so much industrial cannon fodder. However, he does not assume that the future will be without diversity in relation to the organisational forms that emerge. Unlike Peters and Waterman, and to a lesser extent Kanter, he recognises that companies will continue to face differing circumstances and will need to respond in different manners. Therefore, instead of trying to re-establish a new 'one best way' for all organisations, with all the contradictions that arise from such attempts, Handy identifies three generic types of organisation which he argues will dominate in the future:

1 the Shamrock organisation;

2 the Federal organisation;

3 the Triple I organisation.

These are detailed below.

### 1 The Shamrock organisation

This form of organisation, like the plant of the same name which has three interlocking leaves, is composed of three distinct groups of workers who are treated differently and have different expectations: a small group of specialist 'core' workers; a contractual fringe; and a flexible labour force.

The *core workers* are the first leaf, and the main distinguishing feature of the Shamrock form of organisation. These are a group of specialists, professional workers which form the brain, the hub or what we might call the 'nerve centre' of the organisation. These are people who are seen as being essential to the organisation. It is these few intelligent and articulate personnel in whose hands and heads reside the secrets of the organisation. They are both specialists and generalists, in that they run the organisation and control the smart machines and computers that have replaced, to a large extent, much of the labour force. This ' . . . all puts pressure on the core, a pressure which could be summed up by the new equation of half the people, paid twice as much, working three times as effectively' (Handy, 1989: 118–19).

For their well-rewarded jobs, they are expected to be extremely loyal to the organisation, and to live and breathe their work. It is their responsibility to drive the organisation forward to ever greater success; to be flexible enough to meet the constantly changing challenge of competitors and the equally changing and sophisticated needs of customers. Core workers operate as colleagues and partners in the organisation, as opposed to superiors and subordinates. In a very real sense, it is their company, and as such they expect to be recognised and rewarded for their roles and achievements, rather than the position they occupy on the organisation's ladder. It follows that they are managed differently – by consent: asked and not told what to do.

The *contractual fringe* is the second leaf of the Shamrock. A central feature of Shamrock organisations is their smallness in relation to their productive capacity. This is achieved by two methods: first, as mentioned above, the use of machines to replace people; and second, the contracting-out to individuals and other organisations of services and tasks previously done in-house. This leads to the creation of a contractual fringe, who may or may not work exclusively for the company in question. They are contracted to carry out certain tasks, for which they are paid a fee based on results, rather than a wage based on time taken. The arguments put forward in favour of such arrangements are numerous, but tend to boil down to three main ones:

- *It is cheaper* – companies only pay for what they get.

- *It makes management easier* – why keep the people on the payroll with all the attendant human management problems if it is not necessary?

- *Workload balancing* – when business is slack, it is the contractor who bears the impact of the reduced workload.

The *flexible labour force* is the third and fastest-growing leaf of the Shamrock and comprises a pool of part-time workers available for use by organisations. These are people with relevant skills who are not in need of, or who cannot obtain, full-time employment, but who are prepared to work on a part-time basis.

Increasingly, among this group of flexible workers are women who left their skilled jobs to raise families, but who are willing to return to work on a part-time basis, while still maintaining their child-rearing commitments. Included in this also is the growing army of young or retired executives, who prefer to hop from one job to another, doing bits and pieces of work on a part-time basis. These workers are sometimes referred to as temps (temporaries) or casuals. The growth of this group can be measured by the proliferation of employment agencies, catering solely for these groups, which have been established in the United Kingdom since the early 1980s. However, the flexible workforce never

> ...have the commitment or ambition of the core. Decent pay and decent conditions are what they want, ... They have jobs not careers and cannot be expected to rejoice in the organisation's triumphs any more than they can expect to share in the proceeds, nor will they put themselves out for the love of it; more work, in their culture, deserves and demands more money. (Handy, 1989: 80–1)

The picture, therefore, of the Shamrock organisation is one where structure and employment practices allow it to be big in terms of output, whilst being small in terms of the number of direct employees. For the latter reason, it is lean with few hierarchical layers and even less bureaucracy. It achieves this by the application of smart machines and a combination of part-time staff and subcontractors, whose work can be turned on and off as circumstances dictate. However, in a departure from past practice, the people involved may be highly skilled and competent. This also has the advantage of requiring much less office and factory accommodation than more traditionally organised companies. Other than the core staff, the rest are all scattered in different organisations or their own homes, often linked through sophisticated communication systems.

Such organisations, with their flexibility and skills, are well-suited to the provision of high-performance products and services to demanding and rapidly changing markets. The beauty of it all, as Handy argues, is that they do not have to employ all of the people all of the time or even in the same place to get the work done. According to Handy, small is not only beautiful but also increasingly preferable.

## 2 The federal organisation

This is the second type of generic organisation which Handy sees as becoming dominant in the future. He defines this type of organisation as a collection or network of individual organisations allied together under a common flag with some shaped identity. Federations arise for two reasons. The first is that, as Shamrock organisations grow bigger, the core workers begin to find the volume of information available to them to make decisions increasingly difficult to handle. Second, they constitute a response to the constantly changing and competitive environment of the business world. Modern organisations need not only to achieve the flexibility that comes from smallness, but also to be able to command the resources and power of big corporations.

As Handy (1989: 110) puts it:

> It [Federalism] allows individuals to work in organisation villages with the advantages of big city facilities. Organisational cities no longer work unless they are broken down into villages. In their big city mode they cannot cope with the variety needed in their products, their processes, and their people. On the other hand, the villages on their own have not the resources nor the imagination to grow. Some villages, of course, will be content to survive, happy in their niche, but global markets need global products and large confederations to make them or do them.

Federalism, therefore, implies the granting of autonomy to Shamrocks. Autonomy requires that Shamrocks are headed by their own separate chief executives, supported by a team of core workers, who take full responsibility for running the company. In such situations the Shamrocks become separate, but related entities, under the umbrella of the Federal Centre. With the devolving of power to the Shamrocks, who still remain in the Federal portfolio, the Federal Centre is left to pursue the business of providing a common platform for the integration of the activities of the Shamrocks. The Federal Centre has the role of generating and collating ideas from the different Shamrocks and making them into concrete, achievable strategic objectives. Therefore, the Federal Centre is concerned mainly with the future; with looking forward, generating ideas, and creating scenarios and options of what the future will look like. All this is done with the ultimate aim of moving the organisation forward and keeping it ahead not only of its rivals, but also of its time.

Another feature of the Federal organisation is what Handy refers to as the 'inverted do'nut'.

> The do'nut is an American doughnut. It is round with a hole in the middle rather than the jam in its British equivalent ... This, however, is an inverted American do'nut, in that it has the hole in the middle filled in and the space on the outside; ... The point of the analogy begins to emerge if you think of your job, or any job. There will be a part of the job which will be clearly defined, and which, if you do not do, you will be seen to have failed. That is the heart, the core, the centre of the do'nut ... [but] ... In any job of any significance the person holding the job is expected not only to do all that is required but in some way to improve on that ... to move into the empty space of the do'nut and begin to fill it up. (Handy, 1989: 102)

Through this approach, the Federal organisation seeks to maximise the innovative and creative potential of staff members. It does this by specifying the core job, the target and the quality standard expected of a given product or service. Outside of this specified domain, within the do'nut's empty space, however, staff members are given enough room and latitude to challenge and question existing ideas, to experiment and to come up with new methods of doing things, and new products or services. The aim is to encourage enquiry and experimentation that lead to higher standards. It follows from this that the essence of leadership under a Federal system is to provide a shared vision for the organisation; one which allows room for those whose lives will be affected by it – either directly or indirectly – to modify it, ponder over it, expand it, accept it and then make it a reality. Leadership in such situations is about providing opportunities for staff to grow and test their potential to the limit.

### 3 The Triple I organisation

This is the third of Handy's new organisational forms, although in fact it comprises a set of principles rather than a structural model. From the above, it is clear that both Shamrock and Federal organisation types introduce new dimensions into the world of work. Traditional perspectives are being transformed, and the established criteria for judging organisational effectiveness are being re-evaluated. Issues such as the definition of a productive contribution to work, reward systems, managerial skills and many more are being examined in the light of new management ideas. Indeed, according to Handy, we appear to be on the verge of a revolution in management thought and practice.

An examination of the attributes of the core workers in both Shamrock and Federal organisations gives an indication of what will constitute the new formula for success and effectiveness in tomorrow's companies. The core workers, as seen by Handy, use their *Intelligence* to analyse the available *Information* to generate *Ideas* for new products and services. Thus we find that Handy's first two organisational forms contain the seeds to produce his third form, the Triple I – organisations based on Intelligence, Information and Ideas. Since the three Is constitute the prime intellectual capital of the new organisations, clearly the Triple I principle applies most importantly to the core group of workers who are in a position to possess these attributes.

In future, it is argued, the equation for organisational success will be Triple I = AV, where Triple I = Intelligence, Information and Ideas, and AV = Added Value, either in cash or kind. This will be an organisation 'obsessed with the pursuit of truth, or, in business language, of quality' (Handy, 1989: 113). This will not depend solely on human ability but will be a combination of smart people and smart machines. Therefore, organisations of the future will increasingly have to (a) invest in smart machines to remain competitive and effective; (b) recruit skilled and smart people to control the machines; and (c) ensure that this group of skilled people is rewarded equitably.

For the Triple I organisation to emerge and remain successful, it must keep the skills, knowledge and abilities of its staff up to date. This means that it must become a learning organisation; one that provides a conducive environment for the development of its intellectual capital. Time and effort must be consciously and officially devoted to learning and study, at all levels of the organisation. The core, especially, must spend more time than their equivalents in more traditional companies on thinking and study: meeting with other external professionals and experts, going on study tours and listening more to 'partners' within the organisation, all with the objective of improving the organisation's human capital. The new organisations will be dynamic, interactive societies where information is open to all, freely given and freely received. In the Triple I organisation, everyone will be expected to think and learn as well as to do.

Nevertheless, it is the core worker from whom most will be demanded. Such people will be increasingly:

> ... expected to have not only the expertise appropriate to his or her particular role, but will also be required to know and understand business, to have the technical skills of analysis and the human skills and the conceptual skills and to keep them up to date. (Handy, 1989: 124)

This is one of the key features that make the Triple I organisation unique; it is a hotbed of intellectual discourse, where the prevailing culture is one of consent rather than instruction. Staff are unsupervised in the traditional sense, and instead are trusted to do what is right and given room to experiment with new ideas and concepts. Finally, the flexibility of such organisations, and the unpredictability of the environments in which they operate, mean that careers will become more variegated and less permanent.

As can be seen, therefore, Handy's view of the future shape of organisations does not appear dissimilar to that of Kanter, and Peters and Waterman. However, he does depart from their views in at least two crucial respects. First, he explicitly acknowledges that not all organisations will adopt the same form or move at the same pace. His three generic forms indicate that organisations will have to exercise choice and judgement in order to match their particular circumstances to the most suitable form. Also, it is clear that he views this as an evolutionary as well as a revolutionary process: companies cannot immediately become a Triple I type of organisation; they have to develop into one over time. Second, he explicitly states what is only hinted at by the other writers, namely that in the new organisations where everyone is to be treated as an equal 'partner', some will be more equal than others, i.e. the core workers will be treated and rewarded in a more preferential manner than the contractual fringe or the flexible labour force.

Handy does not give specific guidance as to how existing organisations can adapt themselves to take on these new forms, although he does indicate that a lack of empowerment and self-belief amongst individuals in organisations presents a major obstacle to change. However, in an earlier work (Handy, 1986), he does state very clearly that fundamental change is a long-term process and that people tend to react emotionally rather than rationally to change.

After the publication of *The Age of Unreason*, Handy appeared to grow increasingly concerned with the unanticipated consequences of his prescriptions for the world of work. This is made clear in the first paragraph of his 1994 book, *The Empty Raincoat*:

> Four years ago, my earlier book, *The Age of Unreason*, was published. In that book I presented a view of the way work was being reshaped and the effects which the reshaping might have on all our lives. It was, on the whole, an optimistic view. Since then, the world of work has changed very much along the lines which were described in the book. This should be comforting to an author, but I have not found it so. Too many people and institutions have been unsettled by the changes. Capitalism has not proved as flexible as it was supposed to be. Governments have not been all-wise or far-seeing. Life is a struggle for many and a puzzle for most.

> What is happening in our mature societies is much more fundamental, confusing and distressing than I had expected. (Handy, 1994: 1)

In *The Empty Raincoat*, Handy returns to and restates many of the themes of his earlier work, but with two differences. First, he explicitly acknowledges that the types of careers that these new organisational forms will create will have a severely adverse effect on the home life of employees, especially senior managers. They will be called on to be company men and women above all else, including their families.

Second, there is an almost evangelical feel to the book. This is especially noticeable in the latter section of the book, where Handy argues that the modern world has taken meaning out of people's lives and that, whilst the pursuit of profit may motivate senior managers:

> Not many in the lower realms of the organisation can get excited by the thought of enriching shareholders. 'Excellence' and 'quality' are the right sort of words, but they have been tarnished by repetition in too many organisations. (Handy, 1994: 265)

This more pessimistic view of the future is still there in his 1997 book, *The Hungry Spirit* (Handy, 1997: 3):

> Many of us are, I believe, confused by the world we have created for ourselves in the West ... the new fashion for turning everything into a business, even our own lives, doesn't seem to be the answer. A hospital, and my life, is more than just a business.
> What good can it possibly do to pile up riches which you cannot conceivably use, and what is the point of the efficiency needed to create those riches if one third of the world's workers are now unemployed or under-employed as the ILO calculates? And where will it end, this passion for growth? ... I am angered by the waste of so many people's lives, dragged down by poverty in the midst of riches. I am concerned by the absence of a more transcendent view of life and the purposes of life, and by the prevalence of the economic myth which colours all we do. Money is the means for life and not the point of it.

In the book, Handy argues that, in the West, people's spiritual needs have been sacrificed to the pursuit of their material needs; and he examines the options, and where the responsibility lies, for putting balance back into people's lives. In particular he is concerned with the distribution of wealth, the role that education can play in giving everyone a good start in life, and how we can look after ourselves whilst having a care for others as well. He even touches on, perhaps, the biggest question of all: 'What, ultimately, is the real purpose of life?' (Handy, 1997: 5). In addressing these issues he ranges widely, looking at markets, organisations and the role of business, government and religion. He believes the answer lies in the pursuit of 'Proper Selfishness'. This is a redefinition of individualism; he sees individuals as moving away from the pursuit of narrow self-interest, and instead realising that it is in their best interests to pursue a fairer society for all. Though he identifies a role for government and business in creating Proper Selfishness, he believes it is individuals themselves who bear the main responsibility for its achievement. In particular, he draws attention to the role of individual entrepreneurs in changing the world:

Entrepreneurs, whether social or commercial, often discover aspects of themselves in the pursuit of something beyond themselves. Such people are not content to let the status quo be the way forward. They itch to make a difference ... Almost accidentally, corporations have become the nursery for frustrated entrepreneurs. They should turn this to a positive account and do it more deliberately, in the hope that they can retain some of the best for themselves, including women, while seeding the community with the others. The work-place has always been the real school for life. Perhaps it just needs to change its curriculum a little to tune in with the new age of personal initiative. (Handy, 1997: 262)

Handy calls for a new sense of purpose for individuals, organisations and society. He wants to see a strong ethical approach to business and society, and a recreation of the concept that people exist to help and serve each other as well as themselves. These are sentiments which many of us would probably share but, unfortunately, he fails to show how the unleashing of individual entrepreneurship and the creation of the new organisational forms he advocates will aid this search for meaning. Instead, he asks us to put our faith in the goodness of people and to be optimistic about the future. However, a recurrent theme in Handy's work has been the many paradoxes thrown up by contemporary society, especially the presence of dire poverty amidst extreme wealth, and the potential of technology for creating meaningful work compared with the increasing tendency for the quality of life to decline. Therefore, it seems strange that the one paradox that Handy appears to ignore is that the forms of organisations that he advocates may well be creating the poor jobs and poverty he deprecates.

## Culture–Excellence: summary and criticisms

That the Culture–Excellence approach has had a major impact on the thinking of Western businesses, especially in the UK and USA, is beyond question. *In Search of Excellence* has sold over six million copies, making it the best-selling management book of all time. Largely as a result of its success, its authors, especially Tom Peters, have become successful and influential consultants. Rosabeth Moss Kanter and Charles Handy have likewise achieved the pre-eminence in business circles that they had previously only occupied in academia. A look in the business section of any bookshop will show that there are also many more authors who have jumped on the bandwagon. Indeed, barely a day seems to go by without the publication of yet another blockbuster proclaiming that it has discovered the recipe for success. Some of these achieve a degree of prominence in business circles, though many seem to disappear without trace. Nevertheless, the fact that publishers keep publishing them, and that in different ways and shapes they repeat and project the Culture–Excellence message, emphasises the thirst by managers for the message.

Nor is it just a case that managers buy them to leave them on the shelf. Over the last two decades, on both sides of the Atlantic, managers have been attempting to re-shape their companies along the Culture–Excellence lines. In 1997, a survey by the Industrial Society showed that in the UK alone some 94 per cent of respondent organisations either had recently been through or were going through a culture change programme (Industrial Society, 1997).

The reason for its emergence, and for its continuing popularity, was that in a world where old certainties had disappeared, where new and more dangerous competitors seemed to appear every day, it rejected the communal and corporatist approach of the Japanese, and offered instead a recipe for success that was in tune with the free market liberalism, with its stress on individualism, which has dominated much of the West for the last two decades. Nor was it merely a rehash of what had gone before. The Culture–Excellence approach to organisations is significantly different from previous approaches; although we might note that the new forms, especially Handy's Shamrock type, bear an interesting resemblance to the first budding of organisational life during the Industrial Revolution. The entrepreneurial style of management, the stress on a privileged core of skilled workers, and the contracting-out of whole areas of organisational activities are all hallmarks of the early industrial organisations. However, the big differences between then and now relate to the level of sophistication and complexity of the new organisations that are emerging, the degree of integration of both internal functions and external relationships, the grade of intelligence and skill required of all staff, whether they be core or periphery – and, of course, the conditions of employment. For Watson (1986: 66), who coined the term Culture–Excellence school to describe proponents of this approach, there is one further and crucial difference:

> [In these new organisations] What brings the activities of the organisational members to focus upon those purposes which lead to effective performance is the existence of a strong and clearly articulated culture. (Watson, 1986: 66)

It is this which makes it clear that the Culture–Excellence approach that has been developing over the last two decades is remarkably different from most of the theory and practice that has grown up in the last 100 years.

Peters, Kanter and Handy argue that organisations are entering a new age, where familiar themes are taking on different meanings and are being expressed in a new language. Contrasting the old with the new, they argue that what is important in the new is not muscle power, but brain power: the ability to make intelligent use of information to create ideas that add value and sustain competitiveness. The new organisation is flatter in structure, though it might be more accurate to say that structure is decreasing in importance and that its role as a directing and controlling mechanism is being taken over by cultures that stress the need for, and facilitate, flexibility and adaptation (though in passing we should note that Peters (1993) also sees the dismembering of hierarchical structures as an important step in creating these new cultures). The Culture–Excellence approach is sounding the death knell of hierarchical organisations and the concept of promotion through the ranks. Careers and skills are taking on new meanings, as are established ideas of reward.

In future, it is argued, careers are likely to depend on the individual and his/her ability to remain employable. In turn, the skills needed for 'employability' will tend to be generic and broad-based rather than organisation- or function/specialism-specific. Likewise, career paths and promotion will no longer be shaped by the particular employing organisation and its structures and criteria, but will be driven more by individuals creating their own opportunities by taking on new roles and responsibilities, either in one organisation or, more likely, by moving from company to company. As for pay, it seems that this will take the form not so much of a wage related to the particular post occupied, but more that of a fee paid for actual performance.

On human relations, the message being transmitted is that the new forms of organisations will treat their employees in a more responsible and humane fashion than has been the norm. Employees will be seen and treated as 'partners', capable of making a substantial contribution to the growth of the organisation. This approach, it is argued, will manifest itself in a tough-minded respect for the individual, who will receive training, be set reasonable and clear objectives, and be given the autonomy to make his/her own contribution to the work of the organisation. The new organisations will seek to develop open, flexible and pragmatic cultures, which help to maintain a learning environment that promotes creativity and entrepreneurship amongst all employees.

Another feature of the new organisational forms, it is claimed, will be their ability to grant autonomy and encourage flexibility and initiative whilst at the same time keeping tight control of their operations. Like so much else, this is to be achieved through culture rather than structure, and values rather than rules. Everything is to be monitored closely, not by the watching eye of superiors, but by the creation of a homogeneous environment in which all take an equal responsibility for, and legitimate interest in, the work of their colleagues.

Clearly, the new organisation forms which are being promoted offer much that is admirable and worth supporting. Equally clearly, their adherents and promoters raise more questions than they answer. To an extent this is inevitable when dealing with something that is emerging rather than an existing and concrete reality. However, as this concept has been around for nearly two decades, this is no longer the case. Therefore, it would be remiss to ignore or gloss over the questions and dilemmas that seem apparent. Many writers have drawn attention to the shortcomings of the Culture–Excellence approach. Carroll (1983) and Lawler (1985) were both scathing about the methodological shortcomings of the research on which Peters and Waterman's (1982) book was based; Wilson (1992) went further, claiming that it lacks any apparent empirical or theoretical foundations. Though Wilson's criticisms may seem somewhat exaggerated, it is certainly arguable that the Culture–Excellence approach does have serious weaknesses, especially in three areas that are crucial to the operation of organisations:

1 **People**. There are serious concerns and contradictions regarding the role and behaviour of people in the new organisations. On the one hand, they are proclaimed as the chief asset of the new organisations. On the other hand, there are clearly different grades of employee, from core to periphery, and these

different grades will be treated and rewarded in a markedly dissimilar manner; furthermore, none of the different grades can expect any real job security. The new organisations will only value employees as long as they and their areas perform to the highest of standards. Not only does this pit individual against individual, but also one part of the organisation against another. Whilst healthy competition may enhance organisational competitiveness, from what we know of motivation theory (Arnold *et al*, 1998) it is not clear that the Culture–Excellence approach is that healthy. The Culture–Excellence approach also encourages teamwork, yet the pursuit of individual advancement and reward often leads to conflict rather than co-operation (Schein, 1988).

2 **Politics**. Though Western companies traditionally either deny the existence of internal struggles or argue that such behaviour is perverse, it is clear that the struggle for resources, power and survival is as great within organisations as it is between them (Kanter *et al*, 1992; Pfeffer, 1981; Robbins, 1986). As stated above, the recommendations of the Culture–Excellence school would seem to exacerbate this tendency between individuals and groups, yet in the main they ignore this drawback to their approach, even though it is potentially damaging to both organisational and individual performance.

3 **Culture**. The proponents of Culture–Excellence are advocating a 'one best way' (one best culture) approach for all organisations, irrespective of their size, environment and other circumstances. Also, as Wilson (1992) pointed out, it assumes a simple causal relationship between culture and performance.

Nevertheless, for the proponents of the Culture–Excellence school, culture is the great cure-all – the creation of a culture of excellence is seen as answering all questions and solving all problems. This assumes that the creation of new cultures will itself be unproblematic. However, as the next chapter will show, culture and politics appear to be the Achilles' heel of approaches to managing organisations.

It would also be remiss of us if we ignored the differences between the main proponents of Culture–Excellence. Peters is a free market liberal in the classic American mould. He believes that individual and organisational competition untrammelled by government is what makes societies strong. Kanter agrees with most of this, but believes that local communities, working with big business, have a positive role to play in attracting and keeping well-paid jobs for their communities. Handy is also committed to the free market, but has become increasingly concerned with the outcome of his prescriptions. He appears to be turning his back on pure individualism, arguing instead for a less rapacious, more caring capitalism, driven by what he terms 'Proper Selfishness' and more concerned with the collective good than individual wealth creation. Though Peters and Kanter may continue to hold to the Culture–Excellence line, it is difficult to see that the direction which Handy is now taking is consistent with it.

There is one final concern that is wider than the Culture–Excellence approach *per se* or its impact on organisations, but which is reflected in the differences between Peters, Kanter and Handy. The move towards creating segmented workforces of the type described by Handy (1989) and the emphasis on the temporary nature of employment championed by Peters and Waterman (1982) and Kanter (1989) is part of a continuing trend in the West, driven by neo-liberal economic and social policies, towards worsening job security and conditions of service, in order to create a vast pool of under-employed, especially part-time, labour that can be turned on or off as the situation dictates.

In the UK in 1993, for example, some 9.7 million workers (38 per cent of all UK workers) were either part-time, temporary, self-employed, on a government training scheme, or unpaid family workers – an increase of 1.25 million since 1986. Similarly, the proportion of men in employment who were part of the flexible workforce rose from 18 per cent in 1981 to 27.5 per cent in 1993 (Watson, 1994). This tallies with Hutton's (1995) argument that the UK is now more socially divided than at any time since the Industrial Revolution. In particular, he maintains that the UK is a 30/30/40 society – the marginalised, the newly insecure and the advantaged – and that this not only raises the spectre of increased social tensions, but is a positive disadvantage to wealth creation. Hutton's attack on the adverse effects of neo-liberal market policies is supported by others, notably Saul (1997), who points out that the income gap between the highest- and lowest-paid workers in the UK is greater now than at any time since 1880, when records began. Figures published by the UK government (Brindle, 1998a) show that since 1979, whilst the richest 10 per cent of the population have seen their incomes grow by 70 per cent in real terms, the bottom 10 per cent of the population have suffered a cut in real income of 9 per cent. In the same period, poverty in the UK has almost tripled. As White (1999) noted, this increase in poverty has had an especially adverse impact on children. In 1979, 1 in 10 children lived in poverty. In 1996/7, the figure was 1 in 3. The reason for this increase appears to be very clear: 32 per cent of children now live in families without a full-time worker. Nor is this bleak picture restricted to the UK. As Dunphy and Griffiths (1998) point out, in 1980, the Chief Executive Officers of the 300 largest US companies had incomes 29 times that of the average manufacturing worker; 10 years later, their incomes were 93 times greater. Indeed, the founder of Microsoft, Bill Gates, has a personal fortune which is greater than the combined wealth of the 106 million poorest Americans (Elliott and Brittain, 1998). Much of the economic and labour market liberalisation in the 1980s was justified by 'trickle-down' economics – the view that as the rich got richer, then some of this wealth would trickle down to the rest of society and, therefore, society as a whole would become wealthier. This clearly does not appear to be the case. Not surprisingly, if one looks at the poorest nations in the world, especially in Africa and South and South-East Asia, the situation is much worse, with malnutrition, poverty and disease on the increase (Gittings, 1998). In terms of the USA, Robert Reich, who was Secretary of Labor in the first Clinton Administration, and other leading figures have warned of the dangers of a social chasm opening up between an ever-increasing rich elite, holed up in guarded compounds, and a jobless, impoverished majority (Elliott, 1997; Reich, 1997). Indeed, as a sign of this, there are now more private security guards in the

USA than there are publicly employed police (Dunphy and Griffiths, 1998). Contrast this with the case of Japan, discussed next, where, traditionally, at government and organisation level, full employment takes precedence over profit and underpins its voracious appetite for economic expansion (Holden and Burgess, 1994).

Despite these concerns and criticisms, the Culture–Excellence approach has become increasingly influential in the USA and Europe, as is apparent from the many articles on its merits and case studies of its use that appear regularly in management journals. However, since the 1950s, the Japanese have been developing an alternative approach to structuring and managing organisations that is not only markedly different from the Culture–Excellence one but also has a proven track record of success.

## THE JAPANESE APPROACH TO MANAGEMENT

The last 50 years have seen the rebirth of Japan. Reduced almost to ashes at the end of the Second World War, by the 1980s Japan had built an industrial empire second to none. As Morgan (1986: 111) stated:

> With virtually no natural resources, no energy, and over 110 million people crowded in four small mountainous islands, Japan succeeded in achieving the highest growth rate, lowest level of unemployment and, at least in some of the larger and more successful organizations, one of the best-paid and healthiest working populations in the world.

Though writers suggested many reasons for Japan's success, ranging from culture to economic institutions, time and again, its approach to managing organisations was cited as the key factor (Hunter, 1989; Laage-Hellman, 1997; Sako and Sato, 1997; Schonberger, 1982; Smith and Misumi, 1989; Whitehill, 1991).

Before proceeding to examine what is meant by the Japanese approach to management, it is useful briefly to trace Japan's development as an industrial nation. Up to the middle of the nineteenth century, Japan was an intensely nationalistic society which practised a deliberate policy of isolating itself from the outside world. Therefore, for most of its inhabitants, Japan was the world. It was a feudal country which laid strong emphasis on obligation and deference, and where obedience to authority in general, and to the Emperor in particular, was unquestioned (Sheridan, 1993).

For all its deliberate isolation, Japan was a sophisticated and well-educated country with a high degree of literacy. Education was based on a set of Confucian principles which stressed unquestioning obedience to the family; total loyalty to one's superiors; and reverence for education and self-development. The abiding influence of these can still be seen in Japanese society today, and underpins the strength of Japanese organisations (Smith and Misumi, 1989). However, from the mid-nineteenth century, Japan began to experience internal tensions. The feudal aristocracy experienced escalating financial difficulties whilst the merchant class, considered social inferiors, began to prosper. At the same time, it became clear that the growing military might of other countries posed a potential threat to Japan. In response to these developments, Japan adopted a twin-track policy of economic and military growth, not dissimilar to that being developed in Germany at this time (Hunter, 1989).

Missions were dispatched abroad to study and bring technologies and practices back to Japan. On one such visit in 1911, Yukinori Hoshino, a director of the Kojima Bank, became acquainted with the work of Frederick Taylor and obtained permission to translate his work into Japanese. Following this, Taylor's Scientific Management principles, and allied approaches to work study and production management, were rapidly and enthusiastically adopted by the Japanese (McMillan, 1985). Indeed, such was the impact of Taylor's work that, according to Wren (1994: 205), it '... led to a management revolution, replacing the entrepreneur-dominated age'. By the 1920s, Japan had moved from being an agrarian economy to one dominated by industry. Like many Western countries, industrialisation was accompanied by considerable industrial conflict, sometimes violent (Urabe, 1986). However, unlike most Western countries, this was not accompanied by a growing democratisation of society. Instead, democratic tendencies were quashed by a growing coalition between industry and the military which promoted intense nationalism and led, almost inexorably, to the Second World War. After Japan's defeat, its shattered society was occupied by the USA, which stripped the Emperor of his traditional powers and established a Western-style democracy (Sheridan, 1993; Whitehill, 1991).

Given the state of the Japanese economy after the Second World War, the success of its reconstruction is nothing short of miraculous. The Korean War in the 1950s proved a stroke of good fortune for Japan, in that the USA used Japan as an important staging post for troops and supplies. This injected billions of American dollars into Japan's economy. However, perhaps much more important was America's contribution to management education in Japan. In the immediate post-war years, Japanese companies acquired a reputation for bitter industrial disputes, shoddy workmanship and poor quality. The main responsibility for tackling these problems lay with American engineers working for the Civilian Communications Section of the Occupation Administration (Sheldrake, 1996). Four men in particular have been credited with turning this situation around and creating the basis of Japan's fearsome reputation for the productivity of its workforce and quality of its products: Charles Protzman, Homer Sarasohn, Joseph Juran and W Edward Deming. Interestingly, the last three of these had all worked at Western Electric's Hawthorne Works and were, therefore, familiar, though not necessarily always in agreement, with the Human Relations approach. All of them were far removed from the narrow concept of the engineer. They took a wide view of how enterprises should be run and in particular of the need for managers to show leadership and gain the commitment of their workforces. Their approach, which covered business policy and organisation as well as production methods and techniques, was enthusiastically received, adopted and disseminated by the senior managers who attended their courses and lectures. As Horsley and Buckley (1990: 51) noted, Deming, especially, met with enormous success:

> W E Deming became a legend in Japan. He gave hundreds of lectures ... to eager managers on the vital importance of statistical quality control ... Among his pupils were many who were to become captains of Japanese industry in the 1960s and 1970s, heading firms like Nissan, Sharp and the Nippon Electric Company (NEC). The annual Deming Prize for good management was highly coveted in the 1950s, and is still being awarded today.

Nevertheless, despite the economic and technical assistance of the USA, there is little doubt that the main credit for the country's success can be attributed to the hard work, commitment and intelligence of Japanese managers and workers. Under the umbrella of a supportive economic and political framework, Japanese enterprises overcame their severe industrial relations and quality problems of the 1950s and created the distinctive and hugely successful Japanese approach to developing and managing their businesses which allowed them to take the world by storm in the 1970s and 1980s (Fruin, 1992; Pascale and Athos, 1982; Sako and Sato, 1997; Sheldrake, 1996; Smith and Misumi, 1989).

## What is the Japanese approach to management?

As one might expect, it is difficult to find an all-embracing definition of the Japanese approach to management that satisfies all commentators or can be found in all Japanese companies. In particular, there are distinct differences between larger and smaller enterprises in Japan, and in the treatment of full-time and part-time, and male and female employees in all enterprises (Cole, 1979; Laage-Hellman, 1997; Sako and Sato, 1997). Indeed, such are these differences that some argue there is either no such thing as a distinctive Japanese approach to management or that, if it does exist, no one has been able to capture it accurately (Dale, 1986; Keys and Miller, 1984; Sullivan, 1983). Nevertheless, the vast majority of observers do seem to agree that it exists and can, broadly, be defined (Abegglen and Stalk, 1984; Ackroyd et al, 1988; Hatvany and Pucik, 1981; Holden and Burgess, 1994; Pascale and Athos, 1982; Smith and Misumi, 1989).

Perhaps the most influential work, and still the best-selling book, on Japanese management was William Ouchi's (1981) Theory Z: How American Business Can Meet the Japanese Challenge. Drawing on the theoretical insights of Douglas McGregor and Chris Argyris, Ouchi argued that Japanese success stemmed from the involvement and commitment of the entire workforce. In turn, he argued, this was built upon a set of internally consistent norms, practices and behaviours based on trust and strong personal ties between the individual and the organisation, particularly their immediate workgroup. Ouchi drew particular attention to practices such as lifetime employment, slow evaluation and promotion and collective decision-making. Many other writers have also tried to capture the essence of Japanese management.

McKenna (1988) believes that the key elements are lifetime employment, the seniority principle with regard to pay and promotion, and enterprise unionism. Pang and Oliver (1988) agree with McKenna but also draw attention to training and education, company-based welfare schemes, quality circles and manufacturing methods such as Just-in-Time production. Keys and Miller (1984) point to long-term planning, lifetime employment and collective responsibility as being the hallmarks of Japanese management. Laage-Hellman (1997) emphasises the presence of a consensus-seeking decision-making process, incremental planning through the development of a long-term vision and the use of short-term action plans, passive owners who do not usually interfere with managers, strategies that give priority to long-term growth and survival, and the effective use of external resources through partnerships with suppliers and customers. Other commentators have also come up with similar lists.

One of the most quoted of these is by Pascale and Athos (1982) who used the McKinsey Seven S Framework (strategy, structure, systems, staff, style, shared values, and skills), which they had developed jointly with Tom Peters and Robert Waterman, to analyse Japanese management. Like Peters and Waterman's Culture–Excellence approach, Pascale and Athos stressed the four 'soft' Ss (staff, style, shared values, and skills). This was not to dismiss the 'hard' Ss (strategy, structure and systems), but to emphasise that the real difference between Japanese companies and their Western counterparts was that the latter tended to concentrate on the 'hard' Ss and ignore the 'soft' Ss. Pascale and Athos argued that, in contrast, Japanese companies had developed the ability to combine and blend the 'soft' and 'hard' Ss to their competitive benefit. Their work differed from other studies of Japanese management at the time by examining the management style of Japanese companies operating in the USA. In a similar vein, Peter Wickens, who was Personnel Director of Nissan Motor Manufacturing (UK) Ltd for over 10 years, also commented on the transfer of Japanese management to the West. In his 1987 book, *The Road To Nissan*, written when he was still at Nissan, he argued that the Japanese approach can be characterised by three factors: teamwork, quality-consciousness and flexibility. Interestingly, after he left Nissan, Wickens (1995) commented that Ouchi and others tended to miss, or underplay, one very important element of Japanese companies – their very strong control culture, especially in relation to shopfloor workers.

The factors identified by the above writers can be separated into two categories: those relating to personnel/industrial relations issues and those relating to business/manufacturing practices.

### Personnel issues

The dedication, commitment and ability of Japanese workers is seen as a major factor in the success of Japanese companies. Though much credit for this has been given to the culture of Japanese society, especially its Confucian tradition of obedience and loyalty, similar levels of motivation have been reproduced in Japanese companies operating in the West (Wickens, 1987), which would imply that other factors are also at work. Chief among these is the crucial role played by the personnel policies prevalent in many Japanese enterprises, especially the larger ones. The core of the Japanese approach to personnel comprises a combination of practices and policies designed to socialise and bind employees to the organisation, and promote their long-term development and commitment. The principal practices and policies concerned are as follows:

1 **Lifetime employment**. Many employees are recruited straight from school or university, and expect, and are expected, to spend the rest of their working lives with the same organisation. This 'guarantee', based as it is on an age-old sense of mutual obligation and belonging, creates an intense sense of loyalty to and dependence on the organisation. Indeed, Holden and Burgess (1994) observed that whilst a Japanese worker might survive the loss of his family, the collapse of his employing organisation would be unbearable. Therefore, lifetime employment is a central feature of the Japanese approach and supports so much else, including a willingness to change and the maintenance of a stable organisational culture. However, the fact that organisations prefer to recruit school or university leavers also makes it difficult for individuals to move between companies once they have accepted an appointment. It follows that if someone is fired, their chances of securing other employment are negligible.

2 **Internal labour markets**. Most positions are filled from inside the company. This is a corollary to lifetime employment which demonstrates to the employee that satisfactory performance will bring promotion, and it eliminates the potential for tension which can be brought about by the recruitment of outsiders.

3 **Seniority-based promotion and reward systems**. Employees are ranked and rewarded primarily, but not exclusively, on their length of service, and independent of the precise nature of the job they perform.

4 **Teamwork and bonding**. Although Japanese employees are made to feel part of the organisation and see it as some sort of extended family, they are first and foremost a member of a particular workgroup or team. The group is not just a collection of individuals; it is constructed and developed in such a way that it comprises a single entity which takes collective responsibility for its performance. Japanese companies use a variety of techniques, both at work and in a social setting, for bonding team members to each other and to the organisation.

5 **Enterprise (single company) unions**. Unlike the West, Japanese companies tend to allow only one union to represent the interests of the workforce. In addition, Japanese unions tend to be single company or enterprise unions. Indeed, from a Western point of view, they are not so much trade unions as company associations. This is illustrated by the practice of senior managers, at some stage in their careers, being expected to serve as union officials.

6 **Training and education**. Extensive and continuous training and education form an integral part of Japanese personnel policies. This emphasis on the

continual development of employees to enable them to carry out their work better and to prepare them for promotion represents a significant investment by Japanese companies in their human capital. Much of the training is done on the job and is always geared to the twin aims of improving organisational perform-ance and individual development. Though encouraged by the company, employees are expected to take responsibility for their own self-development.

7 **Company welfarism**. Many Japanese companies provide a wide range of welfare benefits for their employees. These can cover medical treatment, education for children and even housing. Some of the larger companies are almost mini welfare states in themselves.

Many other practices and policies could be added to the list, but these appear to be at the core. They are designed to instill the following in employees:

- loyalty and gratitude to the company and a commitment to its objectives;
- a sense of security;
- a strong commitment to hard work and performance improvement;
- an atmosphere of co-operation and not conflict;
- a belief in self-development and improvement.

These are the cornerstone of Japanese company life; their presence is the reason why Japanese national culture is often cited as being at the heart of Japan's ability to compete in a world market. These operate within organisation structures which, to Western eyes at least, appear complex, highly formalised and very hierarchical (Whitehill, 1991). However, these personnel issues cannot be seen in isolation from the working practices that Japanese companies use or the objectives they pursue. It is the combination of the two that makes Japanese companies so effective (Wood, 1991). Without overall direction and the appropriate work systems, even the best skilled and motivated workers are ineffective. This is why Japanese business practices and work systems should receive as much attention as personnel issues.

### Business practices and work systems

The Japanese ability to satisfy customers, and thereby capture markets, by developing and producing products to a higher specification and at a lower cost than their competitors, is staggering considering the state of their industry in the 1940s and 1950s. Indeed, even as recently as the 1960s, 'Made in Japan' was synonymous with poor quality. What has changed, or rather what has come to fruition, has been the methods they apply to all aspects of business, but especially to manufacturing (Hannam, 1993). The fact that some of these methods have, quite naturally, Japanese names (such as *Hoshin Kanri* – policy deployment; *Genba Kanri* – workshop management; *Kaizen* – continuous improvement; *Kanban* – a paperless form of scheduling) tends, for the Western audience, to cloak and mystify the core principles and systems being used, and also to disguise how much of these have been adopted from the West. Leaving aside the jargon and terminology, Japanese business practices and work systems can be characterised by three interrelated elements: long-term planning, timeliness and quality.

**Long-term planning**. This will be discussed further in Chapters 5 and 6, but for now, in brief, let us say that the timescale on which Japanese enterprises operate is far longer than many of their Western competitors, and their focus on building a strong market position similarly contrasts with the short-term profit maximisation objectives prevalent in the USA and UK in particular (Hamel and Prahalad, 1989). Needless to say, this is an enormous advantage when considering investment decisions, whether this be for products, processes or people (Smith and Misumi, 1989).

**Timeliness**. The Japanese are seen as having a crucial competitive edge in their ability to develop products and bring them to market faster than their competitors. Part of the explanation for this relates to teamwork. Whilst many Western companies are still designing and developing products on a sequential basis (whereby one part of the design is completed before another is begun), the Japanese work in teams to undertake these tasks simultaneously. This form of teamwork extends to working jointly with customers and suppliers as well (Laage-Hellman, 1997). Not only does this cut the overall time required, but it also leads to fewer errors and misunderstandings because all the relevant parties are involved (Womack *et al*, 1990). Another major contribution to the timeliness of the Japanese is a series of practices designed to cut manufacturing lead times. The main one is *Just-in-Time* production. Under Just-in-Time, parts are supplied and used only as and when required. This method reduces stock and work-in-progress and thus reduces cost. However, to achieve this (as proponents of lean/agile manufacturing have stressed) requires everything to be 'right first time', otherwise such a system would quickly grind to a halt for lack of usable parts (Kidd and Karwowski, 1994; Lamming, 1993). Therefore, it is necessary to drive waste and inefficiency out of the system, and the key mechanism for achieving this is the Japanese commitment to quality (Dale and Cooper, 1992).

**Quality**. The Japanese commitment to quality is now legendary. Their approach owes much to the inspiration of three Americans: MacArthur, Deming and Juran (Wilkinson, 1991). General MacArthur, who (on behalf of the USA) virtually ruled Japan in the early post-war years, encouraged Japanese industry to improve production quality as part of the rebuilding of their shattered industrial base. Deming (1982) showed the Japanese that statistical process control (SPC), and other such techniques, are powerful methods of controlling quality. Juran (1988) showed the Japanese that quality was determined by all departments in an organisation, and thus set them on the road to developing Total Quality Management. Though imported, the Japanese developed the original concepts considerably. In particular, they introduced the concept of continuous improvement – *kaizen*. Despite the widespread acceptance of the need for improved quality in the West, the Japanese appear to be the only nation so far capable of diffusing successfully the ideas and practices throughout their industry (Dale and Cooper, 1992; Hannam, 1993; Schonberger, 1982; Womack *et al*, 1990).

In any investigation of the Japanese approach to long-term planning, timeliness and quality, it is necessary to recognise the role played by employees in decision-making. Most discussions of Japanese management emphasise the occurrence of upward influence, particularly through the *ringi* system. This is a procedure whereby proposals for new policies, procedures or expenditure are circulated throughout the firm for comment. The proposal is circulated in written form, and is then sent to all who might be affected if it were to be implemented, in ascending order of seniority. The proposal is modified in line with comments, and only when all agree is it implemented. This joint approach to decision-making is also operated through production councils and quality circles, and covers the planning and scheduling of production, work allocation, changes to production methods, problem-solving, etc. (Inagami, 1988). This system of involving large numbers of people in decision-making is the reason why the Japanese are notorious for the slowness with which they make decisions, and famous for their ability to get it right first time (Hannam, 1993; Smith and Misumi, 1989). However, the *ringi* system also has another equally important benefit, as Morgan (1986: 93) states:

> The ringi is as much a process for exploring and reaffirming values as it is for setting a direction . . . In the American view objectives should be hard and fast and clearly stated for all to see. In the Japanese view they emerge from a more fundamental process of exploring and understanding the values through which a firm is or should be operating. A knowledge of these values, the limits that are to guide actions, defines a set of possible actions. An action chosen from this set may not be the very best, but it will satisfy parameters deemed crucial for success.

One factor only mentioned briefly so far is the importance – or not – of culture to the Japanese approach to management. Certainly, early studies laid great stress on the relationship between Japanese culture and business success (Abegglen, 1958). The argument emerged that it was the nature of Japanese society and its impact on individuals and companies that gave Japan its competitive edge. For this reason, it was argued, the West would never be able to replicate Japanese practices and competitiveness successfully. Indeed, one reason why Pascale and Athos (1982) chose to study Japanese companies operating in America was that Pascale doubted whether American companies could learn much from the Japanese in Japan because their cultures were so different (Crainer, 1995). Obviously, as Hofstede (1980, 1990) showed, national cultures do impinge on organisational practices. However, whether or not this means that such practices cannot successfully be adopted in other societies is another question. Recent work has undermined the argument for considering the Japanese approach to management to be dependent on Japanese culture. It has been shown that many of the distinctive practices of Japanese companies are relatively new and not embedded in Japanese history, that the role of culture is less influential than other factors, and that the Japanese approach can be successfully replicated outside Japan (Ackroyd *et al*, 1988; Buckley and Mirza, 1985; Cole, 1979; Marsh and Mannari, 1976; Pascale and Athos, 1982; Smith and Misumi, 1989; Urabe, 1986; Wickens, 1987).

## The future of the Japanese approach

In discussing the distinctive Japanese approach to management, we must not forget the strong reciprocal links between government and business, especially the importance of Japanese industrial policy in stimulating and guiding the country's economic progress. This is seen most clearly in the close links between business and the Ministry of International Trade and Industry (MITI). As part of its remit to establish Japan as a leading industrial nation, MITI played a crucial role in establishing national programmes in key industries to encourage joint action, to develop the country's science and technological base, amongst companies and public research institutions. The ultimate goal of these programmes has been to create a strong, competitive and world class industrial base for Japan. These collaborative programmes have not been at the expense of competition between companies; rather they have helped to improve the competitiveness of all the companies in relation both to each other and, importantly, in relation to international rivals (Laage-Hellman, 1997).

Nevertheless, despite the competitiveness of Japanese firms and the active support of the Japanese government, the economy is not as strong as it was. After successfully coping with the second oil crisis of 1979 and the effects of a rapidly appreciating currency in the mid-1980s, Japan enjoyed sustained economic growth until the early 1990s. However, since then the economy has been in protracted recession, unemployment has increased to record levels (although at 4 per cent it is still low by international standards), and successive banking and political scandals have undermined the stability of the political and financial system on which Japan's industrial might was built (Barrie, 1999; Shirai, 1997). This has led to a flurry of political and business reforms, and attempts to introduce Western-style deregulation in order to foster competition and cut costs.

Despite these unsettling developments, low inflation, low interest rates and, in 1997 and 1998, a once again rapidly increasing balance of payments surplus with the rest of the world of nearly US$100 billion mean that stories of the demise of Japanese industrial might are somewhat far from the truth. Even in the worst years of the 1990s, Japan's economy, and its leading industrial companies, generally continued to outperform those of its competitors in the West (Shirai, 1997). This can be seen most clearly in the continued conflict between Japan and the USA over the former's huge trade surplus. However, low growth, domestic recession, increasing international competition, technological developments that have led to changes in industrial and job structures, and an ageing population have all created pressures to change the Japanese approach to management (Harukiyo and Hook, 1998; Sako and Sato, 1997).

In the larger Japanese companies, these pressures have led to structural changes designed to flatten the hierarchy and create greater flexibility (Koji, 1998). In the motor industry, in particular, there has also been a weakening of the previously strong supply chain links, with second- and third-tier suppliers being exposed to greater levels of competition (Masayoshi, 1998). Looking at the Japanese approach to production systems, here too there have been changes; but these do not seem to have radically changed the main characteristic of the Japanese approach which has been one of blending mass production with flexibility (Masayuki, 1998).

Perhaps the area where the pressures for change have been the greatest is in personnel practices, especially those relating to lifetime employment, seniority-based promotion and rewards systems, and the treatment of female workers (Sako and Sato, 1997). As far as lifetime employment is concerned, there is some evidence that the economic, industrial and technological changes of the 1980s and 1990s have had an effect on this (Barrie, 1999). For white-collar workers, especially the older and higher-paid ones, there is evidence that continuous employment within one enterprise is giving way to continuous employment within a group of enterprises (Inagami, 1995; Sako, 1997). In the past, if a worker's job was eliminated, they would be given another one in the same workplace. Increasingly, the tendency is now to transfer redundant workers to another job within the same group or affiliated group of companies but not necessarily the same workplace. In some cases, this can be hundreds of miles away, and can also involve a reduction in pay (Watts, 1998). However, for blue-collar male workers, where the distinctions between East and West were always the most marked, job security seems to have improved, if anything. This is because of the falling birth rate, which has also led to an increase in the retirement age from 55 to 60 or even 65 (Seike, 1997). Research has also shown that whilst the use of part-time (mainly women) and contract labour may be increasing, job security in this area is also increasing (Wakisata, 1997). Therefore, overall, it appears that stability of employment may actually be increasing. In terms of lifetime employment, though there have been some changes to the system, most Japanese managers, as well as workers, do seem to believe it is desirable and feasible to maintain it, especially as it is seen as essential to manager–worker co-operation (Ohmi, 1997; Sako, 1997; Sugeno and Suwa, 1997). As the Finance Director of a large Japanese corporation commented:

> To secure our employees living life in good shape is one of the corporation's duties . . . We cannot believe in cutting employees to sustain profitability. It is a kind of failed management philosophy. (Quoted in Barrie, 1999: 13)

In the area of the seniority principle, there does seem to be a greater willingness to make changes. There is growing pressure from both employers and unions to consider other criteria, such as ability, as well as seniority when determining pay and promotion (Sugeno and Suwa, 1997). In a 1995 survey, two-thirds of responding managers saw the introduction of ability-based reward and promotion systems as a priority in order to create greater flexibility, although very few managers seemed prepared to abandon the seniority principle totally (Kawakita, 1997; Sako, 1997). Also, it must be remembered that though seniority plays an important part in promotion and reward, ability has always been taken into account as well. Therefore, what seems to be being proposed is fine-tuning of the system rather than its dismantling.

Significant changes do, however, seem to be taking place with regard to female workers. As in the West, there has been a significant increase in the proportion of women in the workforce in Japan in the last 40 years. In 1960, there were 18.1 million working women (40.8 per cent of the workforce); by 1992, this had grown to 26.2 million (75.4 per cent) (Wakisata, 1997). This growth was accompanied by legal changes to promote equal opportunities and practical assistance with child care arrangements. Like men, women have also benefited from greater security of employment. The average length of service of women workers increased from 4.5 years in 1970 to 7.4 years in 1992; the respective figures for men are 8.8 and 12.5 years. In addition, there seems to be a gradual reduction in the very significant gap between male and female rates of pay: in 1970, women earned on average some 50 per cent of male wage levels; by 1992, this had increased to around 60 per cent. However, for female university graduates in their 20s, the figure was over 90 per cent (Wakisata, 1997).

Therefore, there have been and remain significant pressures on the Japanese economy, which have led to changes in how companies are structured and run, and in their relations with customers and suppliers. However, these do not seem designed to undermine or alter significantly the core of the Japanese approach to management (Harukiyo and Hook, 1998). The strong ties which bind workers and Japanese enterprises together and which lie at the heart of the Japanese approach to management have not weakened (Sako and Sato, 1997). As Shirai (1997: xv) commented, '. . . it appears from all the indicators that the foundations of stable labour–management relations in Japan remain unshaken and intact.'

## The Japanese approach: summary and criticisms

It can be seen, therefore, that there are distinctive practices and policies which have a coherence and can be described as 'the Japanese approach to management'. However, it is not simply the merits of the individual practices that have given the Japanese their competitive edge. Rather it is that they are devised and adopted in such a way that they are integrated and mutually supportive of each other; in particular, Japanese companies have a unique way of combining hard and soft practices (Laage-Hellman, 1997; Ouchi, 1981; Pascale and Athos, 1982; Sako and Sato, 1997). This is not to say that this approach is universal in Japan or that all elements are present in those companies who do practise it. However, there is sufficient evidence available to justify stating that it is the dominant approach in Japan at the moment, and has been since at least the 1960s.

This does not imply that it will not change. Indeed, given that most of these practices have been evolving over the last 50 years, it would be surprising if they did not continue to evolve (Smith and Misumi, 1989; Whitehill, 1991). Already, as described above, there is strong evidence to show that changes are taking place. Even in large companies, such as Toyota and Honda, policies of lifetime employment and the reluctance to recruit staff mid-career are being modified, owing to the need to recruit skills that are in short supply, and because of economic and social pressures. These include especially the pressures for equal opportunities for men and women, the implications of an ageing population, and the need to recruit foreigners (Dawkins, 1993, 1994; Thomas, 1993; Wakisata, 1997).

Given that lifetime employment is central to the notion of the Japanese enterprise as an extended family, its elimination, as averse to its modification, could shatter the very basis of Japanese corporate life. For this reason, as the evidence shows, although the dynamic and innovative nature of Japanese organisations and their passionate devotion to competitiveness are likely to lead to changes in the way organisations are run, it is unlikely that these changes will undermine the core construct of mutual obligation between organisation and employee that lies at the heart of the Japanese system (Ohmi, 1997; Sako, 1997; Sugeno and Suwa, 1997). It also seems more than likely that the changes which are taking place and will take place in the future will enhance, rather than detract from, Japan's economic strength.

The Japanese approach has delivered impressive economic results, but there are those who would question the social cost involved. Japanese workers work longer hours than their Western counterparts, and in addition are expected to participate in many work-related social events (Clark, 1979). There is also considerable evidence to show that Japanese workers are less satisfied with their lot than their Western counterparts, especially in relation to working hours and pay (Kamata, 1982; Lincoln and Kalleberg, 1985; Luthans *et al*, 1985; Naoi and Schooler, 1985; Odaka, 1975).

In many respects this is not surprising. From a Western standpoint at least, Japanese companies appear to operate very oppressive and authoritarian regimes which, through the combination of personnel practices and work systems discussed above, together with peer group pressure, leave workers little option but to conform and perform to very high standards (Kamata, 1982; Smith and Misumi, 1989). This accounts, in part at least, for the common observation that the Japanese are a nation of workaholics. However, there are other serious criticisms of the Japanese approach:

- Most companies operate a two-tier labour market, whereby a significant minority of the workforce have good conditions and lifetime employment, at the expense of less well-paid and less secure jobs for the majority, especially women. However, there is now some evidence that this is changing, especially for women (Wakisata, 1997).

- Even those with lifetime employment are little more than slaves to the corporation because they cannot move to other jobs (Morgan, 1986).

- The merits of teamwork are only gained thanks to the unremitting peer group pressure on individuals continually to improve their performance (Kamata, 1982).

- The lack of independent trade unions leaves workers defenceless in the face of managerial pressure to work ever harder (Kazunori, 1998; Yutaka, 1998).

Whatever the merits or demerits of the Japanese approach, there is little doubt that it has had an enormous impact on organisational performance; consequently, many attempts have been made to introduce 'Japanisation' into Western companies (Ackroyd *et al*, 1988; Hannam, 1993; Pang and Oliver, 1988; Pascale and Athos, 1982; Schonberger, 1982; Turnbull, 1986). Despite some reservations about how well the system might travel, Japanese companies have shown that they can transfer their approach to the West. Nissan's Sunderland car assembly plant in the UK was judged by the Economist Intelligence Unit to be the most productive in Europe for the second year running in 1998, whilst in the same year its Smyrna, Tennessee plant was cited as the most productive in North America by the Harbour Report.

However, transferring the Japanese approach to indigenous Western companies appears to have been more problematic. Even the UK car components industry, which, owing to the presence of Nissan, Honda and Toyota, has received more support and encouragement than probably any industry outside Japan, seems to have failed to adopt the Japanese approach successfully (Hines, 1994; Lamming, 1994). This may be a major reason why many companies in the West, whilst not rejecting the lessons of Japanese management *per se*, are now turning to other approaches to increase their competitiveness, especially organisational learning.

## ORGANISATIONAL LEARNING

Though Culture–Excellence and the Japanese approach continue to exert a powerful influence over Western companies, in the 1990s a third approach to organisational success came to the fore: organisational learning. Despite its new-found popularity in the 1990s, organisational learning is not a new concept. Indeed, the much-respected American academic Chris Argyris has been writing about organisational learning for over 40 years (Argyris, 1992). However, there can be no doubt that interest in the concept of organisational learning, or the learning organisation as it is sometimes called, grew considerably in the 1990s. As Crossan and Guatto (1996) noted, there were as many academic papers published on the topic in 1993 as in the whole of the 1980s. Many of these articles are dotted with emotive statements such as, '...the rate at which individuals and organizations learn may become the only sustainable competitive advantage...' (Stata, 1989: 4). Though statements such as this have the power to attract the attention of business leaders, there are really two factors which appear to have moved organisational learning from being a subject for serious academic study to a hot board room topic: the pace of change, and the rise of corporate Japan.

There appears to be considerable support for the view that the pace of change is accelerating as never before, and that organisations have to chart their way through an increasingly complex environment. Organisations are having to cope with the pressures of globalisation, changes in technology, the rise of e-commerce, situations where customers and suppliers can be both competitors and allies, and a change in emphasis from quantity to quality and from products to services. To cope with this growing complexity, organisations are recognising the need to acquire and utilise increasing amounts of knowledge if they are to make the changes necessary to remain competitive (Chawla and Renesch, 1995). As Pautzke (1989) stated:

> Careful cultivation of the capacity to learn in the broadest sense, i.e. the capacity both to acquire knowledge and to develop practical abilities, seems to offer a realistic way of tackling the pressing problems of our time. (Quoted in Probst and Buchel, 1997: 5)

The second, and perhaps main, factor that has generated such interest in organisational learning is the rise of corporate Japan. In attempting to explain and/or combat Japanese penetration of Western markets, many commentators argued that one of the main strengths of Japanese companies is the speed with which they gather information on markets and competitors and disseminate and act upon this information internally (Nonaka, 1988; Pascale and Athos, 1982). However, Japanese companies' ability to learn, adapt and develop also extended to their commitment to continuous improvement, in processes as well as products, both internally and jointly with customers and suppliers (Laage-Hellman, 1997; Sako and Sato, 1997). The result, as described earlier in this chapter, is their fearsome reputation for producing the right product, in the right time and at the right price. Underpinning this is an ability to translate a commitment to individual learning into organisational learning (Hedlund and Nonaka, 1993; Nonaka, 1988; Ouchi, 1981; Whitehill, 1991). This idea, that the promotion of collective learning is crucial to organisational success, has not only led to the upsurge in interest in organisational learning, but it also provides a bridge between Western and Eastern approaches to managing organisations. For these reasons, Probst and Buchel (1997: 1) argue that 'Organizational learning offers an alternative paradigm by which systems can change, thus permitting us to redefine the economy and society.'

## What is organisational learning?

The term 'organisational learning' is often used interchangeably with the term 'learning organisation'. The difference, as Tsang (1997: 74–5) points out, is that:

> Organizational learning is a concept used to describe certain types of activity that take place in an organization while the learning organization refers to a particular type of organization in and of itself.

In effect, the difference appears to be between 'becoming' and 'being'. Organisational learning describes attempts by organisations to become learning organisations by promoting learning in a conscious, systematic and synergistic fashion which involves everyone in the organisation. A learning organisation is the highest state of organisational learning in which an organisation has achieved the ability to transform itself continuously through the development and involvement of all its members (Argyris and Schon, 1978; Burgoyne *et al*, 1994; Chawla and Renesch, 1995; West, 1994). Though the term 'learning organisation' was much promoted in the early 1990s, 'organisational learning' now seems to have been adopted as a more appropriate phrase because very few, if any, appear to have achieved learning organisation status (Easterby-Smith, 1997; Probst and Buchel, 1997; Tsang, 1997).

Having said that, one of the problems in coming to grips with organisational learning is that its advocates appear to offer a multitude of definitions or models of what it is; for example:

**Organizational learning is the process by which the organization's knowledge and value base changes, leading to improved problem-solving ability and capacity for action.** (Probst and Buchel, 1997: 15)

**A learning organization is an organization skilled at creating, acquiring and transferring knowledge, and at modifying behavior to reflect new knowledge and insights.** (Garvin, 1993: 80)

**Organizational learning means the process of improving actions through better knowledge and understanding.** (Fiol and Lyles, 1985: 803)

**An entity learns if, through its processing of information, the range of its potential behaviors is changed.** (Huber, 1991: 89)

**Organizational learning occurs through shared insight, knowledge and mental models and builds on past knowledge and experience, that is, on memory.** (Stata, 1989: 64)

These are only a sample of the definitions that have been advanced. Indeed, it is probably not an over-exaggeration to say that there are nearly as many definitions of organisational learning as there are writers on the topic (Tsang, 1997).

Easterby-Smith (1997) attempts to explain this confusion of definitions by identifying the different disciplinary backgrounds of those writing on organisational learning. He argues that most writers come from one of six disciplines: psychology, management science, sociology, organisation theory, production management and cultural anthropology. He also points out that there is a distinct difference between long-established contributors to the field who have been attempting to analyse, describe and understand learning processes within organisations, without necessarily wishing to change them (e.g. Argyris, 1992; Bateson, 1972), and the relatively newer entrants who are attempting to prescribe what an organisation should do to maximise learning (e.g. Pedler *et al*, 1989; Senge, 1990). This is a point also made by Tsang (1997), who notes that, up to the 1980s, it was the analytical writers who dominated the field, but in the 1990s, with the upsurge in interest in organisational learning, it was the prescriptive writers who came to the fore. Though the variety of disciplinary backgrounds and perspectives of those writing about organisational learning helps to explain the plethora of definitions, it does not help to resolve them. For this reason, as Probst and Buchel (1997) state, there is as yet no comprehensive theory of organisational learning.

Although many writers have contributed to the concept of the organisational learning, those who have done most to popularise the concept in the UK are Pedler, Boydell and Burgoyne (1989). However, perhaps the most influential writer of the 1990s was Peter Senge in the US, whose book *The Fifth Discipline* (1990) caught the imagination of corporate America. Its success motivated a whole host of consultants and academics to follow suit and produce books and articles extolling the virtues of the learning organisation, and the steps necessary to become one (Tsang, 1997). Part of the success of his book lies in the fact that it combines the individualism of the Culture–Excellence approach with the knowledge-generating ability of the Japanese approach. In the book, Senge argues that there are five interrelated disciplines which organisations need to foster amongst individuals and groups in order to promote learning and success:

1 **Personal mastery** – individual growth and learning.

2 **Mental models** – deeply ingrained assumptions which affect the way individuals think about people, situations and organisations.

3 **Shared visions** – the development of a common view of the organisation's future.

4 **Team learning** – the shift from individual learning to collective learning.

5 **Systems thinking** – the 'Fifth Discipline' which links the others together and which, he argues, is missing in most organisations:

> The art of systems thinking lies in being able to recognise increasingly (dynamically) complex and subtle structures ... amid the wealth of details, pressures and cross-currents that attend all real management settings. In fact, the essence of mastering systems thinking as a management discipline lies in seeing patterns where others see only events and forces to react to. (Senge, 1990: 73)

In contrast to Senge, who stresses the attributes an organisation needs to possess in order to learn, others stress the learning styles of individuals and organisations. Perhaps the most influential in this area are Argyris and Schon (1978) who, building on the work of Bateson (1972), proposed a three-level evolutionary model of learning:

- **Level I – Single-loop learning.** This is adaptive learning which involves detecting and rectifying errors or exceptions within the scope of the organisation's existing practices, policies and norms of behaviour in order to ensure its objectives are met. Typical examples of this would be the monitoring of quality standards or adherence to sales targets in order to detect and correct variance. However, this would not feed back into the questioning of, or amendment to, the organisation's original objectives.

- **Level II – Double-loop learning**. This concerns going beyond correcting variance in standards and targets and, instead, involves challenging the appropriateness of the organisation's basic norms, values, policies and operating procedures that create these standards and targets in the first place. This is reconstructive learning which involves reconstructing basic aspects of an organisation's operations. Typically, this might involve questioning whether some functions should be outsourced rather than continuing to be performed in house or if the organisation should adopt a flatter, more open structure to remain aligned with its environment. Out of such changes, new practices, policies and norms of behaviour are generated.

- **Level III – Triple-loop learning**. This involves questioning the rationale for the organisation and, in the light of this, radically transforming it. A typical example of this might be a traditional manufacturing organisation attempting to reinvent itself as a service company with all the implications for culture, structure and practices that such a move would require.

Burgoyne (1995) suggests that, at Level III, the organisation creates its environment at least as much as it adapts to it. He also considers that this is reflected in the ability of the organisation to stabilise the context in which it operates and/or its relationship with it. It is also at this level that the concept of the learning organisation can fully emerge.

Probst and Buchel (1997: 16), on the other hand, take a very different view, claiming that 'Organizational learning is unique to an institution.' That is to say that each organisation can and should find its own way to become a learning organisation. They argue that there are at least four different generic approaches:

- Learning by developing a strategy – shaping the organisation's future through a participative and practical learning exercise.

- Learning by developing a structure – developing structural forms, such as matrix and network structures, which promote learning.

- Learning by developing a culture – the creation of shared values, norms and attitudes that promote collective success over individual attainment.

- Learning by developing human resources – developing staff through participative and group-orientated learning.

Despite the diversity and contradictions evident in those promoting the concept of organisational learning, one thing is clear: they all see the main purpose of learning as facilitating organisational change. As with the Culture–Excellence and the Japanese approaches, its popularity owes much to its posited beneficial link to organisation performance. However, unlike them, it is the only organisation theory whose main purpose is to enable organisations to cope with and promote change. As Probst and Buchel (1997: xi) comment:

> ...learning is attracting increasing attention both in academic circles and business practice. One of the main reasons for this is the increasing pressure of change on

companies as they move towards the close of the twentieth century. The rate of change accelerates steadily, and companies must find their bearings in an increasingly complex environment. The ability to learn is thus of paramount importance. Companies which do not successfully implement organizational changes, and which fail to cultivate their potential to develop, may soon find themselves amongst the losers.

## Organisational learning: summary and criticisms

Though there has been a considerable interest in the concept of organisational learning over the past decade, this does not seem to have created the clarity one might have wished for. It is, therefore, difficult to summarise a concept that has been defined in so many different ways and from so many different perspectives. However, there are perhaps four characteristics of organisational learning that most writers would agree upon:

- An organisation's survival depends on its ability to learn at the same pace as or faster than changes in its environment.
- Learning must become a collective and not just an individual process.
- There must be a fundamental shift towards systems (or triple-loop) thinking by an organisation's members.
- This gives an organisation the ability to adapt to, influence and even create its environment.

Presented in this way, it is easy to appreciate the attractiveness of organisational learning. However, there are also a number of major criticisms that need to be taken into account:

1 As is apparent from the above review, there is no agreed definition of organisational learning (Easterby-Smith, 1997; Probst and Buchel, 1997; Tsang, 1997). Even Tom Peters (1993: 385), who might be expected to be attracted to the concept, stated that: 'Most talk about "learning organisations" is maddeningly abstract or vague – and perpetually falls short on the specifics.'

2 Despite the volume of publications on the subject, there is a scarcity of rigorous empirical research in the area. As Tsang (1997) pointed out, one of the main reasons for this is that many of those writing on organisational learning are practitioners and consultants seeking to prescribe and sell rather than describe or analyse. He argues that, as well as promoting the concept, they are also trying to promote themselves and the organisations they work for. A similar point was also made by Easterby-Smith (1997: 1107):

> Much of the existing research into *learning organizations* is based on case studies of organizations that are said to be successful, and these sometimes seem to rely more on public relations than on any rigorous and grounded studies.

If this is the situation, then much of the research on organisational learning, and the recommendations and conclusions that flow from it, have to be treated with a degree of scepticism.

3 As Thompson (1995) pointed out, 'The term organizational learning is actually a misnomer. In fact an organization itself doesn't learn – people learn.' It follows that, in most organisations, the achievement of a high level of organisational learning will necessitate a fundamental shift in how individuals learn. This is not just a case of collecting and sharing information in new ways but, crucially, of thinking in new ways (Argyris and Schon, 1978). This requires individuals to undergo difficult and sometimes painful changes involving unlearning old ways of thinking and the redrawing of their cognitive maps – the way they perceive and make sense of the world around them. Many writers have commented on the serious obstacles to achieving such changes (Argyris, 1990; Hedberg, 1981; Probst and Buchel, 1997). However, above and beyond these difficulties lies a further issue. In engineering such changes in an individual's thought processes, it is not just their perception of the organisation that is being changed, but their perception of the world outside work and how they relate to it and to others around them. What are being tampered with are deep-rooted personality traits and constructs which are fundamental to an individual's psychological make-up. In such cases, one has to question not only the extent to which such attempts can ever be successful, but also whether it is even ethically justifiable to try.

4 Probst and Buchel (1997) maintain that organisational learning requires the generation of diversity of opinion and, at the same time, the creation of consensus. They argue that these contradictory tasks can be reconciled and achieved through the development of a collective view of reality. This view assumes that it is in everyone's interest to participate in organisational learning and the ensuing changes. Although some writers, especially Argyris (1990), recognise that there are major barriers to organisational learning, the assumption is that these can be overcome. However, as Chapter 1 demonstrated, much of our organisational experience since the Industrial Revolution has shown that managers view knowledge and control as almost synonymous. To this end, managers have systematically attempted to reduce workers' knowledge and increase their own (Rose, 1988). We also know that, as will be discussed further in the next chapter, organisations are riven by political battles and that the possession and selective use of knowledge is a potent weapon in such situations (Pfeffer, 1981). Therefore, to say the least, one should not assume that reconciling diversity and consensus will necessarily be successful or even welcome.

5 Though Japanese companies are often held up as exemplars of organisational learning, most theory and practical advice in this area has been developed in the West, especially the US. The proponents of organisational learning argue that the recipes they have developed are applicable to all organisations and cultures; nevertheless, many writers have drawn attention to the problem of transferring theories and practices developed in one culture to another (Hedlund and Nonaka, 1993; Hofstede, 1993; Rosenzweig, 1994). For example, openness and

the encouragement of public debate and criticism are seen as an essential part of organisational learning (Chawla and Renesch, 1995). Although US managers might not find this too difficult to accept, it is doubtful whether, for example, Chinese managers, with their tradition of preserving face, would find it so easy. Face involves both maintaining one's own dignity and decorum and, at the same time, not undermining or attacking the dignity and decorum of others. Therefore, Chinese managers find it very difficult openly to challenge and criticise the behaviour and ideas of others or for others to do this to them (Ho, 1976; Tsang, 1997). Similarly, as was noted in the previous chapter, proponents of Contingency Theory argued against universal approaches to organisational effectiveness and in favour of a context-based approach (Burns and Stalker, 1961; Woodward, 1965; Child, 1984). In particular, they maintain that theories and practices developed with one sort of organisation/situation in mind may be much less effective in a different set of circumstances (Burnes, 1991).

In conclusion, we can perhaps agree with Probst and Buchel (1997: xi) who warn that:

> **We should be wary of dismissing it [organisational learning] as the latest fad, since the topic of learning is attracting increasing attention both in academic circles and in business practice.**

At the same time, we should also be wary of accepting it as a valid new paradigm unless and until it develops a sharper definition, a more robust empirical base and a theoretical perspective that can explain how it can be all things to all organisations and all cultures.

## CONCLUSIONS

This chapter has examined the three main approaches to managing and structuring organisations that have dominated Western thinking and practice over the last two decades. The proponents of all three approaches claim that theirs is a new paradigm that contrasts sharply and favourably with the organisational theories discussed in Chapters 1 and 2. This does not mean there are not some similarities with what has gone before. For example, the Japanese use the industrial engineering concepts developed by Taylor and his contemporaries to study and design jobs. However, the context in which they are deployed (the lack of payment by results, the use of teamwork and worker involvement, and above all else, guaranteed jobs) is markedly different. In a similar way, the Culture–Excellence approach can be seen to bear some similarities with the Human Relations movement, especially in its emphasis on leadership and communication. However, the emphasis on culture, individual achievement and all-round excellence make it a distinct approach. The same can be said of organisational learning, which builds on, but develops in a wider context, past practices for encouraging individual and group learning.

There are also points of contact between the three approaches themselves. Organisational learning consciously draws on the methods used by the Japanese to gather and use information speedily. In addition, it stresses, as with Culture–Excellence, the importance of individuals in promoting innovation. However, it also clashes with the other two approaches. Advocates of organisational learning stress that it can enable companies to shape and create their environment, whilst supporters of Culture–Excellence stress that organisations have no choice but to adapt to their environment. It is at odds with the Japanese approach in terms of change. The Japanese favour directed continuous incremental change, whereas the organisational learning approach encourages continuous but often undirected adaptation and also transformational change.

There are also points of contact between the Japanese approach and the Culture–Excellence approach (the emphasis on excellence, the importance of culture); but, again, there are marked differences. Lifetime employment and loyalty to the organisation contrast strongly with the stress on the temporary nature of jobs proposed by the proponents of Culture–Excellence. As an example, contrast the threat to thousands of jobs posed by the merger of the Halifax and Leeds building societies in the UK (in order to form the UK's fourth largest bank) with the case of the merger of the Mitsubishi Bank and the Bank of Tokyo in Japan (to form the world's largest bank), where it was stated that maintaining all jobs was a matter of honour (Hughes, 1995; Rafferty, 1995). Likewise, payment by seniority and payment by performance are significant points of departure (though there is an increasing, but still small-scale, use of performance pay in Japan). It is noticeable as well that neither the Culture–Excellence nor the organisational learning approaches really concern themselves with the sort of hard, manufacturing/ quality practices so common in Japan.

Finally, the Culture–Excellence school seem obsessed with downsizing and arguing for smallness. The Japanese, on the other hand, are committed to growth. As Ferguson (1988: 57) remarked, in the 1970s and 1980s the USA was not outperformed by small, nimble organisations, but by 'high industrial complexes embedded in stable, strategically co-ordinated alliances often supported by protectionist governments...'.

On balance, though there are similarities, these three approaches conflict with, rather than complement, each other. The Japanese approach, with its combination of tried and tested, hard and soft techniques, provides a coherent and comprehensive approach to organisations which stresses both innovation and stability. The Culture–Excellence approach is newer and tends to emphasise soft techniques, innovation, dynamism and unpredictability, but leaves unanswered questions regarding its coherence and future development. Organisational learning, as an attempt to provide a coherent paradigm for organisational competitiveness, is the newest and least concrete of the three. At one level it has affinities with the other two approaches, but its emphasis on learning as the principal source of competitiveness also distinguishes it from them. This does not mean that if Western organisations become more adept at adopting Total Quality

Management and other such techniques, and if Japanese companies broaden their use of external labour markets and adopt more flexible structures, the three may not coalesce, especially given the common emphasis on learning. However, at the moment, they remain competitors rather than collaborators.

Needless to say, none of the three approaches is without its drawbacks or criticisms. In particular, there are five concerns that should be highlighted, relating to 'one best way', people, politics, culture and change management.

**One best way**. Much of Part 1 of this book has been concerned with approaches to managing and structuring organisations. The one clear message that has emerged so far is to beware of any theory or proposition which claims that it is the 'one best way' for all situations and all organisations. Yet all three of the approaches we have discussed in this chapter appear to advocate just that.

**People**. The Culture–Excellence and the Japanese approaches also leave much to be desired with regard to people. Both approaches rely on a workforce split into a privileged core and a relatively unprivileged periphery. Under both approaches there is a strong emphasis on commitment to the organisation taking precedence over all else, even family life. Therefore, long hours and short holidays are the norm under both systems. The Japanese approach appears to offer more job security, at least for the privileged core. However, the price of this is that competition for jobs in the better organisations begins, quite literally, at birth. To get a job with the best companies, applicants have to have been to the best universities; to enter those, they have to have been at the best schools; and to enter the best schools, they have to have been at the best nurseries (Bratton, 1992; Fruin, 1992). The lack of clarity of the organisational learning concept makes it difficult to be certain what the implications of it are for people. However, it does project an intensity of work and commitment that aligns it with the Culture–Excellence approach. Also, its emphasis on restructuring individuals' cognitive processes in order to overcome their resistance to learning is, potentially at least, very worrying. Therefore, taking all three approaches together, one cannot escape the conclusion that the social cost of achieving excellence, in either West or East, is high.

**Politics**. The issue of organisational power and politics has received extensive attention over the last 20 years (Kotter, 1982; Minett, 1992; Pfeffer, 1981, 1992; Willcocks, 1994) and will be explored in Chapter 4. Given that organisations are social entities and not machines, power struggles and political infighting are inevitable. They may not always be prominent, but tend to come to the fore in situations where resources are scarce or organisations are in transition (Morgan, 1986). It is perhaps here that Peters and Waterman, with their notion of total openness and trust to the extent of employees effectively allowing others to monitor their work, could most easily be accused of being out of touch with reality. There is a tendency in the West to treat politics and conflict as illegitimate;

but, as Pascale (1993) and Thompkins (1990) argued, conflict is part and parcel of the creative process, and political skills may be a key competence for managers if they are to be successful leaders and persuaders. To ignore the presence of conflict or underestimate its tenacity is usually a recipe for disaster (Kanter *et al*, 1992; McLennan, 1989; Pfeffer, 1992; Robbins, 1986).

However, in the Japanese, organisational learning and Culture–Excellence approaches, little is said on the subject of organisational politics and conflict. As far as the Culture–Excellence and organisational learning perspectives are concerned, there appears to be an assumption that employees working in smaller business units, having greater autonomy and more satisfying jobs, will work with each other, pursuing a common purpose. As the next chapter will show, this is perhaps an unrealistic expectation. It may well be that in Japanese organisations, with their consensual and open approach to decision-making, strong commitment to organisational goals, high peer group pressure and, for some at least, lifetime employment, conflict is either minimised or channelled into creative directions; though Ishizuna (1990), Kamata (1982) and Sakai (1992) have shown that this is not always the case. However, in the West, with companies re-shaping their businesses, where job security is being eroded, where an individual's current performance outweighs all other considerations, and where only the fittest and fleetest of foot can expect to survive, it is foolish to deny or underestimate the importance of power and politics or to believe that culture can act as a cure-all.

**Culture**. This brings us to the next concern to which these three approaches give rise. Proponents of all three approaches treat culture in a rather subordinate fashion. For the Culture–Excellence school, all problems are resolved through the creation of strong, flexible, pragmatic cultures which promote the values of trust, co-operation and teamwork. A similar point can also be made with regard to the creation of a learning culture. In neither approach is there any real discussion or acknowledgement of the difficulties in defining or changing culture, despite much evidence to the contrary (Allaire and Firsirotu, 1984; Schein, 1985; Wilson, 1992). Nor do those who seek to promote the Japanese approach treat the subject of culture any more thoroughly. Either it is portrayed as an immutable feature of Japanese companies which prevents the West from adopting the Japanese approach or, more frequently these days, the Japanese approach is seen as somehow independent of culture (Sheldrake, 1996; Smith and Misumi, 1989). Very few writers acknowledge that Japanese companies, like their Western counterparts, can find themselves with apparently inappropriate cultures which they wish to change (Ishizuna, 1990). Therefore, all three approaches clearly leave themselves open to the accusation that they gloss over the difficulty of changing culture. The role of organisational culture will be examined in the next chapter.

**Change management**. There is one last issue that should be touched on: the management of change. Organisation theories are also theories of change. Most organisation theories claim to show organisations how to identify where they are and where they should be. They also, either explicitly or implicitly, address the issue of change management.

For the Classical school, change management is relatively easy: it tells organisations what they should be and, because managers and workers are rational beings, they should accept any concomitant changes because it's the logical thing to do! A similar approach is adopted by the Contingency Theorists. The Human Relations movement, on the other hand, sees change as more problematic. Organisations are social systems, change is not a rational process, emotions come into play as well. Therefore, persuasion and leadership play a key role in changing organisations.

The Culture–Excellence approach has little to say about how change should be achieved, despite acknowledging the radical transformation it is advocating. Peters (1993) advocated a 'Big Bang' approach to change: 'change radically and do it quickly' seems to be his advice. Handy (1986), on the other hand, seemed to adopt a more gradualist approach to change – big changes over long periods. Kanter *et al* (1992) advocated a combination of both; they argue that major changes, especially in behaviour, can only be achieved over time. However, they also believe that dramatic gestures are also necessary to improve performance in the short term. Therefore, their approach to change is a combination of 'Bold Strokes and Long Marches'. Taken as a whole, the message from the Culture–Excellence school is somewhat mixed and the process and details are lacking, notwithstanding Kanter *et al*'s (1992) book on change.

Though organisational learning is explicitly directed at enabling organisations to change, its proponents are vague and inconsistent in specifying how one leads to the other, and particularly how the ultimate goal, of becoming a learning organisation, can be achieved (Probst and Buchel, 1997). Nor is it clear how the plethora of change initiatives generated by learning will lead to effective, co-ordinated and complementary overall change (Easterby-Smith, 1997; Tsang, 1997).

The Japanese approach, however, is more specific. They advocate creating a vision of the future and moving towards it in incremental steps (*Kaizen*) at all levels of the organisation. The Japanese are extremely able at this process, which has given them a reputation as a nation that makes ambitious long-term plans which are slowly, relentlessly and successfully achieved. However, it is debatable whether this approach could work in many Western countries. In the USA and UK in particular, competitive pressures appear to require radical change over a short timescale, and at the same time there appears to be a built-in aversion to long-term thinking, especially amongst the financial institutions who play a pivotal role in the life of most firms.

Therefore, though the organisational learning, Japanese and Culture–Excellence approaches have their strong points, they also have their drawbacks, at least as far as Western companies are concerned. For this reason, none have achieved the same intellectual or practical dominance enjoyed by past paradigms, though the Culture–Excellence approach has exerted a powerful influence on managerial attitudes for nearly two decades. However, this lack of a dominant paradigm is not necessarily a cause for despair. Developing paradigms by their very nature will contain dilemmas and contradictions that can only be resolved with experience and the passage of time. This is not a case for ignoring them; rather the reverse. The future is not, hopefully, immutable. Managers are not powerless, they do have some freedom of choice and action, and the possibility does exist to influence the future shape of work by promoting the good and avoiding the bad.

Parts 2, 3 and 4 of this book will further consider managerial choice and the degree to which organisations are free to shape their own future. However, before moving on to this, the final chapter in Part 1 will round off the review of organisation theory by examining the postmodern perspective on organisations and, in particular, the role of culture, power and politics in constraining and enabling organisational choice.

## TEST YOUR LEARNING

### Short answer questions

1 What is a paradigm?

2 Why did *In Search of Excellence* become an instant best-seller when it was first published?

3 List the main tenets of the Culture–Excellence approach.

4 What is a Shamrock organisation?

5 What are the main personnel and business issues that make up Japanese management?

6 What are seen as the main benefits of the Japanese approach?

7 Define organisational learning.

8 State the key arguments in favour of organisational learning.

9 For each of the following, briefly state its implications for organisational change: (a) Culture–Excellence, (b) the Japanese approach and (c) organisational learning.

### Essay questions

1 What are the main similarities and differences between the Culture–Excellence approach and Japanese management?

2 What are the core tenets of organisational learning and what difficulties might an organisation encounter in introducing it?

### SUGGESTED FURTHER READING

1 Peters, TJ and Waterman, RH (1982). *In Search of Excellence: Lessons from America's Best-Run Companies*. Harper and Row: London.
In terms of understanding the essence of Culture–Excellence, there is no better book to read than the one that began it all.

2 Wilson, DC (1992). *A Strategy of Change*. Routledge: London.
David Wilson's book provides a pithy and critical analysis of the shortcomings of the Culture–Excellence approach.

**3** Sheldrake, J (1996). *Management Theory: From Taylorism to Japanization*. International Thompson Business Press: London.
Michael Sheldrake provides a brief but good review of the work of Charles Handy and also of the rise of Japanese management.

**4** A more comprehensive and up-to-date review of Japanese management can be found in Sako, M and Sato, H (eds) (1997). *Japanese Labour and Management in Transition*. Routledge: London.

**5** Probst, G and Buchel, B (1997). *Organizational Learning*. Prentice Hall: London.
For a brief, comprehensive and comprehensible look at organisational learning, this book is excellent.

# Chapter 4

# CRITICAL PERSPECTIVES ON ORGANISATION THEORY

## Postmodernism, culture, power and politics

### Learning objectives

After studying this chapter, you should be able to:

1 discuss the contribution of postmodernism to organisational theory;

2 list the strengths and shortcomings of postmodernism with regard to the design and management of organisations;

3 understand the main tenets of organisational culture;

4 discuss the strengths and weaknesses of the cultural approach to organisations;

5 describe the role of power and politics in organisations;

6 state the main advantages and disadvantages of the power-politics perspective on organisations;

7 appreciate the shortcomings of rational approaches to organisations;

8 understand the scope for the exercise of choice in terms of organisational design and change.

## INTRODUCTION

Many writers, from a wide range of perspectives, have been arguing for some years now that our world is changing significantly and that we are entering a new era (Cooper and Jackson, 1997; Handy, 1997; Hassard, 1993; Hatch, 1997; Kanter *et al*, 1997; Peters, 1997a). Whether we refer to this development as 'the Information Age', 'the Age of Innovation', 'the Age of Unreason', 'Post Industrial Society', or 'the Postmodern Age', the message is the same: what worked in the past will not work in the future, and organisations, like society at large, will have to change in unprecedented and unanticipated ways if they are to survive.

The previous three chapters have described the development of organisations and organisation theory from the Industrial Revolution through to the present day, in order to show the various approaches to and options for designing and running organisations so as to meet the challenges they face. What has emerged is a somewhat confusing picture of theories which claim, each in their own way, to be the answer to all organisational ills, yet which are all open to potentially damning criticisms. All the theories we have examined are aimed at giving practical and coherent advice to managers on how to structure and run their organisations. Yet it is in their limited applicability to the range and complexity of situations found in everyday organisational life that these theories are most open to criticism:

- The tendency to assume a unitary frame of reference, in which the interests of workers and managers, blue-collar and white-collar staff, male and female employees either coincide or can be easily reconciled, is a clear shortcoming in all these theories.

- The belief of the Classical school and the Human Relations movement that contextual factors – the external environment, size, technology, etc. – are either irrelevant or easily accommodated is another obvious flaw.

- Similarly, the assumption by both the Contingency theorists and the proponents of Culture–Excellence that managers are powerless to change the situational variables they face, and have no choice but to accept the prevailing recipe for success, is not borne out in reality.

- In addition, there has been growing scepticism regarding the ability of rational, objective science to provide an explanation for the many and fundamental changes taking place in organisations and society in general.

- One of the most serious drawbacks is that only the Culture–Excellence school, and to a lesser extent the Organisational Learning and Japanese approaches, give any importance to the role of organisational culture – and even then it is treated in a simplistic fashion.

- Lastly, none of the theories give serious consideration to the role of power and politics in influencing decision-making in organisations. Not only does this go against a great deal of research that has been produced over the last 20 years, but it also runs counter to most people's own experience of organisational life.

This chapter will address these issues, especially the final two points, by undertaking a review of organisational culture, power and politics, in order to understand the role they play in shaping the structure and behaviour of organisations.

In preparing the ground for this review, the chapter begins by introducing and discussing the concept of postmodernism. Postmodernism is a loosely defined philosophical movement which, though based in the arts, has become increasingly influential in the social sciences over the last 20 years. It is a way of looking at the world that rejects rationality and the construction of systematic explanations for human activity. Instead, it concentrates on the ways in which human beings attempt to shape reality and invent their world. In organisational terms, postmodernism draws especial attention to the role of culture and power.

The review of postmodernism is followed by a discussion of organisational culture. It is shown that many organisations lack a cohesive culture which bonds them together in a common purpose. However, contrary to the arguments of the Culture–Excellence school, even where strong cultures exist, they may not always be appropriate; they may also be undermined owing to the absence of clear or uncontested organisational goals. The review of culture concludes that, first, although organisational culture may have important implications for organisational performance, there is little agreement about the nature of culture, whether it can be changed or the benefits to be gained from attempting to do so. Second, instead of culture being seen as an all-important and malleable determinant of performance, organisational life in many cases is dominated by political-power battles which may be more influential than culture in shaping key decisions. Consequently, the review of culture leads on to an examination of the nature and role of power and politics in organisations. This view of organisations maintains that they are essentially political entities whose decisions, actions and major developments are influenced and determined by shifting coalitions of individuals attempting to protect or enhance their own interests.

In summing up the implications of postmodernism, culture and power-politics for organisations, it is argued that, rather than being the prisoners of organisational theories or contingencies, managers (potentially) have considerable, though by no means unconstrained, freedom of choice over the structure, policies and practices of their organisations, and even over the environment in which they operate. In exercising choice, managers are influenced less by organisational theories than by their concern to ensure that the outcome of decisions favours, or at least does not damage, their personal interests. The conclusion to this chapter – and indeed of Part 1 of the book – is that, whether illegitimate or useful, political behaviour is an ever-present part of organisational life, and that such behaviour is particularly prevalent when major change initiatives are being considered or implemented.

## THE POSTMODERN PERSPECTIVE

### What is postmodernism?

As was described in Chapter 3, a sea-change has taken place over the last 20 years in terms of how we view organisations. The Culture–Excellence model, the Japanese approach and Organisational Learning all have links with the past but they also represent a distinct break with what has gone before. Running alongside these developments and to a large extent giving them a theoretical respectability, albeit mainly an unacknowledged one, is the view that we have moved from the modern to the postmodern world.

For Alvesson and Deetz (1996: 191–2), it was the changing nature of work and competition in the 1980s that forced organisation theorists to question existing and entrenched assumptions about the world:

The increased size of organizations, rapid implementation of communication/information technologies, globalisation, changing nature of work, reduction of the working class, less salient class conflicts, professionalization of the workforce, stagnant economies, widespread ecological problems and turbulent markets are all part of the contemporary context demanding a research response.

Initially, in the 1980s, much of the debate about the changing nature of the modern world revolved around the posited move from 'Fordist' to 'post-Fordist' or 'neo-Fordist' forms of work organisation. This debate, over the move from mass production to flexible specialisation, initially centred on the work of Piore and Sabel (1984). Their argument was that the age of Taylorism and Fordism, the age of mass production, was dead. Mass production was concerned with the production of standardised goods for stable mass markets using a form of work organisation that was characterised by the intense division of labour, the separation of conception from execution and the substitution of unskilled for skilled labour (Tomaney, 1990). However, it is now argued that the market conditions that allowed Fordism to thrive have passed. The emergence of segmented and highly volatile markets, brought about by changes in consumer tastes and technological innovation, require organisations to be highly flexible in order to succeed in these post-Fordist conditions (Laudon and Starbuck, 1997).

According to Piore and Sable (1984), in the present day only decentralised, worker-run firms have the flexibility, skills and commitment to cope with sudden shifts in consumer demands, volatile input prices and rapid changes in technology. They drew on the operation of loose alliances of small firms in Italy to substantiate their case. Though an attractive proposition to some, as Williams *et al* (1987) showed, there does not appear to have been any great movement to create the decentralised worker co-operatives envisaged by Piore and Sable. Instead, other writers began to argue in favour of the emergence of neo-Taylorist or neo-Fordist organisational forms (Smith, 1994; Whitaker, 1992). Rather than the age of industrial bureaucracy coming to an end, it was argued that it was going through a two-pronged programme of change. On the one hand, computerised automation was linking together machines and processes and thus eliminating labour. On the other hand, where this was not possible, managers were shifting production to low-wage regions of the world (Froebel *et al*, 1980).

As Smith (1994) argues, the problem with this perspective is that though it fits, for example, General Motors, it does not fit Toyota, which has proved by far the more successful company. Sayer (1989) complains that the post-Fordist literature is confused, riddled with speculation and is selective in its use of evidence. Piore and Sable (1984) in particular have come in for much criticism, especially in relation to what some see as their over-optimistic view of the developing nature of work (Amin and Robins, 1990). Therefore, though their supporters can point to examples of flexible specialisation and post- and neo-Fordism, the explanations they gave for these and the implications they drew from them seem both partial and particularistic (Whitaker, 1992). Indeed, given the breadth and magnitude of the new organisational developments and forms discussed in Chapter 3, terms such as flexible specialisation, post-Fordism and neo-Fordism seem to have only a limited ability to explain the many changes taking place in organisational life. Nevertheless, what this debate did was to create a receptivity amongst a wider audience for the work of the postmodernists, who provided a more substantial and complex explanation for the changes taking place in the world around us.

Depending on whom one reads, postmodernism is either a relatively new concept or it has been around at least since the 1930s (Appignanesi and Garratt, 1995; Featherstone, 1988a). Certainly, the term became fashionable among young writers, artists and critics in New York in the 1960s. In the 1970s and 1980s, the term became more widely used in architecture, music and the visual and performing arts (Hassard, 1993). However, its adoption by organisation theorists stems from the work of the poststructuralist movement in French philosophy which emerged in the 1960s. The interest in meaning and interpretation by symbolic-interpretive organisation theorists, drawing on linguistic, semiotic and literary theory, also served to increase interest in postmodernism (Hatch, 1997). In the 1970s and 1980s, it became most closely associated with the work of Jean Baudrillard (1983), Jacques Derrida (1978), Michel Foucault (1977) and Jean-François Lyotard (1984).

Researchers in organisation and management studies came relatively late to postmodernism. It was only in the late 1980s, with, for example, the work of Smircich and Calás (1987) and Cooper and Burrell (1988) that postmodernism started to impact on organisation theory. The interest in postmodernism by many social scientists and organisation theorists stemmed from their growing belief that existing, modernist, theories, such as the Contingency approach, could no longer account for the changes taking place in the world of work and society in general. In particular, there was an increasing scepticism concerning the ability of rational, objective science to provide absolute and unitary knowledge of the world. In its place, postmodernists argue for a relativist position which emphasises multiple realities, fragmentation and subjectivity (Linstead, 1993).

Postmodernism, as the term implies, is something that carries on from, succeeds or takes its frame of reference from modernism. Therefore, it is necessary to understand how the proponents of postmodernism define modernism in order to appreciate their arguments. Modernism is a term used to describe the values, rationale and institutions that have dominated Western societies since the Age of Enlightenment in the eighteenth century. This was the period in which European thought, led by France and Great Britain, is seen as making a decisive break with the superstition, ignorance and tradition of the Middle Ages. In its place emerged a passionate belief in progress, economic and scientific rationality, a search for the fundamental rules and laws which govern both the natural world and human nature, and a commitment to a secular, rationalist and progressive individualism (Gergen, 1992; Hassard, 1993). As Hobsbawm (1979: 34) noted, 'Liberty, equality and (it followed) the fraternity of all men were its slogans.' Linstead (1993: 99) commented that the Enlightenment:

...produced a commitment to the unfolding of progress through history, the incremental growth of knowledge through science and the resulting inevitable subordination of nature to culture and the control of man.

Also, as Gergen (1992: 211) stated, modernist 'presumptions remain vital throughout contemporary culture, and have left an indelible mark on theories of organization from early in the century to the present.' Modernists, therefore, assume that the world, both social and natural, and its structuring principles, are accessible through the correct (scientific) methods of observation and analysis. In relation to organisational life, the term modernism is used to describe the form of organisation that has dominated both the public and private sectors over the past 100 years (Biberman and Whitty, 1997). In the previous chapters, we have termed this the Classical or bureaucratic model, though others use terms such as Taylorist, Fordist or machine era paradigm (Fox, 1994; Smith, 1994; Tomaney, 1990). It is an organisational form which, its proponents argue, is based on rationality, logic and the pursuit of scientific rules and principles. Such organisations are characterised by mechanistic and hierarchical structures based on the extreme division of labour, and control systems that suppress people's emotions and minimise their scope for independent action.

Postmodernism opposes or denies the validity of the Enlightenment's emphasis on reason, logic and rationality as the foundation of scientific method and the basis for the establishment of truth. Postmodernism challenges the claim of science to establish authoritative or absolute knowledge. Instead, it argues that scientific knowledge is a social construction by the scientific community, and that new scientific paradigms are brought about by changes in the community of scientists rather than scientific discoveries *per se* (Hassard, 1990).

Therefore, for postmodernists, knowledge is relative, not absolute. It is, as Watson (1997: 383) states:

A way of looking at the world which rejects attempts to build systematic explanations of history and human activity and which, instead, concentrates on the ways in which human beings 'invent' their worlds, especially through language and cultural innovations.

Perhaps the crucial distinction between modernists and postmodernists is how they view the nature of language:

For the modernist, language was simply a tool for the logical representation of the real ... Within the postmodernist view, language ... gains its meaning and significance through its placement within social interchange. Words fail to make sense (they remain nonsense) until there is at least one other person to give assent to their meaningfulness.
(Gergen, 1992: 213–14)

Therefore, if language is a social construct, one cannot take the statements, rules and practices of particular groups and organisations at face value. Instead, taking their cue from Derrida (1978), postmodernists often begin their analysis of a situation or event by 'deconstructing' the language used. Deconstruction is an approach that seeks to reveal and overturn the assumptions underlying an argument, proposition or theory. Overturning assumptions opens up space for previously unconsidered alternatives. In the postmodernist approach, alternatives are left open to multiple interpretations, and the acceptance of multiple, fragmented realities is seen to displace the idea of one unitary transcendent reality (Hatch, 1997). Like many others, the postmodernists recognise that the various stakeholders in an organisation each have different perceptions of what the organisation should do and whose views and interests should be paramount. However, where they differ is that they do not believe that there is a correct view or that one view has a right to be paramount. Instead, postmodern management and organisation theory, beginning with a process of deconstruction, '...seeks to reconstruct organizations by restoring a sense of harmony and balance in our species, our institutions, and our theories' (Gephart *et al*, 1996: 364).

This leads on to another prevailing theme within postmodernism: self-reflexivity – a critical suspicion of one's own suppositions. If reality and language are social constructs, then, so the postmodernist argument goes, to avoid the modernist error of believing they have discovered a fundamental truth or reality, postmodernists must constantly question and be suspicious of their own assumptions, statements and actions (Lawson, 1985).

Moving on to the links between postmodernism and organisation theory, the concept of self-reflexivity has similarities to Argyris and Schon's (1978) notion of double- and triple-loop learning, which promotes the questioning and challenging of existing organisational assumptions (*see* Chapter 3). Other aspects of Argyris' work also show postmodernist leanings, particularly his questioning of the inner contradictions of research methods (Argyris, 1980). We can also see postmodernist tendencies in Morgan's (1986) *Images of Organizations*, in which he treats existing organisation theories as literary metaphors.

Moving into the heartland of organisation theory, Linstead (1993) argues that under postmodernism, hierarchies of merit, legitimacy and authority give way to networks, partnerships and organisational structures of a shifting, fluid and social nature. These are driven by external forces, such as markets or competition, and are *ad hoc*, short-term, fragmentary and localised. According to Daft (1998), necessity will force postmodern organisations to develop more flexible and decentralised organisation structures with fuzzy boundaries both internally and externally. In such organisations, he believes, leaders will become facilitators who will communicate through informal, oral and symbolic channels, control will be exercised through self-regulation, planning and decision-making will be inclusive and egalitarian principles will hold sway. In a similar vein, Clegg (1990) suggests clear distinctions between modernist and postmodernist organisational forms (*see* Table 4.1).

Clegg acknowledges that postmodern forms of organisation are somewhat ill-defined. Nevertheless, he argues that they are associated with developments such as flexible specialisation and post-Fordism, and that examples of postmodern organisations can be found in Japan, Sweden, East Asia and Italy. However, he does point out that whilst they can be associated with progressive developments, such

**Table 4.1 Comparison of modernist and postmodernist organisational forms**

|  | *Modernist organisations* | *Postmodernist organisations* |
|---|---|---|
| **Structure** | Rigid bureaucracies | Flexible networks |
| **Consumption** | Mass markets | Niche markets |
| **Technology** | Technological determinism | Technological choice |
| **Jobs** | Differentiated, demarcated and deskilled | Highly de-differentiated, de-demarcated and multi-skilled |
| **Employment relations** | Centralised and standardised | Complex and fragmentary |

as the extension of industrial democracy in Sweden, they can also be linked to more repressive and elitist developments, such as the segmented labour force policies adopted by many Japanese companies. Therefore, for Clegg, and an increasing number of organisation theorists, postmodernism has arrived, it is having a major impact on the nature and functioning of organisations, and it will continue to do so.

There are two areas of organisational life that the postmodernists have paid particular attention to: culture and power. The postmodern approach to organisational culture rejects both the integrationist perspective, which sees culture as being shared by all members of an organisation, and the differentiation perspective, which sees organisational unity as being broken by coherent and stable subcultures. Instead, it takes a fragmentation perspective, believing that organisational cultures are inconsistent, ambiguous, multiplicitous and in a constant state of flux (Martin, 1992; Meyerson and Martin, 1987). Hatch (1997: 231) observes of the postmodern perspective on culture that:

> In this view, alliances or coalitions can never stabilize into subcultures and certainly not into unified cultures because discourse and its focal issues are always changing – hence the image of fragmentation.

Therefore, for postmodernists, organisational culture is important, and indeed is clearly linked to their interest in symbols and language. However, postmodernists are sceptical of attempts to manipulate and change culture, as Hatch (1997: 235) points out:

> When you attempt to change organizational culture, while it is true that something will change, generally the changes are unpredictable and sometimes undesirable (e.g., increases in employee cynicism towards cultural change programs) ... Do not think of trying to manage culture. Other people's meanings and interpretations are highly unmanageable.

Where power is concerned, postmodernists take a very different view from most other writers on organisations. They are less concerned with the power that individuals or groups possess, acquire or deploy. Rather they believe that power resides in the combination of linguistic distinctions, ways of reasoning and material practices which make up the body of taken-for-granted knowledge that exists in society and organisations (Alvesson and Deetz, 1996). Perhaps the most influential postmodernist writer on power has been the French philosopher, Michel Foucault (1983). Foucault argues for a strong link between knowledge and power. He believes that knowledge, when it becomes socially legitimised and institutionalised, exerts control over what we think and do. However, there is a power struggle between different bodies of knowledge each fighting for legitimacy and supremacy. For Foucault, though these bodies of knowledge are seeking to represent reality, at the same time they socially create it. He argues that power moulds everyone, both those who use it and those who are used by it. He maintains that power and knowledge depend on each other, so that the extension of one is also the extension of the other (Appignanesi and Garratt, 1995). Gergen (1992: 221) takes a similar perspective, arguing that:

> ...power is inherently a matter of social interdependence, and it is achieved through the social coordination of actions around specified definitions.

The postmodernist perspective on power has important implications for how a particular view of reality comes to the fore and is maintained in an organisation. Rather than being the product of an objective and rational process, it is the product of power and politics in an organisation. In some organisations, there does not appear to be a settled and generally agreed view of reality; rather what we see are competing interpretations put forward by competing groups and individuals. However, in other organisations, a definite view does appear to be held and does appear to be maintained. This is achieved when a coalition of groups and forces is able to wield power and use political processes to achieve a dominant position over others in the organisation. When this occurs, it is their view of reality which takes shape and comes to be accepted. Therefore, not only is power deployed to legitimate their view of the world, but, in turn, its legitimacy bolsters their power.

## Postmodernism – some reservations

Perhaps the main reservation and drawback of postmodernism is, as Alvesson and Deetz (1996) point out, the difficulty in defining the concept. In the social sciences, the term has acquired a wide and often conflicting set of definitions, including a social mood, a historical period filled with major social and organisational changes, and a set of philosophical approaches to organisational and other studies (Featherstone, 1988b; Hassard and Parker, 1993). Hatch (1997: 43) believes postmodernism has been defined in so many different ways that:

> It is impossible to choose a core theory, or a typical set of ideas, to exemplify postmodernism – the incredible variety of ideas labelled postmodern defies summarization, and the postmodern value for diversity contradicts the very idea of unifying these different understandings into a single, all-encompassing explanation.

As Appignanesi and Garratt (1995: 4) observe:

> The confusion is advertised by the 'post' prefix to 'modern'. Postmodernism identifies itself by something it isn't. It isn't modern anymore. But in what sense exactly is it post...
> - as a result of modernism?
> - the aftermath of modernism?
> - the afterbirth of modernism?
> - the development of modernism?
> - the denial of modernism?
> - the rejection of modernism?
>
> Postmodern has been used in a mix-and-match of all these meanings.

The confusion and variety of postmodernism is best summed up by the following list of terms used by postmodern theorists, compiled by Featherstone (1988a: 197):

| modern | postmodern |
|---|---|
| modernity | postmodernity |
| modernité | postmodernité |
| modernization | postmodernization |
| modernism | postmodernism |

Not only, as Featherstone shows, do postmodernists attribute different meanings to each of the above terms, but also they do not share common agreement about what the individual terms mean either. Indeed, Burrell (1988: 222) remarked of one of the key influences on the postmodernist debate, Michel Foucault, that:

> ... it is important to note that Foucault's iconoclasm takes him into positions which are not readily defensible and his refusal to retain one position for longer than the period between his last book and the next is certainly problematic.

As well as the difficulty in defining postmodernism, there are also powerful voices who defend modernism and attack postmodernism as a form of intellectual nihilism or of neo-conservatism (Aronovitz, 1989; Callinicos, 1989). Hassard (1993: 119) states that:

> The most influential critic of postmodernism, however, is Jürgen Habermas ... [he] argues that theories of postmodernism represent critiques of modernity which have their ideological roots in irrationalist and counter-Enlightenment perspectives ... Habermas suggests that as many French writers [especially Derrida, Foucault and Lyotard] take their lead from the counter-Enlightenment statements of Nietzsche and Heidegger, this can be interpreted as a disturbing link with fascist thinking ... Habermas wishes to defend robustly 'a principle of modernism', which he suggests is an unfinished project that holds great, unfulfilled emancipatory potential.

Therefore, there are a number of serious reservations which have been expressed regarding the validity of postmodernism. These range from its lack of consistency and clarity to its alignment on the far right of the political spectrum. Certainly, even its proponents do not maintain that the postmodernist message is always clear and consistent. As to its political leanings, though most of its proponents would dispute that it is an ideology of the right, there can be little doubt that the postmodernist message has provided some justification and encouragement for the neo-liberal policies, such as privatisation and deregulation, adopted by most Western governments in the last 20 years.

## The implications for organisations

What we can see from this review of postmodernism is the influence that both modernism and postmodernism have had on organisational theory and practice in the twentieth century. Clearly, the Classical approach, and especially Weber's contribution, with its emphasis on rationality and scientific knowledge is very much within the tradition of modernism. Indeed, one can also say that much of the Human Relations literature, with its use of scientific methods to identify the 'one best way', and certainly the literature on Contingency Theory would appear to fall squarely into the modernist camp. On the other hand, the Culture–Excellence approach seems much more comfortable with the rhetoric of post-modernism. Not only does it share a similar view of the current state of the world, i.e. chaotic and unpredictable, but it also shares some of the same language. For example, Charles Handy (1989) entitled one of his books *The Age of Unreason*, whilst Rosabeth Moss Kanter (1989) writes of 'post-entrepreneurial' organisations. Though Tom Peters does not necessarily use the language of the postmodernists, the essence of his message, and often the way it is delivered, sits comfortably with postmodernism. The same can be said of organisational learning, with its emphasis on knowledge acquisition, rapid change and, most importantly, the ability of organisations to create their own realities (Hatch, 1997). The Japanese approach, with its inclusion of hard and soft elements, on the other hand, seems to contain happily elements of modernism and postmodernism. Indeed, it may be that one of the main criticisms of modernism and postmodernism is that both come from a Western, especially European, intellectual and cultural tradition and, consequently, do not lie easily with other, particularly Eastern and Islamic, intellectual and cultural traditions (Appignanesi and Garratt, 1995). Nevertheless, at least in the West, postmodernism does appear to be having a powerful impact on both theory and practice in organisations.

In summary, despite the somewhat impenetrable and contradictory nature of the literature, the core of postmodernism concerns the nature of reason and reality. For postmodernists, reason and logic have proved illusory and reality is a social construct. In organisational terms, an organisation, or rather those individuals and groups who dominate it, create their own reality – their own view or views of the world. Whether they see themselves as successful or not, whether they view the world as chaotic, whether they believe they can shape their own future, is to a large part determined not by any objective data or what is happening in their environment as such, but by their own ability to shape their own reality.

The extent to which they can impose their view of reality on others both inside and outside will, to a large degree, determine whether they and the organisation are seen as successful or not.

Seen in this light, postmodernism has three important implications for the organisation theories and practices discussed in the previous three chapters. The first implication concerns the nature of organisational culture. As we saw in Chapter 3, the Culture–Excellence school has been highly influential in bringing the issue of organisation culture to the forefront of management thought and practice over the last two decades. In essence, what they argue is that, in order to achieve excellence, managers need to create a strong, unified and appropriate culture for their organisation. A core component of this approach is to manipulate and use language and symbols to create a new organisational reality. Though acknowledging the importance of culture, and sharing a concern with symbols and language, postmodernists, however, view the results of attempts to manipulate and change culture as generally unpredictable and sometimes undesirable. This is because the outcomes depend upon the multiplicity of meanings and interpretations that others in the organisation put on such attempts, and which are inherently unmanageable (Hatch, 1997). The second implication concerns the issue of how a particular view of reality comes to the fore and is maintained in an organisation. The answer concerns the role of power and politics. In some organisations, there does not appear to be a settled and generally agreed view of reality; rather what we see are competing interpretations put forward by competing groups and individuals. However, in other organisations, a definite view does appear to be held and does appear to be maintained. This is achieved when a coalition of groups and forces is able to wield power and use political processes to achieve a dominant position over others in the organisation. When this occurs, it is their view of reality that takes shape and comes to be accepted. The final implication relates to organisational choice. As we saw in the three previous chapters, most organisational theorists and practitioners believe that there is a 'one best way' to run organisations. However, the postmodernist debate has raised significant questions about whether these 'one best ways' represent some form of objective knowledge, or whether they are socially constructed realities which pertain to particular times, countries, industries and organisations. If organisational reality is socially constructed, then, in theory at least, it is open to organisations to construct whatever reality they wish. From this perspective, organisations have a wide degree of choice about what they do, how they do it and where they do it.

In the conclusion to Chapter 3, and the introduction to this chapter, it was argued that the validity of newer management theories was undermined by the way they treated or ignored organisational culture, power and politics, and choice. The postmodern perspective, in questioning the assumptions underlying existing organisation theories, raises particular concerns over these issues. Therefore, the remainder of this chapter will further explore these in order to round off our review and discussion of organisation theory.

# THE CULTURAL PERSPECTIVE

## What is organisational culture?

As can be seen from the discussion in the previous chapter of the Culture–Excellence school, and, to a lesser extent, Organisational Learning and Japanese Management, many writers point out that managers and employees do not perform their duties in a value-free vacuum. Their work and the way it is done are governed, directed and tempered by an organisation's culture – the particular set of values, beliefs, customs and systems that are unique to that organisation. So influential has this view become that, as Wilson (1992) noted, culture has come to be seen as the great 'cure-all' for the majority of organisational ills.

The continuing fascination of business with organisational culture began in the 1980s with the work of writers such as Allen and Kraft (1982), Deal and Kennedy (1982), and above all Peters and Waterman (1982). Academics, however, had drawn attention to its importance much earlier; as Allaire and Firsirotu (1984) and Albrow (1997) have shown, there was already a substantial academic literature on organisational culture well before the work of Peters and Waterman (*see* Eldridge and Crombie, 1974; Turner, 1971). Blake and Mouton (1969), for example, were arguing that there was a link between culture and excellence in the late 1960s. For all this, organisational culture remains a highly contentious topic whose implications are far-reaching.

Turner (1986) traced the 'culture craze' of the 1980s to the decline of standards in manufacturing quality in the USA, and the challenge to its economic supremacy by Japan. He commented that the concept of culture holds out a new way of understanding organisations, and has been offered by many writers as an explanation for the spectacular success of Japanese companies in the 1970s and 1980s. Bowles (1989), amongst others, observed that there is an absence of a cohesive culture in advanced economies in the West, and that the potential for creating systems of beliefs and myths within organisations provides the opportunity for promoting both social and organisational cohesion. The case for culture was best summed up by Deal and Kennedy (1982), who argued that culture, rather than structure, strategy or politics, is the prime mover in organisations.

Silverman (1970) contended that organisations are societies in miniature and can therefore be expected to show evidence of their own cultural characteristics. However, culture does not spring up automatically and fully-formed from the whims of management. Allaire and Firsirotu (1984) considered it to be the product of a number of different influences: the ambient society's values and characteristics, the organisation's history and past leadership, and factors such as industry and technology. Others writers have constructed similar lists but, as Brown (1995) noted, there does seem to be some dispute over what factors shape organisational culture and those which are an integral part of it. Drennan (1992), for example, lists company expectations as a factor that shapes culture, but these might just as easily be seen as a reflection of an organisation's values which, as Cummings and Huse (1989) point out, are a key component of an organisation's culture. However, the difficulty in distinguishing between the factors which shape culture and those which comprise culture is a reflection, as Cummings and Huse (1989: 421) also point out, of the 'confusion about what the term culture really means when applied to organizations'. Brown (1995: 6–7) estimated that there are literally hundreds of definitions of culture. These include the following:

> The culture of the factory is its customary and traditional way of thinking and doing things, which is shared to a greater or lesser degree by all its members and which new members must learn, and at least partially accept, in order to be accepted into service in the firm. (Jacques, 1952: 251)

> Culture ... is a pattern of beliefs and expectations shared by the organization's members. These beliefs and expectations produce norms and powerfully shape the behaviour of individuals and groups in the organization. (Schwartz and Davis, 1981: 33)

> A quality of perceived organizational specialness – that it possesses some unusual quality that distinguishes it from others in the field. (Gold, 1982: 571–2)

> By culture I mean the shared beliefs top managers in a company have about how they should manage themselves and other employees, and how they should conduct business(es). (Lorsch, 1986: 95)

> Culture represents an interdependent set of values and ways of behaving that are common in a community and that tend to perpetuate themselves, sometimes over long periods of time. (Kotter and Hesketh, 1992: 141)

> Culture is 'how things are done around here'. (Drennan, 1992: 3)

Whilst there is a similarity between the above definitions, there are also some distinct differences: is culture something an organisation is or something it possesses? Does it mainly apply to senior managers or does it embrace everyone in the organisation? Is it a weak or a powerful force? Perhaps the most widely accepted definition is that offered by Eldridge and Crombie (1974: 78), who stated that culture refers 'to the unique configuration of norms, values, beliefs, ways of behaving and so on, that characterise the manner in which groups and individuals combine to get things done'. Culture defines how those in the organisation should behave in a given set of circumstances. It affects all, from the most senior manager to the humblest clerk. Their actions are judged by themselves and others in relation to expected modes of behaviour. Culture legitimises certain forms of action and proscribes other forms. This view is supported by Turner (1971), who observed that cultural systems contain elements of 'ought' which prescribe forms of behaviour or allow behaviour to be judged acceptable or not. Other writers have suggested a wide variety of different aspects of culture as being important in shaping behaviour. Martin *et al* (1983) pointed to the role of organisational stories in shaping the actions and expectations of employees. They identified seven basic types of story prevalent in organisations which provide answers to fundamental questions of behaviour:

1 Can employees break the rules?

2 Is the big boss human?

3 Can the little person rise to the top?

4 Will I get fired?

5 Will the organisation help me if I have to move?

6 How will the boss react to mistakes?

7 How will the organisation deal with obstacles?

Alongside stories, much attention has been paid to the role of ceremonies, rites and rituals in reinforcing behaviour. As Trice and Beyer (1984) found, these include the following:

- **Rites of passage** – designed to facilitate and signal a change in status and role through events such as training and induction programmes.

- **Rites of questioning** – to allow the status quo to be challenged through the use of, for example, outside consultants.

- **Rites of renewal** – to enable the status quo to be updated and renewed through participative initiatives including strategy development, vision building and job redesign programmes.

Another common theme in the literature is the role of 'heroes'. Peters and Waterman (1982) stressed the importance of corporate heroes in shaping the fortunes of their 'excellent' companies. Deal and Kennedy (1982) likewise saw the corporate hero as the great motivator, the person everyone looks up to, admires and relies on. Indeed, in the USA especially, much of business success seems to be attributed to the actions and personality of individuals, such as Andrew Carnegie, Henry Ford and Alfred Sloan. Present-day corporate heroes include Bill Gates at Microsoft, Steve Jobs at Apple and Jack Welch at General Electric.

Brown (1995) compiled a long list of these various elements of culture which have been identified by writers in the field. Identifying these separate elements of culture helps us to flesh out and better understand how organisational culture manifests itself and impacts on individual and group behaviour. Nevertheless, as Brown shows, producing lists of elements or focusing on the role of particular elements tends to present a confusing and partial picture of culture. It becomes difficult to determine which are the more and which are the less important elements and, in terms of changing culture, which elements can be easily altered and which are more immutable.

To overcome this lack of clarity, there have been a number of attempts to identify and categorise the constituent elements of culture. Hofstede (1990) developed a four-layered hierarchical model of culture which ranged from *values* at the deepest level through *rituals*, *heroes* and, at the surface level, *symbols*. In a similar way, Schein (1985) suggested a three-level model, with *basic assumptions* being at the deepest level, *beliefs*, *values and attitudes* at the intermediate level, and *artifacts* at the surface level. Based on an analysis of the different definitions of culture, Cummings and Huse (1989: 421) produced a composite model of culture, comprising four major elements existing at different levels of awareness, as follows:

1 **Basic assumptions. At the deepest level of cultural awareness are unconscious, taken-for-granted assumptions about how organisational problems should be solved ... They represent nonconfrontable and nondebatable assumptions about relating to the environment, as well as about the nature of human nature, human activity and human relationships. [ ... ]**

2 **Values. The next higher level of awareness includes values about what *ought* to be in organizations. Values tell members what is important in the organization and what they need to pay attention to. [ ... ]**

3 **Norms. Just below the surface of cultural awareness are norms guiding how members should behave in particular situations. These represent unwritten rules of behavior. [ ... ]**

4 **Artifacts. At the highest level of cultural awareness are the artifacts and creations that are visible manifestations of the other levels of cultural elements. These include observable behaviors of members, as well as the structures, systems, procedures, rules, and physical aspects of the organization.**

However, while the various hierarchical models of culture elements are useful, we should always remember that, as Brown (1995: 8–9) notes, '... actual organisational cultures are not as neat and tidy as the models seem to imply'.

As well as the numerous attempts to define organisational culture, there have also been a number of attempts to categorise the various types of culture. Deal and Kennedy (1982) identified four basic types of culture: the *Tough Guy, Macho culture*, characterised by individualism and risk-taking, e.g. a police force; the *Work-Hard/Play-Hard culture*, characterised by low risks and quick feedback on performance, e.g. McDonald's; the *Bet-Your-Company culture*, characterised by high risks and very long feedback times, e.g. aircraft companies; and the *Process culture*, characterised by low risks and slow feedback, e.g. insurance companies. Quinn and McGrath (1985) developed their own four types of culture: the *Market*, characterised by rational decision-making and goal-orientated employees, e.g. GEC under Arnold Weinstock; the *Adhocracy*, characterised by risk-orientated and charismatic leaders and value-driven organisations, e.g. Apple and Microsoft in their early days; the *Clan*, characterised by participation, consensus and concern for others, e.g. voluntary organisations; and the *Hierarchy*, characterised by hierarchical, rule-based authority which values stability and risk avoidance, e.g. government bureaucracies.

Perhaps the best-known typology of culture, and the one which has been around the longest, is that developed by Handy (1979) from Harrison's (1972) work on 'organization ideologies'. Handy (1986: 188) observed that 'There seem to be four main types of culture ... *power, role, task* and *person*'. He relates each of these to a particular form of organisational structure:

• A **power culture**, he states, is frequently found in small entrepreneurial organisations such as some property, trading and finance companies. Such a culture is associated with a web structure with one or more powerful figures at the centre, wielding control.

- A **person culture** is, he argues, rare. The individual and his or her wishes are the central focus of this form of culture. It is associated with a minimalistic structure, the purpose of which is to assist those individuals who choose to work together. Therefore, a person culture can be characterised as a cluster or galaxy of individual stars.

- A **role culture** is appropriate to bureaucracies, and organisations with mechanistic, rigid structures and narrow jobs. Such cultures stress the importance of procedures and rules, hierarchical position and authority, security and predictability. In essence, role cultures create situations in which those in the organisation stick rigidly to their job description (role), and any unforeseen events are referred to the next layer up in the hierarchy.

- **Task cultures**, on the other hand, are job- or project-orientated; the onus is on getting the job in hand (the task) done rather than prescribing how it should be done. Such types of culture are appropriate to organically structured organisations where flexibility and teamworking are encouraged. Task cultures create situations in which speed of reaction, integration and creativity are more important than adherence to particular rules or procedures, and where position and authority are less important than the individual contribution to the task in hand.

Handy (1986) believes that it is these last two forms of culture, role and task, which are most frequently found in Western organisations. Relating these two types of culture to Burns and Stalker's (1961) structural continuum, with mechanistic structures at one end and organic at the other, we can see that Handy is in effect seeking to construct a parallel and related cultural continuum, with role cultures at the mechanistic end and task cultures at the organic end. This categorisation certainly accommodates the five Western approaches to organisation theory discussed in the previous chapters. However, it is difficult to accommodate Japanese organisations within this framework, as their cultures contain elements of each extreme. As was described in Chapter 3, Japanese companies have very tightly structured jobs, especially at the lower levels; they are very hierarchical and deferential, whilst at the same time achieving high levels of motivation, initiative and creativity in problem-solving. They tend to be heavily group/team-orientated, with such teams having a great deal of autonomy.

Indeed, perhaps the main criticism of these various attempts to categorise culture is that they fail to give sufficient weight to the influence of national cultures on the types of organisational culture that predominate in particular countries. Over the last decade, strong reservations have been expressed about the generalisability of management theories developed in one culture or society to another culture or society (Rosenzweig, 1994). In particular, a number of commentators have shown that the strong cultural differences between Western and Asian countries and companies make it difficult to apply typologies of management developed in one to the other (Ho, 1976; Sullivan and Nonaka, 1986). Given that the various typologies of organisational culture all come from a Western, and predominantly North American, perspective, this is an especially serious criticism.

The most comprehensive work on the differences between national cultures was carried out by Hofstede (1980, 1990). He suggested that national cultures can be clustered along the lines of their similarities across a range of dimensions, as follows:

• the prevailing sense of individualism or collectivity in each country;

• the power distance accepted in each country (the degree of centralisation, autocratic leadership and number of levels in the hierarchy);

• the degree to which uncertainty is tolerated or avoided.

Based on these dimensions, Hofstede's research found that industrialised countries could be classified into four broad clusters:

1 Scandinavia (primarily Denmark, Sweden and Norway): these cultures are based upon values of collectivity, consensus and decentralisation.

2 West Germany (prior to unification), Switzerland and Austria: these are grouped together largely as valuing efficiency – the well-oiled machine – and seeking to reduce uncertainty.

3 Great Britain, Canada, the USA, New Zealand, Australia and the Netherlands: these lie somewhere between 1 and 2 but cluster on the value they place on strong individuals and achievers in society.

4 Japan, France, Belgium, Spain and Italy: these are clustered on bureaucratic tendencies – the pyramid structure – favouring a large power distance.

Wilson (1992: 90) observed that, 'The similarity of the factors in [Hofstede's] national culture study to Handy's (1986) four organizational forms is striking.' However, whilst one can see that Scandinavia can be classed as exhibiting task culture characteristics, and the group containing West Germany can be seen as exhibiting role culture characteristics, the other two groupings (Great Britain *et al* and Japan *et al*) are more difficult to place. Rather than placing Great Britain and the USA in one category, according to where they are positioned on Hofstede's dimensions, it might be more accurate to follow Handy's own lead and say that both task and role cultures are prevalent. This still leaves us with where to place Japan *et al*. From the point of view of Hofstede's dimensions, Japan appears to exhibit characteristics of Handy's role culture. However, as pointed out above, this is only part of the story of Japanese organisational life.

Handy's categorisation of types of culture is nevertheless very useful, in that it takes us beyond vague generalisations and gives us a picture of differing cultures. However, like the other work discussed, it serves to highlight both the difficulty of defining cultures clearly, and also the profound implications of the cultural approach to organisations. These implications fall under four main headings.

First, Deal and Kennedy (1982) argued that behaviour, instead of reacting directly to intrinsic and extrinsic motivators, is shaped by shared values, beliefs and assumptions about the way an organisation should operate, how rewards should be distributed, the conduct of meetings, and even how people should dress.

Second, if organisations do have their own identities, personalities or cultures, are there particular types of cultural attributes that are peculiar to top-performing organisations? As discussed in Chapter 3, the Culture–Excellence school reply to this question with a resounding *yes*!

Third, Sathe (1983) argued that culture guides the actions of an organisation's members without the need for detailed instructions or long meetings to discuss how to approach particular issues or problems; it also reduces the level of ambiguity and misunderstanding between functions and departments. In effect, it provides a common context and a common purpose for those in the organisation. However, this is only the case when an organisation possesses a strong culture, and where the members of the organisation have internalised it to the extent that they no longer question the legitimacy or appropriateness of the organisation's values and beliefs.

Fourth, one of the most important implications is that, as Barratt (1990: 23) claimed, 'values, beliefs and attitudes are learnt, can be managed and changed and are potentially manipulable by management'. O'Reilly (1989) is one of those who clearly believes this is the case. He argued that it is possible to change or manage a culture by choosing the attitudes and behaviours that are required, identifying the norms or expectations that promote or impede them, and then taking action to create the desired effect.

This last implication is particularly contentious, with many writers supporting this view but others arguing strongly against it.

## Changing organisational culture: the arguments in favour

That cultures do change is not in question. No organisation's culture is static: as the external and internal factors that influence culture change, so culture will change. But given that culture is locked into the beliefs, values and norms of each individual in the organisation, and because these are difficult constructs to alter, this type of organic cultural change will be slow, unless perhaps there is some major shock to the organisation (Brown, 1995; Burnes, 1991). This in itself may not be problematic for organisations, provided that other factors change in an equally slow fashion. However, the argument put forward by the proponents of Culture–Excellence is that a successful culture is one based on values and assumptions appropriate to the environment in which it operates. In addition, like Handy (1986), Allaire and Firsirotu (1984) argued that, to operate effectively and efficiently, an organisation's culture needs to match or be appropriate to its structure. Given that an organisation's environment can change rapidly, as can its structure, situations will arise where an organisation's culture may be out of step with changes that are taking place in the environment, structure and practices of the organisation. As Handy (1986: 188) commented:

> Experience suggests that a strong culture makes a strong organisation, but does it matter what sort of culture is involved? Yes, it does. Not all cultures suit all purposes or people. Cultures are founded and built over the years by the dominant groups in an organisation. What suits them and the organisation at one stage is not necessarily appropriate for ever – strong though that culture may be.

Flynn (1993) described how, with the introduction of a more market-orientated philosophy, such a situation has arisen across organisations in the public sector in Britain. Many similar cases can be found in the private sector (*see* Brown, 1995; Cummings and Worley, 1997; Dobson, 1988; Industrial Society, 1997). In such situations, rather than facilitating the efficient operation of the organisation, its culture may obstruct it.

Therefore, for a variety of reasons, organisations may decide that their existing culture is inappropriate or even detrimental to their competitive needs. In such a situation, many organisations have decided to change their culture. A survey of the UK's 1000 largest public and private sector organisations, carried out in 1988 by Dobson (1988), revealed that more than 250 of them had been involved in culture change programmes in the preceding five years. A similar survey by the Industrial Society in 1997, covering over 4000 organisations, found that over 90 per cent of respondents were either going through or had recently gone through a culture change programme (Industrial Society, 1997). The survey found that culture change was promoted through a variety of methods including strategic planning, training, organisation redesign to promote teamwork, and changes to appraisal systems. Based on his 1988 survey, Dobson states that the organisations involved sought to change culture by shaping the beliefs, values and attitudes of employees.

Based on the actions taken by these companies, Dobson identified a four-step approach to culture change:

*Step 1*: Change recruitment, selection and redundancy policies to alter the composition of the workforce so that promotion and employment prospects are dependent on those concerned possessing or displaying the beliefs and values the organisation wishes to promote.

*Step 2*: Reorganise the workforce to ensure that those employees and managers displaying the required traits occupy positions of influence.

*Step 3*: Effectively communicate the new values. This is done using a variety of methods such as one-to-one interviews, briefing groups, quality circles, house journals, etc. However, the example of senior managers exhibiting the new beliefs and values is seen as particularly important.

*Step 4*: Change systems, procedures and personnel policies, especially those concerned with rewards and appraisal.

Cummings and Huse (1989: 428–30) identified what they considered to be the crucial steps necessary to bring about cultural change. Though wider in scope in that their approach sets change in a strategic context, the actual mechanics are very similar to those adopted by the organisations Dobson studied:

1 **A clear strategic vision**: effective cultural change should start from a clear vision of the firm's new strategy and of the shared values and behaviour needed to make it work. This vision provides the purpose and direction for cultural change.

2 **Top management commitment**: cultural change must be managed from the top of the organisation. Senior managers and administrators need to be strongly committed to the new values and the need to create constant pressure for change.

3 **Symbolic leadership**: senior executives must communicate the new culture through their own actions. Their behaviours need to symbolise the kind of values and behaviours being sought.

4 **Supporting organisational changes**: cultural change must be accompanied by supporting modifications in organisational structure, human resource systems, information and control systems, and management style. These organisational features can help to orientate people's behaviours to the new culture.

5 **Organisational membership**: one of the most effective methods for changing culture is to change organisational membership. People can be selected in terms of their fit with the new culture, and provided with an induction clearly indicating desired attitudes and behaviour. Existing staff who cannot adapt to the new ways may have their employment terminated, for example, through early retirement schemes. This is especially important in key leadership positions, where people's actions can significantly promote or hinder new values and behaviours.

Many writers advocating culture change adopt a similar approach. Some of these, including Peters and Waterman (1982) with their eight steps to excellence, take a very prescriptive line. Others appear to underestimate greatly the difficulty involved in changing culture. An example of this is an article in *Management Today* (Egan, 1994) which took just four pages to show how organisations could quickly, and with apparent ease, identify and change their cultures. However, regardless of how its supporters interpret or apply it, this type of generic approach to culture has been criticised as being too simplistic, and putting forward recommendations which are far too general to be of use to individual organisations (Brown, 1995; Gordon, 1985; Hassard and Sharifi, 1989; Nord, 1985; Uttal, 1983).

There are other writers who, whilst sharing the belief that culture can be changed, take a more considered view. Brown (1995) warns that organisations must be sure that the problems they wish to address through cultural change are actually caused by the existing culture. He warns that there is a tendency to assume that culture is the root cause of organisational problems, when in fact they might arise from inappropriate organisational structure. He also points out that senior managers may use the issue of culture to redirect blame for poor perform-ance away from themselves and onto the rest of the organisation. In addition, Brown warns against taking an overly simplistic view of culture by believing that organisations have a single unitary culture, or by assuming that all employees can be made to share a single purpose or vision. This was also a point made by Hatch (1997) on behalf of the postmodernists. One of the most influential writers on the subject of culture, Schein (1985), takes a similarly cautious view. He warns that before any attempt is made to change an organisation's culture, it is first necessary to understand the nature of its existing culture and how this is sustained. According to Schein, this can be achieved by analysing the values that govern behaviour, and uncovering the underlying and often unconscious assumptions which determine how those in the organisation think, feel and react. Difficult though he acknowledges this to be, he argues that it can be achieved by:

- analysing the process of recruitment and induction for new employees;
- analysing responses to critical incidents in the organisation's history, as these are often translated into unwritten, but nevertheless very strong, rules of behaviour;
- analysing the beliefs, values and assumptions of those who are seen as the guardians and promoters of the organisation's culture;
- discussing the findings from the above with those in the organisation, and paying especial attention to anomalies or puzzling features which have been observed.

Schein's approach, therefore, is to treat the development of culture as an adaptive and tangible learning process. His approach emphasises the way in which an organisation communicates its culture to new recruits. It illustrates how assump-tions are translated into values and how values influence behaviour. Schein seeks to understand the mechanisms used to propagate culture, and how new values and behaviours are learned. Once these mechanisms are revealed, he argues, they can then form the basis of a strategy to change the organisation's culture.

In a synthesis of the literature on organisational culture, Hassard and Sharifi (1989) proposed a similar approach to that advocated by Schein. In particular, they stress two crucial aspects of culture change:

> Before a major [cultural] change campaign is commenced, senior managers must under-stand the implications of the new system for their own behaviour: and senior management must be involved in all the main stages preceding change.
>
> In change programmes, special attention must be given to the company's 'opinion leaders'. (Hassard and Sharifi, 1989: 11)

Schwartz and Davis (1981), on the other hand, adopted a different stance with regard to culture. They suggest that, when an organisation is considering any form of change, it should compare the strategic significance (the importance to the organisation's future) of the change with the cultural resistance that attempts to make the particular change will encounter. They term this the 'cultural risk' approach. They offer a step-by-step method for identifying the degree of cultural risk involved in any particular change project. From this, they argue, it is then possible for an organisation to decide with a degree of certainty whether to ignore the culture, manage round it, attempt to change the culture to fit the strategy, or change the strategy to fit the culture. Although Schwartz and Davis' method relies heavily on managerial judgement, they maintain that it constitutes a methodical approach to identifying, at an early stage, the potential impact of strategic change on an organisation's culture, and vice versa.

It should, of course, be pointed out that though Schein's approach and Schwartz and Davis' approach are different, this does not mean they are in conflict or are not compatible. Indeed, both could be considered as different aspects of the same task: deciding whether culture needs to be changed, and, if it does, in what way.

No one should dispute the difficulty of changing an organisation's culture. The work of Schein (1985), Schwartz and Davis (1981), Cummings and Huse (1989) and Dobson (1988) provides organisations with the guidelines and methods for evaluating the need for and undertaking cultural change. Schein's work shows how an organisation's existing culture, and the way it is reinforced, can be revealed. Schwartz and Davis' work shows how the need for cultural change can be evaluated and the necessary changes identified. Finally, the work of Cummings and Huse (1989) and Dobson (1988) shows how cultural change can be implemented.

## Changing organisational culture: some reservations

One of those who sounded a cautious note regarding the feasibility or advisability of culture change was Edgar Schein. Though he believes that culture can be changed, he also argues that there is a negative side to creating (or attempting to create) a strong and cohesive organisational culture (Schein, 1984, 1985). Such shared values, particularly where they have been seen to be consistently successful in the past, make organisations resistant to certain types of change or strategic options, regardless of their merit.

Schein, in conversation with Luthans (Luthans, 1989), was also critical of the idea that culture change can be achieved by a top-down, management-led approach. Schein (1989) appears to advocate a contingency or context-specific view of culture. He argues that an organisation may need a strong culture in its formative years to hold it together whilst it grows. However, it may reach a stage where it is increasingly differentiated geographically, by function and by division. At this stage, managing culture becomes more a question of knitting together the warring factions and subcultures. In such a case, a strong culture may outlive its usefulness.

Salaman (1979) also pointed out that whilst there may be a strong or dominant culture in an organisation, there will also be subcultures, as in society at large. These may be peculiar to the organisation or may cut across organisations. An example of the latter are professional groups, such as accountants, who have their own cultures which extend beyond the organisation. Davis (1985) examined the culture of white- and blue-collar lower-level employees. He found that not only do these groups have their own distinctive cultures, but these can often be in conflict with the dominant (managerial) culture of their organisation. Therefore, sub-cultures exist in a complex and potentially conflicting relationship with the dominant culture. If that dominant culture is seen by some groups to have lost its appropriateness (and thus legitimacy), then potential conflicts can become actual conflicts. The reverse can also be the case; cultural values and methods of operation which one group adopts may be seen as being out of step with 'the way we've always done things'. This in turn can lead to an undermining of the authority of managers and specialists – endangering the efficient operation of the organisation (Morieux and Sutherland, 1988).

Uttal (1983) is another who expressed caution with regard to the difficulties and advisability of culture change. In particular, he observed that even where it is successful, the process can take anywhere from 6 to 15 years. Meyer and Zucker (1989) went further, arguing that whilst managing cultural change may result in short-term economic benefits, in the longer term it may result in stagnation and demise. Another difficulty in achieving culture change is that, as Brown (1995: 153) notes:

> ... most employees in an organisation have a high emotional stake in the current culture. People who have been steeped in the traditions and values of the organisation and whose philosophy of life may well be caught up in the organisation's cultural assumptions will experience considerable uncertainty, anxiety and pain in the process of change ... Even if there are personal gains to be made from altering the habits of a lifetime these are likely to be seen as potential or theoretical only, as against the certainty of the losses.

Therefore, any attempt to change an organisation's culture is inevitably going to be met with resistance. Sometimes this will be open and organised; often it will be covert and instinctive with people trying to hold on to old ways and protect the old order. Unlike many other forms of change, the main resistance may well come from middle and, especially, senior managers who see their status, power and personal beliefs challenged. This is a point made by Cummings and Huse (1989), who observed that culture change programmes often result in or require the removal of managers from key leadership positions.

As can be seen, there are many writers who draw attention to the difficulties inherent in attempting culture change; however, there are also writers who believe that culture cannot be changed or managed at all. Meek (1988: 469–70) commented that:

> Culture as a whole cannot be manipulated, turned on or off, although it needs to be recognised that some [organisations] are in a better position than others to intentionally influence aspects of it ... culture should be regarded as something an organisation 'is', not something it 'has': it is not an independent variable nor can it be created, discovered or destroyed by the whims of management.

In a similar vein, Filby and Willmott (1988) also questioned the notion that management has the capacity to control culture. They point out that this ignores the ways in which an individual's values and beliefs are conditioned by experience outside the workplace – through exposure to the media, through social activities, as well as through previous occupational activities.

From a postmodernist perspective, Hatch (1997: 235) is very dubious of attempts to change organisational culture:

> Do not think of trying to manage culture. Other people's meanings and interpretations are highly unmanageable. Think instead of trying to culturally manage your organization, that is, manage your organization with cultural awareness of the multiplicity of meanings that will be made of you and your efforts.

A further reservation expressed by a number of writers relates to the ethical issues raised by attempts to change culture. Van Maanen and Kunda (1989) argued that behind the interest in culture is an attempt by managers to control what employees feel as well as what they say or do. Their argument is that culture is a mechanism for disciplining emotion – a method of guiding the way people are expected to feel. Seen in this light, attempts to change culture can be conceived of as Taylorism of the mind. Frederick Taylor sought to control behaviour by laying down and enforcing strict rules about how work should be carried out. Van Maanen and Kunda in effect argue that culture change programmes attempt to achieve the same end through a form of mind control. Willmott (1995) expresses similar concerns. He believes that the overriding aim of culture change is to win the 'hearts and minds' of employees by achieving control over the 'employee's soul'. Watson (1997: 278) concludes that:

> Employers and managers engaging in these ways with issues of employees' self-identities and the values through which they judge the rights and wrongs of their daily lives must be a matter of serious concern. To attempt to mould cultures – given that culture in its broad sense provides the roots of human morality, social identity and existential security – is indeed to enter 'deep and dangerous waters'.

## Changing organisational culture: conflicts and choices

As in so much else to do with organisations, there is no agreement amongst those who study culture as to its nature, purpose or malleability. Certainly, few writers doubt its importance, but beyond that there is little agreement. The result, as Brown (1995: 5) notes, is that we are presented with 'an embarrassment of definitional riches'. The Culture–Excellence proponents argue that there is only one form of culture that matters in today's environment – strong and flexible – and that organisations should adopt it quickly or face the consequences. To a lesser extent, the proponents of the Japanese approach to management and the Organisational Learning camp adopt a similar, though less strident, view. Schein (1984, 1985, 1989) agreed that culture is important and that in certain cases a strong culture is desirable. However, in other situations, shared values and strong cultures may have a negative effect by stifling diversity and preventing alternative strategies arising. He also doubts that managers acting in isolation from the rest of an organisation have the ability themselves to change the existing culture or impose a new one. Salaman (1979) also drew attention to the presence and role of subcultures, particularly their potential for creating conflict. Meek (1988) took the view that culture is not amenable to conscious managerial change programmes at all. The postmodernists adopt a similar view. Though they consider organisational culture to be important, they are sceptical of attempts to manipulate and change culture, believing that the outcomes of such attempts are unpredictable and can alienate rather than motivate employees. This is reflected in the warning by Hatch (1997: 235): 'Do not think of trying to manage culture. Other people's meanings and interpretations are highly unmanageable.'

Despite the lack of consensus amongst writers, there are two main conclusions we can draw from the above review of the culture literature. First, in the absence of unambiguous guidelines on organisational culture, managers must make their own choices based on their own circumstances and perceived options as to whether to attempt to change their organisation's culture.

Second, in the absence of strong or appropriate cultures which bind their members together in a common purpose and legitimate and guide decision-making, managers may find it difficult either to agree amongst themselves or to gain agreement from others in the organisation. As Robbins (1987) argued, in such a situation, there is a tendency for conflict and power battles to take place.

Therefore, in understanding how organisations operate and the strengths and weaknesses of the theories we have been discussing in the previous chapters, it is necessary to examine the power-politics perspective on organisations.

## THE POWER-POLITICS PERSPECTIVE

### Political behaviour in organisations

The cultural perspective on organisational life reinforces the argument developed earlier in this chapter and in previous chapters that organisations are not rational entities where everyone subscribes to, and helps to achieve, the organisation's overarching goals. The power-politics perspective puts forward a similar view, arguing that organisations often act irrationally, that their goals and objectives emerge through a process of negotiation and influence, and that they are composed of competing and shifting coalitions of groups and individuals (Brown, 1995; Robbins, 1986, 1987). This perspective began to emerge strongly in the late 1970s and early 1980s, and is especially associated with Jeffrey Pfeffer's (1981) book *Power in Organizations*. Before then, as Gandz and Murray (1980) discovered when they reviewed the literature on organisational politics, there was very little general interest in the topic, and very few publications on it.

Nevertheless, of the early work in the field, Lindblom's (1959) work on the 'science of muddling through' and Cyert and March's (1963) book, *A Behavioral Theory of the Firm*, can be said to have really laid the basis for the later explosion of interest in power and politics in organisations. Writing from the viewpoint of public sector organisations, Lindblom argued that political constraints on policy make a rationalist approach to decision-making impossible. Cyert and March (1963) extensively developed Lindblom's work, showing that private sector firms were no less political entities than public sector organisations. The intention behind their work was to provide a better understanding of decision-making by supplementing existing theories, which tended to focus on market factors, with an examination of the internal operation of the firm. In their book, Cyert and March characterise firms as competing and shifting coalitions of multiple and conflicting interests, whose demands and objectives are constantly, but imperfectly, reconciled and where rationality is limited or bounded by uncertainty over what is wanted and how to achieve it (Mallory, 1997). Under such circumstances, managers 'satisfice': rather than searching for the best solution, they select one that is satisfactory and sufficient (Simon, 1957).

Cyert and March's work on the political dimension of decision-making and the nature of organisational life now forms part of the received wisdom on organisational behaviour. This is not to refute or marginalise the role of organisational culture. As Handy (1993) observed, the extent to which agreement exists about the tasks an organisation undertakes, how it undertakes them, and the extent to which members of the organisation are committed to achieving them, will be affected by the strength and the perceived legitimacy or suitability of the organisation's culture. Willcocks (1994: 31) took the view that diverse interests are part of organisational culture. They include, he argues, 'for example, the goals, values and expectations of the organizational participants and have been described as cognitive maps or personal agendas'. The importance of the power-politics perspective is that it shows that, even where a strong culture may be present, the cohesiveness, willingness and stability of an organisation's members is unlikely to be uniform either across an organisation or over time. Rather the degree of co-operation and commitment they exhibit will vary with the degree to which they perceive the goals they are pursuing as broadly consistent with their own interests (Mullins, 1993). Therefore, as Pfeffer (1978: 11–12) commented:

> It is difficult to think of situations in which goals are so congruent, or the facts so clear-cut that judgment and compromise are not involved. What is rational from one point of view is irrational from another. Organizations are political systems, coalitions of interests, and rationality is defined only with respect to unitary and consistent ordering of preferences.

It might be comforting to believe that individuals and groups within organisations are supportive of each other, that they work in a harmonious and co-operative fashion. Such a non-political perspective portrays employees as always behaving in a manner consistent with the interests of the organisation. In contrast, as Robbins (1986: 283) remarked, 'a political view can explain much of, what may seem to be, irrational behaviour in organizations. It can help to explain, for instance, why employees withhold information, restrict output, attempt to "build empires"...'

174

Handy (1986) also observed the tendency for individuals and groups to pursue courses of action that promote their interests, regardless of the organisation's formal goals and objectives. He notes that where individuals perceive that the actual or proposed goals of the organisation or the tasks they are asked to perform are out of step with their own interests, they will seek where possible to bring the two into line. In some cases, individuals and groups may be persuaded to change their perceptions; in others, they may seek to change or influence the goals or tasks. It is this phenomenon of individuals and groups, throughout an organisation, pursuing differing interests, and battling with each other to shape decisions in their favour, that has led many commentators to characterise organisations as political systems (Mintzberg, 1983; Morgan, 1986; Pettigrew, 1985, 1987; Pfeffer, 1981, 1992).

Zaleznik (1970) stated that where there are scarce resources (which is the case in most organisations), the psychology of scarcity and comparison take over. In such situations, possession of resources becomes the focus for comparisons, the basis for self-esteem and, ultimately, the source of power. Such situations will see the emergence not only of dominant coalitions but also, Zaleznik argues, of unconscious collusion based on defensive reaction. Therefore, whilst some individuals will perceive their actions as 'political' or self-interested, others may act in the same manner, but believe they are pursuing the best interests of the organisation.

Drory and Romm (1988) argued that those in managerial positions are less likely than those in non-managerial positions to define (or recognise) their actions as political. This may be explained by the findings from a survey of 428 managers carried out by Gandz and Murray (1980). They found that managers are more involved in political behaviour, and therefore tend to see it as a typical part of organisational life. If this is the case, it could be argued that the more individuals and groups are involved in political behaviour, the more it becomes the norm, and they become blind to its political nature and see it merely as 'standard' practice. Those less involved in such behaviour, on the other hand, recognise its political nature because it stands out from their normal practices. It is also the case that those lower down the organisation, whilst affected by resource allocation decisions, are less likely, on a regular basis, to be in a position to influence such decisions. For managers, however, arguing for additional resources or allocating existing resources is the normal currency of everyday life. This is reflected in Gandz and Murray's survey, where 89 per cent of respondents thought that successful executives had to be good politicians. Despite this, over 50 per cent of respondents also thought that organisations would be happier places if they were free of politics, and a similar number thought that political behaviour was detrimental to efficiency. As Kanter (1979) and Pfeffer (1992) note, this ambivalent attitude, i.e. believing that political behaviour is necessary but deploring its use, is rife in organisations.

As mentioned earlier, postmodernists take a very different view of power and politics to that of most other writers on organisations. They are not greatly concerned with the way individuals and groups acquire and hold on to power as such. Instead, they focus on the relationship between power and knowledge, and on the way that power is used to promote particular views of reality and to legitimate particular forms of knowledge in organisations.

## Power and politics: towards a definition

Though it is relatively easy to provide simple definitions of power (the possession of position and/or resources) and politics (the deployment of influence/leverage), it is more difficult to distinguish between the two, as was shown by Drory and Romm (1988). They argue that the two concepts are often used interchangeably and that the difference between the two has never been fully settled. Indeed, a brief examination of each shows the difficulty, and perhaps danger, in separating them. First, however, it is also necessary to understand the difference between power and authority.

Robbins (1987: 186) drew an important distinction between authority and power:

> ...we defined authority as the right to act, or command others to act, toward the attainment of organizational goals. Its unique characteristic, we said, was that this right had legitimacy based on the authority figure's position in the organization. Authority goes with the job. .... When we use the term power we mean an individual's capacity to influence decisions. ... the ability to influence based on an individual's legitimate position can affect decisions, but one does not require authority to have such influence.

In support of his view, Robbins quotes the example of high-ranking executives' secretaries, who may have a great deal of power, by virtue of their ability to influence the flow of information and people to their bosses, but have very little actual authority. Pfeffer (1992), whilst agreeing with this view, points out that power can stem from three sources: control over information; formal authority to act; and control over resources. However, he believes this latter source of power is particularly important. We must, Pfeffer (1992: 83) argues, recognise the truth of the 'New Golden Rule: the person with the gold makes the rules.'

On the other hand, Robbins (1987: 194) defines organisational politics as the:

> ...efforts of organizational members to mobilize support for or against policies, rules, goals, or other decisions in which the outcome will have some effect on them. Politics, therefore, is essentially the exercise of power.

Robbins' argument, then, is that power is the capacity to influence decisions whilst politics is the actual process of exerting this influence. This view, that politics is merely the enactment of power, is held by many writers. Gibson *et al* (1988: 44), for example, stated that organisational politics comprises 'those activities used at all levels to acquire, develop or use power and other resources to obtain individual choices when there is uncertainty or disagreement about choices'.

Many writers refer to organisational politics as games. Pfeffer (1981), in his major work on power in organisations, took the view that decisions in organisations are the result of games among players with different perceptions and interests. This was a theme developed by Mintzberg (1983) in his comprehensive review of power and politics in organisations. He lists 13 political games that are common in organisations, the key ones being games to resist authority, games to counter resistance, games to build power bases, games to defeat rivals, and games to change the organisation.

Like all games, political ones have their particular tactics associated with them. Research into political behaviour has identified the seven most common ploys used by managers when seeking to influence superiors, equals and subordinates (Kipnis *et al*, 1980, 1984; Schilit and Locke, 1982), which are as follows:

- **Reason** – facts and information are used selectively to mount seemingly logical or rational arguments.

- **Friendliness** – the use of flattery, creation of goodwill, etc., prior to making a request.

- **Coalition** – joining forces with others so as to increase one's own influence.

- **Bargaining** – exchanging benefits and favours in order to achieve a particular outcome.

- **Assertiveness** – being forceful in making requests and demanding compliance.

- **Higher authority** – gaining the support of superiors for a particular course of action.

- **Sanctions** – using the promise of rewards or the threat of punishment to force compliance.

Robbins (1986) observed that the most popular tactic or ploy is the selective use of reason, regardless of whether the influence was directed upwards or downwards. Although cloaked in reason, arguments and data are deployed in such a way that the outcome favoured by those using the tactic is presented in a more favourable light than the alternatives. Therefore, though reason may be deployed, it is not done so in an unbiased or neutral fashion; it is used as a screen to disguise the real objective of the exercise. In deciding which tactic to use, Kipnis *et al* (1984) identified four contingency variables that affect the manager's choice: the manager's relative power; the manager's objectives in seeking to influence others; the manager's expectations of the target person's/group's willingness to comply; and the organisation's culture.

Having gained a clearer picture of power and politics, we can now move on to examine one of the central issues that arises from this: the distinction between the legitimate and illegitimate use of power and politics.

## Power, politics and legitimacy

Thompkins (1990) firmly believed that the use of politics is a direct contravention of or challenge to the legitimate rules of an organisation. Many, however, see organisational politics as existing in a grey area between prescribed and illegal behaviour (Drory and Romm, 1988). Porter *et al* (1983) differentiated between three types of organisational behaviours: prescribed, discretionary and illegal. They believe that political behaviour falls within the discretionary rather than the illegal category. Therefore, the most common view is that the use of politics in organisations can best be described as non-sanctioned or informal or discretionary behaviour, rather than behaviour that is clearly prohibited or illegal (Farrell and Petersen, 1983; Mayes and Allen, 1977). This definition of politics helps to distinguish between the formal and legitimate use of officially sanctioned power by authorised personnel, and power that is exercised either in an illegitimate manner by authorised personnel or used by non-authorised personnel for their own ends.

Most organisations and many writers see political behaviour as dysfunctional (Drory and Romm, 1988). Batten and Swab (1965), Pettigrew (1973) and Porter (1976) believed that political behaviour goes against and undermines formal organisational goals and interests. Thompkins (1990), though, argued that political manoeuvring in organisations is due to a failure by senior managers to set and implement coherent and consistent goals and policies in the first place. This results in uncertainties, which in turn lead to conflict between groups and individuals. In such a situation, Thompkins (1990: 24) argues:

> Management is then left without top level guidance to run company operations. They will, then, by their own nature of survival, over a period of time, make decisions that will perpetuate their own safety and security. This is the beginning of political power, where legitimate discipline begins to decline and illegitimate discipline begins to strangle the organisation. In short, the tail begins to wag the dog. 'Politics' in this form is created by the neglect of top executive management.

Pfeffer (1981) took a different view of organisational politics. Rather than their being caused by the lack of clear-cut goals and policies, he suggests that the construction of organisational goals is itself a political process. Nevertheless, this does not always mean that political behaviour is detrimental to organisational effectiveness. Mintzberg (1983) maintains that, when used in moderation, political games can have a healthy effect by keeping the organisation on its toes. Mayes and Allen (1977) took a similar view. Pascale (1993) went further, putting forward the view that conflict and contention are necessary to save an organisation from complacency and decline. However, Mintzberg cautions that, when carried too far, such behaviour can turn the whole organisation into a political cauldron and divert it from its main task.

To an extent, the degree to which the balance between positive and negative benefits is tipped one way or the other in an organisation is dependent on the type of power deployed and how it is used. Etzioni (1975) identified three distinct types of power used in organisations:

- **Coercive power** – the threat of negative consequences (including physical sanctions or force) should compliance not be forthcoming.
- **Remunerative power** – the promise of material rewards as inducements to co-operate.

- **Normative power** – the allocation and manipulation of symbolic rewards, such as status symbols, as inducements to obey.

Robbins (1986) developed this further by identifying not only types of power but also the sources of power. To Etzioni's three types of power, he adds a fourth: *knowledge power* – the control of information.

> We can say that when an individual in a group or organization controls unique information, and when that information is needed to make a decision, the individual has knowledge-based power. (Robbins, 1986: 273)

Robbins suggests that these four types of power stem from four separate sources: a person's position in the organisation; personal characteristics; expertise; and the opportunity to influence or control the flow of information.

All four types of power can be and are deployed in organisations. However, the degree to which they will be effective is likely to depend upon the source from which they spring. Coercive power is usually the prerogative of those in senior positions, whilst even quite junior members of an organisation may, in particular circumstances, control or possess information that enables them to exert knowledge power. The interesting point to note is that the use of knowledge power – the selective and biased use of information (often deployed under the guise of reason) – is shown to be effective in gaining willing compliance and co-operation from those at whom it is directed. However, as argued by many observers, the use of remunerative and coercive power is often counter-productive because those on the receiving end of such power tend to view it negatively and resent it (Bachman *et al*, 1968; Ivancevich, 1970; Robbins, 1986; Student, 1968).

This is perhaps why the most detrimental outcomes from the deployment of power arise when people feel they are being coerced into a particular course of action that goes against their beliefs or self-interest. Therefore, irrespective of the source or type of power, it is perhaps the willingness to use it in situations where there will be clear winners and losers, and where the covert activities of warring coalitions turn into open warfare, that leads to the more dysfunctional and damaging consequences. Such battles, where groups and individuals fight to influence key decisions and in so doing bolster their own position, especially where the stakes are high, can end with senior figures either leaving or being forced out of the organisation.

This was the case with BMW, where the battle over the future of Rover's Longbridge plant in the UK led to both Bernd Pischetsrieder, BMW's Chairman, and his long-time boardroom rival, Wolfgang Reitzle, BMW's Marketing Director, being forced to resign (Gow, 1999a; Gow and Traynor, 1999). A similar situation occurred with Pehr Gyllenhammar, the man who ran Volvo for more than two decades. His 1993 attempt to merge Volvo with Renault, the French state-controlled car company, was opposed by a coalition of shareholders and managers, who felt that it was not so much a merger of equals as a takeover by Renault. Both shareholders and managers felt that in such a situation their interests would be damaged, and a very public power struggle ensued, with both sides claiming to act in Volvo's best interests (Done, 1994). Both these cases could be classed as battles between individuals fighting to maintain their own power. However, the reality was that in both cases major issues concerning the future viability of these organisations were at stake. The irony in Volvo's case was that six years after rejecting a merger with Renault because it was seen as disadvantageous to the company's interests, the company sold its car division to Ford Motors, whose work practices were seen as the antithesis of all that Volvo held dear. The battle for control of the advertising agency Saatchi & Saatchi, which resulted in the founders leaving, also shows how a power struggle can leave an organisation damaged (Barrie, 1995; Donovan, 1995). Another very public example of a power clash was the on–off merger of SmithKline Beecham and Glaxo. In 1998, the two companies announced that they planned to merge and form the largest pharmaceutical company in the world, worth an estimated US$165 billion. However, the merger was quickly called off owing to a rumoured clash between SmithKline's Chief Executive, Jan Leschley, and Glaxo's Chairman, Sir Richard Sykes, over who would run the merged company (although given that it later emerged that Mr Leschley's pay, perks and shares package was worth over £90 million, one can understand why he would be reluctant to step down in favour of Sir Richard Sykes (Buckingham and Finch, 1999)). It was only when Leschley and Sykes both announced their retirements that the merger could proceed. In some cases, such clashes can become endemic and linger on even after the initial cause has long gone. Lonrho is a case in point. After the successful battle to oust Tiny Rowland from the company he founded and for so long dominated, Lonrho was split up and sold off. Yet the political battles for control still rumbled on even amongst its demerged parts (Laird, 1998).

Clearly, as the above examples show, the deployment of coercive power can be very damaging; however, other forms of power can also have adverse effects, though perhaps in a more insidious fashion. Thus the use of remunerative power by senior managers in the UK's privatised utilities (gas, water and power) is a good example. On the one hand, they used their power to give themselves extremely generous remuneration packages; whilst on the other hand, they cut jobs and wages for many staff elsewhere in their organisations (Smithers, 1995). The issue is not so much whether the way they distributed the rewards in their organisations was fair or not, but the corrosive effect such a blatant use of power has on employee morale and customer support.

These very public manifestations of power battles in organisations represent merely the tip of the iceberg. They illustrate the tendency for such battles to be fought under the banner of 'the best interests of the organisation'. Political in-fighting, the seeking of allies, the influencing of decisions, and the protection or promotion of one's own or one's group's interests are nearly always justified by recourse to the best interests of the organisation (just as the parties involved in any armed struggle always seem to justify it on the grounds that they have justice on their side). It is not that the participants necessarily believe their own propaganda, though often they do; it is that, without it, they would find it very difficult to justify, to themselves and their allies, the use of blatantly illegitimate tactics such as challenging, undermining or explicitly ignoring their organisation's official goals and policies.

Therefore, in opposing or promoting a particular decision or development, those indulging in even a low level of political behaviour rarely openly declare their own personal interest in the outcome. As Pfeffer (1981) maintained, a major characteristic accompanying political behaviour is the attempt to conceal its true motive. This is because, as Allen *et al* (1979), Drory and Romm (1988) and Frost and Hayes (1979) observed, those involved believe that it would be judged unacceptable or illegitimate by others in the organisation and as such resisted. Accordingly, a false but acceptable motive is presented instead.

The picture of power and politics which emerges from the above tends to be a negative one, portraying individuals and groups as using power and politics purely to pursue their own selfish interests. However, others take a more positive view. Morgan (1986) offered a model of interests, conflicts and power, accepting that diversity of interests can create conflict. In such circumstances, power and influence are, he suggests, the major means of resolving conflict. Buchanan and Boddy (1992) argue that the use of power and politics is a necessary component in the toolkit of those responsible for managing change in organisations. Seen in this light, political behaviour can have a positive effect on improving the working of organisations by enabling them to manage change more effectively. Pfeffer (1992), in a similar vein, maintains that the use of power is an important social process that is often required to get things done in interdependent systems. In fact, he maintains that a failure to deploy power and politics is harmful:

> By pretending that power and influence don't exist, or at least shouldn't exist, we contribute to what I and others (such as John Gardner) see as the major problem facing many corporations today, particularly in the United States – the almost trained or produced incapacity of anyone except the highest-level managers to take action and get things accomplished. (Pfeffer (1992: 10)

Perhaps Gardner (1990: 57) sums up the issues involved in the power-politics debate most succinctly when, in relation to those who possess and deploy power, he argues that, 'The significant questions are: What means do they use to gain it? How do they exercise it? To what ends do they exercise it?'

We can see from the above why writers have found it difficult to separate power from politics. Whilst it is possible to examine the potential for power without also examining how power is or might be exercised, for students of organisational life this is rather a sterile endeavour. For the purpose of understanding what makes organisations tick, how decisions are arrived at, why resources are allocated in a particular way and why certain changes are initiated and others not, we have to comprehend both the possession and exercise of power, whether it be by official or political means.

Though Robbins rightly draws a distinction between formal authority and the possession/deployment of power, we should not fall into the trap of assuming that there is not a close relationship between the two. An examination of the ability to exert influence (power) over key decisions and the possession of position (authority) shows that these tend to lie within dominant coalitions rather than being spread evenly across organisations (*see* Pfeffer, 1978, 1981, 1992; Robbins, 1987). The dominant coalition is the one which has the power to affect structure. The reason why this is so important is that the choice of structure will automatically favour some groups and disadvantage others. A person or group's position in the structure will determine such factors as their influence on planning, their choice of technology, the criteria by which they will be evaluated, allocation of rewards, control of information, proximity to senior managers, and their ability to exercise influence on a whole range of decisions (Morgan, 1986; Perrow, 1983; Pfeffer, 1981, 1992; Robbins, 1987). Though the postmodernists would not disagree with this analysis *per se*, as mentioned earlier, their view of power in organisations is a much broader one. For them, power is the mechanism by which groups in organisations create and reinforce their view of reality. In turn, postmodernists maintain, it is this shaping and construction of reality which, in the main, allows dominant groups in organisations to impose their will on others rather than the use of sanctions and other control mechanisms (Reed and Hughes, 1992).

## MANAGING AND CHANGING ORGANISATIONS: BRINGING BACK CHOICE

This chapter began by looking at the postmodernist perspective on organisational life. The loose, though formidable, grouping of theorists who espouse this view argue that reason and logic have had their day, and that organisations are social organisms in which individuals and groups construct their own views of reality based on their own perceptions of the world and their place in it. Postmodernism challenges taken-for-granted managerial assumptions about how organisations should be run and, instead, argues that there are a wide range of equally possible and valid alternatives. In such a situation, the proponents of postmodernism maintain, a search for the 'best way' (i.e. the most rational) is both unrealistic and itself irrational. This was followed by a review of the literature on organisational culture, which showed that, despite its popularity as a promoter of organisational excellence, culture is difficult to define, change and manipulate. Strong cultures may have a positive effect on organisations, in that they can bond disparate groups together in a common purpose; and weak cultures may have a negative impact, in that individuals and groups can pursue separate and conflicting objectives. However, in some situations, especially where there is major environmental disruption, the reverse may also be true, with strong cultures being a straitjacket on innovation and weak ones allowing new ideas and new leaders to come to the fore. Therefore in such cases, where a clash of interests and a clash of perspectives is present, where the status quo is being challenged, major decisions about the future direction, structure and operation of an organisation are likely to be dominated by issues of power and politics (Pfeffer, 1992).

Murray (1989: 285), reporting on a major study of the introduction and use of information technology, commented that:

> ...the use of new technology is subject to processes of organizational decision-making and implementation characterized by often conflicting managerial objectives, rationalities and strategies developed through the mobilization of organizational power.

Therefore, as far as Morgan (1986), Murray (1989), Robbins (1987) and many others are concerned, the process of organisational change is inherently a political one.

Though the postmodern, cultural and political perspectives on organisational life are very different, there are also strong overlaps. In particular, the management of meaning and the creation of legitimacy through the construction and manipulation of symbols is an area of common ground. This can be seen in Pettigrew's (1987) work on organisational change. He maintains that the process of change is shaped by the interests and commitments of individuals and groups, the forces of bureaucratic momentum, significant changes in the environment, and the manipulation of the structural context around decisions. In particular, Pettigrew (1987: 659) argues:

> The acts and processes associated with politics as the management of meaning represent conceptually the overlap between a concern with the political and cultural analyses of organizations. A central concept linking political and cultural analyses essential to the understanding of continuity and change is legitimacy. The management of meaning refers to a process of symbol construction and value use designed to create legitimacy for one's ideas, actions and demands, and to delegitimate the demands of one's opponents ... [Therefore] structures, cultures and strategies are not just being treated here as neutral, functional constructs connectable to some system need such as efficiency or adaptability; those constructs are viewed as capable of serving to protect the interests of the dominant groups. ... The content of strategic change is thus ultimately a product of a legitimation process shaped by political/cultural considerations, though often expressed in rational/analytical terms.

This view that the choice and use of structure, and other key decisions, is the outcome of a political process rather than the application of rational analysis and decision-making has significant implications for organisation theory. Whilst it does not necessarily invalidate the appropriateness or otherwise of particular approaches, it does mean that managerial aspirations and interests are seen as more important than might otherwise be the case. It also means that, rather than being the prisoners of organisation theory (as some might suppose or hope), managers do exercise significant choice with regard to structure and other organisation characteristics.

In his review of the influence of power and politics in organisations, Robbins (1987) noted that no more than 50 to 60 per cent of variability in structure can be explained by strategy, size, technology and environment. He then went on to argue that a substantial portion of the residual variance can be explained by those in positions of power choosing a structure that will, as far as possible, maintain and enhance their control. He points out that proponents of other determinants of structure, size, technology, etc., assume that organisations are rational entities: 'However, for rationality to prevail an organisation must have either a single goal or agreement over the multiple goals. Neither case exists in most organisations' (Robbins, 1987: 200). Consequently, he argues that structural decisions are not rational. Such decisions arise from a power struggle between special-interest groups or coalitions, each arguing for a structural arrangement that best suits them. Robbins (1987: 200) believes that whilst strategy, size, technology and environment define the minimum level of effectiveness and set the parameters within which self-serving decision choices will be made, 'both technology and environment are chosen. Thus, those in power will select technologies and environments that will facilitate their maintenance of control.'

Many other writers have also challenged the view of management as rational and neutral implementers of decisions determined by objective data. In particular, the detailed case studies of organisational decision-making and change at ICI and Cadbury Ltd carried out, respectively, by Pettigrew (1985, 1987) and Child and Smith (1987) lend a great deal of weight to the view that management in general, and the management of change in particular, is inherently a political process. Murray (1989) made the telling point that, given the insecurity of many managers' positions, particularly during periods of major upheaval and change, it is not surprising that managers and other groups attempt to influence decisions in order to protect, enhance or shore up their position in the organisation.

Nevertheless, one needs to be wary of ascribing the purpose of all organisational decisions and actions to self-interest. Politics plays a part but, to view Robbin's (1987) finding from another perspective, so too do strategy, size, technology and environment. These can act as a constraint on the freedom of action of groups and individuals, as can the need to be seen to act in the organisation's best interests, in line with agreed goals and in a rational manner. Therefore, though the political perspective has become very influential in the last 20 years, it does not explain all actions and all decisions in organisations. We need to see power and politics as an important influence on organisations but not the only influence. Indeed, we need to remember the original objective of Cyert and March's (1963) work on organisational politics. They sought to show that external factors were not the only factors that affected decision-making in organisations. This is not, of course, the same as saying that external factors do not matter. As Child and Smith (1987) have shown with their firm-in-sector perspective, the external environment does matter. In a whole host of concrete and symbolic ways, it constrains and impinges on organisational decision-making and behaviour. It may well be, as Robbins (1987) commented, that strategy, size, technology and environment only define the minimum level of effectiveness and set the parameters within which decisions are taken, but this is still a very important constraint on managers. It is also an important rejoinder to those management theorists who have become, as Hendry (1996: 621) noted, '... overfocused on the political aspects of the change [decision-making] process'.

In summary, therefore, power and politics are amongst the most important factors influencing decision-making in organisations. Indeed, by linking the arguments of Robbins, Pettigrew and Murray regarding managerial choice of structure to the discussion on culture, two very interesting points arise. First, it was argued by Allaire and Firsirotu (1984), and others, that culture and structure need to be mutually supportive if an organisation is to operate efficiently and effectively. If, as the power-politics perspective argues, structure is in part at least the outcome of self-interested choice by the dominant coalition, the degree of congruence between the two may be due more to accident than choice. Second, it was also argued earlier that organisational culture is the product of long-term social learning in which dominant coalitions play a key role. This clearly opens up scope for choices over both structure and culture. However, the development of culture and approaches to changing it are long-term processes. Dominant coalitions, on the other hand, change their composition and priorities over time, sometimes over quite short periods of time. Therefore, although it can be argued that the possibility exists for managers to choose both the structure and culture that best suit their own self-interests, this is only likely to result in a balanced and effective structure–culture nexus if the dominant coalition holds sway and is consistent in its aims over time.

As many observers have noted, whilst these conditions may exist in some Western companies (e.g. News International under Rupert Murdoch, General Electric under Jack Welch), these are the exception. In any case, as the departure of Arnold Weinstock from GEC showed, such situations often rely on dominant individuals to hold coalitions together; when they go, the dominant coalition falls apart and a new one emerges with a radically different vision for the organisation (Brummer and Cowe, 1998; Brummer, 1999). Sometimes the departure of such individuals can even bring an organisation perilously close to collapse, as was the case with Apple Computers when Steve Jobs was fired in 1985, and with Tiny Rowland's forced departure from Lonrho in 1995 (Laird, 1998; Morgan, 1986). Indeed, in some companies, so forceful and coercive is the personality of a dominant individual that their will cannot be questioned, and fundamental problems are only discovered once they depart, as was the case with Robert Maxwell and Mirror Group Newspapers (Bower, 1996).

The Japanese experience seems at first glance to follow a similar pattern of dominant coalitions relying on one key person for their legitimacy and direction. However, in their case, when such a person departs, the dominant coalition appears to maintain the unity of purpose (Fruin, 1992; Pascale and Athos, 1982; Whitehill, 1991). Yet even the Japanese are not immune from problems when changing leaders. For example, Nissan's appointment of a new chief executive in 1985 was followed by an attempt to change its culture in order to overcome what were seen as major mistakes by the previous incumbent (Ishizuna, 1990).

To sum up, therefore, what we can see is that managers have a degree of choice or influence over major organisational variables such as structure, technology, environment and perhaps even culture. However, their freedom of action is constrained by a whole host of factors such as organisational goals, policies, performance, their own and other people's self-interests, and the need to portray their actions as being rational and in the best interests of their organisation. In addition, in a reciprocal way, some of the factors over which they have a degree of choice, such as structure and culture, can also limit managers' freedom of manoeuvre. These constraints will vary from organisation to organisation at any one time and, within and between organisations, over time but will never be fully absent. However, strong though these constraints may be, neither will choice ever be totally absent either.

## CONCLUSIONS

In reviewing the main approaches to organisation theory, the first four chapters of the book have shown that, by succeeding stages, these have moved from the mechanical-rational outlook of the Classical school to the, arguably, culture-based perspectives of the Culture–Excellence, Japanese and Organisation Learning approaches (passing through the social perspective of the Human Relations school and the rational perspective of the Contingency theorists). They all argue for a 'one best way' approach (though the Contingency theorists believed in this for 'each' rather than 'all' organisations). Because of this approach they all, in effect, seek to remove choice from managers: do as we tell you, or else! Indeed, it was one of the main claims of the Classical school that it removed discretion not only from workers, but also from managers. The role of managers, from these perspectives, is to apply rationally the dictates of the particular theory promoted. To do otherwise would be sub-optimal and irrational.

What this chapter has sought to do is to move managerial choice back to centre stage. The first part of the chapter examined the postmodernist perspective on organisational life. This, in particular, questioned the use of reason and logic and argued that, instead, human beings use language and symbols to create (or impose) meaning for themselves and others. In effect, the postmodernists argue, human beings invent their own worlds rather than experiencing them as some objective reality. Following on from this, the concept of organisational culture was explored: is it important? Can it be changed? Should it be changed? What emerged was that culture is a more elusive and less malleable concept than the advocates of the Culture–Excellence school would have us believe. In particular, important though it is in influencing behaviour, there are those who question the usefulness of strong cultures in all situations; diversity and conflict rather than uniformity and consensus may be necessary for organisational survival. Also, the degree to which culture influences behaviour is dependent upon the presence of clear and consistent organisational goals. If these are not present, which appears to be the case in many companies, conflict and disagreement emerge regardless of the nature of the culture. In such situations, it is the political perspective on organisational life that offers the better opportunity for understanding how and why organisations manage and structure themselves in particular ways, or follow particular courses of action.

The examination of organisational politics and power that has been covered in the third section of this chapter added further weight to the criticisms of the approaches to organisation theory considered in previous chapters, particularly concerning the scope for decision-making and choice. To an extent, the key issue was raised when discussing Contingency Theory, namely the question as to whether managers are the prisoners of the situational variables they face, or whether they can influence or change these. Certainly the critics of Contingency Theory argue that managers can, partly at least, influence or choose the contingencies they face. This casts doubts not only on the deterministic nature of Contingency Theory, but also on all organisational theories, because – either openly or implicitly – they are all founded on the notion that organisations face certain immutable conditions which they cannot influence and to which they must therefore adapt.

This does not necessarily mean that the various theories and their attendant structures and practices we have discussed so far in this book are invalid, unhelpful or inapplicable. It does, however, mean that it may be possible for organisations, or rather those who control organisations, to decide upon the structure and behaviours they want to promote, and then shape the conditions and contingencies to suit these, rather than vice versa. Indeed, as far as the public sector in the UK is concerned, this appears to be exactly what successive governments have done. From 1979 to 1996, successive Conservative governments took the view that they wanted managers in the public sector to be cost-focused and entrepreneurial, and shaped the conditions in which the public sector operates (i.e. its environment) in order to promote those attributes (Ferlie *et al*, 1996; Flynn, 1993). Following its election in 1996, the 'New Labour' government similarly manipulated the public sector environment to influence managerial behaviour. This can be seen in terms of significant alterations to the NHS Internal Market, the replacement of Compulsory Competitive Tendering with the notion of 'Best Value' in local government, and the reversal of the previous government's policy of contracting out central government activities through the creation of semi-autonomous agencies and the Next Steps initiative (Salauroo and Burnes, 1998).

Clearly, if decisions are not formulated on the basis of objective theories or measurable contingencies, one then has to ask what factors do influence the decisions taken. The review of the power-politics literature showed organisations as shifting coalitions of groups and individuals seeking to promote policies and decisions that enhanced or maintained their position in the organisation. From the literature, a persuasive argument is mounted for seeing politics and power – usually promoted under the cloak of rationality, reasonableness and the organisation's best interests – as central, though not exclusive, determinants of the way organisations operate.

In particular, though political behaviour appears to be an ever-present feature of organisational life, politics comes to the fore when major issues of structural change or resource allocation are concerned. Such decisions have crucial importance for achieving and maintaining power or position, or even – when the chips are down – for keeping one's job when all around are losing theirs.

Therefore, it is surprising that organisational theory, which after all is primarily concerned with major decisions concerning structure and resource allocation, seems to dismiss or gloss over power and politics. Nevertheless, what is clear from this chapter is that managers, despite the constraints they face, have a far wider scope for shaping decisions than most organisation theories acknowledge, and that the scope for choice and the deployment of political influence is likely to be most pronounced when change, particularly major change, is on the managerial agenda.

Having examined the merits and drawbacks of the main organisational theories, and in particular having raised the issue of the way in which major decisions are decided upon and implemented, we can now turn our attention to an in-depth examination of change management.

## TEST YOUR LEARNING

### Short answer questions

1 What is flexible specialisation?

2 Give three definitions of postmodernism.

3 Using Clegg's (1990) distinction between modernist and postmodernist organisation forms, identify the significant differences between job design under a modernist regime and that under a postmodernist regime.

4 What are Cummings and Huse's four elements of culture?

5 Briefly describe Handy's four types of culture.

6 What does the term 'satisfice' mean?

7 Define organisational power.

8 Define organisational politics.

9 For each of the following, briefly state their implications for organisational change: (a) postmodernism, (b) organisational culture and (c) power and politics.

### Essay questions

1 What are the implications of postmodernism for the design and operation of organisations?

2 Discuss the following statement: organisational culture is the prime determinant of organisational performance.

# SUGGESTED FURTHER READING

1  Hassard, J and Parker, M (eds) (1993). *Postmodernism and Organizations*. Sage: London.
   Hatch, MJ (1997). *Organization Theory: Modern, Symbolic and Postmodern Perspectives*. Oxford University Press: Oxford.
   Taken together, these two books provide a good overview of the postmodernist slant on organisations.

2  Brown, A (1995). *Organisational Culture*. Pitman: London.
   Andrew Brown's book gives a useful introduction to the uses and abuses of organisational culture.

3  Pfeffer, J (1992). *Managing with Power: Politics and Influence in Organizations*. Harvard Business School Press: Boston, Massachusetts, USA.
   This is an entertaining and very useful guide to the power-politics perspective on organisations.

# Part 2

---

## THEORETICAL PERSPECTIVES ON STRATEGY DEVELOPMENT AND CHANGE MANAGEMENT

# Chapter 5

# APPROACHES TO STRATEGY

## Managerial choice and constraints

### Learning objectives

After studying this chapter, you should be able to:

1 discuss the origins, development and popularity of organisation strategy;

2 describe the main features of the Prescriptive stream of strategy;

3 list the strengths and weaknesses of the Prescriptive stream;

4 discuss the key elements of the Analytical stream of strategy;

5 state the major advantages and shortcomings of the Analytical stream;

6 understand the key differences between the Prescriptive and the Analytical streams of strategy;

7 describe the constraints faced by organisations and how these can be manipulated or overcome;

8 appreciate the relationship between strategy and change.

## INTRODUCTION

It has become the accepted view that, for society at large, the magnitude, speed, unpredictability and impact of change are greater than ever before. Certainly, over the last 20 years especially, new products and processes have appeared at an ever-increasing rate. Local markets have become global markets. Protected or semi-protected markets and industries have been opened up to fierce competition. Public bureaucracies and monopolies have either been transferred to the private sector or, as in the case of the UK National Health Service, have had the market transferred into them.

But is it actually true that the degree and magnitude of change are the greatest yet? The Industrial Revolution led to enormous changes in society. The rapid growth of welfare provision and the advent of 'Big Government' was a phenomenon experienced by most Western countries before and, especially, just after the Second World War. In Scandinavia, it was connected with the advent of social democracy; in the USA it came through Roosevelt's New Deal; and in the UK, the creation of the Welfare State was the major work of the post-war Labour government. Whatever the cause, though, in each case it transformed the role of government and led to an unparalleled expansion of the public sector. In the 1950s and 1960s, the rapid growth of industry and competition, particularly at an international level, also saw large-scale changes in societies. This was most noticeable in South-East Asia where some countries, such as South Korea, Malaysia, Hong Kong and Singapore, industrialised at a furious pace. Though the recent economic crises experienced by these countries have severely affected the pace of industrialisation, they seem to have done little to alter the pace of social change. Rather it has taken a more nationalist and protectionist direction.

So although we egotistically tend to see the present level of change as being unprecedented, the history of the past 200 years could well be characterised as successive periods of unprecedented change. Indeed, given that it was the ancient Greeks who coined the phrase, 'change is the only constant', we should perhaps remember that the history of the human race is one of massive change and dislocation. Each generation seems to yearn for some golden past which has been swept away by progress, and each generation, building on past knowledge, develops new ways of coping with and managing change. Therefore, perhaps we should be less concerned with the overall level of change and instead be asking:

- Are all organisations affected to the same degree by their environment?

- How can each organisation best cope with the degree of turbulence it faces?

- What degree of choice can managers exert in such circumstances?

In Part 1 of this book, we discussed the options open to organisations in terms of their structures, cultures and practices. By examining the development of organisational theory in the 200 years since the Industrial Revolution, we saw that, in the beginning, management was almost exclusively concerned with strict labour discipline and long working hours. The methods used to pursue these were *ad hoc*, erratic, short-term and usually harsh and unfair. As the period progressed, more structured and consistent approaches came to the fore. Up to the 1960s, it was the Classical and Human Relations approaches that dominated organisational thinking. With the advent of these two approaches, the emphasis moved to the effectiveness and efficiency of the entire organisation, rather than focusing purely on discipline and hours of work.

Both these approaches tended to dwell on internal arrangements and to assume that organisation structures and practices were in some way insulated from the outside world. The development of Contingency Theory in the 1960s, with its underlying Open Systems perspective, changed all this. The nature of the environment (both internal and external) in which organisations operate emerged as a central factor in how they should structure themselves. This theme has been continued with the development of new paradigms in the 1980s and 1990s, and the importance of situational variables, especially environmental turbulence, which organisations face is seen by many as an unchallengeable fact (Kanter *et al*, 1997; Peters, 1997a).

However, as argued in Part 1, the degree to which organisations are the prisoners of these situational variables (as averse to being able to exercise influence and choice) is certainly open to debate. Similarly, the credibility of the rational approach to decision-making has been considerably undermined in the last two decades. The postmodern, cultural and political perspectives, discussed in Chapter 4, are increasingly influential in explaining how and why decisions are taken in organisations. The increasing appreciation of the complexity of organisational life has been paralleled by a growing recognition that organisations cannot cope successfully with the modern world and all its changing aspects purely on an *ad hoc* and piecemeal basis. Whether decision-makers operate on the basis of rationality or are influenced by personal considerations or organisational cultures, the received wisdom is that for organisations to succeed there must be a consistency and coherence to the decisions taken – which is another way of saying that they must have a strategy (Johnson and Scholes, 1993).

In this chapter, we shall examine the development and shortcomings of the main approaches to strategy that have been put forward in the last 50 years. It will be shown that, since the end of the Second World War, organisations have begun to take a strategic perspective on their activities. They have increasingly sought to take a long-term overview in order to plan for and cope with the vagaries of the future. In many respects, the development of strategic management has tended to mirror the development of organisational theory. In the 1940s and 1950s, the strategy literature only considered one aspect of an organisation's activities – the external environment. It tended to seek rational, mathematical approaches to planning. With the passing of time, more intuitive and less rational approaches to strategic management have been developed which claim to incorporate the totality of organisational life.

The chapter concludes by arguing that, rather than managers being the prisoners of mathematical models and rational approaches to decision-making, they have considerable freedom of action and a wide range of options to choose from. However, they are not totally free agents; their freedom of action is seen as being constrained or shaped by the unique set of organisational, environmental and societal factors faced by their particular organisation. Fortunately, these constraints are not immutable. As argued in Part 1, it is possible for managers to manipulate the situational variables they face with regard to structure. Similarly, managers can also exert some influence over strategic constraints and, potentially at least, can select the approach to strategy that best suits their preferences.

## The origins of strategy

It is commonly believed that our concept of strategy has been passed down to us from the ancient Greeks. Bracker (1980: 219) argued that the word strategy comes from the Greek *stratego*, meaning 'to plan the destruction of one's enemies through the effective use of resources'. However, they developed the concept purely in relation to the successful pursuit of victory in war. The concept remained a military one until the nineteenth century, when it began to be applied to the business world, though most writers believe the actual process by which this took place is untraceable (Bracker, 1980; Chandler, 1962). Chandler (1962) put forward the view that the emergence of strategy in civilian organisational life resulted from an awareness of the opportunities and needs – created by changing population, income and technology – to employ existing or expanding resources more profitably.

Hoskin (1990) largely agreed with Chandler's view of the development of modern business strategy since the Industrial Revolution. However, he does take issue with both Chandler and Bracker on two crucial points. First, he argues that the modern concept of organisational strategy bears little resemblance to military strategy, at least as it existed up to the First World War. Second, he challenges the view that the origins of business strategy are untraceable. When investigating the emergence of modern strategy he did find a link with the military world, though it was not quite the link that Bracker and Chandler proposed. Like Chandler, Hoskin argues that one of the most significant developments in business management in the nineteenth century occurred in the running of the US railways. However, unlike Chandler, Hoskin gives the credit for initiating business strategy to one of the Pennsylvania Railway's executives, Herman Haupt. He states that Haupt:

> ... changes the rules of business discourse: the image in which he reconstructs business, on the Pennsylvania Railroad, is that of the proactive, future-oriented organization, which is managed by the numbers ... How does he do so? By importing the practices of writing, examination and grading ... On the Pennsylvania Railroad we find for the first time the full interactive play of grammatocentrism [writing and recording] and calculability [mathematical analysis of the recorded data]. (Hoskin, 1990: 20)

This approach created the bedrock on which strategic management grew in the United States, especially after the Second World War. It also ensured that strategic management became a quantitatively orientated discipline, whose focus was on the use of numerical analysis to forecast market trends in order to plan for the future. Hoskin also points out that Haupt was a graduate of the US military academy at West Point, which pioneered the techniques of 'writing, examination and grading' in the military world. From there its graduates, particularly Haupt, took them out into the business world – hence the link between military and civilian management techniques.

Thus it is possible to see why strategic management developed in the way it did – as a quantitative, mathematical approach. We can also see that there are links between the military and business world, but that they are not as some have claimed. Management strategy has not developed from the approach to military campaigns of the ancient Greeks; instead it has adopted and made its own the techniques of record-keeping and analysis that were developed at West Point in order to measure the performance, and suitability for military life, of the US army's future officer class.

The contribution of the American armed forces to this quantitative approach to strategy did not end with West Point or in the nineteenth century. In 1945, with the end of the Second World War, America experienced an extraordinary trading boom. McKiernan (1992) commented that this forced many American companies to rethink their business planning systems. In order to justify and implement the capacity expansion necessary to cope with the boom, companies began to abandon short-term, one year, budgeting cycles in favour of more long-range planning techniques. The development of this strategic approach to planning and investment was given a significant impetus when some of the people involved in the USAAF's wartime strategic planning activities returned to civilian life – most notable amongst whom was Robert McNamara, who became Chairman of the Ford Motor Company, Secretary of State under John F Kennedy and President of the World Bank (Moore, 1992). Their main vehicle for influencing business was the Harvard Business School's approach to business policy teaching, which steadily moved the focus of management away from a preoccupation with internal organisational issues (as proposed by the Classical and Human Relations schools) towards an external orientation. This was best exemplified by the development of two important concepts: marketing, with its emphasis on analysing demand and tailoring products to meet it; and systems theory, with its emphasis not only on the interconnectedness of different parts of an organisation, but also the links between internal and external forces.

In the intervening years, first in the USA and later across the Western world, these techniques and approaches have become more widely disseminated and used (Bracker, 1980). Much credit for this must go to three key figures, Kenneth R Andrews, Alfred D Chandler and H Igor Ansoff, for their work in developing and fleshing out the concept of strategic management, and especially for demonstrating the importance of product–market mix. Nevertheless, in highlighting the importance of the outside world, and thus breaking managers' Classical school-inspired fixation with internal structures and practices, they can be criticised for not making the link between the two. So managers moved from believing that internal arrangements alone would bring success to believing that an external, market focus was the key.

## The rise and fall of long-range planning

In order to cope with the new and rapidly changing technological, economic and organisational developments that followed the end of the Second World War, American organisations, which were at the forefront of these developments, began to adopt long-range planning techniques. This necessitated first defining the organisation's objectives, then establishing plans in order to achieve those objectives, and finally, allocating resources, through capital budgeting, in line with the plans. A key aim of this process was to reduce the gap that often occurred between the level of demand that a firm expected, and planned for, and the level of demand that actually occurred (Fox, 1975). Therefore, long-range planning was a mechanism for plotting trends and planning the actions required to achieve the identified growth targets, all of which were heavily biased towards financial targets and budgetary controls. However, this process proved incapable of accurately forecasting future demand and the problem of the gap between the level of expected demand and actual demand remained.

Long-range planning failed for a variety of internal and external reasons (McKiernan, 1992). Internally, many planning systems involved little more than an extrapolation of past sales trends. Little attention was paid to wider external economic, technological or social changes, or even changes in the behaviour of competitor firms. Externally, in the 1960s, the relatively comfortable conditions of high market growth gave way to lower levels of growth which led to increased competition as companies tried to increase, or at least maintain, their market share to compensate for lower levels of growth. One outcome of this was that strategic planners had to adapt to a world where growth was not steady; it could slow down, increase or be interrupted in an unpredictable and violent manner. Also, unforeseen opportunities and threats could and did emerge. Furthermore, it became evident that closing the gap between the plan and what actually occurred was not necessarily the most critical aspect of strategy formulation. Indeed, since the early 1970s, volatile markets, over-capacity, and resource constraints have taken over as dominant management considerations.

Long-range planning techniques could not cope with such environmental turbulence which, to say the least, limits forecasting accuracy. In addition, the nature of American business had begun to change. Slower growth and increased competition led to a situation where large single-business firms which in the past might have dominated a single industry were being replaced by multinational conglomerates operating in a wide range of increasingly competitive industries and markets. Therefore, rather than managing a single, unified enterprise, corporate managers found themselves managing a diverse portfolio of businesses. In response to the failure of long-range planning and the emergence of conglomerates, in the late 1960s, the concept of strategic management began to emerge.

Unlike long-range planning, strategic management focuses on the environmental assumptions that underlie market trends and incorporates the possibility that changes in trends can and do take place, and is not based on the assumption that adequate growth can be assured (Elliot and Lawrence, 1985; Mintzberg and Quinn, 1991). In addition, strategic management focuses more closely on winning market share from competitors, rather than assuming that organisations can rely solely on the expansion of markets for their own growth (Hax and Majluf, 1996). This concept sought to take a broader and more sophisticated view of an organisation's environment and, initially at least, was closely associated with a number of portfolio planning techniques which also emerged in the late 1960s (Hax and Majluf, 1996; McKiernan, 1992). As will be described in Chapter 6, these were developed to assist managers in running large, diversified enterprises operating in complex environments. Much of this work was sponsored and used by large American corporations, such as General Electric, in order to identify the market position and potential of their strategic business units and decide on whether to develop, sell or close them down. This 'positioning' approach to strategic management, the latest variant of which is Porter's (1980, 1985) 'competitive forces model', dominated the practice of strategic management from the 1960s onwards, and to a large extent still does. It has also led many companies to adopt a harsh, and to an extent unthinking, approach to business success which is epitomised by the words of Jack Welch, who became General Electric's Chief Executive in 1981: 'We will run only businesses that are number one or two in their markets' (quoted in Kay, 1993: 339). Therefore, if businesses are not, or do not have the potential to become, leaders in their field, they are sold off or closed down (Koch, 1995).

As Kay (1993), and many others, point out, this approach to strategic management portrays strategy as a rational process whereby managers gather hard, quantitative data on their companies, and from this information come to rational decisions regarding their future. However, from the late 1970s onwards, the rational perspective on strategy has come under increasing attack, not least by the leading management thinker of his generation, Henry Mintzberg (1976, 1978, 1983, 1987, 1994). The main criticisms of the rational approach to strategy are threefold: that hard data are no more reliable, and in some cases less so, than qualitative data; that organisations and managers are not rational entities and do not apply a rational approach to decision-making; and that an organisation's strategy is as likely to emerge from unplanned actions and their unintended consequences over a period of time as it is from any deliberate process of planning and implementation (Child and Smith, 1987; Mintzberg *et al*, 1998; Pettigrew *et al*, 1992; Stacey, 1993; Whittington, 1993).

## Defining strategy

As the above shows, like many other concepts in the field of management, there is no agreed, all-embracing definition of strategy. Indeed, even one of the pioneers of business strategy, Igor Ansoff (1987), warned that strategy is an elusive and somewhat abstract concept. This must be expected when dealing with an area that is constantly developing. Nor should this inhibit the search for a definition, or definitions, because in doing so we can see how the debate on strategy is developing and where the main areas of dispute lie.

Rather than leading to clarity, the eclipse of long-range planning merely heralded the arrival of a wide range of different perspectives on strategy. As early as the 1960s, two schools of thought vied with each other: the Planning school and the Design school (Mintzberg *et al*, 1998). The Planning school was based on formal procedures, formal training, formal analysis and a large dose of quantification. Its underlying assumption was that a strategy could be put together and work in the same way as a machine. It led to the creation of strategic planning departments in large organisations, reporting directly to the chief executive; that person's role – though notionally to be the architect of strategy – was to approve the planners' plan. The chief proponent of the Planning school was Igor Ansoff. Ansoff was a Russian-American engineer, mathematician, military strategist and operations researcher whose *Corporate Strategy* was published in 1965 to great acclaim (Koch, 1995). In this book he assumes that the purpose of a firm is profit maximisation, and he portrays strategic management as being primarily concerned with the external, rather than internal, concerns of the firm, especially the matching of products to markets (the product–market mix). The book provides managers with a plethora of checklists and charts to enable them to derive objectives, assess synergy between different parts of an organisation, appraise its competence profile and decide how, where and in which way to expand. Nevertheless, as Koch (1995) remarked, from today's viewpoint, the book, and indeed the precepts of the Planning school as a whole, have not aged well.

The Design school, though sharing some common features with the Planning school, adopted a different, less formal and machine-like approach. It proposed a model of strategy which emphasises the need to achieve a fit between the internal capabilities of an organisation and the external possibilities it faces. Flowing from this, the Design school places primary emphasis on the appraisal of an organisation's external and internal situations. To facilitate this, it developed the now-famous SWOT technique – the assessment of the internal Strengths and Weaknesses of the organisation in the light of the Opportunities and Threats posed by the environment in which it operates. One of the main architects of the Design school was Alfred Chandler. Chandler was one of the most eminent and influential American economic historians of his generation. His main contribution to the Design school is encapsulated in his 1962 book, *Strategy and Structure*, which was based on a major study of US corporations between 1850 and 1920. In the book, Chandler defined strategy as the determination of the basic long-term goals and objectives of an enterprise, and the adoption of courses of action and the allocation of resources necessary for carrying out these goals. The book also suggested three important precepts for running organisations which challenged the conventional wisdom of the time: first, that an organisation's structure should flow from its strategy rather than being determined by some universal 'one best way'; second, that the 'visible hand of management' was more important than Adam Smith's 'invisible hand of the market' in meeting customer needs; and third, that large organisations need to decentralise and divisionalise in order to remain competitive. Chandler's work proved very influential in shaping the strategy debate over the next three decades.

Nevertheless, like Ansoff, Chandler has attracted his fair share of criticism, especially with regard to his view that structure should follow strategy. Tom Peters (1993: 148), for example, remarked that, 'I understand Chandler's reasoning, but I think he got it exactly wrong. For it is the structure of the organization that determines, over time, the choices that it makes about market attacks' (i.e. its strategy).

The crucial difference between Ansoff and Chandler is that the former regards strategy as almost exclusively concerned with the relationships between the firm and its environment, whilst Chandler takes a broader view. His definition includes internal as well as external factors. In particular, he sees issues such as organisational structures, production processes and technology as being essentially strategic. The point he makes is that the external and internal cannot be separated, as the Open Systems theorists would be the first to point out (*see* Scott, 1987). The external affects the internal, and vice versa. Therefore, strategic management must encompass the totality of the organisational domain and must not be restricted to one aspect, such as determining the product–market mix (Andrews, 1980).

This brings us a little nearer a definition but still leaves us with a hazy concept. This is not surprising given that even Henry Mintzberg argued that we need at least five definitions of strategy to gain a full understanding of what the concept is. According to Mintzberg *et al* (1988), the five interrelated definitions of strategy are as follows: *plan*, *ploy*, *pattern*, *position* and *perspective*.

- **Strategy as a plan**. According to this view, strategy is some form of consciously intended course of action which is created ahead of events. This can be either a general strategy or a specific one. If specific, it may also constitute a ploy.

- **Strategy as a ploy**. This is where strategy is a manoeuvre to outwit an opponent. An example of this is when a firm threatens to lower its prices substantially to deter new entrants into its market. It is the threat to lower prices that is the consciously intended course of action, and not any actual plan to do so.

- **Strategy as a pattern**. This is where we observe, after the event, that an organisation has acted in a consistent manner over time; i.e. whether consciously or not, the organisation exhibits a consistent pattern of behaviour. We can say from this that an organisation has pursued a particular strategy. It could be argued that this reflects a conscious plan. However, this is often not the case.

- **Strategy as a position**. From this perspective, strategy is about positioning the organisation in order to achieve or maintain a sustainable competitive advantage. Mintzberg *et al* argue that most organisations try to avoid head-on competition. What they seek to achieve is a position where their competitors cannot or will not challenge them. In this sense, strategy is also seen as a game: groups of players circling each other, each trying to gain the high ground.

- **Strategy as perspective**. This definition sees strategy as a somewhat abstract concept that exists primarily in people's minds. For members of an organisation, the actual details of its strategy, as such, are irrelevant. What is important is that everyone in the organisation shares a common view of its purpose and direction which, whether people are aware of it or not, informs and guides decision-making and actions. Consequently, without the need for detailed plans, the organisation, through a shared understanding, pursues a consistent strategy/purpose.

In a manner that has a postmodernist feel to it, Mintzberg *et al* (1988) do not argue that one definition should be preferred to the others. In some senses they can be considered as alternatives or complementary approaches to strategy. Also, they are useful in adding important elements to the discussion of strategy. They draw our attention to the distinction between conscious and unconscious strategy, and between emergent and planned strategy. They also highlight the role of the organisation's collective mind in developing and implementing strategy.

In a similar way to Mintzberg *et al*, Johnson (1987) also distinguishes between different views of the strategic management process. He argues that there are three basic views which reflect more general distinctions in the social sciences. These are as follows:

- The **rationalistic** view – which sees strategy as the outcome of a series of preplanned actions designed to achieve the stated goals of an organisation in an optimal fashion.

- The **adaptive** or **incremental** view – which sees strategy evolving through an accumulation of relatively small changes over time.

- The **interpretative** view – which sees strategy as the product of individual and collective attempts to make sense of, i.e. interpret, past events.

One way of considering these various definitions, following on from Morgan (1986), is as metaphors. Morgan (1986: 12–13) comments that metaphors:

> ...lead us to see and understand organizations in distinctive yet partial ways. ... By using different metaphors to understand the complex and paradoxical nature of organizational life, we are able to manage and design organizations in ways that we may not have thought possible before.

In a similar way to Morgan's use of metaphors, it could also be argued that, drawing on the postmodernist viewpoint discussed in Chapter 4, the varying definitions of strategy can be seen as competing realities which managers attempt to impose on their organisations. By seeing Mintzberg *et al*'s five definitions and Johnson's three definitions of strategy as metaphors or alternative realities, rather than as totalities in themselves, we can arrive at a fuller picture of strategic management.

These multiple definitions can also help us to make sense of the confusion of terms which litter the strategy literature and which different writers use in different ways. Many writers seem to treat corporate planning, long-range planning, strategic planning and formal planning as synonymous. However, not all would agree. Naylor (1979), for example, defined strategic planning as long-range planning with a time horizon of three to five years. Litschert and Nicholson (1974) disagreed: they state that strategic and long-term planning are not synonymous. They argue that strategic planning is a process which involves making a sequence of interrelated decisions aimed at achieving a desirable future environment for an organisation. Andrews (1980), similarly, defined strategy as a:

> ...pattern of decisions in a company that determines and reveals its objectives, purposes, or goals, produces the principal policies and plans for achieving those goals, and defines the range of business the company is to pursue, the kind of economic and human organisation it is, or intends to be, and the nature of the economic and non-economic contribution it intends to make to its shareholders, employees, customers and communities. (Quoted in Smith, 1985: 10)

What we can see from the above is that, knowingly or not, writers are using different definitions of strategy and thus interpreting particular terms or phrases in the light of their own implicit or explicit definition. Nevertheless, in the use of these various terms, a certain consensus of opinion does emerge with regard to the basic features of strategic management and strategic decisions. Most of the writers would agree with Johnson and Scholes (1993), who described strategy as:

- concerning the full scope of an organisation's activities;
- the process of matching the organisation's activities to its environment;
- the process of matching its activities to its resource capability;
- having major resource implications;
- affecting operational decisions;
- being affected by the values and beliefs of those who have power in an organisation;
- affecting the long-term direction of an organisation.

## Approaches to strategy: the Prescriptive versus the Analytical stream

In defining strategy, especially bearing in mind Mintzberg *et al*'s (1988) and Johnson's (1987) various definitions, there are two further issues which need to be considered:

1 Is strategy a process or the outcome of a process?

2 Is strategy an economic/rational phenomenon or is it an organisational/social phenomenon?

Taking these two questions together, it can be seen that there are two parallel, competing and, to an extent, interacting streams of ideas. The first, the Prescriptive stream, sees strategy as a controlled, intentional, prescriptive process, based on a rational model of decision-making, which produces complete deliberate strategies (Ansoff, 1965; Argenti, 1974; Steiner, 1969). The second, the Analytical stream, which is more interested in understanding how organisations actually formulate strategy rather than prescribing how they should formulate it, argues that it is the outcome of the complex social and political processes involved in organisational decision-making (Hamel and Prahalad, 1989; Miles and Snow, 1978; Mintzberg, 1987; Pettigrew, 1980; Quinn, 1980a).

The Prescriptive stream grew out of the long-range planning initiatives of the 1940s and 1950s, and is aimed primarily at the practitioners of strategy. Through the work of the Planning and Design schools, this stream dominated the practice of strategy in the 1960s and 1970s. They not only saw strategy as an economic-rational process, but also considered its options and usefulness as primarily restricted to issues relating to market share and profit maximisation (Ansoff, 1965; Porter, 1980). However, with growing disillusionment amongst academics and practitioners over the ability of this approach to deliver competitiveness, a new variant of this approach came to the fore in the 1980s: the Positioning school. This school is most closely identified with Michael Porter (1980, 1985) whose competitive forces framework reinvigorated the prescriptive approach and allowed it to maintain its dominance on the practice of strategy in the 1980s and 1990s (Teece *et al*, 1997). The main difference between the Positioning school and the earlier Planning and Design ones was that:

> Both the planning and design schools put no limits on the strategies that were possible in any given situation. The positioning school, in contrast, argued that only a few key strategies – as positions in the economic market place – are desirable in any given industry: ones that can be defended against existing and future competitors. Ease of defense means that firms which occupy these positions enjoy higher profits ... By thereby dispensing with one key premise of the design school – that strategies have to be unique, tailor-made for each organization – the positioning school was able to create and hone a set of analytical tools dedicated to matching the right strategy to the conditions at hand ... (Mintzberg *et al*, 1998: 83)

The work of Porter and the Positioning school will be discussed in more detail in Chapter 6. However, for now, the key points to note are that the three schools that comprise the Prescriptive stream have dominated the practice of strategy within organisations since the 1960s. The reason for this is threefold. First, its proponents set out deliberately to address the needs of industry and commerce by providing them with a blueprint for strategy formulation and implementation. Second, the Prescriptive stream interacted closely with a number of leading consultants, notably the Boston Consultancy Group, and business schools, notably Harvard, to promote their work and tailor it to the needs of organisations. By reinforcing and promoting each other, this triple alliance of researchers, consultants and educators created an iron orthodoxy which organisations, especially large ones, felt they ignored at their peril. Finally, because all three groups in this triple alliance were in effect engaged in a business activity, selling strategy as a product, they were able to invest in promoting and developing their product in a way that others were not. As the following examination of the Analytical stream of strategy will show, though, this did not mean that other important perspectives on strategy were not developed or did not achieve acceptance by a wide audience. It did, however, mean that these alternative perspectives have never had the same impact on practice within organisations as those promoted by the Prescriptive stream.

The Analytical stream, which began to appear in the 1970s and represents a more sceptical and more academically orientated face of strategic management, views strategy not as a process, but as an outcome of a process. Its proponents' emphasis is not on the construction of detailed plans, which in any case they believe to be a misdirected approach, but on the organisational and social aspects of strategy formation. Their argument is that the capabilities of an organisation, in terms of its structure, systems, technology and management style, restrict the range of strategic options the organisation can pursue. Consequently, in a very real sense, it is the day-to-day stream of decisions regarding the development of its capabilities that determines an organisation's strategic direction, rather than the reverse (Mintzberg, 1994).

One of the oft-cited examples for this view is that of Japanese management. Pascale and Athos (1982) and Hamel and Prahalad (1989) argued that Japanese business success is not based on well-thought-out strategies *per se*, but on the commitment of Japanese managers to create and pursue a vision of their desired future. The vision is then used to bind an organisation together and give it a common purpose to which all can contribute. A key part of this common purpose is the identification and development of the core competences and capabilities necessary for the achievement of the organisation's vision.

This theme has been taken up by other Western writers on strategy. Kay (1993) used the term 'distinctive capabilities' rather than 'core competences', but is clearly describing the same thing. He argues that a firm's distinctive capabilities fall under four headings: reputation, architecture (i.e. internal and external structures and linkages), innovation and strategic assets. Kay believes that an organisation's competitiveness is dependent not upon any strategic plan *per se*, but upon the uniqueness and strength of its capabilities. It is these that allow an organisation to take advantage of opportunities and avoid threats, whether foreseeable or not. In a similar way, Stalk *et al* (1992) used the term 'core capability' in referring to an organisation's practices and business routines; and Grant (1991a) proposed a framework for analysing a firm's competitive advantage in terms of its resources and capabilities.

To an extent, the case made by Kay, Stalk *et al* and Grant is complementary to Mintzberg's (1987) concept of emergent strategy. Based on the many Western companies he had studied, Mintzberg argued that successful companies do not start out with detailed strategic plans. Instead, their strategies emerge over time from the pattern of decisions they take on key aspects of their activities. Mintzberg *et al* (1998: 189–90) draw a distinction between planned or deliberate strategies and emergent ones:

> Deliberate strategy focuses on control – making sure that managerial intentions are realized in action – while emergent strategy emphasizes learning – coming to understand through the taking of actions what those intentions should be in the first place. ... The concept of emergent strategy ... opens the door to strategic learning, because it acknowledges the organization's capacity to experiment. A single action can be taken, feedback can be received, and the process can continue until the organization converges on the pattern that becomes its strategy.

Clearly, there are similarities between the Japanese approach, Mintzberg's and that of Kay, etc. However, the Japanese consciously work out their shared vision and consciously pursue it. The Emergent approach, at least in its pure form, lacks the concept of 'vision' and doubts the presence of conscious intent. However, Mintzberg (1994: 25) does recognise that in practice some organisations pursue:

> ...umbrella strategies: the broad outlines are deliberate while the details are allowed to emerge within them. Thus emergent strategies are not bad and deliberate ones good;

effective strategies mix these characteristics in ways that reflect the conditions at hand, notably the ability to predict as well as the need to react to unexpected events.

Kay (1993) took a similar view. Whilst doubting the efficacy of corporate vision *per se*, he does stress that the development of capabilities is, or at least can be, a conscious and planned process.

A further approach which has attracted a great deal of interest in recent years is *Chaos Theory* (Stacey, 1993). Though it has been adopted by some organisation theorists, it was originally a concept developed in the physical sciences, which maintains that disequilibrium is a necessary condition for the growth of dynamic systems (Prigogine and Stengers, 1984). As Lessem (1998) comments, these systems are called 'dissipative structures' because they dissipate their energy in order to re-create themselves into new forms of order. Faced with increasing levels of disturbance, these systems possess innate properties to reconfigure themselves so that they can deal with new information. For this reason, they are frequently referred to as self-organising or self-renewing systems, one of whose distinguishing features is resilience rather than stability.

The applicability of Chaos Theory to organisations is based on the notion that the environment in which organisations operate has become more and more chaotic and unpredictable, and that organisations have to develop self-renewing or self-organising properties if they are to survive (Nonaka, 1988). In such a situation, it is dubious whether organisations possess the ability to plan their future in any meaningful way. For Chaos Theorists, strategy is about achieving beneficial change. Stacey (1993) argued that change falls into two categories: closed and contained change, where outcomes are predictable and achievable; and open-ended change, where the process is unpredictable and outcomes are unknowable. In the case of closed and contained situations, structured approaches to strategy and change are appropriate and can be effective. When it comes to rapid, open-ended situations where outcomes are unpredictable and unknowable, planned and structured approaches are impractical. Instead, what is necessary is an approach which can create 'organisational order' out of 'environmental chaos'.

The Chaos Theorists argue that organisations can only counter a situation of environmental chaos by creating internal chaos (Stacey, 1993). Weick (1987: 56) argued that:

> ...it may be necessary for the organizational process to be chaotic in order to match adequately the chaotic nature of the environment. We can understand what we have done only through meaningful experiments, ie acts.

Stacey (1990) stated that visions and plans are counter-productive in trying to manage open-ended change; they merely lead to unintended and counter-productive consequences. For companies to succeed in a chaotic environment, according to Stacey (1990: 15), they must:

> ...focus on single strategic issues and challenges, usually one by one, they develop explicit dynamic strategic agendas, they focus organizational attention on issues and

challenges at many levels, they make experimental energy and resources. In this way, they develop their business organically and dynamically.

Though Chaos Theory has become fashionable in the social sciences, a number of serious criticisms have been raised about whether or not, and how, theories developed in one research domain can be transferred to another (Gersick, 1991). Though some proponents of Chaos Theory, such as Wheatley (1992a), clearly do believe that it can cross the disciplinary boundary, others are much more cautious about its literal adoption by management theorists, believing its value lies as a metaphor which allows us to see organisations and the challenges they face in a different light (Zimmerman, 1992). Stickland (1998) put this point to the speakers at a seminar on the use of Chaos Theory in the social sciences. The speakers were split between those who treated it as transferable in its entirety and those who saw it as a useful metaphor. Apart, that is, from 'One individual [who] declared after some thought, that he honestly did not know and had never considered the point' (Stickland, 1998: 162).

Another point against Chaos Theory, and indeed most approaches to strategy, arises from the work of population ecologists such as Hannan and Freeman (1988). They take issue with the notion that success can be assured by consciously matching strategies to circumstances. Their argument is that the modern business environment is so unpredictable, unstable and hostile that survival cannot be planned; luck may be more important than good judgement.

As with Chaos Theory, population ecology is borrowed from the physical sciences. It is a Darwinist-type approach that focuses on how organisations adapt and evolve in order to survive within the general population of organisations to which they belong (Carroll, 1988; Morgan, 1990). Watson (1997: 273) comments that:

> One way of considering the relationship of organisations to other organisations in the environment is to regard them as involved in a process of natural selection: a fight for survival within the ecological system of which they are part. ... They go through both planned and unplanned 'variations' in their form, and, largely through processes of competition, the environment 'selects' the form which best suits the organisation. Organisations then 'retain' the form which best suits their particular 'niche' or 'domain' ...

Population ecologists do not, therefore, challenge the importance of the fit or correspondence between an organisation and its environment. They do, though, question the extent to which achieving this is a conscious and planned process. In particular, as Pettigrew *et al* (1992: 25) maintain: 'Ecologists are unimpressed by the possibility that managers can turn their organizations round, and instead stress organizational inertia.' This argument echoes Hannan and Freeman's (1977: 957) assertion that:

> ... for wide classes of organizations there are very strong inertial pressures on structure arising from both internal arrangements (for example, internal politics) and from the environment (for example, public legitimation of organizational activity). To claim otherwise is to ignore the most obvious feature of organizational life.

Population ecologists argue that an organisation's survival, the extent to which it achieves a fit with its environment, depends on a combination of the organisation's own (planned and unplanned) actions, the activities of other organisations in its field and a strong element of luck (i.e. being in the right place, with the right combination of characteristics and at the right time).

The stress on luck or serendipity is also present in the work of writers such as Williamson (1991) and Weick (1979). Weick, in particular, views the world as an essentially ambiguous place in which it is unrealistic, and indeed impossible, to make detailed plans. This is clearly a strong challenge to those who emphasise the need for, and ability of, organisations to pursue environmental match or correspondence. However, Child's (1972) concept of equifinality takes this challenge even further. Equifinality, as (Sorge, 1997: 13) notes:

> ... quite simply means that different sorts of internal arrangements are perfectly compatible with identical contextual or environmental states. The principle goes against the idea of a quasi-ideal 'match' which is inherent in the principle of correspondence. Whereas correspondence [i.e. Contingency] theory suggests that rigid and bureaucratic structures are not a good match for volatile and shifting product markets, equifinality theorists claim that it may very well turn out to be a good match but only if the level and diversity of the workforce is large and organization culture produces motivated and flexible actors.

As Mintzberg *et al* (1998) note in relation to equifinality, managers need to recognise that achieving a successful outcome is more important than imposing the method of achieving it.

Pettigrew (1985, 1987) and Child and Smith (1987), through their respective studies of ICI and Cadbury, also offered important insights and perspectives on approaches to strategic management and environmental fit. Pettigrew argues that there is a need for a change theory which sees organisations and how they operate in their entirety, one that recognises the importance and influence of the wider environment and appreciates the dynamic and political nature of strategy development and change. He is critical of theories which assume that organisations are rational entities pursuing agreed goals that reflect their best interests. Instead, he argues that organisations have to be understood in the context of the constraints and possibilities offered by the environment in which they operate and in relation to the self-interests of the individuals and groups which comprise them.

Pettigrew, therefore, sees organisations primarily as political systems in which groups and individuals, under the guise of rationality, seek to mobilise support for, and legitimate the pursuit of, strategies and actions that promote or sustain their personal or sectional interests. Particular groups or individuals may achieve a position of dominance, but that dominance is always subject to prevailing intra-organisational and environmental conditions. Therefore, Pettigrew rejects the view that strategy is a rational process of deliberate calculation and analysis. Instead he believes that organisational strategy – though often cloaked in rational and analytical terms – is in reality the outcome of a combination of internal political struggles, between groups and individuals seeking to influence policy in their favour, and external environmental pressures and constraints (this argument was examined in more detail in Chapter 4).

Child and Smith's (1987) firm-in-sector perspective had some similarities with Pettigrew's work; however, they argue for a stronger determining link between the individual firm and the sector in which it operates, and a lesser role for organisational politics. They suggest three areas of firm–sector linkage which shape and constrain the strategies organisations pursue:

1 *The 'objective conditions' for success.* Though each firm within the sector may pursue a different strategy, these will all tend to focus on or be determined by similar success factors such as customer satisfaction, quality, profitability, etc.

2 *The prevailing managerial consensus.* Within and across a sector, regardless of the organisation in which they work, managers are likely to develop a common and (implicitly at least) agreed view of how firms should operate, the key factors in their industry and the basis on which they compete with one another.

3 *The collaborative networks operating in the sector.* These may be with customers, suppliers, outside experts or even competitors.

Child and Smith's (1987) view draws on economic theories of the firm and suggests that the sector, particularly when strongly competitive, determines the path a firm must take for its future success. Though not denying a role for organisational politics, they claim that, unless the strategic decisions a firm takes are consistent with the conditions prevailing in its sector, success may be jeopardised. Therefore, though falling in the analytical stream, Child and Smith appear to exhibit a greater faith in a rational and linear progression from market sector analysis to strategy formulation and implementation than Pettigrew and many other writers.

The Analytical stream also has a number of other variants, most notably those who see the role and personality of leaders as being the key determinants of successful strategy (Bennis and Namus, 1985). Leadership will be touched on later in this chapter, and covered more extensively in Chapter 14; nevertheless, merely mentioning here it serves to emphasise the somewhat disparate nature of the Analytical stream of strategy. Proponents of this stream are united by a number of factors such as their attempt to understand rather than prescribe strategy, their orientation, mainly, to an academic rather than a business audience, and their view of organisations as complex social entities operating within dangerous, dynamic and unpredictable environments. On the other hand, the proponents of the elements which make up the Analytical stream are divided by their emphasis on different aspects of strategy, such as politics, the industry sector, the general environment, organisational and national cultures, leadership, etc. So, although it is true to say that proponents of the strategic intent/competence argument came to the fore in the 1990s, it is also true to say that they are challenged by the proponents of the other elements in this stream who still exert a powerful influence on the debate over strategy. It follows that their differences with each other are as important as their differences with proponents of the Prescriptive stream of strategy.

## UNDERSTANDING STRATEGY: CHOICES AND CONSTRAINTS

Whilst the above identifies key themes in the debate over organisational strategy, it still presents a somewhat confusing picture. Clearly there is a distinction between those who adhere to the Prescriptive stream of strategy, which arose from the long-range planning approach of the 1940s and 1950s, and the Analytical stream as represented by, amongst others, the strategic intent/competences approach of the 1980s and 1990s. However, what is not clear is the degree to which a common understanding and perspective exists amongst those collected under the Analytical umbrella. Certainly, a number of writers have tried to argue that a common perspective does exist. Brown and Jopling (1994) believed that the main distinction lies between the writers of the 1950s and 1960s who, they argue, saw strategy as basically concerned with fitting the organisation to its environment, and the writers of the 1980s and 1990s who, they argue, see strategy as focusing on internal issues, mainly to do with the development of core competences. They base their case on a contingency perspective. The earlier approach, they argue, was suitable to organisations operating in relatively stable and predictable environments, who had a limited product range, and where competition was restricted. With the advent of greater competition and more unstable environments, this approach was no longer viable, and firms had to look internally at how they could organise themselves to cope with the new situation. To an extent, this is an attractive analysis. However, though it is true that the earlier writers on strategy – such as Ansoff and company – did concentrate on product–market mix issues, it is also true that later they came to appreciate the link between the outside and the inside (Moore, 1992). Also, whilst Mintzberg and others have concentrated on internal capabilities, the Japanese approach has been to see the internal and external as two sides of the same coin, which is why they emphasise the importance of the strategic outward-looking vision driving the development of internal capabilities.

Nevertheless, such a simple distinction, based on one dimension of organisational life, cannot resolve the complex differences between and within these Prescriptive and Analytical streams. As Mintzberg *et al* (1998) noted, the strategy field is more eclectic and more populous, in terms of different approaches, than ever before. In such a situation, attempts to fit writers into two camps, whether they be early and late, external and internal, are bound to fail. The multiple-definition view of strategy argued by Mintzberg *et al* (1988), and particularly their proposition that the various definitions of strategy are both competing and complementary, offers another perspective. Strategy can be considered as either a process or an outcome. It can also be considered as either a rational approach or a political/social phenomenon. The various approaches to strategy do not reflect some underlying truth; rather they are different approaches which organisations can choose (consciously or not) to adopt, depending on their circumstances, objectives and management.

If this is the case, it may be that instead of looking for a theory of or approach to strategy that unifies and encompasses all the others, we should turn the argument on its head and ask, as we did with organisational theory, whether there is a 'one best way' for strategy?

In approaching this question, it is valuable to return to Child's (1972) concept of equifinality. As stated earlier, by Sorge (1997: 13), equifinality 'quite simply means that different sorts of internal arrangements are perfectly compatible with identical contextual or environmental states'. To paraphrase this definition, and to stretch the concept a little further than Child might have intended, it could be argued that different approaches to strategy formulation may be perfectly compatible with positive outcomes. This may especially be the case if one takes account of the growing opinion, as expressed in this and the previous chapter, that organisations can manipulate and even create their own environment or reality. If this is the case, then, as Mintzberg *et al* (1998: 365) maintain, 'the question is not whether there exists strategic choice, but how much'. In order to approach this question, we need to attempt to classify the various approaches to strategy in order to establish the degree to which they incorporate or exclude choice.

Though the above review of approaches to strategy cannot claim to be all-embracing, it does cover the key protagonists in the area. However, whilst it separates the main approaches into two streams, it does not provide a classification or taxonomy of the various approaches. Whittington (1993) attempted to make sense of the many definitions and categories of strategy by identifying four generic approaches to strategy: the Classical, Evolutionary, Processual and Systemic.

- **The Classical approach**. This is the oldest and most influential approach to strategy. It portrays strategy as a rational process, based on analysis and quantification, and aimed at achieving the maximum level of profit for an organisation. It argues that, through rigorous analysis and planning, senior managers can predict future market trends and shape the organisation to take advantage of these.

- **The Evolutionary approach**. As the name implies, this uses the analogy of biological evolution to describe strategy development. It believes that organisations are at the mercy of the unpredictable and hostile vagaries of the market. Those organisations which survive and prosper do so not because of their ability to plan and predict, which is impossible, but because they have been lucky enough to hit on a winning formula. From this perspective, successful strategies cannot be planned, but emerge from the decisions managers take to align and realign their organisations to the changing environmental conditions.

- **The Processual approach**. This perspective concentrates on the nature of organisational and market processes. It views organisations and their members as shifting coalitions of individuals and groups with different interests, imperfect knowledge and short attention spans. Markets are similarly capricious and imperfect but, because of this, do not require organisations to achieve a perfect fit with their environment in order to prosper and survive. Strategy under these conditions is portrayed as a pragmatic process of trial and error, aimed at achieving a compromise between the needs of the market and the objectives of the warring factions within the organisation.

- **The Systemic approach**. This approach sees strategy as linked to dominant features of the local social system within which it takes place. The core argument of this perspective is that strategy can be a deliberate process, and planning and predictability are possible, but only if the conditions within the host society are favourable. Therefore, to an extent, this is a contingency approach to strategy which can accommodate situations where firms do not seek to maximise profit or bow to market pressures. If the conditions within the host society are supportive, markets can be manipulated, financial considerations can become a secondary issue and stability and predictability can be achieved. Also, under such conditions, the objectives managers seek to pursue may be related more to their social background, degree of patriotism or even professional pride, than to profit maximisation. Therefore, from the Systemic perspective, the strategy an organisation adopts and the interests managers pursue reflect the nature of the particular social system within which it operates.

Whittington's categorisation of generic approaches to strategy is extremely useful in making sense of the plethora of approaches on offer. As one would expect, it is not perfect; some writers, such as Mintzberg, could fall under more than one heading, whilst others, like Child and Smith, are difficult to locate. Nevertheless, the Classical approach would clearly incorporate the work of the Planning, Design and Positioning school and the early Western writers on strategy. The Evolutionary approach is akin to the work of population ecologists such as Hannan and Freeman (1988); Mintzberg's (1994) work on emergent strategy might also fall under this heading. The Processual approach could also cover Mintzberg's work and certainly includes Pettigrew's (1985, 1987) work on organisational politics. The Systemic perspective clearly owes much to the Japanese approach to strategy as described by Hamel and Prahalad (1989).

Whittington (1993) also categorises these four approaches to strategy in terms of how they view outcomes and processes. He argues that the Classical and Evolutionary approaches see profit maximisation as the natural outcome of strategy. The Systemic and Processual approaches, on the other hand, believe other outcomes are both possible and acceptable. With regard to processes, the groupings change. Here the Classical and Systemic both agree that strategy can be a deliberate process. The Evolutionists and Processualists, though, see strategy as emerging from processes governed by chance and confusion.

Whittington's four categories of strategy can be summarised as follows:

- Classicists see strategy as a rational process of long-term planning aimed at maximising profit.
- Evolutionists also believe that the purpose of strategy is profit maximisation, but regard the future as too volatile and unpredictable to allow effective planning. Instead, they advise organisations to focus on maximising chances of survival today.
- The Processualists are equally sceptical of long-range planning, and see strategy as an emergent process of learning and adaptation.
- The Systemic perspective argues that the nature and aims of strategy are dependent upon the particular social context in which the organisation operates.

To an extent, the four approaches to strategy have some symmetry to the Western approaches to organisation theory discussed in Part 1. The Classical, Evolutionary and Processual approaches are clearly 'one best way' or 'only possible way' approaches, whereas the Systemic approach offers a Contingency perspective on strategy. They also share some common ground with organisation theory on the issue of rationality. The Classical and Systemic approaches argue that strategy is or can be rational and intentional in its development and objectives. The Processualists believe that it is rational in neither aspect; the Evolutionists take a similar view to them of process, but appear to adopt a rational perspective on outcomes, in that profit maximisation is seen as the only outcome that guarantees survival.

In their view of the scope for managerial choice and judgement, three of these four approaches to strategy do appear to be more permissive than organisation theory. Clearly, the Classical strategy theorists leave little scope for either: their instruction seems to be to follow the textbook in terms of outcomes and processes or else. However, both the Evolutionists and the Processualists emphasise the need for managers to be fleet of foot and percipient in making key decisions responding to opportunities or threats; although the Evolutionists (rather like Napoleon in his view of generals) appear to believe that, at the end of the day, a lucky manager may be more desirable than an able one. For advocates of the Systemic approach, choice and judgement are important, but tend to be constrained by the limits and objectives of the society in which they are located.

It would appear, therefore, that managerial choice, preference and judgement, for all but the Classicists, do have a role to play in determining not just the organisation's strategy, but also the particular approach to strategy it adopts. However, in our examination of the strategy literature, it is clear that choice is constrained and can only be exercised within limits (from some perspectives, very narrow limits indeed). As Figure 5.1 shows, these limits or constraints, which are suggested by or inferred from the literature, can be classified under four headings.

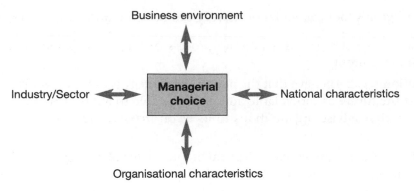

Figure 5.1 Constraints on managerial choice

### National objectives, practices and cultures

The case for country-specific constraints very much follows the argument of the Systemic perspective on strategy. This view sees the operation of organisations as strongly influenced by the social system in which they operate. In some cases, such as in Japan and Germany, patriotism, national pride and a collectivist ethos have created a business environment that supports the pursuit of long-term national objectives. This is reflected in the behaviour of individual firms and financial institutions that favour stable growth over the medium to long term, rather than short-term profit maximisation. In Britain and the USA, on the other hand, the climate is far more supportive of individual endeavour and short-term profit maximisation rather than the national interest *per se*.

The difference between these two approaches is neatly summed up in the old saying that 'What's good for General Motors is good for America'. The Japanese would, of course, transpose this to read 'What is good for Japan is good for Toyota'. This view also draws support from Hofstede's (1980, 1990) work on national cultures discussed in Chapter 4. The implication, therefore, is that organisations ignore national norms at their peril: the pursuit of short-term profit maximisation in Japan and Germany is likely to be as difficult, and perhaps counter-productive, as the pursuit of a long-term strategy of growing market share, which ignores short-term profitability, would be in the UK or the USA. Nevertheless, these constraints are open to manipulation and avoidance. The move by many British companies – GEC, GKN, Lucas Verity – to manufacture outside the UK and/or to form international alliances is an example of this, as is the Japanese trend to establish manufacturing plants in the USA and Europe in order to avoid high production costs on the one hand and import quotas on the other. Another example is the lobbying of governments and national and international bodies for changes in laws and regulations that particular organisations or industries see as operating against their interests.

### Industry and sector practices and norms

This follows from Child and Smith's (1987) firm-in-sector perspective. As discussed earlier, they believe that the objective conditions operating in a sector, managers' understanding of the dynamics of the sector, and the nature and degree of inter-firm collaboration all combine to determine the path a firm must take for its future success. This is especially the case where the sector is highly competitive. In effect, Child and Smith's argument is that firms must stick to the rules of engagement in their sector or perish. However, they do concede that, where competition is less intense, then managers have a greater degree of freedom with regard to the selection of strategy. Indeed, the low level of competition may explain how Japanese companies were able to change the rules of engagement to their advantage in many industries in the 1960s and 1970s (Hamel and Prahalad, 1989); although it is also the case that Japanese companies pay less attention to today's sectoral constraints than to re-shaping the rules of the game to create competitive conditions more favourable to themselves (Turner, 1990). Another method of overcoming sectoral constraints and conditions is, as illustrated by Allaire and Firsirotu (1989), by diversifying into new products and different sectors.

### Business environment

For nearly all the approaches to strategy that we have discussed, their proponents assume, explicitly or implicitly, that they are operating in a particular type of environment. The Classical approach to strategy is clearly predicated on the existence of a relatively stable and predictable environment. If this exists, then predicting the future and planning accordingly is a much less hazardous exercise than would otherwise be the case. The Systemic view also seems to assume a degree of environmental stability. However, as Japan and Germany show, stability needs to be actively promoted by government–industry co-operation rather than relying on the invisible, and often volatile, hand of the market. For Processualists and even more so for Evolutionists, the environment is a hostile, unpredictable and uncertain place. Planning is almost impossible, and success comes either from continuously adapting to changes in the environment, or from being in the right place at the right time.

For three of these perspectives, the environment is a given, even if they disagree about exactly what is given. However, for those advocating a Systemic approach, the environment is not a given: it can be changed. As this chapter and Part 1 have argued, there is now a considerable body of evidence from a number of different perspectives to this effect (Hatch, 1997; Morgan, 1986). Shapiro (1989) utilises the tools of game theory to show how firms influence the behaviour and actions of their competitors, and in so doing change the environment in which they operate. In a similar way, Teece *et al* (1997) argue that investments in production capacity, R&D and advertising can all be used to alter an organisation's environment favourably. Weick (1979) takes a different perspective. He argues that the world is so complex and ambiguous that an organisation cannot possibly 'know' its environment. Instead, organisations have to 'enact' their environment; that is to say, they have to develop and act upon their own interpretation of their environment. This is very similar to the learning organisation and postmodernist perspectives, as discussed in Chapters 3 and 4, that organisations have the ability to 'invent' their own reality. The implication from these different perspectives is that though many companies may have to adjust their strategic approach to environmental conditions, some companies may be able to do the reverse. The UK National Health Service is a good example of this. As Burnes and Salauroo (1995) noted, the NHS operated prior to 1990 as a typical government bureaucracy. The government allocated resources and gave policy direction, whilst the NHS centrally planned how resources would be allocated and policies operationalised (i.e. the Classical approach to strategy). This meant that there was considerable stability and predictability in its environment. However, the government of the day wanted the NHS to operate in a more cost-conscious and entrepreneurial mode. To facilitate and encourage this, it changed the way funds were provided and distributed. Rather than funds being given as of right to service providers (e.g. hospitals), they were reallocated to service purchasers (e.g. local doctors) who could decide what to buy and from whom. This creation of a market for the provision of medical services destabilised the environment and made planning and prediction very hazardous exercises (thus making an Evolutionary or Processual approach to strategy more relevant). However, with a change of government in 1997, the pendulum began to swing back. Whilst wishing to retain some of the perceived benefits of a market system, the new government announced that it would modify the purchaser–provider system to create greater stability (Salauroo and Burnes, 1998).

Normally, attempts at manipulating the environment aim to reduce, or at least cope with rather than increase, uncertainty. Allaire and Firsirotu (1989) identified three ways of coping with uncertainty. The first of these is through predicting and planning (the Classical approach). The second is to restructure for flexibility (the Contingency approach). The third, however, is to manipulate or control the environment. Allaire and Firsirotu cite the examples of Boeing and IBM, who created and subsequently dominated their environments. Another major approach they identify is the use of co-operative strategies – collusion, market-sharing and other methods of reducing competition. An example of this in the UK was the agreement by the main companies in the milk industry to 'carve up the country so they stop competing with each other' for doorstep sales (Cowe, 1995: 40). Perhaps the most famous recent example is Microsoft's attempt to dominate the market for internet products by providing its web browser 'free' to everyone who bought its Windows operating system. Therefore, as can be seen, there is certainly sufficient evidence to show that it is possible to change or control or manipulate the environment in which an organisation operates, and thus either necessitate or make possible a particular approach to strategy.

### Organisation characteristics

Obviously, there are many organisation characteristics that act to constrain or facilitate managerial choice. However, there do appear to be four that have particular importance: structure, culture, politics and managerial style. Apart from the latter, these have been reviewed extensively in Chapters 3 and 4 and can be discussed relatively briefly. An organisation's structure and culture have clear implications for managerial choice in the area of strategy. Organisations with organic structures and task cultures are likely to be resistant to or incapable of operating a Classical form of strategy. Similarly, organisations with mechanistic structures and role cultures are likely to have a somewhat hostile attitude towards Processual or Evolutionary approaches to strategy. Moving on to the issue of organisational politics: where decisions are heavily influenced by individual and/ or group self-interest, as averse to organisational objectives, it is unlikely that a Classical or Systemic approach to strategy would be successful. A Processual or Evolutionary approach, though, would have clear applicability.

There remains the subject of managerial or leadership style. There has been considerable interest in recent years in applying Burns' (1978) pioneering work on political leadership to leadership in organisations (Burnes and James, 1995; Beatty and Lee, 1992; and Gibbons, 1992). Burns identified two basic organisational states: *convergent* – a stable state; and *divergent* – where predictability and stability are absent. For each of these states, he argued, there is an appropriate managerial style. Convergent states require managers with a *transactional style* – ones who are good at optimising the performance of the organisation within the confines of existing policy. Divergent states, however, require managers with a *transformational style* – ones who challenge the status quo and create new visions. It follows from this that transactional managers will prefer approaches to strategy that stress continuity and predictability (i.e. the Classical or, in some circumstances, Systemic approach), whilst transformational managers will be more comfortable with a Processual or Evolutionary type of approach. Managerial style will be further discussed in Chapter 14.

As was the case with the other three forms of constraint, organisational characteristics can be amended. The debate on structure and culture has been well covered already, but the level of political behaviour is also open to change. As Pfeffer (1981, 1992) showed, though political behaviour is never absent from organisations, there are situations where it is likely to be more prevalent. In particular, political behaviour is likely to be most evident where major structural changes are taking place that affect the power distribution in organisations. By recognising that this is the case, by taking steps to reduce ambiguity and by trying to increase the transparency and openness of the decision-making process, the ability of individuals to pursue their own interests can be reduced. This is demonstrated by the Japanese *ringi* system, which promotes extensive and open debate over decisions in order to ensure that they fit in with the company's objectives rather than those of sectional interests. As far as changing managerial styles is concerned, although there is evidence that these are shaped and changed by the organisations in which managers work, there is also considerable evidence that senior managers tend to change organisations to fit their style (Morgan, 1986).

It should be borne in mind that the particular mix of these four forms of constraint will vary from organisation to organisation, even where these operate in the same country and industry. Also, it needs to be recognised that these constraints are as likely to conflict with each other as they are to complement each other: for example, car companies operating in the UK may find that the culture of the UK's financial institutions favours short-term profit maximisation, whilst the car industry appears to require long-term investment in building market share. This may be one reason why the UK motor industry is now foreign-owned. In addition, it should be noted that whilst managers are not obliged to take account of the constraints they face, they may well pay a price for this in terms of the performance of their organisation. Successful firms are likely to be ones which have managers who are aware of, and can balance, the various constraints they face. This obviously raises the issue of managerial ability and competence, an issue we shall explore in some depth in Chapter 14.

Therefore, the key point to recognise from the above review is that the type of strategic approach adopted is a matter of managerial choice, but that choice is constrained by a variety of organisational, environmental, sectoral and national factors. As was argued in Part 1, organisations and managers may be able to influence or change the constraints they face.

However, both the case for managerial choice and the argument for manipulating constraints need to be taken with a pinch of salt. The fact of the matter is that in the West, as Teece *et al* (1997) and Whittington (1993) noted, the Classical approach to strategy, latterly through the work of the Positioning school, is still dominant. Also, as noted in Chapter 4, there is a tendency for decision-makers to 'satisfice'. That is to say, rather than undertaking an extensive examination of the issues involved and searching for all the possible solutions, decision-makers tend to accept the first satisfactory solution to a problem (Butler, 1997). This equates to Argyris and Schon's (1978) concept of single-loop learning (*see* Chapter 3). It is also similar to Cohen *et al*'s (1972) comment that decisions are often not taken but happen. They suggest that decisions occur when four independent streams meet: problems, solutions, participants and choice opportunities; the so-called Garbage Can model of decision-making. They argue that when a problem becomes severe it demands attention. Solutions, on the other hand, are answers looking for a problem. Participants are the people in the organisation possessing problems and/or solutions, while choice opportunities are occasions when organisations are required to make a decision. When these four elements come together, decisions occur. Seen in this way, decision-making is not conscious, rational or systematic; on the contrary, decisions are haphazard, accidental and unplanned. From a slightly different perspective, Nelson and Winter (1982) argue that in many cases decision-making is an unconscious and automatic process, based on a repertoire that individuals develop over time of responses to particular situations. This is similar to Ashforth and Fried's (1988) observation that there is a tendency in some organisations for behaviour to become almost mindless – employees and managers, as a result of organisational socialisation and experience, respond automatically to events in a programmed way. Consequently, though the potential for choice exists, the reality is that many managers appear not to exercise it, preferring instead to stick to tried-and-tested, routine, orthodox, textbook approaches – regardless of their suitability.

Nevertheless, it is important to note that, in the academic world, the weight of the argument appears to be shifting from seeing strategy as a rational, mathematical process, to seeing it as the outcome of the ability of an organisation's management to utilise its strengths and competencies in the competitive pursuit of success. However, there are some writers who believe the reverse is true of the business world, and that more and more firms are opting for rational decision-making approaches to strategy based on value-maximising financial techniques and quantitative analysis of market positions (Grant, 1991b; Teece *et al*, 1997). Whatever the truth or otherwise of this view, as the following chapter will show, the main strategies favoured by organisations are still, though no longer exclusively, market- and quantitatively-orientated, and certainly give greater credence to rational decision-making than to more qualitative approaches.

## CONCLUSIONS

As can be seen from this chapter, the concept of strategy has developed considerably since it began to be widely used in America in the 1950s and 1960s. No longer is strategy purely about the external world, no longer is it solely seen as a rational, quantitative process. Indeed, writers and practitioners from different backgrounds and countries, such as Hamel and Prahalad (1989), Mintzberg and Quinn (1991), Ohmae (1986) and Stacey (1993), have argued that it is not a process at all, but the outcome of a process: an outcome that is shaped not by mathematical models but by human creativity.

The move towards this new, more emergent, perspective on strategy has been brought about by the mounting criticisms against the Classical or prescriptive approach to strategy. The main criticisms are that it is mechanistic, prescriptive, inflexible, and reliant on quantitative tools and techniques of dubious validity. The result is that organisations who attempt to construct strategies using the Classical approach fall foul of what Peters and Waterman (1982) described as 'Paralysis Through Analysis' and 'Irrational Rationality'. In effect, organisations contort themselves in a vain attempt to make the real world fit the constraints and limitations of their mathematical models, rather than vice versa.

The alternative view, and one that is gaining adherents, is that organisations should move away from exclusive reliance on mathematical models. Instead, human creativity should be brought into play. Senior managers should create a vision of the organisation's future – establish its strategic intent. This should then be pursued relentlessly by the organisation. In the process of doing so, the strategy emerges from the decisions that are taken with regard to resource allocation, organisation structure and the other key areas of operation. From different perspectives, a number of writers have come to the same conclusion. For successful companies, strategy does not appear to be a preconceived and detailed set of steps for achieving a coherent package of concrete goals within a given timescale. Neither does it seem to be a rational process which is amenable to mathematical modelling. Rather, it is the outcome of a process of decision-making and resource allocation that is embarked upon in pursuit of a vision (though even here there is disagreement about how conscious this process is). Such an approach is inherently irrational, inherently unplannable – it cannot be modelled or quantified, though it can and must be pursued with rigour and determination.

In this chapter, we have suggested a third approach, one which sides with neither the quantitative nor qualitative schools of thought. Instead, it has been argued that the approach to strategy that organisations adopt is or can be the outcome of managerial choice and preference. However, choice in this respect, as in most others, is constrained. The key constraints identified were societal, sectoral, environmental and organisational. Whilst on the face of it this appears to impose severe limitations on the degree of freedom managers have with regard to the choice of strategy, it was also argued that managers can influence or manipulate the constraints they face in order to create their own preferred organisational reality.

This follows on from Part 1, where it was claimed that managers are not the passive creatures portrayed by much of organisation theory. Instead of having to adapt their organisations to the circumstances in which they find themselves, they can attempt to amend or even reinvent the circumstances. So, managers in organisations faced by a dynamic and unpredictable environment could seek to change markets and/or products, influence the behaviour of competitors, or change customers' perceptions, in order to reduce uncertainty and increase predictability. By so doing, an organisation could still function efficiently at the more mechanistic end of the mechanistic–organic spectrum, if that was the type of structure preferred by its managers.

This argument would seem equally applicable to the constraints managers face when choosing an approach to strategy. Some managers might prefer an Evolutionary or Processual approach to strategy, either because it suits their own temperament or because they believe that a hostile and turbulent environment suits them better than their competitors (the move by Rupert Murdoch's newspapers in the UK in the 1990s to start a price-cutting war was an example of this). On the other hand, constraints might be manipulated or changed for ideological reasons, such as the attempt by most Western governments to privatise or introduce market forces into the public sector. The point is that the possibility does exist for managers to choose not only the approach to strategy but also, to an extent at least, the constraints they face.

To choose an approach to strategy is one thing; to apply it is an entirely different matter. Therefore, just as this chapter has reviewed the main arguments with regard to strategy, so the remaining chapters in Part 2 will review the strengths and weaknesses of the main approaches to applying strategy and implementing change.

## TEST YOUR LEARNING

### Short answer questions

1 What does Hoskin (1990) see as being the origins of modern business strategy?

2 Define long-range planning.

3 What technique did the Design school develop for assessing an organisation's potential?

4 How do Johnson and Scholes (1993) define strategy?

5 What is the Prescriptive school of strategy?

6 What is the Analytical school of strategy?

7 What is emergent strategy?

8 What is umbrella strategy?

9 What are the main constraints on organisational choice?

10 Describe the relationship between organisational strategy and organisational change.

### Essay questions

1 How do Whittington's four generic approaches to strategy relate to the Prescriptive and Analytical schools of strategy?

2 Discuss the following statement: strategy development and implementation can never be a rational process.

## SUGGESTED FURTHER READING

1 Mintzberg, H, Ahlstrand, B and Lampel, J (1998). *Strategy Safari*. Prentice Hall: Hemel Hempstead.
Almost anything with Henry Mintzberg's name on it is worth reading and this book is no exception. It provides a succinct and pertinent review of the main perspectives on strategy.

2 Whittington, R (1993). *What is Strategy and Does it Matter?* Routledge: London.
In this short and eminently readable book, Richard Whittington challenges much of the orthodox thinking on strategy.

# Chapter 6

# APPLYING STRATEGY

## Models, levels and tools

**Learning objectives**

After studying this chapter, you should be able to:

1 describe the three basic approaches to strategy that organisations can adopt;

2 discuss the three levels of strategic decision-making in organisations;

3 list the main strategic planning tools;

4 state the strengths and weaknesses of quantitative tools;

5 list the advantages and disadvantages of qualitative tools;

6 understand why quantitative tools have tended to be preferred to more qualitative ones;

7 appreciate the growing interest in vision-building techniques;

8 identify the implications for organisational change of both quantitative and qualitative tools and techniques.

## INTRODUCTION

This chapter begins where the previous one ended. Chapter 5 reviewed the main perspectives on strategy. In seeking to understand and define strategy formulation, it identified two streams of thought, the Prescriptive and the Analytical. As the name implies, the Prescriptive stream comprises approaches which seek to 'prescribe' how organisations should undertake strategy but, in so doing, tends to ignore or downplay the irrational and highly convoluted nature of organisational life. The Analytical stream, on the other hand, rather than telling organisations how they should build strategy, seeks to analyse – to understand and describe – the complexity and range of forces that affect how organisations do build strategy. This divergence is reflected in their respective views of strategy. The Prescriptive stream, which was the first on the scene and is very much practitioner-orientated, sees strategy formulation as an economic-rational process based on mathematical models. The Analytical stream, which began to appear in the 1970s, represents the more reflexive and more academically orientated face of strategy. It views strategy not as a process, but as an outcome of a process. Its proponents' emphasis is not on the construction of detailed plans, which in any case they believe to be an unworkable approach, but on the organisational, social and political aspects of strategy formulation.

The two streams represent markedly different perspectives on strategy formulation and whilst the Analytical stream has tended to win the academic arguments over the last 20 years, the Prescriptive one has had considerably more impact and influence on the practice of strategy.

It is on this latter aspect, the application of strategy in practice, that this chapter will concentrate. The chapter begins by examining the three basic types or models of strategy that organisations can adopt: the Competitive Forces model; the Strategic Conflict model; and the Resource-Based model. The chapter then moves on to look at the three levels of strategic decision-making in organisations: corporate, business and functional. This is followed by a review of the main strategic planning tools.

The chapter ends by arguing that one of the principal reasons for the dominance of prescriptive approaches to strategy has been the alliance between leading consultancies and business schools in America to develop, market and update these. In so doing, the Prescriptive school has established itself as the orthodox, safe and practical approach to strategy formulation. Nevertheless, with the take-up of more analytically based types of strategy, this is beginning to change. As Chapter 5 maintained, the model or type of strategy an organisation should adopt, and the associated planning tools that accompany it, are dependent upon the constraints the organisation faces. However, organisations do not have to fit themselves and their strategies to these constraints. Rather, they have a choice; they can seek to influence or mould the constraints they face in order to make them more amenable to the type or model of strategy they wish to pursue. Therefore, the approach to strategy an organisation adopts may have less to do with the merits of the different models on offer and more to do with the type of organisation it is and the orientation of its managers.

## TYPES OF STRATEGIES

As the previous chapter demonstrated, there is a wide, and often confusing, variety of approaches to strategy development which organisations can adopt. It follows that the same comment can be made with regard to the types of strategy that organisations do actually adopt. However, Teece *et al* (1997) argue that, in the main, there are only three basic types or models that organisations do adopt in practice, which are as follows.

### The Competitive Forces model

This stems from the Positioning school and, in the 1980s and 1990s at least, this was the dominant approach to strategy. The central tenet of this approach is the need to align the organisation with its environment, the key aspect of which is the industry or industries in which it competes. Proponents of this view believe that industry structure strongly influences the competitive rules of the game as well as the range of strategies open to the organisation. This model is most closely associated with the work of Michael Porter (1980, 1985) and his 'five forces' framework. Porter argues that there are five industry-level forces which determine the inherent profit potential of an industry: entry barriers; threat of substitution; the bargaining power of buyers; the bargaining power of suppliers; and rivalry amongst the firms in the industry. Based on this, Porter (1980) argues that there are only three basic generic strategies a firm can adopt: *cost leadership*, *product differentiation*, and *specialisation by focus* (these are discussed in more detail below). Porter believes that a firm's ability to increase its profits is dependent on its ability to influence the competitive forces in the industry or to change its market position in relation to competitors and suppliers. This approach obviously has links to Contingency Theory (*see* Chapter 2), given that it is based on a systematic empirical search for relationships between external conditions and internal strategies. In addition, because of its focus on the importance of sector and industry factors, it has an affinity with Child and Smith's (1987) firm-in-sector perspective discussed in Chapter 5.

There is little doubt that the Positioning school in general, and Porter's work in particular, has had a huge influence on the practice of strategy within organisations. However, as one would expect, it has also attracted considerable criticism. Miller (1992) criticised it as too narrow and inflexible, and thus likely to leave organisations vulnerable if social, technological or economic developments lead, as can happen, to rapid changes in the market place. Mintzberg *et al* (1998) noted that the Positioning school's assumption of rationality ignores the political nature of organisations; that it is biased towards big business, where market power is greatest, and therefore has little to say to small and medium-sized enterprises; and that its dependence on analysis and calculation impedes both learning and creativity. A further and telling criticism is that the big competitive battles of the last 30 years, especially between Japanese and American firms, tend not to have been won by those who have identified and defended their market position, but by those, such as Toyota and Cannon, who have changed the rules of the game itself (Hamel and Prahalad, 1989). This is perhaps why there has been growing interest in the Strategic Conflict model.

## The Strategic Conflict model

This model harks back to the military metaphor, and portrays competition as war between rival firms. This approach draws on game theory to understand the nature of competitive interaction between rival firms. It came to prominence with the publication of Carl Shapiro's (1989) article, *The Theory of Business Strategy*. Central to this approach is the view that a firm can achieve increased profits by influencing the actions and behaviour of its rivals and thus, in effect, manipulate the market environment. This can be done in a number of ways, such as by investment in capacity (Dixit, 1980), R&D (Gilbert and Newberry, 1982) and advertising (Schmalensee, 1983). However, such moves will have little impact if they can be easily undone; therefore, to be effective, they require irreversible commitment.

Also, it is argued, these various manoeuvres are crucially dependent on what one firm thinks another firm will do in a particular situation. Therefore, the model incorporates the role of strategic signalling as an important mechanism for influencing or intimidating rivals. This includes such practices as predatory pricing (Kreps and Wilson, 1982) and limit pricing (Milgrom and Roberts, 1982). In addition, more recently, the model has come to embrace issues relating to the role of commitment and reputation (Ghemawat, 1991) and the simultaneous use of competition and co-operation (Brandenburger and Nalebuff, 1996).

Therefore, from the strategic conflict perspective, an organisation's ability to increase its profits is dependent on its ability to outwit, out-bluff and out-manoeuvre its rivals. This argument has been underpinned by game theory, which has allowed established intuitive arguments concerning various types of business tactics and strategy (e.g. predatory pricing) to be explained and formalised. In terms of the Prescriptive and Analytical streams of strategy, although Porter (1980) acknowledges the benefits of strategic manoeuvring, it does not fit in with his or the rest of the Positioning school's work. Instead, its emphasis on quick-wittedness, gut instinct and the more emotional elements of decision-making means it sits better with the Analytical stream.

Given that conflict-based strategies do not take account of the wide range of external and internal factors which also contribute to an organisation's competitiveness, its usefulness may well be limited. As Teece *et al* (1997) noted, strategic conflict is likely to be more appropriate in situations where there is an even balance between rivals in an industry (e.g. Coca-Cola and Pepsi) rather than in situations where one organisation has a substantial competitive advantage over its rivals (e.g. Microsoft). In these latter situations, it is perhaps the Resource-Based model of strategy that is of most interest.

## The Resource-Based model

This perspective sees profitability as coming from superior systems and structures which allow firms to have lower costs or better quality, rather than from tactical manoeuvring or product market positioning. This approach focuses on the benefits of scarce firm-specific resources or capabilities. The resource-based perspective echoes observations made in the 1960s about the need for firms to have distinctive competences and strengths (Learned *et al*, 1965). However, it came to the fore in the 1980s and 1990s as an explanation for the rise of corporate Japan. It was out of the research into the competitiveness of Japanese firms that Prahalad and Hamel (1990) produced their article, *The Core Competence of the Corporation*. In it, they argue that real competitive advantage comes from the ability to build at lower cost and more speedily than competitors the core competences which spawn unanticipated products. They also argue that senior managers should spend a significant proportion of their time developing a corporation-wide architecture for establishing objectives for competence-building. The influential study of the car industry by Womack *et al* (1990), *The Machine That Changed The World*, came to a similar view of Japanese competitiveness. Support for this perspective has also come from a number of studies of Western firms. Cool and Schendel (1988) showed that there are systematic and significant performance differences among firms in the same industry sectors. Rumelt (1991) showed that intra-industry profit differentials are greater than inter-industry differentials. Kay's (1993) work on strategy also comes to the conclusion that an organisation's success comes from developing distinctive capabilities.

Hax and Majluf (1996: 10) state that:

> The essence of the resource-based model ... [is] that competitive advantage is created when resources and capabilities that are owned exclusively by the firm are applied to developing unique competencies. Moreover, the resulting advantage can be sustained due to the lack of substitution and imitation capabilities by the firm's competitors.

Proponents of the Resource-Based model view organisations as being hetero-geneous in respect of their resources, capabilities and endowments, i.e. no two firms possess exactly the same combination of these. In addition, because resources, capabilities and endowments cannot easily or quickly be acquired or developed, in the short run, firms are stuck with the ones they possess. Therefore, depending on the circumstances, and how they change, these firm-specific assets can be either a boon or a curse. Perhaps the main criticism of this approach comes from population ecologists who argue that, because these competences take so long to develop and environments change so quickly, any beneficial match between an organisation's competences and its environment is more likely to be accidental or fortuitous rather than the result of deliberate or foresightful actions by managers (Hannan and Freeman, 1988).

Nevertheless, the influence of the resource-based perspective can be seen in the fact that it is now the received wisdom that organisations should, in Peters and Waterman's (1982) phrase, 'stick to the knitting' and discard activities that are not part of their core business and which do not build on their core competences (Hax and Majluf, 1996).

These three types or models of strategy are all currently fashionable, though Porter and the Positioning school are by far the more dominant. They are, however, very different in their emphasis and timescales. The Strategic Conflict model is very much about out-manoeuvring the opposition, and tends to have a short-term focus, although a number of its tactics do have longer-term implica-tions. The Competitive Forces model is concerned with identifying and occupying a defensible market position, and thereby achieving higher profits than others in the industry. This tends to have a medium-term focus. The Resource-Based model has a much longer-term focus than either of the other two. Its proponents believe that organisations need to build strategic competences which, almost through a process of serendipity, will allow it to meet future and unanticipated market needs.

## LEVELS OF STRATEGY

It is easier to see how the three types of strategy above are applied in practice by examining the three levels of strategic decision-making in organisations:

- **The corporate level**. Strategy at this level concerns the direction, composition and co-ordination of the various businesses and activities that comprise a large and diversified organisation, such as GEC or Richard Branson's Virgin empire.
- **The business level**. Strategy at this level relates to the operation and direction of each of the individual businesses within a group of companies, such as Nissan's car assembly plant at Sunderland.
- **The functional level**. Strategy at this level concerns individual business functions and processes such as finance, marketing, manufacturing, technology and human resources.

Each of these levels has its own distinct strategic concerns and each can draw on a different battery of strategic tools, techniques and approaches to aid them. Nevertheless, it is important to remember that they are interrelated. Traditionally, it has been assumed that the corporate level sets the direction for each of its constituent businesses and, in turn, these set the direction for their various functions. Though this is true for some organisations, it is now recognised that these three levels interact in an iterative and dynamic fashion (Johnson and Scholes, 1993; Lynch, 1997). Therefore, as Mintzberg (1994) argues, just as business level and functional level strategy can be seen as being imposed or driven by corporate level decisions, so corporate level strategy can be seen as emerging from, or being shaped by, functional level and business level decisions and actions. Consequently, it follows that although there are strategies at the corporate level which have their counterparts at the business and the functional levels, it would be wrong to assume that this is always a product of a top-down rather than a bottom-up process.

Moving on to look at these three levels in more detail: at the corporate level, strategy is said to deal with the 'game plan' for managing diversified enterprises whose activities cut across a number of different areas of business. It concerns itself with the following questions:

- What is the mission of the organisation?
- What are its unique attributes?
- How should the business portfolio be managed?
- Which existing businesses should be disposed of and which new ones acquired?

- What priority and role should be given to each of the businesses in the current portfolio?

The central strategic concerns at the individual business level are as follows:

- How should the firm position itself to compete in distinct, identifiable and strategically relevant markets?
- Which types of products should it offer to which groups of customers?
- How should the firm structure and manage the internal aspects of the business in support of its chosen competitive approach?

Functional level strategy concerns itself with the following issues:

- How can the strategies formulated at the corporate and business levels be translated into concrete operational terms in such a way that the individual organisational functions and processes (marketing, R&D, manufacturing, personnel, finance, etc.) can pursue and achieve them?
- How should the individual functions and processes of the business organise themselves in order not only to achieve their own aims, but also to ensure that they integrate with the rest of the business to create synergy?

Given the different concerns of these three levels, it is easy to appreciate the need to integrate the strategies and structures at these three levels. Otherwise, for example, the corporate level may pursue a strategy of diversification whilst the individual businesses are busy concentrating their efforts on fewer products and markets. However, it is also easy to appreciate why in practice it is so difficult for large diversified organisations to identify and pursue a consistent strategy through all areas of their activities (Johnson and Scholes, 1993; Lynch, 1997). As argued in the last chapter, strategy formulation and implementation is not a mechanical process which begins at the corporate level and moves in a linear and logical fashion through to the functional level. Strategy formulation is inherently iterative, and aims to optimise the operation of the organisation in its entirety rather than maximising the product of any one particular part. These issues, and the main differences in scope and focus of the individual levels, can clearly be seen by a brief examination of the types of strategy that are pursued at the corporate, business and functional levels.

## Corporate level strategy

Broadly speaking, there are six basic forms of strategy which organisations pursue at this level:

- **Stability strategy** (also known as maintenance strategy). As its name implies, strategies under this heading are designed to keep organisations quiet and stable. They are most frequently found in successful organisations, operating in medium-attractiveness industries, who are faced with unpredictable circumstances outside the range of their normal business experience. Because of their markets and products, such organisations believe they have no need to make sudden changes and have the time and position to allow events to unfold before making any response (Wheelen and Hunger, 1989).

- **Growth strategy**. This is possibly the most common form of all corporate strategies, and involves either concentrating on dominating one industry or growing by diversification across a number of industries (e.g. Microsoft and Virgin respectively). As a number of writers have suggested (*see* Argenti, 1974; Byars, 1984), its basic attraction is twofold. First, it is claimed that there is a strong and proportional correlation between increased turnover and increased profit. Second, the performance of senior managers tends to be measured in terms of the annual increase in turnover and profit. However, there are those who point out that increases in turnover are not necessarily matched by increases in profits and that, given the need to invest to achieve growth in turnover, growth may actually weaken a company's financial health (Byars, 1984; Drucker, 1974).

- **Portfolio extension**. This is another variant of the growth strategy, but is achieved through mergers, joint ventures or acquisitions, rather than through internally generated organic growth. The first two of these, mergers and joint ventures, allow growth or development to take place, without the organisations involved having to invest the level of resources that would be necessary if they were operating in isolation. The latter, acquisition, is usually resource-intensive but brings immediate gains in the form of an established and, hopefully, profitable business (Byars, 1984; Little, 1984; Leontiades, 1986).

- **Retrenchment strategy**. This strategy is usually only embarked upon when an organisation is in trouble or, because of adverse market conditions, sees trouble ahead. It usually involves a process of downsizing, i.e. cutting back on numbers employed and activities undertaken. In some situations this may lead to selling off the entire enterprise. However, the general aim is to cut back in order to match expenditure to projected income, and refocus the organisation so as to be able once again to attain prosperity in the future (Bowman and Asch, 1985; Thompson and Strickland, 1983).

- **Harvesting strategy**. This involves reducing investment in a business or area of activity in order to reduce costs, improve cashflow and capitalise on whatever residual competencies or areas of advantage still remain. This approach can be implemented at different rates depending on the urgency of the situation. Slow harvesting means to reduce financial support at such a slow rate that it almost appears to be a maintenance strategy; at the other extreme, fast harvesting can result in budgets being cut at such a rate that it seems almost indistinguishable from liquidation (Harrigan, 1980; Kotler, 1978; Porter, 1980).

- **Combination strategy**. The above strategies are not mutually exclusive, and can be linked together in whatever combination seems appropriate given the circumstances of the organisation in question. However, combination strategies are clearly more appropriate, or at least more necessary, in large multi-divisional organisations where the circumstances faced by the different activities are likely to vary. Therefore, in such situations, organisations may experience a constant flurry of change, where some parts are being run down and/or disposed of whilst new units are being acquired and other areas of the business rapidly expanded (Glueck, 1978; Pearson, 1977).

The above list is not exhaustive, nor can it be, given that each organisation is free to develop its own strategic variant in relation to its own circumstances. As argued in Chapter 5, it is the circumstances of the particular organisation in question that should dictate the type of strategy adopted by its managers, rather than any attempt to copy what has been successful elsewhere. Though Porter's Competitive Forces model can be applicable to all these forms of strategy, the Strategic Conflict and Resource-Based models appear to be more suitable to situations where growth is being pursued or where companies have a strong market position. Nevertheless, it needs to be remembered that it is the precepts and assumptions of Porter and the Positioning school which dominated the practice of strategy in the 1980s and 1990s. A further point to note is that all except the first, maintenance strategy, imply fundamental restructuring of the internal operations of the organisation. In such situations, there are likely to be winners and losers, and managers may be more concerned with preserving their jobs and power than choosing the best strategy for the organisation.

Nevertheless, in both America and Europe, over the last 20 years, the tide has been turning against corporate strategy, or rather against the large corporate centres responsible for developing corporate strategy and which wielded so much power in the 1970s and 1980s. The case against them is summed up by Koch (1995: 78) who maintains that:

> Anything other than a minimal [corporate] Centre can only be justified if the Centre adds more value than it costs and subtracts from the business. ... Yet it should be clear that ... independent of their cost, most corporate Centres destroy more value than they add.

This negative view of corporate strategy has, perhaps, been most vociferously championed by Peters and Waterman (1982), but has also received strong support from academic researchers (Goold *et al*, 1994). The result of this is that there has been an increasing tendency to devolve responsibility for strategy from the corporate to the business level.

## Business level strategy

Whilst corporate level strategies are mainly concerned with managing diversified enterprises whose activities span a number of different areas, business level strategies relate to the different ways that an individual business unit can compete in its chosen market(s). However, it must be remembered that they are chosen and deployed within the framework of an overall corporate strategy and not in isolation from it, though the degree of freedom allowed to individual business units in this respect will vary from organisation to organisation. To this end, the strategic concerns of managers at the business level tend to be, as Hax and Majluf (1996: 46) note:

> ...the mission of the business, the attractiveness of the industry in which the business belongs, and the competitive position of the business unit within the industry. These are the inputs that determine the strategic agenda of a business and lead to the formulation and implementation of its strategy.

Just as at the corporate level, the available business level strategies are many and varied. Rather than attempt to describe them all, we shall examine main variants by addressing Porter's (1980, 1985) work in this area.

Porter (1985: 11) argues that there are only two 'basic types of competitive advantage a firm can possess: low cost or differentiation'. He adds to these the 'scope' of the business (i.e. the range of its markets) to create 'three generic strategies for achieving above average performance'. As mentioned earlier, these are cost leadership, product differentiation and specialisation by focus.

### Cost leadership

The aim of this strategy is to achieve overall lower costs than one's competitors, without reducing comparable product quality. To do this requires a high volume of sales in order to allow organisations to structure themselves in such a way that they can achieve economies of scale. This strategy, to quote Porter (1980: 15), requires the:

> ...aggressive construction of efficient scale facilities, vigorous pursuit of cost reductions from experience, tight cost and overhead control, avoidance of marginal customer accounts, and cost minimisation in areas like R&D, services, sales force and so on.

### Product differentiation

This strategy attempts to achieve industry-wide recognition of different and superior products and services compared to those of other suppliers. This recognition can be accomplished through the design of special brand images, technology features, customer service or higher quality, all of which have implications for the structure and operation of companies. Achieving differentiation is likely to result in insulation against competitive rivalry due to securing customer loyalty. The resultant competitive advantage also leads to increased returns, sometimes through making customers less sensitive to high product price.

### Specialisation by focus

In this case the strategy is concerned with selecting (focusing upon) only certain markets, products or geographical areas in which to compete. Porter argues that by focusing in this way, it becomes feasible for a firm to dominate its chosen area(s).

The method of achieving domination could either be through cost advantage or product differentiation. According to Porter (1980: 15), however, such niche markets must have certain characteristics which separate them out from the market in general:

> ... the target segment must either have buyers with unusual needs or else the production and delivery system that best serves the target must differ from that of the other industry segments.

If the niche market grows, or is incorporated, into a larger market, then market dominance is unlikely to be retained. In such circumstances, the previously dominant organisation will find itself having to compete for market share with others. In effect, the rules of the game will have changed and a different strategy is required – either attempting to gain cost leadership across the entire market, or adopting a product differentiation policy which neutralises other competitors' cost advantage.

Porter's assertion concerning these three strategies is that they are distinct and cannot be mixed. That is to say, it is not possible to pursue successfully a cost leadership strategy and a product differentiation strategy at the same time because each requires different organisational arrangements to be successful. Also, if a firm does not achieve cost leadership, product differentiation or specialisation in its products, services or market, it is bound to produce low profitability and have below-average performance. He refers to these sorts of firms as 'stuck in the middle'. Many others share Porter's view (*see* White, 1986). Nevertheless, a study by Dess and Davis (1984), though broadly supporting Porter, did question his assertion concerning the negative effects of mixing strategies. They found that there is some evidence to show that businesses with both a low cost and a high differentiation position can be very successful.

Miller (1992) also questioned Porter's assertion that firms should pursue only one strategy. He points out that such strategic specialisation can lead to inflexibility and narrow an organisation's vision. In addition, Gilbert and Strebel (1992) point to the success of 'outpacing' strategies. This is where firms enter a market as low-cost producers and then, once established, differentiate to capture a larger slice of the market. This was the approach, i.e. moving from one successful form of strategy to another, used by Japanese companies to capture Western markets in the 1970s and 1980s. In so doing, Japanese firms used a Strategic Conflict approach, but this was underpinned by their commitment to building and developing their core competences. Therefore, though Porter's work has tended to dominate the practice of strategic management in Western firms, both the Strategic Conflict and Resource-Based models have shown their worth. Nevertheless, regardless of which business level approach to strategy organisations have followed, prompted by the success of Japanese companies, there has been a growing interest in the importance of functional level strategy (Hax and Majluf, 1996; Schonberger, 1982).

## Functional level strategies

The main functional level strategies concern marketing, finance, R&D, technology, human resources, manufacturing/operations and purchasing. Of the three levels of strategic decision-making, the functional level has probably been the most neglected by Western organisations. This is for three reasons. First, the concentration at both the corporate and business levels on the external world, i.e. the market, led to a lack of interest in the internal operation of organisations. The assumption was that the internal world was malleable, and could and should adjust to the priorities set by corporate and business strategists (Schonberger, 1982). Second, key elements of functional level strategy, especially concerning finance, marketing, R&D and technology, were in effect determined and constrained by corporate strategists. Indeed, in many organisations, even the human resource strategy was determined at the corporate level. Finally, even though the 1980s saw a renewed interest in functional level strategy, this tended to be one-sided, tending to stress soft, personnel-type issues. As discussed in Chapter 3, in seeking to understand and emulate Japanese success, Western researchers created the Seven S Framework: strategy, structure, systems, staff, style, shared values, and skills (Peters and Waterman, 1982; Pascale and Athos, 1982). Though acknowledging that the Japanese were strong in and integrated all the Seven Ss, the tendency in the West was to stress the so-called soft Ss: staff, style, shared values and skills. This not only continued to neglect areas such as manufacturing/operations and purchasing, but also, in so doing, failed to produce the sort of integrated corporate, business and functional level strategies that were seen as lying at the core of Japanese competitiveness. Once again, this highlights the difficulty that Western strategy practitioners, consultants and theorists have with creating an approach to strategy that goes beyond focusing on particular aspects and takes an all-encompassing view (Mintzberg *et al*, 1998).

In examining the corporate, business and functional levels, it can be seen that there are only a limited number of forms of strategy that organisations tend to adopt and which flow from the Competitive Forces, Strategic Conflict and Resource-Based models of strategy discussed earlier. However, the appropriateness of any of these for a particular organisation is, as maintained in Chapter 5, related to the nature of the societal, sector, environmental and organisational constraints it faces. These include the stage of product–market evolution, the competitive position the firm has, the competitive position it seeks, the business strategies being used by rival firms, the internal resources and distinctive competencies at a firm's disposal, the prevailing market threats and opportunities, the type and vigour of competition, customer needs, and the conditions which financial institutions place on capital availability, to mention only the more obvious ones (Hax and Majluf, 1996; Johnson and Scholes, 1993; Koch, 1995; Thompson and Strickland, 1983). In addition, it must be acknowledged that generic strategies will always give rise to a host of variants and, therefore, at any one time the choice of the most suitable strategy will be a highly complex task. Indeed, this is what one would expect. If choosing and implementing strategy was easy, then all firms would be successful. But, given that success is usually measured in relative terms, by definition not everyone can be successful; therefore, strategy formulation will and must remain fraught with danger and complexity.

A major point to note, though, is that almost without exception, whatever form of strategy is adopted, it will require the organisation to achieve a fit between its external environment and internal structures, culture and practices. Contrary to the views of earlier writers on strategy (such as Ansoff, 1965), if organisations are driven by their external environment, internal arrangements may, and probably do, need to change, often radically, in order to achieve the desired market-place objectives. This once again emphasises the importance of functional level strategy and shows why it should not be treated as a lesser issue. Nevertheless, it should also be borne in mind, as argued in previous chapters, that the possibility does exist for organisations to shape the external environment to fit in with their internal arrangements. The fact that many do not, may say more about the type of organisation they are than the constraints they face.

## Types of organisation

Miles and Snow (1978) developed an important variant of the argument on types of strategy. Rather than attempting to classify the types or levels of strategy that organisations can adopt, they classify the organisations themselves as strategic types, based on the rate at which an organisation changes its products or markets. Miles and Snow identified four strategic types:

- **Defenders**. These seek internal stability and efficiency by producing only a limited set of products, directed at a narrow but relatively stable segment of the overall market, which they defend aggressively. Such organisations are characterised by tight control, extensive division of labour and a high degree of formalisation and centralisation.

- **Prospectors**. These are almost the opposite of defenders. They aim for internal flexibility in order to develop and exploit new products and markets. To operate effectively in a dynamic environment they have a loose structure, low division of labour and formalisation, and a high degree of decentralisation.

- **Analysers**. These types of organisation seek to capitalise on the best of both the preceding types. They aim to minimise risk and maximise profit. They move into new markets only after viability has been proved by prospectors. Their internal arrangements are characterised by moderately centralised control; with tight control over current activities but looser controls over new undertakings.

- **Reactors**. This is a residual strategy. These types of organisation exhibit inconsistent and unstable patterns caused by pursuing one of the other three strategies erratically. In general, reactors respond inappropriately, perform poorly, and lack the confidence to commit themselves fully to a specific strategy for the future.

Though Miles and Snow's classification has received empirical support from some researchers (e.g. Shortell and Zajac, 1990), others have questioned its applicability across industries (e.g. Hambrick, 1983). Notwithstanding this, as Waldersee and Sheather (1996) point out, there are some similarities between Miles and Snow's work and Porter's work. They argue that successful firms pursue one of two basic types of strategy – innovative or stability.

Organisations pursuing innovative strategies, which embrace both Porter's product differentiators and Miles and Snow's prospectors, seek to achieve success through reducing price competition by offering products and services that are considered unique in terms of their design, brand image and features. On the other hand, organisations pursuing stability strategies, which embrace Porter's cost leaders and Miles and Snow's defenders, seek to achieve success by locating and maintaining secured niches in stable product areas where they can produce higher-quality or lower-price products than their competitors.

Covin (1991) agrees with the proposition that successful organisations pursue one of two forms of strategy, though he labels them entrepreneurial and conservative. The former falls within Waldersee and Sheather's innovative category, whilst the latter falls with their stability category. Covin argues that the strategy an organisation adopts reflects its basic nature (i.e. its culture). Therefore, for Covin, the selection and pursuit of strategy is driven by managerial style and organisational culture. However, Waldersee and Sheather dispute this. Their work sought to examine the relationship between strategy and managerial style, and whether one drove the other. Their conclusion, which was tentative, was that different types of strategy may predispose managers to act in different ways (i.e. managerial style follows strategy type) rather than managers' styles predisposing them to a particular type of strategy. Yet, recalling Chapter 5's discussion of strategy and the constraints on managerial choice, it could be argued that these writers are taking too narrow and deterministic a view. It might well be that, depending on the constraints faced by managers and their perceptions of these, in some situations strategy does require managers to adopt a particular style of working, whilst in other situations managerial style does influence the nature of the strategy adopted. This discussion of the relationship between managerial style and organisational context will be returned to in the concluding chapter of this book.

Before moving on to examine the strategic tools that organisations have at their disposal, it is important to remember that the concept of strategy (whether at the functional, business or corporate level) is contentious. Chapter 5 showed that there are many influential writers who do not believe in strategy as a conscious and planned process (e.g. Mintzberg, 1994; Pettigrew, 1985; and Stacey, 1993). This does not invalidate corporate, business or functional strategies *per se*, but it does mean that they occupy a problematic and contested terrain.

## STRATEGIC PLANNING TOOLS

This section briefly reviews the main tools that organisations use to select and construct their strategies. By and large, these tools tend to have either a quantitative or a qualitative bias. In the past, and to a major extent even now, it was the quantitative tools (mathematical models) that tended to dominate. This is largely a reflection of the types of strategy organisations adopt, and a (not unrelated) preference for quantification, especially in the financial arena, in the USA, where many of the leading tools of and approaches to strategy originated (Grant, 1991b; Hax and Majluf, 1996; Moore, 1992). It should be noted, though, that other leading industrial nations, especially Germany and Japan, place less reliance on financial and other quantitative measures in determining strategy (Carr *et al*, 1991; Whittington, 1993). For example, the Japanese electronics giant, NEC, never uses discounted cash flow; and though Toyota does calculate cash flows, it does not take account of them for decision-making purposes (Williams *et al*, 1991). Nevertheless, even in the USA and the UK where financial considerations appear paramount, there has been some movement away from the sole reliance on quantitative techniques, and a growing interest in softer, qualitative tools such as scenario/vision-building. In part, this interest in more qualitative techniques is a result of the perceived failure, especially in the face of Japanese competition, of more quantitative approaches favoured by proponents of the Positioning school to deliver a genuine and sustainable competitive advantage. This interest in qualitative techniques has also received a boost from the growing interest in the Strategic Conflict and Resource-Based approaches to strategy. In addition, it forms part of, and has been given impetus by, the move away from quantification and towards the use of more qualitative techniques in organisation theory in general.

As one would expect, there are an enormous range and number of tools and techniques available to the strategist. However, perhaps the ones that have attracted most attention are, in chronological order:

1 the PIMS (Profit Impact on Marketing Strategy) model;

2 the Growth-Share Matrix;

3 the Scenario construction approach.

The first two focus on corporate and business level strategies and are biased towards large organisations that have an established and significant presence in the markets they serve. The third, though, has no such restrictions or biases and can be applied to a wide range of situations.

### PIMS

The PIMS (Profit Impact on Marketing Strategy) programme was launched in 1972 and derived from research by Sidney Schoeffler. This was put into practice by

General Electric, who wanted to analyse their operations with the aim of identifying those factors determining business success (Schoeffler, 1980). In 1975, Schoeffler founded the Strategic Planning Institute (SPI), which is linked to Harvard Business School, to provide a permanent base for the PIMS work. Since then, PIMS has grown to become the largest privately owned database in the world, comprising over 200 major corporations and some 2,600 individual business units (McNamee, 1985; Moore, 1992).

The rationale underlying the PIMS model is that certain characteristics of a business and its markets determine profitability. Consequently, understanding these characteristics and acting upon them will aid a company to become more profitable. The model is based upon the belief that there are three major factors which determine a business unit's performance: its strategy, its competitive position, and the market/industry characteristics of the field in which it competes (Moore, 1992). Underpinning the model are two key assumptions. The first is that all business situations are basically alike and obey the same laws of the market place (Schoeffler, 1980). The second is that the future will resemble the past, i.e. if certain linkages between strategy and performance resulted in profitability in the past, they will do so again in the future (Buzzell and Gale, 1987).

PIMS operates as a form of club. It collects information from its member companies relating to such factors as market share, profitability, product quality and investment. This information is fed into the PIMS database and is then used to provide individual members with answers to questions such as:

- What profit rate is 'normal' for a given business?
- What strategic changes are likely to improve performance?
- What are the likely effects on profitability, cash flow, etc., of adopting a particular strategy?

There has been much discussion as to the success of the PIMS. Certainly, some of its users, as well as academic observers, regard it as having only a limited use (Ford, 1981; Mitroff and Mason, 1981). The main criticisms levelled against PIMS are as follows:

- It is flawed because it uses historic data, without consideration for future changes. The argument is that, as organisations operate in a dynamic environment, to use the past to predict the future can be a dangerous exercise. Indeed, PIMS seems to be useful only in a stable environment, where companies stick to doing what they know best. It is even questioned whether PIMS can be regarded as a tool for policy in a strategic sense, since it can be argued that the 'variables' it so relies on, such as market share, are performance variables, not strategic ones (Abell, 1977).
- It is highly analytical, but very limited in solving problems. In addition, because PIMS has to use a very large database for its analysis, it is argued that this creates a major problem for managers in terms of absorbing all the data generated. In

turn, since the statistical errors in its output are rarely openly discussed, there is a tendency for managers not to question its findings because 'the computer is always right' (Andrews, 1980).

- Its most famous, and contentious, assertion that profitability is closely linked to market share, and that an improvement in market share can be associated with a proportionate increase in return on investment, is of dubious validity. As Smith (1985) maintains, it could equally be argued that both are due to common factors, such as low costs and good management. It is also said to be responsible for inculcating in managers and consultants a belief that low market share businesses are bad and must either increase their market share or withdraw from the industry in question, regardless of profitability (McKiernan, 1992).

- Most of the factors which govern the forecasts of the model are beyond the control of individual companies. Therefore, since PIMS relies heavily on this data, whatever conclusions it reaches about the fate of a company are final. It is neither comforting nor particularly useful to be told that you cannot do anything to turn a negative forecast around, because the factors responsible are out of your hands (Anderson and Paine, 1978).

- It assumes that a rather large set of quantitative variables, primarily of a financial nature, are sufficient to capture the state of a business and from this determine a realistic strategy (Naylor, 1981). Also, as Mintzberg *et al* (1998: 99) comment, '. . . finding a correlation between variables . . . is one thing; assuming a causation, and turning that into an imperative, is quite another.'

- It is based on the premise that business problems are orderly or well-structured. PIMS thus assumes that the determination or classification of the level of the organisation or business unit, the customer group, the competition, the market and the product line to which the analysis applies are all either well-known or well-specified. It is, therefore, not equipped to handle imprecise, let alone conflicting, definitions of business problems (Koch, 1995; Naylor, 1981).

In summary, the main criticisms of PIMS are that it is too mechanistic, overly complex, based on unreliable data, and cannot cope adequately with dynamic and unpredictable environments. Yet, despite the criticisms levelled against it, many researchers still believe that PIMS is a useful tool. The PIMS method has also been praised for the insight it has given into the true nature of the relationships between strategic variables such as profit and market share. Obviously, managers deal with these variables and their relationships on a daily basis, but attempts at conceptualising these relationships had been lacking until the advent of the PIMS research programme (Anderson and Paine, 1978; Ford, 1981; Mitroff and Mason, 1981).

This is not, however, to minimise the shortcomings of the PIMS model. It is biased towards, and contains data almost exclusively provided by, large and well-established corporations who already occupy significant positions in their markets. Therefore, as Mintzberg *et al* (1998: 99) observe, its emphasis is on 'being there' or 'staying there' rather than 'getting there'. It follows that its prescriptions may have little relevance for new, small or innovative businesses seeking to enter new markets.

## The Growth-Share Matrix

This was the brainchild of the Boston Consulting Group (BCG) in the USA and is arguably the most famous strategic tool ever developed (Koch, 1995). BCG was formed in 1963 by Bruce Henderson, and it is generally considered to be the pioneer of business strategy analysis. The Growth-Share Matrix, or 'Boston Box' as it is colloquially referred to, arose from two concepts developed by BCG: the experience curve and the sustainable growth formula (McKiernan, 1992).

The experience curve, which Henderson claims to have discovered in the 1960s, suggests that 'as the cumulative production of a product doubles, the cost of producing it seems to decrease by a constant percentage (usually 10 to 30 percent)' (Mintzberg *et al*, 1998: 97). From this, BCG concluded that if costs fall in relation to production volume (i.e. experience), then cost must also be a function of market share. Therefore, the company with the largest market share should also have the greatest competitive advantage and, it follows, the highest profit margin.

The sustainable growth formula, which was developed by BCG in the early 1970s, is based on the relationship between growth, investment and returns. It maintains that companies with the highest rate of returns on investments can, theoretically, grow the fastest (McKiernan, 1992).

It was bringing together these two concepts (that the company with the highest returns can grow the fastest and that the company with the highest market share should have the highest profit margin) that created the basis for the Growth-Share Matrix. The matrix is based on the assumption that all except the smallest and simplest organisations are composed of more than one business. The collection of businesses within an organisation is termed its business portfolio. Using pictorial analogies, it posits that businesses in an organisation's portfolio can be classified into stars, cash-cows, dogs and problem children (Smith, 1985).

- **Stars** are business units, industries or products with high growth and high market share. Because of this, stars are assumed to use and generate large amounts of cash. It is argued that as they, generally, represent the best profit and investment opportunities, then the best strategy for stars, usually, is to make the necessary investments to maintain or improve their competitive position.

- **Cash-cows** are defined as former stars whose rate of market growth is in decline. They were once market leaders, during the early days when the market was rapidly growing, and have maintained that position as the growth tapered off. They are regarded as businesses with low growth but high market share. Because they are entrenched in the market, they have lower costs and make higher profits than their competitors. These businesses are cash-rich; therefore the appropriate strategy for such businesses is to 'milk' them in order to develop the rest of the organisation's portfolio.

- **Dogs** are businesses that have low market share and which operate in markets with low growth potential. Low market share normally implies poor profit, and because the market growth is low, investment to increase market share is frequently prohibitive. Also, in such situations, the cash required to maintain a competitive position often exceeds the cash generated. Thus, dogs often become cash traps. It follows from this that, generally, the best strategy is for dogs to be sold off.

- **Problem children** or **question marks**, as they are sometimes labelled, are regarded as having a high growth rate and low market share. They have high cash requirements to keep them on course, but their profitability is low because of their low market share. They are so named because, most of the time, the appropriate strategy to adopt is not clear. With their high growth rate, it might be possible to turn them into stars, by further investment. On the other hand, because of the uncertainty that surrounds this type of business, the best strategy might be to sell them off altogether.

The originators of the Growth-Share Matrix see it as a dynamic tool for assessing and planning market and business developments. For example, the matrix predicts that as growth in their industries slows down, the original stars will move into the position of cash-cows, as long as they keep maintaining their high market share; otherwise they will become dogs. It also claims to predict how cash-cows and dogs will develop as their markets change. Therefore, the Growth-Share Matrix can be used to forecast the development of a business portfolio over a period of time. There are two basic assumptions underlying the matrix: first, that those industries, products or businesses that have a high growth rate can be differentiated from those that have a low growth rate; and second, that those that have a high competitive position/market share can be differentiated from those that have a low competitive position/market share. Based on these assumptions, the matrix classifies business units or activities according to the growth rate of the industry of which they are part and by their market share (Koch, 1995; McKiernan, 1992; Moore, 1992).

The matrix was widely and rapidly adopted by American corporations in the 1970s. This was for two reasons: first, the matrix's simplicity and ease of construction; and second, because most large corporations were busy splitting their organisation into strategic business units focusing on particular industries and products. The corporate centres were looking for a simple means of categorising and directing the activities of these units, and the matrix was seen by them as an ideal tool for this purpose. McKiernan (1992), however, argues that its advantages go far beyond merely its simplicity and ease of construction. He maintains that it aids strategic planning, balancing cash flow between businesses, investment decisions, and competitive benchmarking.

Nevertheless, as many commentators note, over the years, the Growth-Share Matrix has attracted its fair share of criticisms as well as praise (Koch, 1995; McKiernan, 1992; Mintzberg *et al*, 1998). One of the obvious objections to the matrix is the labels it employs for the classification of businesses. Andrews (1980) described these labels as a 'vulgar and destructive vocabulary'. There are, however, other more serious criticisms concerning the assumptions underlying, and the operation of, the 'Boston Box'. The main one is that the uniqueness of an organisation and its problems may not be adequately captured by this or any other tight classification scheme. This is reflected in the views of Mitroff and Mason (1981), who argue that the critical assumptions underlying the matrix are tautologous and simplistic. They summarise these assumptions as follows:

- that the classification scheme applies to all businesses, because all businesses can be classified as one of the four basic types;
- that the classification scheme is relevant to all businesses, meaning that all businesses should be able to be classified as one of the four types;
- that the model and its recommendations for action are universally applicable to all businesses, no matter what the characteristics of a particular business may be.

In addition, a wide range of researchers have drawn attention to the difficulty in defining and measuring the major variables on which the matrix relies. In this respect, the criticisms are similar to those raised against PIMS. As examples, Hax and Majluf (1982) argue that the definition of market share used in the matrix is unrealistic. Similarly, Hax and Nicholson (1983) point out that a product/market segment can be defined in a variety of ways, and that, in reality, there is a whole hierarchy of product/market segments. Another reservation, expressed by Fawn and Cox (1985), is the difficulty of defining what constitutes a single business.

There is also some concern as to the validity of the indicators of profitability used: market share and industry growth. Hax and Nicholson (1983) pose two interesting and vital questions in this respect: 'Is market share really the major factor determining profitability?' and 'Is industry growth really the only variable that fully explains growth opportunities?' These reservations are echoed by Smith (1985). A further concern is that the matrix assumes that a good portfolio analysis should identify the competitive strengths and the industry attractiveness of each business unit. Alternatives to the Growth-Share Matrix, however, reject this assertion. Instead they start by assuming that these two dimensions cannot be revealed by a single measurement, but require a wider set of critical factors for reliable positioning of the business units (Hax and Majluf, 1982; Hofer and Schendel, 1978). One of the most telling criticisms is that many of the companies who have used the matrix found, to their alarm, that all their component businesses were classed as dogs even though these businesses were actually profitable!

Perhaps the key and most common criticism relates to the way the matrix, and other similar tools, have been used. As Hax and Majluf (1996: 313) observe:

> ...matrices tend to trivialise strategic thinking by converting it into simplistic and mechanistic exercises, whose final message is dubious at best. Also the matrix methodology has tended to take strategic analysis and, subsequently, strategic thinking away from managers and into the realms of planning departments.

In the face of such criticisms, a number of modifications were made to the original Growth-Share Matrix. General Electric, for example, in association with management consultants McKinsey, developed a nine-way matrix instead of the original four-way classification (Hax and Nicholson, 1983). A similar system called the Directional Policy Matrix (DPM) was also developed by Shell Chemicals in the UK (Hussey, 1978). Many other organisations, in their turn, developed or employed similar schemes to meet their organisational needs (Koch, 1995; McKiernan, 1992; Patel and Younger, 1978). Nevertheless, portfolio models, possibly because they seek to cover all possible types of businesses, do seem severely flawed (Turner, 1990).

Regardless of the merits of these criticisms, few would dispute that, like PIMS, the Growth-Share Matrix is primarily suited to well-structured planning problems in which the basic definition of a business unit, product or competition is not an issue (Bowman and Asch, 1985). Unfortunately, because of the uncertain and rapidly changing nature of business today, such situations are becoming less and less common. This, to an extent, may account for the increase in the popularity of the next approach.

## The scenario/vision-building approach

As a way of overcoming some of the criticisms of the above quantitative approaches, the use of scenario-building techniques emerged in the 1970s. The use of scenarios is based on the assumption that if you cannot predict the future, then by considering a range of possible futures, an organisation's strategic horizons can be broadened, managers can be opened up to new ideas and, perhaps, the right future can even be identified (Porter, 1985). The aim, therefore, of the scenario approach is to enable an organisation to picture and make various assumptions about future events and trends that might affect its operation. Organisations, like individuals, are unique and complex. As argued above, this can undermine the effectiveness of models or general principles as tools for strategic planning. If this is the case, rather than applying standard, but inappropriate, tools, each organisation must consider its own individual requirements. This process should be based on an intensive examination of its unique features and needs by a personally concerned, involved and experienced analyst. It is this that scenario-building attempts to do (Linneman and Klein, 1979).

The scenario approach has been defined in a number of ways. McNulty (1977) defined it as a quantitative or qualitative picture of a given organisation or group developed within the framework of a set of specified assumptions. Kahn and Weiner (1978) defined it as a hypothetical sequence of events constructed for the purpose of focusing attention on causal processes and decision points. To Kahn and Weiner, the purpose of scenarios is to display, in as dramatic and persuasive a fashion as possible, a number of possibilities for the future. To Norse (1979), scenarios are a means of improving our understanding of the long-term global, regional or national consequences of existing or potential trends or policies and their interaction. All these definitions are useful in the sense that they portray the different uses (national, international, corporate level, business level) to which scenarios can be put.

Essentially, building scenarios can be regarded as making different pictures of the future (business or otherwise) through the construction of case studies, either quantitatively or qualitatively. The quantitative variant of scenario-building, sometimes called the hard method, uses mathematics, models and computers to make pictures of the future, through the production of a vast array of numbers and figures. However, the main approach is the qualitative, or soft, method which is essentially intuitive and descriptive; it is based on the resources of the human mind and derived from the methods of psychology and sociology.

The two main scenario-building approaches that have become well-established are the *Delphi Method* and the *Cross Impact Method*. However, in recent years, a third approach has become increasingly influential: *vision-building*. Though this bears some relation to other scenario-building techniques, it comes from a different tradition. The scenario approach and especially vision-building have some similarities with the postmodernist view that organisations exist in and represent multiple realities which compete with each other for supremacy (*see* Chapter 4). From the postmodernist perspective, organisations have the ability to create their own reality and, therefore, both scenario- and vision-building can be viewed as processes which assist organisations, or the dominant group within an organisation, to select or construct the reality that most suits their needs.

Underpinning scenario/vision-building is the concept of double- and triple-loop learning (*see* Chapter 3). Double- and triple-loop learning occurs when, in response to organisational problems or environmental changes, individuals and groups question the efficacy and appropriateness of existing strategies, norms and even the organisation's rationale for existing (Argyris, 1977; Bateson, 1972). Therefore, one of the main functions of scenario-type approaches is that they enable organisations to question the very foundations of their existence, to examine the usefulness of their values and norms. Instead of asking how they can improve what they are doing, they begin to ask: Why are we doing this at all? What alternatives are there? This questioning of basic assumptions is something that is alien to the quantitative tools discussed above, especially given that most managers do not understand the assumptions built into such models in the first place. Indeed, quantitative models appear to remove the necessity for managers to think by providing them with 'answers' rather than information on which to base their own decisions (Hax and Majluf, 1996). The three main qualitative approaches, on the other hand, are designed specifically to make managers think radically about their organisation, its purpose and its future.

## The Delphi Method

This uses a panel of experts, who are interrogated about a number of future issues within their area of expertise. In the classic application, the interrogation is conducted under conditions whereby each respondent is unknown to the others, in order to avoid effects of authority and the development of a consensual bandwagon. After the initial round of interrogations, the results are reported to the panel and another round of interrogations is conducted. Several rounds may be carried out in this manner.

Results produced from these interrogations may be amenable to statistical treatment with a view to yielding numbers, dates and ranges from them. At the end of the process, depending on whether a quantitative or qualitative approach is taken, either a detailed numerical forecast of the future is obtained, or a more descriptive and richer picture. In both cases, the central tendencies of majority opinion and the range of minority disagreements will also be included (McNulty, 1977; Zentner, 1982).

### The Cross Impact Method

This is a variation to the Delphi Method. It uses essentially the same interrogation method as the Delphi, i.e. a panel of experts; the difference, however, lies in what they are asked to do. The Delphi requires the experts to identify a number of future issues that they think will affect the organisation or business within their area of expertise. The Cross Impact Method, on the other hand, asks its panel of experts to assign subjective probabilities and time priorities to a list of potential future events and developments supplied by the organisation. The emphasis is on identifying reinforcing or inhibiting events and trends, to uncover relationships and to indicate the importance of specific events. The accruing data from this exercise are processed to yield curves of the probabilities for each event as a function of time (Lanford, 1972).

### Vision-building

This has gained in popularity in the last 10 to 15 years, especially in the United States. Whilst it certainly bears a resemblance to the other scenario-building techniques, it is influenced more by Japanese management practices than by those in the West (Cummings and Huse, 1989; Hamel and Prahalad, 1989). It is a much less structured approach than the other two scenario-building techniques, and relies more on a company's own management. The major elements of vision-building are as follows:

- the conception by a company's senior management team of an 'ideal' future state for their organisation;
- the identification of the organisation's mission, its rationale for existence;
- a clear statement of desired outcomes and the desired conditions and competences needed to achieve these.

Vision-building is an iterative process which is designed to move from the general (the vision) to the specific (desired outcomes and conditions), and back again. By going round the loop in this manner, according to Cummings and Huse (1989), an ambitious yet attainable future can be constructed and pursued. This owes much to the Japanese, who pioneered the concept of strategic intent on which vision-building is based. The work of Hamel and Prahalad (1989) is of particular importance in this respect. They argued that the strategic approach of Japanese companies is markedly different to that of their Western counterparts. Rather than attempting to lay down a detailed plan in advance, Japanese companies operate within a long-term framework of strategic intent. They create a vision of their desired future – their 'intent' – which they then pursue in a relentless but flexible manner. Hamel and Prahalad quote examples of leading Japanese companies who, in the 1960s, when they were insignificant in world terms, set out to dominate their markets. Honda's strategic intent was to be the 'Second Ford', Komatsu's to 'Encircle Caterpillar' and Canon's to 'Beat Xerox'. These companies then mobilised their resources towards achieving their individual strategic intent. In this, the prime resource they deployed was the commitment, ingenuity and flexibility of their workforces.

Like all approaches to strategic planning, these scenario/vision-building approaches have attracted criticism. One criticism is their reliance on subjectivity. The fact that any five management specialists can interpret the same situation in totally different ways is an oft-quoted example of this type of criticism. Also, this approach is prone to retrospection. People's ideas of the future are informed by their knowledge and experience of the past. Since experience is not always the best teacher, scenarios and visions may be based on false assumptions. A further criticism is that, because competing views of the future direction and shape of the organisation are being considered, participants will be strongly influenced in their preference of scenario by their own sectional and personal interests.

Another claimed drawback is that scenario development cannot be carried out by novices. It requires experts in the field concerned to be able to look into the future and make judgements about the likelihood of what might happen. In a survey of US industrial companies using scenarios in 1979, a senior Vice-President claimed that 'The major problem is the amount of time and quality of personnel required to prepare meaningful scenarios'. Others in the same survey complained that 'multiple anything is more work than single anything, especially if the need for the multiple is questionable'. A further respondent said, 'As no one is clairvoyant, to develop more than a most probable scenario is counter-productive and an exercise of mental gymnastics'. Most concluded that 'it is a waste of time and effort, since it mostly deals with the improbable' (Keshavan and Rakesh, 1979: 57–61).

A further set of criticisms relates to how many scenarios to construct and what to do with scenarios once they are constructed. Porter (1985) suggests that organisations need sufficient scenarios to cover the important possible contingencies, but not so many that they are unmanageable. He also argues that managers have to select and act on the most probable or most beneficial but, at the same time, hedge their bets and remain flexible. However, as Wack (1985) argues, based on his experience at Shell, getting managers to accept radical scenarios which challenge their worldview is a much more demanding task than actually building scenarios themselves.

In a similar way, there are those who warn that the use of visions, or over-reliance on them, can be harmful. Stacey (1992) is particularly critical of this approach, claiming that the available guidance on how to create a vision is neither concrete enough to be useful, nor possible to use when dealing with a future that is unknowable. Stacey also argues that visions fix managers too tightly in one direction and put an unrealistic burden on leaders. Collins and Porras (1991) suggest that, in any case, the role of charismatic leaders in establishing visions is much over-rated.

Nevertheless, in a study conducted in 1984 to review the extent of the use of multiple scenarios in Europe, the researchers discovered that 46 per cent (of a sample of 100 companies) said they would increase their use of the method in the future and only 12 per cent stated that they would make less use of the method. Companies in the same report stated that scenario construction was useful in controlling the 'uncertainty and unpredictability of the corporate environment'. It also helped them to 'organise co-operation between different levels of management and participation in creating the company's future, and thus improved not only planning, but the whole strategic management' (Malaska *et al*, 1984: 48). Finally, Shell, a company which pioneered the use of scenarios in corporate strategy and which has, since 1973, adopted it as a permanent strategy tool, regards the use of scenarios as a way out of the ills associated with predicting the future. Shell asserts that the use of scenarios in planning has provoked better strategic thinking throughout the company and has increased flexibility (Leemhuis, 1990; Smith, 1985). It has also, according to Wack (1985: 89), created more cohesive management at Shell because:

> When the world changes, managers need to share some common view of the new world. Otherwise, decentralized strategic decisions will result in management anarchy. Scenarios express and communicate this common view, a shared understanding of the new realities to all parts of the organization.

This may be a major reason why the popularity of the vision-building approach grew at such a tremendous rate in the 1980s and 1990s (Cummings and Worley, 1997).

Therefore, to summarise, there are a wide range of strategic planning tools and techniques available to organisations. In reviewing the main quantitative and qualitative ones, it can be seen that none are without their weaknesses. However, in tandem with the increased use of less prescriptive and more qualitative models of strategy, more qualitative tools and techniques are increasing in popularity.

## CONCLUSIONS

Just as the aim of Chapter 5 was to examine the main approaches to understanding strategy, the aim of this chapter has been to examine the main approaches to applying strategy. The chapter began by describing the three main models of strategy which organisations have tended to utilise over the last 20 years: the Competitive Forces model; the Strategic Conflict model; and the Resource-Based model. This was followed by an examination of the different organisational levels at which strategy is applied and the main forms of strategic planning tools on offer.

What the examination of these areas has shown is that, in the West at least, it is the approaches, tools and techniques of the Prescriptive stream of strategy which organisations have tended to favour. The continuing prominence of the Positioning school, through the work of Michael Porter, clearly demonstrates the enduring influence of the Prescriptive stream. This of course should not be surprising. After all, the livelihood of those who comprise the Prescriptive stream, whether they be consultants, consultancies, business schools or academics, is dependent to a large extent upon creating a market for its strategic planning products. It is also, probably, the case that when leading consultancies, business schools and large corporations are all arguing for a particular approach, there is enormous pressure on managers elsewhere to follow. To paraphrase the old slogan that 'no one ever got fired for buying IBM', one could also say, 'no one ever got fired for calling in the Boston Consultancy Group or Michael Porter'.

Nevertheless, as this chapter has also shown, the Strategic Conflict model and the Resource-Based model have been growing in importance in the last 15 years. Both tend to be located in and draw support from the Analytical stream of strategy. The Strategic Conflict model has its roots in the perspective of strategy as a battle between warring organisations. However, as explained, its renewed prominence has come both from practical concerns about the applicability of the Competitive Forces model, and, from new theoretical insights from areas such as game theory. The Resource-Based approach, on the other hand, owes much to those, such as Prahalad and Hamel (1990), who have sought to understand and explain the Japanese approach to strategy. In both cases it can be seen that strategy is conceived of as an emergent rather than a planned process. Therefore, though the Prescriptive stream of strategy is still extremely influential in determining how managers develop and implement strategies, the influence of the Analytical stream is also growing.

To return, however, to the argument developed in Chapter 5, it would be wrong to fall into the trap of seeing the Analytical stream as being the 'right' way to apply strategy and the Prescriptive as the 'wrong' way, or vice versa. Instead, it may be that approaches from both the Prescriptive and Analytical streams have much to offer organisations, depending on their circumstances or constraints. For organisations with a dominant position in a relatively stable market, an approach from the Prescriptive stream, such as the Competitive Forces model, may be suitable. Likewise for organisations seeking to enter new markets or grow their business over a long time-frame, an approach from the Analytical stream, such as the Resource-Based model, has much to commend it. Similarly, in evenly balanced competitive situations, the Strategic Conflict model may be more appropriate. This is not, though, to propose a Contingency model of strategy. Rather, as was argued in Chapter 5, what is being suggested is that organisations have a choice; they can seek to influence or mould the constraints they face in order to make them more amenable to the type or model of strategy they wish to pursue. Therefore, as indicated earlier in this chapter when looking at the work of Miles and Snow (1978), the approach to strategy an organisation adopts may have less to do with the merits of the different models on offer and more to do with the type of organisation it is and the orientation of its managers.

Nevertheless, choosing the type or model of strategy to pursue is one thing; implementing it is an entirely different matter. This is especially so if one recognises that the Prescriptive and Analytical streams of strategy have distinctly different, indeed almost opposite, perspectives on implementation. For the former, implementation flows from the organisation's strategic plan. For the latter, the strategy emerges from and is given shape by the actions and decisions organisations make on a day-to-day basis to change and adapt themselves to their circumstances. But no matter which model of strategy one subscribes to, it is only when organisations implement changes that strategies come alive. This highlights the crucial importance of organisational change. Consequently, just as this chapter and the previous one have reviewed the main arguments with regard to strategy, so the next two chapters will review the strengths, weaknesses and implications of the main approaches to change management.

## TEST YOUR LEARNING

### Short answer questions

1 What is the Competitive Forces model of strategy?

2 Define the Strategic Conflict model of strategy.

3 Briefly discuss the case for the Resource-Based model of strategy.

4 What are the three levels of strategic decision-making in organisations?

5 Give Miles and Snow's four strategic types of organisations.

6 Describe the Growth-Share Matrix.

7 What is scenario construction?

8 Briefly discuss the implications for organisational change of the following: (a) the PIMS model and (b) vision-building.

### Essay questions

1 Contrast and compare the strengths and weaknesses of quantitative and qualitative approaches to strategy.

2 To what extent can vision-building be seen as a postmodern approach?

## SUGGESTED FURTHER READING

1 Hax, CA and Majluf, NS (1996). *The Strategy Concept and Process* (2nd edition). Prentice Hall: New Jersey, USA.

Koch, R (1995). *The Financial Times Guide to Strategy*. FT Pitman: London.

There are a vast number of books on strategy but, unfortunately, no one book covers all the main tools and techniques. However, these two books do cover the main quantitative approaches to strategy.

2 Cummings, TG and Worley, CG (1997). *Organization Development and Change* (6th edition). South-Western College Publishing: Cincinnati, Ohio, USA.

Though primarily about organisational change, Cummings and Worley's book does provide a good description of and guide to vision-building.

# Chapter 7

# APPROACHES TO CHANGE MANAGEMENT

| Learning objectives |

After studying this chapter, you should be able to:

1 appreciate the importance of organisational change;

2 understand the different perspectives on the speed and magnitude of organisational change;

3 describe the main theoretical foundations of change management;

4 discuss the contribution of Kurt Lewin to managing change;

5 state the core elements of the Planned approach to change;

6 show how the Organisation Development movement has sought to improve the Planned approach;

7 list the strengths and weaknesses of the Planned approach to change.

## INTRODUCTION

This chapter follows on from the discussion of approaches to strategy in the two previous chapters. Chapters 5 and 6 were essentially concerned with approaches to determining and charting an organisation's strategic direction. Underpinning both chapters was the division between the Prescriptive stream of strategy, whose members seek to tell organisations how they should formulate strategy, and the Analytical stream of strategy, whose members seek to understand what organisations actually do to formulate strategy. The former tend to see strategy as a formal, rational and pre-planned process. The latter tend to see strategy as a more messy, less rational, emergent process. Therefore, for the Prescriptive stream, organisational change flows from, and is concerned with implementing, an organisation's predetermined strategy. For the Analytical stream, organisational change is not an outcome of strategy but the process by which it is created and given form. For both streams, change management is vitally important, whether it be for strategy implementation or development.

Consequently, this and the next chapter will focus on the approaches to planning and implementing the changes required to achieve, or shape, strategic objectives. The chapter begins by discussing the importance of change management. Following this, it goes on to examine the main perspectives on the nature of organisational change: the incremental, punctuated equilibrium, and continuous transformation models. The chapter then continues by describing the theoretical foundations of change management. In particular, it is shown that the three main schools of thought that underpin approaches to change management can be distinguished by their respective concentration on individual, group and organisation-wide issues. This leads on to an examination of the Planned approach, which was developed by Kurt Lewin in the 1940s. This approach dominated both the theory and practice of change management from then until the 1980s, when it met with increasing levels of criticism, especially from those questioning its suitability for organisations operating in dynamic and unpredictable environments. The chapter concludes by arguing that, though some of the criticism may be unjustified, the Planned approach is limited in the types of situations in which it can be applied.

## THE IMPORTANCE OF CHANGE MANAGEMENT

Neither strategy nor change management would be considered particularly important if products and markets were stable and organisational change was rare: however, that is not the case, nor – as Chapter 1 showed – has it ever been so. Change is an ever-present feature of organisational life, though many would argue that the pace and magnitude of change have increased significantly in recent years. The Institute of Management, formerly the British Institute of Management, which regularly carries out surveys of its members, has certainly found this to be true. In 1991, the Institute reported that 90 per cent of organisations in its survey were becoming 'slimmer and flatter' (Coulson-Thomas and Coe, 1991: 10). In 1992, it reported that 80 per cent of managers responding to its survey had experienced one or more corporate restructurings in their organisations in the previous five years (Wheatley, 1992b). In its 1995 survey, 70 per cent of respondents reported that their organisations had restructured in the previous two years (Institute of Management, 1995). A similar picture emerged from a study carried out around the same time by the University of Manchester Institute of Science and Technology (UMIST). This study found that 51 per cent of respondents' organisations were experiencing major transformations (Ezzamel *et al*, 1994). In 1997, surveys by both the Institute of Management (Worrall and Cooper, 1997) and the Industrial Society (1997) showed that there was no slackening in the pace of change. Indeed, the Industrial Society survey showed that some 94 per cent of respondent organisations were going, or had gone, through some form of culture change in the 1990s. Therefore, we can see that over a very short timespan, most organisations and their employees have experienced or are experiencing substantial changes in what they do and how they do it.

Undoubtedly, the way such changes are managed, and the appropriateness of the approach adopted, have major implications for the way people experience change and their perceptions of the outcome. In the various Institute of Management surveys, managers reported considerable levels of dissatisfaction with the outcome of change. The 1995 survey found that, as a result of organisational changes, managers' workloads had increased greatly and that one in five was working an extra 15 hours per week. Many also reported that increased workloads were preventing them from devoting adequate time to long-term strategic planning or to their own training and development needs. Indeed, the Institute's 1997 survey of managers concluded that 'the restructuring that has taken place in UK businesses in the last 12 months has had a massively negative effect on employee loyalty, morale, motivation and perception of job security' (Worrall and Cooper, 1997: 33). In addition, the Institute's 1998 survey found that, for a majority of respondents, 'the impact of restructuring had been to deplete the organisation of people with key skills and experience' (Worrall and Cooper, 1998: 34).

Given the vast literature on the topic, it may appear strange that many managers have doubts about both the approach to and outcome of change. Yet the reality, according to these surveys, is that organisations can and do experience severe problems in managing change effectively. It is clear that to manage change successfully, even on a small scale, can be complex and difficult. The literature abounds with evidence and examples of change projects that have gone wrong, some disastrously so (*see* Brindle, 1998b; Burnes and Weekes, 1989; Bywater, 1997; Cummings and Worley, 1997; Howarth, 1988; Kanter *et al*, 1992; Kelly, 1982a, b; Kotter, 1996; Stace and Dunphy, 1994; Stickland, 1998). Therefore, there is substantial evidence that managers have good reason to be anxious about organisational change.

Change comes in all shapes, sizes and forms and, for this reason, it is difficult to establish an accurate picture of the degree of difficulty organisations face in managing change successfully. However, there are three types of organisational change which, because of their perceived importance, have received considerable attention: the introduction of new technology in the 1980s; the adoption of Total Quality Management (TQM) over the last 15 years; and, from the early 1990s, the application of Business Process Re-engineering (BPR). All three, in their time, were hailed as 'revolutionary' approaches to improving performance and competitiveness.

The impact of the (so-called) Microelectronics Revolution of the 1980s, which saw the rapid expansion of computers and computer-based processes into most areas of organisational life, was the subject of a great many studies. These found that the failure rate of new technology change projects was anywhere between 40 per cent and 70 per cent (AT Kearney, 1989; Bessant and Haywood, 1985; Burnes and Weekes, 1989; McKracken, 1986; New, 1989; Smith and Tranfield, 1987; Voss, 1985). Nor do the problems in this area appear to be limited to the 1980s. In 1998, the UK government had to admit that its £170 million programme to replace the computer system which holds the National Insurance records of everyone in the country was in such a mess that the system had collapsed, throwing its social security system into turmoil (Brindle, 1998b, 1999).

The move by European countries to adopt Total Quality Management began in the mid-1980s. At its simplest, TQM is an organisation-wide effort to improve quality through changes in structure, practices, systems and, above all, attitudes (Dale and Cooper, 1992). Though seen as pre-eminently a Japanese innovation, the basic TQM techniques were developed in the USA in the 1950s (Crosby, 1979; Deming, 1982; Juran, 1988; Taguchi, 1986). Though TQM appears to be central to the success of Japanese companies, the experience of Western companies has been that it is difficult to introduce and sustain. Indeed, one of the founders of the TQM movement, Philip Crosby (1979), claimed that over 90 per cent of TQM initiatives by American organisations fail. Though a 90 per cent failure rate seems incredibly high, studies of the adoption of TQM by companies in the UK and other European countries show that they too have experienced a similarly high failure rate – perhaps as much as 80 per cent or more (AT Kearney, 1992; Cruise O'Brien and Voss, 1992; Dale, 1999; Economist Intelligence Unit, 1992; Whyte and Witcher, 1992; Witcher, 1993; Zairi *et al*, 1994).

Business Process Re-engineering was hailed as 'the biggest business innovation of the 1990s' (Mill, 1994: 26). Wastell *et al* (1994: 23) stated that BPR refers to 'initiatives, large and small, radical and conservative, whose common theme is the achievement of significant improvements in organizational performance by augmenting the efficiency and effectiveness of key business processes.' Though newer, and therefore less well documented, than either new technology or TQM, Wastell *et al* (1994: 37) concluded from the available evidence that 'BPR initiatives have typically achieved much less than they promised'. A study by Breslin and McGann (1998) estimated the failure rate at 60 per cent, and one by Bywater (1997) put the figure at 70 per cent; other studies of BPR have come to similar conclusions (Coombs and Hull, 1994; Short and Venkatraman, 1992). Indeed, Michael Hammer, who is credited with starting the BPR craze, agrees with Bywater and concedes that 70 per cent of BPR initiatives ultimately fail (Stickland, 1998).

Therefore, even these three types of well-established change initiatives, for which a great deal of information, advice and assistance was and is available, are no guarantee of success. This is perhaps why, throughout the 1990s, managers consistently identified the difficulty of managing change as one of the key obstacles to the increased competitiveness of their organisations (Hanson, 1993; Industrial Society, 1997; Worrall and Cooper, 1997). As the following will show, one of the reasons why successful change is such an elusive creature may be because there is a great deal of dispute about how often and to what degree organisations need to change.

## THE FREQUENCY AND MAGNITUDE OF ORGANISATIONAL CHANGE

As has been mentioned often in this book, the view which many leading commentators take is that organisations are changing at a faster pace and in a more fundamental way than ever before (Kanter *et al*, 1997; Kotter, 1996; Peters, 1997a). These commentators judge the present level of organisational change to be unprecedented, although – as Chapter 5 noted – the history of the past 200 years could well be characterised as successive periods of unprecedented change. Obviously, an appreciation of whether organisational change is to be a continuing feature or a one-off event and whether it is on a small or large scale play a key role in judging the appropriateness of particular approaches to managing change. It is, therefore, important to go beyond the tabloid-like headlines thrown up by writers such as Tom Peters and to examine the main models of organisational change that are currently being promoted and, also, to recognise that there are strong disagreements about the nature and pace of change that organisations experience. In this respect, there are three current models that are prominent in the literature.

## The incremental model of change

Advocates of this view see change as being a process whereby individual parts of an organisation deal incrementally and separately with one problem and one goal at a time. By managers responding to pressures in their local internal and external environments in this way, over time, their organisations become transformed. As Miller and Friesen (1984: 222) state:

> The incrementalist perspective on change has been around a, relatively, long time. It stems from the work of Lindblom (1959) and Cyert and March (1963), and was further developed by Hedberg et al (1976) and especially Quinn (1980b and 1982). Quinn argues that strategic change is best viewed as 'muddling through with purpose,' using a continuous, evolving and consensus building approach.

As Pettigrew *et al* (1992: 14) note, 'The received wisdom therefore is that change will take place through successive, limited and negotiated shifts'. Though Quinn (1980b, 1982) and others have marshalled considerable support for the increment-alist perspective from Western sources, in recent years the pre-eminent exemplars of incremental change have been Japanese companies (Hamel and Prahalad, 1989). As described in Chapter 3, Japanese companies have an enviable track record of achieving fierce competitiveness through pursuing incremental change year in, year out. Dunphy and Stace (1992) also advocated this approach for Western companies, arguing for a form of managed incrementalism that avoids both the stagnation engendered by fine tuning and the brutality associated with rapid corporate transformations. However, as Mintzberg (1978) argued, though organisations do go through long periods of incremental change, these are often interspersed with brief periods of rapid and revolutionary change. Indeed, given the turbulence of the last 20 years, some writers have argued that it is now the periods of stability which are brief and the revolutionary change periods which are long, at least in Western firms (Handy, 1989). Not surprisingly, this has led to an increased interest in how organisations move between periods of stability and instability.

## The punctuated equilibrium model of organisational transformation

This somewhat inelegantly titled approach to change:

> ...depicts organizations as evolving through relatively long periods of stability (equilibrium periods) in their basic patterns of activity that are punctuated by relatively short bursts of fundamental change (revolutionary periods). Revolutionary periods substantively disrupt established activity patterns and install the basis for new equilibrium periods.
> (Romanelli and Tushman, 1994: 1141)

The punctuated equilibrium model is associated with the work of Miller and Friesen (1984), Tushman and Romanelli (1985), and Gersick (1991). The inspiration for this model arises from two sources: first, from the challenge to Charles Darwin's gradualist model of evolution in the natural sciences: Steven Jay Gould (1989), in particular, mounted a case for a punctuated equilibrium model of evolution; and second, from the assertion that whilst most organisations do appear to fit the incrementalist model of change for a period of time, there does come a point when they go through a period of rapid and fundamental change (Gersick, 1991). However, as even Romanelli and Tushman (1994: 1142) admit, 'Despite the growing prominence and pervasiveness of punctuated equilibrium theory, little research has explored the empirical validity of the model's basic arguments.' This has led some to reject both the incremental and punctuated models of change (Brown and Eisenhardt, 1997).

## The continuous transformation model of change

The argument put forward by proponents of this model is that, in order to survive, organisations must develop the ability to change themselves continuously in a fundamental manner. This is particularly the case in fast-moving sectors such as retail where, as Greenwald (1996: 54) notes, 'If you look at the best retailers out there, they are constantly reinventing themselves.' Brown and Eisenhardt (1997: 1) maintain that:

> For firms such as Intel, Wal-Mart, 3M, Hewlett-Packard and Gillette, the ability to change rapidly and continuously, especially by developing new products, is not only a core competence, it is also at the heart of their cultures. For these firms, change is not the rare, episodic phenomenon described by the punctuated equilibrium model but, rather, it is endemic to the way these organizations compete. Moreover, in high-velocity industries with short product cycles and rapidly-shifting competitive landscapes, the ability to engage in rapid and relentless continuous change is a crucial capability for survival...

The underpinning rationale for the continuous transformation model is that the environment in which organisations operate is changing, and will continue to change, rapidly, radically and unpredictably. Only by continuous transformation will organisations be able to keep aligned with their environment and thus survive. Though this view has many adherents, there are two groups who are its main promoters. The first is the Culture–Excellence school. This group, especially

Tom Peters (1997a, b) and Rosabeth Moss Kanter *et al* (1997), have been arguing for a continuous transformation model of change since the early 1980s. However, as argued in Chapter 3, they provide little solid empirical evidence to support their view. The second group are those who seek to apply Chaos Theory, which was developed in the physical sciences, to organisation theory (e.g. Stacey, 1993). The basis of Chaos Theory, which was discussed in Chapter 5, lies in the assumption that all organisations operate in an environment that is chaotic (dynamic and unpredictable). In order to cope with external chaos, it is argued, they must promote continuous internal chaos. The problems with this perspective, as Stickland (1998) shows, are that (a) it is not clear that one can readily apply theories from the physical sciences to the social sciences, as is demonstrated by the fact that even proponents of its use in the social sciences are equivocal on this point; and (b) there is little strong evidence to support the chaos view.

Nevertheless, as the popularity of the work of Peters and Kanter has shown, there is growing support for the continuous change model. However, there does seem to be some confusion as to what continuous change is. Is it very fast incremental change or more frequent punctuated change? Perhaps the most cogent description of the continuous change model is put forward by Brown and Eisenhardt (1997: 28) who, in looking at a number of firms in the computer industry, argued that:

> The rate and scale of innovation within the industry and our firms was such that the term 'incremental' seemed, in retrospect, stretched. Yet it was not radical innovation such as DNA cloning, either. As one manager observed, 'I don't know if I'd call this innovation or breakthrough, but it's probably somewhere in between that and next generation.' Similarly, managers described 'constantly reinventing' themselves. This too seemed more than incremental ... but also not the massive, rare, and risky change of the organizational strategy literature. And so we realized that we were probably looking at a third kind of process that is neither incremental nor radical and that does not fit the punctuated equilibrium model...

In attempting to bring more precision to their 'third kind' of change, Brown and Eisenhardt (1997: 29) use the analogy of complex systems in nature:

> Like organizations, complex systems have large numbers of independent yet interacting actors. Rather than ever reaching a stable equilibrium, the most adaptive of these complex systems (e.g., intertidal zones) keep changing continuously by remaining at the poetically termed 'edge of chaos' that exists between order and disorder. By staying in this intermediate zone, these systems never quite settle into a stable equilibrium but never quite fall apart. Rather, these systems, which stay constantly poised between order and disorder, exhibit the most prolific, complex and continuous change...

Though the incremental, punctuated equilibrium and continuous change models all have some appeal, and some empirical support, it is difficult to find evidence, other than gut instinct, that supports one above the others. Also, it has to be acknowledged that the main proponents of these three models gather their data in different ways and for different purposes. In developing the incremental model, Quinn, for example, gathered his data from individual executives and was interested in their intentions and perceptions. Miller and Friesen, though, in developing the punctuated equilibrium model, tracked the behaviour, actions and outcomes of firms. Peters appears to cite selectively those individuals and organisations whose actions and views support the case for continuous transformation. Therefore, it is perhaps not surprising that they came up with different models of change.

Another, complementary, explanation as to why it is difficult to find support for one of these three models above the others is offered by the concept of 'organisational life cycles' (Kimberley and Miles, 1980). As Pettigrew *et al* (1992: 23) comment:

> In the most schematic form of the [organisational life cycle] model, birth, early development, maturity, decline and death can all be seen as distinct organizational stages which may be characterized by different organizational processes.

If this is the case, then it may well be that the three models of change apply to different stages in an organisation's life cycle. Support for this view might also come from the population ecologists (*see* Chapter 5) who would expect that, in the general population of organisations, some would be changing slowly, some would exhibit periodic bouts of large-scale change, and others would appear to be changing continuously and fundamentally.

There are, of course, other explanations for the variance between these three models; for example, the evidence to support them comes from organisations operating in different industries with different rates of change, or who are at different phases of the economic cycle. So, there is no shortage of explanations as to why we are presented with different models of change; what there is, though, is a shortage of evidence which might help us resolve the conflict between them. Indeed, it might prove very difficult to assemble the research necessary to provide any convincing evidence. It would need to be longitudinal, perhaps over 20, 30 or even 40 years. The research would also need to cover a large group of diverse organisations covering a number of industries and countries. Another problem lies in the thorny issue of terminology. For example, is Total Quality Management an incremental process, a revolutionary change or merely a passing fad (Van der Wiele, 1998)? A further issue, from the postmodernist perspective, is that all three models may be equally valid but represent competing realities or versions of events; there is no one absolute truth, as interpretations will vary depending on the interpreter (Hassard, 1993; Hatch, 1997).

This is not to argue that the three models of change should be dismissed. On the contrary, they draw our attention to serious issues and debates. The models make us aware, importantly, of the broad range of change situations that organisations experience and, equally, of the need to judge approaches to change management according to their appropriateness for the different forms of change. Also, whatever particular form change takes, and whatever objectives it seeks to achieve, organisations cannot expect to achieve success unless those responsible for managing it understand the different approaches on offer and can match them to their circumstances and preferences. On this basis, understanding the theory and practice of change management is not an optional extra but an essential requisite for survival.

## THEORETICAL FOUNDATIONS

Change management is not a distinct discipline with rigid and clearly defined boundaries. Rather, the theory and practice of change management draws on a number of social science disciplines and traditions. Though this is one of its strengths, it does make the task of tracing its origins and defining its core concepts more difficult than might otherwise be the case.

The task is complicated further by the simple fact that the social sciences themselves are interwoven. As an example, theories of management education and learning, which help us to understand the behaviour of those who manage change, cannot be fully discussed without reference to theories of child and adult psychology. Neither can these be discussed without touching on theories of knowledge (epistemology), which is itself a veritable philosophical minefield.

The challenge, then, is to range wide enough to capture the theoretical foundations of change management, without straying so far into its related disciplines that clarity and understanding suffer. In order to achieve this delicate balance, the examination will be limited to the three schools of thought that form the central planks on which change management theory stands:

- the Individual Perspective school
- the Group Dynamics school
- the Open Systems school

### The Individual Perspective school

The supporters of this school are split into two camps: the Behaviourists and the Gestalt-Field psychologists. The former view behaviour as resulting from an individual's interaction with their environment. Gestalt-Field psychologists, on the other hand, believe that this is only a partial explanation. Instead, they argue that an individual's behaviour is the product of environment and reason.

In Behaviourist theory, all behaviour is learned; the individual is the passive recipient of external and objective data. Among the earliest to work in the field of conditioning of behaviour was Pavlov (1927). In an experiment which has now passed into folklore, he discovered that a dog could be 'taught' to salivate at the ringing of a bell, by conditioning the dog to associate the sound of the bell with food. Arising from this, one of the basic principles of the Behaviourists is that human actions are conditioned by their expected consequences. Behaviour that is rewarded tends to be repeated, and behaviour that is ignored tends not to be. Therefore, in order to change behaviour, it is necessary to change the conditions that cause it (Skinner, 1974).

In practice, behaviour modification involves the manipulation of reinforcing stimuli so as to reward desired activity. The aim is to reward immediately all instances of the wanted behaviour, but to ignore all instances of the unwanted behaviour (because even negative recognition can act as a reinforcer). This is based on the principle of extinction; a behaviour will stop eventually if it is not rewarded (Lovell, 1980). Not surprisingly, given the period when it emerged, the Behaviourist approach mirrors in many respects that of the Classical school, portraying humans as cogs in a machine, who respond solely to external stimuli.

For Gestalt-Field theorists, learning is a process of gaining or changing insights, outlooks, expectations or thought patterns. In explaining an individual's behaviour, this group takes into account not only a person's actions and the responses these elicit, but also the interpretation the individual places on these. As French and Bell (1984: 140) explain:

> Gestalt therapy is based on the belief that persons function as whole, total organisms. And each person possesses positive and negative characteristics that must be 'owned up to' and permitted expression. People get into trouble when they get fragmented, when they do not accept their total selves ... Basically, one must come to terms with oneself, ... must stop blocking off awareness, authenticity, and the like by dysfunctional behaviours.

Therefore, from the Gestalt-Field perspective, behaviour is not just a product of external stimuli; rather it arises from how the individual uses reason to interpret these stimuli. Consequently, the Gestalt-Field proponents seek to help individual members of an organisation change their understanding of themselves and the situation in question, which, they believe, in turn will lead to changes in behaviour (Smith *et al*, 1982). The Behaviourists, on the other hand, seek to achieve organisational change solely by modifying the external stimuli acting upon the individual.

Both groups in the Individual Perspective school have proved influential in the management of change; indeed, some writers even advocate using them in tandem. This is certainly the case with advocates of the Culture–Excellence school, who recommend the use of both strong individual incentives (external stimuli) and discussion, involvement and debate (internal reflection) in order to bring about organisational change (*see* Chapter 3).

This combining of extrinsic and intrinsic motivators owes much to the work of the Human Relations movement, who (through the work of Maslow, 1943) stress the need for both forms of stimuli in order to influence human behaviour. However, though acknowledging the role of the individual, the Human Relations movement also draws attention to the importance of social groups in organisations, as do the Group Dynamics school.

## The Group Dynamics school

As a component of change theory, this school has the longest history (Schein, 1969). Its emphasis is on bringing about organisational change through teams or work groups, rather than individuals (Bernstein, 1968). The rationale behind this, according to Lewin (1947a, b), is that because people in organisations work in groups, individual behaviour must be seen, modified or changed in the light of groups' prevailing practices and norms.

Lewin (1947a, b) postulated that group behaviour is an intricate set of symbolic interactions and forces which not only affect group structures, but also modify individual behaviour. Therefore, he argued that individual behaviour is a function of the group environment or 'field', as he termed it. This field produces forces, tensions, emanating from group pressures on each of its members. An individual's behaviour at any given time, according to Lewin, is an interplay between the intensity and valence (whether the force is positive or negative) of the forces impinging on the person. Because of this, he asserted that a group is never in a 'steady state of equilibrium', but is in a continuous process of mutual adaptation which he termed 'quasi-stationary equilibrium'.

To bring about change, therefore, it is useless to concentrate on changing the behaviour of individuals, according to the Group Dynamics school. The individual in isolation is constrained by group pressures to conform. The focus of change must be at the group level and should concentrate on influencing and changing the group's norms, roles and values (Cummings and Huse, 1989; French and Bell, 1984; Smith *et al*, 1982).

*Norms* are rules or standards that define what people should do, think or feel in a given situation. For the Group Dynamics school, what is important in analysing group norms is the difference between implicit and explicit norms. Explicit norms are formal, written rules which are known by, and applicable to, all. Implicit norms are informal and unwritten, and individuals may not even be consciously aware of them. Nevertheless, implicit norms have been identified as playing a vital role in dictating the actions of group members.

*Roles* are patterns of behaviour to which individuals and groups are expected to conform. In organisational terms, roles are formally defined by job descriptions and performance targets, though in practice they are also strongly influenced by norms and values as well. Even in their work life, individuals rarely have only one role. For example, a production manager may also be secretary of the company's social club, a clerical officer may also be a shop steward, and a supervisor may also be the company's safety representative. A similar situation exists for groups. A group's main role may be to perform a particular activity or service, but it might also be expected to pursue continuous development, maintain and develop its skills, and act as a repository of expert knowledge for others in the organisation. Clearly, where members of a group and the group itself are required to conform to a number of different roles, the scope for role conflict or role ambiguity is ever-present. Unless roles are both clearly defined and compatible, the result can be sub-optimal for the individual (in terms of stress) and for the group (in terms of lack of cohesion and poor performance).

*Values* are ideas and beliefs which individuals and groups hold about what is right and wrong. Values refer not so much to what people do or think or feel in a given situation; instead they relate to the broader principles which lie behind these. Values are a more problematic concept than either norms or roles. Norms and roles can, with diligence, be more or less accurately determined. Values, on the other hand, are more difficult to determine because group members are not always consciously aware of, or can easily articulate, the values that influence their behaviour. Therefore, questioning people and observing their actions is unlikely to produce a true picture of group values. Nevertheless, the concept itself is seen as very important in determining, and changing, patterns of behaviour.

Despite its limited focus, the Group Dynamics school has proved to be very influential in developing both the theory and practice of change management. This can be seen by the very fact that it is now usual for organisations to view themselves as comprising groups and teams, rather than merely collections of individuals (Mullins, 1989).

As French and Bell (1984: 127–9) pointed out, the importance given to teams is reflected in the fact that:

> ... the most important single group of interventions in OD [Organisation Development] are team-building activities, the goals of which are the improved and increased effectiveness of various teams within the organization. ... The ... team-building meeting has the goal of improving the team's effectiveness through better management of task demands, relationship demands, and group processes. ... [The team] analyzes its way of doing things, and attempts to develop strategies to improve its operation.

In so doing, norms, roles and values are examined, challenged and, where necessary, changed.

Nevertheless, despite the emphasis that many place on groups within organisations, others argue that the correct approach is one that deals with an organisation as a whole.

## The Open Systems school

Having examined approaches to change which emphasise the importance of groups and individuals, we now come to one whose primary point of reference is the organisation in its entirety. The Open Systems school (as mentioned in Chapter 2) sees organisations as composed of a number of interconnected sub-systems. It follows that any change to one part of the system will have an impact on other parts of the system, and, in turn, on its overall performance (Scott, 1987). The Open Systems school's approach to change is based on a method of describing and evaluating these sub-systems, in order to determine how they need to be changed so as to improve the overall functioning of the organisation.

However, this school does not just see organisations as systems in isolation; they are 'open' systems. Organisations are seen as open in two respects. First, they are open to, and interact with, their external environment. Second, they are open internally: the various sub-systems interact with each other. Therefore, internal changes in one area affect other areas, and in turn have an impact on the external environment, and vice versa (Buckley, 1968).

The objective of the Open Systems approach is to structure the functions of a business in such a manner that, through clearly defined lines of co-ordination and interdependence, the overall business objectives are collectively pursued. The emphasis is on achieving overall synergy, rather than on optimising the performance of any one individual part *per se* (Mullins, 1989).

Miller (1967) argues that there are four principal organisational sub-systems:

- **The organisational goals and values sub-system**. This comprises the organisation's stated objectives and the values it wishes to promote in order to attain them. To operate effectively, the organisation has to ensure that its goals and values are compatible not only with each other, but also with its external and internal environments.

- **The technical sub-system**. This is the specific combination of knowledge, techniques and technologies which an organisation requires in order to function. Once again, the concern here is with the compatibility and appropriateness of these in relation to an organisation's particular circumstances.

- **The psychosocial sub-system**. This is also variously referred to as organisational climate and organisational culture. In essence, it is the fabric of role relationships, values and norms that binds people together and makes them citizens of a particular miniature society (the organisation). It is influenced by an organisation's environment, history and employees, as well as its tasks, technology and structures. If the psychosocial sub-system is weak, fragmented or inappropriate, then instead of binding the organisation together, it may have the opposite effect.

- **The managerial sub-system**. This spans the entire organisation. It is responsible for relating an organisation to its environment, setting goals, determining values, developing comprehensive strategic and operational plans, designing structure and establishing control processes. It is this sub-system that has the responsibility for consciously directing an organisation and ensuring that it attains its objectives. If the managerial sub-system fails, so does the rest of an organisation.

The Open Systems school is concerned with understanding organisations in their entirety; therefore, it attempts to take a holistic rather than a particularistic perspective. This is reflected in its approach to change. According to Burke (1980), this is informed by three factors:

1 *Sub-systems are interdependent*. If alterations are made to one part of an organisation without taking account of its dependence or impact on the rest of the organisation, the outcome may be sub-optimal.

2 *Training, as a mechanism for change, is unlikely to succeed on its own*. This is because it concentrates on the individual and not the organisational level. As Burke (1980: 75) argues, 'although training may lead to individual change and in some cases to small group change, there is scant evidence that attempting to change the individual will in turn change the organisation'.

**3** *In order to be successful, organisations have to tap and direct the energy and talent of their workforce.* This requires the removal of obstacles which prevent this, and the provision of positive reinforcement which promotes it. Given that this is likely to require changes to such things as norms, reward systems and work structures, it must be approached from an organisational, rather than individual or group, perspective.

Though the Open Systems perspective has attracted much praise, attention has also been drawn to its alleged shortcomings. Butler (1985: 345), for example, while hailing it as a major step forward in understanding organisational change, points out that, 'Social systems are extremely dynamic and complex entities that often defy descriptions and analysis. Therefore, one can easily get lost in attempting to sort out all the cause-and-effect relationships.' Beach (1980: 138), in a similar vein, argues that Open Systems theory:

> ... does not comprise a consistent, articulated, coherent theory. Much of it constitutes a high level of abstraction. To be really useful to the professional practice of management, its spokesmen and leaders must move to a more concrete and operationally useful range.

Despite these criticisms, the level of support for this approach, from eminent theorists such as Burns and Stalker (1961), Joan Woodward (1965) and Lawrence and Lorsch (1967), is formidable. This is why, as explained in Chapter 2, it has proved so influential.

## Summary

In looking at the three schools which form the central planks of change management theory, three major points stand out. First, with the exception of the Behaviourists, not only do they stand, generally, in sharp contrast to the mechanistic approach of the Classical school towards organisations and people, but also, in their approach to individuals, groups and organisations as a whole, they form a link to the emerging organisational paradigms that were discussed in Chapter 3. Indeed, it might be possible to go further and say that these three schools provide many of the core concepts of the new paradigms, especially in respect to teamwork and organisational learning. If this is so, the claim (by Kanter, 1989; Senge, 1990; and others) that these new forms of organisation are a radical break with the past may have to be reconsidered.

Second, the three theoretical perspectives on change focus on different aspects of organisational life and, therefore, each has different implications for what change takes place and how it is managed. It follows that, as with the three models in the previous section, any approach to managing change should be judged by whether or not it is applicable to all or only some of the types of change covered by the Individual, Group and Systems schools.

Third, though each school puts itself forward as the most effective, if not the only, approach to change, they are not necessarily in conflict or competition. Indeed, it could well be argued that they are complementary approaches. The key task, which will be examined in more detail later in this and the next chapter, is to identify the circumstances in which each is appropriate: does the problem or the objective of change lie at the level of the organisation, group or individual? Can any of these levels be tackled in isolation from the others?

The Open Systems perspective may be correct: change at one level or in one area should take into account the effect it will have elsewhere in the organisation. However, whether the perspective adopted is organisation-wide, or limited to groups and individuals, in the final analysis, what is it that is being changed? The answer, surely, is the behaviour of individuals and groups, because organisations are, as the proponents of these perspectives admit, social systems. To change anything requires the co-operation and consent, or at least acquiescence, of the groups and individuals who make up an organisation, for it is only through their behaviour that the structures, technologies, systems and procedures of an organisation move from being abstract concepts to concrete realities. This is made even plainer in the remainder of this chapter and in the next chapter, where we examine the main approaches to managing organisational change.

## THE PLANNED APPROACH TO ORGANISATIONAL CHANGE

Change has always been a feature of organisational life, though many would argue that the frequency and magnitude of change are greater now than ever before. Planned change is a term first coined by Kurt Lewin to distinguish change that was consciously embarked upon and planned by an organisation, as averse to types of change that might come about by accident, by impulse or that might be forced on an organisation (Marrow, 1969). However, just as the practice of change management is dependent on a number of factors, not least the particular school of thought involved, so, not surprisingly, even amongst those advocating Planned change, a variety of different models of change management have arisen over the years. Though these were devised to meet the needs of particular organisations, or arose from a specific school of thought, nevertheless, the Planned approach to change is most closely associated with the practice of Organization Development (OD) and indeed lies at its core. According to French and Bell (1995: 1–2):

> Organization development is a unique organizational improvement strategy that emerged in the late 1950s and early 1960s. ... [It] has evolved into an integrated framework of theories and practices capable of solving or helping to solve most of the important problems confronting the human side of organizations. Organization development is about people and organizations and people in organizations and how they function. OD is also about planned change, that is getting individuals, teams and organizations to function better. Planned change involves common sense, hard work applied diligently over time, a systematic, goal-oriented approach, and valid knowledge about organizational dynamics and how to change them. Valid knowledge derives from the behavioural sciences such as psychology, social psychology, sociology, anthropology, systems theory, and the practice of management.

Underpinning OD is a set of values, assumptions and ethics which emphasise its humanistic orientation and its commitment to organisational effectiveness. These values have been articulated by many writers over the years (Conner, 1977; Gellerman *et al*, 1990; Warwick and Thompson, 1980). One of the earliest attempts was by French and Bell (1973), who proposed four core values for OD:

- The belief that the needs and aspirations of human beings provide the prime reasons for the existence of organisations within society.
- Change agents believe that organisational prioritisation is a legitimate part of organisational culture.
- Change agents are committed to increased organisational effectiveness.
- OD places a high value on the democratisation of organisations through power equalisation.

In applying these core values, in a survey of OD practitioners, Hurley *et al* (1992) found there were five clear values that they espoused:

1 empowering employees to act,
2 creating openness in communications,
3 facilitating ownership of the change process and its outcomes,
4 the promotion of a culture of collaboration,
5 the promotion of continuous learning.

Within the OD field, there are a number of major theorists and practitioners who have contributed their own models and techniques to its advancement (e.g. Argyris, 1962; Bechard, 1969; Blake and Mouton, 1976; French and Bell, 1973). OD also shares some common concepts with, and sits easily alongside, the Human Relations movement. Indeed, Douglas McGregor, a key figure in the Human Relations movement, also played a significant role in the early stages of OD (*see* McGregor, 1967). However, despite this, there is general agreement that the OD movement grew out of, and became the standard bearer for, Kurt Lewin's pioneering work on behavioural science in general, and his development of Action Research and Planned change in particular (Cummings and Worley, 1997).

## Kurt Lewin and Planned change

Though there has been an increasing tendency in recent years to play down the significance of his work for contemporary organisations, few social scientists can have received the level of praise and admiration that has been heaped upon Kurt Lewin. As Edgar Schein (1988: 239) enthusiastically commented:

> There is little question that the intellectual father of contemporary theories of applied behavioural science, action research and planned change is Kurt Lewin. His seminal work on leadership style and the experiments on planned change which took place in World War II in an effort to change consumer behaviour launched a whole generation of research in group dynamics and the implementation of change programs.

Indeed, in his memorial address for Kurt Lewin delivered at the 1947 Convention of the American Psychological Association, Edward C Tolman said, 'Freud the clinician and Lewin the experimentalist – these are the two men whose names will stand out before all others in the history of our psychological era' (quoted in Marrow, 1969: ix).

Before we discuss Lewin's contribution to the development of organisational behaviour, it is necessary to know something of the man. Lewin was born on 9 September 1890 in the small village of Mogilno in the Prussian province of Posen, now a part of Poland. For a Jew growing up in Germany, especially Prussia, at this time, officially approved anti-semitism was a fact of life. Few Jews, even if they met the educational requirements, could expect to achieve a responsible post in the civil service or universities. Despite this, and even though his chances of becoming a full professor with tenure were extremely small, in 1910 Lewin registered at the University of Berlin, was awarded a doctorate in 1916 and, after the First World War, he went on to teach at the University. Though he was never awarded tenured status, in the 1920s Lewin achieved a growing international reputation as a leading thinker, and especially as an experimentalist in the field of psychology. However, with the rise of the Nazi Party, Lewin recognised that the position of Jews in Germany was increasingly threatened. The election of Adolf Hitler as Chancellor in 1933 was the final straw for him, so he resigned from the University and moved to America (Marrow, 1969).

In America, Lewin had a growing body of supporters who managed to find him a job, first as a 'refugee scholar' at Cornell University and then, from 1935 to 1945, at the University of Iowa. Having already built a reputation as a theorist and experimenter, during the 14 years up to his death in 1947, as Schein indicated, he was credited with laying the foundations for behavioural science.

In the period leading up to and during the Second World War, Lewin was interested in the behaviour of individuals and groups in society at large rather than within the confines of organisations. For most of his life, Lewin's main preoccupation was the resolution of social conflict and, in particular, the problems of minority or disadvantaged groups, whether they be Jews in Germany or blacks and Asians in America. Underpinning this preoccupation was a strong belief that only the permeation of democratic values into all facets of society could prevent the worst extremes of social conflict.

During the years of the Second World War, much of Lewin's work was focused on the American war effort. This included his famous study aimed at persuading American housewives to buy cheaper cuts of meat (Lewin, 1943). With the end of the Second World War, Lewin set out to pursue his work through two new institutions, both launched in 1945. First, he secured financial support to establish his own research centre: the Research Center for Group Dynamics at the Massachusetts Institute of Technology. The aim of the Center was to look at all aspects of group behaviour, especially the conditions and forces which bring about change or resist it. At the same time, he was also chief architect and senior consultant to the Commission on Community Interrelations (CCI). Founded and funded by the American Jewish Congress, it was originally envisaged as a body directed at identifying the roots of, and eradicating, anti-semitism; however, partly at Lewin's insistence, when it was launched its aim was the eradication of discrimination against all minority groups. As Lewin wrote at the time, 'We Jews will have to fight for ourselves and we will do so strongly and with good conscience. We also know that the fight of the Jews is part of the fight of all minorities for democratic equality of rights and opportunities...' (quoted in Marrow, 1969: 175).

In the two years from 1945 until his death in 1947, Lewin worked tirelessly at both the Center for Group Dynamics and the CCI. He was also influential in establishing the Tavistock Institute in the UK and its journal, *Human Relations* (Jaques, 1998; Marrow, 1969). In addition, in 1946, the Connecticut State Inter-Racial Commission asked Lewin to help train leaders and conduct research on the most effective means of combatting racial and religious prejudice in communities. This led to the development of sensitivity training and the creation, in 1947, of the now famous National Training Laboratories (Marrow, 1969). However, his huge workload took its toll on his health, and on 11 February 1947 he died of a heart attack. His close friends and colleagues had little doubt that, at the age of 56, he had literally worked himself to death.

## Lewin's work

Though he died relatively young, his output and influence were substantial. Lewin was a humanitarian and a fierce believer in the power of democracy to improve people's lives. The driving force behind his work was his belief that only by resolving social conflict, whether it be religious, racial, marital or industrial, could the human condition be improved. In developing an approach to resolving social conflict, Lewin believed that the key issue was to facilitate learning and so enable individuals to understand and restructure their perceptions of the world around them. Though a psychologist by training, Lewin rejected the idea that an individual could only be understood in relation to his or her individual personality. Instead, a unifying theme of much of his work is the view that, as Allport (1948: vii) commented, 'the group to which an individual belongs is the ground for his perceptions, his feelings and his actions'.

It is Lewin's attempt to understand and explain the interdependence of the individual and the group, and the forces which maintain the group's status quo, that underpins most of Lewin's work. Out of this he developed the concept of 'field theory' (or topological psychology, as he also referred to it). As mentioned when discussing Group Dynamics earlier, he argued that to understand any situation it was necessary that: 'One should view the present situation – the *status quo* – as being maintained by certain conditions or forces' (Lewin, 1943b: 172). As stated earlier, Lewin (1947b) believed that group behaviour is an intricate set of symbolic interactions and forces, that create a 'field' or group environment. These forces not only affect group structures, but also modify individual behaviour.

According to Lewin, an individual's behaviour at any given time is an interplay between the intensity and valence (whether the force is positive or negative) of the forces impinging on the person.

Lewin's view was that if one could identify, plot and establish the potency of these forces, then it would be possible not only to understand why individuals and groups act as they do, but also what forces would need to be diminished or strengthened in order to bring about change. However, Lewin believed that though a field existed and could be measured, it was also in a state of flux. Because of this, he asserted that a group is never in a 'steady state of equilibrium', but is in a continuous process of mutual adaptation which he termed 'quasi-stationary equilibrium', i.e. never fully stable but nevertheless exhibiting a certain degree of constancy in terms of key behaviours and beliefs. Though field theory is probably the least understood element of Lewin's work, it provides the theoretical underpinning for the other main areas of his work, especially Group Dynamics, as discussed earlier.

In terms of organisational change, Lewin's key contributions came in the form of Action Research and the Three-Step model of change.

### Action Research

This term was coined by Lewin (1946) in an article entitled 'Action Research and Minority Problems'. Though originally conceived of as a collective approach to solving important social problems such as racial and religious prejudice, it rapidly began to be applied mainly to organisational problems. In the UK, soon after its emergence, it was adopted by the Tavistock Institute, and used to improve managerial competency and efficiency in the, then, newly nationalised coal industry. Since then it has acquired strong adherents on both sides of the Atlantic (Elden and Chisholm, 1993; Marrow, 1969). According to French and Bell (1984: 98–9):

> Action Research is research on action with the goal of making that action more effective. Action refers to programs and interventions designed to solve a problem or improve a condition ... action research is the process of systematically collecting research data about an ongoing system relative to some objective, goal, or need of that system; feeding these data back into the system; taking action by altering selected variables within the system based both on the data and on hypotheses; and evaluating the results of actions by collecting more data.

Action Research is based on the proposition that an effective approach to solving organisational problems must involve a rational, systematic analysis of the issues in question. It must be an approach which secures information, hypotheses and action from all parties involved, as well as evaluating the action taken towards the solution of the problem. It follows that the change process itself must become a learning situation: one in which participants learn not only from the actual research, the use of theory to investigate the problem and identify a solution, but also from the process of collaborative action, problem-solving (Bennett, 1983).

In organisational terms, the classic Action Research project usually comprises three distinct groups: the organisation (in the form of one or more senior managers), the subject (people from the area where the change is to take place), and the change agent (a consultant who may or may not be a member of the organisation). These three distinct entities form the learning community in and through which the research is carried out, and by which the organisation's or group's problem is solved. Indeed, it was Lewin's view that it was primarily the learning, which would then feed into behaviour, that was important rather than any resulting organisational changes as such.

The three entities must all, both individually and collectively, agree to come together, as a group, under mutually acceptable and constructed terms of reference. This usually small face-to-face group constitutes the medium through which the problem situation may be changed, as well as providing a forum in which the interests and ethics of the various parties to this process may be investigated. It is a cyclical process, whereby the group analyses and solves the problem through a succession of iterations. The change agent (consultant), through skills of co-ordination, links the different insights and activities within the group, so as to form a coherent chain of ideas and hypotheses (Heller, 1970).

The method of data gathering, analysis and diagnosis is dependent on the nature of the problem; but in all cases, these are carried out participatively. The change agent provides the methods of investigation in accordance with her understanding of the problem. The organisation contributes its understanding of the specific situation and its idiosyncrasies. These data are then presented to the subject for consideration. The response is fed back to the other two parties, and a series of iterations begins. The knowledge and understanding gained from this exchange of views and perceptions of the issues often result in a redefinition of the situation and of the problem. This in turn demands new action planning, if the outcome is to be followed up, fed back and evaluated. From this fact-finding process, hypotheses are framed, and the line of action decided upon, implemented and evaluated. All this happens within the group and with the consent of every member.

Action Research is, therefore, a two-pronged process. First, it emphasises that change requires action, and is directed at achieving this. Second, it recognises also that successful action is based on analysing the situation correctly, identifying all the possible alternative solutions (hypotheses) and choosing the one most appropriate to the situation at hand (Bennett, 1983). This two-pronged approach, by stressing action as well as research, overcomes the 'paralysis through analysis' syndrome that can occur with some techniques (see Peters and Waterman, 1982). In part, the theoretical foundations of this approach lie in Gestalt-Field theory, which stresses that change can only successfully be achieved by helping individuals to reflect on and gain new insights into their situation. However, Action Research also has a strong affinity with Group Dynamics, given that it uses teams to solve problems and stresses the involvement of all those concerned. This, of course, is not surprising given Lewin's central role in developing both Action Research and Group Dynamics.

Nevertheless, though Action Research has enjoyed a large following over the years, one of the barriers to its use is the need to gain the commitment of both those who manage the organisation and those who are the subject of the change. This becomes especially difficult when dealing with large organisations. Therefore, a key strategy is to use a top-down approach, establishing senior management agreement as a first step. But this does not always work, as compliance at the top does not always guarantee co-operation at other levels in the organisation (Clark, 1972).

Co-operation, though, is not enough. There also has to be a 'felt-need', as Lewin termed it. Felt-need is an individual's inner realisation that change is necessary. The need must be felt by all those involved if progress is to be made. If felt-need is low in the organisation, introducing change becomes problematic – especially where the principles of Action Research are being applied. Also, even when the need for change is accepted, this may not override anxieties about the implications of change. This can be particularly so when there exists a close relationship between personal identity, position at work and social standing, which is threatened by the proposed change (Bennis, 1966).

Even taking these drawbacks into consideration, Action Research is still a highly regarded approach to managing change and resolving social conflict, not only within organisations but within society at large (Cummings and Worley, 1997; Elden and Chisholm, 1993). However, this did not prevent its originator, Kurt Lewin, from seeking to improve upon it.

### The Three-Step model of change

In developing this model, Lewin (1947a: 228–9) noted that:

> A change towards a higher level of group performance is frequently short lived; after a 'shot in the arm', group life soon returns to the previous level. This indicates that it does not suffice to define the objective of the planned change in group performance as the reaching of a different level. Permanency at the new level, or permanency for a desired period, should be included in the objective. A successful change includes therefore three aspects: unfreezing (if necessary) the present level..., moving to the new level ... and [re]freezing group life on the new level. Since any level is determined by a force field, permanency implies that the new force field is made relatively secure against change.

For Lewin, therefore, successful change involves three steps:

1 *unfreezing* the present level;
2 *moving* to the new level;
3 *refreezing* the new level.

This recognises that before new behaviour can be successfully adopted, the old has to be discarded. Only then can the new behaviour become accepted. Central to this approach is the belief that the will of the change adopter (the subject of the change) is important, both in discarding the old, 'unfreezing', and the 'moving' to the new. This once again stresses the importance of felt-need.

Felt-need is not the only similarity that the Three-Step model shares with Action Research. Indeed, it is not too much to argue that the first two steps of the model, unfreezing and moving, roughly approximate to Action Research. This can be seen from the techniques used.

Unfreezing usually involves reducing those forces maintaining the organisation's behaviour at its present level. According to Rubin (1967), unfreezing requires some form of confrontation meeting or re-education process for those involved. This might be achieved through team-building or some other form of management development, in which the problem to be solved (changed) is analysed, or data presented, to show that a serious problem exists (Bowers *et al*, 1975). The essence of these activities is to enable those concerned to become convinced of the need for change. Unfreezing clearly equates with the research element of Action Research, just as the next step, moving, equates with the action element.

Moving, in practice, involves acting on the results of the first step. That is, having analysed the present situation, identified alternatives and selected the most appropriate, action is then necessary to move to the more desirable state of affairs. This requires developing new behaviours, values and attitudes through changes in organisational structures and processes. The key task is to ensure that this is done in such a way that those involved do not, after a short period, revert back to the old ways of doing things.

Refreezing is the final step in the Three-Step model and represents, depending on the viewpoint, either a break with Action Research or its logical extension. Refreezing seeks to stabilise the organisation at a new state of equilibrium in order to ensure that the new ways of working are relatively safe from regression. It is frequently achieved through the use of supporting mechanisms that positively reinforce the new ways of working; these include socialisation processes, such as recruitment and induction, reward systems, and cultural reinforcement through the creation of new norms of behaviour (Cummings and Huse, 1989).

The Three-Step model provides a general framework for understanding the process of organisational change. However, the three steps are relatively broad and, for this reason, have been further developed by OD practitioners in an attempt to enhance the practical value of this approach to change.

## Phases of Planned change

In attempting to elaborate upon Lewin's Three-Step model, writers have expanded the number of steps or phases. Lippitt *et al* (1958) developed a seven-phase model of Planned change, whilst Cummings and Huse (1989), not to be outdone, produced an eight-phase model. However, as Cummings and Huse (1989: 51) point out, 'the concept of planned change implies that an organization exists in different states at different times and that planned movement can occur from one state to another.' Therefore, in order to understand Planned change, it is not sufficient merely to understand the processes that bring about change; there must also be an appreciation of the states that an organisation must pass through in order to move from an unsatisfactory present state to a more desired future state.

Bullock and Batten (1985) developed an integrated, four-phase model of Planned change based on a review and synthesis of over 30 models of Planned change. Their model describes Planned change in terms of two major dimensions: change phases, which are distinct states an organisation moves through as it undertakes Planned change; and change processes, which are the methods used to move an organisation from one state to another.

The four change phases, and their attendant change processes, identified by Bullock and Batten are as follows:

1 **Exploration phase**. In this state an organisation has to explore and decide whether it wants to make specific changes in its operations and, if so, commit resources to planning the changes. The change processes involved in this phase are becoming aware of the need for change; searching for outside assistance (a consultant/facilitator) to assist with planning and implementing the changes; and establishing a contract with the consultant which defines each party's responsibilities.

2 **Planning phase**. Once the consultant and the organisation have established a contract, then the next state, which involves understanding the organisation's problem or concern, begins. The change processes involved in this are collecting information in order to establish a correct diagnosis of the problem; establishing change goals and designing the appropriate actions to achieve these goals; and persuading key decision-makers to approve and support the proposed changes.

3 **Action phase**. In this state, an organisation implements the changes derived from the planning. The change processes involved are designed to move an organisation from its current state to a desired future state, and include establishing appropriate arrangements to manage the change process and gaining support for the actions to be taken; and evaluating the implementation activities and feeding back the results so that any necessary adjustments or refinements can be made.

4 **Integration phase**. This state commences once the changes have been successfully implemented. It is concerned with consolidating and stabilising the changes so that they become part of an organisation's normal, everyday operation and do not require special arrangements or encouragement to maintain them. The change processes involved are reinforcing new behaviours through feedback and reward systems and gradually decreasing reliance on the consultant; diffusing the successful aspects of the change process throughout the organisation; and training managers and employees to monitor the changes constantly and to seek to improve upon them.

According to Cummings and Huse (1989), this model has broad applicability to most change situations. It clearly incorporates key aspects of many other change models and, especially, it overcomes any confusion between the processes (methods) of change and the phases of change – the sequential states which organisations must go through to achieve successful change.

The focus of Bullock and Batten's model, just as with Lewin's, is change at individual and group level. However, OD practitioners have recognised, as many others have, that 'Organizations are being reinvented; work tasks are being reengineered; the rules of the marketplace are being rewritten; the fundamental nature of organizations is changing', and, therefore, Organization Development has to adapt to these new conditions and broaden its focus out beyond individual and group behaviour (French and Bell, 1995: 3–4).

## The changing nature of organization development

In the USA at least, OD has become a profession with its own regulatory bodies, to which OD practitioners have to belong, its own recognised qualifications, a host of approved tools and techniques, and its own ethical code of practice (Cummings and Worley, 1997). The members of this profession, whether employed in academic institutions, consultancy practices or private and public organisations, exist to provide consultancy services. As with any profession or trade, unless they provide their customers with what they want, they will soon go out of business. Therefore, to appreciate the current role and approach of Planned change, it is necessary to say something of how OD has responded to the changing needs of its customers.

As stated earlier, Organization Development is a process that applies behavioural science knowledge and practices to help organizations achieve greater effectiveness. The original focus of OD was on work groups within an organisational setting rather than organisations in their entirety, and it was primarily concerned with the human processes and systems within organisations. However, as French and Bell (1995) and Cummings and Worley (1997) have noted, in recent years there has been a major shift of focus within the OD field from the group to the organisation setting, and even beyond. Three developments in particular caused it to broaden out its perspective:

- With the rise of the Job Design movement in the 1960s (*see* Chapter 2), and particularly the advent of Socio-Technical Systems Theory, OD practitioners came to recognise that they could not solely concentrate on the work of groups and individuals in organisations but that they needed to look at other systems. Gradually, OD has adopted an Open Systems perspective which allows it to look at organisations in their totality and within their environments.

- This organisation-wide perspective has caused OD practitioners to broaden out their perspective in two interrelated ways. First, and not surprisingly, they have developed an interest in managing organisational culture. Given that, when working with groups, OD consultants have always recognised the important of group norms and values, it is a natural progression to translate this into an interest in organisational culture in general. Second, they have developed an interest in the concept of organisational learning. Once again, as derived from Lewin's work, OD practitioners tend to stress that their interventions are as much about learning as change. Therefore, it is a natural extension to move from group learning to organisational learning. However, in both cases, these developments have tended to reflect and follow on from a general interest in such issues by organisations and academics rather than necessarily being generated by the OD profession itself.

• The increasing use of organisation-wide approaches to change (e.g. culture change programmes), coupled with increasing turbulence in the environment in which organisations operate, have drawn attention to the need for OD practitioners to become involved in transforming organisations in their totality rather than focusing on changes to their constituent parts.

Therefore, as can be seen, OD has attempted to move considerably away from its roots in Group Dynamics and Planned change and now takes a far more organisation- and system-wide perspective on change. This has created something of a dilemma for proponents of OD. As Krell (1981) pointed out, much of what can be conceived of as traditional OD (e.g. Action Research, t-groups, etc.) had become accepted practice in many organisations by the early 1980s. Even some of the newer approaches, such as job design and self-managed work teams, have become mainstream practices in many organisations (Beer and Walton, 1987). By and large, these tried-and-tested approaches still tend to focus on the group level rather than on the wider organisation level. However, the more organisation-wide transformational approaches which are seen as crucial to maintaining OD's relevance for organisations are less clear, less well-developed and less well-accepted (Cummings and Worley, 1997; French and Bell, 1995). In addition, the more that OD becomes focused on macro issues, the less it can keep in touch with and involve all the individuals affected by its change programmes and the less able it is to promote its core humanist and democratic values.

It would indeed be an irony if at this time, in pursuit of what is perceived as continued relevance, OD lost sight of its core values. This is because, as Wooten and White (1999) argue, the core values of OD – equality, empowerment, consensus-building and horizontal relationships – are ones which are particularly relevant to the postmodern organisation. If this is the case, rather than loosening its ties with its traditional values in order to retain its relevance, OD should be strengthening them in order to create the 'framework for a postmodern OD science and practice' (Wooten and White, 1999: 17).

## Planned change: summary and criticisms

Planned change is an iterative, cyclical, process involving diagnosis, action and evaluation, and further action and evaluation. It is an approach which recognises that once change has taken place, it must be self-sustaining (i.e. safe from regression). The purpose of Planned change is to improve the effectiveness of the human side of the organisation. Central to Planned change is the stress placed on the collaborative nature of the change effort: the organisation, both managers and recipients of change, and the consultant jointly diagnose the organisation's problem and jointly plan and design the specific changes. Underpinning Planned change, and indeed the origins of the OD movement as a whole, is a strong humanist and democratic orientation and an emphasis on organisational effectiveness.

Nevertheless, as Planned change has developed over the years, although the emphasis on organisational effectiveness has remained, a difference has emerged with regard to the participatory and democratic nature of its approach. This is particularly the case with the role of the change consultant. In the original version, Lewin, both in Action Research and the Three-Step model, stressed the need to solve problems through social action (dialogue). He believed that successful change could only be achieved through the active participation of the change adopter (the subject) in understanding the problem, selecting a solution and implementing it. Lewin, and the early OD practitioners, saw the change agent as a facilitator, not a director or a doer. More important even than the solution to the problem, Lewin believed that the consultant's real task was to develop those involved, and to create a learning environment that would allow them to gain new insights into themselves and their circumstances. Only through this learning process could people willingly come to see the need for and accept change.

Bullock and Batten's model, as with other more recent variants of Planned change, gives the consultant a more directive and less developmental role. Their model seems to place a greater emphasis on the consultant as an equal partner rather than as a facilitator; the consultant is as free to direct and do as the others involved. Those involved are more dependent on the change agent, not just for her skills of analysis but also for providing solutions and helping to implement them. Therefore, the focus is on what the change agent can do for those involved, rather than on seeking to enable the subjects to change themselves. This tendency for consultants to have a more directive role, and for employees to have a less participatory one, has become even more pronounced as OD practitioners have shifted their focus from individuals and groups to organisations in their entirety.

Action Research and the Three-Step model, as mentioned earlier, comprise an off-shoot of the work of the Gestalt-Field theorists, who believe that successful change requires a process of learning. This allows those involved to gain or change insights, outlooks, expectations and thought patterns. This approach seeks to provide change adopters with an opportunity to 'reason out' their situation and develop their own solutions (Bigge, 1982). The danger with Bullock and Batten's approach, and certainly later developments in OD, is that they appear to be moving more in the Behaviourist direction. As French and Bell (1995: 351) observed, from the 1980s onwards, there has been a growing tendency for top managers to focus less on people-oriented values and more on 'the bottom line and/or the price of stock. ... [Consequently] some executives have a 'slash and burn' mentality'. Clearly, this tendency is not conducive to the promotion of democratic and humanistic values. Instead, the emphasis is on the consultant as a provider of expertise that the organisation lacks. The consultant's task is not only to facilitate but also to provide solutions. The danger in this situation is that the learner (the change adopter) becomes a passive recipient of external and, supposedly, objective data: one who has to be directed to the 'correct' solution. Reason and choice do not enter into this particular equation; those involved are shown the solution and motivated, through the application of positive reinforcement, to adopt it on a permanent basis (Skinner, 1974). This appears to be especially the case with the newer, organisation-wide and transformational approaches about which even supporters of OD admit there is some confusion (Cummings and Worley, 1997).

Therefore, the move away from its original focus and area of expertise, i.e. the human processes involved in the functioning of individuals and groups in organisations, coupled with a more hostile business environment, appear to be eroding the values which Lewin and the early pioneers of OD saw as being central to successful change.

As might be expected, these developments in OD, as well as newer perspectives on organisations, have led many to question not only particular aspects of the Planned approach to change but also the utility and practicality of the approach as a whole. The main criticisms levelled against the Planned approach to change are, as Burnes and Salauroo (1995) point out, as follows.

First, as Wooten and White (1999: 8) observe, 'Much of the existing OD technology was developed specifically for, and in response to, top-down, autocratic, rigid, rule-based organizations operating in a somewhat predictable and controlled environment'. Arising from this is the assumption that, as Cummings and Huse (1989: 51) pointed out, 'an organization exists in different states at different times and that planned movement can occur from one state to another'. However, an increasing number of writers argue that, in the turbulent and chaotic world in which we live, such assumptions are increasingly tenuous and that organisational change is more a continuous and open-ended process than a set of discrete and self-contained events (Garvin, 1993; Nonaka, 1988; Peters, 1989; Stacey, 1993).

Second, and on a similar note, a number of writers have criticised the Planned approach for its emphasis on incremental and isolated change and its inability to incorporate radical, transformational change (Dunphy and Stace, 1993; Harris, 1985; Miller and Friesen, 1984; Schein, 1985).

Third, the Planned change approach is based on the assumption that common agreement can be reached, and that all the parties involved in a particular change project have a willingness and interest in doing so. This assumption appears to ignore organisational conflict and politics, or at least assumes that problem issues can be easily identified and resolved. However, given what was said of organisational power, politics and vested interests in Chapter 4, such a view is difficult to substantiate. Also, as Stace and Dunphy (1994) have shown, there is a wide spectrum of change situations, ranging from fine-tuning to corporate transformation, and an equally wide range of ways of managing these, ranging from collaborative to coercive. Though Planned change may be suitable to some of these situations, it is clearly much less applicable to situations where more directive approaches may be required, such as when a crisis, requiring rapid and major change, does not allow scope for widespread involvement or consultation.

Fourth, it assumes that one type of approach to change is suitable for all organisations, all situations and all times. Dunphy and Stace (1993: 905), on the other hand, argue that:

> Turbulent times demand different responses in varied circumstances. So managers and consultants need a model of change that is essentially a 'situational' or 'contingency model', one that indicates how to vary change strategies to achieve 'optimum fit' with the changing environment.

In supporting and adding to this list of criticisms, we can also refer back to the discussion of the frequency and magnitude of change and the theoretical under-pinnings of change management. What this shows is that whilst the Planned approach may be applicable to incremental change, it is less relevant to trans-formational change, whether it be punctuated or continuous. The same can be said of the theoretical underpinnings. Planned change is certainly applicable to the individual and group context, but seems less appropriate for system-wide change.

Leading OD advocates, as might be predicted, dispute these criticisms and point to the way that Planned change has tried to incorporate issues such as power and politics and the need for organisational transformation (Cummings and Worley, 1997; French and Bell, 1995). Also, as Burnes (1998b) argues, there is a need to draw a distinction between Lewin's original analytical approach to Planned change and the more prescriptive and practitioner-orientated variants which have been devel-oped by the OD profession subsequently. Nevertheless, even taking these points into account, it has to be recognised that Planned change was never intended to be applicable to all change situations and it was certainly never meant to be used in situations where rapid, coercive and/or wholesale change was required.

## CONCLUSIONS

This chapter began by presenting the case for the importance of studying and understanding change. In particular, it showed that a large percentage of change projects are seen to fail. The chapter then moved on to examine the three main views regarding the frequency and magnitude of change: the incremental, punctuated equilibrium and continuous transformation models. The argument made was that though in combination they might cover all forms of organisa-tional change, individually they did not. Consequently, in judging any approach to managing change, it would be necessary to identify whether it was applicable to all or only some change situations embraced by these models. In the review of the three theoretical foundations of change management which followed, a similar point was made with regard to judging the applicability of approaches to managing change; one should assess whether they apply to individual, group or system-wide change.

The chapter then proceeded to examine the origins and development of the Planned approach to change, which dominated the theory and practice of change management from the 1940s to the 1980s. It was shown that the foundations of Planned change were laid by Kurt Lewin. However, after his death it was taken up by and became the central focus of the Organization Development movement in the USA. In its origins, it is an approach to change that focuses upon improving group performance by bringing together managers, employees and a change consultant. Through a process of learning, those involved gain new insights into their situation and are thus able to identify more effective ways of working together. Advocates of Planned change, especially the earlier ones, believe that group learning and individual development are at least as important as the actual change process itself. This, in part, arises from the humanist and democratic values that underpin Planned change and which derive from Kurt Lewin's background and beliefs.

Under the auspices of Organization Development, however, the influence of these values has lessened. The focus of Planned change has moved from conflict resolution to performance enhancement, as Organization Development has grown into a thriving consultancy industry aimed almost exclusively at resolving problems within client organisations. Therefore, as was the case with the approaches to strategy discussed in Chapters 5 and 6, it is possible to draw a distinction between those proponents of Planned change, especially Lewin and early pioneers, who take an analytical approach, and those who take a more prescriptive approach, especially those whose livelihood depends upon their selling their services as change consultants.

In the 1960s and 1970s, Planned change, with its increasing array of tools, techniques and practitioners, became the dominant approach to managing organisational change. However, from the 1980s onwards, Planned change has faced increasing levels of criticism; the main ones relating to its perceived inability to cope with radical, coercive change situations or ones where power and politics are dominant. In its defence, as described earlier, there are proponents of Planned change who would argue that these criticisms are not valid, that it is a more flexible and holistic approach than its detractors would acknowledge and that it is capable of incorporating transformational change (Cummings and Worley, 1997; French and Bell, 1995; McLennan, 1989; Mirvis, 1990). Perhaps partly as a consequence of these criticisms of the Planned approach, a new approach to change has been gaining ground in recent years. Though aspects of it have been given a number of different labels, such as continuous improvement or organisational learning, it is more often referred to as the *Emergent* approach to change. The Emergent approach tends to see change as driven from the bottom up rather than from the top down; it stresses that change is an open-ended and continuous process of adaptation to changing conditions and circumstances; and it also sees the process of change as a process of learning, and not just a method of changing organisational structures and practices (Dawson, 1994; Mabey and Mayon-White, 1993; Wilson, 1992). Therefore, the next chapter will examine the principles and merits of the Emergent approach to change.

## TEST YOUR LEARNING

### Short answer questions

1 What is the incremental model of change?

2 Describe the punctuated equilibrium model of change.

3 Briefly discuss the continuous transformation model of change.

4 What are the main theoretical foundations of change management?

5 What does the term 'Planned change' mean?

6 Define Action Research.

7 What are the three steps in the Three-Step model of change?

8 What are the main criticisms of the Planned approach?

9 Discuss the main implications of the Planned approach for managerial behaviour.

### Essay questions

1 What was Kurt Lewin's main contribution to change management?

2 How has the OD movement sought to update its approach to organisational change? To what extent has it been successful?

## SUGGESTED FURTHER READING

1 Cummings, TG and Worley, CG (1997). *Organization Development and Change* (6th edition). South-Western College Publishing: Cincinnati, Ohio, USA.
French, WL and Bell, CH (1995). *Organization Development* (5th edition). Prentice Hall: Englewood Cliffs, New Jersey, USA.
Taken together, these two books provide a comprehensive guide to the origins and practices of Planned change.

2 Marrow, AJ (1969). *The Practical Theorist: The Life and Work of Kurt Lewin*. Teachers College Press (1977 edition): New York, USA.
Though now only available through interlibrary loan, for anyone interested in knowing more about the life and work of Kurt Lewin, this is the book to read.

# Chapter 8

# DEVELOPMENTS IN CHANGE MANAGEMENT

## The emergent approach and beyond

### Learning objectives

After studying this chapter, you should be able to:

1 list the reasons for the decline in popularity of the Planned approach to change;

2 identify the alternatives to the Planned approach;

3 discuss the main elements of the Emergent approach to change;

4 state the strengths and weaknesses of the Emergent approach;

5 appreciate the role of the change agent;

6 understand the range of approaches to change and the situations in which they are most appropriately used;

7 describe how organisations can increase their degree of choice when undertaking change.

## INTRODUCTION

As was described in Chapter 7, the Planned approach dominated the theory and practice of change management from the late 1940s to the early 1980s, when the Emergent approach came to the fore. The Emergent approach to change starts from the assumption that change is a continuous, open-ended and unpredictable process of aligning and re-aligning an organisation to its changing environment. Advocates of Emergent change argue that it is more suitable to the turbulent environment in which modern firms now operate because, unlike the Planned approach, it recognises that it is vital for organisations to adapt their internal practices and behaviour to changing external conditions. Furthermore, and just as importantly, it sees change as a political process whereby different groups in an organisation struggle to protect or enhance their own interests.

This chapter begins by presenting the case against the Planned approach. It then goes on to examine the main characteristics of Emergent change, and to introduce its proponents. This will show that, although they do not always agree with each other, the advocates of Emergent change are united by the emphasis they place on organisational structure, culture and learning, and their perspective on managerial behaviour and the role of power and politics in the change process. Following this, the chapter presents the recipes for change put forward by proponents of Emergent change. It also examines their neglect of the role of change agents. In summarising the Emergent approach, it is argued that, though it has a number of distinct strengths, like Planned change it is a flawed and partial approach to change.

Therefore, despite the large body of literature devoted to the topic of change management, and the many tools and techniques available to change agents, there is considerable debate regarding the most appropriate approach. In an effort to bring clarity to the issue, the chapter concludes by arguing that neither the Emergent approach nor the Planned approach is suitable for all situations and circumstances. Instead, it proposes a model of change which incorporates, and goes beyond, both approaches and, similarly to Chapters 4 and 5, stresses the potential for organisations to influence the constraints and conditions under which they operate in order to have genuine choice over what to change and how to change.

## THE CASE AGAINST THE PLANNED APPROACH TO ORGANISATIONAL CHANGE

As was shown in Chapter 7, the Planned approach to change has been, and still is, highly influential. From the late 1940s to the early 1980s, it was certainly the dominant approach to change, especially in the USA. Even today, it is still far and away the best developed, documented and supported approach to change. This is because of the custodianship of the Organization Development movement in the USA. OD has taken Kurt Lewin's original concept of Planned change and turned it into a thriving consultancy industry with its own standards, accreditation procedures and membership (Cummings and Worley, 1997). Nevertheless, from the early 1980s onwards, it has faced increasing levels of criticism as to its appropriateness and efficacy, especially from the Culture–Excellence school, the processualists and the postmodernists.

The rise of Japanese competitiveness and the apparent eclipse of Western industry from the late 1970s led to a questioning of existing approaches to structuring, managing and changing organisations (e.g. Pascale and Athos, 1982; Peters and Waterman, 1982). The proponents of Culture–Excellence were the most vociferous critics of the existing order, arguing that Western organisations were bureaucratic, inflexible, and stifled innovation. Their view of Planned change is, probably, best summed up by Kanter *et al*'s (1992: 10) scathing comment that:

> Lewin's model was a simple one, with organizational change involving three stages; unfreezing, changing and refreezing ... This quaintly linear and static conception – the organization as an ice cube – is so wildly inappropriate that it is difficult to see why it has not only survived but prospered. ... Suffice it to say here, first, that organizations are

never frozen, much less refrozen, but are fluid entities with many 'personalities'. Second, to the extent that there are stages, they overlap and interpenetrate one another in important ways.

In place of Lewin's 'wildly inappropriate' model of change, the Culture–Excellence proponents have, as described in Chapter 3, called for organisations to adopt flexible cultures which promote innovation and entrepreneurship and that encourage bottom-up, flexible, continuous and co-operative change. However, Culture–Excellence advocates recognised that top-down coercion, and rapid transformation, might also be necessary to create the conditions in which this type of approach could flourish.

At the same time, other new perspectives on organisations, especially concerning the role of power and politics in decision-making, were also coming to the fore. As Chapter 4 argued, writers such as Jeffrey Pfeffer (1981, 1992) maintained that the objectives, and outcomes, of change programmes were more likely to be determined by power struggles than by any process of consensus-building or rational decision-making. This paved the way for the development of a processual approach to organisational change, which highlights the continuous, unpredictable and political nature of change (Dawson, 1994; Pettigrew and Whipp, 1993; Wilson, 1992). Looking at Planned change versus a processual approach, Dawson (1994: 3–4) comments that:

> Although this [Lewin's] theory has proved useful in understanding planned change under relatively stable conditions, with the continuing and dynamic nature of change in today's business world, it no longer makes sense to implement a planned process for 'freezing' changed behaviours. Implementing stability and reinforcing behaviour which conforms to a rigid set of procedures for new work arrangements does not meet the growing requirements for employee flexibility and structural adaptation to the unfolding and complex nature of ongoing change processes. ... The processual framework ... adopts the view that change is a complex and dynamic process which should not be solidified or treated as a series of linear events. ... central to the development of a processual approach is the need to incorporate an analysis of the politics of managing change.

For the postmodernists, power is also a central feature of organisational change, but it arises from the socially constructed nature of organisational life:

> In a socially-constructed world, responsibility for environmental conditions lies with those who do the constructing. ... This suggests at least two competing scenarios for organizational change. First, organization change can be a vehicle of domination for those who conspire to enact the world for others ... An alternative use of social constructionism is to create a democracy of enactment in which the process is made open and available to all ... such that we create opportunities for freedom and innovation rather than simply for further domination. (Hatch, 1997: 367–8)

As can be seen, from the early 1980s, a powerful consensus built up against the Planned approach to change. However, it is a consensus that criticises Planned change from very different perspectives; ranging from the free market neo-liberalism of Tom Peters to the neo-Marxism of some of the postmodernists. Therefore, they are certainly a much less coherent group than the advocates of

Planned change and, rather than being united by a shared belief, they tend to be distinguished by a common disbelief in the efficacy of Planned change. Nevertheless, they do share at least two common beliefs: first, instead of seeing change as a phenomenon that can be pre-planned and has a finite end point, they see change as an 'emerging' and ongoing process of organisational transformation. Second, they adopt an open systems perspective. That is, they see individual organisations as interdependent parts or sub-systems of a much larger environment; though they disagree about whether the environment is a concrete reality or a socially constructed phenomenon. The environment impacts upon and affects the actions and decisions of organisations, but they also impact on the environment. Proponents of the Emergent approach see change as emerging from the day-to-day actions and decisions of members of an organisation. In this sense, change can emerge from attempts by members of organisations to align the organisation with its environment, or as the result of different groups battling for domination, or even from attempts to construct a new, or challenge an old, social reality.

Having identified what separates it from the Planned approach to change, we can now move on to examine the Emergent approach in more detail.

## THE EMERGENT APPROACH TO CHANGE

The rationale for the Emergent approach stems from the belief that change cannot and should not be solidified, or seen as a series of linear events within a given period of time; instead, it is viewed as a continuous process. Dawson (1994) and Wilson (1992) both challenged the appropriateness of Planned change in a business environment that is increasingly dynamic and uncertain. They argue that those who believe that organisational change can successfully be achieved through a pre-planned and centrally directed process of 'unfreezing', 'moving' and 'refreezing' ignore the complex and dynamic nature of environmental and change processes, and do not address crucial issues such as the need for employee flexibility and continuous structural adaptation. Wilson (1992) also believes that the Planned approach, by attempting to lay down timetables, objectives and methods in advance, is too heavily reliant on the role of managers, and assumes (perhaps rashly) that they can have a full understanding of the consequences of their actions and that their plans will be understood and accepted and can be implemented. In addition, Buchanan and Storey (1997: 127) maintain that the main criticism of those who advocate Planned change is:

> ... their attempt to impose an order and a linear sequence to processes that are in reality messy and untidy, and which unfold in an iterative fashion with much backtracking and omission.

Pettigrew (1990a, b) argues that the Planned approach, as exemplified by the OD movement, is too prescriptive and does not pay enough attention to the need to analyse and conceptualise organisational change. He maintains that it is essential to understand the context in which change takes place. In particular he emphasises the following:

- the interconnectedness of change over time;
- how the context of change shapes and is shaped by action;
- the multi-causal and non-linear nature of change.

For Pettigrew (1987), change needs to be studied across different levels of analysis and different time periods. This is because organisational change cuts across functions, spans hierarchical divisions, and has no neat starting or finishing point; instead it is a 'complex analytical, political, and cultural process of challenging and changing the core beliefs, structure and strategy of the firm' (Pettigrew, 1987: 650).

The Emergent approach, therefore, stresses the developing and unpredictable nature of change. It views change as a process that unfolds through the interplay of multiple variables (context, political processes and consultation) within an organisation. In contrast to the pre-ordained certainty of Planned change, Dawson (1994) in particular adopts a processual approach to change which is less prescriptive and more analytical and, he argues, better able to achieve a broader understanding of the problems and practice of managing change within a complex environment.

This processual approach to change is akin to the processual approach to strategy discussed in Chapter 5. Advocates of Emergent change who adopt this perspective tend to stress that there can be no simple prescription for managing organisational transitions successfully, owing to time pressures and situational variables. Neither, as Dawson (1994: 181–2) argued, can change be represented as 'the results of objective rational decision-making on the part of managers. ... [nor] as a single reaction to adverse contingent circumstances'. Therefore, successful change is less dependent on detailed plans and projections than on reaching an understanding of the complexity of the issues concerned and identifying the range of available options. Processualists also stress the central role played by power and politics in initiating and managing change (Pettigrew, 1987). This point is further emphasised by the postmodernists, for whom the struggle for power and domination is the central feature of change in organisations (Hassard, 1993; Hatch, 1997). However, as Finstad (1998) notes, the difference is that, for the processualists, the political nature of change tends to close off options, whereas for the postmodernists, the presence of conflicting interests can present new possibilities.

Despite their difference in emphasis, proponents of the Emergent approach do agree that power and politics play a central role in the process of organisational change. This is a major point of departure between them and proponents of Planned change. In commenting on the failure to incorporate the political nature of change into the traditional and more prescriptive literature on change, Hardy (1996) argues that this 'aversion' to discussing power has restricted our understanding of change and impeded our ability to manage it effectively. Pugh (1993) makes a similar point by emphasising that organisations are occupational systems and political systems as well as systems for allocating resources through rational decision-making. However, he also argues that members of an organisation operate in all three systems simultaneously and, therefore, the rational and occupational systems need to be considered alongside, and not subordinate to, the political system. This clearly conflicts with the processualists who see the political system as being paramount.

Moving on to examine the change process itself, Dawson (1994) sees change as a period of organisational transition characterised by disruption, confusion and unforeseen events that emerge over long time-frames. Even when changes are operational, they will need to be constantly refined and developed in order to maintain their relevance. Genus (1998: 51) uses an 'interpretive' perspective to explain the messy nature of organisational change, arguing that the ' ... various political, symbolic and structural factors [involved in the change process] condition the perceptions of individuals or groups...'. Finstad's (1998) view of organisational change, whilst being consistent with the perspectives of Dawson and Genus, does, however, draw an important distinction between the concrete elements of change, such as structures and practices, and the more symbolic elements, such as people's basic understandings and assumptions about their organisations. He observes, based on his own research, that it is the symbolic aspects which dominate the change process rather than the more concrete changes. The importance of symbolism and ritual in the change process is also emphasised by Schuyt and Schuijt (1998), who argue that the management of these is not only central to achieving successful change, but also plays a crucial role in reducing the uncertainty which change generates.

It is because change is so complex and multifaceted that Clarke (1994) suggested that mastering the challenge of change is not a specialist activity to be facilitated or driven by an expert but an increasingly important part of every manager's role. To be effective in creating sustainable change, according to McCalman and Paton (1992), managers will need an extensive and systemic understanding of their organisation's environment, in order to identify the pressures for change and to ensure that, by mobilising the necessary internal resources, their organisation responds in a timely and appropriate manner. Dawson (1994) claims that change must be linked to developments in markets, work organisation, systems of management control and the shifting nature of organisational boundaries and relationships. He emphasises that, in today's business environment, one-dimensional change interventions are likely to generate only short-term results and heighten instability rather than reduce it. This is a point emphasised by many other writers (Genus, 1998; Hartley *et al*, 1997; Senior, 1997).

As can be seen, though they do not always openly state it, advocates of Emergent change tend to adopt a Contingency perspective. Implicit in their argument is the assumption that if organisations operated in more stable and predictable environments, the need for change would be less and it might be possible to conceive of it as a process of moving from one relatively stable state to another. Consequently, for advocates of Emergent change, it is the uncertainty of the environment that makes Planned change inappropriate and Emergent change more pertinent. This is a point emphasised by Stickland (1998: 14) who draws on systems theory to emphasise the way that organisations are separate from but connected to their environment:

> A system has an *identity* that sets it apart from its environment and is capable of preserving that identity within a given range of environmental scenarios. Systems exist within a *hierarchy* of other systems. They contain subsystems and exist within some wider system. All are interconnected . . .

From this systems perspective, Stickland (1998: 76) raises a question which many of those studying organisational change appear not to acknowledge: 'To what extent does the environment drive changes within a system [i.e. organisation] and to what extent is the system in control of its own change processes?' Finstad (1998: 721) puts this issue in a wider context by arguing that 'the organization is . . . the creator of its environment and the environment is the creator of the organization.'

This reciprocal relationship between an organisation and its environment clearly has profound implications for how organisations conceptualise and manage change. It also serves to emphasise that a key competence for organisations is the ability to scan the external environment in order to identify and assess the impact of trends and discontinuities (McCalman and Paton, 1992). This includes exploring the full range of external variables, including markets and customers, shareholders, legal requirements, the economy, suppliers, technology, and social trends. This activity is made more difficult by the changing and arbitrary nature of organisation boundaries: customers can also be competitors; suppliers may become partners; and employees can be transformed into customers, suppliers or even competitors for scarce resources.

To cope with this complexity and uncertainty, Pettigrew and Whipp (1993) maintain that organisations need to become open learning systems, with strategy development and change emerging from the way the company as a whole acquires, interprets and processes information about its environment. Clarke (1994) took a similar view, arguing that an organisation's survival and growth depend on identifying environmental and market changes quickly, and responding opportunistically. However, as Benjamin and Mabey (1993: 181) pointed out:

> . . . while the primary stimulus for change remains those forces in the external environment, the primary motivator for how change is accomplished resides with the people within the organization.

Changes in the external environment, therefore, require appropriate responses within organisations. Such responses, the supporters of the Emergent approach state, should promote extensive and deep understanding of strategy, structure, systems, people, style and culture, and how these can function either as sources of inertia that can block change, or alternatively, as levers to encourage an effective change process (Dawson, 1994; Pettigrew and Whipp, 1993; Wilson, 1992).

A major development in this respect is the move to adopt a 'bottom-up' rather than 'top-down' approach to initiating and implementing change. The case in favour of this move is based on the view that the pace of environmental change is so rapid and complex that it is impossible for a small number of senior managers effectively to identify, plan and implement the necessary organisational responses. The responsibility for organisational change is therefore of necessity becoming more devolved. As described in Chapter 2, this is very much what the advocates of Contingency theory would expect in such a situation.

Nevertheless, the need for a bottom-up approach does not just arise from external pressures. As Stickland (1998: 93) notes, organisations are continually experiencing 'natural changes', i.e. the unintended consequences of deliberate decisions and actions:

> Within any organisation at a given point in time there are a number of continual shifts and changes playing out at various levels. These are not planned changes with a defined beginning and end, but rather reflect the natural dynamics which take place internally.

Such events may present organisations with unexpected and unlooked for opportunities, such as new product ideas, but may also present unwelcome threats, such as the departure of key staff. Given that such changes are continually happening at all levels and across all functions, organisations would quickly become paralysed if it was left solely to senior managers to identify and resolve them. Therefore, if they are to be dealt with speedily, these local problems or opportunities have to be dealt with locally. As Senior (1997) comments, this requires organisations to empower their employees to make changes at a local level. As Mintzberg (1994) suggests, it is from these local and bottom-up actions that the direction of the organisation emerges and is given shape.

Therefore, a bottom-up approach requires a major change in the role of senior managers. Instead of controlling employees, they have to empower people. Instead of directing and controlling change, they have to ensure that the organisation's members are receptive to, and have the necessary skills and motivation to take charge of, the change process. Wilson (1992) believed that to achieve this, senior managers must not only change the way they perceive and interpret the world, but achieve a similar transformation amongst everyone else in the organisation as well. Pettigrew and Whipp (1993) contend that the degree to which organisations can achieve such a difficult task, and create a climate receptive to change, is dependent on four conditioning factors:

- the extent to which key players in the organisation are prepared to champion methods for gathering and assessing information on the organisation's position that increase openness;
- the degree to which such information gathering occurs and how effectively it is integrated with central business operations;
- the extent to which environmental pressures are recognised;
- the structural and cultural characteristics of the organisation.

As can be seen, the advocates of Emergent change come from a wide variety of backgrounds and each offers their own distinct view on how organisations should and should not manage change. However, as the following section will show, there are some core similarities which link them.

## The Emergent approach to successful change

Though the proponents of the Emergent approach reject the concept of universally applicable rules for change, the guidance they do provide tends to stress five features of organisations which either promote or obstruct success: structures, cultures, organisational learning, managerial behaviour, and power and politics.

### Organisational structure

This is seen as playing a crucial role in determining where power lies, in defining how people relate to each other and in influencing the momentum for change (Clarke, 1994; Dawson, 1994; Hatch, 1997; Kotter, 1996). Therefore, an appropriate organisation structure can be an important lever for achieving change, but its effectiveness is regarded as dependent upon the recognition of its informal as well as its formal aspects.

The case for developing more appropriate organisational structures in order to facilitate change very much follows the arguments of the Contingency theorists (discussed in Chapter 2) and the Culture–Excellence school (discussed in Chapter 3), i.e. that dynamic and chaotic environments require organisations to adopt more flexible, less hierarchical structures. Those favouring an Emergent approach to change point out that the 1990s witnessed a move to create flatter organisational structures in order to increase responsiveness by devolving authority and responsibility (Senior, 1997). As Kotter (1996: 169) remarks, the case for such structural changes is that:

> An organization with more delegation, which means a flat hierarchy, is in a far superior position to manoeuvre than one with a big, change-resistant lump in the middle.

One aspect of this is the move to create customer-centred organisations with structures that reflect, and are responsive to, different markets rather than different functions. Customer responsiveness places greater emphasis on effective horizontal processes and embodies the concept that everyone is someone else's customer.

One result of attempts to respond rapidly to changing conditions by breaking down internal and external barriers, disseminating knowledge and developing synergy across functions is the creation of network organisations, or to use Handy's (1989) term, federal organisations. Snow *et al* (1993) suggested that the semi-autonomous nature of each part of a network reduces the need for and erodes the power of centrally managed bureaucracies, which, in turn, leads to change and adaptation being driven from the bottom up rather than from the top down. They further argue that the specialisation and flexibility required to cope with globalisation, intense competition and rapid technological change can only be achieved by loosening the central ties and controls that have characterised organisations in the past (Genus, 1998; Kanter *et al*, 1997; Kotter, 1996). However, is it clear that every organisation will have to adopt such structural changes in order to survive? The premise that they will have to is based on the assumption that all organisations experience similar levels of environmental turbulence and cannot do anything other than adapt their internal arrangements to these external conditions. As argued in previous chapters, there are three flaws to this argument. First, environmental instability is not uniform; it varies from industry to industry and organisation to organisation. Second, even where instability is present, organisations can choose to take action to reduce it rather than merely having to adapt to it. Lastly, as Child's concept of equifinality discussed in Chapter 5 suggests, there are a range of internal arrangements that are compatible with external turbulence, of which flattened hierarchies are only one.

### Organisational culture

Johnson (1993: 64) suggested that the strategic management of change is 'essentially a cultural and cognitive phenomenon' rather than an analytical, rational exercise. Clarke (1994) states that the essence of sustainable change is to understand the culture of the organisation that is to be changed. If proposed changes contradict cultural biases and traditions, it is inevitable that they will be difficult to embed in the organisation. Kotter (1996) takes a similar view, arguing that for change to be successful it must be anchored in the organisation's culture.

Dawson's (1994) work echoes this theme. He suggests that attempts to realign internal behaviours with external conditions require change strategies that are culturally sensitive. Organisations, he points out, must be aware that the process is lengthy, potentially dangerous, and demands considerable reinforcement if culture change is to be sustained against the inevitable tendency to regress to old behaviours. Clarke (1994) also stressed that change can be slow, especially where mechanisms which reinforce old or inappropriate behaviour, such as reward, recruitment and promotion structures, continue unchallenged. In addition, if these reinforcement mechanisms are complemented by managerial behaviour which promotes risk aversion and fear of failure, it is unlikely to create a climate where people are willing to propose or undertake change. Accordingly, as Clarke (1994: 94) suggests, 'Creating a culture for change means that change has to be part of the way we do things around here, it cannot be bolted on as an extra.'

Therefore, for many proponents of the Emergent approach, an essential factor in successful change is for organisations to possess or to be able to develop an appropriate organisational culture. However, Senior (1997) notes that many writers and researchers take a different view. Beer *et al* (1993), for example, suggested that the most effective way to promote change is not by directly attempting to influence organisational behaviour or culture. Instead, they advocate restructuring organisations in order to place people in a new organisational context which imposes new roles, relationships and responsibilities upon them. This, they believe, forces new attitudes and behaviours upon people. This view, as discussed in Chapter 3, is also shared by Tom Peters (1993) who advocates rapid and complete destruction of existing hierarchical organisation structures as a precursor to behavioural change.

In Chapter 4 we discussed the difficulty and relevance of achieving cultural change, by whatever means. It was argued that many writers are highly sceptical about seeing culture as a promoter of change. This view is, perhaps, best summed up by Wilson (1992: 91), who claims that:

> ... to effect change in an organization simply by attempting to change its culture assumes an unwarranted linear connection between something called organizational culture and performance. Not only is this concept of organizational culture multi-faceted, it is also not always clear precisely how culture and change are related, if at all, and, if so, in which direction.

## Organisational learning

This was discussed extensively in Chapter 3. For advocates of the Emergent approach, learning plays a key role in preparing people for, and allowing them to cope with, change. A willingness to change often only stems from the feeling that there is no other option (Pettigrew *et al*, 1992). Therefore, as Wilson (1992) suggests, change can be precipitated by making impending crises real to everyone in the organisation (or perhaps even engineering crises) or encouraging dissatisfaction with current systems and procedures. The latter is seen as being best achieved through the creation by managers of mechanisms which allow staff to become familiar with the market place, customers, competitors, legal requirements, etc., in order to recognise the pressures for change.

Clarke (1994) and Nadler (1993) suggested that individual and organisational learning stem from effective top-down communication and the promotion of self-development and confidence. In turn, this encourages the commitment to, and shared ownership of, the organisation's vision, actions and decisions that are necessary to respond to the external environment and take advantage of the opportunities it offers. Additionally, as Pugh (1993) points out, in order to generate the need and climate for change, people within organisations need to be involved in the diagnosis of problems and the development of solutions. Carnall (1990) took this argument further, maintaining that organisational effectiveness can only be achieved and sustained through learning from the experience of change.

Clarke (1994: 156) believes that involving staff in change management decisions has the effect of 'stimulating habits of criticism and open debate' which enables them to challenge existing norms and question established practices. This, in turn, creates the opportunity for innovation and radical change. Benjamin and Mabey (1993) argue that such questioning of the status quo is the essence of bottom-up change. They consider that, as employees' learning becomes more valued and visible within a company, then rather than managers putting pressure on staff to change, the reverse occurs. The new openness and knowledge of staff puts pressure on managers to address fundamental questions about the purpose and direction of the organisation which previously they might have avoided. Pettigrew and Whipp (1993: 18) also contended that 'collective learning' is one of the main preconditions for sustainable change. They argue that 'collective learning' ensures that the full implications of an organisation's view of its environment can then inform subsequent actions over the long-term and, in turn, the way in which future shifts in the environment are tackled. Nevertheless, as Easterby-Smith (1997) and Tsang (1997) noted, organisational learning is a somewhat imprecise and elusive concept which appears to vary from author to author. The result of this diversity of opinion may be to make organisational learning a more difficult concept to apply than its supporters acknowledge.

### Managerial behaviour

As was argued in Chapter 1, the traditional view of organisations sees managers as directing and controlling staff, resources and information. However, the Emergent approach to change, as with the Culture–Excellence approach to managing organisations, requires a radical change in managerial behaviour (Kanter *et al*, 1997; Kotter, 1996; Peters, 1997a). Managers are expected to operate as leaders, facilitators and coaches who, through their ability to span hierarchical, functional and organisational boundaries, can bring together and motivate teams and groups to identify the need for, and achieve, change (Mabey and Mayon-White, 1993).

To be effective in this new role, Clarke (1994) believes that managers will require knowledge of and expertise in strategy formulation, human resource management, marketing/sales and negotiation/conflict resolution. But the key to success, the decisive factor in creating a focused agenda for organisational change is, according to Clarke, managers' own behaviour. If managers are to gain the commitment of others to change, they must first be prepared to challenge their own assumptions, attitudes and mindsets so that they develop an understanding of the emotional and intellectual processes involved (Buchanan and Boddy, 1992).

For supporters of the Emergent approach, the essence of change is the move from the familiar to the unknown. In this situation, it is essential for managers to be able to tolerate risk and cope with ambiguity. Pugh (1993) took the view that, in a dynamic environment, open and active communication with those participating in the change process is the key to coping with risk and ambiguity. This very much follows Clarke's (1994: 172) assertion that: 'Top-down, unilaterally imposed change doesn't work. You need bottom-up change, early involvement and genuine consultation.' This in turn requires managers to facilitate open, organisation-wide communication via groups, individuals, and formal and informal channels (Kanter *et al*, 1992; Senior, 1997).

An organisation's ability to gather, disseminate, analyse and discuss information is crucial for successful change, from the perspective of the Emergent approach. The reason for this, as Wilson (1992) argues, is that to effect change successfully, organisations need consciously and proactively to move forward incrementally.

Large-scale change and more formal and integrated approaches to change (such as Total Quality Management) can quickly lose their sense of purpose and relevance for organisations operating in dynamic and uncertain environments. However, if organisations move towards their strategic vision by means of many small-scale, localised incremental changes, managers must ensure that those concerned, which could potentially be the entire workforce, have access to and are able to act on all the available information. Also, by encouraging a collective pooling of knowledge and information in this way, a better understanding of the pressures and possibilities for change can be achieved, which should enable managers to improve the quality of strategic decisions (Boddy and Buchanan, 1992; Quinn, 1993).

As well as ensuring the free flow of information, managers must also recognise and be able to cope with resistance to, and political intervention in, change. They will, especially, need to acquire and develop a range of interpersonal skills that enable them to deal with individuals and groups who seek to block or manipulate change for their own benefit (Boddy and Buchanan, 1992). In addition, supporting openness, reducing uncertainty, and encouraging experimentation can be power-ful mechanisms for promoting change (Mabey and Mayon-White, 1993). In this respect, Coghlan (1993) and McCalman and Paton (1992) advocated the use of Organization Development (OD) tools and techniques (such as transactional analysis, teamwork, group problem-solving, role-playing, etc.) which have long been used in Planned change programmes. However, there is an enormous and potentially confusing array of these; Mayon-White (1993) and Buchanan and Boddy (1992) argue that managers have a crucial role to play in terms of identifying and applying the appropriate ones. The main objective in deploying such tools and techniques is to encourage shared learning through teamwork and co-operation. It is this which provides the framework and support for the emergence of creative and innovative solutions and encourages a sense of involvement, commitment and ownership of the change process (Carnall, 1990; Kanter *et al*, 1997; McCalman and Paton, 1992; Peters, 1997a).

Nevertheless, it would be naïve to assume that everyone will want to work, or be able to function effectively, in such situations. The cognitive and behavioural changes necessary for organisational survival may be too large for many people, including, and perhaps especially, managers. An important managerial task will, therefore, be to identify sources of inertia, assess the skill mix within their organisation and, most of all, consider whether their own managerial attitudes and styles are appropriate.

### Power and politics

Though the advocates of Emergent change tend to view power and politics from differing perspectives, they all recognise their importance and that they have to be managed if change is to be effective. Dawson (1994: 176), for example, concluded that 'The central argument is that it is important to try and gain the support of senior management, local management, supervisors, trade unions and workplace employees.' Pettigrew *et al* (1992: 293) state that 'The significance of political language at the front end of change processes needs emphasizing. Closures can be labelled as redevelopments. Problems can be re-coded into opportunities with ... broad positive visions being articulated to build early coalitions...'. Kanter *et al* (1992: 508) argue that the first step to implementing change is coalition-building: '... involve those whose involvement really matters ... Specifically, seek support from two general groups: (1) power sources and (2) stakeholders.' In a similar vein, Nadler (1993) advocates the need to shape the political dynamics of change so that power centres develop that support the change rather than blocking it. Senior (1997), drawing on the work of Nadler (1988), proposes four steps which organisations need to take to manage the political dynamics of change:

*Step 1* Ensure or develop the support of key power groups.

*Step 2* Use leader behaviour to generate support for the proposed change.

*Step 3* Use symbols and language to encourage and show support for the change.

*Step 4* Build in stability by using power to ensure that some things remain the same.

Important though power and politics are in the change process, as Hendry (1996) and Pugh (1993) argue, they are not the be-all and end-all of change and it is important not to focus on these to the exclusion of other factors. Nevertheless, the focus placed on the political dynamics of change does serve to highlight the need for those who manage change to be aware of and control this dimension of the change process. To this end, Carnall (1995: 129) offered a model of the political skills that can be utilised to manage change (*see* Table 8.1). Carnall's argument is not that one individual will possess all these skills, but that those managing change will have to gain the support of those who do.

As can be seen, therefore, there are a number of core issues on which the advocates of Emergent change share similar views. Having identified the beliefs which distinguish them as a group, it is equally important to understand what advice they offer for putting their approach into practice.

**Table 8.1 Political skills and the management of change**

| *Resources* | *Process* | *Form* |
|---|---|---|
| Formal authority | Negotiation | Politics of: |
| Control of resources | Influencing | budgets |
| Control of information | Mobilising support | careers |
| Control of agenda | Mobilising bias | succession |
| Control of access symbols | Use of emotion | information |
| | Ceremony and rituals | organisational structures |
| | Professional 'mystery' | appraisal |

## Recipes for Emergent change

Pettigrew and Whipp (1993: 6) maintain that there are no universal rules with regard to leading change; rather it involves 'linking action by people at all levels of the business'. However, this has not prevented most of the advocates of Emergent change from suggesting sequences of actions which organisations should follow. Pettigrew and Whipp (1993), for example, propose a model for successfully managing strategic and operational change which involves five interrelated factors:

- **Environmental assessment**: organisations, at all levels, need to develop the ability to collect and utilise information about their external and internal environments.

- **Leading change**: this requires the creation of a positive climate for change, the identification of future directions and the linking together of action by people at all levels in the organisation.

- **Linking strategic and operational change**: this is a two-way process of ensuring that strategic decisions lead to operational changes and that operational changes influence strategic decisions.

- **Human resources as assets and liabilities**: just as the pool of knowledge, skills and attitudes possessed by an organisation is crucial to its success, it can also be a threat to the organisation's success if the combination is inappropriate or managed poorly.

- **Coherence of purpose**: this concerns the need to ensure that the decisions and actions that flow from the above four factors complement and reinforce each other.

For his part, not to be outdone by Pettigrew and Whipp's five factors, Dawson (1994: 179) puts forward 15 'major practical guidelines which can be drawn from a processual analysis of managing organizational transitions'. These guidelines range from the need to maintain an overview of the dynamics and long-term process of change, to the need to take a total organisational approach to managing transitions. On the way, he makes the case for understanding and communicating the context and objectives of change, and ensuring managerial and employee commitment. Wilson (1992: 122) also draws attention to the complex and long-term nature of change, writing that:

> This book has deliberately taken a particular stance towards the question of organizational change. The argument has largely been against skill-based approaches, ready-made models of good organizational practice (for example, the 'excellence' models) and reliance upon analysing change as primarily the outcome-oriented pursuit of great and charismatic individuals. The arguments have, rather, favoured the potency of organizational structures, of economic determinism, of institutionalization within which the manager must operate. To operate successfully (and in the long term) he or she must understand and learn from the wider context or organization. This is not to say that individual skills are unimportant, only that they cannot be considered in isolation from the wider factors of strategic change.

Unfortunately, the problem with much of the advice for managing change offered by advocates of the Emergent approach is that it tends to be relatively cursory or abstract in nature and difficult to apply on a day-to-day basis. It can sometimes also, as with Dawson's list, appear almost as an afterthought. However, there are those whose work offers much more substantial guidance to managers and organisations. Inevitably, as one might expect, these tend to come from the prescriptive camp rather than the analytical camp and are more concerned with telling organisations what they should do than in providing detailed analyses of what they do do. The two leading exponents of change in this respect are Rosabeth Moss Kanter and John P Kotter. Kanter's work has already been discussed extensively in Chapter 3, but to recap briefly, she proposes 'Ten Commandments for Executing Change' (Kanter *et al*, 1992: 382–3):

1 Analyse the organisation and its need for change.
2 Create a shared vision and a common direction.
3 Separate from the past.
4 Create a sense of urgency.
5 Support a strong leader role.
6 Line up political sponsorship.
7 Craft an implementation plan.
8 Develop enabling structures.
9 Communicate, involve people and be honest.
10 Reinforce and institutionalise change.

Looking at approaches to change, Kanter *et al* (1992) distinguished between 'Bold Strokes' and 'Long Marches'. The former relate to major strategic decisions or economic initiatives, usually of a structural or technological nature. These, they argue, can have a clear and rapid impact on an organisation, but they rarely lead to any long-term change in habits or culture. The Long March approach, on the other hand, favours a host of relatively small-scale and operationally focused initiatives, each of which can be quickly implemented but whose full benefits are achieved in the long term rather than the short term. However, the Long March approach can, over time, lead to a change of culture. Bold Strokes are initiatives taken by a few senior managers, sometimes only one; they do not rely on the support of the rest of the organisation for their success. In contrast, the Long March approach requires widespread commitment throughout an organisation. Without the involvement and commitment of the majority of the workforce, Kanter *et al* argue, such initiatives cannot succeed. They do maintain that Bold Strokes and Long Marches can be complementary, rather than alternative, approaches to change; though in practice companies appear to favour one or the other. Nevertheless, companies may need both if they are to succeed in transforming themselves.

Like Kanter, Kotter is a professor at the Harvard Business School and runs his own highly successful consultancy – Kotter Associates. He is the author of a wide range of books and articles on management and change, including his highly influential 1995 *Harvard Business Review* article, 'Leading Change: Why Transformation Efforts Fail'. This article jumped to first place among the thousands of reprints sold by the *Review* which, considering the quality of the articles in its reprint base, is a considerable achievement. Spurred on by the reception of his views on change, Kotter went on to write his 1996 book, *Leading Change*. This elaborates and expands on the ideas in his *Harvard Business Review* article. The book begins by identifying eight key errors which Kotter believes cause transformation efforts to fail, which are as follows:

*Error 1*   Allowing too much complacency.

*Error 2*   Failing to create a sufficiently powerful guiding coalition.

*Error 3*   Underestimating the power of vision.

*Error 4*   Undercommunicating the vision by a factor of 10 (or 100 or even 1000).

*Error 5*   Permitting obstacles to block the new vision.

*Error 6*   Failing to create short-term wins.

*Error 7*   Declaring victory too soon.

*Error 8*   Neglecting to anchor changes firmly in the corporate culture.

Kotter (1996: 16) maintains that the consequences of these errors are that:

- New strategies aren't implemented well.
- Acquisitions don't achieve expected synergies.
- Reengineering takes too long and costs too much.
- Downsizing doesn't get costs under control.
- Quality programs don't deliver hoped-for results.

In order to eliminate these errors and their consequences, the book then proceeds to present Kotter's Eight-Stage Process for successful organisational transformation:

*Step 1*   Establishing a sense of urgency.

*Step 2*   Creating a guiding coalition.

*Step 3*   Developing a vision and strategy.

*Step 4*   Communicating the change vision.

*Step 5*   Empowering broad-based action.

*Step 6*   Generating short-term wins.

*Step 7*   Consolidating gains and producing more change.

*Step 8*   Anchoring new approaches in the culture.

Kotter (1996: 23) stresses that his eight stages are a process and not a checklist, and that 'Successful change of any magnitude goes through all eight stages ...

skipping even a single step or getting too far ahead without a solid base almost always creates problems.' He also points out that most major change efforts comprise a host of small and medium-sized change projects which, at any one point in time, can be at different points in the process. Kotter (1996: 24–5) cites the example of a telecommunications company where:

> The overall effort, designed to significantly increase the firm's competitive position, took six years. By the third year, the transformation was centred in steps 5, 6 and 7. One relatively small reengineering project was nearing the end of stage 8. A restructuring of corporate staff groups was just beginning with most of the effort in steps 1 and 2. A quality program was moving along, but behind schedule, while a few small initiatives hadn't even been launched yet. Early results were visible at six to twelve months, but the biggest payoff didn't come until near the end of the overall effort.

A further key point made by Kotter is the need to distinguish management from leadership. Management, he argues, concerns a set of processes, such as budgeting and planning, for ensuring that organisations run smoothly. Leadership, on the other hand, is a set of processes for creating or transforming organisations: 'Leadership defines what the future should look like, aligns people with that vision, and inspires them to make it happen . . .' (Kotter, 1996: 25). He also stresses the need to develop learning organisations.

As can be seen, there is a reassuring similarity between Kanter *et al*'s Ten Commandments and Kotter's eight-stage process. Taken together, they provide detailed guidance for implementing change. However, there is one area where both they and the other advocates of the Emergent approach are strangely silent. Though advocates of Emergent change place a great deal of emphasis on leadership and the ability to manage change, what most of them put to one side is the role of the change agent. Indeed, as the next section will show, though this is a crucial, complex and skilled role, there is a tendency to assume that it is not a specialist role but one that most managers should be able to embrace.

## The role of the change agent

Whether one takes a Planned or Emergent approach to change, it has to be managed; someone has to take responsibility for ensuring that change takes place. Whether this person is a team leader, facilitator, coach or even a dictator, there is usually one individual who bears the responsibility of being the change agent. One of the strengths of the Planned approach is that it not only offers a well-developed change process, but it also provides a blueprint for the role and attributes of change agents who, in turn, are buttressed and supported by a host of tools and techniques for analysing organisations and managing change (Cummings and Worley, 1997). The Emergent approach, whilst stressing the issue of process, tends to play down or ignore the role of the change agent. This is based on the view, as articulated by Clarke (1994), that change is not a specialist activity driven by an expert, but an increasingly important part of every manager's role. The drawback with this perspective is that it deflects attention from the specialist skills which are necessary to manage change, whether this is being done by a manager or by a change specialist. It may also be one reason why, as Hartley *et al* (1997) observe, there has been relatively little empirical research on the roles played by change agents. However, Buchanan and Boddy (1992: 27) sought to redress the balance by analysing the skills needed to be a successful change agent and, in particular, by drawing attention to the change agent's need to:

> ...support the 'public performance' of rationally considered and logically phased and visibly participative change with 'backstage activity' in the recruitment and maintenance of support and in seeking and blocking resistance. ... 'Backstaging' is concerned with the exercise of 'power skills', with 'intervening in political and cultural systems', with influencing and negotiating and selling, and with 'managing meaning'.

Buchanan and Boddy suggest a model of the expertise of the change agent which identifies the skills and competences necessary to achieve successful change. Their model begins by listing the diagnostic skills required to identify the organisation type; change category; personal vulnerability; agenda priorities; and public performance and backstage skills. The model then goes on to list 15 competences under five clusters: goals; roles; communication; negotiation; and managing up. The last two elements of their model relate to process outcomes and personal and organisational outcomes. What emerges from their work is a picture of the change agent as a highly skilled and well-trained political operator who has not only an in-depth knowledge of change processes and tools, but also the personal qualities and experience to use them both in the open and, especially, behind the scenes. In contrast to this, the Planned approach sees the change agent's role as being mainly an up-front activity and working with a transparent agenda (French and Bell, 1995).

Buchanan and Boddy (1992: 123) also draw attention to the social construction of the process of change which, they argue, is a creative activity:

> Expertise does not simply involve the mechanical deployment of diagnostic tools, competences and stereotyped solutions, but involves also the innovative and opportunistic exploitation of other dimensions of the organizational context.

Mirvis (1988) is another who drew attention to the crucial role played by innovative and creative skills of change agents in achieving successful change. In an article entitled 'Grace, Magic and Miracles', Lichtenstein (1997) investigated this side of the change agent's role further by examining the work of three leading change practitioners: Peter Senge, William Torbert and Ellen Wingard. In the article, the three consultants described their approach to change and the theories which underpin it. They also described how, in applying their approaches, it was insufficient just to follow the steps laid down. Success required the consultants to overcome major obstacles, and, in so doing, to adopt novel and experimental methods. Senge, Torbert and Wingard use terms such as 'grace', 'magic' and 'miracles' to describe the moment of breakthrough; the point where serious obstacles were overcome and genuine progress made. In fact, what they describe is the ability of the change agent to recognise the need to depart from the 'script' and to experiment with the unknown in order to make progress. Just as Buchanan and Boddy (1992) identified the need for change agents to be able to present and utilise the rational face of change, whilst being adept at the less rational 'back-stage' skills, so Lichtenstein (1997: 407) also concludes that:

> ...there is a logical framework that produces rational actions in the first stages of an intervention effort. However, at a critical threshold it is non-linear logic and spontaneous felt action – grace, magic and miracles – that actually supports organizational (and personal) transformation.

Drawing on the work of cultural anthropologists, Schuyt and Schuijt (1998) use the analogy of the change agent as a magician. They point out that magicians, witch doctors and medicine men in non-Western cultures use symbols and rituals to smooth the various transitions in life cycles: birth, puberty, marriage and death. In the same way, Schuyt and Schuijt (1998: 399) pose the following question: are not consultants and change agents 'also, in a certain sense, magicians who guide and structure important transitions through the use of rituals and symbols?' These rituals and symbols have a number of key functions: to establish the change agent's credentials, to prepare the participants mentally for change, to guide them through the transition, and to reinforce the 'participants' feeling that they are taking part in a controlled and well-managed process of change ... but ultimately the crux is to reduce the client's uncertainty' (Schuyt and Schuijt, 1998: 405).

The argument of most of the Emergent school is that the complexity and multi-level nature of change mean that it cannot be left to a few experts or a few managers. However, what the work of Buchanan and Boddy, Lichtenstein, Schuyt and Schuijt, and, indeed, the Organization Development movement would seem to show is that the more complex the change process, the more difficult it is to achieve and the greater the need to utilise the skills and experience of a specialist change agent.

## EMERGENT CHANGE: SUMMARY AND CRITICISMS

The proponents of Emergent change are a somewhat disparate group who tend to be united more by their scepticism regarding Planned change than by a commonly agreed alternative. Nevertheless, there does seem to be some agreement regarding the main tenets of Emergent change, which are as follows:

- Organisational change is a continuous process of experiment and adaptation aimed at matching an organisation's capabilities to the needs and dictates of a dynamic and uncertain environment.
- Though this is best achieved through a multitude of (mainly) small- to medium-scale incremental changes, over time these can lead to a major re-configuration and transformation of an organisation.

- Change is a multi-level, cross-organisation process that unfolds in an iterative and messy fashion over a period of years and comprises a series of interlocking projects.

- Change is a political-social process and not an analytical-rational one.

- The role of managers is not to plan or implement change *per se*, but to create or foster an organisational structure and climate which encourages and sustains experimentation, learning and risk-taking, and to develop a workforce that will take responsibility for identifying the need for change and implementing it.

- Though managers are expected to become facilitators rather than doers, they also have the prime responsibility for developing a collective vision or common purpose which gives direction to their organisation, and within which the appropriateness of any proposed change can be judged.

- The key organisational activities which allow these elements to operate success-fully are information-gathering – about the external environment and internal objectives and capabilities; communication – the transmission, analysis and discussion of information; and learning – the ability to develop new skills, identify appropriate responses and draw knowledge from their own and others' past and present actions.

Though not always stated openly, the case for an Emergent approach to change is based on the assumption that all organisations operate in a turbulent, dynamic and unpredictable environment. Therefore, if the external world is changing in a rapid and uncertain way, organisations need to be continuously scanning their environment in order to adapt and respond to changes. Because this is a continuous and open-ended process, the Planned approach to change is inappropriate. To be successful, changes need to emerge locally and incrementally in order to respond to environmental threats and take advantage of opportunities.

Presented in this manner, there is an apparent coherence and validity to the Emergent approach. However, it is a fragile coherence and a challengeable validity. As far as coherence is concerned, some proponents of Emergent change, especially Dawson (1994) and Pettigrew and Whipp (1993), clearly approach it from the processual perspective on organisations. However, it is not clear that Buchanan and Boddy (1992) and Wilson (1992) would fully subscribe to this view. In the case of Carnall (1990), Clarke (1994), Kanter *et al* (1992) and Kotter (1996), it is clear that they do not take a processual perspective. They do not doubt the importance of power and politics in the change process, but for them the issue is one of legitimacy and pragmatism. Managers and change agents have the legitimate right to introduce changes, but to do so they must use political skills in a pragmatic way to build support and overcome or avoid resistance. For the processualists, change is about dominant coalitions trying to impose their will on the rest of the organisation in order to bolster or improve their position. Partly, this is explained by the fact that some of these writers (especially Dawson, 1994; Pettigrew and Whipp, 1993; Wilson, 1992) are attempting to understand and analyse change from a critical perspective, whilst others (notably Kanter *et al*, 1992; Kotter, 1996) are more concerned with prescribing recipes and checklists for successful change. Therefore, though the advocates of Emergent change have a number of common bonds, their differing objectives and perspectives do put a question mark against the coherence of the Emergent approach.

In terms of the validity or general applicability of the Emergent approach to change, this depends to a large extent on whether or not one subscribes to the view that all organisations operate in a dynamic and unpredictable environment to which they have to adapt continuously. The issue of the nature and posited immutability of the environment in which organisations operate has been discussed extensively in previous chapters. The conclusion reached was that not all organisations face the same degree of environmental turbulence and that, in any case, it is possible to manipulate or change environmental constraints. This does not necessarily invalidate the Emergent approach as a whole, but it does indicate that some organisations, by accident or action, may find the Planned approach to change both appropriate and effective in their particular circumstances.

Obviously, the above raises a major question mark over the Emergent approach; however, even without reservations regarding its coherence and validity, there would still be serious criticisms of this approach. For example, many of its supporters seem to advocate the same approach to organisations as the Culture–Excellence school and are, therefore, open to the same criticisms (*see* Chapters 3 and 4). Given this link to Culture–Excellence, not surprisingly, a great deal of emphasis is placed on the need for appropriate organisational cultures. But, as the writers on Emergent change seem to sway between advocating the need for culture change (Kanter *et al*, 1992) and advocating the need to work with existing cultures (Kotter, 1996), it is not clear what they perceive the role of culture to be. In any case, as is noted in Chapter 4, the whole issue of the role and the manipulability of organisational culture is a veritable minefield. Indeed, as mentioned earlier, even Wilson (1992), who supports the Emergent perspective, was sceptical about the case for culture. Similar points can be made regarding the 'learning organisation' approach. As Whittington (1993: 130) commented:

> The danger of the purely 'learning' approach to change, therefore, is that ... managers [and others] may actually recognize the need for change, yet still refuse to 'learn' because they understand perfectly well the implications for their power and status. Resistance to change may not be 'stupid' ... but based on a very shrewd appreciation of the personal consequences.

A variant of this criticism relates to the impact of success on managerial learning. Miller (1993: 119) observed that, whilst managers generally start out by attempting to learn all they can about their organisation's environment, over time, as they gain experience, they 'form quite definite opinions of what works and why' and as a consequence tend to limit their search for information and knowledge. So experience, especially where it is based on success, may actually be a barrier to learning, in that it shapes the cognitive structures by which managers, and everyone else, see and interpret the world. Nystrom and Starbuck (1984: 55) observed:

> What people see, predict, understand, depends on their cognitive structures ... [which] manifest themselves in perceptual frameworks, expectations, world views, plans, goals ... myths, rituals, symbols ... and jargon.

This brings us neatly to the topic of the role of managers. Though this will be discussed extensively in Chapter 14, for now it should be noted that managers are the ones who appear to have to make the greatest change in their behaviour. However, as the above quotations indicate, they may neither welcome nor accept such a change, especially where it requires them to challenge and change their own beliefs, and where it runs counter to their experience of 'what works and why'. Also, if the possibility exists (as mentioned above) to manipulate environmental variables and constraints rather than having to change their behaviour, managers may perceive this as a more attractive or viable option.

Though the above reservations regarding the coherence and validity of the Emergent approach are fairly damning, there are three further criticisms which are equally serious. The first relates to the difference between their approach and the Planned approach. The Planned approach is attacked because of its reliance on Lewin's Three-Step model of unfreezing, moving and refreezing. It is argued that in a turbulent environment, organisations are in a constant state of change and that, therefore, to speak of unfreezing and refreezing is nonsense (Kanter *et al*, 1992). However, if one examines the process of change advocated by, for example, Dawson (1994), Kotter (1996) and Pettigrew *et al* (1992), though they argue to the contrary, they do speak of change as a 'transition' process which does have a beginning, middle and end. Indeed, Hendry (1996: 624), who worked with Pettigrew at Warwick Business School, comments:

> Scratch any account of creating and managing change and the idea that change is a three-stage process which necessarily begins with a process of unfreezing will not be far below the surface.

The second criticism concerns the emphasis placed on the political and cultural aspects of change. Advocates of the Emergent approach have undoubtedly provided a valuable contribution to our understanding of change by highlighting the neglect of these important issues in the past. However, they have also been criticised from a number of perspectives for perhaps going too far the other way. Hendry (1996: 621) argues that 'The management of change has become ... overfocused on the political aspects of change', whilst Collins (1998: 100), voicing concerns of his own and of other researchers, argues that:

> ...in reacting to the problems and critiques of [the Planned approach], managers and practitioners have swung from a dependence on under-socialized models and explanations of change and instead have become committed to the arguments of, what might be called, over-socialized models of change.

Lastly, though the Emergent approach undoubtedly raises key issues, and offers valuable insights and guidance, it does not appear to be as universally applicable as its advocates imply. At the beginning of Chapter 7, we identified three categories of change: incremental, punctuated equilibrium and transformational. We also identified three different perspectives on change: the individual, group and system. The Emergent approach is specifically founded on the assumption that organisations operate in a dynamic environment which requires continuous, large-scale change. It is, then, by its own definition, not applicable to organisations operating in environments which require incremental, or perhaps even punctuated equilibrium change programmes. The focus of Emergent change tends to be the organisation and its major sub-systems rather than individuals and groups *per se*. It is also the case that, both implicitly and explicitly, the Emergent approach advocates co-operative change rather than coercive or confrontational change. Though this is to be applauded, it is also clear that there are many situations where change is pushed through in a rapid and confrontational manner (*see* Dunphy and Stace, 1992; Edwardes, 1983; Franklin, 1997; Grinyer *et al*, 1988).

Therefore, it can be seen that Emergent change is limited in terms of both what it can be applied to and how it can be applied. Though it has apparent advantages over the Planned approach, or rather it is applicable to situations for which Planned change is not suitable, an examination of the Emergent approach reveals that there are serious question marks over its coherence, validity and general applicability. In response to this, the next section of this chapter will examine the range of change situations and put forward a framework for choosing which approach to apply.

# A FRAMEWORK FOR CHANGE: APPROACHES AND CHOICES

## Varieties of change

As Stickland (1998: 14) remarks:

> ... the problem with studying change is that it parades across many subject domains under numerous guises, such as transformation, development, metamorphosis, transmutation, evolution, regeneration, innovation, revolution and transition to name but a few.

This and the previous chapter have reviewed the two dominant approaches to managing change, identifying their strengths, weaknesses and the situations they are designed to address. It has become clear that, even taken together, neither the Planned nor Emergent approach cover the broad spectrum of change events organisations encounter. In order to address this deficiency, the following will seek to identify the range of change situations organisations face and match these to a wider group of approaches. This will enable the construction of a framework that will allow different change situations to be matched to appropriate approaches to managing change. It will then be argued that, by manipulating key variables in this framework, it is possible for organisations to have genuine choices in what to change, how to change and when to change.

As noted in Chapter 7, types of change can be categorised as to whether their primary focus applies to individuals, groups or systems and sub-systems. As far as models of change are concerned, once again as noted in Chapter 7, the three main ones are the incremental model; the punctuated equilibrium model; and the continuous transformation model. As shown in Figure 8.1, bringing these together creates a change matrix which, as the examples illustrate, appears to cover most situations. However, there are other types, models and forms of change which expand on, cut across or are not included in this matrix. Senior (1997), drawing on the work of Grundy (1993), identifies three categories of change: *smooth incremental*, covering slow, systematic, evolutionary change; *bumpy incremental*, pertaining to periods where the smooth flow of change accelerates; and *discontinuous change*, which is similar to the punctuated equilibrium model. Kanter *et al* (1992), addressing the issue of transformational change, have noted that it can be achieved either by a Bold Stroke approach (rapid overall change) or a Long March approach (incremental change leading to transformation over an extended period of time). Cummings and Worley (1997) identify a continuum running from incremental change to quantum change. Whereas their definition of quantum change could include both Kanter *et al*'s Bold Stroke and their Long March, incremental change, for them, is about fine-tuning an organisation that is already working well. Dunphy and Stace (1992), in a similar but more detailed way, identify a four-stage change continuum that comprises the following: fine-tuning, incremental adjustment, modular transformation and corporate transformation. Looking at the latter, Stace and Dunphy (1994) argue that corporate transformations can take four forms: developmental transitions; task-focused transitions; charismatic transformations; and turnarounds. For Peters (1989), rapid, disruptive and continuous change is the only appropriate form of change there is. With echoes of Peters, Quinn (1996) differentiates between incremental change, which he sees as leading to slow death, or deep, radical change leading to irreversible transformation. Pettigrew *et al* (1992)

|  | Incremental | Punctuated | Continuous |
|---|---|---|---|
| **Individuals** | Learning | Promotion | Career Development |
| **Groups** | *Kaizen* | Team Building | Changes in Composition and Tasks |
| **Systems** | Fine Tuning | BPR | Culture |

Figure 8.1 Varieties of change

distinguish between types of change by their scale and importance. Their change continuum spans operational change (small-scale, relatively unimportant) and strategic change (major and important structural changes). Buchanan and Boddy's (1992) classification is almost the same as Pettigrew *et al's*, but they use two dimensions: incremental change to radical change; and changes which are of central importance to the organisation to those which are peripheral to its purpose. Kotter (1996) ignores the notion of a continuum of change as such and, instead, argues that organisations need to be continuously transforming themselves through a series of large and small interlinked change projects spanning different levels and functions and having different timescales.

One could of course extend this review further by including other writers (e.g. Dawson, 1994; Strickland, 1998; Wilson, 1992); however, the end product would be the same: change can be viewed as running along a continuum from incremental to transformational. Incremental or fine-tuning forms of change are geared more to changing the activities/performance/behaviour/attitudes of individuals and groups, whereas transformational change is geared towards the processes/structures and culture of the entire organisation. Obviously, there are differences in how these writers construe these concepts. Some writers see fine-tuning or incremental change as being relatively isolated and/or relatively unimportant (i.e. Dunphy and Stace, 1992; Pettigrew *et al*, 1992), whilst others see it as being part of an overall plan to transform an organisation (e.g. Kanter *et al*, 1992; Senior, 1997). In contrast, all seem to view transformational change as being strategic and important; though there are those who see it as being a relatively slow process (Kotter, 1996), those who see it as being a relatively rapid one (Peters, 1989), and those who argue that it can take both forms (Kanter *et al*, 1992; Stace and Dunphy, 1994).

Regardless of these differences, the overall view as shown by Figure 8.2 is that change can be seen as running along a continuum from small-scale incremental change to large-scale transformational change. This of course is no surprise; intuitively, one would expect change to range from small-scale to large-scale and from operational to strategic. The important consideration is perhaps not the type of change but how it should be conceived and managed. Implicit in the arguments of the Emergent approach is the view that Planned change stands at the left-hand end of this spectrum and Emergent change at the right-hand end, and that what separates them is the nature of the environment (*see* Figure 8.3). Planned change is considered suitable for (relatively) stable environments, with Emergent change being better suited to more turbulent environments. However, as shown in this and the previous chapters, these two approaches to change are more limited than their advocates claim. In particular, both the Planned and

**Small scale**                       **Large scale**

**Operational**                       **Strategic**

Figure 8.2 Change continuum

**Figure 8.3 Approaches to change**

Emergent approaches tend to stress the collaborative and consultative approach to managing change. Dunphy and Stace (1992), however, identify four approaches to managing change based on the degree to which employees are involved in planning and executing change, as follows: collaborative, consultative, directive and coercive. They also argue that consultative and directive approaches tend to dominate, except where rapid organisational transformations are required, when more coercive approaches come into play. Kotter (1996) takes a different view, seeing the overall direction of change as being decided by senior managers, but its implementation being the responsibility of empowered managers and employees at all levels. Boddy and Buchanan (1992) believe that the way in which a change should be managed will be viewed differently, depending on whether it is central or peripheral to the organisation's purpose. Davenport (1993) expands on these two issues by constructing a list of five principal factors that influence how a project will be managed: the scale of change; the level of uncertainty about the outcome; the breadth of change across the organisation; the magnitude of change in terms of attitudes and behaviour; and the timescale for implementation. Storey (1992), taking a slightly different tack, begins by identifying two key dimensions. The first concerns the degree of collaboration between the parties concerned: varying from change that is unilaterally constructed by management, to change brought about by some form of joint agreement with those involved. The second dimension concerns the form that change takes: ranging from change that is introduced as a complete package, to change comprising a sequence of individual initiatives. From these two dimensions, Storey constructs a fourfold typology of change:

1 **Top-down systemic change** aimed at transforming the organisation.
2 **Piecemeal initiatives** devised and implemented by departments or sections in an unconnected fashion.
3 **Bargaining for change** where a series of targets are jointly agreed between managers and workers, but are pursued in a piecemeal fashion.
4 **Systemic jointism** where managers and workers agree a total package of changes designed to achieve organisational transformation.

As with the earlier review of the types of change, to make sense of this review of the nature of change and how it should be managed, we need to find a way of categorising and tabulating the various viewpoints. However, this is a far from straightforward exercise. Dunphy and Stace's (1992) fourfold categorisation of approaches to change, ranging from co-operative to coercive, is useful in that it appears to cover most of the managerial approaches on offer. However, it is the circumstances in which each of these might best be used that is perhaps of most concern. Boddy and Buchanan's categorisation of central–peripheral is interesting but, in most instances, this appears to boil down to an issue of project size. Almost by definition, all major projects can be considered as central by virtue of their size and, for a similar reason, most smaller projects are, relatively speaking, peripheral. Davenport's five factors are perhaps more useful in helping us to categorise change, especially those concerning uncertainty, behaviour and attitudes, and timescale. As we have noted frequently in this book, uncertainty tends to be present when the environment is changing in a rapid and unpredictable fashion. This requires organisations to respond quickly; advocates of the Emergent approach believe this is best done by small- to medium-scale local or cross-functional or process changes. However, the ability to do this is dependent on having appropriate structures, attitudes and cultures in place. If this is not the case, then change will be delayed or not quick enough and, as Stace and Dunphy (1994) showed, will be likely to require rapid transformational change undertaken in a directive or coercive fashion. Nevertheless, both Kanter *et al* (1992), and our review of culture in Chapter 4, argue that changes in attitudes and culture cannot be achieved in a rapid and coercive manner. That type of approach tends to be effective in changing structures and processes, but achieving attitudinal and/or cultural change is a much slower process.

If we summarise the above views, we can create yet another change continuum. At one end is slow change, where the focus is on behavioural and cultural change. At the other end of the continuum is rapid change, where the focus is on major changes in structures and processes. If we merge this together with Figures 8.2 and 8.3, what we get, as Figure 8.4 shows, are four quadrants, each of which has a distinct focus in terms of change. Quadrants 1 and 4, on the left-hand side of the figure, identify situations where the primary focus is on cultural and attitudinal/behavioural change. As argued above, these are likely to be best achieved through a slow, participative approach, rather than a rapid and directive or coercive one. For relatively small-scale initiatives whose main objective is performance improvement through attitudinal and behavioural change at the individual and group level, the Planned approach, with its emphasis on collaboration and participation, is likely to be most appropriate. For those relatively large-scale initiatives, whose main focus is culture change at the level of the entire organisation or large parts of it, the Emergent approach (Kanter *et al*'s Long March), which emphasises both the collaborative and political dimensions of change, is likely to be most appropriate.

The right-hand side of Figure 8.4 identifies situations where the primary focus is on achieving changes in structures, processes, tasks and procedures. Quadrant 2 relates to situations where the focus is on achieving major changes in structures and processes at the level of the entire organisation (i.e. Kanter *et al*'s Bold Stroke). Situations where such changes are required arise for a variety of reasons. It may be that an organisation finds itself in serious trouble and needs to respond quickly to realign itself with its environment. Alternatively, it may be that an organisation is

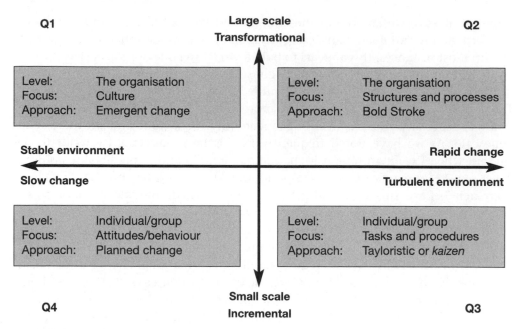

**Figure 8.4 A framework for change**

not experiencing a crisis, but that it needs to restructure itself for the future or in response to a merger or acquisition. In such cases, it may not be possible or advisable to change the structure slowly and on a piecemeal basis and, therefore, a major and rapid reorganisation is necessary. Because it involves the entire organisation or major components of it, this is likely to be driven by the centre and to be the focus of a political struggle, given that major structural changes are usually accompanied by major shifts in the distribution of power. Therefore, the new structure will be imposed from the top in a directive or even coercive way, depending on the balance between winners and losers. Quadrant 3 presents a different picture. This is where the changes tend to be small-scale and of a relatively technical nature, and have few (if any) implications for behaviour and attitudes. Such changes take place at the individual and group level rather than at the level of the entire organisation. How these are managed will depend on the culture of the organisation. In a traditional, bureaucratic organisation, a Taylor-istic approach may be adopted, i.e. specialist managers and engineers will identify the 'best way of working' and impose it. In a more participative culture, such as a Japanese company, a more collaborative approach may be appropriate, such as a *kaizen* initiative which brings together a team comprising workers and specialists. But either is possible.

Of course, it could be argued that it is difficult to identify situations that involve solely cultural changes or involve solely structural changes. This is true to an extent, but the real issue is to identify the main focus of the change. Chapter 3 examined the work of the Culture–Excellence approach. Here it was shown that writers such as Tom Peters and Rosabeth Moss Kanter were arguing for structural change in order to promote the values and behaviours necessary for organisations to survive in an increasingly complex world. Therefore, though significant structural changes were recommended, these were part of the process of culture change and not an end in themselves. John Kotter, as noted in this chapter, advocates the need for organisations to restructure themselves on a continuous basis in order to meet the challenges of the future. However, in many cases, where organisations already have an appropriate culture, he sees structural changes as working with and reinforcing the existing organisational culture rather than leading to its replacement.

Where does this leave us? First, drawing on the work of Davenport (1993), we need to distinguish between initiatives that focus on fundamental attitudinal change and those aimed at fundamental structural change. As mentioned by Allaire and Firsirotu (1984) and as argued in Chapter 4, there is a strong relationship between organisational structures and organisational cultures, and so changes in one may require corresponding changes in the other. However, as was also argued earlier, it is much easier and quicker to change structures than to change cultures. Consequently, we need to take into account the timescale for change. Rapid change is only likely to be effective or necessary where the main changes are structural changes, or where the organisation is in such trouble that delay is not an option. In the former case, change may involve some consultation but is likely to have a large element of direction from the centre. In the latter case, because of the speed and nature of the situation, change is likely to be directive and, probably, coercive.

There is one further point which needs to be noted, and that relates to how these various approaches can be used in combination. In a manner reminiscent of Mintzberg's (1994) definition of 'umbrella' strategies, Pettigrew et al (1992: 297) write of instances where change is both 'intentional and emergent'. Storey (1992) identifies the need for change projects whose outlines are decided at corporate level with little or no consultation, but whose implementation comprises an interrelated series of change initiatives, some or all of which could be the product of local co-operation and consultation. Kotter (1996) takes a similar perspective. He sees strategic change as comprising a series of large and small projects aimed at achieving the same overall objectives but which are begun at different times, which can be managed differently and which vary in nature. Buchanan and Storey (1997) also hint at this when criticising Planned change for attempting to impose order and a linear sequence to processes which are untidy, messy, multi-level and multi-function, and which develop in an iterative and backtracking manner. This is also identified by Kanter et al (1992) when speaking of Long Marches and Bold Strokes. They argue that Bold Strokes often have to be followed by a whole series of smaller-scale changes over a more extended timescale in order to embed the changes brought about by the Bold Stroke. Therefore, when examining the management of major change projects, one should not see them as solely co-operative or solely coercive. They may have elements of both but at different levels, at different times and managed by different people. They may also, indeed probably will, unfold in an unexpected way which will require rethinking and backtracking from time to time.

## A framework for choice

As can be seen from Figure 8.4, what appears to be on offer is a menu approach to change whereby organisations, or more accurately those who manage them, can choose the approach which fits their circumstances. This conception of a multiplicity of approaches is in line with the call by Dunphy and Stace (1993: 905) for 'a model of change that is essentially a "situational" or "contingency model", one that indicates how to vary strategies to achieve "optimum fit" with the changing environment'. If we were to stop at this point, it might be considered that we had indeed made significant progress in our understanding of change; yet there would still be one essential question outstanding: what about choice? We have identified situations where these various approaches seem appropriate or not, but does that mean they cannot be used in other situations and does that mean that the context cannot be changed? Supposing organisations, whose management prefer a co-operative approach, find themselves seriously out of alignment with their environment: is their only option rapid and coercive structural change? Or, alternatively, where managers prefer a more directive, less participative style, are they compelled to adopt a more participative style and culture?

These questions revolve around two issues. The first issue concerns the extent to which an organisation can influence the forces driving it to change in one direction or another. If we accept that the speed and nature of the changes that organisations are required to make are dependent upon the nature of the environment in which they are operating, then choice will relate to the extent that organisations can influence, manipulate or recreate their environment to suit their preferred way of working. This is a subject that has been examined a number of times so far, especially in Chapters 4 and 5. The conclusion reached was that organisations could influence their environment, either to stabilise or to destabilise it. If this is the case, then the important question is not just how organisations can do this, but whether, finding themselves in trouble, they have the time to influence their environment?

This leads on to the second issue: to what extent and for how long can an organisation operate with structures, practices and cultures that are out of line with its environment? The answer to this question revolves around Child's (1972) concept of equifinality. As discussed in Chapter 5, equifinality 'quite simply means that different sorts of internal arrangements are perfectly compatible with identical contextual or environmental states' (Sorge, 1997: 13). This does not imply that any structure is suitable for any environment. What it does suggest, though, is that total alignment between structure and environment is not always necessary. The duration for which this non-alignment is sustainable will clearly vary with the degree of non-alignment and the circumstances of the organisation in question; however, at the very least, it does offer organisations the potential to stave off realignment for some time during which they can influence or change their circumstances. It follows that Figure 8.4 depicts not only a framework for change but also a framework for choice.

In summary, therefore, what we can see is that the debate between Planned change and Emergent change is too narrow. It is too narrow in the sense that there are other approaches to change which organisations have available to them; especially it tends to ignore the more coercive and directive approaches to change that, in many organisations, may be more prevalent than more co-operative ones. It is also too narrow in the sense that it assumes that change is unidirectional, i.e. is driven by the environment. Organisations do have the opportunity to make choices about what to change, how to change and when to change. This does not mean that all organisations will exercise such choices or that those which do will be successful. Nor, as Chapter 5 argued, does it mean that choice is not severely constrained. However, it does mean that those who do not recognise that choice exists may be putting themselves in a worse competitive position than those who do.

## CONCLUSIONS

This and the previous chapter have examined the Planned and Emergent approaches to change which have successively dominated the theory and, to a large extent, the practice of organisational change over the past 50 years. Chapter 7 was devoted to the Planned approach to change. It was argued that, though elaborated upon and supported by a considerable number of very useful tools and techniques, it has remained essentially true to Kurt Lewin's original 'unfreezing', 'moving' and 'refreezing' approach. However, in the increasingly dynamic and unpredictable business environment of the 1980s, writers began to question the appropriateness of a top-down approach which saw the process of change primarily in terms of a 'beginning, middle and end' framework. In place of the Planned approach, as this chapter has shown, the Emergent approach began to gain support. With its emphasis on bottom-up and open-ended change, it appeared to offer a more appropriate method of accomplishing the stream of adaptations organisations believed they needed to make in order to bring themselves back into line with their environment. However, this chapter has shown that Emergent change may have as many shortcomings as Planned change.

Nevertheless, the two approaches appear to have some striking similarities, especially the stress they place on change as being a learning process. They also share a common, and major, difficulty which is that whilst both claim to be universally applicable, they were developed with particular change situations, organisation types and environments in mind. The Planned approach is clearly predicated on the assumptions that organisations operate in stable or relatively predictable environments, that managers can identify where change is required, that change projects are concerned primarily with group attitudes and behaviours, and that change is about moving from one fixed point to another fixed point and that the steps or phases in between are relatively clear and realisable. The Planned approach also appears to assume that organisations, managers and employees are open, frank, welcome involvement, and are willing to change, or that these attributes can be achieved with the application of the appropriate tools and techniques.

The Emergent approach, on the other hand, assumes that organisations are open and fluid systems which operate in unpredictable and uncertain conditions over which they have little control. It further assumes that change is a continuous process of adaptation and transformation which, because of its speed and frequency, managers cannot either fully identify or effectively control centrally. Therefore, from the Emergent perspective, identifying and managing change has to be the responsibility of everyone in the organisation. This view portrays managers, who are seen as highly competent and adaptable, as capable of changing themselves from outmoded controllers and co-ordinators to new style facilitators and partners; and employees are seen as willing to take responsibility for identifying deficiencies and implementing change. Above all, and somewhat contradictorily, change is seen as being a political process whereby different groups and individuals strive to protect or enhance their power and position. As mentioned earlier, it is on this last point – that change revolves around power and politics – that Emergent theorists and postmodernists are most in agreement.

As Chapter 7 showed, the Planned approach has had a considerable impact on organisation practice since its inception in the 1940s. However, despite its undoubted merits, as has been argued, it does appear limited in terms of the situations in which it can successfully be applied. In particular, the Planned approach has been criticised for its lack of suitability to situations requiring large-scale change and/or ones where political and power considerations are prevalent. However, as this chapter has demonstrated, the Emergent approach, which is seen as being suitable to such situations, also has major drawbacks, especially its over-emphasis on the political dimension of change and its contradictory tendency, both implicitly and explicitly, to characterise change as a slow and co-operative process. It has also been argued that, even taken together, the Planned and Emergent approaches do not cover all change situations. In particular, neither approach seems suitable for situations where the primary focus is rapid and radical structural change.

Instead of portraying the argument regarding the most appropriate approach to change as a contest between the merits of the Planned and Emergent approaches, a change framework has been developed (*see* Figure 8.4) that provides an overview of the range of change situations and approaches organisations face or are offered and the types of situations in which they can best be applied.

Though this Contingency-type approach to change appears to have some merit, it is subject to the same sort of criticisms levelled at Contingency Theory in Chapter 2. However, this chapter has also argued that, if we adopt the perspective developed in previous chapters and see the environment and other organisational constraints as manipulable or subject to managerial choice, many of these criticisms can be answered and new possibilities opened up. Some organisations will find that the organisational adjustments required to accommodate their position on the environment continuum coincide with the dominant view in the organisation of how it should operate. In that case, whether the approach to change adopted is Planned or Emergent, directive or co-operative, it will fit in with both how the organisation wishes to operate and the needs of the environment. Some organisations will, obviously, find that the dominant view internally of how they should operate is out of step with what is required to align or re-align them with their environment. Such organisations face a number of choices ranging from whether to attempt to change their structures, cultures or style of management to accommodate the environment, or whether to attempt to manipulate the environment and other constraints so as to align them more closely with the dominant view within the organisation of how it should operate. Still further, there will be other organisations who face severe problems either because they failed to respond quickly enough or in an appropriate manner to changes in their environment, or because the environment moved too rapidly for an incremental approach to respond adequately. Nevertheless, by showing that a more conducive environment can be brought about, the framework also provides those who wish to promote more co-operative approaches to change with the means to argue their case in situations where previously more directive and coercive measures appeared to be the only option.

The concept of a change framework which allows approaches to change to be matched to environmental conditions and organisational constraints is clearly attractive. The fact that it incorporates the potential for managers, and others, to exercise some choice or influence over their environment and other constraints allows the model to move beyond the limitations of mechanistic and rational perspectives on organisations, and into the heartland of organisational reality. In addition, though not by accident, it is in harmony with the approach to strategy developed in Chapters 5 and 6.

Nevertheless, though such a model of change has its attractions, its usefulness depends on how well it accommodates the reality of organisational life. To investigate this, the next part of the book (Chapters 9–11) presents ten case studies of strategy development and change. This is then followed, in Chapter 12, by a comparison of the case studies with this and the previous three chapters (5, 6 and 7) dealing with change management and strategy. The intention in Chapter 13 is to present a model of change management that incorporates both theory and practice.

## TEST YOUR LEARNING

### Short answer questions

1 Briefly discuss the Processual approach to change.

2 List the main attributes of the Emergent approach to change.

3 How do proponents of the Emergent approach view the nature of the environment in which organisations operate?

4 What is a 'bottom-up' approach to change?

5 From the Emergent perspective, what are the five features of organisations that promote or hinder successful change?

6 What do Buchanan and Boddy (1992) describe as the core skills of change agents?

7 List the main criticisms of the Emergent approach.

8 What are the implications of the Emergent approach for managerial behaviour?

### Essay questions

1 What are the main differences and similarities between the Emergent and Planned approaches to change?

2 To what extent is the Emergent approach based on the premise that change is a process of political manipulation?

3 In what circumstances might the Planned approach be used in combination with the Emergent approach?

### SUGGESTED FURTHER READING

1 Dawson, P (1994). *Organizational Change: A Processual Approach*. Paul Chapman Publishing: London.
   Patrick Dawson's book is an excellent guide to the processual and more analytical wing of Emergent change.

2 Kotter, JP (1996). *Leading Change*. Harvard Business School Press: Boston, Massachusetts, USA.
   John Kotter's work represents the more prescriptive and pragmatic wing of Emergent change.

3 Buchanan, D and Boddy, D (1992). *The Expertise of the Change Agent*. Prentice Hall: London.
   This book provides a useful guide to the role of the change agent. In particular, it describes the political skills that such individuals need to develop and deploy.

# Part 3

## CASE STUDIES IN STRATEGY DEVELOPMENT AND CHANGE MANAGEMENT

# Chapter 9

# CASE STUDIES IN STRATEGIC CHANGE

### Learning objectives

After studying the case studies in this chapter, you should be able to:

1 understand how real-life organisations develop and implement strategy;

2 describe how organisations can reinvent themselves;

3 discuss the traps that organisations can fall into when seeking to bring about strategic change;

4 show how staff can be motivated or demotivated by different approaches to strategic change;

5 appreciate that managers can exercise considerable choice in terms of their organisations' strategy;

6 identify the positive and negative roles played by managers in developing and implementing strategy;

7 understand the limitations of adopting a purely rational approach to change.

## INTRODUCTION

The four chapters in Part 2 of this book examined approaches to strategy development and change management by leading theorists and practitioners. Chapters 5 and 6 described the origins and development of strategic management, showing how it had moved from being considered as a rational perspective solely concerned with product–market issues, to a situation where there are radically differing perspectives on its purpose, function and efficacy. The quantitative rationality of the Classical approach is still very much in evidence, but it has been challenged by the fatalism of the Evolutionists, the pragmatism of the Processualists and the societal perspective of the Systemicists – though no one now appears to doubt the need to view organisations in their entirety, rather than being merely concerned with external variables. In a similar way, Chapters 7 and 8 described the development of change management, showing that many theorists and practitioners see it as having moved from being a planned, predictable and rational process to one that is inherently unpredictable and where politics and power have a major role to play. However, in concluding Part 2, it was argued that the various approaches to strategy development and organisational change all have their drawbacks as well as benefits. It was also argued that none of these approaches has universal applicability; all are situation-dependent. Successful change, therefore, requires organisations to choose the right approach to their circumstances or, as was emphasised, to change their circumstances to accommodate their favoured approach.

This chapter presents four case studies of organisations that have embarked on strategic change. It describes the experiences of these four organisations and relates these to issues discussed in Part 2. The case studies cover a wide range of situations, from rapid and apparently successful transformational change to more hesitant and less successful planned change. They also cover different time-frames, ranging from 5 to 20 years.

The chapter begins with the case of the Danish hearing-aid manufacturer, Oticon, which literally overnight reinvented itself. This is a company singled out as an outstanding example of transformational change by no less a person than Tom Peters (1992: 206): '...the transition at Oticon to a radically new form of organization has been smoother than almost anyone would have imagined'. Oticon's story is one that highlights the importance of visionary leadership that is prepared to break out of the industry standard approach and, *de facto*, change the rules of the game.

Case Study 2 could have been invented, though it was not, to show the applicability in the West of the Japanese long-term approach to strategy. It illustrates how a strong leader, with a clear vision, can move an organisation from an apparently hopeless position to one where, 20 years later, it employs nearly six times as many people, has increased turnover more than fortyfold, and is considered an international leader in its field. It demonstrates how a combination of consistency of purpose, the adoption of industry best practice, trial and error and, possibly, good fortune can transform an organisation – but not, in this case, overnight.

The third case study concerns the privatisation of the Property Services Agency (PSA). It shows that, increasingly, the PSA lost touch with and became alienated from its clients in the public sector. This, combined with an ideological aversion on the part of the government at the time to the concept of public sector bodies carrying out commercial activities, eventually led to its privatisation. The case study reveals the difficulty faced by managers, used to operating in the relative stability of the public sector, who are obliged to move their organisation into an uncharted and potentially hostile environment.

The concluding case study, Midshires College of Midwifery and Nursing, concerns the attempt to merge five organisations into one entity. It illustrates the problems that can arise when a manager with a traditional, transactional approach to strategy attempts to apply this approach in a rapidly changing and unpredictable environment. The result was a constant chopping and changing of plans and initiatives, which not only demoralised staff but increased rather than reduced the level of uncertainty.

The chapter concludes by discussing the implications of the case studies in the light of the constraints on managerial choice identified in Chapter 5. It is argued that breaking out of constraints and exercising choice, especially where this challenges the status quo, requires special qualities from a manager.

## Case study 1

# OTICON – THE DISORGANISED ORGANISATION [1]

## Background

Oticon, a Danish company founded in 1904, was the first hearing instrument company in the world. In the 1970s, it was the world's number one manufacturer of 'behind the ear' hearing aids. However, as the market for 'in the ear' products grew in the 1970s and 1980s, its fortunes plummeted and it lost money and market share. In 1987, so poor was the company's performance that it lost half of its equity. The basic problem was that Oticon was a very traditional, departmentalised and slow-moving company. It had a distinguished past but it was a small company operating in a global market. Though it had 15 sites around the world and 95 distributorships, the Head Office, its largest site by far, only employed 145 people. Yet it was operating in a market which had come to be dominated by Siemens, Phillips, Sony, 3M and Panasonic. More importantly, it had the wrong products. Oticon manufactured the standard 'behind the ear' hearing aids but customers increasingly preferred the 'in the ear' variety. Also, Oticon was strong in analogue technology, whilst the market and its customers were moving towards digital technology. In addition, though the company was strong in the state-subsidised markets of Scandinavia and Northern Europe, it was weak in the more buoyant markets of America and the Far East.

This began to change with the appointment of Lars Kolind as President of the company in 1988. The fact that he was only the third person to hold this post in the company's history helps to explain its strong attachment to tradition. In his view the company had 'been sleeping for ten years'. In the next two years, he worked hard to turn the situation round through cost-cutting measures: he pared the company down, cut staff and increased efficiency, and reduced the price of a hearing aid by 20 per cent. By 1990 Oticon made a profit of some £16 million on a turnover of £400 million with sales growing at 2 per cent per annum. However, the market was growing at 6 per cent. More importantly, Kolind did not think the company had a future. He had been searching for a sustainable competitive advantage for Oticon: 'I looked at technology, audiology. I looked at distribution strength. I looked at everything, but there was nothing we could do

---

[1] I am grateful for the help of Ronnie Stronge of Stronge Communications in preparing this case study. Further information on Oticon can be obtained from its web site (http://www.oticon.com).

better than the competition'. That he arrived at this view is hardly surprising. When competing against the world's leading electronics companies, it is very difficult to see how a small Danish company could, for example, design a better microchip for digital sound processing than Sony.

Nevertheless, he did not give up. Instead, Kolind resolved to 'think the unthinkable'. On New Year's Day 1990, the solution came to him:

> Maybe we could design a new way of running a business that could be significantly more creative, faster, and more cost-effective than the big players, and maybe that could compensate for our lack of technological excellence, our lack of capital, and our general lack of resources.

## The vision – a knowledge-based organisation

Kolind realised that the industry was totally technology-focused, and that the main thrust was to make hearing aids smaller. He, on the other hand, thought this exclusive focus on technology was short-sighted. He believed Oticon was not in the hearing-aid business *per se*; they were in the business of 'making people smile' – restoring the enjoyment of life that hearing-impairment can destroy. Making people smile, he reasoned, means not only giving them a wonderful piece of technology but actually changing people's lives for the better. To this end, the company adopted a new mission statement:

> To help people with hearing difficulties to live life as they wish, with the hearing they have.

To achieve this requires a knowledge of people's lifestyle and how hearing impairment affects this, and an understanding of the social stigma associated with hearing impairment and the use of hearing aids. He saw that what would allow Oticon to compete and thrive was not selling hearing aids, but providing a new holistic approach to customer care – a system that would allow a hearing clinic to assess hearing loss, to discuss the lifestyle needs of the person concerned, to select the appropriate hearing aid, to programme it, and to interpret the feedback from the user in order to fine-tune the hearing aid. The intent would be to allow people with hearing difficulties to lead the sort of life they wanted in their situation, whether they preferred classical music or rock music, whether they worked in a noisy environment or a quiet one, whether sound was central to their work or peripheral.

Kolind had the vision for Oticon's role in meeting customers' needs, but he still had to find a way of implementing it. He believed the key lay in the mix of expertise necessary to produce a hearing aid: micro-mechanics, microchip design, audiology, psychology, marketing, manufacturing, logistics, and all-round service capability. If Oticon were to move away from merely making hearing aids and instead provide a total package of support for people with hearing difficulties, it would have to develop a whole new concept in hearing-aid service. It would need to combine this expertise in a new way and add new areas of expertise to the organisation. In short, they would have to move from a technological orientation to a knowledge orientation, from a technology-based manufacturing company to a knowledge-based service business. They had to build a learning organisation where experts put aside their expertise and work as a team to 'make people smile'.

For Kolind, a knowledge-based or learning organisation:

> ... should not work like a machine, it should work like a brain. Brains do not know hierarchies – no boxes – no job descriptions; what there is is a very chaotic set of thousands of relationships tangled in with each other based on certain knowledge centres, with an interaction which may seem chaotic. It is the reflection of the brain into the organisation that creates companies that are able to manage that knowledge process.

Kolind began by redefining his role as CEO. Instead of seeing himself as the captain that steers the ship, he saw himself as the naval architect who designs it. He believed that it was more important to design the organisation to act in a clever and responsible way than to control every action. On this basis, he drafted plans for the company's future which he first presented in April 1990. He wanted to create 'the spaghetti organisation' – a chaotic tangle of relationships and interactions that would force the abandonment of preconceived ideas and barriers to innovation and competitiveness.

## The strategy

Having identified the vision for the organisation, the next step was to set about fleshing out and implementing his strategy for change. Beginning with the Head Office, which comprised the finance, management, marketing and product development functions, he decided to abandon the concept of a formal organisation; instead he wanted to create a 'disorganised organisation'. Formal structures, job descriptions and policies were seen as creating barriers to co-operation, innovation and teamwork rather than facilitating it. Kolind's new disorganised organisation would be founded on four principles:

- Departments and job titles would disappear and all activities would become projects initiated and pursued informally by groupings of interested people.
- Jobs would be redesigned into fluid and unique combinations of functions to suit each employee's needs and capabilities.
- All vestiges of the formal office would be eradicated and replaced by open space filled with workstations which any one could use.
- Informal, face-to-face dialogue would replace memos as the acceptable mode of communication.

Therefore, Oticon got rid of departments, departmental heads and other managerial and supervisory positions. Job descriptions and titles and anything else that created a barrier between one member of staff and another were also eliminated. The company wanted to get rid of everything associated with traditional organisations, including budgets. The intent was to see what happened when staff were 'liberated' to do what they thought best. They wanted everyone in the organisation, from secretaries to technical experts, to work much more closely together to make things happen more creatively, faster and more cost-effectively.

After 15 months of preparation, the change to the new way of working took place at 8 am on 8 August 1991. Two old buildings were abandoned and the Head Office moved into a refurbished former factory in the northern part of Copenhagen. The heart of the new Head Office was a state-of-the-art electronic infrastructure, costing nearly £30 million.

The reason for beginning with the Head Office was relatively simple: this was not just where the largest percentage of Oticon's costs were but, more importantly, where the core of its competence lay. The belief was that if it could get the Head Office functioning effectively, the rest of Oticon's somewhat scattered organisation would follow.

The concept of creating chaos out of organisation and expecting anything other than a disaster to follow seems far-fetched, if not downright lunatic. Oticon also recognised the dangers in the course it was embarking upon. The company realised that if success was to follow, above all else, there were two elements it needed to get right: direction and human values.

### Direction

Oticon's management was convinced that without a clear direction which everyone understood and believed in, the company would fragment and collapse into a disorientated mass of individuals each pursuing their own course of action. To avoid this, the management and staff openly and at length discussed and debated the new strategy for the company, and the implications for how Oticon would be structured and operate. Kolind commented that:

> . . . the entire staff discussed not only where we were going but why we were doing so, and we created a consensus among staff that not only made them know why we were doing it and what we were doing, but we also got as far as having everybody think that this fundamentally made a lot of sense . . . so there was consensus on the strategy.

### Human values

As well as a consensus about the strategy, Oticon realised it also needed to get a 'fundamental consensus about the basic human values' of its business. After much debate, these were summed up in one sentence:

> We build this company on the assumption that we only employ adults, and everything we do will rest on that assumption, so we will not treat our staff as children – we will treat them as responsible adults.

Underlying this simple statement was a view that adults do not have to be told when to come to work and go home or that those dealing with, for example, the Japanese market will come in later and go home later than those servicing the American market. In a similar way, Oticon's management believed that staff would not overspend or misspend budgets and, therefore, there was no need continually to remind them of this fact or harp on about other company rules or practices.

## Implementing the strategy

Oticon now operates on a project basis. Anyone can start a project, provided they have the permission of one of five senior managers. Some projects are also initiated by management. Whomsoever the idea comes from, the main criterion for acceptance is that a project is customer-focused. Anyone can join a project, provided they have the agreement of the project leader. The basic idea, going back to the concept that Oticon treats everyone as an adult, is that it is the individual's responsibility to fill their day usefully. If people do not have anything to do, it is their job to find something useful to do – either by starting a project or by joining one.

Kolind's view of Oticon would send shivers down the spine of most traditional CEOs: 'Hearing aids are not the core of what this company is about. It's about something more fundamental. It's about the way people perceive work. We give people the freedom to do what they want.' This is perhaps why, as well as the 100 or so 'authorised' projects, as Kolind comments, 'We have a lot of skunk work going on that's not in any official priority.' There is a saying in Oticon that 'It's easier to be forgiven than to get permission.' Basically, this means, 'If in doubt do it. If it works, fine. If it doesn't, we forgive you.'

Communication is at the centre of this new approach to work. Partly this is facilitated by computer. Each desk has a computer, and these list all the projects 'on offer' and the team leader's name along with the tasks involved. Usually the team leader will try and 'recruit' the skills he or she needs, but individuals are also expected to seek out opportunities as well. There are no demarcation lines; if an R&D specialist or a secretary wants to work with a marketing group, then all they have to do is have a chat with the project leader in order to sign on.

The physical embodiment of this new 'structureless' structure is the workplace. Gone are individual offices, gone are corridors – all the walls were taken out and everyone works in the same open-plan office. Staff gather where they wish to work. Instead of individual offices, everyone has a little filing cabinet on wheels. Staff come in each morning, pick up their mobile office and trundle it to where they are working that day. Oticon is also a genuinely 'paperless office'. All incoming mail is scanned into the computer and then shredded. The reason for this is simple: Oticon wants staff to move around from project group to project group as work requires. It does not want this process hindered by staff having to transport masses of paper as happens in most offices – the solution is to get rid of the paper.

This requires everyone to have access to and to be able to use a computer. However, the emphasis at Oticon is on face-to-face, informal communication (although, for example, e-mail is used but not extensively). This is why the office is littered with stand-up coffee bars to encourage small, informal (but short) meetings. Three or four people will meet to discuss an issue or exchange ideas and information and then return to where they are working that day and follow up ideas and suggestions. These are usually fed straight into the computer and are available to everybody else. There is also an expectation not only that all information is open to staff in this manner, but that staff actually want to know the information. Therefore, rather than putting up barriers or operating on a need-to-know basis, Oticon tries to be transparent about all aspects of its business, whether it be new products, staff salaries or finance in general. The view is that the more a person knows, the more valuable they are to the company.

Staff did not take to this radically new way of working overnight. This is perhaps not surprising. Staff were not originally recruited for their teamworking and project management skills, and some found it hard to come to terms with these new arrangements. Nor did they welcome the loss of routine and clear authority relationships or find the resultant uncertainty easy to adjust to. This was especially the case with managers for whom the loss of their power base, information monopoly and status symbols was difficult to accept.

In addition, under the new arrangement, managers were reclassified as project leaders and had to compete for the best staff, rather than having their own dedicated subordinates. Some groups of staff also found it difficult to find a role in the project team environment; for some time, receptionists, for instance, still answered the telephone. It was also some years before this new approach was adopted outside the Head Office, though the Danish manufacturing operation, which is on a different site, did show some interest quite early.

Kolind anticipated resistance and sought to overcome this by involving staff in planning the transformation of the company. Small groups of staff were selected to handle such projects as designing the new electronic infrastructure, locating a site for the new Head Office and selecting an architect. Also, all staff were given IT skills training. Indeed, they were all given a home PC and encouraged to identify their own training needs. One result of this was that staff formed their own PC club to work together to develop their skills. Despite this, prior to the move to the new building, Kolind found it necessary to issue an ultimatum to staff: accept the new arrangements or leave.

Regardless of this carrot and stick approach, the biggest boost to the new arrangements came when staff could see they actually worked better than the old ones. One immediate benefit was that Oticon 'found' that it had already developed the industry's first automatic, self-adjusting hearing aid in the 1980s. However, owing to technical problems (the solution to which was given a very low priority), lack of communication between the R&D and sales staff, and a lack of imagination, nobody seemed to have realised that they had developed a potentially world-beating product. In the transformed Oticon, this new type of hearing aid quickly resurfaced, the technical problems were rapidly ironed out, and the MultiFocus hearing aid, as it became known, was launched in late 1991. In the next two years, three more powerful variants of the MultiFocus were developed and its size reduced by half.

To set the seal on this transformation, in December 1994, after a seminar with staff, Oticon (1994: 6) published a statement of fundamental human values (*see* Table 9.1).

**Table 9.1  Oticon's statement of fundamental human values**

| *Oticon's fundamental human values* | *How do we implement them?* |
|---|---|
| We assume that Oticon employees want to take responsibility if they get the opportunity. | Whenever possible (especially within a project), an employee chooses his task, work hours and place of work. |
| We assume that Oticon employees want to develop and grow in their jobs and experience new challenges within the company. | We make it possible for an employee to assume several tasks at the same time, if he is interested and qualified – possibly with the support of colleagues. |
| We assume that Oticon employees want the greatest possible freedom... | This freedom is possible because Oticon has the fewest rules practicable, and because we encourage staff to use their common sense instead of slavishly complying with rules. |
| We assume that Oticon employees want to have qualified and fair feedback to their work and a salary corresponding to their contribution. | All levels of management – technical, staff and project managers – should give honest feedback to their employees – negative as well as positive. |
| We assume that Oticon employees want to be partners in Oticon, and not adversaries. | At intervals, we offer staff in Oticon shares at favourable rates so that they benefit financially from the success to which they have contributed. |
| We assume that Oticon employees want the security that derives from improving themselves in their current jobs so that they are able to get another job if they – for one reason or another – should leave Oticon. | We make it possible for staff to improve themselves in their jobs and assume other tasks in the company wherever relevant. |
| We assume Oticon employees want to be treated as grown-up, independent people. | Oticon's entire way of operating is based on this. |
| We assume that Oticon's employees want to understand how their tasks fit into the context of the whole company. | Oticon is an open company where all employees have access to as much information as possible. |
| We assume that Oticon employees are more interested in challenging and exciting tasks than in formal status and titles. | We have a minimum of titles and no formal career planning. We seek, however, to give each employee the possibility of personal and professional development through varied and ever more challenging tasks. |

## Sustaining and extending change

The changes to – or rather the transformation of – Oticon started at 8 am on 8 August 1991. At the beginning, all was chaos. It took months before everyone understood their new roles, and for the organisation to cast off its old ways and begin to operate in the manner Kolind had envisaged. However, by 1994, the results were impressive:

- 15 new products had been launched (twice as many as the company had previously);

- new product lead time had been halved;

- the company's sales were growing at 20 per cent per year, after a period of 10 years without real growth and at a time when the market had begun shrinking by 5 per cent per year;

- Oticon's market share increased from 8 per cent in 1990 to 12 per cent in 1993.

Nor did the progress stop there. In 1995, Oticon launched the world's first digital hearing aid, the DigiFocus. This is, in effect, a four-gram computer which fits in the ear but has the processing power of a desk-top machine. Not only was this a technological breakthrough for which Oticon has won a number of major innovation awards, but it also allowed Oticon to regain its position as one of the world's top three hearing aid producers. Also, by 1995 turnover had increased by 100 per cent on 1990 and profits had increased tenfold.

For some, this would have been a time to sit back and feel satisfied. Yet Kolind was becoming increasingly dissatisfied. The launch of the DigiFocus had dominated 1995 and the long-standing project teams created to develop and launch the product had taken on an air of permanency. He believed the company was in danger of slipping back into a traditional departmental organisational form. His response to this was to 'explode the organisation'.

In a uncharacteristically directive way, Kolind instructed people and teams to re-locate within the Head Office. Teams devoted to short-term business goals (such as sales, marketing, and customer service) were moved to the top floor. People working on medium-term projects (upgrading existing products, for example) and long-term research were put on the second floor. Those dealing with technology, infrastructure and support were located on the first floor. In Kolind's words, 'It was total chaos. Within three hours, over 100 people had moved.' He justified this new bout of chaos by arguing that 'To keep a company alive, one of the jobs of top management is to keep it dis-organised.'

As can be seen, Oticon went through major and substantial changes in the 1990s; nor were these solely restricted to its Head Office. In the early 1990s, Oticon began to extend the new working arrangements to its two factories in Denmark, and laid plans for their extension to its sales operations throughout the world. By 1997, all of its major subsidiaries in Europe, the USA and the Pacific Rim had moved into purpose-built offices designed to replicate the arrangements in its Danish HQ. The intention was to:

> ...set the standard for the knowledge-based sales company of the future ... [Through the] concept of a flat organisation, which stimulates openness, flexibility and informal communication...

Though Oticon believes that its approach can be replicated in other countries, it is not blind to cultural differences. The company realised that Denmark, with a culture characterised by equality and lack of formality, provided fertile ground for its approach to work. Therefore, in extending this approach to its operations in other countries, Oticon recognised the need for cultural sensitivity.

In addition to its own organisation, Oticon also developed partnership-style arrangements with both its component suppliers and the 5000 or so hearing care centres who distribute its products throughout the world.

Such has been its perceived success that Oticon's approach has been copied by many other organisations in Denmark, including a government ministry.

In 1998, after 10 years at the head of Oticon, Lars Kolind decided it was time to move on. He left the company in a far, far stronger position than it had been when he first arrived. In almost every sense, whether financial, technological, structural and most of all philosophical, he transformed the company. His leaving was very amicable. As he said:

> I am quitting Oticon now because I feel that both the company and I will benefit from a change. There is a whole new generation of young people who are ready to run with the ball – and why shouldn't I let them?

Kolind's departure highlights the dilemma of transformational managers: what do you do when you have transformed the company? For Oticon, success did not end with Kolind's departure, nor does it appear to have led to any rethinking of his approach to work. Rather the reverse. Oticon is now more than ever stressing the wider ethical and social role it wishes to play. As his successor, Niels Jacobsen, stated when receiving the prestigious Employee Empowerment Pioneer Award in New York in 1998:

> Our goal is to do business in a manner that positively contributes to society in every country where we do business. We support the principle that industry has a responsibility for society and that we have a collective responsibility to the environment.

## Summary

Quite obviously, Oticon must be doing something right, but what? The key to its success appears to lie in seven factors:

- *Changing the rules of the game.* Oticon created a vision of where it wanted to be. Like Japanese companies such as Cannon and Honda, this was based not only on ambition but also on a deep understanding of the nature of the market in which it operates. This allowed Oticon to spot the chink in the armour of the big players, and in effect to change the rules of the game – recognising that service delivery in total, and not technological development in isolation, is what customers really want.

- *Moving to a project-type structure which fits the strategy and vision of the business.*

- *Creating a whole-hearted commitment from everyone to working co-operatively and proactively*. In effect, there appears to have been a wholesale cultural change at Oticon, from the senior management down.

- *Creating a learning organisation*. The restructuring (or rather, de-structuring) of Oticon removed hierarchical, horizontal and cultural barriers to information flows, and created a situation where people genuinely want to exchange ideas and learn from each other. This is supported by the emphasis on informality, experimentation, innovation and risk-taking.

- *Leadership*. The Oticon story appears to be one of those rare cases of genuine visionary leadership that transformed an organisation over a relatively short space of time and then continued to support, drive and reinforce the transformation.

- *Consistent vision*. Lars Kolind had a vision of what he wanted Oticon to become. He pursued this consistently and with passion. Nor, after the new Oticon had been working for some years, and was very successful, did he hesitate to take decisive action when he felt that the company was slipping back into old ways.

- *Societal values*. As has been mentioned previously, Scandinavia has a long history of industrial and social democracy. Denmark in particular has led the way with the creation of a strong co-operative movement. The changes that have taken place at Oticon appear to be a classic, if somewhat extreme, form of Scandinavian industrial democracy. As such, Oticon's new way of working fits in with the societal values espoused by Denmark and other Scandinavian countries.

## Case study 2

# FLAIR ENGINEERING LTD

## Background

This UK company is a leading supplier of automotive components to car plants throughout Europe and has a turnover of over £100 million. It began life in the 1940s as a manufacturer of pressed steel products. In the 1950s it ceased to be an independent company and joined a small, family-owned conglomerate. By the 1960s and early 1970s, it had ceased to produce its own products and tended to specialise in providing pressed parts for the white goods industries. However, with the increasing penetration of the UK market by foreign companies, this work declined. By the late 1970s, it was operating as a 'seller of capacity' to whoever was prepared to buy. Throughout the previous 40 years, it had remained a small company; employment fluctuated between 50 and 150. Its turnover never exceeded £4 million and its profits were equally modest, though even in difficult periods it never made significant losses, nor did it require its parent company to provide much in the way of capital investment.

Therefore, like many small companies, it survived rather than thrived, and it reacted to events rather than seeking to control its own destiny. However, this all began to change in 1980 with the promotion of an existing manager to the post of Managing Director. On taking over, he carried out a strategic review of the company, the first in its history. The review confirmed his worst fears: turnover for 1979/80 was down from £4 million to £2.5 million and the company's main customers were continuing to cut back their orders. Furthermore, in the midst of a world economic recession, there did not seem to be much likelihood of alternative customers filling the gap.

The Managing Director concluded that the company lacked:

- product differentiation;
- distinct competitive strengths;
- a low cost base;
- modern equipment and manufacturing methods.

## A strategy emerges

The future looked bleak and, as proved to be the case for many companies in a similar state in the early 1980s, the most likely outcome was that they would go out of business. However, the Managing Director was determined that this would not happen. He believed that the company did have a prosperous future, but only if it could be transformed into a modern, competitive manufacturing organisation. This required it to face up to four major challenges:

- to develop a distinctive product and industry focus;
- to reduce its cost base;
- to improve quality;
- to invest in people and equipment.

These four challenges went hand-in-hand. Flair could not survive any longer merely as a seller of capacity to whoever required it. It needed to provide a coherent range of products, built around its core competence in pressed metal parts, to an industry or industries whose long-term prospects were secure. In order to achieve this, the company needed to reduce its cost base, improve quality and modernise its production equipment and methods. In addition, they had a loyal, though somewhat apprehensive workforce, whose goodwill and commitment they had to maintain if they were to transform the company.

The first steps to achieving these challenges were as follows:

1 *To undertake a market survey in order to identify potential and desired customers and products.* This took approximately six months; in the end, they targeted the motor vehicle industry as their preferred market. The UK industry was in a poor state at the time – Talbot Motors was about to fold and Rover Group (at that time still called British Leyland) looked as though it could follow. However, they believed its long-term future was secure. This industry proved to be a particularly judicious choice, given the arrival of the Japanese transplants in the UK in the latter half of the 1980s.

2 *To establish how best to organise the company in order to become a credible force in its chosen field.* In effect, the company undertook a benchmarking exercise to identify world-class performance. Though benchmarking activities and the search for world-class performance are now commonplace, this was not so in 1980, and shows how the company was beginning to become a trendsetter rather than a follower. In order to establish benchmarks, the Managing Director visited leading companies in Germany and Japan. Whilst he was impressed by the engineering skills of German companies, the way that the Japanese organised and applied themselves was a revelation to him. He found their commitment to quality, and the way the whole workforce was involved in eliminating waste and increasing effectiveness, particularly impressive. It was clear from this point onwards that if the company was to achieve its vision of becoming a world-class automotive supplier, it was to Japanese standards of excellence that they should aspire.

Having established where they wanted to go, the company now needed to win orders from its target market and establish a long-term relationship with customers. Though Ford and Rover were impressed enough with Flair's plans to give them work on forthcoming models, it was made clear that they would share this work with other suppliers and that future work depended on the company's ability to meet the cost, quality and delivery performance of these other suppliers.

With the Ford and Rover work, the company set itself two objectives: first, to exceed the performance of the other suppliers; and second, to become the single-source supplier for these components. This in essence became the company's strategy for developing partnerships with customers: outperform the opposition and on that basis take 100 per cent of the available work.

Though it had won the work, it now needed to deliver. The Ford and Rover models were both due to come on stream in 1983. This meant that Flair had two years to organise production. The company had already convinced its parent company of the worth of the strategy; now it needed to get its agreement to raise and spend the £1 million necessary to make this happen. Though reluctant to invest such a large sum in an ailing company, the parent agreed. Persuading the financial institutions to lend the money was even more difficult, but this was also achieved.

The new equipment was then installed and though there were continuing teething troubles, the company began delivering parts to Ford and Rover as planned in 1983. In the financial year 1983/4, company turnover increased fivefold over its 1979/80 level, which appeared to justify the relatively large investment.

It was at this point that the parent company, worried about raising the capital for Flair's ambitious plans, agreed to a management buy-out. Finance for this was raised partly from the Directors' own resources, but mainly from venture capitalists. Though this freed the hands of the managers (now the owners) to pursue their own plans, it did not make raising capital for investment any easier. No British banks were prepared to put up money for their investment needs. As a last resort, Flair approached a French bank who were prepared to advance the necessary capital for Flair's investment programme.

## The mid-1980s: increasing the pace of change

Despite the success with the Ford and Rover work, the Managing Director still felt that the company's performance was well below what it should be. Once again the senior managers undertook a full review of the company and came to the following conclusions:

- Senior managers were still operating in a reactive rather than proactive mode.
- Key operational problems were being 'worked round' rather than analysed and solved.
- Costs had grown faster than turnover.
- Quality was poor and they were still relying on inspection to detect and correct this.

Nevertheless, there was good news. The company's reputation as a reliable and innovative supplier was growing and they were attracting additional work from both existing and new customers. Also, the motor industry was beginning to change its view of customer–supplier relationships. Based on the Japanese experience, vehicle manufacturers were coming to see the merits of developing long-term partnerships. In particular, preferred supplier status was emerging, and customers were urging such suppliers to invest in new equipment and processes in order to enhance their competitiveness. Given that the company was already re-shaping itself along these lines, it was in advance of many of its competitors.

However, this did not obviate the need to tackle the serious issues identified above. Therefore, the management team set itself six key objectives for 1985/6:

1 reduce costs;
2 reduce stocks and work-in-progress;
3 acquire new customers in order to gain full utilisation of capital equipment;
4 reorganise sales and purchasing into one operation;

5 move to Just-in-Time manufacturing;

6 adopt the Deming/Juran approach to quality, beginning with the introduction of Statistical Process Control (SPC).

The adoption of these objectives, especially the last, began to move the company away from being just another company who had introduced new technology towards one which was truly committed to transforming itself into a world-class performer. In 1985/6 the company's turnover exceeded £12 million, and profits were in excess of £500,000. In addition, it had been chosen as a supplier to the new car factory being established in the UK by Nissan. Statistical Process Control had been introduced throughout the factory, work was continuing on getting processes right, and targets were now in place for all key areas of activity.

The progress made so far had been driven by senior managers, mainly the Managing Director. The management team believed the company needed to move from having a workforce that accepted management initiatives to one that understood and took a proactive approach to its strategic aims. Without this, the Managing Director believed, they would never match Japanese performance levels, especially in terms of quality.

What was to prove the crucial initiative in gaining employee participation began in 1986, with the introduction of cellular manufacture and the move to team-working at all levels. On the shopfloor, separate cells (process teams) were created, and these were to be supported by the other key processes in the company, i.e. engineering, purchasing and finance. The intention was that, eventually, the cells would be given responsibility for their own quality, methods and costs. From the outset, though, they were encouraged to examine critically all aspects of how the cell operated in order to make improvements.

In retrospect, the cellular approach turned out to be a key move in terms of achieving a step change in performance, although it was nearly a decade before it began fully to work as anticipated. The main difficulties lay in developing a team mentality and, in particular, appointing suitable team leaders. Also, a major retraining effort was needed to ensure the multi-skilling necessary for this approach. A further problem was the need to change the relationship between the shopfloor cells and the various staff functions. In the past, staff in engineering and purchasing had been more used to telling the shopfloor personnel what to do rather than vice versa. As for the finance section, previously they had had little to do with the shopfloor, whereas under the new arrangement they had a central role in supplying information to the cells. Therefore, though the move to cellular manufacture could be characterised as shopfloor reorganisation, it was in fact a sea change for the entire company. The locus of power ceased to be fragmented amongst the various staff functions and moved to the cells. In particular, the cell managers came to play a pivotal role in orchestrating the day-to-day life of the company.

Not surprisingly, such wholesale changes took a long time to implement. They were made even more difficult because in the late 1980s the company went through a period of rapid and sustained growth. New products and equipment were introduced and staff recruited at an unprecedented rate for the company. The result was that, though Flair was making progress, there were worrying trends in terms of both delivery and quality performance. By 1990, some four years after its introduction, the benefits the company anticipated from cellular manufacture had still not been realised. Indeed, in 1990, Flair was near the bottom of Nissan's league table of supplier performance – although, given Nissan's exacting standards, this made them rather good compared to most companies. However, Flair did not want to be compared with most companies, they wanted to be compared with the best and, if they were to continue to win orders from the likes of Nissan, Ford and Rover, they needed to be able to compete with the best.

## 1991/2: A turning point

Three key events occurred in 1991/2 which were to have a significant impact on the company's strategy and performance. The first was the appointment of a new Operations Director. The Managing Director had taken personal responsibility for operations in the past, but it was clear that the volume of work involved would not allow this to continue. It was also clear that many of the problems associated with making the cellular approach work were due to a lack of consistent managerial focus. The new Operations Director was both experienced and progressive. Almost his first action was to visit Japan to benchmark the company against the best in · the world.

The second event was that one of their key customers, Nissan, asked them to take part in a strategy development programme for senior managers. This took place over six months and allowed them (a) to undertake a rigorous review of their plans for the company's future; (b) to set clear targets, based partly on the Operations Director's benchmarking exercise; and (c) to focus on achieving world-class status.

One outcome of these first two events was a renewed determination to make the cellular approach work. There were changes to the overall structure of the company to make it more customer-focused and to ensure that the shopfloor cells received the necessary support. Customer teams were created in the commercial and operations functions led by product group managers who had a broad portfolio of responsibilities. The medium-term intention was for these product group managers to become mini general managers. As Table 9.2 shows, these changes and the focus given by the appointment of the Operations Director resulted, over the next four years, in significant improvements in the company's performance.

The third major event was that the Directors, with a great deal of reluctance, decided to sell the company. Flair's ever greater need for capital, for its ambitious expansion programme, was becoming increasingly difficult to sustain. During this period, capital investment was running at nearly 50 per cent of turnover. Not surprisingly, the venture capitalists who owned a large part of the company were becoming concerned about this. After much debate and many offers – the

**Table 9.2 Flair's performance indicators over a four-year period**

| Performance indicators | End 1992 | End 1994 | End 1996 |
|---|---|---|---|
| Quality (PPM) | 600 | 50 | 25 |
| Die change time (min) | 240 | 30 | 10 |
| Days of inventory | 20 | 10 | 5 |
| On-time delivery (%) | 90 | 100 | 100 |
| Cost reduction index | 100 | 90 | 80 |
| Design capability (%) | 20 | 70 | 100 |

company was seen as a prize catch in the industry – Flair was sold to a German conglomerate.

The sale of the company did not materially alter Flair's strategy or approach. Nor did the management change; indeed, it was a condition of the sale that they remain in place. What it did do was to remove the financial uncertainty from the company and allow managers to concentrate on building a world-class organisation.

By 1996 the company had been totally transformed from what it was in 1980. Turnover was £80 million (compared to £2.5 million in 1980) and it employed 850 staff (compared to 150 in 1980). Its customer base was exclusively leading vehicle builders, and its reputation in the industry for quality and performance was high. In addition, an independent survey had shown that it was one of the few UK-based companies that was approaching world-class status.

In some organisations this would have led to complacency, or at least a slackening of the rate of change. Not so for Flair. In 1996, the company's Operations Director spent a month in Japan in order, once again, to benchmark the company against the best in the world. As Table 9.2 shows, Flair had made significant progress since his first visit in 1992; however, the Japanese had not stood still either, and what had appeared to be exceptional performance four years earlier had now become the industry standard. In particular, quality and delivery performance were no longer considered as differentiators – these were now prerequisites for doing business with the leading car companies. The Operations Director identified the new differentiators as cost focus, design capability and flexibility. He believed that whilst Flair could achieve these, it would require the total commitment of the whole organisation to continuous improvement. Indeed, one of the key lessons it learned from acting as a supplier to Nissan was the need to incorporate continuous improvement (*kaizen*) into all its activities.

In 1993, the company had begun to develop shopfloor improvement programmes; these were later extended to all aspects of Flair's activities. The standard approach was developed from Nissan's 2-day and 10-day improvement programmes (as described in Chapter 11). By 1999, the company had undertaken some 400 improvement activities, which had played a significant part in allowing it to double its output whilst not increasing its workforce. As an example, over a two-year period, one of their major product lines underwent 52 separate improvement activities which, as well as increasing productivity and reducing quality concerns, reduced the number of staff needed to operate the line from 12 to 6.

Nevertheless, though in European terms Flair had moved from being a nobody to become one of the leading companies in its field, in global terms (which is the arena in which it must compete) it recognised there was much to do. This was especially the case given that its main customer, Ford, was by then looking for suppliers who could supply on a global and not merely a regional basis. This was why, in 1997, it reached an agreement with an American company jointly to build and operate a new plant in the US to supply Ford and other US-based car plants. The opening of this plant in 2000 marks the 20-year transformation of Flair from a company with a £2.5 million turnover that was going bust, to a company with a £100 million turnover that has gone global.

## The outcome

Any case study that covers such a lengthy period is bound to raise a wide range of issues. Looking at strategy development and change management, there are five areas which seem particularly important:

- *Constancy of purpose.* From 1980 onwards, Flair developed, continued to revisit and consistently pursued its strategic objectives, which enabled it to take charge of its own destiny.

- *A sense of urgency.* No matter what it has achieved, there seems to have been no point in the last 20 years when Flair has attempted to rest on its laurels; rather the reverse. It has been aware of how strong the competition is, how much ground it has had to catch up, and the need to spread learning and development throughout the organisation if it is to compete against the best in the world.

- *Redefining managerial roles.* Flair redefined the role of senior managers. No longer do they expect, or are they expected, to involve themselves in routine day-to-day decision-making or problem-solving. Instead, they focus on strategic issues rather than operational fire-fighting.

- *Delegation and empowerment.* The new role for senior managers can only be maintained because of the company's move to focus on processes, and to organise on a cellular basis. This gives front-line managers and their teams both the responsibility and the authority to deal with day-to-day issues, thus freeing senior managers to concentrate on longer-term strategic issues.

- *Managerial stability.* For 20 years, the process of change was driven by the vision, ambition and commitment of the Managing Director. Though there is little doubt that it was this man who, in a somewhat autocratic manner, dragged and pushed the company along in pursuit of his vision, he was not alone. For all this period he was accompanied by the Finance Director and Engineering Director who, together with the Operations Director who joined in 1991, have proved to be a formidable, stable and coherent managerial team.

There are three points to note with regard to these issues. First, the transformation of Flair took place over a 20-year period. The changes involved were not easily devised or implemented, nor did they always work first time. In essence, they emerged from a combination of predetermined strategic objectives, best practices from elsewhere, trial and error, and sheer determination to succeed.

Second, though major organisational and technical changes have been achieved, the key changes have been in the behaviour and attitudes of staff at all levels in the company. In effect, the company has experienced a culture change. Changes in attitudes and behaviour throughout the company were not quickly or easily achieved and tended to follow changes in structure, objectives, personnel (the company has taken on over 700 new staff), and senior management behaviour. The two key changes in this respect are that (a) staff now work co-operatively in teams rather than individually in isolation, and (b) they are proactive completers rather than reactive buck-passers. Though this change of culture was necessary in order to achieve greater internal effectiveness, it was not planned as such. It arose from the actions taken to improve competitiveness.

Finally, let us examine the company's approach to strategy. As discussed in Chapters 5 and 6, there are many approaches to strategy, but the tendency in the West has been to pursue quantitatively based, resource-driven strategies as averse to the more vision- and ambition-driven approach of the Japanese. What is interesting in this case is that the company, apparently unconsciously, adopted a Japanese approach. It identified a long-term, ambitious vision for itself. As part of this vision, it determined the core technologies and competencies it would need to develop in order to make this vision a reality. The company did not attempt to plot out its strategy in detail, which would have been impossible given the dynamic environment in which it chose to operate. Rather, it laid down key objectives and milestones which were reviewed and updated on a regular basis. By identifying its preferred customers and products, and determining and developing its core competencies and skills, it put itself in a position to take advantage of opportunities and avoid threats. As Hamel and Prahalad (1989) argued, this approach is the classic Japanese recipe for success. It also, incidentally, fits in with Mintzberg's (1987) theory of emergent strategy.

That the company's approach was appropriate for (or at least worked in) its situation is demonstrated by its dramatic growth in turnover and improvement in all-round performance.

# THE PROPERTY SERVICES AGENCY – PRIVATISATION AND BEYOND[2]

## Background

Claims of bureaucratic inefficiency and waste in the UK public services have, over the years, attracted much attention and occasioned a number of official enquiries (Chapman, 1978; Fulton, 1968; Osborne and Gaebler, 1992; Plowden, 1961). However, it was not until the election of the first Thatcher government in 1979 that tackling 'bloated, wasteful, over-bureaucratic, and underperforming' public services became the centrepiece of government policy (Ferlie *et al*, 1996: 11). Subsequently, successive Conservative governments attempted to deliver better value for money in public services through measures such as privatisation, outsourcing and compulsory competitive tendering (Flynn, 1993; Horton, 1996). Not surprisingly, given its size and importance, but most of all the fact that it seemed to be carrying out a role that in other sectors of the economy was carried out by the private sector, the Property Services Agency (PSA) was a prime target for reform.

The origins of the PSA can be traced to 1962 when the Ministry of Public Buildings and Works was made responsible for maintaining all the government's civil buildings. A year later, the Ministry was merged with the Works Directorates of the Admiralty, War Office and Air Ministry. The merger increased the Ministry's workforce to over 60,000. With the creation of the Department of the Environment (DoE) in 1970, it was decided that the responsibility for construction and maintenance services should become the responsibility of a separate agency and thus the Property Services Agency was born. Its role was to:

> ...provide, manage, maintain, and furnish the property used by the government, including defence establishments, offices, courts, research laboratories, training centres and land. (PSA, 1988: inside cover)

Prior to 1981, most of these services were carried out by the PSA's own staff and included all activities within the construction cycle, such as feasibility studies, preliminary and final design plans, construction/installation and maintenance. In 1981, the government introduced a policy of contracting-out 70 per cent of construction services to private sector consultants, although these services remained under the overall supervision of the PSA.

In the mid-1980s, the government's Efficiency Unit recommended that departments should start to take responsibility for commissioning and managing their own construction contracts and services (Horton, 1996). This policy was enshrined

---

[2] This case study is based on the PhD thesis of Dr Ron Coram, which I supervised. I am grateful to Dr Coram for permission to use this material. Further information on the PSA's privatisation and its aftermath can be found in Coram (1997).

in the Standard Agreement on Payment and Untying which was agreed in July 1987. In effect, it allowed departments to break away from the PSA, and many quickly took the opportunity to do so. Following this, in 1988, the Secretary of State for the Environment stated that the PSA would have to operate as a commercial concern and bid for government work on the same basis as the private sector. This, in effect, sounded the death knell of the PSA. In 1989, the Secretary of State for the Environment announced that the PSA would be privatised (PSA, 1989). The privatisation was carried out in two phases: PSA Projects was sold in December 1992; and PSA Building Management was split up into five separate companies and sold to four different private sector companies in September and October 1993. This was not a sale that made money for the taxpayer. Indeed, it was estimated that the eventual cost to the taxpayer of the sale could exceed £500 million, owing to restructuring costs prior to privatisation, and employment and contract guarantees provided to ex-government employees and the new companies (Flynn, 1993).

To understand why government departments were so keen to abandon the PSA and take responsibility for their own construction activities, it is necessary to examine how the PSA operated.

## The PSA – before privatisation

The PSA acted as an intermediary between government departments (customers) and the construction industry (suppliers). In theory, this was a cost-effective and efficient method of commissioning construction services. Rather than each department employing their own experts to carry out these tasks, there would be one body whose sole function was to commission and oversee construction projects and services. In practice, however, according to government departments, this was far from the case. Government departments were compelled, through the Allied Service Agreement, to use the PSA for all their construction requirements. Therefore, government departments had no choice but to use the PSA and because the PSA had all the expertise, departments found themselves in a subservient position. It was the PSA who told them what they could have, when they could have it, how much it would cost and who would get the contract to carry out the work. Nor did the departments carry a great deal of weight with the contractors. The PSA had the monopoly for allocating all government construction contracts relating to buildings and facilities, from the largest buildings to the smallest maintenance contracts. Therefore, as far as the contractors were concerned, it was the PSA who was in charge, and not government departments.

Government departments were, therefore, unable to control their funding arrangements on construction and maintenance issues, and were prevented from approaching alternative sources of supply. It was also very much an 'arms length' relationship. One senior civil servant said of the PSA that it was '... distant, in an ivory tower somewhere, and there wasn't the human contact and input there'. Similar comments were made by officials in other departments:

It was a poor service in that we weren't treated as customers. Our requirements and needs were not taken into account. They [their requirements] were driven almost like a central diktat if you like.

Though the PSA was providing a service for government departments, because departments had neither the power to withdraw from the Allied Service Agreement nor the necessary technical expertise to challenge its judgement, there was very little onus on the PSA to develop anything other than a distant relationship in which the departments were in a subordinate position. This one-sided relationship led to both complacency and conflict between the PSA and its customers. The process of construction or maintenance took place without any real collaboration or input from client departments. Because they had no control or power, many departments chose to sit back and let the PSA take the responsibility, and any blame, for projects. Some departments, though, found the entire process frustrating. From the mid-1970s onwards, and increasingly after 1979, there was great pressure on departments to demonstrate that they were offering value for money (Flynn, 1993). Yet in a major area of capital and revenue expenditure, the construction and maintenance of buildings departments felt they had very little control.

It was, therefore, perhaps inevitable that when Mrs Thatcher's Efficiency Unit turned its attention to expenditure on construction contracts, the PSA's role would be seen in an unfavourable light and, given the ideological inclinations of the government, that the PSA should ultimately be privatised.

## The process of privatisation

In retrospect, it is possible to see that the process of privatising the PSA went through six key stages and began well in advance of the actual announcement that it was to be privatised.

- *Stage 1*. In order to increase the commercial efficiency of the PSA, in 1986 the government appointed the consultancy firm Deloitte to develop and introduce new accounting and management information systems. These new systems were designed to allow the PSA to operate along private sector lines and to abandon public sector practices which were seen as uncommercial.

- *Stage 2*. In 1987, it was announced that, from April 1988, civilian departments of government could take responsibility for commissioning their own construction projects with a value of over £150,000. The Ministry of Defence was allowed to follow suit in April 1990. In effect, this meant that the PSA had to bid alongside private sector companies for government work.

- *Stage 3*. In 1988, the Secretary of State for the Environment announced that the PSA would in future operate on a commercial basis. This is to say that its income, and indeed its survival, would depend on gaining work from other government departments, in the face of private sector competition. To facilitate this, the PSA was restructured into a number of separate business functions, the main ones being property ownership, property services (major contracts and new work) and estate services (minor works and maintenance). In addition, in order to promote a more commercial orientation, a Business Development Directorate was established within the PSA. The consultants Price Waterhouse were appointed to operate alongside the new Directorate to assist the PSA's commercial development by, among other things, training staff in business accounting, financial management, business planning, people management, customer care and marketing.

- *Stage 4*. In September 1989, the government announced that the PSA was to be privatised. In June 1990, the legislation necessary to enable this to take place was passed.

- *Stage 5*. In October 1990, in preparation for privatisation, the PSA was restructured into three main businesses: PSA Projects, PSA Building Management (which was eventually split into five separate companies), and PSA International (which, in the end, was closed down rather than sold).

- *Stage 6*. PSA Projects was privatised in 1992. This was followed in 1993 by the sale of the five companies that comprised PSA Building Management.

The above presents the privatisation of the PSA as a relatively straightforward and structured process. However, this is far from the reality of what happened. First, it must be recognised that most of the above actions were imposed on the PSA rather than arising from the decisions of its own management. Second, the six stages focused very much on changes to structures and procedures whilst paying little attention to the reaction of the PSA's staff to the notion of privatisation. Finally, as the following will explain, the move to privatise the PSA was far slower and much messier than either the government or the PSA's management had allowed for.

## The pace of privatisation

It is generally agreed that the privatisation process was longer and more painful than expected. As a director of one of the privatised companies remarked:

> The privatisation process was a very lengthy process. It was much longer than it was originally intended to be and meant that the natural unease and nervousness that occurs during such periods was prolonged.

The main reasons for this slowness were twofold.

### Lack of strategic direction

At first, the PSA's Board appeared to treat privatisation as a standard public sector change programme which could be planned in advance, executed in a straightforward way with few unforeseen problems, and which staff would accept, even if they did not like it. However, this proved to be far from the case.

As mentioned above, in advance of privatisation the PSA had to try to operate as a commercial concern. Given this situation, it might be expected that the PSA's

Board would have adopted a twin-track strategy of developing a commercial culture whilst accelerating the privatisation process. However, the Board tended to focus on the, mainly, structural changes necessary to prepare the PSA for sale and to ignore or downgrade the importance of cultural change. Even in relation to structural change, little sense of urgency or strategic direction was apparent. Indeed, there were claims that there was a total lack of leadership from the top, in terms of both the direction and pace of change. This is perhaps not totally surprising. The Board were attempting to introduce commercial practices with which they themselves were unfamiliar. In addition, their planned approach to change, which focused on structures and procedures, whilst possibly suitable for changes within the public sector, was totally unsuitable for the level of un-certainty, unpredictability and hostility that the privatisation process was bringing. The reality was that the Board found itself bogged down in unfamiliar territory. Perhaps not surprisingly, one senior engineer described the PSA at this time as 'a ship without a rudder'. The situation was made worse by the departure of the PSA's Chief Executive and other senior staff. To many of those remaining, it appeared that they were leaving a sinking ship.

The PSA's Board brought in a firm of consultants to help them to clarify the PSA's strategic direction. However, as the following quotation from the PSA's then Deputy Chief Executive demonstrates, the result seemed somewhat unfocused:

> For example, we did a lot of work on objectives. I don't think I can remember what we boiled it down to in the end, ... something like: to preserve the maximum number of viable long-term jobs.

Whatever the merits or not of the work the Board did, it was clear that the middle and lower reaches of the PSA were more alarmed than consoled by developments. It was also the case that even where positive decisions were taken by the top, such as a commitment to provide retraining and outplacement support for staff, they found it difficult to put them into practice. One former PSA Director stated that:

> There were a few things like that [the training] where I think the best intentions at the top were weakened by people underneath, and I didn't know why.

There seem to have been three main reasons why top management found it difficult to develop a new strategy for the PSA and to push forward the pace of change. The first was that though, as civil servants, they had been brought up in a stable environment which operated by well-understood rules, they found them-selves having to transform the organisation into a commercial entity that could be successful whilst not understanding the nature of competition nor ever feeling in control of the pace of change.

Second, having been used to running a bureaucratic organisation with com-pliant staff, they found themselves attempting to construct a more flexible and entrepreneurial body with an increasingly disgruntled and worried workforce.

Last, their actions were being dictated and judged by their political masters, whose sole concern appeared to be to privatise the organisation as quickly as possible, no matter what it cost or who was offended. Therefore, senior managers found themselves caught between the politicians' desire for speed and their staff's desire for reassurance and clarity, all of which clashed with their own cautious and rule-driven approach to change.

### Resistance by PSA employees

The majority of PSA employees did not want their organisation privatised. Not only did they value the stability and certainty that working for a government body gave them, but also most believed that the PSA had little chance of survival in the private sector. As one of their trade union officials put it:

> The implications of privatisation for staff, in respect of pensions, severance terms, general pay and conditions, were enormous. What happens if the organisation who took them over went bust at some later date?

The result of this uncertainty and fear for their future was that staff sought to resist and delay privatisation. On an individual basis, many staff resisted by withholding information and slowing down the process wherever possible. For example, some staff basically gave up work and devoted all their time to searching for another job, whilst others fabricated rumours. There was also a general increase in union militancy.

The PSA staff trade union decided to oppose the privatisation. As one union official commented:

> ...we felt and still feel that if you are providing a service for the public sector and using taxpayers' money, that it's quite inappropriate to have this work carried out by organisations making a profit.

The official also went on to state that it was union policy to delay the privatisation:

> ...the idea was that the longer it took, the longer people were in the public sector. There were issues about information, about negotiation over what the implications of the sale would be for staff, and obviously, from that point of view, the idea of slowing the process down wasn't one that we were objecting to.

Eventually this resistance became overt and staff took industrial action, including working to rule and strikes. In an attempt to defuse staff opposition to privatisation, the government devised a staff choice scheme whereby PSA staff could choose to transfer fully to the privatised companies, to be seconded to them for a limited period, or to take early retirement. Though this defused some of the opposition, it was not until after the 1992 General Election, where many people – mistakenly as it turned out – expected a change of government, that staff finally accepted the inevitability of privatisation.

As can be seen, the planning and execution of the PSA's privatisation was characterised overall by uncertainty, delay, backtracking and a lack of any clear strategic direction. The entire process was driven by one unquestionable aim:

privatisation. The process, cost and consequences of privatisation were all subordinate, and, in some senses, irrelevant to achieving that one aim. Though clear in itself, the aim provided no guidance as to how it was to be achieved nor, importantly, did it offer any direction for what was to take place afterwards. As for the PSA's strategy, instead of clarity and purpose, what developed was a stream of unplanned, *ad hoc* and muddled decisions made in reaction to events, rather than in anticipation of them.

## After privatisation

Once the PSA was in private hands, and needing to win work from both public and private sector organisations, the purchasers began to re-shape the new companies to cope with the rigours of the private sector. As might be expected, different companies used different approaches. Three of the privatised companies adopted a slow and considered approach based on a process of communication, education and involvement. The others preferred a much more direct and rapid approach, designed to introduce attitudinal and behavioural change. These companies deliberately brought about disruption and confusion in order to shake staff out of their old habits. A director of one of these companies explained this approach by stating that:

> Quick forceful changes often have dynamic impacts. Slow, incremental changes tend to get dissipated. Things done with pace often carry with it force, and although you may waste a bit of money, or some of the energy gets dissipated, it often has the most poignant effect on the business.

Despite the different approaches to change, all the new companies made significant structural changes in their first six months of life. These included creating flatter organisational structures, wider spans of control, and emphasising leadership as averse to managerial skills. Also, the new management style tended to be more directive, to stress individual accountability and to encourage employees to be proactive. One company director commented that:

> It's certainly more autocratic than it was, and less democratic. That's one of the differences between the private and public sectors. The PSA had a very convoluted hierarchy. My impression of them was that the way to succeed in the PSA was never to be responsible for any of your actions. . . . Now, it's the exact opposite. I tell them, 'Don't just come to me and see me with a problem, think about it before you come to me, and think about the solution, and I'll discuss the solution with you, but take ownership of it, you take the initiative.'

All the companies also had to move to new premises, as the old ones were government-owned. Though forced on the new companies, as one ex-PSA employee stated, the move had its benefits:

> They took us over on the 1st September, and on the 2nd we were sitting in this new office here. We marched in here on the 2nd September and everybody had a desk with their name on it. Psychologically that says to people, you're different now.

Many of the staff claimed that the new environment, company name, new logo, etc., helped to create a new sense of identity and confidence in their abilities to survive in the private sector.

Over the following two years, the purchasing companies began to assess the quality and suitability of the staff they had inherited. This resulted in some staff being promoted, others demoted and some made redundant. Many of those who had agreed to move to the new companies on a 'seconded' basis were returned to government employment because they were judged to have insufficient loyalty to the new organisations. One company director remarked:

> Over fifty percent chose to second, so over this last two years, those people have been replaced by new recruits. Now, that has had the biggest impact of change, because you're bringing in private sector people to balance up the old civil service mentality, and that has been the biggest agent of change rather than trying to go off and formalise a programme of change.

Despite this, the companies also tried to enlist, relatively successfully, the trade unions in winning staff over and in neutralising potential resistance to change. For example, a senior manager in one company commented:

> They [the trade unions] have to come and stand on the podium alongside us as well, and they have to explain and sell the concepts that we've jointly agreed in negotiation to their members, our staff, and that is the stance that we've adopted.

Another major area where the new companies needed to engineer an attitudinal change was in their staffs' attitude towards their former colleagues in the civil service, with whom they now had to develop a new relationship in order to win business.

## The new customer–supplier relations

For government departments, the privatisation created clearer lines of demarcation between themselves and contractors. In addition, the advent of market testing (HMSO, 1991) forced departments to undertake a more rigorous analysis of what they could effectively provide in-house and what should be contracted out to the private sector. In recognition that departments were entering unfamiliar territory in taking responsibility for purchasing, the government provided guidelines designed to make the roles of customers and suppliers clearer. According to the senior civil servants, government departments were much happier with the new arrangements.

The other side of the coin, though, was that the former PSA organisations lost much of their superior status and power following privatisation, and were less favourably inclined to the new arrangements. This led them to examine ways to pull back some of their former influence. In particular, they examined the various ways that had been advocated for developing partnership-style relationships with the public sector (Bennett and Jayes, 1995). For instance, some companies attempted to implement 'value added' and 'magnanimous' service cultures to strengthen relationships with their customers by creating greater trust and, ultimately, more interdependency.

Companies attempted to measure what they are giving to government clients above and beyond what they were contracted to provide. As one privatised company director commented:

> ...people have got to report on what we call added value. That is, what have you done to the client in the last month that is additional to what you're contracted to do? In other words, what are you giving for nothing if you like? People are actually required to report on that ... What we say is that, provided it doesn't cost you anything, we want you to give the client as much added value as you possibly can.

Some former PSA companies even went to the extent of producing short training courses for customers, in an effort to educate them in their new role as property managers. Nevertheless, though there was general agreement about the need to move away from the construction industry's adversarial and litigious culture, the public sector remained sceptical that long-term relationships provided value for money.

## Outcomes

Though it is not the purpose of this case study to evaluate the merits or otherwise of the decision to privatise the PSA, it is important to recognise that the wave of privatisation seen in the UK in the 1980s and 1990s was essentially based on a political belief that the private sector, driven by competitive pressures, was far better at delivering value-for-money services than the public sector (Ferlie *et al*, 1996; Flynn, 1993). Consequently, the privatisation of the PSA, like other privatisations, was not driven by some form of rational-economic decision-making process, but by a political agenda aimed at transferring parts of the public sector to the private sector. Therefore, successive governments were less concerned with the process of change, or indeed the cost, and much more concerned with ensuring that the transfer took place.

This put the senior managers of the PSA in a situation for which they were ill-prepared and had little experience. They had to plan for, and sell to staff, a proposition for which they probably had little sympathy and over which, in the final analysis, they felt they had little control. The result of this was that they attempted to apply the sort of rational and planned approach to privatisation that had worked in the past in a relatively stable public sector environment with a compliant workforce and where, by and large, there were few potential losers.

Unfortunately, the government's policy in this instance was driven by ideology, not rationality, and the workforce were afraid and hostile rather than compliant. It was also the case that the senior echelons of the PSA were themselves apprehensive and lacking in support for the privatisation. Therefore, senior managers found it difficult to put their plans into practice when faced with an uncertain environment and staff hostility.

As time passed, three factors came to the fore which ensured that privatisation was completed:

1 In order to achieve its objective, the government was prepared to be pragmatic as to how the PSA was privatised and its cost, but not in the objective itself.

2 After the 1992 General Election produced no change of government or policy, it was clear to staff that privatisation of the PSA was inevitable.

3 The PSA management abandoned its planned approach to change and, basically, adopted a reactive and *ad hoc* approach to overcoming the barriers to privatisation – dealing with them as they arose and prepared to be flexible in most aspects of the process, but not the objective.

Therefore, in terms of strategic change, this was an instance where there was a clear, though limited, objective, but no clear or consistent strategy for achieving it. It is highly debatable whether or not the privatisation of the PSA has produced any measurable benefits to the UK taxpayer. Certainly the government's own National Audit Commission (NAO, 1995, 1996) was critical of the cost and process of the PSA's privatisation. Also, whilst most organisations in the private sector appear convinced that closer, less hostile and longer-term working relationships between customers and suppliers are the way to achieve best value for money, this does not seem to be the case in terms of the public sector's relations with the construction industry (Burnes and Coram, 1999).

# MIDSHIRES COLLEGE OF MIDWIFERY AND NURSING[3]

## Background

The cornerstone of the British welfare state, since its inception after the Second World War, has been the National Health Service (NHS). Such is, or at least was, the NHS's standing that it was often referred to as 'the envy of the world'. However, since the early 1980s, it has experienced successive waves of increasingly contentious change. One of the most far-reaching changes was heralded by the then government's 1989 White Paper 'Working for Patients' (HMSO, 1989), which came into operation in 1991. This was aimed at creating an internal market within the NHS, primarily through the division of 'purchasers' and 'providers' of medical and other services into separate, semi-autonomous bodies, e.g. GP Fundholders and NHS Hospital Trusts. The rationale behind the internal market was, according to two senior figures in the NHS (Carr and Donaldson, 1993: 23):

---

[3] The research for this case study was undertaken with Mohammad Salauroo of the University of Hertfordshire School of Nursing.

> ...the belief that a market system of care would induce positive behaviour [by managers and professionals] which would work in the interests of patients, and that it would bring accountability and value for money within a proper management framework.

Nor, it should be said, did the advent of a New Labour Government in 1997 appear to alter this approach, despite talk of modifying or eliminating the internal market (Cook, 1998; Salauroo and Burnes, 1998).

This case study describes how the management and staff within one particular part of the NHS, colleges of midwifery and nursing, coped with the new NHS. In line with the market-led approach, the NHS Executive Board decided that colleges of nursing needed to be able to offer a wider range of services and expertise than in the past, and therefore a programme of merging colleges of midwifery and colleges of nursing to form larger organisations was initiated. In the case in question, it was decided to merge five existing colleges to form the new Midshires College of Midwifery and Nursing. These colleges, between them, serviced hospitals in ten different Health Authorities.

The Health Authorities, in consultation with the Regional Health Authority, appointed a Steering Group of senior managers, drawn from the Boards of Governors of the five colleges, to oversee the merger. The Steering Group comprised General Managers from hospitals (NHS Hospital Trusts) within the Health Authorities, Chief Nursing Officers, and representatives from the Regional Health Authority, some 24 members in all.

The remit of the Steering Group was fairly straightforward: to oversee the amalgamation of the five colleges. There seems to have been no formal acknowledgement that this amalgamation was in any way different from previous ones. However, there were a number of issues related to the changing nature of the NHS which made this process significantly different and inherently more complicated than past amalgamations:

- There was uncertainty over the demand for nurse education in the future (both in terms of numbers and function).

- A potential conflict of interest existed between the General Managers on the Steering Group on the one hand and the new college on the other. The General Managers, under the new purchaser–provider system in the NHS, would in future not be tied to a particular college of nursing in terms of nurse education. They could, if they so wished, put their requirements out to open tender to any college in the country, as one Trust elsewhere in the UK had already done. In addition, and in the short term more probably, they could seek alternative suppliers for post-experience courses, or even provide these courses themselves in competition with the new college. Indeed, two of the Health Authorities had already established their own organisation for delivering post-experience nurse education in competition with the new college. This is perhaps why some members of the Steering Group suggested that the new college should not have in its remit the provision of post-experience courses (with implications for the jobs of some 30 per cent of existing staff in the five colleges to be amalgamated).

Therefore, key players in establishing the college found themselves placed in a somewhat ambiguous position with regard to its purpose and remit.

- It was expected that qualifications gained at the new college would be validated by a higher education institution and that eventually, as similar colleges were doing, it would actually merge into the university sector.

It might have been expected that the Steering Group would seek to clarify these key issues before proceeding to resolve the structure and organisation of the new college. After all, how could decisions regarding its structure and functioning be resolved in advance of key decisions on student numbers, course content, areas of operation, and whether or not it would merge with a higher education institution? Nevertheless, the Steering Group avoided consciously tackling these issues prior to commencing the merger process.

## Developing the strategy

The Steering Group decided that merging the five colleges could and should be managed as a straightforward and uncomplicated, almost mechanical, process. In November 1992, they appointed a Project Leader, on a fixed-term contract of two years, to complete the task of merging the colleges by October 1994.

The appointee was the Principal of one of the colleges being merged. He had no direct experience of merging colleges, but had only two years' service left prior to retirement. This meant that, unlike the other four college principals, he would not be a potential candidate for the principal's post in the new college. Surprisingly, the Project Leader was given no budget or dedicated secretarial or administrative support. He could, though, call on the resources of the five colleges, provided that the principals agreed.

Within 48 hours of his appointment, the Project Leader contacted the principals of the other colleges, by fax, and announced both the formation of a Project Board and its membership. The membership included the Project Leader and the principals of the five colleges, including the acting principal from his own college. There were also three external members brought in as advisers to the project group. These were a Finance Manager and a Personnel Manager from the Regional Health Authority and the Education Officer from the English National Board for Nursing.

By the time of the Project Board's first meeting, the Project Leader had produced a plan which, amongst other objectives, proposed the immediate integration of some administrative processes and the centralisation of student recruitment. The core of the plan was the establishment of four sub-projects aimed at integrating the major functions of the five colleges: pre-registration courses for nursing; post-registration courses for nursing; midwifery education; and education support services.

The first meeting of the Project Board discussed its own membership, the Project Leader's project plan, the roles of the Project Board members, communications, the development of new courses, and the accountability of the Project Board to the Steering Group. The Project Leader stated that he had been given clear instructions by the Steering Group, and that the task of the Project Board was to get on with the job of integrating the five colleges as laid down in his project plan. This first meeting set the pattern for the future; the Project Leader would act as the only conduit between the Steering Group and the Project Board, and questions relating to the pace, purpose and form of the proposed merger were not part of the Board's remit. Within these constraints, scope for questions and initiatives existed, but the Project Leader had the final say on all matters.

## Time for a rethink

In February 1993, some four months after the first Project Board meeting, a one-day staff conference was organised for everyone employed at the five colleges. The purpose of the day was to brief staff on developments and get feedback from them. It was apparent as the day progressed that, although staff in the colleges were enthusiastic about the change, and indeed appeared to have more enthusiasm and ideas than the Project Board itself, there were key issues which were not being addressed and which were causing increasing concern. The obvious issue for staff was that no one seemed to have a clue as to how many staff would retain their posts in the new college, or what mix of skills would be required. However, staff were just as concerned, if not more so, by the lack of any clear direction for the new college: What was its mission? What products/services would it provide? How would it be structured? Who would make these decisions, when and on what basis? What seemed to shock and dismay many of the staff was that the Project Leader seemed as uncertain and powerless as themselves regarding these issues.

The conference brought home to the Project Leader the lack of progress made towards amalgamation. The sub-groups had met frequently and produced extremely detailed plans; but the ability to turn these plans into actions seemed to elude them, partly because key issues had still not been resolved. For the Project Leader, the conference had crystallised a number of his concerns regarding both the pace of the amalgamation and the effectiveness of the Project Board system.

He also, privately, expressed the view that he had become a 'piggy in the middle' between the Project Board and the Steering Group; having critics in both camps but supporters in neither. In addition, some members of the Project Board were meeting informally but regularly to discuss and promote alternative ideas to those of the Project Leader, though whether he was aware of this was unclear. Similarly, Board members were seeing members of the Steering Group informally as well. So a great deal of behind-the-scenes lobbying and jockeying for position was taking place. This was hardly surprising, given the uncertainty – particularly over jobs – that was present.

Shortly after the staff conference, the Project Leader called a one-day Project Board meeting to discuss progress, and he invited the Chair of the Steering Group to part of the meeting. Though members were told that the meeting was to examine the situation and discuss options, they were in effect presented with a *fait accompli* by the Project Leader. He made a number of major announcements at this meeting which in effect tore up the previous four months' work:

1 The Project Board was to be disbanded and replaced by an interim Management Committee for the new college.

2 The four existing principals would become part of the Management Committee with specific areas of responsibility.

3 The role of the existing principals in the five individual colleges would be replaced by the appointment of heads of sites.

4 The sub-projects were to be abandoned; in their place, the Project Leader announced a structure for the new college which would, he stated, be fully operational by October 1993.

Despite these changes, decisions had still not been taken regarding the number of students the new college would have in the future, whether it would be allowed to offer post-registration courses, or whether it would be moving into higher education. Without this information, it was almost impossible to determine staffing levels and the skill mix for the new college, or judge the appropriateness of the proposed structure. In such a situation, inevitably, staff morale continued to decline, especially amongst staff on short-term contracts. One example of this was the high number of staff, especially in managerial positions, who were on long-term sick leave with stress-related illnesses.

## An exit strategy

The creation of the Management Committee appeared to have had little positive impact upon the new college. The new structure still only existed on paper. The reports from the Management Committee were vague, irregular and fragmented. However, the appointment of a new Chair of the Steering Group began to clarify some major issues, especially staffing levels. The new Chair came in with a sense of urgency to resolve staffing issues because it had been decided by the Regional Health Authority that his Trust would take over formal responsibility for the college in April 1995. This meant that any redundancies that might arise, and any associated costs, would be borne by his Trust.

As a condition of his Trust taking over the college, he got the Regional Health Authority to guarantee the new college the same level of pre-registration work (training student nurses) in 1994 as in 1993. However, in 1995, the guarantee would be reduced to 50 per cent, and in 1996 it would be eliminated altogether. This did not mean that the new college's workload in this area would necessarily decline. It did mean, though, that it could expect to face competition for the work. The situation with regard to post-registration courses (up-grading the skills of practising nurses), however, was still unresolved, as was the question of the link with higher education. On this latter issue, it had been understood informally that the final decision would be known in December 1993 but, like other deadlines for this decision in 1993 – May, June, July and September – it came and went with no decision being made.

Therefore, nearly two years after the merger process officially began, key issues around which the future of the college revolved had still not been resolved. Most staff still did not know if they would have jobs with the new college, although those on short-term contracts were informed by open fax messages to each of the college's sites that their contracts would not be renewed (this was later rescinded). In a similar vein, a leaked letter from the Project Leader to the Regional Health Authority discussed redundancy arrangements for permanent staff. Not surprisingly, as 1994 progressed, the climate in the organisation deteriorated drastically and any sense of optimism had all but evaporated.

In October 1994, the Project Leader was replaced by a Principal, an outsider, appointed to take charge of the new college. However, he was only appointed on a two-year contract and his main remit was not to complete the formation of the new college, nor to resolve the outstanding staffing and workload issues *per se*. Instead, his priority was to negotiate the incorporation of the new college into a university and thus remove responsibility for its running and funding from the NHS.

In effect, the Chair of the Steering Committee, along with the Regional Health Authority, appeared to have decided that the exit of the college from the NHS was preferable to attempting to resolve the issues facing the college. As with everything else to do with the college, this took longer than expected, and was not finally accomplished until November 1997 when the college became part of a local university. In the interim, the original Principal left and was replaced. Even then, the College's future seemed somewhat vague. Unlike other colleges of nursing which amalgamated with universities, it did not become part of the university proper. Instead, a separate, arms-length relationship was maintained. It had its own structures and practices, which remained unsettled for some time, and the college's staff were not appointed on the same basis as other university staff.

## The outcome

This case study shows that the market-orientated environment in which the NHS is now operating has brought about significant changes in relationships between all parts of the NHS, and not just between purchasers and providers of patient care, although for obvious reasons it is the latter which has been the focus of most attention. The creation of the NHS internal market was not just an attempt to create a more efficient method of distributing resources. It was also seen as a key element in creating a more entrepreneurial culture in the NHS (Carr and Donaldson, 1993; Fullerton and Price, 1991; Rothwell, 1994). However, the process of creating such a culture brings with it a large degree of uncertainty, dislocation and conflict, as the case study illustrates.

In this study, we can see how this conflict of interests, together with a failure to appreciate the implications of the new arrangements within the NHS, acted to undermine the effectiveness of an approach to the management of change which assumed that stability was possible and conflict was absent, or at least easily resolvable. In particular, there are three issues which seem of major significance in understanding the development of the change process in this instance:

1 *The move from a stable to an uncertain environment.* The NHS was no longer operating in a stable environment. Even leaving aside the question of the level of overall funding, the introduction of the internal market was likely to have an enormous impact on the location and flow of resources in the NHS. It was also apparent that no one could predict who would be the winners and losers in that particular game, or when – if ever – a stable state would again emerge. Therefore, the environment for the NHS was becoming increasingly uncertain and unpredictable. In such a situation, the assumption by the Steering Group that the merger of the colleges could be conducted in a planned and almost mechanical way was clearly flawed.

2 *The Project Leader.* Many of the problems which then arose in merging the colleges can be traced to the Steering Group's misconception regarding the nature of the change process in this instance, and especially the choice of Project Leader. This job was given to a man who could have been expected to amalgamate the separate colleges efficiently, almost as if dealing with model building blocks, if he had been operating in a stable environment with a bureaucratic culture amenable to his autocratic style. When it became clear to him that this was not the case, the Project Leader lacked the aptitude either to win over his own colleagues (who in some cases were apparently actively working against him) or to confront the Steering Group with its own indecision. This was not a shortcoming on his part; rather the fault lay with those who had chosen a manager with a traditional bureaucratic approach to change to undertake a complicated exercise in an uncertain and, as it transpired, hostile situation. Nor did this situation end with his replacement or the College's incorporation into the university sector. Instead of lessening, it appears to have become endemic. This was not because it was inevitable. As Salauroo and Burnes (1998) showed, other colleges and other parts of the NHS did find themselves able to create a more stable climate. Rather it was because those responsible for developing and implementing the College's strategy did not take the steps necessary to resolve the issues causing the uncertainty.

3 *Conflict of interests.* It can be seen that the potential conflict of interests both among and between members of the Steering Group led to key issues concerning the college's future workload, and thus staffing needs, not being addressed in advance of (or even during) the merger process. Instead of resolving issues regarding student numbers and the scope of its activities, the Steering Group appointed a Project Manager whose style and track record could almost guarantee that these issues would not be raised or resolved. Small wonder,

therefore, taking into account the absence of any firm decision about the new college's role and workload, and the turbulent environment in which it would be operating, that this approach failed. Nor, perhaps, is it surprising that those who found themselves responsible for the College's future within the NHS should find it easier to develop an exit strategy for the College than to resolve the problem issues, which would have been necessary if it were to remain part of the NHS.

The lesson for the NHS, and for other public sector organisations in the UK, is that conflict and ambiguity are an inevitable outcome of the changing environment in which they now operate; and that these adjustment difficulties, and the culture change which is accompanying them, cannot be dealt with as though they either do not exist or do not matter. Different situations do call for different approaches; a style of management suited to a stable state situation may, as in this instance, be totally unsuited to a more dynamic situation. Yet the culture of organisations in the UK, as Hofstede (1980, 1990) noted, tends to be one where organisations are seen as well-oiled machines which pursue rational ends and where personal conflicts and ambitions are subjugated to the needs of the organisation. In such situations, it is frequently not seen as legitimate to acknowledge conflicts of interest.

## CONCLUSIONS

In Part 2, it was argued that the potential exists for managers to exercise a wide degree of choice with regard to almost all aspects of their business, whether that be products, structures, personnel policies or culture. However, this potential freedom is limited by societal, environmental, industry-specific and organisational constraints, many of which may conflict with each other.

This chapter has demonstrated that, despite the formidable constraints on managerial freedom of action, it is possible for organisations to throw off the shackles, strike out in new directions and, in some cases, literally reinvent themselves. The Oticon case study shows how a determined manager can break out of the standard patterns of competition that exist in an industry and re-write the competitive rule book to his company's advantage. The second case study, Flair Engineering, shows, once again, the ability of a determined manager to transform his organisation: not, this time, by changing the rules, but by changing its markets, products and technologies. In effect, he chose to move into an industry where the Japanese had already changed the rules in order to favour the type of organisation he wished to create. He also broke out of the financial straitjacket that limits so many UK companies' freedom to manoeuvre by borrowing from a French bank and eventually selling the company to a German conglomerate. Nevertheless, though both the Oticon and Flair cases show the importance of leadership, they also show that this is not enough. Without support from other managers, and the ability and willingness of the rest of the organisation to develop the necessary competences and take responsibility for their own actions, both organisations would have failed.

The last two case studies illustrate what happens without clear leadership and a well-motivated workforce. The PSA case study described how, in a relatively short period of time, the PSA found itself moving from being an intrinsic part of the public sector to become a privatised commercial enterprise. It could be argued that the PSA's senior management ought to have seen the risk after the election of Mrs Thatcher in 1979 and taken steps to make itself less vulnerable. Nevertheless, the fact still remains that in 1989, much against its will, the PSA's Board were made responsible for transforming it from a public body underwritten by the taxpayer to a commercial organisation dependent for its survival on achieving a profit. Given that the Board were steeped in a public sector ethos, with little experience of how to operate a commercial concern, it is perhaps not surprising that they struggled to achieve this. Also, unlike other privatisations, the PSA had neither a monopoly position in its market nor a unique product to sell. It is also not surprising that they found it difficult to convince their workforce that privatisation would be of benefit to them. Therefore, for the PSA, the strategic change process was certainly not driven by a sunny vision of the future, but by a government determined that, literally, whatever the cost it would happen. Once the PSA had been split up and privatised, and new commercially orientated managers were in place, a much more considered and longer-term pattern of changes began to take place driven by a clearer view of what the organisations needed to achieve and what structures, behaviours and relationships needed to be developed.

Case Study 4 demonstrates that even where strategic change takes place within the boundaries of the public sector, old ways of managing it are no longer proving successful. The case of Midshires College illustrates the problems that arise when a situation which apparently warrants radical change is designated the responsibility of a manager who lacks the ability or aptitude to challenge and change the status quo. The manager, with a brief which assumed that change could be approached in a mechanical, bureaucratic manner, failed to recognise, or could not cope with, the uncertainties and unpredictability of an environment that was diverging from the stable state conditions that he had come to expect as the norm. Nor could he cope with the political dimension of change or reconcile the conflicting interests of the various stakeholders. The result was a constant chopping and changing of initiatives but very little progress.

The case studies raise a number of important issues regarding strategic change in general and managerial choice in particular:

- The particular strategic approach that an organisation (or rather its management) adopts is limited by, and to an extent must accommodate, societal, environmental, sectoral and organisational constraints. However, because these can conflict with each other, or be manipulated or changed for more favourable conditions, managers do have the freedom to adopt a strategic approach that is more in keeping with their own interests or beliefs. That is to say, under certain conditions and certain circumstances, the world in which they operate can be shaped by their views, rather than vice versa. This certainly appears to be one interpretation of events in the Oticon and Flair case studies.

- Nevertheless, as the PSA and Midshires cases show, there are situations where managers either have to accept an approach to strategy that would not be their first choice, or flounder because they cannot adapt their style or beliefs to the needs of the situation.

- A clear vision of the future and the strength of character to challenge existing norms seem essential attributes for achieving radical change; yet these are not enough. Managers must also be capable of winning over other managers and the workforce as a whole. In Oticon this seems to have taken approximately 18 months (though much remained to be done after this). In Flair, managerial co-operation seems to have been achieved at an early stage, but convincing the rest of the workforce, particularly those in support functions, was a much longer process. However, both cases were aided initially by the apparently parlous state of the organisations in question. In the PSA, managers found themselves, or allowed themselves, to be trapped between a determined government and a hostile workforce. Only once privatisation had taken place, and new owners were in charge, were managers able to begin charting a new strategic direction and shape for the dismembered PSA. In the Midshires case, it took managers some time to realise – or at least openly acknowledge – all the dangers the new organisation faced, by which time the manager in charge appeared to have lost support. Even then, many of the issues that caused uncertainty and disaffection were never resolved.

- In terms of implementing strategy, it is not necessary to work out all the details in advance, but the first few steps must be clear and consistent with the vision. It also helps if they are seen to succeed! This appears to have been the situation for Oticon and Flair, despite the fact that, in Oticon's case, the initial steps also resulted in a degree of chaos – although this may well have been deliberate. For the PSA, there appears to have been no strategy *per se*, merely an aim: to privatise it. This was something which managers moved uncertainly towards in an *ad hoc*, reactive and far from effective way. Similar criticisms regarding clarity of purpose and quality of management can be drawn from the Midshires study.

## TEST YOUR LEARNING

### Short answer questions

1 Identify three ways in which it could be said that Oticon had reinvented itself.
2 List three ways in which it could be said that Oticon had changed its culture.
3 State the main organisational constraints faced by Flair.
4 What was Flair's vision?

5 Briefly describe why the PSA lost the confidence of its customers.

6 Identify the main reasons why the PSA failed to win over its staff.

7 What was the main conflict of interest in the Midshires case study?

8 State the two main factors that destabilised Midshires' environment.

## Essay questions

1 To what extent does the Oticon case study support the argument for managerial choice?

2 Is it valid to describe the Flair case study as a prime example of the merits of Emergent change?

3 Discuss the following statement: the PSA case study shows the limitations of the Planned approach to change.

4 Briefly discuss whether the Midshires case study provides conclusive evidence for the need for change agents to be equipped with political skills.

# Chapter 10

# CASE STUDIES IN CHANGING INTERNAL RELATIONSHIPS AND ATTITUDES

## Learning objectives

After studying the case studies in this chapter, you should be able to:

1 list the main pressures on organisations for change;

2 understand how real-life organisations manage change;

3 appreciate that individual change projects can either be viewed as isolated and finite events or as one of a stream of events which can, over time, shape and re-shape an organisation;

4 identify different approaches to managing change;

5 discuss the strengths, weaknesses and suitability of different approaches to change;

6 show the respective roles of managers and staff in planning and executing change;

7 describe how environmental uncertainty influences the process of change;

8 understand why employees might resist change and how this can be avoided or coped with;

9 show how managers can exercise choice in what to change, when to change and how to change.

## INTRODUCTION

This chapter presents three case studies of organisations who, for varying reasons of efficiency, effectiveness and competitiveness, attempted to change internal relationships and attitudes across functions and between hierarchical levels. Drawing on the arguments developed in Part 2, the case studies examine why and how the particular decisions relating to change were taken and, especially, whether the resultant implementation programmes could be described as Planned or Emergent.

Case Study 5 recounts the attempts by Volvo, over a period of more than 25 years, to break with the assembly-line approach to car production and move to a more human-centred approach. The study shows that it is unclear to what extent the move to Job Design precepts could be construed as part of a vision or concerted strategy for the organisation. Other strategic developments within Volvo were certainly in tune with and helped to encourage the move to Job Design. It is nevertheless apparent that, both in its conception and execution, the move to reorganise work at Volvo was Emergent rather than Planned. Subsequent job redesign initiatives were obviously informed by, and built on, what went before to the extent that a general orientation towards group work and the creation of more satisfying jobs appears to have become embedded in Volvo. However, the particular form of work reorganisation varied from case to case, and was heavily influenced by local circumstances and the orientation of the parties involved; the same applied to implementation and development. Though much effort went into planning the actual changes, it does not appear as though a settled pattern of working arrangements developed on any of the sites. Rather, as circumstances changed, and perhaps the balance of forces shifted, so too did the actual characteristics of jobs and relationships between groups and individuals, groups and other functions, and groups and management. Therefore, the move to Job Design at Volvo, though driven by a general predisposition, can be characterised as a process of development, experimentation and learning.

The Rover Group study, Case Study 6, is another attempt by a car company to change internal relationships and attitudes. However, unlike Volvo, the main focus was not on changing job content or moving away from the assembly line, it was on developing a learning organisation – creating a skilled, committed and empowered workforce. In the Rover case, one can see successive strategies emerging which moved the emphasis away from seeing workers as liabilities and threats, towards seeing them as the company's main competitive edge. This process of change was consciously open-ended and experimental. In its attempts to create a learning organisation, Rover was prepared to embark upon some initiatives almost as an act of faith rather than in the pursuit of concrete and measurable objectives and ends.

Not all Rover's change projects share this open-ended nature. Rover has also adopted an approach to managing operational changes which very much exemplifies the beginning, middle and end approach developed by Kurt Lewin. Therefore, at Rover we can see that the company operated a range of approaches to change depending on the issues and circumstances involved; key to these developments was a consistent approach by senior managers. However, the takeover by BMW precipitated the departure of a number of senior managers and the chain of consistency was broken. The result was that Rover appeared to lose its way, especially in terms of its commitment to organisational learning. Eventually, in the face of mounting losses, BMW dismembered and sold off Rover.

GK Printers, Case Study 7, is now an efficient and forward-looking company but is a prime example of an organisation which so nearly 'snatched defeat from the jaws of victory'. The company put a great deal of collective effort into turning around its fortunes, only to see the gains threatened by inertia and conflict between managers. Fortunately, it managed to rescue the situation in time, but it could so easily have been different. In many respects, it is a company where only in a crisis can existing norms and concepts be challenged and new strategies emerge. The actual implementation process tends towards Planned rather than Emergent or open-ended change. GK operates in a changing and highly competitive environment, and though it was inclined to view change as a one-off activity rather than a process of continuous improvement, this view has been evolving. GK is also showing that it can be innovative, and has extended the range of its capabilities to develop a lucrative business in developing and designing web sites for its customers.

The chapter concludes by arguing that in modern organisations, facing uncertain and changing environments, it is not just strategy that is Emergent but also, in many cases, the implementation process. This does not invalidate the Planned approach to change, and certainly not the many tools and techniques associated with it. However, it does mean that, for change projects which are rather experimental in nature and/or open-ended, the concept of some form of settled pattern being established, and thus the process of change being concluded, is not valid.

## Case study 5

# VOLVO'S APPROACH TO JOB DESIGN[1]

## Background

In Chapter 3, we examined the emergence of new organisational paradigms. In reviewing the Culture–Excellence school, the Japanese approach and organisational learning, the emphasis placed on team or group work was striking. Though the importance of group work for individual well-being, organisational performance and collective learning has been a central feature of the Job Design literature for many years (*see* Chapter 2), its actual influence on work and organisational design in Western companies has been relatively small. One of the few exceptions to this has been Volvo, the Swedish motor vehicle manufacturer, which has been seen as a leader in innovations in work organisation since the 1970s. Indeed, it is probably not an exaggeration to say that in the 1970s, when it began moving away from traditional methods of car assembly, Volvo was more famous for its commitment to work humanisation than for the actual vehicles it manufactured (Blackler and Brown, 1978).

As will be described below, Volvo's approach to reorganising vehicle production has evolved through a number of distinct phases: the abandonment of the assembly line in favour of group-based static assembly; the extension of group

---

[1] The term Job Design is fully explained in Chapter 2. In essence it is the antithesis of Taylorism and involves designing work to fit human needs and abilities.

roles to include more collective responsibility and some decision-making auto-nomy; and the introduction of self-paced assembly work (Pontusson, 1990). It is also worth noting that the process of change was initially entirely management-driven (though the unions were involved or consulted on some aspects). The Swedish Co-determination Law, which came into effect in 1976, obliged firms to involve unions more but, in this instance, it may also have encouraged Volvo to be more radical in extending group work than might otherwise have been the case. However, through the 1980s in particular, the trade unions took a more proactive role.

The move to more flexible forms of work organisation at Volvo went hand-in-hand with its move away from corporate bureaucracy and to more decentralised, localised management of its various vehicle operations. In addition, the last 25 years have seen repeated attempts at diversification and alliances by Volvo, aimed at spreading the risks and costs of operating in a highly cyclical and very capital-intensive industry. In 1993, Pehr Gyllenhammar, Volvo's long-serving Chief Executive, attempted to merge Volvo with Renault, the French state-controlled car company. This move was defeated by a coalition of shareholders and managers with the result that Gyllenhammar resigned from the company. With his departure in 1994, Volvo tried to construct a new direction for itself. It began selling off its interests in other industries and businesses in order to concentrate on vehicle production (Done, 1994). However, as the wave of takeovers and mergers that swept the industry in the 1990s showed, as far as car production is concerned, size matters. In 1999, Volvo finally recognised that it did not have the financial resources to operate as an independent automotive company. In what must be one of the industry's great ironies, after rejecting a merger with Renault five years earlier, Volvo sold its car division to the Ford Motor Corporation.

Although Ford's takeover does not invalidate Volvo's unique approach to building cars, it does threaten it. Despite the benefits of good design and leading-edge technologies, vehicle producers tend to stand or fall by the effectiveness and efficiency of their assembly operations (Womack et al, 1990). Ford's opinion of the efficiency of Volvo's assembly operations will be crucial in determining whether the Volvo approach survives or is replaced by more traditional Fordist ways of work.

What this highlights, though, is that Volvo's move to end assembly-line production was not and is not a marginal activity – it strikes at the very core of its competitiveness. The decision to adopt Job Design at Volvo was and remains driven by management, regardless of later union and legislative encouragement, though to what extent they foresaw how extensively it would develop is not known. What is clear is that, in the 1960s, Volvo was as committed as any car company to the Classical approach to work organisation espoused by Taylor and embodied in the assembly-line approach to car production devised by Henry Ford. Yet, in the 1970s, it chose to break away from this industry-standard approach and embark on (what has turned out to be) a long-term programme of increasingly radical work reorganisation.

There are two complementary explanations for Volvo's actions. The first is the explanation given by Pehr Gyllenhammar (1977: 73), until 1994 Volvo's Chief Executive, identifying the need to reduce labour turnover, which the company believed was caused by boring and monotonous jobs:

> The company has to bear the costs of recruiting labour and training employees. The absenteeism and turnover rates also increase the costs for quality control, for maintaining buffer stocks of semifinished goods and components, and for adjustments, tools and machinery. Administrative costs go up when a company must maintain pools of reserve labour to fill requirements during peak periods of absenteeism.

To flesh Gyllenhammar's explanation out a little, Pontusson (1990) pointed out that Volvo's freedom of manoeuvre in tackling its recruitment and retention problems was limited by the labour market conditions of the time. There was full employment, which made it easier for workers to move jobs; and very effective wage bargaining by unions, establishing industry and sectoral pay rates which made it very difficult for Volvo to offer higher wage rates than other employers. In the presence of full employment and the absence of wage flexibility, Volvo chose to tackle labour turnover and absenteeism by attempting to create more satisfying and varied jobs.

The second explanation was offered by Karlsson (1973). He pointed out that Volvo was one of Sweden's largest and most successful companies. As such, its actions and practices were always in the public eye. With the increasing interest in Job Design in Scandinavia in general and Sweden in particular in the 1960s and 1970s, it was hardly surprising that Volvo's work organisation methods were the subject of much attention. In particular, Karlsson (1973: 34) pointed out that the company was heavily criticised for its 'inhuman principles of organisation' based 'entirely on the scientific management method'.

So it appears that Volvo's conversion to Job Design was inspired by commercial considerations relating to the costs of absenteeism and labour turnover, allied to pressure from public opinion in Sweden for it to embrace a less 'inhuman' form of work organisation. Although these appear to be the principal reasons for Volvo's management embarking on its commitment to Job Design, since then the process has developed its own momentum, to the extent that (as noted by Auer and Riegler, 1990: 14): 'group work is the basic concept for all changes in the organisation of production work at Volvo'. However, this did not come about overnight, without hesitation and backtracking, or in a fully planned and co-ordinated fashion; rather it has evolved or emerged through a number of distinct phases.

## Phases of change

Volvo's adoption of Job Design principles began over 25 years ago. It has now reached a stage where group work has become the standard approach to work design, and assembly-line working is not considered appropriate for any new Volvo plant. When dealing with events spanning such a long period, it is often difficult to form an accurate picture of what has taken place and why; particularly when, as in this case, these events have been played out on different sites by different groups of managers and workers. Nevertheless, as Auer and Riegler (1990) and Pontusson (1990) pointed out, by examining major change programmes involving large investments in new or remodelled plants, it is possible to identify a number of distinct phases in the evolution of Volvo's approach to Job Design.

These phases are related to major investment projects which occurred in the 1970s, 1980s and 1990s, namely:

- **Kalmar** – This plant opened in 1974 and was the company's first, and most cited, attempt to move away from assembly-line work.

- **Torslanda** – This is Volvo's main car plant which, since the late 1970s, has seen a number of increasingly radical attempts to move away from the traditional assembly-line approach to car production.

- **Uddevalla** – This new assembly plant opened in 1990, and exemplifies Volvo's decisive break with traditional motor industry jobs.

- **Gent and Born** – The introduction of new cars in these existing plants in the late 1980s allowed Volvo the opportunity to introduce the methods developed in its other plants, thus showing Volvo's commitment to extending its Job Design philosophy across all areas of its operations.

### Phase One – Kalmar

Those committed to challenging the 'inhuman' approach to work, epitomised by the Classical school in general and Henry Ford's moving assembly line in particular, came to look on Volvo's Kalmar car plant as a sort of promised land – a blueprint for the future of work. This was not only because Kalmar was seen as a model of human-centred work organisation, but also because it struck at the very heart of the industry which, through its use of the moving assembly line with its severe division of labour and short cycle times, had taken Taylorist work practices to their ultimate extremes. In addition, and just as importantly, it was heralded as a commercial success. Indeed, Kalmar was famous throughout the world for its 'revolutionary' approach to Job Design even before it opened (Blackler and Brown, 1978).

Perhaps the main reason for the perception that Kalmar was making a decisive break with the past was due to the way Volvo approached its design. The original management concept for Kalmar attempted to incorporate many of the progressive Job Design ideas circulating in the early 1970s. A project team composed of managers, engineers and architects was given responsibility for designing and building the plant. However, each decision of this team had to be approved by a committee which included trade union representatives, health and safety experts, doctors and outside Job Design experts, including colleagues of Einar Thorsrud, the noted Norwegian work psychologist.

However, the 'revolutionary' image of Kalmar also owed much to the efficiency of Volvo's own publicity machine. This can be seen from statements about the ethos of the plant made by Pehr Gyllenhammar, Volvo's former Chief Executive, before it opened:

> The objective of Kalmar will be to arrange auto production in such a way that each employee will be able to find meaning and satisfaction in his work.
>
> This will be a factory which, without any sacrifice of efficiency or the company's financial objectives, will give employees opportunities to work in groups, to communicate freely among themselves, to switch from one job assignment to another, to vary the pace of their work, to identify with the product, to be conscious of a responsibility for quality, and to influence their own working environment.
>
> When a product is made by people who find meaning in their work, it must inevitably be a product of high quality. (All quotes are from Aguren *et al*, 1984: 13)

Opened in 1974, Kalmar was Volvo's second largest final assembly plant (the much bigger Torslanda being the largest). It had been planned for an annual capacity of 30,000 cars with around 600 employees. In 1976, it produced 22,000 cars but production fell to 17,000 when demand slumped after the second oil shock in 1977. Production rose again in 1979 but fell back in 1980, when a four-day week was briefly introduced. In 1985, Kalmar produced 32,500 cars, representing about 16 per cent of Volvo's Swedish output of cars. In 1988 the plant had around 960 employees (Aguren *et al*, 1984; Auer and Riegler, 1990).

The differences between Kalmar and a traditional car plant are that, in the latter, the pace of work is determined by the moving assembly line, jobs are extremely fragmented and have cycle times of a few minutes or less, and workers are dedicated to one task only. At Kalmar there is no assembly line, workers operate in teams, with each team having its own dedicated area of the factory. Within the team, workers can move between tasks, and each task has a cycle time of between 20 and 30 minutes. In place of the assembly line, cars are mounted on automated carriers which move around the plant and serve both as a means of transport and as a work platform. This arrangement allowed Kalmar originally to operate two alternatives to the moving assembly line:

- **Straight-line assembly**. Work within each team area is split up into four or five work stations placed in a series along the production flow. Two team members work at each station, following the carrier through all the stations and carrying out all the necessary assembly operations.
- **Dock assembly**. This is where one carrier at a time is guided into the 'dock' assembly areas where all of the team's tasks are carried out on the stationary carrier by two or three people.

The main difference between the two approaches is that the first, straight-line assembly, still bears some relation to the moving assembly line in that the car carriers move automatically from station to station thus determining the pace of work. In the second approach, the dock system, the car is stationary all the time giving workers more control over the pace of work. Nevertheless, both forms revolve around teamwork and offer variety and task completeness.

There can be very little doubt that, for its time, Kalmar represented a significant break with the past. However, there are those who question whether the original high hopes for the plant, in terms of the humanisation of work, have been met. Pontusson (1990) argued that the economic consequences of fluctuations in output levels led the plant management to retreat from its original ambitions and, in the latter part of the 1970s, to tighten managerial control over the work process. It was certainly the case that, compared to its conventional plants, there was no significant improvement in output. Also, as Berggren (1992: 123) noted, the ability of work teams to change the pace of work led to some 'mischief', and a team might change the pace of work of another team 'for fun'. For these reasons, according to Pontusson (1990), dock assembly was abandoned, and the potential for workers to influence the pace of work by taking automated carriers out of the main flow was ended.

Blackler and Brown (1978) argued that, with the abandonment of dock assembly, and despite longer cycle times, some fundamental elements of the assembly line (i.e. machine-paced work) have been maintained. Auer and Riegler (1990) made a similar point. They argued that, over time, changes such as new work evaluation methods, the removal of time buffers between stages and the general speeding up of the carriers (which are controlled by a central computer) have intensified the pace of work and have returned the production process much closer to the assembly-line concept than was originally intended.

Before it opened, Kalmar was being hailed as a revolution in Job Design. The reality is that Kalmar does not appear to have represented the dramatic break with the Fordist–Taylorist production process that many had hoped for (Auer and Riegler, 1990; Blackler and Brown, 1978; Pontusson, 1990). However, this does not mean that Kalmar was a failure. Given that Volvo, hitherto very much a traditional car company, were trying to invent a new concept in car assembly, it would have been surprising if they had managed to rewrite the rules of car production at the first attempt. It must be remembered that, although Kalmar was a social experiment, it was also expected to be an economic success. If the social dimension appeared to threaten financial performance, it was the former rather than the latter that would be sacrificed. The true measure of Kalmar's success lies not in the degree to which it achieved its 'revolutionary' goal, but in the extent to which it encouraged Volvo's management to continue with and accelerate the move away from Fordist–Taylorist approaches to work. As Auer and Riegler (1990: 27) concluded, despite some disagreement among managers over the effectiveness of the organisation of Kalmar plant, there were sufficient supporters for Volvo to proceed with the development of 'far more progressive' and 'radical' attempts to distance itself from the traditional assembly-line approach to car production. This is a point also made by Gyllenhammar:

> Volvo Kalmar is no final solution. It is the first step on the road. But much remains to be done in the field of work organisation. I could imagine much greater freedom and independence at work. (Quoted in Berggren, 1992: 127)

Nevertheless, in 1992, at the time of a major recession in the European car industry, Kalmar was closed.

### Phase Two – Torslanda

As well as Kalmar, the late 1970s and early 1980s saw Volvo experimenting with alternatives to the traditional assembly line at a number of plants. In the main, these were small-scale, and tended to concentrate on bus or truck production rather than car assembly. However, from the late 1970s onwards, a series of increasingly radical attempts were made to transform work organisation at Torslanda, Volvo's main car assembly plant. In 1976, at the central assembly plant, Torslanda management experimented with the use of large, autonomous work groups to assemble an entire car using a dock-assembly approach similar to that being attempted at Kalmar. Owing to poor productivity, this was abandoned within six months. Management believed that the workforce lacked the necessary skills to make such an approach work, whilst the metal workers' trade union felt the experiment was too risky.

In 1979/80, with the opening of the TUN facility at Torslanda to assemble the new 700 series car, management attempted to revive group-based assembly. The TUN workforce was selected from the existing production personnel at Torslanda. The original plan for TUN, initially drawn up without union involvement, envisaged car assembly being carried out by autonomous work groups who would be responsible for their own quality and pace of work. It was planned that work groups would also have responsibility for job rotation, managing material supplies and some maintenance tasks.

The reality though was somewhat less ambitious than originally conceived. The unions, who – when eventually involved – played a larger part in the design of TUN than they had at Kalmar, were highly sceptical of the original concept and this, together with certain practical difficulties in trying to mix indirect tasks, such as maintenance and material control, with direct production work, led to the scaling-down of the original proposals. TUN is still organised around group-based assembly, and job rotation is still practised, but the pace of work is centrally controlled and workers no longer perform indirect tasks. Nevertheless, workers at TUN see it as being a clear improvement on the traditional approach to car assembly (Auer and Riegler, 1990).

In 1986, once again management began to consider major changes to the organisation of work at Torslanda's central assembly plant. At this time, the plant employed 4,000 workers and was mainly organised around Fordist–Taylorist principles. This time the trade unions were involved much earlier and played a more central role. In February 1986, management and unions agreed an 'action plan' which emphasised the transformation of car assembly into an 'attractive alternative' to the traditional methods of car manufacture. In particular, learning from the earlier failure, the plan stressed the need for high-quality training and continuing education to allow workers to gain the skills necessary for effective group work. The action plan appeared to revive many of the original plans for TUN (including the provision for direct production workers to carry out indirect tasks). In addition, it envisaged working time being adjusted to employee needs.

Though the reorganisation of Torslanda is a continuing process, some of the individual sections, such as motor and axle assembly, have been operating along new lines for some time. The changes envisaged in the action plan have been introduced, especially those relating to workers controlling the pace of work and undertaking indirect tasks. Staff turnover and absenteeism is very low at Torslanda, which reflects both the work environment and the rigorous recruitment methods designed to select well-educated staff who are team-orientated. It is a very clean plant with good recreational facilities, such as a gym and swimming pool, and also provides a creche for the children of all staff. At Torslanda, upward and downward communication is considered vital, and staff are encouraged to show initiative through formal and informal discussion groups.

As might be expected, there have been some difficulties in implementing these new working arrangements at Torslanda. The main problem appears to relate to trade union attempts to protect traditional demarcations between direct and indirect tasks and between work groups and supervisors. Maintenance staff still work outside the work group structure, and the foremen's trade union successfully resisted their partial replacement by rotating team leaders. The metal workers' union also wanted to maintain a more hierarchical structure in order to preserve a job ladder between the shopfloor and management.

By the late 1990s, the workforce at Torslanda had increased to 5,500 and the plant was producing 580 vehicles a day. Multi-skilling was a fact of life and, in some parts of the factory, jobs were rotated every hour. Such was the perceived success of the factory that it was given responsibility for assembling Volvo's C70 car which was launched in 1997. Therefore, progress has been made and, though the final form that Torslanda will take is still uncertain, it does appear to promise a more radical break with tradition than occurred at Kalmar (Auer and Riegler, 1990; Pontusson, 1990).

### Phase Three – Uddevalla

This was the first all-new car assembly plant built by Volvo in Sweden since Kalmar. It was designed to employ 1,000 people and have the capability to produce 40,000 cars per year. Many observers believe the plant goes far beyond Volvo's previous attempts at Job Design: 'the only one [car plant] in the world where workers build cars from start to finish rather than on an assembly line' (McIvor, 1995: 37). The design of the plant was the result of a 'modernisation pact' between the plant's management and the metal workers' union, many of whose extensive demands were incorporated into the plant's design (Auer and Riegler, 1990). In accordance with Sweden's Co-determination Law (and Volvo's practice at Torslanda), the unions were involved in the steering group responsible for designing and building the Uddevalla plant. Indeed, three union officials worked full-time on the project between 1985 and 1987.

The completed plant comprised six mini-factories, each containing eight dock assembly areas, each with its own autonomous work group. Therefore, in total, there were 48 assembly groups. Each work group has 10 fully-trained assembly workers, each of whom can, again in theory, perform all the tasks necessary to assemble an entire car. The work groups are responsible for determining their own pace of work and internal job rotation. In addition, the groups have responsibility for maintenance, administration and quality control. The role of group leader rotates among the members of each group. The incorporation of so many functions within each group resulted in a very flat hierarchy; there are no layers between the groups and the factory managers. To facilitate these working arrangements, the process of car assembly had to be re-thought in order to refine and simplify it. The plant also adopted an equal opportunities policy which reserved at least 40 per cent of production jobs for women and at least 25 per cent for workers over 45 years old.

The plant is clearly at the leading edge of Job Design, at least as far as the car industry is concerned. As Karlsson (1996: 11) remarked:

> What was created was an extremely horizontal organisation, but also some vertical integration. This included responsibilities for quality and some integration with sales, because in the result-oriented team the idea was that the worker should be able to experience what he delivered to the customer. Hence the members of the assembly group could meet and talk directly to the customer.

Nevertheless, as other such initiatives by Volvo have shown, economic and operational concerns can lead to its more radical elements, especially self-paced work, being modified over time. Indeed, the original plan for the plant very much followed the practices adopted at Kalmar. It was only with considerable pressure from the trade unions, and the intervention of Volvo's top management, that more radical ideas were eventually adopted, though even the unions took some convincing that machine-paced assembly might be abandoned altogether (Pontusson, 1990).

Unfortunately, the plant opened at a time when car demand was falling dramatically. Despite attempts to keep it open, along with the Kalmar plant, Volvo closed Uddevalla in 1992 in the face of mounting losses, and notwith-standing the fact that, in productivity terms, it was the most efficient of Volvo's Swedish plants (Cressey, 1996). However, in 1995 the plant was re-opened as a joint venture. Though operating on a smaller scale than originally envisaged, Uddevalla's new Chief Executive appeared determined to stick to its original Job Design concept (McIvor, 1995).

### Phase Four – Gent and Born

By the late 1980s, Volvo's approach to Job Design was widely accepted and practised throughout the company, especially wherever new developments were taking place. When Volvo's Gent plant was chosen to build the 850 series (known internally as the VEC – Volvo European Car), it was natural for Volvo to adopt team-based assembly. The VEC teams operated very much as at the Uddevalla plant but with even greater emphasis on continuous improvement. There was also a great deal of emphasis on the teams to carry out their own maintenance as well as other support tasks. Indeed, so successful was this that Gent became the first plant outside Japan to gain the Total Productive Maintenance Award. In 1996, similar developments took place in Volvo's Belgium plant at Born. The plant was chosen as the site of a joint venture between Volvo and Mitsubishi called Nedcar. The objective was to make cars for both companies that share the same chassis, and have one-third of the parts in common. In essence, it was an attempt to blend Japanese lean production techniques with Volvo's job design approach. The aim was to achieve world class efficiency, and the plant quickly became one of Europe's most efficient car plants.

Both Gent and Born demonstrate Volvo's on-going commitment to develop, extend and experiment with alternative forms of job design to those used elsewhere in the car industry. As Karlsson (1996) suggests, Volvo is continually looking for new and different ways to organise production, in the case of Gent and Born by adopting a lean production philosophy, but ensuring that group work lies at the heart of any new developments.

## The outcome

The progress of redesigning jobs at Volvo has been remarkable in comparison with the Tayloristic–Fordist nature of the company in the 1960s. The fact that it has continued and intensified over a period of 25 years, and that any organisational changes at Volvo are expected to revolve around group work, speaks volumes for the degree to which it has become embedded in the culture of the company. This is not to say that the result is perfect. It must be remembered that assembling cars and trucks will always be a physically demanding job. Also, Volvo are not an altruistic organisation; they exist to make a profit, and the way they organise work must reflect and facilitate this (regardless of pressures from trade unions, government legislation and public opinion). Nevertheless, as Pontusson (1990: 315) observed of Volvo, the 'stages of workplace reform involve a cumulative process of innovation, with a trajectory which adds up to a more or less definitive break with Fordism'. This conclusion, of course, makes the takeover of Volvo by Ford in 1999 all the more ironic.

Some might also point out that though Volvo have led the way, many other companies have followed – including much of the car industry. However, this would be to miss two important points. First, Volvo's approach is not a copycat or 'flavour of the month' one. Rather, it is long-standing and still developing approach which appears to be fundamental to the way the company operates. Second, though most other car companies have adopted, to a lesser or greater extent, the autonomous/semi-autonomous work group concept, especially the Japanese, no one else has abandoned the assembly line or gives workers the degree of autonomy and control that Volvo do, especially over the pace of work. Indeed, given the output of the leading car plants, if anything the pace of work on assembly lines, and rigid control over what assembly workers do, seemed more intense in the 1990s than in the supposedly bad old days of the 1960s and 1970s (Milner, 1998).

The changes at Volvo have taken place over an extended timescale, at different sites and under different conditions and, therefore, have been influenced by a wide range of factors. Despite the subsequent advent of the Culture–Excellence approach and the Japanese approach, what has successfully taken place at Volvo is the adoption of practices and principles associated with the Human Relations school as operationalised by the Job Design movement. The key factors which appear to have influenced Volvo to adopt this approach are as follows:

- For sound economic and business reasons, Volvo needed to reduce absenteeism and high labour turnover.

- Full employment and a lack of wage flexibility precluded more traditional 'stick and carrot' measures for dealing with absenteeism and labour turnover. Therefore, Volvo had to look at alternative methods of reducing absenteeism and labour turnover and, instead of trying to alleviate the symptoms, they chose to tackle the boredom and dissatisfaction that gave rise to labour problems in the first place. The decision by Volvo's management to adopt a Job Design approach appears to have come about owing to a combination of intense public pressure on the company to move to a more human-centred approach to assembly work, and managerial preference. It should be noted, though, that Volvo's management have never been unanimous in supporting the more radical aspects of Job Design, as was demonstrated by the disagreement over the success of Kalmar and the need for senior managers to intervene to ensure a more radical approach at Uddevalla.

- The parallel move by Volvo to adopt a strategy of decentralising control to plant level (as averse to its previous centralised, bureaucratic control procedures) gave local management some freedom to experiment with new ways of working, and also allowed management to experience the lessening of control which they were advocating for workers.

- Though originally the move away from Fordist–Taylorist work practices was entirely management-inspired, trade unions came to play an increasingly active role in encouraging its adoption. In this, they were aided by both the Co-determination Law which came into effect in 1976 and the generally favourable climate towards Job Design in Sweden. However, as Torslanda demonstrated, the trade unions – like Volvo's management – are capable of exhibiting conservative tendencies and need to be convinced that some of the more radical elements of group work should be adopted.

- Whilst these changes have taken place on different sites and at different times, both management and workers appear to have found a way of capturing the knowledge gained at other plants and lessons learnt for future projects. This process of organisational learning appears to be fundamental to understanding how Volvo has moved (not always in an easy or deliberate fashion) from the limited, though significant, structural changes at Kalmar to the genuine expansion of workers' control seen at Uddevalla. Auer and Riegler (1990: 52), who carried out a comprehensive review of work organisation changes at Volvo, commented that:

> Interviews with managers, representatives of trade unions and researchers all confirmed ... Volvo is one of the few companies where management, employees, and trade unions have found broad opportunities for gathering experience in changing the organisation of work and that the company is a place of learning...

Evidently, the case of Volvo's attempts to move to a radical change in its internal relationships, one which passes significantly greater control of production to workers than had hitherto been considered wise and efficient, is by no means straightforward. Though the intent was there from the start, though we can argue about why the move to Job Design came about, the actual details have been subject to a process of pragmatism, revision and trial and error over more than 25 years. The new approach to work organisation coincided with Volvo's granting of greater autonomy to plant-level managers, the introduction of the Co-determination Law, and considerable public support for Job Design in Sweden; clearly, these were all influential in what happened at Volvo. However, it should be remembered that Volvo was, at the time, a large and relatively successful private company. If it had wanted to, it could have chosen another course of action: indeed, Volvo's management itself disagreed about the need for and extent of Job Design. The fact that Volvo chose to break the car industry mould at Kalmar, and to keep breaking it at other plants, shows that no matter how powerful or dominant a particular paradigm is, alternatives are always possible. It is also true that, if the move to new ways of working had not allowed the company to develop its competitiveness, the initiative would not have flourished. It may well have been the case that in the atmosphere of the 1970s, Volvo was under great pressure from a number of sources to develop a more human-centred approach to work. However, with the easing of this pressure in the 1980s and 1990s, the company could have chosen quietly to abandon this approach. That it did not clearly demonstrates the belief, especially by Volvo's management, that job redesign works. Whether or not this commitment will survive the introduction of Ford management, only time will tell. However, given the stark disparity between Ford's approach to work organisation and Volvo's, it is difficult to see how the two can co-exist.

# ROVER GROUP – THE RISE AND FALL OF A LEARNING ORGANISATION[2]

## Background

In June 1999, it was announced that BMW would invest over £3 billion in its Rover plants over the next six years and that, in addition, the UK government would provide industrial aid of £152 million (Gow, 1999b). This appeared to have brought to an end yet another crisis for the company, whose history is punctuated with such crises. This crisis erupted in early 1998, when BMW announced that its Rover subsidiary would lose over £600 million that year and that its future, particularly that of its Longbridge plant, was in jeopardy. BMW threatened plant closures if unions did not bow to management demands for new, flexible working patterns and if the UK government did not provide huge amounts of taxpayers' money to keep plants open. The crisis also cost the jobs of Bernd Pischetsrieder, BMW's Chairman, and his long-time boardroom rival, Wolfgang Reitzle, BMW's Marketing Director, who were forced to resign because of the conflict between them over Rover's future (Gow, 1999a; Gow and Traynor, 1999). However, within a year of BMW's declaration that the crisis was over, it announced the dismemberment and sale of Rover owing to continuing heavy losses.

This all seemed a far cry from April 1995, the year after BMW took over, when it was announced that the Rover Group had made record profits and that its domestic and export sales were continuing to forge ahead. This appeared to confirm what many observers believed – that Rover had turned itself into one of Europe's leading car companies, and was approaching a position where it could challenge the best in the world. It was this belief in its potential for world-class performance which lay behind BMW's purchase of Rover in February 1994. As the BMW Chairman, Bernd Pischetsrieder, commented on BBC TV's *Money Programme* at the time, 'The objective is that BMW and Rover together will be the largest specialist manufacturer worldwide'. The purchase of the company by a German firm renowned for its commitment to quality, flair and financial soundness was a major vote of confidence in Rover, and seemed to set the seal on what appeared to be one of the most remarkable turnarounds in British corporate life.

By any stretch of the imagination, Rover Group should not have survived into the 1990s. Its troubled history of the 1970s and early 1980s, both in terms of industrial relations and serious financial problems, would have been enough to sink many an organisation. However, it was also plagued with an image of poor quality and design, and high costs, at a time when the Japanese had taken the world motor industry by storm. General Motors and Ford were in serious trouble and Chrysler, once regarded as one of the three leading motor companies in the world, looked likely to sink without trace. If these companies were in trouble, how could Rover survive?

---

[2] This case study is based on research carried out with Dr Penny West of Edge Hill College.

The short answer was that it could not. In 1975, when it was still called British Leyland, it was nationalised by the then Labour government to save it from collapse. Nevertheless, it still continued to make substantial losses. By the early 1980s, it had received state aid of £2 billion and had still accumulated losses of £2.6 billion. Margaret Thatcher, then Prime Minister and no supporter of state aid, wanted the company broken up and sold off. Nevertheless, she did not get her way. Though Unipart (the spares business) and Jaguar were floated off as separate companies (the latter eventually purchased by Ford), and the bus and truck operations were sold to Volvo and DAF respectively, the car business remained intact and continued the task of re-shaping itself for future prosperity.

In 1988, to most people's surprise, Rover Group was sold to British Aerospace for £150 million, which, given that the BMW deal valued it at £1 billion, appeared something of a bargain. Between 1989 and 1994, Rover's transformation continued apace. Partly thanks to collaboration with its long-time partner Honda, it launched a series of best-selling and award-winning cars (the 200, 400, 600 and 800 series and the Discovery were especially successful).

Though this transformation could be attributed to many factors, especially its links with Honda, perhaps its most remarkable aspect is the way that Rover's employees moved from being seen as its greatest liability to its greatest asset.

## The genesis of a learning business

The change in employee relations at Rover came neither overnight nor without accompanying changes in managerial personnel and style. When Michael Edwardes became Managing Director in 1978, the company had become a byword for industrial militancy – a common joke at the time was: 'only Bobby Charlton strikes faster than British Leyland'. One of Edwardes' first priorities was to tackle the industrial relations strife at the company and establish, or re-establish, 'management's right to manage'. Obviously, he did much else, including establishing the link with Honda, but it was his fierce determination to restore managerial authority and end union militancy that characterised his reign.

In 1982, Edwardes left and was replaced by Harold Musgrove. By this time, employee relations were on a less volatile footing. It was under Musgrove that management, strongly influenced by Rover's alliance with Honda, came to recognise that the rapid development of new models and attendant changes in processes and techniques required a substantial retraining of the workforce, and an end to the 'them and us' culture which still dominated the organisation. However, it was not until 1986, with the appointment of Graham Day as Chairman, followed shortly after by the appointment of a new managing director, that 'people' moved to the top of the agenda.

Under Edwardes and Musgrove, Rover's priorities had been profits, products, procedures and people, in that order. Day became convinced that Rover's only hope of long-term survival was to stand the company's objectives on their head. Profit, he argued, would be the result of people concentrating on producing superior products by way of distinctive processes. People came first, profits came later. It is difficult to overestimate how much of a challenge this was to the established view held by managers at Rover. They had spent three or four very painful years in the late 1970s and early 1980s establishing their right to manage, and fully subscribed to the traditional macho management ethos of the British motor industry. Suddenly they were being told that employee initiative was the key to success, that there must be a partnership between managers and workers.

Nevertheless, through a succession of meetings and brainstorming sessions, senior managers began to craft a new personnel approach for the company. The effort began with a new quality initiative within Rover which stressed that 'quality is about people' and a new mission for Rover 'to achieve extraordinary customer satisfaction'. The personnel function also adopted a new mission statement:

> The purpose of personnel within Rover is to achieve success through people and the purpose of the personnel team is to gain success for the business through the success of its people.

From this time, as the following quotations demonstrate, senior managers began to speak a new language: 'we want to change the emphasis from training – people having something done to them, to learning – people doing something for themselves'; 'we want to unlock the potential of everyone to make a contribution to the future'; 'we want to bridge the gap between management and workforce'; 'we want to achieve success through people'; 'it's our people's contribution which will give us our competitive edge'. Also, the emphasis moved from managers managing to managers leading: 'We see excellent leadership as the key to unlock those [employees'] contributions so we focus heavily on encouraging our line managers' leadership skills'.

From 1986 onwards, a whole raft of measures and policies designed to open up the opportunities for and to promote learning were introduced. By the mid-1990s, Rover estimated that, at any one time, over half of all employees were engaged in some form of learning. In order to facilitate this process and create a corporate learning environment, the company attempted to remove barriers which separate one employee from another. It flattened its management structure and removed the bewildering plethora of job titles and job descriptions that used to exist. It committed itself to end the divide between blue-collar and white-collar jobs, and the insecurity that had often been a feature of the former. This commitment was demonstrated in 1992 with the launch of the company's far-reaching 'Rover Tomorrow – The New Deal'. This included the following:

- a company undertaking not to make compulsory redundancies, in return for a commitment from employees to continuous improvement and flexibility;

- the harmonisation of terms and conditions between white-collar and blue-collar staff;

- the coining of a new term – 'associates' – to describe all Rover employees, regardless of what job they did or where they worked;

- the expectation that white-collar staff should be prepared to be redeployed onto assembly-line work;
- a requirement that all new graduate recruits had to spend their first three months with Rover working on the production lines;
- the expectation that all Rover employees, even directors, should wear the same grey overalls.

In order to accelerate that pace of change at Rover, Rover Learning Business was created in 1990 to bring together and give focus to the company's various learning initiatives.

## Rover Learning Business

The idea of creating a separate business within a business to promote organisational learning appears at first strange, especially given the enormous effort Rover put into creating a learning culture between 1986 and 1990. However, senior managers came to believe that the push for continuous improvement through the provision of opportunities for continuous learning could lead to a mass of fragmented and unco-ordinated initiatives, unless a group was established with the sole purpose of directing, co-ordinating and developing the company's learning initiatives. This view was strengthened by the evidence from employee attitude surveys, which the company had conducted for a number of years. These had consistently shown that (a) employees did not feel the best use was being made of their talents, and that they were prepared for faster and more radical change than the company had so far experienced; and (b) employees felt they were not well enough informed about opportunities for involvement, development and progression within Rover. Consequently, there was a strong view amongst both managers and workforce that the pace of change could and should be accelerated and, despite past efforts, that a more coherent, co-ordinated and publicised approach to learning was required. Rover Learning Business (or RLB, as it was generally referred to at Rover) was launched on 14 May 1990. It was given a budget of around £30 million, and a remit to help Rover Group achieve a number of specific objectives:

- to distinguish Rover Group as the best in Europe for attracting, retaining and developing people;
- to emphasise the view that people are its greatest asset;
- to gain recognition by its own employees that the company's commitment to every individual had increased;
- to unlock and recognise employee talents and to make better use of these talents;
- to improve the competitive edge of the company.

In addressing the first RLB Open Conference in 1993, Sir Graham Day, Rover Group's Chairman, summed up the philosophy that underpinned the work of RLB:

Neither the corporate learning process nor the individual one is optional. If the company seeks to survive and prosper, it must learn. If the individual, at a minimum, seeks to remain employed, let alone progress, learning is essential.

The work of RLB was overseen by a Board of Governors, comprising senior managers from Rover and leading educationalists from the UK and beyond. In the six years until its demise in 1996, RLB expanded its activities to include car dealerships and suppliers as well as Rover employees. RLB also received much media attention for its innovative role.

Its main focus, though, was on internal activities and relationships within Rover. Its core learning products, as it referred to them, were as follows:

- **REAL** (Rover Employee Assisted Learning). This programme provided employees with £100 per year to spend on personal development. Originally, staff could spend it on whatever learning activity they chose (many people used it to develop leisure pursuits such as scuba-diving or archery). The reasoning behind it was that people whose experience of education had not been positive, or who had been out of education for many years, needed to gain confidence in their own ability to learn. REAL money was later limited to work-related learning activities (though this was very broadly defined). REAL was increasingly used to fund team-building activities whereby work groups and teams, on their own initiative, combined their REAL money to go on team-building courses together.

- **Personal Development Files** (PDFs). These were launched as a result of the inadequacies of traditional approaches to appraisal and performance review. PDFs were designed not only to review past performance, but also to identify future learning objectives for individuals, and match these to the company's business objectives. By 1996, more than 70 per cent of the workforce had asked for PDFs, though the interest from managers, supervisors and team leaders seemed to be much greater than from shopfloor associates.

- **GLEN** (Group Learning Exchange Network). This comprised an extensive computer database of information and case studies developed to assist Rover associates to improve and develop the manner in which they carried out their work. As well as being able to access GLEN, staff were also expected to put information into it. As an example, when staff carried out an improvement activity, they were encouraged to write it up and put it into GLEN so that others could learn from their experience.

- **The Change Management Process**. RLB put a great deal of effort into assisting staff within Rover to plan and implement change. Out of this, it developed an approach to change that was both rigorous and effective. The approach was based on teamwork, and stressed the need to seek information on best practice and benchmarking, and to involve those most closely affected. The process was driven by business needs, and took the change team step-by-step through the various stages necessary to plan and implement change. It was also a learning tool. Once a project had been completed, the team evaluated what worked and what did not work, and what lessons they could learn for the future.

For example, staff at Land Rover used the process successfully to plan and implement the introduction of a new production line for the Discovery. They assembled a team and went off-site for four days. They were accompanied by a fellow manager who was familiar with the RLB Change Management Process and who acted as a facilitator. At the end of the four days, they not only had a plan for introducing the new Discovery line, including a timetable and resource implications, but had also developed a presentation to explain to managers and other associates what they intended to do. One of the team members commented that it was the smoothest and quickest change project he had ever been involved in. In addition, the team managed to introduce the new line at no cost to the company and with no additional resources or loss of production.

Nevertheless, though many staff were enthusiastic and complimentary about the work of RLB, especially the opportunities for learning, increasingly senior managers were questioning what it had actually achieved.

## The demise of RLB

In 1996, six years after its launch, RLB was closed and its staff transferred elsewhere within Rover. The beginning of the end for RLB seemed to coincide with the takeover by BMW. Previously muted criticisms of RLB began to be more openly voiced. Of particular concern was the lack of rigour with which RLB monitored, assessed and evaluated the cost-effectiveness of its activities. For example, dealer training was making a loss of £500,000 at this time and questions were raised over the tangible benefit to Rover of this costly activity. Also, many of the business units felt that RLB was too close to Rover and lacked the objectivity, and wider expertise, of outside consultants. A further criticism was that, as an internal activity, it put too much effort into playing the political games designed to promote itself and not enough time actually delivering tangible results.

The takeover by BMW also saw a new General Manager appointed to run RLB. His remit was to refocus RLB in order to restore its image with and usefulness to the rest of Rover. Nevertheless, RLB continued to pursue similar activities as before and the level of criticisms of its performance grew. Therefore, it was not surprising that when RLB's General Manager took early retirement in 1996, Rover saw this as an appropriate time to close the business. The official reason for RLB's demise was that it had served its purpose in energising the learning process throughout the Rover Group. As one RLB manager stated:

> By 1996 what we were trying to establish from 1990 onwards had been institutional-ised. People were comfortable with the approach and a learning culture was becoming evident.

However, the events of 1998–2000 suggest a different picture. Though the 1998/9 crisis, and the subsequent demise of Rover, was attributed to many factors – lack of new models, the severing of its links with Honda, inappropriate German management, poor marketing, the strength of the pound – perhaps the most surprising was lack of employee flexibility and low productivity. In comparison with other UK car plants, Rover's Longbridge plant, its main production facility, had the lowest productivity levels in the industry. Compared to Nissan's Sunderland plant which turned out 98 cars per employee in 1998, Ford's Dagenham plant with 62, Toyota's Burniston plant with 58 and GM's Luton plant with 39, in 1998 each Longbridge employee produced only 34 cars (Milner, 1998). Yet one of the prime reasons for RLB's existence was to tackle the productivity issue by promoting organisational learning.

Therefore, though the official explanation for RLB's demise was that it had done its job, the low productivity of Rover's largest plant, Longbridge, clearly suggests that this was not the case. Instead, there are three explanations for its demise. The first is that it failed to deliver the goods. It was excellent at publicising itself, but in terms of instilling a learning culture that would provide a competitive edge for Rover, it failed. The second is that it lost the political power struggle within Rover. When it was launched, RLB had the support of key senior managers. By 1996, most of these had left. In the face of mounting criticisms from the personnel function, who thought they should be doing the work RLB was doing, and business units, who wanted to be free to choose their own consultants, RLB was left without sufficient political support to survive. The last explanation concerns the takeover by BMW and the separation of the link with Honda. Much of Rover's improvement in the 1980s and early 1990s came from its links with Honda. Like most Japanese companies, Honda believed in the power of individual and organisational learning. BMW were more sceptical. They wanted to see hard evidence for RLB's effectiveness. Increasingly, RLB found it difficult to demonstrate the link between its work and improved performance. Where evidence of improved performance did exist, RLB found that it was the business units who took the credit.

Which of the above explanations for RLB's demise is nearest the truth is difficult to say. It may well be that all three combined to create a climate in which it became easier to criticise and close RLB than to keep it open.

## The outcome

Before its takeover by BMW, Rover had a clear strategy that was much influenced by its Japanese partner, Honda. The strategy was to stimulate changes on a broad front, aimed ultimately at achieving a competitive advantage through the efforts of all managers and employees. Rover took the view that in an industry of fast followers, those who learn fastest will be the winners. Therefore, it did not necessarily need to invent new methods and new processes itself; however, it had to be capable of identifying them and utilising them more quickly and better than its competitors. For Rover, the emphasis was not on technology (though that was important to them), production methods (though the Honda link put them at the forefront in these), or design (though their cars were extremely well-thought-out and designed), all of which can be copied relatively quickly. The emphasis was on developing people as the key to achieving a competitive edge, and on creating a learning organisation which could draw on ideas from a wide range of industries and sources and adapt them to Rover's needs.

The result of this was to transform relationships and working practices in the Rover Group. The 'them and us' philosophy which permeated the company was replaced, though probably not in everyone's mind, with a much more team- and company-orientated approach. Perhaps the most dramatic example was that not only was the company prepared to ask white-collar staff to take shopfloor jobs, but some actually did. However, the takeover by BMW, and crucially the loss of Honda's expertise, seemed to bring this process to a halt and create something of a vacuum in terms of Rover's overall philosophy. The end of its relationship with Honda meant that it lost a great deal of practical assistance and, perhaps more importantly, a role model. BMW, on the other hand, was slow to recognise the vacuum and introduce its own way of working. Therefore, instead of continuing to improve its performance by following the Honda path, Rover stood still, or even lost ground.

In cases such as this, where companies receive a great deal of media attention, it is important to try to separate the hype from the reality. What can be seen objectively is that by 1995 Rover had changed out of all recognition since it was rescued by the UK government in 1975. Though the foundations for this were laid in the Edwardes' era (especially the link with Honda), the step change in performance came in the late 1980s and early 1990s with the development of a new attitude towards staff, and the move to creating a learning organisation. Unfortunately, the advent of BMW seemed to bring this to a halt.

A number of important issues can be discerned from the Rover experience:

- The strategic development of Rover as a learning organisation emerged over time in response to the specific needs of the business as perceived by senior managers.

- The move to change management–worker relations (and indeed, manager–manager and worker–worker relations) was not driven by any altruistic belief in the goodness of human nature. Rather it was driven by the commercial reality of the world in which Rover operated. Managers realised that they could not beat the opposition by competing on technology or cost alone. However, they could build a better organisation, one that was smarter and faster than the opposition.

- In effect, Rover chose to compete on different grounds, to focus on different competences, to the opposition. This was by no means the obvious or the easiest route for Rover, but managers chose it because they felt it would give them a genuine competitive edge over the opposition. In effect, they decided to change the organisational environment in which they operated.

- Though driven by management, this strategy also required changes to management. It was developed by successive management teams, each of which found it slightly easier than the last to move down this route: so, just as Musgrove succeeded Edwardes, so co-operation succeeded conflict; and, as Day succeeded Musgrove, so partnership succeeded co-operation. When George Simpson took over from Graham Day, these developments were given a further boost.

Nevertheless, though it is important to note that changes in managerial personnel and style preceded changes in Rover's internal and external relationships, it is also important to note that Rover was pursuing a consistent and developing managerial philosophy.

- Though this was an emergent process, and in some elements experimental, it was neither *ad hoc* nor unplanned. Instead, managers spent considerable time thinking through the implications and planning the implementation of the changes. In particular, because Rover regularly surveyed opinion amongst its workforce, it ensured that changes were geared towards eliminating discontent and promoting desired behaviour. In creating Rover Learning Business, the company was trying to avoid the danger of fragmentation and loss of ownership that can occur if a large number of initiatives are launched in a short space of time. RLB should have allowed Rover to give ownership and focus to its learning initiatives, and ensure that they were driven by business needs. In addition, the RLB Board, with a significant outside representation, could have acted as a ginger group to encourage Rover to take more ambitious and perhaps innovative steps than might otherwise be the case. Unfortunately, it appears that neither of these took place to the extent envisaged.

- The takeover by BMW signalled, though not deliberately, an end to the managerial and philosophical continuity at Rover. George Simpson, Rover's Managing Director, resigned over the sale and was replaced by a senior manager from BMW. Over the next few years, more and more of Rover's senior managers were replaced by BMW managers. Just as the BMW managers found it difficult to come to grips with Rover's culture, so Rover employees found it difficult to understand or adapt to BMW's managerial philosophy. In the absence of a major effort by the new owners to restore or replace Rover's culture, the constancy of purpose it had exhibited since the early 1980s began to be eroded and Rover began to flounder once again.

In conclusion, we can see that in the 1980s Rover transformed itself, especially in terms of employee relations. However, in the 1990s it clearly lost its sense of direction and descended into a crisis from which, this time, it could not escape.

Case study 7

# GK PRINTERS LIMITED – CHANGING SYSTEMS AND ATTITUDES

## Background

GK Printers Limited is a small, family-run printing business. It was established just after the Second World War by the present Managing Director's father. The company was originally a jobbing printers; which is to say they would print anything. 'No job too large or too small' might well have been their motto, although in fact, the mainstay of their business was producing stationery, business cards and publicity brochures for local companies.

This work was moderately profitable and provided a reasonable living for the owners and their workforce, some 20 people. However, by the beginning of the 1980s, this situation was beginning to change. First, the recession at this time had a strong negative effect on their traditional customer base, and orders began to fall off dramatically. Second, the advent of newer, computerised printing techniques, which GK had not adopted, meant that rivals could offer a quicker, cheaper and often better-quality service. Third, the advent of small printing bureaux (such as Prontaprint), often situated in prime city centre locations, and portraying an up-to-date image, further eroded GK's business. Last, it was clear that many of their customers were no longer going to a printer directly. Instead, in the image-conscious 1980s, they were putting their work out to graphic designers who, having finalised the design, would then subcontract out the printing. In such a situation, there was no guarantee that the work from their traditional customers would eventually end up with them. It depended upon the preference of the particular graphic designers concerned.

All these factors combined to threaten the financial viability of GK and, for the first time ever, the company lost money. The loss was only small (£20,000), but it came as a major shock to a company that had grown used to making a reasonable, if not spectacular, profit. The result of this was that the Managing Director and the company's Printing Manager, along with other members of the owning family, formed a 'crisis committee' to review the future of the business.

## Phase One: developing a strategy

It rapidly became clear to the committee that to do nothing was not an option; the result would be to go out of business. The two main options considered were whether to sell the business, or, in some way, to change it to secure a viable future. Without exception, the crisis committee preferred the second option, if only because it was clear that it would be very difficult to find a buyer for the company. However, no one was sure what it was that they needed to do to change the fortunes of the business.

In desperation, almost, they approached a lecturer at the local polytechnic who was a friend of the Printing Manager. His suggestion was that one of his business studies students should undertake a project to examine the company's options. This took two months, during which the Managing Director and Printing Manager worked closely with the student.

The student's final report had a dramatic impact on the company. Its main findings were as follows:

- The printing market was expanding rather than contracting. This was mainly due to companies recognising the need to promote themselves more and in a better way than in the past.

- The market expansion was mainly at the higher value-added end of the market, in the area of high-class, glossy promotional material.

- The newer print bureaux were not as strong competitors as the company had thought. Their product quality was both variable and, at best, no better than GK's. Also, their costs appeared to be higher.

- GK's existing customer base would prefer to continue to do business with them, but perceived them as old-fashioned, lacking in key capabilities (mainly graphic design), slow, and not particularly flexible.

- GK's printing equipment was not capable of producing the higher value-added products that customers were increasingly demanding.

These findings were met with some astonishment and a great deal of relief by the crisis committee. Without exception they had steeled themselves for a report that would be doom-laden. Instead, they could see that a future did exist, and possibly a very profitable one. But some major changes would be required. However, before making any decisions, the Managing Director and Printing Manager insisted that the findings should be discussed with the workforce.

Employee relations were very good in the company and, whilst not being pater-nalistic, the tendency was to see the company almost as an extended family. The print workers, who made up the majority of the workforce, were all union members, and two of them were prominent activists in their local union branch. The work-force knew that a review was taking place; it would have been almost impossible to keep it from them, given the nature of the company, but in any case the manage-ment had been very open about it. Like the crisis committee, the workforce were relieved that the findings were more optimistic than many had believed possible. However, they wanted to know what the management intended to do to change the company in order to take advantage of the opportunities that appeared available.

The Managing Director was slightly taken aback by the workforce's apparent eagerness for change; he had expected some resistance, especially from the print workers. Instead, the reverse was the case: the two union activists were the strongest advocates of new equipment. As one later said: 'We knew what was happening elsewhere; skilled workers were being replaced by glorified typists. But we also knew that we needed new equipment. The deal we struck with manage-ment was that we would accept anything they bought, but we would be trained for it and we would operate it'. Indeed, they went beyond this – they actually told the management what to buy and from whom.

On the basis of the report from the student, the management constructed a strategy for rejuvenating the company. The strategy had three main elements:

1 The appointment of a Marketing and Design Manager to develop the company's customer base and provide a graphic design capability.

2 Upgrading the company's image. The above appointment was part of this process, but it also involved remodelling the company's frontage and reception areas, redesigning its stationery and creating a company logo.

3 Progressively replacing old printing machines with newer, more capable equipment.

Though the company never formally created a 'vision' of its future, the Managing Director later said:

> After the student's report I began to see a picture in my own mind of what I would like the company to be. I wanted it to be a one-stop shop for all our customers' printing needs. In the past, if we could not do it ourselves, or if we were too busy, we turned people away. Not any more. If we could not do it, we subcontracted, just like the graphic designers. But we would ensure that we could do the money business in-house (the high value-added business) and eventually only subcontract out the cheap stuff.

Therefore, the company began its transformation by the appointment of a Marketing and Design Manager and upgrading its image. Initially, it did not buy any new equipment, but took the decision to subcontract work they could not do until such time as the volume of work necessitated new investment. This allowed them to turn round the business without having to borrow large sums of money.

Nevertheless, within 12 months, such was the success of the strategy that the company began buying new equipment. After that, as the economy grew in the 1980s, the company's fortunes also grew. By the late 1980s, GK employed 40 staff (double its previous number) and had quadrupled its turnover to £4 million. In the process, it had managed to improve its profitability substantially.

However, in 1989, it grew concerned that the increased volume of business, made more complicated by the need both to design as well as print, and to co-ordinate their subcontracting activities, was having an adverse effect on customer service. The main problems were controlling paperwork (especially orders and invoices), the company's costing system, and production scheduling. Therefore they undertook a review of these activities to see how they could be improved. Thus began the second phase of the transition of GK into a highly competitive printing company.

## Phase Two: changing systems

### Reasons for change

As mentioned above, market, product and operational changes meant that the company needed to provide a faster and better service to its customers. While much had been done to achieve this, in 1989 it was also realised that better business systems were required, especially in the area of costing, invoicing and production control.

Given that GK is only a small company, it was relatively easy for the Managing Director to bring together the six people who were responsible for these activities and, in effect, to state the problems and give them the authority to come up with their solution.

The people concerned agreed to meet for two hours each Friday afternoon to review the issues involved and come up with options. They were clear that they did not want to rule anything out, but set out instead to identify all the available alternatives, and choose the one that suited them and the company best.

After three weeks they had reached a consensus on the root cause of their problems: they were all being asked to do more and more without any additional resources. Not only did this mean that backlogs occurred, but also that the greater need to communicate across functions, which the company now required, was not taking place.

Given this analysis, their first inclination was to ask for more staff. However, they also looked at other options, the main one being to introduce better systems – ones which reduced duplication. This raised the additional question: manual or computer systems?

Eventually they agreed a number of key objectives which any option must be tested against. These were that any new system should provide the following:

- a faster and better response to customers' requests for quotations;
- speedier invoicing and improved debtor control;
- better record-keeping and a reduction in duplication;
- an increase in productivity of clerical staff;
- better control of production, resulting in reduced lead times, and quicker and more reliable service to customers;
- system integration.

Having decided upon these criteria, the people involved then asked the Printing Manager if he would approach his contact at the local polytechnic for assistance. This he did, and once again the assistance came in the form of a student project. The student evaluated the company's existing operations and looked at alternatives. Her report stated that it was possible to improve the existing systems but that this would not allow them to achieve their objectives. Instead, she advocated introducing computer-based systems.

As they had witnessed the successful introduction of computerised printing equipment during recent years, staff were neither overawed nor complacent about computerising their systems. They discussed with the local polytechnic how best to approach an evaluation of the benefits of computer systems, and selection of a system.

The group then prepared a written report for the Managing Director which detailed their investigations, their initial objectives, and the advice they had received. Their recommendation was that the company should invite a number of computer companies to visit them to discuss their needs. A long discussion took place between the Managing Director and the group, which resulted eventually in their report being accepted. However, the Managing Director did add one proviso. This was that the group should be responsible for deciding whether to computerise, and, if so, what system to select and from whom to purchase it. The Managing Director said he would sit in on any negotiations that took place with computer companies, but that he would not take the decision away from them; rather he would bolster their authority by his presence.

So a number of computer companies were invited to discuss the company's requirements with them. In total, some 20 companies visited them. The upshot of these visits was that the company became convinced that their needs could best be met by purchasing a computerised business system which could perform the necessary work and integrate their existing manual systems. However, the cost of this was likely to be between £20,000 and £30,000, which – for a company of GK's size – was significant. The Printing Manager, and others, pointed out that such an amount spent on printing equipment would greatly extend their capabilities. Nevertheless, after much discussion, the decision was taken to go ahead with the purchase of a computerised business system (CBS).

Though it took a number of meetings to reach this decision, which was subject to much discussion throughout the company, the final decision was almost unanimous. The reason for this was that the company was performing well on all fronts except in the areas covered by the proposed changes. Late and inadequate quotations, poor debtor control and erratic delivery performance were all causing the company problems. These were not as yet major problems, but could be expected to get worse as the company expanded.

**Introduction and development of CBS**

Once the decision had been made, the original group were given the responsibility, as the Managing Director had earlier stated, for specifying and deciding which equipment to purchase. Their task was made difficult because, whilst it was clear that standard software packages were suitable for such tasks as sales ledgers, wages and invoicing, special software would need to be written to accommodate the company's production control needs. The CBS steering group, as they jokingly referred to themselves, spent a number of months identifying and writing a specification of their exact requirements from a production control system. They then asked the computer companies to quote for a CBS on the basis of this specification. However, of the original companies who had shown interest, only two were prepared to provide the bespoke software the company required. The company wished to ensure that both the hardware and software were supplied by the same vendor, not only to avoid any incompatibility problems, but also to have only one organisation responsible for any problem that might arise. Further discussions took place with the two companies, during which the software specification was further refined, and eventually a supplier was chosen. The entire process, from the Managing Director raising the issue, to actually placing the order, took over a year.

The computer for running the systems, and the standard packages, were delivered almost immediately, but it was another six months before the production control package was installed. This was because it had to be specially written. The company ensured that it closely monitored the writing of the software and that the final package met the specification. It then took some three months to bring the production control package on line. During this period, manual records were still kept in parallel to the computerised system. After this, it took a further three months before the total CBS package was up and running satisfactorily. Therefore, in total, it took two years from the inception to the completion of the project. Nevertheless, no one regretted the time spent. As the Managing Director said:

> If you'd told me at the beginning it would take so long I'd have laughed at you. But now we've ended up with a system that gives us all we want – and more. It's a system that 'belongs' to the people who work it – it's not my system, it's theirs.

Though the company only bought one workstation initially, it had specified that the CBS should be capable of networking. This was done with the intention that once the CBS had proved itself, further workstations would be acquired. Since then, three more workstations have been purchased and the company has also doubled the memory capacity of the system. In total, some £35,000 has been spent on the CBS.

As with other aspects of the CBS, the company was careful to ensure that adequate training was provided to those who would use the system. Once again, this was made easier because it was the users who had selected the system, so they knew what it could do and what training they required. This ranged from three days to a week, depending upon the users' requirement. The training was provided by the equipment supplier. Training took place in stages, allowing users to become familiar with one aspect of the system before being trained on another aspect of it. Training was provided for clerical staff who would use and maintain the system, and also to managers who needed to access it for information.

Staff appear to have taken to the CBS very well. Though initially there was an additional workload for them in terms of inputting information into the system, they now find that it is better and faster than the previous manual system. Their workload is no less than before, but they take satisfaction from being more effective by using 'their' system. Obviously, the system has had a knock-on effect elsewhere in the company, both in the collection and use of information. This adjustment appears to have been accomplished with little or no difficulty.

### The benefits

The CBS has not transformed the fortunes of GK; no single system will do that for any company. However, it has made a significant contribution, in the areas it covers, to improving the service GK provides to its customers and meeting its own requirements.

The company believes that computerising its business systems has brought the following benefits:

- better and more accurate records;
- quicker access to information;
- better control of resources;

- a speedier and more accurate response to quotation requests;
- higher productivity from clerical staff;
- reduced lead times;
- faster and more reliable deliveries;
- a greater integration of business functions;
- an improvement in staff morale and skills.

Though this appears to be a case of successful technical change, it would be wrong to perceive it exclusively in this light. Certainly, that is not how those involved saw it. Rather they believed that the main benefit gained was the ability to work together more effectively. The CBS assisted this by automating some of the more routine elements of their work, thus allowing them to put their skills to better use. However, they are the ones who know what customers and the company require, not the CBS. Whether their perception is true or not may not matter: the real issue is that they believed it to be so. This clearly had a substantial effect on their effectiveness, self-esteem and morale.

### Reasons for success

To the outsider, at least, this appears to be an almost textbook case of how to manage change. However, the staff involved, whilst clearly pleased with their role, are also not uncritical of their performance. With hindsight, they say that they should have completed the process in a year rather than two years. They also believe that they should have included additional features in the CBS.

Whilst these criticisms may be true, they are only so from the vantage point of having gone through the process of change and having gained confidence and experience from it. They also reflect a key reason for the success of the process: a willingness to be open and critical about themselves and their requirements, and a belief that they all needed to be convinced of what was required before proceeding.

Nor should the role played by the Managing Director be undervalued. In a company where – a few years earlier – change, of any sort, was very rare indeed, it takes considerable courage for a senior manager to delegate authority to users. Indeed, at one point he openly told the group that 'if you succeed, it's your success – not mine. If you fail, I carry the can – not you.' This created the climate of trust and responsibility which made those involved determined to succeed.

Nevertheless, it would be remiss not to draw attention to several other factors that contributed to successful change in this instance:

- The company had a strategy for its future development (or at least a general view of what it wanted to become) and therefore was able to take an overview of all areas of its business in relation to future objectives.
- Because the company was strategy-driven, it was able to establish not only where problems lay in the company, but also whether the problems were high,

low or medium priority. This meant that the company could establish that there was a need to improve business systems and that this was the priority.

- The company did not rush into making a decision about what exactly was the problem, what solution to adopt or what equipment to purchase.
- The company clearly documented its requirements, and identified where standard packages were sufficient and where bespoke software was required.
- It carefully selected a supplier in whom it had confidence and with whom it could work closely.
- It constructed a timetabled implementation plan with clear objectives for the introduction of the CBS.
- It ensured that the appropriate training was provided.

Two further points should be stressed about the introduction of the CBS. First, the company was attempting to move from being an organisation where change was the exception, to one where it becomes the norm. In such a situation, it is impossible for change to be controlled exclusively by management or 'experts'. The sheer volume of work would overwhelm them. Without devolving the responsibility to those affected, change either would not take place or would be unsuccessful. Nor would it be possible for senior managers to concentrate on the longer-term strategic aspects of their business. Therefore, sustaining the changes in managerial behaviour which promote involvement and team work are essential to GK's prosperity.

Second, devolving responsibility in this way ensures that those who have to live with the change take ownership of the process, and are committed to it. It allows those involved to develop their skills and confidence. It also ensures that once the changes do take place, they become fully operational as rapidly as possible. It should have the additional advantage that it encourages those concerned to continue to search for improvements.

Unfortunately, as business increased, thanks to the changes at GK, there was a tendency to concentrate on output rather than development, and to revert back to old patterns of behaviour. This was particularly the case with the Managing Director, who felt that the priority was to meet customers' requirements rather than to involve other managers in decisions which had always been his responsibility. When an organisation is operating successfully, as GK appeared to be, it is difficult to argue that time should be spent improving what already, apparently, works well. Similarly, though teamworking had proved its usefulness in facilitating major decisions and changes, it was more difficult for managers, especially the Managing Director, to appreciate its effectiveness on a day-to-day basis.

Therefore, though major organisational changes had taken place at GK, changes in managerial behaviour were not sustained. By 1993, it was apparent that the pace of improvement was slowing down under the pressure of work. This situation continued until the beginning of 1994 when, once again, the company recognised that it faced serious problems.

## Phase Three: changing attitudes and behaviour

### Accelerating the pace of change

Unlike many companies, GK's business continued to grow throughout the early 1990s. Though its existing customers were being hit by the recession, it was winning new business which more than compensated for this. Nevertheless, in 1993, GK started to become aware that its customers, old and new, were becoming increasingly demanding with regard to price and delivery. In addition, there were signs that its competitors were beginning to win back some of the work they had lost to GK.

By the beginning of 1994 it was clear that GK was losing a significant amount of business. This was partly due to increased competition, but mainly it was because its customers, in seeking to cut their own costs, were reducing the size and frequency of their orders (though when orders were placed, they were often required far faster than previously). This presented a double threat to GK. First, the fall in overall volumes was having an adverse effect on turnover and profit. Second, the reduction in size of individual print runs was having an adverse effect on costs because, though the actual volume was smaller, the design, order processing and set-up costs remained constant. In effect, as volumes decreased, the cost of each printed item increased. In addition, there were worrying signs that some customers were using word-processing packages and colour printers to produce their own publicity material instead of going to a printer.

At a time when its customers were facing severe pressure to cut their costs, GK were faced with the dilemma of whether to increase its prices to offset rising costs (and risk customers going elsewhere or developing their own facilities), or to maintain or reduce prices and see its profits plunge. This was not a situation unique to GK; practically every company in the UK was experiencing a similar dilemma. However, this knowledge did not make it any less painful or any easier to resolve.

The knee-jerk reaction of many in the company was, 'If customers want smaller runs, the price goes up'. However, the Managing Director and the other managers in GK came reluctantly to accept that, whilst the logic was impeccable, the result could be disastrous. After much seemingly futile discussion, it was the Marketing and Design Manager who eventually came up with a suggestion which, though laughed at initially, later turned out to be the key to GK's survival. He pointed out that to maintain its existing volume of business, and perhaps even increase it, GK needed to improve on its already good level of service. In particular, it needed to cut costs in order to cut prices and improve the efficiency of its internal operations to cut delivery times. The initial reaction to these suggestions was, perhaps predictably, very negative. After all, if volumes decrease, unit costs must increase because set-up costs are constant; also, an increase in the number of smaller print runs actually extends turnaround times for a similar reason – more set ups are required. So the Marketing and Design Manager was attempting to turn the conventional wisdom regarding printing on its head. In addition, in some people's eyes, he was still a newcomer to GK and consequently he was believed to lack an in-depth knowledge of the printing industry. Lastly, GK had made significant strides in improving efficiency and cutting costs, and there was some doubt as to the scope for any real improvements in these areas.

## A false start

Despite the initial adverse comments, the Managing Director began to wonder if it might be possible to reduce set-up times and costs. If it could, he reasoned, the company would be able to attract more business, prevent customers seeking in-house solutions, and undermine their competitors. He considered asking for outside assistance again, but instead asked the Marketing and Design Manager to put forward some suggestions for reducing costs and set-up times. This was for two reasons. First, he wanted to give him a chance to prove himself to the rest of the team who, to an extent, thought he still had to learn the ropes. Second, the Managing Director wanted to demonstrate that they now had the managerial talent to dispense with outside assistance.

The Marketing and Design Manager quickly responded and within a fortnight presented his proposals to the Managing Director and other senior staff. He began by identifying what he saw as the main problem the company faced:

1 Though there had been a slight decline in the number of individual orders, the actual reduction in the volume of business was much greater because customers were ordering shorter print runs.

2 The result of this was that, whilst office staff, marketing, design, administration, etc., were as busy as ever, the print shop was short of work, and it was not unusual to see printers sitting reading the paper with nothing else to do.

3 However, though the printers were underworked, this did not provide much scope for reducing delivery times, because most of GK's lead time was accounted for by non-printing activities – especially design, which could take anything up to two weeks.

Having laid out what he saw as the problem, the Marketing and Design Manager went on to offer a solution. He argued that the key to solving the company's problems lay in speeding up design time. He pointed out that there was always a backlog of design work ranging from one to two weeks. Given that everything, even repeat orders, went through design, total lead time could be anything from three to five weeks. Whilst this was considerably better than in the 1980s, it was no longer acceptable as customers were cutting stock to a minimum. Many customers were asking to have their printing back within seven days, sometimes even sooner where promotional material was concerned. The solution, therefore, he argued, was to have more design staff. If one extra designer was employed and another design workstation purchased, the Marketing and Design Manager believed that design lead time could be reduced to two or three days.

The Managing Director and other managers, especially the Printing Manager, who had been arguing unsuccessfully for new equipment for some time, were taken aback by this proposal. The analysis, they believed, was correct but the solution, they felt, was an outrageous piece of opportunism. The case for more design staff had been raised and rejected in the recent past. The Marketing and Design Manager's colleagues felt that he was blatantly using the company's current problems to empire-build. Not surprisingly, he vigorously denied this. Nevertheless, the meeting ended acrimoniously and no decision was taken.

The Managing Director was particularly infuriated, as he had genuinely been expecting an acceptable solution to emerge from the meeting. Instead, the friendly working atmosphere he valued, and which he felt he did much to promote, had been shattered. Nor did he see an easy way to bring his managers back together to seek a co-operative solution. He was also annoyed because he realised that he had made a mistake in asking only one person to put forward their view. Not only would a team have avoided favouring one area rather than another; it would not even occur to anyone to make the accusation. However, having made the mistake, he was not sure how to remedy it. If a team was set up to examine the options that did not include the Marketing and Design Manager, he would rightly see it as a snub and probably attack any solution that was put forward. If he was included, it was likely that he would continue to push his proposal and the other managers would react badly. His inclination was to impose a solution and tell everyone to get on and implement it. Unfortunately, he did not have a solution to impose.

### Towards a new way of working

After several weeks of indecision, during which tensions within the management team continued to rise, the Managing Director decided once again to seek outside assistance. He approached GK's contact at the local polytechnic and, at length and with some passion, explained the situation. However, rather than proffering help, as expected, the lecturer stated that the situation was outside his area of expertise. He explained that there seemed little point in offering a 'technically appropriate' solution, because relations were so bad in the company that, whatever it was, it would be met by hostility from some quarters. He pointed out that the success of earlier interventions was due to achieving unanimity about both the problem and the solution; at present, this was unlikely. He did, though, refer the Managing Director to a colleague at the polytechnic who was skilled in team-building. Though the Managing Director was sceptical, the lecturer pointed out that, working together, there was enough experience in GK to solve its current dilemma. Therefore, the issue was how to bring people together, rather than seeking outside solutions.

The Managing Director met with the team-builder, who impressed him not only with his general demeanour of professionalism but also with the impressive array of organisations he had worked with. The team-builder said that the process he used was straightforward. First, all the relevant managers had to be involved. Second, he would meet each of them individually and then, as a group, would take them away from the company for two days to work on the problem. Third, each member of the team would have to agree to operate in an open and constructive fashion during the two days. This meant not only responding positively to each other's ideas, but also being honest. Lastly, the team would agree to reach a commonly agreed solution by the end of the two days.

It was on this basis that the team-building exercise went ahead. Though the GK management later admitted that the first day had been decidedly uncomfortable, they also agreed that the two days had been a success. The proceedings began with the team-builder reporting on his findings from the individual interviews. Though he did not reveal who said what, in a small organisation such as GK, it was relatively easy for managers to make a good guess as to the source of particular comments. This was one of the reasons why they found the first day uncomfortable.

The team-builder's report was split into positive and negative findings. On the positive side, there was a strong commitment to making the company a success, and common agreement regarding priorities for change (primarily, cost reduction and increasing responsiveness to customers). On the negative side, there was considerable tension between the managers, especially the Printing Manager and the Marketing and Design Manager. Underlying this, however, was the style of the Managing Director.

Though on a number of occasions the Managing Director had used teams to make crucial decisions and had been prepared to consult widely, this was not his normal mode of operation. He tended to make decisions either by himself or in consultation with one other manager. He justified this on the grounds that most decisions were not related to overall policy but to particular areas of the business. If new printing equipment was to be purchased, then this concerned him and the Printing Manager. If the issue was customers, then the Marketing and Design Manager would be involved. Decisions concerning finance were, the Managing Director felt, mainly his responsibility. The counter-argument to this, identified and articulated by the team-builder, was that it inevitably created suspicion among managers excluded from decisions, and led to accusations of favouritism. All the managers, other than the Managing Director, favoured a more open and collective style of management.

The Managing Director was very upset and said so. He believed he had always acted to promote teamwork and good relations in the company. To be accused of the reverse came as a shock. He wanted, he said, to 'clear the air' there and then. However, the team-builder suggested, and agreement was eventually reached, that they should all reflect on what had been said, and return to the issue at the end of the second day. They then moved on to discuss the immediate problems facing GK: how to reverse the decline in turnover and profitability. With the delicate matter of the Managing Director's approach to decision-making out in the open but put to one side, everyone seemed happy to focus on these problems. For the rest of day one and most of day two, they alternated between working in two groups and working as one team. The result was that they reached an agreement on the way forward which they all accepted.

The main areas of action were very straightforward:

1  GK should meet with its main customers to identify what their needs were and discuss how these could best be met. It was felt that not all of a customer's requirements were urgent, and that what was necessary was to identify those that were and agree that they would be dealt with in a speedy fashion.

2  The company's CBS – computerised business system – was much more efficient than the previous manual system, but all orders, large or small, urgent and non-urgent, were dealt with in the same manner and at the same speed. The same applied to design: though the actual design time varied between orders, they were all scheduled and dealt with in the same fashion. This meant that they all tended to take between one and two weeks, depending on the design office's workload. It was also a similar story when it came to printing and dispatch: everything was in the same queue. It was agreed that the entire process from order intake to dispatch be examined, with the intention of either reducing it for all orders, or possibly shortening it for specific categories of orders.

These actions were to be carried out by two groups comprising managers and employees from the areas involved, who would report directly to the management team.

This then left the thorny issue of the Managing Director's role. Since the issue had been raised on the first day, he had spoken to the team-builder and his colleagues informally, and had come to recognise the strength of feeling on the issue, though he did not fully accept their interpretation of his actions. Nevertheless, he was prepared to amend his management style. He agreed that there would be regular management team meetings which would deal with all major decisions. He also agreed that he would not seek to impose a decision on the team unless the managers themselves could not reach agreement.

### Six months later

The investigation of customer requirements and the order-to-dispatch process resulted in changes which brought significant improvements in the service GK could offer to its customers, and a reduction in lead times and costs.

The company now offers its customers a choice of lead times and prices: normal – a two-week delivery and a 5 per cent reduction on the standard prices; accelerated – a one-week delivery charged at standard prices; and urgent – a one working day delivery charged at 10 per cent above standard prices.

GK was able to achieve these improvements owing to three factors:

1  Understanding what its customers wanted and were prepared to pay for. In speaking to customers, GK also identified what its competitors were offering in terms of prices and deliveries.

2  In examining the order-to-dispatch process, GK came to appreciate that there was a large amount of wasted time involved which could be eliminated with better co-operation between functions, especially design and printing, and a

greater awareness of the need to reduce lead times. In examining the entire process in detail and involving everyone in this, some very glaring examples of wasted time emerged. For convenience, incoming orders were processed in batches. So an order could sit for two days just waiting to be entered on the system. Similar delays were identified in dispatch, with completed orders sitting for one or two days waiting either for collection or for GK to make a delivery in that part of the city where the customer was located. As the dispatch clerk commented, 'No one told me it was a problem'. Once staff realised it was a problem, there was almost a competition to see who could come up with the best suggestion.

Most of this did not require additional expenditure, merely better communication and a willingness to help each other. Reducing set-up time on the printing presses did require some modest expenditure, but this led to reductions in set-up times of between 50 and 80 per cent. Some small expenditure was also required to modify the computer system to cope with the new three-tier delivery price system.

3 The design office made a number of changes to the way it operated which speeded up its activities. Nevertheless, it was recognised that there was also a capacity shortage: they simply had more work than they could cope with. Much of the work was simple and did not need a fully-qualified designer; and only about 50 per cent of a designer's time was actually spent on the computer. Therefore, it was decided to employ someone else to perform the more simple design tasks.

At first, GK was going to recruit a new member of staff for this post, but the printers, who had always wanted to be involved in design, suggested that they might do this. When the suggestion was discussed, a number of possibilities opened up, including that simple but urgent jobs be given straight to a printer who would undertake the entire design and printing process at one go. The actual mechanics of this were difficult to work out, and many practical obstacles were apparent, but GK none the less decided to undertake a trial with one printer in order to identify the difficulties and evaluate the benefits.

In addition to these changes, the management team, after some initial difficulties (such as identifying what constituted a major decision), found that working together and having all information out in the open reduced the tension, not only between individual managers but between the individual functions as well.

## Postscript: the World Wide Web beckons

For the most part, GK's fortunes rose steadily throughout the latter half of the 1990s, despite much talk of an imminent recession. They developed strong partnerships with key customers and attracted new ones. They acquired a reputation as a forward-looking company that was responsive to its customers' needs. However, they developed one area of their business which grew much faster than the rest and which promises much for the future: developing and designing web sites for its customers.

As with so much of GK's development, there seemed to be an almost accidental element to its web site business. In the mid-1990s, one of its main customers decided to conduct much of its business, especially in terms of orders and invoices, electronically. GK had no alternative but to accommodate this. The Managing Director gave the task of developing electronic communications to one of the graphic designers who was very keen on computing; not only did he have his own web site, but he had also developed one for his local athletics club.

Consequently, as well as allowing them to receive and send information electronically, he also constructed a web site for GK. Being a graphic designer, and an enthusiast, what he produced was a state-of-the-art web site which provided an excellent showcase for GK's capabilities. Almost before most people in the company realised they had a web site, or understood what one was, its customers were asking GK to do the same for them. At first the Managing Director thought that this was something of a diversion from the company's main activities. However, when he saw what customers were prepared to pay, and he realised that, in essence, it was a logical extension of printing publicity material, he created a separate department under the graphic designer to develop the web-site business. It is now the fastest-growing part of GK and by far its most profitable.

## The outcome

After the first two phases of changes at GK, the company felt it could rightly take pride in how it had responded to the situation in which it had found itself. Rather than falling into a spiral of decline, as seemed possible, it had reinvigorated itself. It had introduced new equipment and, initially at least, developed a new sense of co-operation. However, its own success began to eat away at some of its gains. The pressures of day-to-day business began to take precedence over both improvement activities and co-operation. In particular, the Managing Director went back to taking decisions either without consulting anyone else or only in consultation with the 'appropriate' manager. In effect, though the company had maintained the operational changes, it had failed to maintain behavioural changes, especially those associated with teamwork, co-operation and delegation. Therefore, the first two phases of the company's turnaround can be characterised by successful operational changes but less successful behavioural changes.

The results of the failure to sustain behavioural changes were as follows:

- GK failed to adopt a continuous improvement approach.
- Poor co-ordination and co-operation led to inefficiencies in the processing and dispatch of work.
- Most importantly, an undercurrent of discontent and fighting for position arose among managers, which made it difficult to reach agreement about how the organisation should respond to its changed circumstances.

For these reasons, the key action in the third phase of the transformation of GK was not any of the operational changes, but the changes in attitudes among managers and other staff regarding co-operation, and in particular, the Managing Director's belated conversion to team-based decision-making. It was the new element of co-operation that allowed GK successfully to identify what to change and how to change it. The greater teamwork, and trust, also created the environment that allowed the company's web-site business to be developed by making people more open to new ideas and less suspicious of others' motives.

## CONCLUSIONS

In the review of strategy and change management in Chapters 5–8, it was argued that whilst approaches to strategy and change needed to be matched to the constraints under which an organisation operated, these constraints were themselves amenable to change and in any case could conflict with each other. This means that the freedom of action or manoeuvre of managers is potentially very significant. In the three case studies we have examined in this chapter, we can see managerial choice in action.

In the Volvo study, we can see that managers made a determined and apparently successful attempt to break away from the industry standard approach to car assembly. However, in challenging and changing a powerful constraint on their freedom of manoeuvre, they were very much in tune with societal, environmental and, at least in some instances, their own orientations. Also, there were parallel changes in the structure of the organisation towards decentralisation and flexibility, which supported and made more appropriate the emergent and open-ended approach to strategy used by Volvo.

The Rover study is another case where managers sought to break out of the constraints on their freedom of action. Recognising that they could no longer operate on a 'them and us' basis, Rover managers set about building a new relationship with its workforce. In order to turn them from the threat they were perceived to be in the early 1980s, to become the organisation's main competitive edge in the 1990s, managers initiated a programme of learning and development for staff. Given the traditional nature of its internal relationships, this constituted a major attempt to restructure the organisational constraints managers faced. However, such a change is clearly in line with the operation of leading car companies such as Honda, Nissan and Toyota. It is also in line with the changing and competitive nature of the environment in which the motor industry operates.

Therefore, to an extent, Rover, as with Volvo, could be seen as making an attempt to harmonise the constraints it faced. In Volvo's case, it attempted to bring internal arrangements into line with societal and environmental constraints (though in so doing they strongly contradicted industry constraints). In Rover's case, changes in internal constraints clearly assisted in bringing Rover into line with industry and environmental constraints (though not perhaps societal). In both cases, the approach to strategy adopted was Emergent and open-ended. The same point can be made with regard to change. Though a role for Planned change can be seen at both Rover and Volvo the implementation of strategy also had elements of experimentation and open-endedness. In Volvo's case, each successive attempt at Job Design built on and developed past projects, but also tended itself to change and develop. Rover's experience was that, in trying to transform itself into a learning organisation, individual initiatives tended to evolve and take on a life of their own. However, the change of ownership at Rover, with the consequent departure of senior managers and the breaking of its relationship with Honda, led to an end to the continuity of management and ideas which had driven the company forward since the early 1980s. Not only did this undermine the support for organisational learning at Rover, but it may also have set the scene for the final demise of Rover.

As far as Volvo is concerned, its takeover has also raised serious questions regarding its future direction. Given that its approach to work organisation represents a clear and decisive break with Fordist methods, it is difficult to see that approach surviving now that Volvo is owned by Ford.

The case of GK Printers is somewhat different. It is much more difficult to perceive any distinct societal or industry constraints on the organisation. However, both environmental and organisational constraints were clearly apparent, and the changes which took place were to a greater or lesser extent aimed at both changing and harmonising these constraints. One reason for the internal changes in the company was to tie customers closer to the company, and thus reduce the uncertainty present in the environment. As with Volvo and Rover, GK's strategy emerged rather than being pre-planned, but it also seems to have been much more stop–go than either of the other companies. Also, its approach to change appears to be more in line with the Planned approach than the Emergent.

Therefore, as far as managerial choice, strategy development and change management are concerned, the case studies provide some interesting and thought-provoking insights:

- Managerial freedom is clearly constrained but this does not mean that managers cannot break out of or change these constraints. However, in so doing, the tendency appears to be to resolve or reduce conflict between constraints rather than necessarily to re-write the managerial rule book completely.

- The process of strategy development and change management in these cases was mainly Emergent, open-ended, and in some instances opportunistic, though some examples of Planned change were also evident. However, managerial conflict and politics also played a part in decision-making and, in the case of Rover, managerial changes preceded attempts to achieve organisational changes.

- Planned change as such appears to be less effective than Emergent change in these instances, though a role for it can be seen in each of the companies. Nor is it the case that some aspects of Planned change are not applicable, especially those relating to problem definition and implementation planning. However, where the two approaches diverge is that Planned change programmes tend to have a finite duration and are an end in themselves. Emergent change, on the other hand, is not only open-ended, but the process of change can itself be seen to be a process of learning as well.

## TEST YOUR LEARNING

### Short answer questions

1 Briefly describe the main reasons for Volvo's original move to Job Design.

2 What were the trade unions' main concerns regarding Volvo's move to Job Design?

3 List three benefits Rover expected to gain from organisational learning.

4 Identify the main factors which contributed to and led to the demise of Rover Learning Business.

5 Briefly discuss one example of employee involvement at GK Printers.

6 Identify three ways in which the managers at GK can be seen to have changed their style from autocratic to participative.

### Essay questions

1 Discuss the following statement: the stages of workplace reform at Volvo involve a cumulative process of innovation, with a trajectory which adds up to a more or less definitive break with Fordism.

2 Before the BMW takeover, to what extent had Rover turned itself into a learning organisation?

3 Does the GK case study represent an example of emergent change, or of *ad hoc* and reactive management?

## Chapter 11

# CASE STUDIES IN CHANGING EXTERNAL RELATIONSHIPS

### Learning objectives

After studying the case studies in this chapter, you should be able to:

1 understand why organisations are seeking to work more closely with their customers and suppliers;

2 appreciate that changing external relationships can require significant changes in internal relationships;

3 describe some of the mechanisms used by organisations to bring about changes in their external relationships;

4 discuss how changes at one level between two firms may not always result in changes at other levels;

5 show how customers and suppliers can overcome suspicion and achieve mutual gains;

6 appreciate the need for strong and consistent management.

## INTRODUCTION

The previous two chapters have presented examples of strategies and initiatives that have resulted in new internal relationships within organisations through structural, operational and behavioural change. However, since the mid-1980s, more and more, companies have also sought to change their external relationships, by developing closer and more harmonious links with their suppliers and customers. As the case studies in this chapter will show, this is usually accompanied or preceded by internal changes within either the supplier, the customer or both. These changes are taking place due to a growing climate of opinion that customers, suppliers and even rivals working co-operatively have considerable advantages over the more traditional adversarial relationships (Hines, 1994; Lamming, 1993; Saunders, 1997). Though this move has been led by the automotive and electronics industries, the concept has spread into many other sectors as well (Burnes and New, 1997; Christopher, 1998; New and Burnes, 1998).

There is little doubt that customer–supplier partnerships are beginning to be seen as the most beneficial and effective method of organising the purchase of goods and services (Burnes and Dale, 1998; Handfield and Nichols, 1999; Waller, 1999). A UK survey conducted in the early 1990s by the University of Manchester Institute of Science and Technology for the management consultants, AT Kearney Ltd, found that over 90 per cent of respondents thought such an approach was relevant to them, and over 60 per cent were using or implementing partnership schemes with their suppliers and/or customers (AT Kearney Ltd, 1994). These results were broadly comparable with a survey at the same time by Partnership Sourcing Ltd (Tett, 1994). Nevertheless, as a follow-up survey in 1996 by UMIST showed, the benefits of this approach to purchasing are often difficult to quantify and can be very customer-biased (Burnes and New, 1996).

The partnership approach to customer–supplier relationships originated in Japan, and is especially prevalent in the Japanese motor and electronics industries (Bhote, 1989; Lloyd et al, 1994; Ishikawa, 1985). In attempting to understand the factors which underpinned the competitiveness of Japanese companies, attention in the West was first directed at their internal arrangements; but it quickly became apparent that this told only half of the story. Typically, bought-in parts and services account for over 70 per cent of the cost of a finished product. Therefore, it became clear that to understand the advantages that Japanese companies had over their Western counterparts, in terms of costs, quality, time to market, etc., it was necessary to understand the unique relationship they had with their suppliers (Francks, 1992; Womack et al, 1990).

A number of European companies, notably Philips with its Co-Makership initiative, tried to emulate the Japanese. However, it was only with the arrival of Japanese transplants, especially the opening of the Nissan car plant in Sunderland in the mid-1980s, that interest in customer–supplier partnerships really took off in the UK, with the rest of Europe some way behind (Burnes and Whittle, 1995; Hines, 1994; Lloyd et al, 1994; NEDC, 1991a, b).

Though there is no universally agreed definition of customer–supplier partnerships, Partnership Sourcing Ltd (1991b: 2), the UK body established by government and industry to promote the concept, appears to have captured its essence by defining it as a situation:

> . . . where customer and suppliers develop such a close and long-term relationship that the two work together as partners. It isn't philanthropy: the aim is to secure the best possible commercial advantage. The principle is that teamwork is better than combat. If the end-customer is to be best served, then the parties to a deal must work together – and both must win. Partnership sourcing works because both parties have an interest in each other's success.

The move to more co-operative and stable relationships between customers and suppliers is not merely a case of adjustments at the organisational interface. Rather, to be successful, it requires more fundamental changes in both customers and suppliers. The three case studies in this chapter show how such partnerships work in practice and, in particular, illustrate how the concept requires not only changes in the relationships between organisations but also attitudinal, behavioural and structural changes within them.

Each of the three studies relates to a different aspect of the partnership process. Case Study 8 deals with the consequences of Rover's decision to outsource the assembly of suspension modules to TRW. It demonstrates that such initiatives, through closer operational integration, can bring great benefits but that these can be jeopardised if they are not also accompanied by closer strategic relationships. Case Study 9 concerns one of the leading advocates of customer–supplier partnerships, the UK plant of the car company Nissan. It focuses upon Nissan's Supplier Development Team (SDT), which is one of its prime mechanisms for cementing partnerships and assisting suppliers to improve their performance. The study describes the purpose and operation of the SDT, and shows how Nissan has moved beyond exhortation to become directly involved in the process of change within its suppliers. Case Study 10 shows that the move to develop new relationships is not just driven by customers. In this instance a supplier, Speedy Stationers, took the first step. It recognised that, in its case, the partnership approach was not just a means of providing a better service to its customers; it could also be an effective mechanism for securing increased business. The case study recounts how Speedy came to this conclusion, the steps it took to convince one of its customers to enter into a partnership and to co-operate, and the resulting changes and benefits.

The chapter concludes by arguing that though much attention has been given to the creation of new internal relationships and structures as a mechanism for coping with environmental turbulence and uncertainty, changes in external relationships can also play an important role in this process. Consequently, partnerships can help organisations to restore, to an extent, a degree of stability and predictability to their lives.

The conclusion also points out that, as the Rover–TRW case illustrates, it is very difficult for organisations to quantify in advance the benefits of developing partnerships. Indeed, as shown in Case Study 9, Nissan believed it would have to wait over ten years before it began to see the real benefits from its partnership activities, though as the Rover and Speedy examples show, early benefits can also accrue. Therefore, the move to new customer–supplier relations is not driven by rational and quantitative decision-making. Rather, the move to partnership requires an act of faith based on an instinctive and philosophical belief that the old methods do not work and that 'the game requires new rules', rules which cannot be written in advance but emerge as the game unfolds.

# ROVER–TRW – OPERATIONAL INTEGRATION[1]

## Background

This case study concerns the relationship between Rover Group and one of its largest suppliers, TRW. The case study focuses on Rover's decision to outsource the assembly of front suspension modules to TRW and the benefits and difficulties which ensued. It shows that outsourcing sub-assemblies can bring great operational benefits when managed effectively by both parties, but that these may be jeopardised if this co-operation fails to extend to a more strategic level.

Details of Rover's history and present situation are given in Case Study 6. However, it should be noted that from the early 1980s, Rover was developing more co-operative internal working relationships and that it gradually began to extend this approach to its suppliers (*see* Grove, 1998, for further details). For its part, TRW is one of the world's largest manufacturing companies. Founded in 1901, and with its Headquarters in Cleveland, Ohio, TRW is an American-owned company with a turnover of some $12 billion. It employs over 80,000 people worldwide. It has recently announced an agreed takeover of LucasVarity, which will increase its turnover to around $19 billion and give it a workforce in excess of 130,000 people. TRW is split into two divisions: Space, Avionics, Defence and Communications; and Automotive. The automotive business is the largest division, accounting for over 60 per cent of sales and employees.

TRW's vision and goals for its European automotive business are as follows:

- to be the leading manufacturer of power steering in Europe;
- to deliver superior value to our customers;
- to achieve total quality management;
- to reduce costs by 30 per cent;
- to achieve a 20 per cent return on assets employed.

TRW Automotive's European sales are well over $1 billion. Some 23 per cent of this comes from its UK business (TRW Steering Systems Ltd) which operates on five sites, the main one being at Resolven in Wales, employs 1,400 people and, as its name states, manufactures steering systems. Its main customers are Rover, Honda, Nissan, Ford and Volvo. Though TRW has a close working relationship with all these companies, it enjoys a particularly strong and long-standing relationship with the Rover Group and is Rover's second biggest supplier.

TRW's steering systems business began supplying the forerunners of Rover over 60 years ago. A major milestone in the relationship came in 1959 when it was

---

[1] The research on which this case study is based was funded by AT Kearney Ltd and carried out jointly with Dr Steve New of Hertford College, Oxford University (*see* Burnes and New, 1996, for further details).

awarded the contract to supply the rack and pinion steering for the then revolutionary Mini. This was the first time rack and pinion steering had been fitted as standard on any mass-produced vehicle. TRW still supplies the steering gear for the Mini. During the 1960s and 1970s, British Leyland (as Rover were then called) had its own in-house facility for manufacturing both power-assisted and manual rack and pinion steering. However, in 1980, this was closed down and TRW took over responsibility for supplying all British Leyland's steering requirements.

In 1989, this relationship was further strengthened when Rover decided to outsource the assembly of front suspension modules, of which the steering gear was the key component. TRW was asked to bid for this work, was awarded the contract and began supplying the suspension modules in May 1989. In order to meet Rover's exacting standards, TRW set up a new assembly facility located at Frankley, about two miles from Rover's Longbridge plant.

## The origins of Frankley

The main reason for Rover's decision in 1988 to outsource the assembly of front suspension modules, and consequently for TRW to establish a new facility at Frankley, was quite straightforward: Rover needed the space. The introduction and success of new models meant that Rover no longer had the space to carry out this assembly operation at its Longbridge plant. A subsidiary reason was that Rover, like most car companies at the time, believed that modular assembly of cars, from outsourced sub-assemblies, was a strong possibility for the future, and this initiative with TRW gave the company the opportunity to assess the benefits of this approach.

Rover invited TRW and one other existing supplier to put forward proposals for running the new facility to assemble front suspension modules. TRW saw this as a major opportunity and responded in a very positive way. The main reasons for this were as follows:

- They wanted to continue to supply direct to Rover rather than through another supplier.
- TRW in the USA had (unsuccessfully) bid for a similar initiative with Ford, and could see the benefits it could bring to the business in terms of future growth and becoming 'essential' to the customer. In addition, TRW also thought that modular assembly was the future for the car industry.

Therefore, not only was TRW responsive to Rover's suggestion, but it could draw on its experience with Ford in preparing its proposal. TRW showed Rover the proposal they had put to Ford in the United States and prepared a business plan for the new operation. A succession of increasingly detailed meetings ensued with both Rover and their (then) partner, Honda.

Rover moved very quickly in making a decision and awarded the contract to TRW. This was mainly because Rover were impressed with TRW's plans and proposals, but also because they felt that its size and resources (of both expertise and money) made it a suitable partner in this instance. An additional factor was that TRW's steering gear was by far the most complex and expensive part of the suspension modules.

## Making a start

Planning and proposing was one thing; getting started was quite another. Rover were working to a very tight timetable and needed both the space and the suspension modules for a range of new cars it was introducing. One of the conditions of the contract was that TRW had to establish an assembly operation within a few miles of the Longbridge Plant. Therefore, in late 1988–early 1989, TRW found itself pursuing two major activities simultaneously:

1 developing its own approach to steering system assembly;
2 finding a site and recruiting staff for the new facility.

### Developing its own approach to suspension module assembly

After a rigorous selection process, three supervisors were recruited from TRW's Cleveden plant to run the new operation. One of the supervisors was appointed as manager for the new facility; however, in essence, the three were jointly responsible for the new product and new facility, and operated very much as a team. This co-operative approach was something new to TRW but it was clear that everyone needed to work closely together if the project was to be successful. TRW had no previous experience of assembling suspension modules and, to a large extent, the manager and two supervisors were thrown in at the deep end. As one of the three put it, 'We were given a bag of parts and told to assemble them.' Initially based at TRW's main UK site at Resolven, they worked closely with an engineer from Rover to learn what Rover's requirements were in terms of the suspension modules and then they began to experiment with different approaches to assembly.

All three had previously been on TRW's First Line Supervisors course, and the Rover work gave them the opportunity to utilise some of the ideas they had learnt. In particular, they chose to adopt a 'greenfield' approach (starting from scratch) rather than building on existing TRW/Rover practices. Despite the tight timetable, they were allowed to experiment, and through a process of trial and error began to see how the assembly process could be best organised. The essence of their approach has been to focus on continuous improvement by developing teams, encouraging initiative and ensuring that change is driven by and with the full support of the people on the assembly line. Since it began production in 1989, the Frankley operation has been transformed out of all recognition. Manual assembly has given way to semi-automation, they have achieved zero defects, costs and assembly times have been reduced considerably and, regardless of the inherent instability of customer schedules, they always deliver what the customer wants, when it wants it and in the correct order.

### Finding a site and recruiting staff

At the same time that TRW were undertaking trial assemblies at Resolven, it located a site at Frankley, near Longbridge, which was ideal for their requirements, and the assembly operation was moved there in May 1989. Though they had tried to recruit from within, the only TRW staff who transferred to Frankley were the manager and the two supervisors. All the rest (some 30 staff initially) were recruited locally. The recruitment procedures were very structured and rigorous. They wanted skilled and flexible staff who would fit into a teamworking environment and who were prepared to contribute ideas and give commitment. Above all, they wanted to build an operation that was dedicated to meeting the customer's requirements fully, no matter how demanding or difficult these might be.

Though they had the advantage of starting out with a greenfield site and a workforce that had few preconceptions or restrictions, it also meant that everyone had to be trained from scratch.

## Frankley – the early years

Mainly drawing on their own ideas and resources but working hard to understand Rover's needs, Frankley began to develop itself into a world-class assembly plant. The Frankley operation started out with two shifts and eventually moved to three in order to match Rover's own assembly operation. In order both to understand the customer's needs and to develop an effective working relationship, a great deal of time (by all concerned) was spent at the Rover plant. Indeed, it is now compulsory for all new recruits to Frankley to spend a period working at Rover before taking up their appointment at Frankley.

Year on year, Frankley has consistently and diligently reduced costs and lead times, and improved quality. The essence of its ability to do this revolves around three core principles:

- understanding what Rover wants and giving it to them;
- teamwork and involvement;
- continuous improvement.

The biggest difficulty Frankley faced was in matching what it produced to Rover's actual build requirements. The steering assembly has 39 derivatives, and it is far from easy to ensure that the mix of derivatives TRW dispatches matches the mix of cars Rover is assembling at any one time. Rover did and does provide Frankley with a monthly schedule and a 10–day rolling programme (five days firm and five tentative). This allows TRW to schedule its suppliers. However, the key information, originally at least, was the mix of cars going into the paint shop (the step immediately prior to assembly). This provided TRW with only 12 hours' notice of the model mix that Rover planned to assemble.

Therefore, initially, Frankley had to gear itself to working on 12 hours' notice. However, owing to damage during painting, what went into the paintshop was not always what went down the assembly line. Therefore, in the first year of operation, though Frankley delivered to the pre-paint shop schedule, it found that what it delivered was not always what Rover was actually assembling.

In many instances, the customer and supplier would have argued about whose fault this was. Instead, Frankley and Rover worked to resolve the problem. It was eventually agreed that instead of informing Frankley of the mix that went into the paint shop, they should tell them what undamaged cars came out. This represented a major step forward in terms of Rover trusting its suppliers. Rover, like most car companies, had been reluctant to give too much information to its suppliers. This was not only because information was seen as power, but also because it would be Rover's line managers who would have to take responsibility if the information was wrong. Nevertheless, Rover did provide the information. It did mean that Frankley only had $4\frac{1}{2}$ hour's notice of Rover's requirements rather than the 12 hours previously, but at least the schedule was much more accurate. However, even this was not foolproof, and eventually they moved to a system whereby Rover would notify them of the build mix just $2\frac{1}{2}$ hours before the parts were required.

Working in this way does give Frankley exact information on what is required and they now know that if they build a particular suspension module it will be used. However, to get to this position has required two major efforts:

- building trust between Rover and Frankley, so that both have faith in each other and are prepared to provide information and make commitments without feeling that either is leaving itself open to abuse;

- establishing an assembly operation that is not only capable of building a wide product range in an efficient and effective manner, but which can also do so at very short notice. To achieve this required a major effort by Frankley staff.

Though this approach has obvious advantages to Rover, it also has considerable advantages to Frankley. First, it means that it must run a lean and efficient operation which operates with a 'right first time' approach. Second, it has no finished stocks and only two days' worth of component stocks (down from eight days in 1994).

The Frankley site has clearly developed an approach to assembly and customer satisfaction that owes more to Japanese than Western methods. However, one recent Japanese visitor was heard to remark that Frankley was not as good as Japanese plants ... it was better!

TRW has not achieved this overnight, and in some instances has had to modify its initial ideas. Originally, TRW looked on the Frankley site merely as an assembly plant. Most of the support services were dealt with by Resolven. Though this made Frankley a very 'lean' enterprise, it also meant that the lack of on-site, dedicated resources restricted its ability to improve, especially in the areas of process improvement and supplier development. Therefore, over time, Frankley came to acquire its own support staff rather than having to rely on Resolven.

The benefits of this are clear in terms of the efficiency of the Frankley assembly operation. However, though less visible, the benefits of materials management being based at Frankley have also been substantial, though this was forced on them by the necessity of having to build the same type of relationship with its suppliers that it enjoys with Rover. Nevertheless, originally this did not look as though it would be necessary.

## Developing suppliers

Taking over an operation from another company and re-creating it from scratch is never going to be easy, but when it also involves managing that company's suppliers on their behalf, some difficulty can be anticipated, to say the least. TRW had few illusions that suppliers selected by and working for Rover, and who would continue to see Rover as their customer, would welcome being managed by an 'intermediary'. However, the reality was even more difficult than TRW anticipated.

Though communication and co-operation between TRW and Rover was constructive from the outset, the one area Rover seemed most reluctant to discuss with TRW was the handover and management of the other suspension module component suppliers. Consequently, when TRW began assembling the suspension modules at Frankley, none of the suppliers had been informed of the change. TRW found that not only had Rover not informed them, but that some companies did not even know who TRW was. The suppliers still considered themselves as working directly for Rover, and were more than somewhat resentful of TRW's new role.

Initially, TRW managed the suppliers from its main site at Resolven, but it soon became apparent that if the supplier–Frankley interface was to operate effectively, responsibility for suppliers would have to reside at Frankley. To achieve this, one of the original Frankley supervisors was made responsible for managing suppliers. His first task was to visit all the suppliers and explain the new arrangement to them. Though some began to adopt a more co-operative attitude to TRW, others still tended to ignore it and liaise with Rover instead. However, with Rover's assistance, Frankley gradually came to build a working relationship with the Rover-nominated suppliers. Nevertheless, when it came to know the suppliers better, two issues emerged:

1 Though Frankley was tailoring its production and deliveries to Rover's assembly programme, suppliers still tended to operate on a 'boom or bust' basis, i.e. they would deliver too much or too little.

2 A number of the suppliers did not meet TRW's quality standards.

Given that the suppliers were nominated by Rover, TRW was not in a position to change them. Therefore, it had no alternative but to work with the suppliers to improve them. Frankley set out to build the same relationship with the suppliers that it was developing with Rover. Initially, presentations were made to all the suppliers explaining who TRW was, what Rover required of the Frankley operation, and what Frankley required of the suppliers. This was followed by reviews of each supplier's performance with action plans being agreed to resolve any problems and concerns. Though no one would pretend that everything always runs smoothly or that continuous improvement is not expected, supplier performance is far better than it was in 1989.

## The new contract

Up to 1994, the relationship between Rover and TRW continued to improve and there were very few operational concerns. However, in 1994 Rover began to discuss the replacement of the 200/400 series cars for which Frankley supplied the suspension modules. Though TRW expected stiff bargaining over the terms of the new contract, it did not expect Rover to question whether TRW should get the contract or not. From TRW's perspective, it had more than exceeded Rover's expectations when the original contract was awarded in 1989. However, in the intervening period, there had been a number of intense and not always good-tempered negotiations regarding the pricing of the contract and TRW had, reluctantly, made a number of downward adjustments to the original contract price.

It should also be said, though Rover did not appear to be fully aware of this, that TRW had made better profits from the Frankley operation than it originally expected. In the main, this was because Frankley was much more efficient than Rover had been at assembling the suspension modules, the volume of products was greater than originally assumed, and the overhead charges were generous. For its part, Rover was more concerned with the latter issue rather than the first two. It felt that TRW's costing system exaggerated the true cost of the Frankley operation. TRW's procedure was to add a management fee to the direct cost of the Frankley operation and so arrive at what they believed was a true cost to themselves. Rover, however, disputed the size of this fee and though, as mentioned, TRW did reduce the price it originally agreed with Rover, when the contract came up for renewal, some senior Rover managers were so concerned at the situation that they wanted to take the work back in-house.

TRW found itself in a position where it had to justify its accountancy system (which was standard throughout TRW), and also convince Rover that it could continue to offer it a better service than could be achieved by taking the work back in-house. Though the latter was not difficult to do, the former took some hard negotiations to achieve. In the end, TRW made a considerable reduction in its Frankley management fee and the new contract was awarded to TRW.

The difficulties did not end there, however. As Rover introduced new vehicles, it redesigned the suspension modules which necessitated changes to component suppliers. As was the case originally, Rover would not let TRW enter a dialogue with suppliers until actual assembly began. Nevertheless, building on its earlier experience, TRW has become extremely proficient at overcoming any resistance amongst new suppliers and is able rapidly to inculcate them in the TRW approach.

## The outcomes

The Rover–TRW case study clearly shows that the outsourcing of major sub-assemblies can bring important benefits to both customers and suppliers, particularly at an operational level. It also shows that the process is far from easy, and that even after many years major misunderstandings can occur which can threaten the relationship. The Rover–TRW experience can be judged at two levels – operational and strategic. At the operational level, it can be viewed as follows:

- The Frankley staff were given a clear, though by no means simple, task: they had to meet Rover's needs for suspension modules. In so doing, they were allowed, and encouraged, to use their own initiative.

- Though Frankley met some initial scepticism from Rover's assembly staff, whose co-operation they needed, it consistently and with real determination set out to identify what Rover needed, to establish where the obstacles lay and to overcome these.

- This was neither a one-off effort nor limited to a few managers. Instead, it was a process of continuous improvement by all concerned.

- There were three key factors in this: (a) the selection and training of staff; (b) allowing staff to interface directly with their customer, thus ensuring rapid performance feedback; and (c) establishing a 'greenfield' mentality which meant that they all started from scratch and without preconceptions regarding how best to organise assembly or the nature of relations with their customer.

At the strategic level, however, a different picture emerged:

- Though one of the original objectives – albeit of secondary importance – was for both parties to assess the benefits of and approach to contracting out major sub-assemblies, this appears to have been quickly forgotten. Instead, the initiative came to be seen as a purely operational matter.

- As the relationship developed, it was clear that neither partner had had any real idea of how to cost such an operation. Originally, Rover had felt that it had negotiated a good deal because it was getting better supplies at lower cost. Likewise, TRW were happy to win the contract and felt that it would make a profit because it would be more efficient than Rover.

- Neither party realised that the Frankley operation would be able to make the large performance improvements that it did. However, when Rover realised how much more efficient Frankley was than it had been itself, it began to question the price it was paying. TRW, for its part, was extremely pleased by the return on its investment, though reluctant to reduce its prices.

- This led to a series of acrimonious confrontations, culminating in Rover seriously considering taking the work back in-house. Fortunately for both parties, the issue was resolved. Nevertheless, it demonstrated that though operationally Rover and TRW were working closely in partnership, at a more senior level they were not. Yet, if they had been, not only might they have avoided much acrimony, but they would also have learned more about how to run such collaborations in the future.

In this instance, it is important to note that neither Rover nor TRW set out to achieve strategic and high-level co-operation *per se*. Rather, Rover were motivated, primarily, by operational considerations and though TRW did see strategic advantage, its main aim was to maintain first-tier supplier status. This may explain why both parties made enormous strides forward in operational integration but failed to make similar progress in terms of strategic integration and trust.

## Case study 9

# NISSAN MOTOR MANUFACTURING (UK) LTD – THE SUPPLIER DEVELOPMENT TEAM APPROACH

## Background

When Nissan established its British operation in the mid-1980s, it recognised that European – especially UK – component suppliers fell far short of Japanese standards of quality, reliability and cost. Measuring suppliers' capabilities on a scale of 0 to 100, Nissan rated Japanese suppliers at 100, suppliers in mainland Europe were rated at 80 and UK suppliers were rated at 65–70. Nissan were required by the European Union to produce cars which contained, by value, 80 per cent local content. Therefore, it needed to improve the capabilities of its European suppliers, if it was to maintain the quality and cost standards achieved by its plants in Japan.

Though Ford had put considerable effort into improving the quality standards of suppliers in the UK and other European countries, Nissan believed that it needed to go further, offering direct assistance to suppliers if major improvements were to be achieved. As one means of helping suppliers to improve their capability, Nissan decided in 1987 to form a Supplier Development Team (SDT) based at its Sunderland plant. The aim of the SDT was and is to help suppliers to develop their business to the stage where they can meet Nissan's present and future performance requirements. A similar function had been in operation for 15 years in Japan, and this was considered to be a suitable model for its UK operation.

Initially, two engineers were sent to Japan for a nine-week training course. This training included extensive practice in undertaking improvement activities within Nissan's Japanese suppliers. On their return, based on the techniques learnt in Japan, the engineers developed a 'ten-day improvement activity' for use with UK suppliers. Their aim was to establish an approach which, whilst achieving immediate productivity and quality improvements, would convince UK suppliers to adopt the Japanese approach to manufacturing. Consequently, though Nissan was concerned that the outcome of any improvement activity should be positive, its ultimate objective was for suppliers to recognise the value and benefits of adopting the Japanese approach, and to continue with it once the SDT had left.

The SDT approach was officially launched in the UK in November 1988, and involved a group of 12 medium-sized suppliers. Since these small beginnings, the size of the SDT has grown, and it has become an established and important part of Nissan's operations. It has worked with the majority of Nissan's suppliers, and has established a reputation amongst them for its expertise and commitment. Though it originally concentrated on shopfloor improvement projects, which still form the core of its work, it also provides a broader range of assistance, such as cost reduction initiatives, joint product development, supervisory training and strategic planning programmes. In essence, it offers a consultancy service to Nissan's suppliers which is, normally, free of charge.

So the role of the SDT is to help suppliers develop and improve their overall capability and performance. It seeks to improve productivity, reduce costs and maintain quality-assured production amongst suppliers. Though the SDT is a dedicated and high-profile resource which is available to help suppliers, it is only one part of Nissan's overall commitment to developing its suppliers. But although other areas of Nissan, such as design, also provide specialist assistance to suppliers, it is the SDT that is charged with assessing the overall requirements and capabilities of suppliers and, where possible, helping them to become capable of meeting Nissan's needs.

Though the assistance given by the team to suppliers is in effect free consultancy with, at least in the early days, no obvious or short-term benefit to Nissan, this is not totally philanthropic. Nissan tends to see supplier development as essentially a long-term process, with payback times of the order of ten years or more. It believes that, by assisting them to develop improved working practices and engendering a continuous improvement mentality, it will enable suppliers to achieve world-class performance standards. Nissan sees this as being necessary in order for it to produce world-beating cars.

## The SDT in action

The SDT approach is to work co-operatively with suppliers to help them identify areas for improvement, and then to assist them to develop and monitor improvement plans. In particular, the SDT will train supplier personnel in quality and production improvement methods, and support supplier initiatives to improve production and reduce defects. The idea of free consultancy by an organisation such as Nissan sounds attractive, but suppliers can also perceive such an offer as either domineering or patronising. Nissan's relations with its suppliers were and are very positive; however, given the history of antagonism between customers and suppliers in the UK car industry – which still persists to some degree (Lamming, 1994; Burnes and New, 1996) – it tends to tread warily and prepare the ground carefully before offering assistance.

## Initial approach

Before undertaking the first improvement activity with a supplier, the SDT makes a presentation to the senior managers of the company concerned. This is because it regards senior management commitment and understanding as an essential precondition for success. Unless this commitment is gained, the SDT cannot and does not proceed further. Though the SDT approach is now well established among and valued by suppliers, in the early days of the SDT, some suppliers were sceptical and resistant to such an approach. Nevertheless, most suppliers respond favourably to the initial presentation.

The SDT's standard presentation begins by describing what continuous improvement (*kaizen*) is and the benefits it brings. The SDT then outlines a typical improvement activity, including the various tools and techniques used. The team stresses that most improvement activities can be carried out at little or no cost, provided that the employees working in the area concerned are involved in planning and making the necessary changes.

If, after the presentation, senior managers are willing to proceed, the SDT briefs other staff and undertakes a factory assessment.

## The factory assessment

The length of time devoted to a factory assessment varies, but typically it takes a day. Assessments are not compulsory, but most suppliers welcome an independent review of their operations, especially by a world-class company such as Nissan. The factory assessment does not form part of Nissan's formal supplier assessment procedure and, therefore, is less threatening than might otherwise be the case.

Factories are assessed under ten headings:

- Company policy
- Quality performance and procedures
- Delivery control methods and performance
- Productivity
- Equipment maintenance procedures
- Stock control
- Production process development
- Housekeeping (how tidy and orderly the factory is)
- Health and safety
- Employee morale

Each heading is scored out of five and the scores recorded on a factory assessment summary sheet. The assessment is then discussed with and explained to the supplier's management. From the assessment, the supplier and the SDT can begin to identify areas of concern and possible targets for improvement. The SDT then proceeds to suggest how it might be of assistance and, if this offer is accepted, agrees an improvement project with the supplier.

### Improvement activities

Though the ten-day improvement activity offered by the SDT is based on the tools, techniques and experience of Nissan in Japan, it has been tailored to meet the specific needs of its European suppliers (who are mainly based in the UK). Improvement activities usually include some or all of the following:

- reducing assembly time and improving methods;
- reducing overhead costs – including reducing inventory and improving equipment availability;
- reducing work-in-process;
- preventing defects;
- improving productivity by reducing throughput times and introducing Just-in-Time scheduling.

As mentioned, most improvement activities are usually achieved at little or no cost to the supplier; however, the supplier does need to commit time and personnel to the activity. The improvement process revolves around a multifunctional team composed of the supplier's own staff, who are assisted by the SDT. The supplier's team includes operators and supervisors from the production area concerned as well as maintenance, process engineering, quality and sometimes administrative staff. The team is led by someone from the supplier. The SDT stress that the most important members of the team are the shopfloor employees working on the process that is to be improved. Not only does this prevent change simply being imposed on those who will be directly affected by it, with all the scope for resentment and mistrust that this can cause, but it also ensures that the valuable knowledge of the shopfloor employees is utilised. Perhaps more importantly, it provides them with the skills and motivation to continue to improve the process even after the SDT have ceased to be involved. An independent study (Lloyd *et al*, 1994) found that this approach led to greater commitment to the activity, and improved morale in the areas concerned. It also found that improvement activities helped to break down functional barriers, and assisted the development of greater co-operation and team spirit.

Once the process or activity that is to be improved has been agreed, targets for the improvement are then established (e.g. reductions in lead time, improvements in quality). The supplier prepares the ground for the activity by briefing staff and making any necessary resources available, such as a dedicated meeting room. If the improvement activity is likely to cause a disruption to production, a stock of components may be built up before the activity commences to compensate for this.

*Day One* of the ten-day improvement activity is devoted to providing training for the supplier's team. If it is the first time the supplier has been involved in such an activity, the SDT will take the lead in this. However, if the supplier has previous experience of SDT improvement activities, then a member of its staff is expected to take the lead. The SDT sees its prime purpose as ensuring that everyone understands the concept of *kaizen*; the procedures for the ten-day activity are clear; and the team becomes familiar with the tools and techniques necessary for its task. In this latter respect, the most frequently used tools and techniques are flow-charts, work-flow diagrams, pareto charts, cause and effect (fish bone) diagrams, brainstorming and critical path analysis. Where necessary, these are reinforced and supplemented as the ten-day improvement activity develops.

On *Day Two* of the improvement activity, the team splits into smaller groups to analyse and discuss the process to be improved. The groups use a combination of hard data, such as scrap rates, equipment down time and stock levels, and more subjective opinions, such as comments about layout, ease of use and the provision of information, to identify causes of waste and possible counter-measures. The SDT encourages the use of stop watches and even video cameras to assist the supplier's team to analyse the process in question, though these can sometimes be viewed with suspicion by operators.

Once the individual groups have completed their deliberations, they reconvene as a team. The team usually makes a flow diagram of the entire process in order that everyone can appreciate what is involved and agree the changes that will bring the best benefits. The data that have been collected by the groups are analysed by the entire team. To make this easier, data are ordered and analysed under a number of standard headings:

| | |
|---|---|
| *Quality* | Are quality problems due to material, process, design or training deficiencies? |
| *Technology* | Is the equipment appropriate, well-maintained, and used correctly? |
| *Ease of operation* | Can work be made easier through ergonomic improvements such as by eliminating the need to bend, or through modifications to the equipment? |
| *Layout* | Does the layout of the process result in time delays or excessive work-in-process? |

For each of the above categories, the team proceeds to identify concerns, causes and counter-measures. Most suppliers' teams find this a demanding approach. In the space of two days, not only do they have to learn new tools and techniques, but they also have to deploy these in a rigorous and constructive fashion. Nevertheless, by the end of the second day, teams have normally identified what the problems are, what is causing them and the measures necessary to correct them. Sometimes, the outcome is a recognition that existing equipment is inadequate for its task, but it is more usually the case that the team comes up with a list of low cost/no cost changes which they can implement themselves. In some cases, other members of the supplier's staff may be called in to discuss the feasibility of some of the ideas generated. However, in the main, the suppliers' teams are usually capable of making their own judgements.

*Days Three to Eight* of the improvement activity are spent implementing the agreed improvements. Though the SDT does come back on day six to observe progress and can be contacted for assistance at any time, the responsibility for this phase of the programme lies firmly with the supplier's personnel. The changes they make may be small and simple, or may involve the re-arrangement of complete areas of a factory. Where feasible, the team makes the changes in conjunction with personnel in the area concerned. The changed process is then tested, re-analysed and, if necessary, fine-tuned. To minimise disruption, any major changes in layout tend to take place during the weekend which falls in the middle of the improvement activity.

For *Days Nine and Ten* of the improvement activity, the SDT returns to help the team review what they have learnt and achieved, and to ensure that all changes are fully documented. They also discuss outstanding issues and concerns, and potential future improvement projects. The final task is to prepare and deliver a presentation to the company's senior managers describing the changes achieved and the benefits gained. Not only does this give staff the opportunity to show senior managers what they have achieved (and receive well-earned praise), but it also helps those unused to public speaking to develop their skills in this area.

The SDT has come to be considered as a valuable resource by Nissan's suppliers, and there is always a queue for its services. From the suppliers' perspective, this is understandable. Improvement activities usually meet or exceed their targets. Productivity increases of between 20 and 40 per cent are quite common, as are similar improvements in quality and reductions in work-in-process. From Nissan's point of view, it is not the individual improvement projects *per se* that are important, but the ability of suppliers to carry on making improvements once the SDT presence is removed. For many, this is the case, and individual improvement projects act as a catalyst to the development of continuous improvement both on and off the shopfloor. Nevertheless, this does not always occur, and some suppliers do appear to find difficulty sustaining and spreading the SDT philosophy. However, though the main focus of the SDT's work is improvement projects with suppliers, it is also involved in a wide range of other educational, training, advisory and development work aimed at enhancing the capabilities of Nissan's suppliers.

## Training for supplier personnel

Over the years, through its work with suppliers, the SDT has identified particular forms of training that it considers crucial for supplier development, which include the following:

- **An improvement manager course**. This is designed for suppliers' staff who, following the SDT lead, are given responsibility for running improvement activities. The course covers all the techniques used during improvement activities. As well as classroom instruction, all course members take part in an improvement activity either in the Nissan plant or with one of its local suppliers.

- **A trouble-shooting course.** This teaches the principles and techniques of problem-solving.

- **A supervisor development course.** SDT members assist in running a development course for Nissan's own supervisors. In the past, the SDT had arranged for suppliers' personnel also to take part in these courses. However, such was the demand from suppliers that the SDT now organises a supervisor development course specifically for suppliers.

## Strategy development activities

In addition to the above SDT activities, the rest of Nissan are involved in a wide variety of activities with its suppliers, ranging from cost reduction exercises to joint product development programmes. Most of these focus on one particular aspect of a supplier's business, usually manufacturing-related. However, in the early 1990s, Nissan began to be increasingly aware that the success of these individual activities in generating a long-term and sustainable improvement in performance depended upon the ability of suppliers to take a strategic approach to their business. In cases where significant progress had been made, it was noticeable that Nissan's efforts formed part of, and were incorporated within, the supplier's own proactive and long-term business plans. In companies where progress was slow and often not sustained, Nissan's efforts did not link in to any overall plan, and remained isolated and fragmented pockets of activity.

Nissan recognised that whilst most suppliers had a strategic plan, in some cases these tended to be short-term, reactive or unambitious. In such instances, they were no more than paper plans which no one appeared to be committed to implementing. The SDT felt that without a workable strategy, no matter how much assistance Nissan gave, suppliers would make little overall progress, though there might be considerable improvements in isolated aspects of their business.

Nissan's response to this was to develop a strategic planning package which it could offer to appropriate suppliers. Though the SDT were responsible for sponsoring and promoting the package, it did not feel it should also deliver it itself. This was for two reasons. First, neither the SDT by itself, nor Nissan in total, had or could make available the time, resources and expertise necessary to provide such assistance. Second, for such an approach to be successful, it required the full co-operation of suppliers, and a willingness to open up all aspects of their business. Given that suppliers usually deal with a number of car manufacturers, this would involve revealing confidential information about Nissan's competitors, not to mention the suppliers' own future intentions. For obvious reasons, it was not considered either reasonable or possible to ask suppliers to reveal this information.

In order to overcome these obstacles, Nissan entered into a partnership with the National Economic Development Office (NEDO) and the University of Manchester Institute of Science and Technology (UMIST) to produce and provide a strategy development package to its suppliers. The package was developed and piloted jointly by the SDT, NEDO and UMIST. However, once it became fully operational, the SDT restricted its role to identifying suitable suppliers and promoting the package. The actual delivery of the programme was the responsibility of NEDO and UMIST, though the SDT still maintained a quality assurance role.

Unlike many other SDT activities, suppliers had to pay for this service. Nevertheless, it appears to have been well-received by suppliers who, often having had a poor experience of using external bodies for such activities in the past, welcomed a strategy development package sponsored by a major customer. For Nissan, it ensured that a supplier, who it felt had a particular need in this area, could use a service in which Nissan had confidence without compromising commercial confidentiality.

The strategy development programme was launched by Nissan in 1992 and offered to all those suppliers who Nissan felt would benefit from such an initiative. The programme was discontinued after some five years when all the suitable suppliers had undertaken it. However, Nissan's other supplier development activities still continue, though, as the 1990s progressed, they came to focus more heavily on cost reduction.

## The outcome

Since it first embarked on the supplier development route, Nissan has moved from trying to sell the concept to a few suppliers to a position where suppliers are queuing up for the services of its Supplier Development Team. At the same time, the SDT has expanded its role from undertaking improvement activities within suppliers, which still accounts for the majority of its time, to offering a range of training courses and even to providing assistance with strategic planning. Given the traditional distrust between suppliers and customers in the car industry, for the former to welcome such levels of 'interference' in their internal affairs is remarkable, and provides clear evidence of partnerships in action.

It is nevertheless important to set Nissan's SDT activities in context. Today, the UK car industry is the second largest in Europe, and the UK provides a base not just for Nissan but for Toyota and Honda as well. However, when Nissan announced its intention to establish a car assembly plant in the UK, the domestic industry was in crisis. All the (then) UK-based producers were experiencing financial difficulties, vehicle imports were at an all-time high, and component suppliers genuinely feared for their future. Therefore, the prospect of one of the mighty Japanese car companies establishing a new plant in the UK was seen not just as a much-needed vote of confidence in Britain's future as an industrial nation, but also as a major opportunity by component suppliers. In addition, Nissan let it be known that it wanted to establish the same sort of long-term, mutually beneficial partnerships with British suppliers as it enjoyed with its Japanese ones. Though many were unsure of what this meant, the prospect of working with a car company whose fortunes were waxing rather than waning was clearly very attractive.

Unlike other producers in the UK at the time, Nissan did not establish a tender list and ask for quotations. It identified the suppliers it wanted; rigorously assessed their capabilities; established cost, quality and delivery targets with them; and awarded them contracts for the lifetime of the car they were supplying components for. It also declared that it expected suppliers to stay with Nissan for the next car it built and the one after, performance and technological factors permitting. In addition, as a customer it was seen to be reliable, predictable and trustworthy – it kept its word.

Accordingly, when Nissan arrived in the UK it met with considerable goodwill and co-operation, which tended to grow rather than diminish as suppliers came to appreciate its approach to purchasing. There was also a great deal of prestige attached to being associated with Nissan, and this applied to its suppliers as much as anyone else. The fact that Nissan was also a good customer who changed the rules of customer–supplier relationships, from an antagonistic relationship based on a win–lose equation to a partnership based on win–win, was almost a bonus.

It was in this context that Nissan launched its Supplier Development Team. Car industry customers seeking to improve suppliers was not new – Ford had been doing it for some years with its quality assurance programmes. The difference was that whilst Ford unilaterally imposed requirements on suppliers, Nissan took a voluntary and co-operative approach and did not seek to penalise those who did not take part. Nissan's aim was, and still is, to transfer to its European suppliers practices and techniques that had proved successful in Japan. The SDT activities should therefore be seen not as an end in themselves, but rather as a catalyst to stimulate the search for continuous improvement.

Despite some early suspicion, there is little doubt that Nissan's Supplier Development Team has proved an effective force for change, not just in terms of the internal arrangements of Nissan's suppliers, but also with regard to customer–supplier relations (Lloyd *et al*, 1994). This change in relationships was reinforced by the arrival of Toyota and Honda.

Regardless of the context in which the SDT was launched and still operates, the approach it adopts when working with suppliers is also extremely important. The key elements of this approach are as follows:

- The team operates as part of Nissan's partnership approach to purchasing.

- Suppliers are at liberty to choose whether or not to invite the SDT into their plant.

- The SDT begins by explaining to senior managers within suppliers that its objective is to help them to develop a continuous improvement philosophy.

- It seeks to train and guide a supplier's personnel to undertake change projects for themselves, rather than doing the work for them.

- The SDT insists that operators and supervisors in the area where change is to take place are involved.

- The SDT's own members are extremely well-trained and proficient and, consequently, are able to win the confidence of the people with whom they work.

- It seeks to ensure that those who carry out the improvement get the credit and praise for it, rather than seeking to take the credit itself.

- Above all, the SDT members see themselves as ambassadors for Nissan and for Nissan's approach to partnership. Therefore, they seek to promote trust and co-operation between themselves and suppliers' personnel.

It would be misleading to give the impression that Nissan was in anyway 'soft' on suppliers. Nissan may have given its 'partners' new rights, but they have also acquired new responsibilities. In return for openness and trust on its part, it expects the same from suppliers, who are expected to open up every aspect of their business to inspection and scrutiny. As Sir Ian Gibson, Nissan's Managing Director, stated, 'Co-operative supply relationships are not an easy option, as many imagine, but considerably harder to implement than traditional buyer–seller relationships' (quoted in Burnes and Whittle, 1995: 10). However, the success of Nissan's approach is demonstrated not only by the fact that its Sunderland plant is now the most efficient car assembly operation in Europe (Milner, 1999) but also that since it initiated the move towards partnerships, all other UK-based car companies have followed suit, as have a considerable number of companies in other industries.

## Case study 10

# SPEEDY STATIONERS LTD AND UTL (TURBINES) LTD – SUPPLIER-DRIVEN CHANGE [2]

### Background

In the vast majority of cases, it is customers who take the initiative to change relationships rather than suppliers. This is for quite obvious reasons to do with power (it is the customer who has the money and who decides what to purchase and from whom) and experience (there are very few examples of how suppliers can influence customers). However, unlike the Rover and Nissan studies, where it was the customers who made the first move and, at least in Nissan's case, attempted to

[2] This case study is based on original research by Dr Steve New of Hertford College, Oxford University.

bring about significant changes in their suppliers, this case study deals with organisational change driven by a supplier.

This case examines the development of a partnership between Speedy Stationers Ltd and UTL (Turbines) Ltd, whereby the former took responsibility for the provision and in-company management of all UTL's stationery requirements.

Speedy Stationers was founded in 1953, and in 1994 had a turnover of roughly £50 million. Originally the firm acted just as a wholesaler selling to distributors and retailers. In the mid-1980s, almost by accident (an acquaintance of the Managing Director happened to be appointed to the same position in UTL) it began dealing directly with a small number of large industrial companies. Typically, these companies' total stationery bill might be over £200,000 per year. However, because Speedy did not deal with printed stationery, letterheads, etc., it rarely did more than £50,000 worth of business with any of these customers. Nevertheless, the Managing Director, whose pet project this was, had high hopes for direct selling.

Partly influenced by the possibility of selling directly to large companies, Speedy embarked on an expansion programme in the late 1980s which doubled its number of distribution centres from three to six. This geographical spreading of risk allowed the company to weather the recession of the early 1990s without any significant loss of business – though its profit margins were squeezed. Nevertheless, by 1993, senior managers came to recognise that the possibilities of continued expansion through the establishment of more distribution centres was limited, as well as expensive. Also, selling stationery directly to end users, whilst potentially attractive, had failed to live up to its initial promise. This was partly because there was a limited number of companies whose stationery bills made it worthwhile dealing with them directly, and partly due to the fact that even the ones they did deal with tended to shop around pursuing, in some cases, extremely small savings. A continuing bone of contention was also the amount of the Managing Director's time taken up with servicing the direct customers. Orders had originally been won on the basis of his contacts, and he felt that they could only be maintained on this basis.

## A strategy emerges

It was in 1993, after much heated debate, that senior managers took the decision to set up the direct sales business as a distinct entity within Speedy. It was given its own manager, and a small team of staff was assembled to run the operation. The intention was to allow the rest of the company to focus on its core business, the provision of stationery to distributors and retailers, whilst giving the direct sales operation one last chance to prove itself. Though this was something of a 'sink or swim' approach, Speedy was not abandoning direct sales to its fate. As a concession to the Managing Director's strong commitment to direct sales, the person given responsibility for its development was a board member who, it was felt, would eventually succeed the present Managing Director.

Before informing its customers of this change, the Direct Sales Division (to give it its official title) set about establishing its strategy. Though this was mainly the work of the Director for Direct Sales, he was careful to involve all his staff and to ensure the continued support of the Managing Director. The strategy that emerged had three objectives:

- to offer a complete stationery service to its existing customers, including printed letterheads, forms, etc.;

- to develop partnerships with its customers whereby the Direct Sales Division would supply and manage their stationery stock;

- to triple turnover in three years whilst maintaining its profit margin.

The thinking behind this strategy stemmed from four characteristics of its present business:

1 The turnover of the direct business was £750,000 (out of Speedy's total turnover of £50 million) from 15 customers. The profit margin on this business was 7.5 per cent (as averse to 5 per cent on Speedy's main business).

2 Direct customers were mainly located near its headquarters in Birmingham and therefore could easily be serviced by one group of staff. A geographical expansion would be proportionately more costly owing to distance.

3 Speedy only accounted for some 20–25 per cent of direct customers' stationery requirements, because it did not provide printed stationery. Once this was on offer, doubling or tripling business with each customer seemed quite possible.

4 In the early 1990s, the concept of partnerships between suppliers and customers began to take off. Already, the wholesale business was discussing managing the inventory for a number of medium-sized distributors, so it did not seem totally unfeasible to offer a similar service to direct customers – especially if Speedy were likely to be supplying the majority of their stationery needs in any case.

In developing the strategy, it was agreed that the first two priorities were to establish a partnership with a printer, and to identify the first customer to approach regarding partnering. The first part of this was relatively easy: they approached the printer who had dealt with all Speedy's own printing requirements over the past 20 years, and with whom they had a very close relationship already. The printer readily agreed to the arrangement – apart from anything else, it did not entail any major cost for them, but did promise additional lucrative business.

Identifying a customer for partnership was more problematic, but eventually they decided to approach UTL (Turbines) Ltd. Not only had UTL been Speedy's first direct customer (thanks to the relationship between the two Managing Directors) but it was well known that it wanted to develop partnerships with its suppliers. Therefore, it was decided to make an approach to them.

## UTL (Turbines) Ltd

In 1992, UTL spent some £200,000 per annum on stationery, but this was small compared to the £30 million it spent on buying components for its turbines. It had a very traditional, distrusting and arms-length approach to purchasing, which it applied to all its purchases. It had at least five suppliers for each commodity and, with some exceptions, it purchased purely on price. Not surprisingly, it had over 1500 suppliers, and the main contact most of these had with UTL was in response to written requests for quotations. Owing to the friendly relations at senior level, Speedy was one of the few suppliers who ever met purchasing staff.

The company is part of a large multinational group, and serves markets worldwide. UTL (Turbines), as its name implies, is the division responsible for the design and manufacture of turbines which are supplied to a wide range of industrial users.

Like many manufacturing operations in the UK, the plant had experienced severe reductions in the number of people employed. From over 1,500 in 1987, the number working at the factory by 1994 had shrunk to about 900. In recent years, purchasing activities had undergone significant reorganisation. In 1992, two different aspects of the business – export and domestic turbines – merged their operations. Purchasing was one of the first functional groups to combine, and a new manager was brought into the company to take charge of the combined department.

As noted above, the company had a very traditional purchasing orientation. However, with the creation of the new purchasing function, a number of important changes were introduced to encourage staff to take a wider view of their role. In particular, the new manager wanted to focus attention on the total cost of doing business with a particular supplier, rather than just favouring those who submitted the lowest tender. The manager recognised that he needed to change staff attitudes towards suppliers, and indeed the Purchasing Department's view of its role in general. As a starting point, several innovations were introduced, including a series of lunchtime seminars which the manager saw as a vehicle for both team-building and idea generation. The seminar programme consisted of outside speakers (including suppliers), presentations from staff in the department who had been on training courses, and videos.

When vacancies in the department arose, these were generally filled from outside the company, with appointments favouring youth and enthusiasm over age and experience. The new manager was keen that the importance of the purchasing group should be recognised in the organisation, and wanted to develop a team with a clear professional focus. He believed that the traditional perceptions of purchasing as merely a bureaucratic support activity had to be challenged.

As might be imagined, most of the Purchasing Department's attention was focused on suppliers of production components. Nor did this change under the new manager; indeed, as far as he was concerned, the less he had to do with non-production suppliers the better. It was this that gave Speedy Stationers its opportunity for building a partnership with UTL.

## Speedy takes the initiative

By 1993, the reorganisation and re-orientation of UTL's Purchasing Department was well under way. In particular, the seminar series, which at first attracted some adverse comment within the company, was proving a key vehicle for introducing new ideas and generating fresh thinking. When the Director for Direct Sales at Speedy heard about the seminar programme, he offered to come and talk about its new approach to working with customers. The Purchasing Manager was at first resistant, as were many of his staff, because this was not the area on which he wished to focus attention. Nevertheless, he finally agreed when the Speedy Director told him that the title of his presentation would be 'Contract Out Stationery Management and Reduce Costs by 10 Per Cent'.

Under the existing system, ordering stationery was a slow, complicated process. When individual departments required stationery, a requisition would be raised which was then translated by the Purchasing Department into a purchase order. On arrival, items would be inspected – which, for stationery, meant that the contents of each delivery would be counted and checked against the delivery note and original order. The items would then be booked into the stores, from which they could be withdrawn to departmental stores after more paperwork. As there were many stationery suppliers, problems with shortages were sometimes difficult to resolve. Each supplier would send invoices, which needed to be checked against orders and delivery notes. In addition, there was a particular problem with printed stationery; it was not unusual for the wording which the originating department thought it had specified to be incorrect when the stationery finally arrived with them. However, tracing where the fault lay could be a tortuous process. It was also the case that departments ordered, and kept, far more stationery than they needed in order to avoid shortages. It was clear to the Direct Sales Division at Speedy, if not to UTL's own purchasing staff, that inefficiencies were rife, and that a 10 per cent reduction in costs should be achievable.

Speedy's proposal for managing all UTL's stationery needs was to establish two or three stationery bunkers in each department, close to the point of use (one for general stationery, e.g. photocopying paper; one for specialist items, e.g. printed forms; and one for consumables, e.g. pens and pencils, printer cartridges, etc.). These bunkers were to be clearly labelled; the average requirement for each type of stationery would be calculated and two week's worth of inventory was to be held in each. Speedy staff would visit weekly and top up the bunkers to the agreed level. Each delivery would be signed for by a designated manager for that area and, at the end of each month, all the supplies would be consolidated onto a single invoice. None of the incoming stationery would go through goods inwards or inspection, and there would be no need to raise individual orders. Indeed, the only work required of the Purchasing Department would be to pay the monthly invoice.

Though the Director for Direct Sales presented a very well-argued case, he met with some incredulity, not to mention hostility. Some staff thought the plan simply would not work. Others felt that UTL would be swindled. Yet another group feared for their jobs if this type of approach spread from stationery to other purchased items. Nevertheless, the prospect of getting rid of stationery purchasing, plus all the complaints it generated, and thus releasing staff for what he considered more important activities, proved too tempting for UTL's Purchasing Manager. The estimated 10 per cent saving, and informal encouragement from his Managing Director, also assisted the decision. In addition, Speedy pointed out that, for the first time, UTL would have accurate and regular figures for stationery consumption broken down by area and type of stationery.

Towards the end of 1993, Speedy and UTL signed a two-year contract covering the provision of all stationery requirements from the beginning of 1994. Though the contract included certain specific details (especially regarding auditing the new system), it was acknowledged that most of the mechanics of the arrangements would only emerge as the system was implemented.

## Implementing the new system

Under the new system, UTL was divided into 20 separate stationery zones, each with three stationery bunkers. The initial target was to set up this system for two of these zones from the beginning of 1994, with the remainder in place by March 1994. Speedy promised a maximum three-hour response time to resolve problems.

The new system entails significant reductions in the bureaucracy of supplying stationery, but also challenges many traditional approaches to buyer–supplier relationships, especially in relation to trust. First, in the absence of direct checks, UTL has to have complete confidence in the quality of the products supplied by Speedy and the reliability of its operation. Second, UTL has to trust that Speedy is actually delivering what it is invoicing for. Finally, UTL has to be sure that a single-source supplier will not exploit its position and introduce opportunistic price rises.

Managers from different functions within UTL needed to be reassured that the system was going to work, and that Speedy were capable of providing the new style of service. Presentations were held at which reservations could be expressed, and the new approach explained. However, it was not only managers within UTL who had some concerns; so did some of the workforce. To set up the new system, Speedy had up to five staff carrying out the initial analysis and making the arrangements for the new stocking locations. It became clear that UTL employees were suspicious and wary of what was going on. A major source of this unease was a fear that a system for delivering items direct to departments and zones would threaten the jobs of those in the goods inward, the incoming inspection and stores activities.

To help overcome these doubts, representatives from all areas concerned, including trade unions, were included in the series of presentations organised jointly by Speedy and UTL. Many of the questions raised related to the logic of the planned arrangement from UTL's point of view, and the potential vulnerability of being dependent on a single source. Other objections reflected the more immediate fear about the loss of jobs. Despite his earlier reservations, UTL's

Purchasing Manager became the main champion for the Speedy initiative. In essence, he pointed to the need for all UTL employees and resources to focus on improving the competitiveness of their core business, rather than 'messing about trying to find an envelope'. This, together with a promise that no one's job was threatened by the initiative, seemed to overcome most of the reservations.

Despite winning staff over to the new arrangements, the practicalities still had to be worked out. One of the major obstacles in implementing the new delivery system was the amount of stationery already held at UTL. The problem was not just the inventory held centrally and in each department's own store, but also the large quantities of stationery 'hidden' in various locations around the factory. These had arisen because staff, especially those working on the shopfloor, frequently took more from the stores than they actually needed in order to avoid 'shortages'.

As part of the implementation programme Speedy staff scoured UTL for these 'private' stationery cupboards. The office of one supervisor on the night shift became known as 'WH Smith' because of the large collection of stationery, much of it years out of date, which was held there. He had been unable to draw stationery from the stores at night, and so had assembled his own supply. In some cases, the unofficial inventory amounted to a year's worth of a particular item.

UTL had estimated that they held about two months' worth of stationery overall. In order to integrate this with the new system, Speedy began sorting this by type into agreed quantities. It transpired, however, when all the existing stationery had been accounted for, that in fact existing stocks were nearer four months' worth of inventory. This meant that for the first few months of the relationship, Speedy delivered relatively little of its own material, and so had little to invoice for. Like many aspects of the new stationery management system, this factor was not covered by the written contract; episodes like this were dealt with on the basis of mutual understanding and trust.

By the end of 1994, the new system was fully up and running. Despite a number of hiccups, the change appears to have been much smoother than anyone really imagined possible. Also, both parties felt that they had obtained major benefits from the change. The benefits to Speedy were as follows:

- It increased its business with UTL from approximately £50,000 per year to over £200,000, and actually improved its profit margin to 8.5 per cent.

- It proved that the new arrangements could work, and had three other customers keen to develop similar arrangements.

For UTL, the benefits were also significant:

- It made a 20 per cent saving on its annual stationery bill – twice as much as anticipated, even taking account of using up old stock.

- Consumption of stationery declined significantly in some areas, partly thanks to better stock control, and partly owing to a decline in 'home usage' – as one manager put it.

- The number of complaints relating to stationery dwindled almost to zero.

However, UTL managers felt there was a more important, if less quantifiable, benefit, which was that managers at UTL (not just in Purchasing) had seen the possibilities for new ways of conducting and organising business. In particular, managers now had a more favourable view of the prospects for achieving change in the company. As one manager commented:

> We've had our eyes opened. No one suspected some of our people would so easily accept such radical changes, especially ones driven by a supplier. The improvements we've made in handling stationery are really secondary to the confidence it's given us in our ability to manage change and make improvements.

One clear sign of this new confidence was that UTL began to examine seriously how it could develop similar links with other suppliers and its own customers.

## The outcome

Though the new direction proved profitable and effective for both Speedy and UTL, it also has important implications for customer–supplier relations in particular, and change management in general:

- Whilst it has been recognised since the 1960s that customers and suppliers can impact on each other's internal operations, the general view has been that this occurs in an unintended and unplanned fashion. What this case study shows is that customers and suppliers can link together consciously to change the nature of the environment in which they operate to their mutual benefit.

- The study also shows the serendipitous and unplanned nature of much of business life. Speedy only moved into the direct sale of stationery because of a friendship between its Managing Director and UTL's. It was only by chance that Speedy's decision to extend its operations into printed stationery and to develop partnerships occurred at a time when UTL were receptive to such an approach. A year earlier, and the approach would undoubtedly have been rejected; a year later, and UTL might have moved away from the idea, or might have been busy developing partnerships with production suppliers.

- The manner in which suspicion and resistance were overcome is also worth noting. From the start, Speedy approached the project in an open and frank manner – it raised the suggestion of a partnership in an open seminar attended by all purchasing staff, and open to all other UTL managers. UTL for their part chose to hide nothing from its workforce; both parties took account of worries and suspicions, and did their utmost to resolve these before embarking on change. Furthermore, UTL gave an assurance that the changed arrangements would not lead to any job losses.

- Another major point is that both parties were prepared to set aside the distrust which permeates so many business relationships, and attempt to establish a partnership based on trust. Nevertheless, the trust was based on adequate checks and a belief, subsequently proved correct, that such an approach was mutually beneficial.

Since 1994, the contract between Speedy and UTL has been renewed twice, and now runs for a four-year period. The benefits to UTL have been considerable. It has dispensed with the need to manage its own stationery requirements and, therefore, can concentrate more effectively on its core business and its core suppliers. In addition, instead of the original 10 per cent savings it expected, it is now making a 20 per cent saving on stationery costs. Speedy has also achieved significant benefits by building on its experience with UTL. It has developed similar relationships with another ten large organisations. The turnover from its Direct Sales Division is now over £2 million and the profit margin is well in excess of that from its other activities. However, since 1998, this area of Speedy's activities has stood still. To develop it further would take a considerable effort in terms of time and money because, having exhausted the possible customers in the Birmingham area, it would need to offer it on a national basis. The current Managing Director, whose original idea this was, is opposed to this; he believes that the time and money would be better spent developing other aspects of Speedy's business. Nevertheless, he is to retire shortly and is expected to be replaced by the Director of Direct Sales. If this is the case, the Director is determined that direct sales will be offered on a national basis.

## CONCLUSIONS

The three case studies in this chapter amply demonstrate the manner in which companies are changing not just their internal relationships, but also their external ones. Though the move towards closer relationships between customers and suppliers clearly makes for a more harmonious atmosphere in which to conduct business, this is little more than a side-effect and not the main reason for the change. Increasingly, companies have come to recognise the need to make major improvements in their performance but, as anything up to 70, 80 or even 90 per cent of the value of their products comprises bought-in goods and services, this cannot be achieved solely on the basis of internal performance improvements. Rather, what is required is that their suppliers also improve their business. As Ford found out in the car industry, seeking to impose improvements has its limitations. Suppliers have to be keen to improve and willing to work with customers. The argument for adopting a partnership approach to purchasing in the UK, and other Western countries, is that this is one of the cornerstones of Japan's success and, therefore, must be beneficial (Womack *et al*, 1990).

What we have seen in this chapter is three aspects of this type of relationship. Case Study 8, Rover–TRW, showed that closer working relationships at an operational level, based on openness and trust, can bring great benefits to both customers and suppliers. However, these benefits can be threatened if a similar degree of openness and trust is not achieved at a more strategic level. The Rover–TRW case also illustrates the emerging, and to an extent unplanned, nature of partnership developments. Nevertheless, the close operational-level relationship could not have prospered unless both companies, especially TRW, had not broken with traditional, Tayloristic, approaches to managing people and allowed their staff the freedom to experiment with and develop new ways of working.

Case Study 9, Nissan's Supplier Development Team, illustrates a different approach to developing partnerships. Nissan, with a long history of working closely with its suppliers in Japan, was intent on doing the same in the UK. It recognised the need to transfer knowledge and practices from Japan to its new suppliers, if they were to meet Nissan's exacting performance standards. A key method of achieving this in Japan is the supplier development approach; so Nissan established a Supplier Development Team, along Japanese lines. However, the team adapted its approach to meet local needs. In Japan, improvement activities tend to average two days; in the UK, the duration tends to be ten days. This reflects the fact that the performance and capabilities of Nissan's UK suppliers are much worse than its Japanese ones. However, as the SDT worked with suppliers to change their internal working arrangements, it recognised a need to offer further assistance. In the first instance, this took the form of training for suppliers' staff. But, as time progressed, Nissan came more and more to appreciate the strategic weakness of some of its suppliers, and began to offer assistance in this area as well. Though the strategic planning package emphasised vision-building and strategic intent, the SDT adopts a much more planned and pre-programmed approach. Each activity has clear objectives and timescales, and is highly focused.

Taking Nissan's activities with its suppliers as a whole, it can be seen that, though Nissan had a clear picture both of how it wished to work with suppliers, and of the end result in terms of improved performance by suppliers, the actual details emerged over time. Nevertheless, this emerging strategy was based less on trial and error than on a well thought out and planned approach. New developments, especially the strategic planning package, were the subject of much discussion and planning, and were piloted before being fully launched. The Nissan approach, therefore, whilst being emergent, was neither *ad hoc* nor trial and error, but the product of a great deal of thought and planning.

The last case study, Speedy Stationers, offers a new twist on the development of closer customer–supplier relationships. Normally, it is the customer who takes the lead in promoting changes in purchasing behaviour. This is for the obvious reason that the customer is usually the one with the power in the relationship (they can generally choose where to purchase and on what terms). However, in this instance, Speedy took the initiative and approached their customer with a suggestion for change. This was for basic commercial reasons: they needed to win additional business and saw partnerships as being the prime vehicle. They believed that the partnership approach would not only be commercially beneficial but would also give Speedy a competitive edge over its rivals. Speedy were fortunate in that they were able to approach a customer responsive to this type of initiative. The process of building the relationship led to many changes, both at Speedy and particularly in its customer. Much information only came to light as the new arrangements were developed and implemented, and it was only by actually putting the new approach into practice that sceptics could come to appreciate its benefits. For both Speedy and its customer, this new approach was something of a leap into the unknown which appeared to succeed, though only time will tell to what extent.

In reviewing these three case studies, what is remarkable is the extent to which organisations have come to recognise that, in pursuit of increased competitiveness, improving their own internal operations and relationships is not enough. The full potential for performance improvement can only be realised when there are also similar developments within their suppliers and customers, and when they develop better working relationships with them. In undertaking such changes, three points stand out from the case studies.

The first is that these companies are changing the rules of the game; they are challenging the prevailing orthodoxy in the UK and the rest of Europe with regard to commercial relationships between customers and suppliers.

The second point is that, although this type of action is based on others' successful experiences, it nevertheless requires a considerable act of faith by the parties concerned. It is not possible in advance to spell out either the exact form of the new relationships or the specific measurable benefits they might bring. Yet dissatisfaction with traditional relationships, and the potential for commercial advantage, have spurred the case study companies described in this chapter to take such decisions. As can be seen, the decision to move towards partnerships cannot be judged solely on the basis of rational analysis and the pursuit of quantified and clear commercial objectives. Actually establishing a partnership may constitute a leap in the dark, requiring boldness, initiative and trust.

The last point to note relates to one of the major benefits or consequences of partnerships. One reason why companies are seeking to develop new ways of working is to help them to cope with the competitive pressures and uncertainty of the modern world. Partnerships appear not only to allow companies to strengthen their competitive position, but also to reduce a major source of environmental uncertainty, by making the actions of customers and suppliers more predictable and transparent. This goes against those, such as Tom Peters, who argue for the benefits of increasing chaos rather than reducing it. It also shows that one of the major constraints or contingencies organisations face, environmental uncertainty, can be managed in such a way that the ability to plan for the future, in terms of product development and production, is increased. As the Contingency Theorists, described in Chapter 2, argued over three decades ago, the external environment does affect the internal workings of an organisation, but an organisation's internal arrangements can also affect the environment. Therefore, if a turbulent environment leads to changed internal relationships, then given that organisations are open systems, we can expect these to be mirrored in changed external relationships. So although internal changes are often seen as mechanisms for coping with environmental uncertainty, the move by suppliers and customers to develop closer links can go one step further, actually reducing uncertainty.

## TEST YOUR LEARNING

### Short answer questions

1 Identify the key reason why Rover developed its partnership with TRW.
2 List the two main benefits that each party gained from the Rover–TRW partnership.
3 What benefits did Nissan expect to gain from its partnership approach to suppliers?
4 How did Nissan's Supplier Development Team seek to overcome potential resistance from managers and staff in the companies where it operated?
5 To what extent can the Speedy case study be seen as supporting the Emergent approach to change?
6 What was the decisive factor in persuading UTL to enter into partnership with Speedy?

### Essay questions

1 To what extent does the Rover–TRW case study show the limitations of continuous improvement?
2 Discuss the following statement: the Nissan case study shows the strength of combining Emergent and Planned change.
3 In moving towards partnerships, how did Speedy overcome potential resistance to change from both its own staff and those of its customers?

# Part 4

---

# MANAGING CHOICE

# Chapter 12

# MANAGING CHANGE

## Lessons from theory and practice

**Learning objectives**

After studying this chapter, you should be able to:

1 analyse the ten case studies in Part 3 in relation to the following:
   (a) how each organisation's strategy developed,
   (b) the constraints on choice,
   (o) managerial behaviour,
   (d) the way change was managed,
   (e) the approach or approaches to change adopted,
   (f) the objectives pursued;

2 describe the main lessons from each of the ten case studies in relation to the above issues;

3 understand the factors which determine the level of employee involvement necessary to bring about successful change;

4 appreciate that there are a multiplicity of approaches to change which can be used separately, sequentially or in combination.

## INTRODUCTION

In the previous three parts of this book, we examined the theory and practice of how organisations develop and change. From the Industrial Revolution to the present day, we can see that the history of organisations is one of change and upheaval. In the light of this, the idea that organisations have ever operated in a stable state or a predictable environment, other than for relatively brief periods, is difficult to sustain. Whether because of economic fluctuations, the development of new products and processes, social change or war, organisations and entire industries tend to face recurrent bouts of upheaval. Some industries still remain strong, though their products and leading players have changed significantly. One clear example of this is the computer industry, which has moved from being dominated by IBM's mainframes to being dominated by Microsoft's operating systems. Other industries though, such as the UK coal industry, have shrunk to a shadow of their former size and importance, and appear doomed to be relegated to the role of bit player on the industrial stage.

Not surprisingly, given the rise and fall of industries and technologies over the last two decades, many writers argue that organisations and society at large are in a period of rapid and unprecedented change: a period where old certainties no longer hold good, and new ones have yet to emerge. An alternative view is that the pace and uncertainty of change varies from company to company, industry to industry and even country to country. As a consequence, at any one point in time, some organisations will be experiencing extreme turbulence whilst others appear to operate in a relatively stable environment. However, whether either of these views offers a suitable explanation of the stability–turbulence question is perhaps irrelevant. The pertinent issue is how organisations can cope with both the environment in which they operate and the constraints, challenges and threats they face. In undertaking this task, one thing is perfectly clear: the amount and diversity of information and advice on offer is certainly greater than ever before.

No longer is business analysis and advice confined to a few specialist publishers and journals, or locked up in business school libraries. Books, magazines and videos on 'how to' management can be found in airports and railway stations as well as almost any bookshop. Newspapers, radio and television also play their part in popularising the latest panacea or giving a platform to business gurus or practitioners. In addition, the ubiquitous management consultant can always be relied upon to offer the latest approach, at a price. Therefore, managers cannot claim to lack advice or offers of assistance. The problem, as this book has shown, is that no two approaches appear to be exactly the same and in some cases they may almost entirely contradict each other. Almost in despair, many managers must ask themselves the simple question: if the experts can't agree, what hope is there for me?

This question illustrates the powerlessness some managers feel when faced with issues which, quite wrongly, appear to have become the territory of the specialist. Though there are managers who adopt an almost fatalistic attitude to their situation, believing that events are beyond their control, others, fortunately, adopt a more positive stance. However, even these managers often give the impression that their job is to implement the particular approach to strategy and change which the specialists recommend, or which other more successful organisations have adopted. This book has sought to argue that this is not only incorrect, but a potentially dangerous notion.

Though many 'experts' claim some sort of universal applicability for their favoured approach or theory, as argued in the first two parts of this book, the reality is that such approaches are developed in particular circumstances, at particular times and often with particular types of organisations in mind. It follows that a key role for organisations and their managers is to understand the approaches on offer, identify their own circumstances and needs, and choose the approach which best suits them. By doing this, in effect, as this book has attempted to show, managers can cease to be prisoners of circumstances and experts, and begin to make their own choices about the future operation, direction and nature of their organisations.

This chapter draws on the review of the literature on organisations, strategy and change presented so far in this book to shed light on the ten case studies present in the last three chapters. The chapter begins by reviewing Chapters 5–8 and identifying a number of key common points, especially with regard to managerial choice. These are then used to examine the case studies presented in Chapters 9–11. This then leads on to a discussion of the nature of and rationale for employee involvement, particularly in cases of rapid transformational change. The chapter concludes by contending that organisations and theorists need to reject the notion that Planned and Emergent approaches to change necessarily stand in opposition to each other, or that they cannot be used in tandem. Instead, it is argued that there are a multiplicity of approaches to change and that managers have genuine choice in how and when they are used, and what to change and when to change it.

# LESSONS FROM THEORY AND PRACTICE

Chapters 5–8 began to develop a model of managerial choice and change management. The case studies which followed showed how ten organisations dealt with these issues. The case studies will now be compared with the findings from Chapters 5–8. First, the four chapters will be reviewed and key issues identified; these issues will then be used to examine the case studies. The intention is to begin to combine theory and practice in order to develop a Choice Management–Change Management model for understanding and implementing organisational change.

## Issues from Chapters 5–8

Chapters 5 and 6 examined the origins and development of approaches to strategy. They showed that strategy was originally conceived of as a rational, quantitative process concerned with an organisation's external environment, especially its products and markets. The key role for managers was to identify trends, establish future objectives or targets, and then implement them. It was shown that as the concept of organisational strategy developed, a distinction emerged between the Prescriptive school of strategy and the Analytical school. The former was and is primarily concerned with telling managers what they should do and promoting a planned, quantitative and rational approach to strategy. On the other hand, the Analytical school tends to focus on what organisations actually do when formulating and implementing strategy, rather than what the experts say they should do. For the Analytical school, strategy is a messy, complex, less rational and more emergent affair than the picture painted by the Prescriptive school.

Though in the 1980s and 1990s the Prescriptive school still tended to dominate the practice of strategy, the insights of the Analytical school had a growing impact. In particular, the emphasis on rationality and quantification began to be seen as less important than intuition, creativity, and power and politics in shaping an organisation's strategy. The impact of this on managers has been that instead of being required to construct detailed and elaborate plans for their organisation's future, they are increasingly being seen as primarily responsible for creating a vision or strategic direction for their organisations, which is pursued, often in a bottom-up fashion, through day-to-day decisions concerning such matters as resource allocation, product/market development and a host of, often, small-scale organisational changes. From this standpoint, an organisation's strategy is not set in advance, but emerges from the decisions taken at all levels in the organisation. Therefore, as Chapters 5 and 6 demonstrated, the Analytical school of strategy, as averse to the Prescriptive school, draws no distinction between strategy development and implementation – an organisation's decisions are informed by its visions or intent, but the nature and details of the strategy they pursue emerge from the decisions they take. Nevertheless, despite the growing interest in the Analytical school, more rational and quantitative approaches to strategy have not been replaced. Rather, as Chapters 5 and 6 show, the situation is that a number of more or less competing perspectives on strategy and change are now available to organisations.

In Chapter 5, it was argued that none of the competing perspectives on strategy were necessarily true or false. Instead, they tended to be appropriate to given situations. The main elements determining their appropriateness were national characteristics, the business environment, industry-specific factors, and the internal characteristics of the organisation in question. However, rather than arguing that the role of managers was to choose the appropriate approach to strategy for their organisation's circumstances, the chapter concluded by arguing that managers could choose to amend these circumstances to fit in with their preferred approach to strategy.

Chapters 7 and 8 moved from examining strategy to reviewing change management. Chapter 7 began by looking at three models dealing with the pace and nature of organisational change – the Incremental, Punctuated Equilibrium and Continuous Change models. These drew attention to the spectrum of change events ranging from small-scale, localised ones to large-scale events designed to transform or reinvent an organisation in its totality. The chapter then proceeded to examine the main theories which underpin approaches to change management. These concerned the behaviour and importance of individuals, groups and systems within organisations. This was followed by a review of what had been the dominant approach to change management – Planned change. The Planned approach tends to concentrate on individuals and groups, but has less to say about the overall organisation and its environment, though there have been attempts by its promoters to rectify this. This approach, as its name implies, regards change very much as a planned and conscious process of moving parts of organisations from one relatively fixed state to another. It is an approach that seeks to improve organisational effectiveness by changing individual and group beliefs and behaviour through a process of participation and learning.

Alternative, and newer, approaches to change management were assembled and reviewed in Chapter 8 under the collective title of the Emergent approach. This approach rejects the concept of a planned change process with a definite and fixed outcome. Instead, it conceives of organisations as operating in a continuous state of flux and turbulence. It tends to be a bottom-up approach which characterises organisational change as an unpredictable, confusing and politically driven process. From this perspective, it is argued that the role of managers is to develop a climate in which everyone in the organisation has a responsibility for identifying the need for and implementing change. The objective is not to achieve a fixed outcome but continually to align and realign the organisation with the changing needs of an unpredictable environment. In particular, the Emergent approach identifies five features of organisational life which either promote or block change: structure, culture, organisational learning, managerial behaviour, and power and politics.

Despite the battle between the promoters of these two approaches, Chapter 8 concluded that neither the Planned nor the Emergent approach provided a comprehensive picture of organisational change. Rather, there are a wide variety of approaches which are suited to different situations. The suitability of any one approach is determined by a range of factors, especially the stability, or otherwise, of an organisation's environment. In this situation, as Chapter 8 argued, a key role for managers is to identify the situation of their organisation and align it to the most suitable approach to change. Nevertheless, it was also argued that, though constraints such as the nature of the environment in which their organisations operate place limitations on managers' freedom of choice, managers can influence or alter these constraints – in line with the arguments developed in Chapter 5 – to make them better suited to their and their organisations' own preferences and needs.

Therefore, to summarise, the evidence and arguments from these four chapters are as follows:

- There are a wide and diverse range of change situations, ranging from small-scale change to the complete transformation or reinvention of organisations. These are not, however, mutually exclusive. They can occur, whether consciously or unconsciously, simultaneously within the same organisation, though not necessarily to achieve the same objectives.

- Though there are a number of valid and well-supported approaches to strategy development and change management available to organisations, there is a tendency for managers, and academics, to focus on a limited range.

- The dominant view is that managers have to adopt the approach which appears to fit in with the constraints, especially environmental ones, they face.

- An alternative perspective, however, is that it is possible for managers to influence these constraints, in effect to change the rules of the game, to make them more appropriate to the particular approach to strategy and change management which suits them and their organisations.

In order to examine the validity of this last point, the ten case studies from Part 3 will now be reviewed to see to what extent the experience of real life organisations supports or contradicts this view. In particular, drawing on Chapters 5–8, for each case study the following key issues will be explored:

1 **Strategy**. How was the organisation's strategy developed?

2 **Constraints**. What were the constraints the organisation faced, and did the strategy seek to work within or influence these?

3 **Managerial behaviour**. What role did managers play in strategy development and change management?

4 **Change management**. How were change projects managed and who was involved?

5 **Planned, Emergent or combined change**. To what extent were strategies and/or change projects fully planned in advance, seen as emergent and open-ended, or exhibiting a combination of approaches?

6 **Objectives**. Was the focus of strategy development and/or change projects to alter individual and group behaviour or to change or reinvent an organisation in its entirety?

## Reviewing the case studies – Chapters 9–11

In examining the 10 case studies against the above six issues, it should be borne in mind that Case Studies 1–4 (Chapter 9) deal specifically with strategy development, and Case Studies 5–10 (Chapters 10 and 11) concentrate on change management projects. Nevertheless, all the case studies, to a lesser or greater extent, contain elements of strategy development and all contain elements of change management. With that proviso in mind, we can now move to a brief examination of the individual case studies. Each case will be reviewed under the six headings above.

### Case Study 1: Oticon

1 **Strategy**. The company's strategy was developed and driven by one person (its then President, Lars Kolind). He created a vision of a service-based organisation and pursued it by, in effect, razing the existing organisation to the ground and starting again.

2 **Constraints**. Though there is no clear evidence that existing constraints influenced the strategy, the new flexible structure which emerged was certainly compatible with Danish norms or expectations regarding job design. As far as

industry norms were concerned, Oticon was at a disadvantage in that competition was based on the technical sophistication of products, and Oticon's capability in this respect was falling behind that of other companies. To counter this disadvantage, Oticon chose to re-write the rules of competition in the industry by moving the focus from technology to service. The business environment in which Oticon operated had been and still remained very turbulent. Indeed, by attempting to change the basis of competition in the industry, Oticon can be seen as adding to rather than reducing uncertainty. In terms of organisation characteristics, Lars Kolind was again attempting to re-write the rule book. The existing structure was demolished, its culture was challenged and the style of management changed drastically. Kolind appeared to face very little overt resistance but, in introducing the changes initially, and taking corrective action when he thought they were failing, he did use the power of his position in a very directive and, perhaps, coercive manner.

3 **Managerial behaviour**. The strategy was developed by Oticon's President and though he explained it to other managers, it is clear that he neither expected nor wanted them to modify it. Their role was to support him and to help sell and implement the idea, rather than necessarily to be part of the process of its development. As these changes took hold, and a more co-operative atmosphere developed in the company, managers moved away from their previous directive style of management and developed a more facilitative role.

4 **Change management**. The approach taken was to prepare the ground carefully but then to change overnight. This part of the approach was, in effect, to use Kanter *et al*'s (1992) phrase, a Bold Stroke. Employees left the company and its old systems and practices on a Friday night, and on Monday walked into a completely different organisation. However, what followed was months of chaos as everyone tried to work out what they were doing and how they should do it. Nor did Kolind appear to wish more settled internal arrangements to prevail. When he felt that the company was in danger of, as Kurt Lewin would say, refreezing, he 'exploded' the organisation again.

5 **Planned, Emergent or combined change**. Though we can see evidence of both Planned and Emergent change, it was the latter which dominated. Lars Kolind had a vision of the organisation's future but the actual details and nature of the change process emerged as the company struggled to implement it. Also, change was open-ended and, given the nature of the new organisation, it is not clear if it will ever settle down into a fixed state. There is also a great emphasis on collective learning, and using this learning to keep the company on the move. To use Kanter *et al*'s (1992) analogy, again, it was a Bold Stroke followed by a Long March.

6 **Objectives**. The aim was no less than a total transformation or reinvention of the organisation in all its aspects, and to move from being a traditionally structured technology-driven organisation to a learning organisation focused on

service delivery. However, central to this was the need to change the attitudes and behaviour of individuals and groups.

### Case Study 2: Flair Engineering

1 **Strategy**. The strategy was driven by the vision of Flair's Managing Director who, though supported by his fellow directors, appeared to make things happen by the force of his personality and the power of his position. His aim was to reinvent the company; to transform it from a small seller of capacity into a leading designer and supplier of components to the motor industry.

2 **Constraints**. Flair faced and overcame a number of major obstacles. The company had neither the experience nor the equipment to manufacture motor components. It had to acquire these rapidly and to continue to develop and accumulate expertise in this area. In addition, the financial needs and objectives of the company, as well as the way it wished to organise itself, stood in sharp contrast to existing financial and industrial practices in the UK. The company used a number of methods to overcome these obstacles including, eventually, becoming part of a German industrial conglomerate. Though philosophically moving in the same direction as the rest of the UK motor component industry, it tended to be in advance of it and, therefore, in the absence of a domestic model, tended to draw on Japanese experience. Throughout the last 20 years, Flair has operated in an uncertain and, to an extent, hostile business environment. Internally, Flair changed its structure, culture and management style. Also, the more extensive the changes became, the more it had to overcome internal resistance, especially from support functions, in order to achieve success.

3 **Managerial behaviour**. Though the Managing Director and his colleagues drove the strategy and early changes, as time progressed more and more day-to-day decisions were devolved to line managers, especially the cell managers and the staff in the cells themselves. Therefore, as with Oticon, though not to the same extent, the behaviour of managers moved from being directive to being co-operative and facilitative. At various times, the company was also assisted by their customers and by outside consultants.

4 **Change management**. Identifying and managing larger change projects is still the prerogative of senior managers. However, more and more change projects, particularly small-scale improvements, are devolved to line managers and their teams.

5 **Planned, Emergent or combined change**. The development of the company's strategy has emerged over the years and has tended to be open-ended. Nevertheless, many of the projects, such as new product introduction, by their very nature have to have specific objectives and a fixed timetable; although this does not mean they were not, and are not, subject to continuous improvement. Also, such improvement activities themselves, as the Nissan study in Chapter 11 showed, tended to have specific objectives and timescales. Therefore, a combination of approaches to change can be seen within Flair whereby Emergent and

open-ended strategic change also embraced more planned, more focused and finite projects.

6 **Objectives**. Though the vision became clarified as the company developed and became successful, the overall objectives tended to be global rather than specific, with particular emphasis on transforming the organisation into something comparable to its Japanese counterparts. This did involve changing the attitudes and behaviour of individuals and groups. Also, although Flair did not explicitly set out to change its culture, this did happen.

## Case Study 3: The Property Services Agency (PSA)

1 **Strategy**. Though the PSA Board were given a clear objective, to privatise the PSA, there is no evidence that the Board, either before or during the process, had any settled or agreed strategy for achieving this. Rather the Board tended to be driven, and in some cases perhaps even paralysed, by events over which it felt it had little control. It also seemed to have little sympathy with the objective it was told to pursue.

2 **Constraints**. The constraints the PSA Board faced in bringing about privatisation were many and obvious. The Board appeared to feel itself trapped between an implacable government, bent on privatisation at all costs, and a hostile workforce, convinced that privatisation would leave them worse off. Once privatisation was accomplished, the management of the new companies faced the task of achieving cultural and structural changes and winning back customers who had been only too glad to see the demise of the PSA, whilst trying at the same time to make a profit in a fiercely competitive industry.

3 **Managerial behaviour**. The PSA's management operated in a bureaucratic culture where command and control were the order of the day. Though its staff did not always agree with the Board's plans, in the past they had tended to comply rather than resist. The skills and approach necessary to manage the privatisation process and win over a hostile workforce were very different ones from those needed to run a bureaucratic organisation with a compliant work-force. Indeed, faced with this task, some of the senior managers preferred to leave the organisation. Nor is there much evidence that those managers who stayed were able to change their behaviour to adapt to the new situation. Once the PSA was privatised, its new owners made it a priority to change the style and behaviour of managers, and staff, to equip them better for life in the private sector.

4 **Change management**. Though the PSA's Board set out to manage the privatisation process, and though it brought in outside consultants to assist it in this, it is difficult to believe that the Board was in control of the situation. Rather the Board acted as if it were the prisoner of events and could only respond to the actions of others. The privatisation took place because the government decreed it would take place and was willing to underwrite the cost. From that point of view, not even the PSA's Board seemed involved in the process, never

mind anyone else in the organisation. After privatisation, change in the new companies was a more proactive and managed affair, with genuine attempts to involve staff.

5 **Planned, Emergent or combined change**. Though the PSA management wanted to have a Planned approach to change, it proved incapable of achieving this. Nor, though, could this be called an Emergent approach to change, as such. Instead, change was imposed from outside by the government and shaped, to an extent, by the resistance and legitimate concerns of the PSA's staff. In the newly privatised companies, on the other hand, a combination of Planned and Emergent change could be seen.

6 **Objectives**. The overriding objective was to transfer the PSA from the public to the private sector. Therefore, primarily it was perceived as a case of restructuring the PSA so that it could be sold to private-sector buyers. Though this was achieved, it was certainly costlier, and took far longer, than the government had anticipated. Nor does it appear to have resulted in government departments receiving a better service; rather that in taking on some of the responsibilities of the PSA, they have also taken on some of its antagonistic characteristics. In so doing, they appear to be missing out on the benefits that working in partnership might bring.

### Case Study 4: Midshires College of Midwifery and Nursing

1 **Strategy**. The most striking feature of the case study was the lack of either a vision or a strategy for creating the new college or determining its future when the college had been established.

2 **Constraints**. The business environment in which the college operated had become markedly less certain and more complex. This clearly had an adverse impact on the ability of the Project Leader to manage change in the directive-mechanical fashion he preferred. The other constraints which seem to have had a significant effect in this case related to the characteristics of the organisation itself and of those bodies that controlled its destiny. Of particular relevance was the combination of managerial style, clashes of interests, and organisational politics, none of which were either openly addressed or really resolved. The transactional orientation of the Project Leader, coupled with the lack of support from his colleagues and the manoeuvring for advantage of some members of the Steering Committee, held back progress considerably.

3 **Managerial behaviour**. Initially the Project Leader attempted to involve the other managers by allocating to them responsibility for particular aspects of the amalgamation process – though even this was done in a very directive manner. When this failed to produce results, he, in effect, pushed them to one side and took most of the decisions himself. When this also failed to show progress, he too was, to an extent, side-lined and decisions imposed from above. Even after his replacement, and later when the college had been taken over by a local university, a directive rather than participative style of management was still in evidence.

4 **Change management**. Initially the Project Leader adopted a very mechanistic approach to change, pursued through a number of planning groups. When he realised that this approach was not working, he switched to the use of more directive means, but the success of this approach was also limited. After the Project Manager's departure, change seemed to be planned, if that is not too strong a word, and imposed from above with little or no consultation.

5 **Planned, Emergent or combined change**. Despite obvious attempts to plan, this was a situation where, for much of the time, change failed to take place at all. The progress that was eventually made arose out of the confusion in which the organisation found itself. Therefore, rather than being an example of either Planned or Emergent change, it is better characterised in this instance as forced on the college's managers by events to which, under pressure, they reacted.

6 **Objectives**. Though the ultimate objective of the change process was clear – to create one entity from the five separate colleges – many of the issues which surrounded this remained unclear and unresolved. Though the Project Leader addressed the structural issues concerned, he seemed incapable of acknowledging or coping with the more behavioural, attitudinal and political issues involved. Even after the running of the college was in the hands of the local university, its purpose and future direction still appeared uncertain.

### Case Study 5: Volvo

1 **Strategy**. Volvo's strategy for Job Design was to reorganise its plants to eliminate the moving assembly line, and replace it with group-based assembly. The strategy originated from a need both to reduce labour turnover and absenteeism, and to respond to societal pressures to eliminate dehumanised forms of work organisation. However, even when these were no longer an issue, the company continued to pursue the move away from assembly-line working. The strategy was driven, and continuity provided, by Volvo's long-serving Chief Executive, Pehr Gyllenhammar. However, even after his somewhat acrimonious departure, the commitment to Job Design survived, though it is difficult to imagine that, had he stayed, Gyllenhammar would have sold Volvo's car business to Ford with all the risks to the Job Design strategy that this implies.

2 **Constraints**. Though public opinion in Sweden favoured a move away from the assembly line, it was and remains the car industry's established mode of operation. Therefore, Volvo was clearly aiming to change industry constraints whilst aligning itself with societal ones. From the perspective of the business environment, Volvo's move to 'humanise' car assembly appeared to bring them much valuable publicity and its approach to building cars was seen as a selling point. However, in the early years, internal constraints and resistance (both attitudinal and technical) acted to limit the radicalness of the initiative. One point to note is that, at least in the early years, there was perhaps more open suspicion and resistance from Volvo's trade unions than from its managers.

3 **Managerial behaviour**. All the change projects involving Job Design were driven by senior managers. Outside experts in Job Design were also involved at the planning stage, and so were trade union representatives, whose enthusiasm grew over the years. Nevertheless, the outcome of successive waves of Job Design was to devolve power from Volvo's headquarters to the individual plants and in the plants to give the shopfloor teams more authority and control. This led to the elimination of middle management layers, the creation of a flatter organisation structure and the progressive development of a much more empowered workforce.

4 **Change management**. Each project was planned in great detail in advance. This involved not only managers, but also trade union representatives and outside experts. However, once in operation, the actual arrangements were modified in order, so it was claimed, to meet business needs and cope with operational difficulties. In most cases these modifications appear to have reduced the ability of workers to set their own pace of work and to expand their range of activities. Nevertheless, whether in new or existing plants, each change project built on the last, and each project resulted in greater levels of shopfloor control. Central to this was organisational learning: the ability collectively to capture and transmit, from one plant to another, the experience of making radical Job Design work. It is also clear that with each project, the confidence of managers, workers and trade unions that Job Design could work grew.

5 **Planned, Emergent or combined change**. Though Volvo's strategy for Job Design was driven by a clear intent, it was implemented on different sites and in different ways over a considerable period of time using a combination of approaches. In terms of the individual Job Design projects, the Volvo case shows that even where changes are planned in detail in advance, the final outcome emerges through a process of iteration, modification and negotiation once the new practices are put into operation. It is this combination of Emergent change within a Planned framework, linked to a willingness to experiment and a commitment to continuous improvement for over 25 years, which makes the Volvo experience unique.

6 **Objectives**. The objectives were twofold. The first was financial – to reduce absenteeism and labour turnover. The second was social – to humanise the assembly of cars. These were pursued through a combination of structural and behavioural change, which led to major changes both in the overall shape of the company and in the attitudes of individuals and groups. However, the social objectives were modified, though not overcome, by the need for the company to operate profitably in a highly competitive market. The impact of Ford has yet to be seen.

### Case Study 6: Rover Group

1 **Strategy**. Rover's vision and strategy – to rebuild itself as a world-class car company – emerged and took shape over a long period of time. In the early

1980s, strategy was driven by a few senior managers and was aimed, originally at least, at restoring managerial authority. By the late 1980s, responsibility for strategy was spread across a wider group of managers, and focused on creating a learning organisation through behavioural and cultural change, and by building involvement and commitment at all levels. However, by the late 1990s, the takeover by BMW, and the departure of key Rover managers, had undermined this strategy without, apparently, replacing it with a new one. Therefore, a period of drift and decline set in.

2 **Constraints**. In the late 1970s, it appeared that Rover faced insurmountable obstacles to its survival. External forces, particularly foreign competition, seemed lined up against it, and internally the company appeared to be at war with itself. Indeed, it was only after managers broke the power of the trade unions that they turned their attention to reinventing Rover as a world-class car company. In building the new Rover, senior managers were helped partly by the link with Honda and partly by large government subsidies. However, one of the most significant factors appeared to be that successive Chief Executives, and their senior colleagues, developed and consistently pursued a vision of Rover's future as a modern and efficient car company. What was perhaps equally remarkable, given Rover's troubled history, was that central to its vision was creating a partnership with its workforce that encouraged commitment, learning and initiative. Therefore, up to the takeover by BMW, Rover appeared to have either coped with or changed the constraints it faced, especially market perceptions and labour force attitudes. It did not, though, try to change the rules of the game in the motor industry, though its attempt to become a learning organisation was aimed at developing its own distinctive competencies in order to compete more effectively than its rivals. What it did attempt to do, however, was to align its internal operations and external image with the needs of the environment and industry in which it operated. Unfortunately, the BMW takeover, which was partly justified by the need to put Rover on a sound financial footing, led to the blurring of Rover's vision.

3 **Managerial behaviour**. The changes at Rover were led by successive waves of senior managers – each wave, seemingly, prepared to become more radical and ambitious than their predecessors. As its strategy progressed, more managers were involved in developing and implementing it. In the process, managerial behaviour changed gradually from one of mistrust of the workforce and the pursuit of tight control to a position where workers were seen as partners in the business, whose abilities and initiative were central to Rover's success. This was exemplified by Rover's wish to see its employees take responsibility for initiating and implementing change. However, towards the end of the BMW era, managers adopted a more aggressive attitude to the workforce, and change began to be driven by imposition and threat.

4 **Change management**. The development of Rover as a learning organisation was driven by a vision, rather than by a list of concrete objectives to be achieved

in a prescribed timescale. This vision was created by a few senior managers, though as time went by, more and more managers were involved in fleshing it out. However, within the framework of the vision, there were change projects that were devised, led and implemented by employees working together in teams.

5 **Planned, Emergent or combined change**. At Rover, it appears that larger projects, particularly ones aimed at behavioural and/or culture change, tended towards an open-ended and emergent nature. However, there were other change projects, generally technical or production-related, which were pre-planned and did have clear objectives and fixed timetables. Therefore, as with some of the other case studies, one can see that Rover used a combination of approaches to change.

6 **Objectives**. There were successive waves of change at Rover aimed at transforming it into a world-class car company. An important emphasis, up to the mid-1990s, was on changing the attitudes of individuals, promoting teamwork and organisational learning, and eradicating the 'them and us' mentality which used to permeate the company. Taken together, these initiatives appear to have led to a culture change at Rover. However, under BMW's ownership the earlier gains made by Rover both in terms of people and performance seemed to be lost. For BMW, the main objective changed from how best to improve Rover to how best to dispose of it.

### Case Study 7: GK Printers

1 **Strategy**. GK's strategy tended to develop in response to potential crises, or latterly opportunities, rather than being proactively led by its management. The company, mainly on a reactive basis, appears to be reinventing itself as a modern, service-orientated company by aligning its internal arrangements with the changing needs of its environment and customers. However, this was not and is not part of any conscious plan or vision; rather it is being revealed by the pattern of actions the organisation has taken over the last decade. Originally, this pattern began to emerge through technological changes within GK, but over time it has become more pronounced by attitudinal and behavioural change, especially among managers.

2 **Constraints**. External considerations, such as societal pressures, business environment and industry-specific factors did not appear to constrain the freedom of action of GK's managers. Indeed, the turbulence and increased competition in the external environment seemed to assist GK with its internal changes. GK's main constraints were internal and related to existing attitudes, technology and practices. Increasingly, however, as the need arose to develop a more collective leadership, it was the directive style of the Managing Director that was seen as a key constraint on progress. Nevertheless, his directive style, and his tendency to play managers off against each other, has gradually changed.

3 **Managerial behaviour** Though originally it was the Managing Director who was responsible for strategy development and change, it became clear over time that a more collective and co-operative style of management was required if GK was to overcome the obstacles it faced and seize the opportunities on offer. Therefore, gradually, all the company's managers became involved in and took responsibility for strategy development, and they even devolved responsibility for some change projects to staff in the areas concerned.

4 **Change management**. A mixture of approaches to managing change projects can be seen at GK. In most instances, managers took responsibility for identifying the need for change, and in some instances actually directed it. However, in the case of the computerised business system, for example, the company left selection and implementation to the staff concerned. Also, in terms of the website business, GK allowed a staff member who was a web enthusiast to develop this area. This demonstrates how far the company had progressed in developing a climate of trust and involvement.

5 **Planned, Emergent or combined change**. A mixture of both Planned and Emergent approaches can be seen at GK. In the early days, the company tried to adopt a Planned approach, especially when introducing new technology, but new developments or improvements to existing arrangements have tended to be reactive and Emergent rather than proactive and Planned. Change at GK still tends to be *ad hoc*, reactive or opportunistic rather than being part of any grand plan.

6 **Objectives**. The original aim was to survive. To this end, GK changed its technology and image in order to improve its competitiveness. However, as events unfolded, it became clear that the key to competing effectively was to change people's attitudes, especially at management level, and create a greater commitment to teamwork and collective decision-making. This has created a climate where managers and staff are more receptive to new ideas, and responsive to new opportunities, than before. Nevertheless, though a pattern of change may be emerging at GK, it is by no means a well-articulated or even conscious one.

### Case Study 8: Rover–TRW

1 **Strategy**. This particular initiative between Rover and TRW did not form part of a strategic plan, or contribute towards a vision. In essence, the objective was an operational one, not a strategic one: to outsource the assembly of suspension modules owing to lack of space. At TRW, those in charge focused on the steps necessary to have the new operation up and running on time, and able to meet Rover's requirements. There was a strategic element to this initiative in that both organisations wished to find out more about modular assembly, but this sub-objective very quickly vanished from sight.

2 **Constraints**. The main constraints tended to be attitudinal and organisational. To be successful, TRW needed to ensure that staff at the Frankley site had the

motivation, initiative and ability to develop a new operation remote from the main TRW site in Wales. There was also a requirement to build a good working relationship with Rover's assembly line personnel. In organisational terms, a new factory and workforce needed to be established, new equipment installed, new practices learned and new skills developed. At an operational level, both in terms of the relationship and the performance, this worked better than anyone had anticipated. However, the persistence of old, less trusting relationships at a more senior level between the two companies did threaten the gains made at the operational level.

3 **Managerial behaviour**. At Frankley, supported by their superiors within TRW, managers created a genuine atmosphere of co-operation which allowed staff to work closely with their counterparts at Rover, and to improve their performance continuously. At a more senior level, though, a less co-operative and more guarded atmosphere prevailed between Rover and TRW.

4 **Change management**. Frankley was created from scratch and, once established, was committed to continuously improving and developing its performance. From the outset, and in contrast to established practices within TRW, the Frankley management sought to ensure that everyone was involved in and could contribute to change. It was only a small organisation, with some 30 to 40 staff initially, and this obviously made it easier to create a team spirit. Nevertheless, the key was the attitude of the management at Frankley, who set out to involve all staff.

5 **Planned, Emergent or combined change**. This was clearly a case where one could see both Emergent and Planned change going on side by side. Originally, there was a clear set of objectives that Frankley had to achieve and a fixed timescale within which to achieve them; these revolved around setting up the new plant and beginning deliveries to Rover. Beyond that, though, was a process of learning, experimentation and development which was central to the major performance improvements made by Frankley.

6 **Objectives**. The original objectives were basically structural and revolved around establishing a new assembly operation capable of meeting Rover's requirements. Though these objectives were met, staff at the Frankley site did not rest on their laurels. Instead, motivated by the desire to improve the service to Rover, they set themselves, and achieved, ever more ambitious targets.

### Case Study 9: Nissan

1 **Strategy**. Based on its experience in Japan, Nissan had a clear strategy for how it wished to work with suppliers and the results it wished to achieve. This strategy was part of its wider plans for how the European arm of its business would contribute to establishing Nissan as one of the world's leading car companies. Nissan's supplier strategy was originally set and driven by its senior managers. One of the main initiatives they took was to establish a Supplier Development Team (SDT) to educate suppliers in the practices and approaches

used successfully in Japan. However, the actual tools and mechanisms used in developing suppliers were determined by the SDT itself in response to Nissan's developing perception of its suppliers' needs.

2 **Constraints**. Though the UK's overall practices and industrial culture did not fit in with the Nissan approach, this seems to have had little effect on how Nissan organised and ran its Sunderland plant or its approach to suppliers. When the plant first opened, it was helped, to an extent, by the stagnant business environment which made suppliers eager for new business, especially from internationally competitive firms such as Nissan. The main constraint it faced was the past history of antagonistic customer–supplier relations which existed in the UK and European motor industries. Though this was an industry characteristic, it was manifested in the behaviour, attitudes, structures and practices of individual supplier companies. In the light of this, Nissan faced a choice: should it work within existing arrangements or should it try to change them? For what appeared to be sound business reasons, Nissan chose to adopt the same partnership approach to its UK and European suppliers as it used in Japan. Therefore, in effect, it chose to change the rules of the game.

3 **Managerial behaviour**. As stated, the original objectives for the SDT had been set by senior managers at Nissan as part of its supplier strategy. However, the actual implementation of the strategy was delegated to the Supplier Development Team, which was expected to develop its own plan of action, though it had to convince colleagues and superiors that its plans constituted the most effective use of resources. As far as the improvement activities were concerned, the role of a supplier's senior management was to give approval, or not, to SDT involvement. However, after an improvement activity had demonstrated the potential of such an approach, the supplier's managers and staff were then expected to initiate and sustain their own programme of improvement activities.

4 **Change management**. The SDT initiative was originally created by senior managers. However, once in operation, it was the SDT's responsibility to continue to develop it. Individual improvement activities were mainly driven by suppliers' own personnel, who (with the SDT's guidance) decided upon and implemented changes.

5 **Planned, Emergent or combined change**. Though Nissan started out with a clear picture of how it wished to work with its suppliers and the results it expected, the actual details and mechanisms for achieving these emerged over time. The improvement activities, on the other hand, were planned in advance and highly focused. Areas of improvement were identified and analysed, and improvement targets set. These activities were all carried out within the framework of a highly structured programme. In many respects – such as short timespan, the educational role of the SDT, and staff involvement – the improvement activities carry the hallmark of the Planned approach to change. Nevertheless, the activities were not seen as ends in themselves, but as a means of promoting wider organisational learning in the companies concerned.

Therefore, the role of the SDT was, in Lewin's words, to unfreeze and move the suppliers; but it did not wish to refreeze them. Instead, its aim was to promote continuous improvement and open-ended change.

6 **Objectives**. Nissan's overall objective was to assemble cars at its Sunderland plant as efficiently as in its plants in Japan. A key factor in achieving this was to develop a co-operative relationship with its suppliers. Looking at individual suppliers, Nissan wished to see major changes in their whole approach to manufacturing, and to promote a teamwork mentality. The catalyst for achieving this was the SDT's ten-day improvement activity. By achieving change to a small part of a company, Nissan believed it could show the potential of the Japanese approach to manufacturing. Linking all this together was Nissan's belief that it needed to change attitudes, perceptions and behaviour in its suppliers. Though not explicitly aimed at changing culture, Nissan's approach did stress the need for teamwork and an end to 'them and us' attitudes in its suppliers.

### Case Study 10: Speedy Stationers

1 **Strategy**. The development of Speedy's vision or strategy tended to be driven by force of events or opportunism rather than necessarily being pre-planned. Each time a major opportunity or concern arose, Speedy examined its options and chose the one which appeared to be more favourable to the development of its business.

2 **Constraints**. The degree to which external or internal factors affected Speedy's strategy is unclear. Certainly, the company did not appear to have faced great restrictions on its freedom of manoeuvre. Nor, except in one case, did it appear to have sought to change or influence the constraints it faced. The exception is its attempt to develop a partnership approach to customers. In this instance it was attempting to change industry practice. Though this met with some resistance internally, it also had to overcome a large degree of scepticism in the customer concerned.

3 **Managerial behaviour**. It was Speedy's Managing Director who originally developed its partnership strategy. Subsequently, and rather reluctantly, he handed responsibility for its continuing development to another director of the company who established his own plans which he then convinced his colleagues, and Speedy's customers, to accept. However, later, when it came to convincing his fellow directors that they should expand direct sales nationally, he was less successful and even the project's original champion, the Managing Director, rejected the suggestion. Therefore, overall, though it wanted to promote more co-operative relationships with customers, there was no discernable move towards more co-operative working within Speedy.

4 **Change management**. The actual implementation of the partnership approach required not only the involvement of Speedy's own staff, but also, as the UTL instance shows, co-operation from its customers' managers and staff at all levels.

5 **Planned, Emergent or combined change**. The development of the strategy itself, the partnership with UTL, and the further expansion of this approach, was and is an open-ended process. Initial implementation of the partnership was carefully planned, but from then on the form and content of the changes emerged on a day-to-day basis.

6 **Objectives**. The objective of Speedy's strategy was to grow its business by developing a new type of relationship with its customers. Implementing this led to changes within both Speedy, though these tended to be limited to its Direct Sales Division, and within the ten customers with whom it developed partnerships. Though some of these changes were structural, most changes concerned the attitudes and behaviour of individuals and groups, especially in terms of greater openness and trust. However, there is little evidence that these have led to any wider cultural changes within Speedy.

Before moving on to discuss the implications of the above for the way in which strategy and change are conceived and executed, there are two outstanding and interrelated issues that still need to be clarified. These concern employee involvement, and rapid and wholesale organisational transformation.

## EMPLOYEE INVOLVEMENT AND ORGANISATIONAL TRANSFORMATION

Dunphy and Stace (1993) argued that Planned change could not incorporate large scale change undertaken in a directive or coercive fashion. Neither, by definition, can the Emergent approach incorporate this type of change. This would seem to call for a new perspective on organisational change which is neither Planned nor Emergent. However, the Oticon study in Chapter 9 appears to offer a different explanation. This was a case of rapid organisational transformation which was based on a vision imposed on the company in a mainly directive fashion by its CEO. However, the planning, execution and subsequent development of the vision was undertaken in a more participative way; within a directive framework, the transformation exhibited both Planned and Emergent elements. It follows that Dunphy and Stace's (1993) argument that rapid change cannot be achieved by a Planned or, by implication, Emergent approach is difficult to sustain in cases such as this where a combination of approaches is evident. In this case, the vision was directive but a more Planned approach was used to achieve the rapid structural change which, in turn, was followed by a period of Emergent change where staff had to develop and adjust to new ways of working with, and behaving towards, each other. This should not be surprising, as we know that structural changes can be achieved quickly and that any concomitant cultural or behavioural changes will take much longer.

Though this Planned–Emergent combination appears to explain part of the issue raised by Dunphy and Stace, it still leaves the question of how such fundamental changes can be achieved without the full co-operation and involvement of the people concerned. Current wisdom, as described in Chapters 7 and 8, regards employee involvement as the key to successful change. However, Schmuck and Miles (1971) argued that involvement is not necessary in all situations. Instead they argue that the level of involvement required is dependent on the impact of the change on the people concerned. Huse (1980) developed this distinction further. Building on earlier work by Harrison (1970), Huse categorised change interventions along a continuum based on the 'depth' of intervention, ranging from the 'shallow level' to the 'deepest level'. The greater the depth of the intervention, Huse argues, the more it becomes concerned with the psychological make-up and personality of the individual, and the greater the need for the full involvement of individuals if they are to accept the changes.

The argument, therefore, is that it is necessary to link levels of involvement to the types of change proposed. The key is that the greater the effect on the individual, especially in terms of psychological constructs and values, the deeper the level of involvement required if successful behaviour change is to be achieved. This appears to explain why, in some cases, involvement can be dispensed with or minimised, whilst in other cases it is vital. It does not, however, explain why major changes at Oticon were successful without a great deal of initial involvement, nor indeed why, in the end, Rover were not successful despite a high level of involvement.

In seeking to understand and explain such apparent contradictions, Burnes and James (1995) draw on the theory of cognitive dissonance. This theory states that people try to be consistent in both their attitudes and behaviour. When they sense an inconsistency either between two or more attitudes or between their attitudes and behaviour, people experience dissonance; that is, they feel frustrated and uncomfortable – sometimes extremely so – with the situation (Jones, 1990). Therefore, individuals will seek a stable state where there is minimum dissonance. This latter point is important. It is unlikely that dissonance can ever be totally avoided, but where the elements creating the dissonance are relatively unimportant, the pressure to correct them will be low. However, where the issues involved are perceived by the individual to be significant, the presence of such dissonance will motivate the person concerned to try to reduce the dissonance and achieve consonance, by changing either their attitudes or behaviour to bring them into line (Robbins, 1986; Smith *et al*, 1982). This may involve a process of cognitive restructuring, which is unlikely to be free from difficulties for the individual concerned (Mahoney, 1974). However, as Festinger (1957), one of the originators of the concept, pointed out, in addition to trying to reduce the dissonance, people will actively avoid situations and information that would be likely to increase the dissonance. Since the emergence of the theory of cognitive dissonance in the 1950s, it has been developed and refined (*see* Cooper and Fazio, 1984; Fazio *et al*, 1977; Jones, 1990).

Applying principles of cognitive dissonance to organisational change, it can be seen that, if an organisation embarks on a change project that is decisively out of step with the attitudes of those concerned, it will meet resistance unless those concerned change their attitudes. On the other hand, where the level of dissonance occasioned by proposed changes is low, attitudinal adjustments will be minor and potential resistance negligible. Therefore, the level and type of involvement should be geared to the level of dissonance that any proposed changes may provoke.

Up to this point, cognitive dissonance supports the work of Schmuck and Miles (1971) and Huse (1980). However, if we apply the theory to situations, such as Oticon's, where old certainties proved inadequate and the very survival of the organisation is at stake, a different picture emerges. The crisis (or potential crisis) raises the level of dissonance in the organisation as it becomes apparent that existing practices are no longer viable and change is required. Not only does this make individuals and groups more receptive to radical change, but in addition, change can be one of the main ways of reducing dissonance. We can also see that this was the case in Midshires College; however, the difference was that although the workforce wanted to change, they lacked a clear sense of direction owing to the inability of the college's management to agree one. Therefore, in such instances, the dissonance is occasioned not by the change, but by the condition of the organisation leading up to the change. This perspective also helps to explain cases where, initially, managers and others were resistant to changes or were only prepared to move slowly. In such situations, the absence of a sense of deep crisis prevents existing certainties being successfully challenged. Only when more severe threats arise are these old certainties challenged, and those involved become more prepared to accept and promote radical solutions that had previously been rejected.

A similar and complementary explanation for the involvement or non-involvement of employees is offered by the notion of the psychological contract. Though this concept has been around since the 1950s (*see* for example Argyris, 1960), it was only in the 1980s and 1990s that it became widely used by organisation theorists, especially in America (Arnold *et al*, 1998). As Schein (1988: 22–3) states:

> The notion of a psychological contract implies that there is an unwritten set of expectations operating at all times between every member of an organization and the various managers and others in that organization. ... The psychological contract implies further that each role player, that is, employee, also has expectations about such things as salary or pay rate, working hours, benefits and privileges ... and so on. Many of these expectations are implicit and involve the person's sense of dignity and worth. ... Some of the strongest feelings leading to labor unrest, strikes, and employee turnover have to do with violations of these aspects of the psychological contract, even though the public negotiations are often over the more explicit issues of pay, working hours, job security, and so on.

We can certainly see why the employees of the PSA, who had joined a public sector organisation with a public sector ethos, might feel as though their psychological contract had been violated when they were suddenly told they were to be transferred to the private sector – particularly as the change represented a considerable threat to their job security. However, why was there not a more adverse reaction from Oticon's staff or GK's employees? The reason offered by proponents of the psychological contract would be that they recognised the need and justification for the changes and therefore the legitimacy of the need to change their psychological contracts.

Consequently, in understanding the employee involvement/non-involvement question, we need to draw on the complementary ideas of levels of involvement, cognitive dissonance and the psychological contract. What these show us is that in many cases where change is proposed, it is necessary to convince staff, through a process of constructive engagement, of the need to challenge their existing beliefs, behaviours and expectations and to renegotiate their 'contracts' with the organisation. However, this questioning of beliefs, behaviours and expectations can also arise in situations of crisis without the need for elaborate involvement techniques, because those concerned can see that, unless major or radical changes are made, their jobs or even the entire organisation may cease to exist.

Having addressed the issue of employee involvement, and particularly the question of how rapid and directive change can be accomplished without it, we can now move on to present the conclusions drawn from the analysis of the case studies.

## CONCLUSIONS: MERGING THEORY AND PRACTICE

One should be wary of drawing any firm conclusions about either theory or practice from such a small number of case studies. However, the case studies presented in Part 3 are rich in detail, cover an extended time period, and do raise some important issues which it would be unwise to ignore. These are as follows.

### Strategy

Though in some cases this was driven by a clear vision, more often it was triggered by perceived opportunities, problems or crises. The actual form of each organisation's strategy emerged from attempts to pursue visions or respond to events. In addition, we should note that there were instances where senior managers, individually or collectively, tried to reinvent their organisations. Whether we refer to this as creating a vision, as the Japanese might, or trying to impose a new reality, as the postmodernists might, is perhaps irrelevant. What is important is that some managers do have the will and the ability to re-shape their organisations and to overcome or modify the constraints they face.

### Constraints

The case studies reveal that external and internal constraints do affect the degree of choice managers have or perceive themselves to have. However, the studies also show that managers can take action either to align their organisation more closely with external demands, or influence or change the constraints they face to suit their personal preferences and/or the organisation's existing arrangements.

Interestingly, in terms of internal constraints, despite what many writers believe, though there were some power struggles and some political battles, overt political behaviour did not feature in most of the case studies. Nevertheless, where such activity was present, as in Midshires and Rover, it tended to have negative outcomes. There are a number of possible explanations as to why politics did not appear to play a more significant role in most of these cases. These include the presence of dominant individuals or coalitions, and the widely recognised need for change in some of the organisations which gave legitimacy to managerial initiatives.

### Managerial behaviour

In all the instances examined, managers played a central role in initiating or developing visions and strategies. Managers also played a leading role in implementing strategies or attempting to create the conditions for their implementation. In some cases they also led change projects. There were, though, instances, as with GK, where managers had to change their behaviour or managerial style in order to achieve successful change. Also, there were instances, as with Midshires College and the PSA, where managers did not change their behaviour or managerial style and as a result change was adversely affected. One crucial point to note is the importance of managerial stability and the continuity of objectives. The importance of these two factors can be seen in the cases of Flair, Volvo and Nissan, for example. It is also noticeable that, in part at least, Rover's problems in the late 1990s appeared to arise from a period of drift caused by the departure of some senior managers after the BMW takeover. However, as the PSA case illustrates, managerial continuity alone is not enough.

### Managing change

A variety of approaches to change management can be seen in the case studies. These range from instances where all the major decisions were taken by one manager, to others where staff in the areas concerned led and planned change projects. The general tendency was for managers to involve employees in planning and implementing smaller, more short-term projects, often of a technical nature, and in some cases even to devolve such responsibility to them. Larger, more strategic and longer-term projects, though, especially those concerned with attitudinal or behavioural change, were very much initiated and under the control of senior managers.

### Planned, Emergent or combined change

Once again, the picture is mixed. Longer-term and larger projects were usually open-ended, with diffuse objectives, and involved large numbers of people; whereas smaller projects, where clearer objectives could be set, were inclined to be more tightly controlled and planned. However, perhaps the main distinction was between those projects aiming to change attitudes and behaviour, which by their nature needed to be more flexible, and those concentrating on structural or technical change, especially at the operational level, which tended to have clearer objectives and required more fixed timescales. Nevertheless, as the cases show, some organisations appeared to use a combination of approaches to change consciously and appropriately, e.g. Nissan and, as time developed, Flair. In some of the case studies, we can see that different approaches were tried, though not always consciously, appropriately or successfully, e.g. GK. Yet again, some of the other organisations tried to stick to one approach to change even where it did not appear to be working, e.g. Midshires and the PSA.

Underpinning the case study companies' preferences as far as change is concerned appear to be two dominant factors. The first concerns their preferred or dominant style of management. The use of a combination of change approaches seems to have been more prevalent and successful in those companies where there was, or there developed, a participative style of management. An example is Nissan, who favoured working co-operatively both internally and externally. This explains not only their wish to develop supplier partnerships but also the way in which they approached this objective. Though their improvement activities had elements of Planned change, these were set within Nissan's overall style, which favoured the Emergent approach and which promoted employee involvement, learning and bottom-up change. In the cases of Midshires and the PSA, on the other hand, managers preferred a much more command-and-control, top-down approach with little involvement from staff. Therefore, the dominant approach to change was mechanistic and directive. Oticon, Flair and Volvo, though, represent different aspects of managerial style again. In these instances, managers set out to change the dominant managerial style of their companies. Initially, in all the companies, managers began to make these changes by imposition rather than through employee involvement. Nevertheless, over time, more quickly in some cases than others, as the changes began to work, a more participative form of management emerged and there was less need for changes to be imposed from above instead of emerging from below. Therefore, what we can see is that a variety and combination of approaches to change were used by the more successful companies.

The second factor concerns the degree to which organisational change was seen as a series of one-off events, or a continuous process. In some of the companies, e.g. GK, each change project arose and was dealt with on its own merit. Indeed, at GK, each new project seemed to involve reinventing the wheel as far as choosing an approach to change was concerned. Consequently, and not surprisingly, there were a number of false starts before the most appropriate approach was chosen. In other companies, however, e.g. Nissan and latterly Flair, where change was considered as – or became – the norm, a battery of approaches, tools and techniques were developed which could be used as and when appropriate.

Therefore, if we take these two factors together, participative managerial style and the need to see change as a continuous process, they not only account for the successful use of a combination of change techniques but also for the successful outcome to change projects.

## Objectives

A variety of objectives could be discerned, ranging from localised structural change to organisation-wide cultural change. However, in all the organisations, either at the outset or over time, changes to the behaviour and attitudes of individuals and groups came to be considered as more important than either technical or structural adjustments.

So we can see that, depending on the circumstances or constraints, strategy development and change management can take many forms. In the case studies, there are examples of deliberate and conscious attempts to shape strategy as well as more unconscious and accidental approaches. We can also see cases where an organisation's strategy or change programme, by design or accident, resulted in the re-shaping or realignment of the constraints the organisation faced. In terms of change management, there were cases where the process of change and the process of strategy development, because of their emergent nature, coincided. However, there were also cases where Planned change followed on from and was determined by a pre-set strategy.

In conclusion, the case studies illustrate the arguments regarding managerial choice, strategy and change developed in Part 2. They show that whilst the Planned and Emergent approaches to change are important, they are not the be-all and end-all of change, or even mutually exclusive. The case studies also show that managers can exercise a high degree of choice about what to change, when to change it and how to change it. In addition, it can be seen that where decisions are taken in an open manner, when those concerned are genuinely listened to and involved, and where serious attempts are made to identify and resolve reservations and resistance, there is less likelihood that political behaviour, individual interests or bias will be able to subvert the process.

Having now reviewed the ten case studies in the light of Parts 1–3, the next chapter will present the Choice Management–Change Management model for strategy development and organisational change.

## TEST YOUR LEARNING

### Short answer questions

1 In terms of its relationship with TRW, what key lesson could Rover have learnt from Nissan's partnership strategy?

2 In what way can it be said that Speedy Stationers failed to overcome the constraints it faced?

3 List three of the main differences between the behaviour of managers within Oticon and the behaviour of managers in the PSA.

4 What lessons can be learned by comparing change management at Midshires with that at GK?

5 Discuss the case for seeing Volvo as an example of combined change.

6 What lessons can be drawn from the fact that Flair's change of culture emerged out of its pursuit of other objectives, rather than being an objective in itself?

7 What did Huse (1980) mean by the 'depth' of intervention?

8 What is cognitive dissonance?

9 What is a psychological contract?

## Essay questions

1 Given that its initial approach to change was somewhat autocratic, explain the level of co-operation and commitment which Oticon received from its staff.

2 Compare and contrast the different approaches of Midshires College and Nissan to the constraints they faced.

# Chapter 13

---

# ORGANISATIONAL CHANGE AND MANAGERIAL CHOICE

**Learning objectives**

After studying this chapter, you should be able to:

1 understand the rationale underlying the Choice Management–Change Management model;

2 discuss the three organisational processes which make up the Choice–Change model;

3 describe how organisations can manage change effectively;

4 identify the range of choices which organisations have when considering change;

5 appreciate how organisations can influence their circumstances to align them with their preferred way of working;

6 understand the need for managers to play a proactive role in the change process.

## INTRODUCTION

From Chapter 12, we can see that whilst organisational change can be a complex, ambiguous and open-ended phenomenon, it can also be relatively straightforward with understandable and limited objectives. This in itself is not a new or radical finding – anyone who works in or studies organisations will have noted that change comes in a wide variety of shapes and sizes. However, it was argued in Chapter 8 that in order to cope with the wide variety of types of change, there is a need for a corresponding variety of approaches to strategy development and change management.

This point, the need to match types of change with appropriate approaches to managing change, is not as prominent in the literature on organisational change and behaviour as one might expect. As Part 2 also showed, despite the widespread influence of Contingency Theory, the majority of writers and practitioners are committed to a 'one best way' approach to strategy and change. The call by Dunphy and Stace (1993) for a situational or contextual approach to these issues has still been taken up by few others. Though there are writers on strategy, such as Mintzberg *et al* (1998) and Whittington (1993), who identify the various approaches to strategy, they tend, eventually, to opt for one as the preferred approach. This is even more pronounced in the change literature, where there is a clear distinction between those who support the Planned approach (such as Cummings and Worley, 1997; French and Bell, 1995) and those who adhere to a more Emergent approach (such as Dawson, 1994; Kotter, 1996; Senior, 1997; Wilson, 1992).

Many of those arguing for their own favoured approach to strategy and change do so, either explicitly or implicitly, on the basis of their perception of the nature of the environment in which organisations operate. Those arguing for a Planned approach to strategy and/or change appear to assume that the environment is relatively stable and predictable. Those who take a more Emergent approach to both seem to operate on the assumption that the environment is turbulent and unpredictable.

Furthermore, most writers seem to assume that the principal role of managers and the ultimate objective of strategy and change is to align or realign an organisation with its environment. In the preceding chapters, a case has been built for rejecting this argument and adopting a different stance. Rather than accepting the view that managers are prisoners of the circumstances in which their organisations operate or find themselves, it was argued that managers can and do exercise a considerable degree of choice. It was further argued, however, that the scope and nature of the choices managers face and make are constrained by a range of external factors (national characteristics, the business environment and industry norms) and internal organisational characteristics (especially structure, culture, politics and managerial style). This argument goes much further than many by challenging the assumption that managers are in some way the passive agents of forces beyond their control, but it still leaves them as prisoners of circumstances – although the prison in this case is much roomier than many of the writers we have discussed would acknowledge.

However, the final arguments in Chapters 4, 5 and 8 challenged even this definition of managerial choice. It was suggested that the constraints on choice are themselves amenable to managerial actions – in effect, organisations can influence or change the constraints under which they operate. This possibility was first suggested when examining Contingency Theory in Chapter 2; it was further developed in subsequent chapters and shown to be more than a possibility. In particular, some managers are even capable of reinventing their organisations or, as the postmodernists would have it, creating a more preferable reality for them. The ten case studies in Part 3 reveal that, though organisations do try to align and realign themselves with their environment, they also attempt to influence and restructure the environment and other constraints in their favour. Sometimes, by accident or design, this results in a reconfiguration of the accepted rules by which the industry in which they operate competes; whilst in other instances, it prevents organisations being forced to undertake more radical internal upheavals.

In the case of Oticon (Chapter 9), it can be seen that the company deliberately set out to change the basis on which it competed by reinventing itself as a service-based rather than a technology-driven organisation. Lacking the technological strength of its competitors, which was the accepted cornerstone of competition in its industry, it proposed to offer a superior level of service instead. By changing the rules of the game in its industry, Oticon hoped to steal a march on its competitors. In the case of Nissan, to accept the antagonistic relationship with suppliers that was the norm in the UK motor industry might have necessitated radical alterations to the culture and practices it wished to promote in its new UK car plant. To avoid this, Nissan sought to build a new type of relationship with its suppliers in the UK and other European countries, one that would increase the element of predictability and stability in its environment and fit in with its own preferred way of working. In effect, they chose to present a different reality to their suppliers; one where co-operation rather than conflict was the norm. Though Flair's development of closer links with its suppliers also increased the stability and predictability of its environment, its main reason for doing so was to provide a better service for its customers and thus increase its own competitiveness. Nevertheless, once again this was a case where an organisation had reinvented itself.

The implications of managerial choice for the nature and focus of change management are, as the above shows, significant. Change management need not be seen as a mechanism for achieving a specified and predicted outcome (the Planned approach). Nor need it be conceived of as a continuing process of aligning and realigning the organisation with its environment (the Emergent approach). Instead, as this chapter will show, by linking managerial choice to the management of change, organisations can open up a much wider spectrum of options. These range from focusing on achieving radical internal change to align an organisation with its external constraints, doing the same in an attempt to restructure such constraints, to influencing or changing external constraints in order to avoid internal upheavals. In such a situation, not only are managers trying to make sense of their situation for themselves and others but they are also seeking to construct a more favourable reality as well. The chapter begins by presenting an overview of the Choice Management–Change Management model for understanding and implementing organisational change. This is followed by a detailed description of the three components of the model: the choice process, the trajectory process, and the change process. The chapter concludes by maintaining that though organisations may choose to restructure their internal operations and practices in order to align them with the external circumstances they face, they can also choose to change or modify external and internal conditions and constraints in order to avoid extensive internal upheaval and/or to bring the constraints into line with their preferred *modus operandi*. Whatever choices are made, it is the role of managers consciously to explore and identify all the available options, however improbable they seem, rather than assuming that they have no, or only limited, choice in the matter.

## THE CHOICE MANAGEMENT–
## CHANGE MANAGEMENT MODEL

As the Choice Management–Change Management Model in Figure 13.1 shows, organisational change can be viewed as the product of three interdependent organisational processes:

- **The choice process** – which is concerned with the nature, scope and focus of organisational decision-making.

- **The trajectory process** – which relates to an organisation's past and future direction and is seen as the outcome of its vision, purpose and future objectives.

- **The change process** – which covers approaches to, mechanisms for achieving, and outcomes of change.

These processes are interdependent because, as Figure 13.1 shows, the change process is itself an integral part of the trajectory process and this, in turn, is a vital part of the choice process. Within each of these processes there are a group of elements, or forces, which interact, clash with and influence each other in subtle and complex ways. It is this interaction of elements or forces which prevents

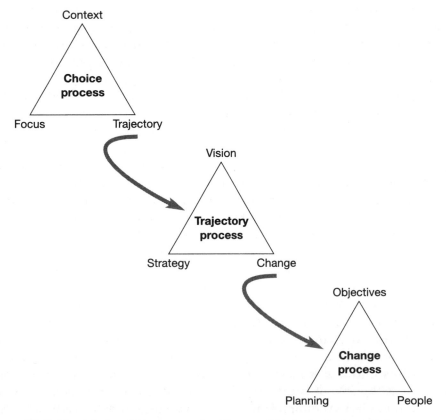

Figure 13.1 The Choice Management–Change Management model

decision-making and change management from being a rational-mechanical process, and ensures that they are based on subjective and imperfect judgement.

Each of these three processes will now be described, not only to show their complexity and interdependence, but also to provide a guide to putting the Choice Management–Change Management model into practice. For this latter reason, the description of the change process, in particular, will dwell on the steps necessary to accomplish change successfully.

## The choice process

The choice process comprises three elements:

- Organisational context
- Focus of choice
- Organisational Trajectory

### Organisational context

One of the standard prescriptions for successful organisations is that they should know their own strengths and weaknesses, their customers' needs and the nature of the environment in which they operate. However, as the case studies show, many organisations appear only to begin collecting this sort of information when they are in trouble. Yet how can organisations hope to understand and appreciate the options open to them unless they develop mechanisms for collecting and analysing information on their performance and general situation?

No one would suggest that assembling information on past, present and future performance is easy or that understanding the nature of the constraints faced by an organisation is simple. However, there are relatively well-established methods for benchmarking an organisation's performance against a range of internal and external comparators (Camp, 1989). There are also a number of tried and tested ways for gathering information on and evaluating the main internal and external organisational constraints. The two most used by organisations are the SWOT analysis (Strengths and Weaknesses, Opportunities and Threats) and the PEST analysis (Political, Economic, Socio-Cultural and Technological) (Lynch, 1997). As discussed in Chapter 5, the main organisational constraints are national characteristics, industry and sector norms, the business environment, and organisational characteristics such as structure, culture, politics and management style.

One advantage to working in this fashion is that organisations can promote openness and reduce, though probably not eliminate, political behaviour and conflict. Nevertheless, some organisations will find that owing to the context in which they operate, teamwork, co-operation and openness are very difficult to achieve without first changing those factors which hinder or prevent these. Perhaps the prime consideration in this respect is the prevalent style of management. Though others can exert pressure, managers are really the only group who can initiate change and will rarely (as a group) voluntarily adopt changes which adversely affect them. It follows that, faced with a mismatch between their organisation and its environment, some managers will seek to achieve realignment by influencing the environment rather than pursuing an internal upheaval which may involve changes in management style and personnel.

Gathering this sort of information, as well as discussing it and agreeing how to interpret it, will require the participation of a wide range of people and functions. Not only should this provide a robust basis for decision-making, it can also develop a sense of teamwork, co-operation and mutual understanding amongst those concerned. Nevertheless, it should also be recognised that no matter how rigorously information is collected, analysed and argued over, there will always be a large element of subjectivity in how it is interpreted. This is why, as a number of writers have commented, one of the key tasks managers perform is 'sensemaking' (Weick, 1995). Sensemaking basically is what the word implies; managers interpreting and explaining, making sense of, their organisation's world for themselves and others in such a way that it guides and provides a rationale for action. Sensemaking is the process by which managers attempt or can attempt to impose their view of reality on others.

### Focus of choice

At any one time, successful organisations appear to focus their attention on only a narrow range of short-, medium- and long-term issues. Some of these will relate to the organisation's performance, whilst others may be more concerned with building or developing particular competencies or technologies. In some cases, the issues may be of passing interest only, whilst in other cases they may be fundamental to the organisation's survival. Certainly, in most instances, organisations will in one way or another focus on aligning themselves with or even influencing or changing the constraints under which they operate.

How an organisation decides upon which issues to focus, and whether this is done in a concerted way (as at Flair), or in a way which allows different groups and individuals to pursue their own agenda (as at Midshires College), is a fundamental factor in any organisation's decision-making process. Certainly, the received wisdom is that a concerted and co-ordinated approach, which focuses upon a small number of issues at any one time, is more effective than a fragmented one (Kay, 1993; Senge, 1990). Japanese organisations are particularly good at identifying the key aspects of their strategy on which they need to focus. The particular technique they use is called *Hoshin Kanri* (Policy Deployment), and it is a structured process, undertaken annually, for ensuring that key strategic objectives are pursued in a rigorous manner and inform decisions at all levels in the organisation (Akao, 1991).

### Organisational trajectory

An organisation's trajectory or direction is shaped by its past actions and future objectives and strategies. As such it provides a guide or framework within which to judge the acceptability, relevance or urgency of issues, concerns and proposed actions. The trajectory process encompasses the determination of and interplay between an organisation's vision, strategies and approach to change.

In some respects, the concept of trajectory comprises both an organisation's 'memory' of past events and its intent in terms of future ones. For some organisations, the trajectory will be clear and unambiguous. In others, making sense of past events and agreeing proposals for future actions will be the subject of dispute and uncertainty.

It will also be the case that some organisations will consciously attempt to plot their trajectory in minute detail, whilst others may adopt a more global and distant set of objectives. Many organisations may find that their trajectory emerges from a set of apparently unrelated actions. Indeed, as the case studies show, it is the interplay between past actions and future intent coupled to the wide variety of approaches to these which makes decision-making so complex.

Each of the three elements of the choice process is complex in itself, but they also interact with each other in an intricate and unpredictable way. An organisation's trajectory, whether it is seen as successful or not, can influence both the focus of its decision-making, and the context within which the organisation operates. Likewise, the context provides a framework within which the trajectory is developed. Similarly, the focus of choice will influence which aspect of the organisation's context its trajectory will be directed towards, not only in the short term but also in the medium and long term.

Given the complex and multifaceted nature of decision-making, it is not, perhaps, surprising that writers have drawn attention to the tendency for managers to 'muddle through' rather than attempt an exhaustive and exhausting examination of all the available options (Lindblom, 1968). Nor is it surprising that some managers prefer 'fire-fighting' to tackling fundamental issues (Burnes, 1991) – at least the objective is immediate and clear, and a favourable outcome can be achieved (though it is usually short-lived).

Appreciating the complexity of decision-making also casts the Japanese *ringi* system (discussed in Chapter 3) in a favourable light. Only by an exhaustive analysis of the issue concerned and the options available is the most appropriate decision likely to be arrived at. However, the *ringi* system is usually aided by and carried out within the framework of a strong corporate vision and clear strategies for its pursuit, which make it easier to identify which decisions and actions are appropriate. By framing decisions within such a framework, or such a perspective on reality, Japanese companies ensure that they do not have to explore all the available possibilities when taking decisions – merely those that are in harmony with their vision/strategy/intent. In this way, the entire choice process is simplified and made more achievable. Japanese companies have shown themselves to be masters of developing visions and strategies which not only make them successful but also, and not incidentally, reduce the uncertainty in their environment, alter the basis of competition in their favour, and narrow the focus of decision-making (Hamel and Prahalad, 1989). The result is that though the choice process remains complex, not only does it have a greater degree of consistency between the elements and people involved, but it is also more focused in the range of issues and decisions required.

Therefore, what can be seen is that whilst the choice process is uncertain, complex and time-consuming, there are approaches which do reduce these factors and can make the process more transparent and effective. In order to understand further how this can be achieved, we shall now examine the trajectory process.

## The trajectory process

Like the choice process, the trajectory process comprises three elements.

### Vision

As described in Chapter 6, the use of scenario-building and 'visioning' techniques has become increasingly popular in recent years. The purpose of these techniques is to generate different organisational futures, or realities, in order to select the one that seems most favourable or appropriate. The ten case studies in Part 3 showed that not all companies have visions, and not all visions find favour with the managers and employees who have to implement them. However, the concept of organisations driving themselves forward by creating an ambitious vision (or intent or scenario) of where they wish to be in the long term has become increasingly influential over the last 15 years (Cummings and Worley, 1997; Johnson and Scholes, 1993; Senge, 1990), though it has also generated increasing levels of cynicism (Collins, 1998; Watson, 1994). The argument, in brief, for this approach is that previous attempts to plan the future have either fallen foul of the difficulty of accurately translating past trends into future projections, or have not been ambitious enough because they have allowed future plans to be constrained by present resources (Hamel and Prahalad, 1989). The process of developing an organisation's vision attempts to overcome this by encouraging senior managers to think freely, without considering present resource constraints, about possible futures for their organisation in the long term.

This can produce very ambitious objectives, such as Honda's declaration in the 1960s (when it was barely more than a motorcycle producer little known outside Japan) that it wanted 'to become the second Ford'. The creation of visions is an iterative process whereby options are identified, an initial vision is created, and the gap between this and the present circumstances is identified. Then the organisation considers its strategic options to bridge the gap, and in so doing refines the vision itself. This refining process serves partly to ensure that the vision is discussed widely within the organisation, and to gain employees' commitment to its objectives, thus using the vision as a motivating and guiding force for the organisation. Over time, by this process of revisiting and refining the vision, loose and intangible ideas become transformed in people's minds into an achievable reality. The process can, and in some cases does, eventually encompass everyone in the organisation. Nevertheless, the vision is usually driven, not to say created by, a few senior managers who use the power of their position and strength of their personalities to get others to accept the vision as a beneficial and achievable reality.

The organisational vision can best be described as a beacon shining from a faraway hillside at night that guides travellers to their destination. Travellers can usually only see a few feet ahead but are prevented from getting lost by the beacon. Occasionally the traveller will have to make a detour, or sometimes even reverse course, but this is done in the certain knowledge that they still know where it is that they are travelling to. The concept of the beacon is a useful analogy, in that it highlights one of the main differences between vision-building and other forms of long-range planning. Normally it is only the leadership of an organisation that has a clear view of where the organisation is going in the long term. However, the vision, like the beacon, should shine clearly for everyone in the organisation to see, so that they can all know where they are heading for, and use it to judge the appropriateness of their actions.

Cummings and Huse (1989) developed guidelines to help organisations construct visions. They argue that there are four aspects to constructing a vision:

1 **Mission**. This states the organisation's major strategic purpose or reason for existing. It can indicate such factors as products, markets and core competencies.

2 **Valued outcomes**. Visions about desired futures often include specific performance and human outcomes the organisation would like to achieve. These can include types of behaviour and levels of skill as well as more traditional outcomes such as turnover and profit. These valued outcomes can serve as goals for the change process and standards for assessing progress.

3 **Valued conditions**. This element of creating a vision involves specifying what the organisation should look like to achieve the valued outcomes. These valued conditions help to define a desired future state towards which change activity should move. Valued conditions can include issues relating to structure, culture, openness and managerial style as well as external issues such as relations with customers and suppliers.

4 **Mid-point goals**. Mission and vision statements are by nature quite general and usually need to be fleshed out by identifying more concrete mid-point goals. These represent desirable organisational conditions but lie between the current state and the desired future state. Mid-point goals are clearer and more detailed than desired future states, and thus, they provide more concrete and manageable steps and benchmarks for change.

By constructing a vision in this manner, the organisation not only has a picture of what it wishes to become but also some concrete targets to aim for. In the case of Nissan (Chapter 11), their vision of what they wanted from suppliers and how they preferred to work with them was clear. The actual details had to be worked out as Nissan developed its supplier base. It recognised the need for supplier development; later, it saw that training would also be required; and then it moved on to offer strategy development packages. The point is that visions (and components of visions such as Nissan's vision for its suppliers) identify the intent, and mid-point goals are then needed to help identify a way forward. These goals will periodically have to be renewed and revisited in the light of their achievement or non-achievement, but this is always within the context of the vision. However, the possibility always exists for the process of implementation to cast new lights on the vision itself and cause this to be rethought. Visions are implemented and brought to life, given reality, through the development of strategy.

### Strategy

In the context of a vision, strategy can be defined as a coherent or consistent stream of actions which an organisation takes or has taken to move towards its vision. This stream of actions can be centrally planned and driven, they can be delegated and distributed throughout the organisation, and they can be either conscious actions in pursuit of the vision, or unconscious or emergent ones resulting from past patterns of decisions or resource allocations, or from current responses to problems and opportunities. In reality, organisations tend to pursue a mixture of these. Therefore, there can be a central strategy, sub-strategies and, influenced by the vision and circumstances, a general awareness of the need to act or respond in a particular way.

Such strategies would usually cover marketing, product development, manufacturing, personnel, purchasing, finance, information technology and quality. The characteristics of conscious strategies are that they generally look five years or more ahead, but only contain firm and detailed plans for the next 12 to 18 months (this is because changing circumstances usually prevent most companies from being firm about their intentions for any longer than this). These strategies are put together in one strategic plan which is, usually, formally reviewed annually, but is frequently reviewed informally and when major and unexpected events occur. Because the strategies are not ends in themselves, but means to an end (the vision), they are by necessity both flexible and pragmatic. They should be constructed and pursued only to the extent that they facilitate the pursuit of the vision.

One way of viewing strategy is to see it as a series of links in a chain which stretch from the present to the indeterminate future where the vision lies. Each link in the chain represents particular strategies or groups of decisions that organisations pursue to move themselves forward, in the light of both their eventual target and the prevailing circumstances of the time. The links (strategies) are continually having to be forged and reforged (to use Mintzberg's (1987) term, 'crafted') over time. So strategy contains both Planned and Emergent elements – the exact balance being determined by the circumstances of the particular organisation in question rather than any intrinsic merit of either the Planned or Emergent approach.

One final point: it follows from this that organisations do not need to be able to see all the links in the strategic chain: merely those that will guide them over the next few years. Nor do they need to dictate centrally or identify what should be done and when. Instead, they need to establish both a climate of understanding and a general willingness to pursue certain courses of action, as the opportunity arises or circumstances necessitate.

### Change

Just as an organisation's trajectory is both an important element of the choice process and a process in its own right, the same applies to change. The change process will be discussed below, but in the context of the trajectory process it is necessary to note that, though visions and strategies can be crucial in shaping the life of organisations, it is only when some facet of the organisation is changed or changes that visions and strategies advance from being mere possibilities to become reality. This is also a two-way street. On the one hand, visions and strategies shape and direct change. They indicate what needs to change and where. They also create the conditions and climate within which change takes place. On the other hand, because visions and strategies only become reality through the actions of the organisation, it is these changes, these actions which shape visions and strategies.

In summary, we can see that the trajectory process, whilst playing a key role in shaping choice, is also itself a complex process comprising vision, strategy and change. Though it is difficult to conceive of any organisation that does not possess some elements of all three, the degree to which they are held in common or are consistent with each other or are part of a conscious effort clearly varies. Partly this relates to the circumstances of the organisation. Under conditions of stability and predictability, even without prompting from senior managers, it is much easier for people to develop a common view of how an organisation should operate, what its future should be and what changes need to be made. However, in rapidly changing circumstances, where certainties and fixed points of reference are few and far between, a common understanding is unlikely to arise automatically. Where it does exist, in such situations, it is likely to be outmoded and inappropriate. This is why senior managers more and more are trying consciously to use visions to create a common cause. They want to reduce uncertainty, make sense of what is happening, and create a broad understanding of what needs doing, and how. For many organisations, the merit of this approach is not only that it makes change easier, but that it also allows staff to judge for themselves what changes need to be made and what approach to adopt. In order to explore this further, we can now examine the change process itself.

## The change process

As argued earlier in this chapter, change can be viewed as something to be dealt with on a one-off, issue-by-issue basis or as a continuous process. As the case studies in Part 3 illustrated, where change is dealt with on a one-off basis, organisations tend to have difficulty in choosing the most appropriate approach and there also tends to be no structured, or even informal, procedure for capturing the lessons from one change project and making them available for future projects. In organisations such as Nissan, where change is seen as a continuous process, not only do they have structures and procedures for learning from each change project, but they also have a formalised and documented set of tools, techniques and approaches to change which allows them to select the most appropriate approach for each situation. In such organisations not only is change seen as an everyday event, but the management of it is also seen as a core capability that needs to be developed and in which staff receive training.

In terms of the change process itself, as with the choice and trajectory processes, this comprises three interlinked elements:

- Objectives and outcomes
- Planning the change
- People

### Objectives and outcomes

It was noted in Chapter 7 that a high proportion of change efforts end in failure. Burnes and Weekes (1989) found that, in many cases, change projects failed because their original objectives or the desired outcomes were ill-thought-out and inconsistent. In addition, it was suggested in Chapter 4 that organisational change, because it affects the distribution of power and resources, is an inherently political process driven by sectional interests rather than organisational needs.

Though it is difficult to envisage a situation where political interests are not present, Burnes (1988) suggested an approach to assessing the need for and type of change which attempts to make the process of establishing objectives and outcomes more rigorous and open. Openness and rigour not only make it harder to disguise political considerations, they also allow assumptions regarding the merits (or lack of them) of particular options to be tested. Burnes' approach has four phases – the trigger, the remit, the assessment team and the assessment:

**The trigger**. Organisations should only investigate change (other than relatively minor projects that can be easily accommodated) for one of the following reasons:

- The company's vision/strategy highlights the need for change or improved performance.
- Current performance or operation indicates that severe problems or concerns exist.
- Suggestions or opportunities arise (either from the area concerned or elsewhere) which potentially offer significant benefits to the organisation.

If one or more of the above arises, then this should trigger the organisation to assess the case for change, which leads to the next phase.

**The remit**. This should state clearly the reasons for the assessment, its objectives and timescale, and who should be involved and consulted. The remit should stress the need to focus as much on the people aspects as the technical considerations involved. In addition, it must make clear that those who will carry out the assessment must look at all options rather than merely considering one or two alternatives. Organisations need to be clear who draws up such remits and who has the final say on the assessment team's recommendations. As was shown by Burnes and Weekes (1989), this responsibility is often unclear. In traditional organisations, this responsibility would lie with senior managers. In many of today's organisations, the responsibility for such activities is devolved. However, there is usually a requirement to inform senior managers of change, and certain types of major change remain the responsibility of senior managers. Also, where change affects more than one area or activity, co-ordination between areas will be essential. The important point is that there must be clarity and agreement about who has the responsibility and authority to initiate change before an assessment begins.

**The assessment team**. This is the body who will assess the need for change. In most cases, this should be a multi-disciplinary team consisting of representatives from the area affected (both managers and staff), specialist staff (finance, technical and personnel), and, where appropriate, an outside consultant or change facilitator. It may also require the involvement of senior managers.

**The assessment**. The first task of the assessment team is to review and if necessary clarify or amend its remit. Only then can it begin the assessment, which should comprise the following four steps:

1 **Clarification of the problem or opportunity**. This is achieved by gathering information, especially from those involved. In some situations it might be found that the problem or opportunity is redefined, or does not exist, or can be dealt with easily by those most closely concerned. If so, this is reported back and probably no further action needs to be taken. However, if the clarification reveals that a significant problem or opportunity does exist, then the remaining steps need to be completed.

2 **Investigate alternative solutions**. A wide-ranging examination should take place to establish the range of possible solutions. These should be tested against an agreed list of criteria covering costs and benefits, in order to eliminate those solutions which are clearly inapplicable and to highlight those which appear to offer the greatest benefit. However, it should be recognised that not all changes, particularly those of a strategic nature, can be assessed on purely financial criteria, e.g. Oticon's restructuring and Flair's move into the car industry. In any case, changes rarely have single benefits. For example, a change in technology which brings financial benefits may also offer opportunities to increase team-working and to develop the skill and knowledge base of the organisation. Similarly, though, where there are benefits there are disbenefits. Where new

skills are gained, old ones are discarded. Greater teamworking can threaten the authority of line managers and middle managers. If such disbenefits are to result from change, it is better to recognise this in advance and prepare for them rather than finding out later when the damage is done. This then leads on to the next step.

3 **Feedback**. The definition of the problem or opportunity and the range of possible solutions should be discussed with interested or affected parties, particularly those from whom information was collected in the first place. This helps to counter the tendency to fit solutions to problems, and it also helps to prepare people for any changes that do take place. In addition, it helps to establish the criteria for selecting the preferred solution or solutions.

4 **Recommendations and decision**. The team should present their recommendations in a form that clearly defines the problem/opportunity, identifies the range of solutions, establishes the criteria for selection and makes recommendations. These recommendations should include not only the type of change, but also the mechanics and timescale for making such changes and the resource implications, as well as performance targets for the new operation.

This then leaves those responsible for decision-making in a position to assess, modify, defer or reject the assessment team's recommendations in the light of the vision and strategic objectives of the organisation. Indeed, some change programmes and projects are so complex that it is only possible to judge their worth in relation to an organisation's long-term intent. Such changes are more an act of faith than a racing certainty, though managers may choose to present them as closer to the latter in order to garner support. If the decision is to proceed with the proposed changes, then it becomes necessary to begin planning the implementation process.

### Planning the change

Whether the need for change arises from an organisation's strategy or emerges in some other way, once it has been established that it should take place and what form it should take, it is then necessary to plan how this will be achieved and then to implement the plan. As argued earlier in this chapter and also in Chapter 8, there are many different approaches to change and their appropriateness depends on what is to be changed. As the case studies in Part 3 showed, small-scale, technical changes can usually be planned and executed relatively quickly, and may not require extensive consultation with or the involvement of all the staff affected. However, it can be dangerous to seek to apply this type of approach to larger-scale changes, particularly where people's attitudes and behaviours are the prime object of the change process. Therefore, planning and execution, and consequent development, in such cases can be extensive, span hierarchical levels and horizontal processes and include a high degree of ambiguity. For these reasons, their success will depend, to a large extent, on the involvement and commitment of all those concerned with and affected by it. The range of change situations and approaches, therefore, needs to be borne in mind when considering the following six interrelated activities which make up the planning and change process:

1 **Establishing a change management team**. To maintain continuity, the team should include some, if not all, of those responsible for the original assessment of the need for change. However, it will usually also have a greater user input, especially at the implementation stage. Sometimes, for large change projects, sub-groups responsible for discrete elements of the change programme may be established. These will generally comprise those most closely affected by the changes, both managers and others. Their role is to handle the day-to-day implementation issues. Although it must be recognised that all the people in the change management team, and its sub-groups, are in effect 'change agents', change specialists should also be involved, i.e. people, whether insiders or outside consultants, whose primary input is their experience in managing change. As was discussed in Chapter 8, the role of change agents is not just a technical one concerned with establishing plans and ordering their implementation. Change agents need a wide range of skills, not least of which is what Buchanan and Boddy (1992: 27) refer to as the ability to deploy 'backstage activity':

> 'Backstaging' is concerned with the exercise of 'power skills', with 'intervening in political and cultural systems', with influencing and negotiating and selling, and with 'managing meaning'.

Therefore in choosing members of the change management team, depending on the nature of the change being undertaken, it is especially necessary to ensure that some, if not all, have the requisite 'backstage' skills.

2 **Management structures**. Because larger change projects, especially organisational transitions, are wide-ranging, have multiple objectives and can have a high degree of ambiguity, existing control and reporting systems are unlikely to be adequate for managing them. For example, the more that a change project challenges existing power relations and resource allocation procedures, the more it is likely to encounter managerial resistance. In such cases, unless the change management team has a direct line to, and the public support of, senior managers or the CEO, the change process is likely to become bogged down or even abandoned. Therefore, effective reporting and management structures need to be put in place in advance in order to provide direction, support and resources.

3 **Activity planning**. This involves constructing a schedule for the change programme, citing the main activities and events that must occur if the transition is to be successful. It must be recognised that not all the elements of a large change programme can be planned in detail in advance. Such programmes are by their nature multi-level, multi-stage and can stretch over an extended time-frame. However, as a change programme proceeds, it becomes

possible for successive levels and stages to become clearer and plans more detailed. It follows that, in order to stay on course, activity planning should clearly identify and integrate key change events and stages and ensure they are linked to the organisation's change goals and priorities. Activity planning should also gain top management approval, should be cost-effective, and should remain adaptable as feedback is received during the change process. Activity planning therefore comprises the final and intermediate objectives, and ensures that where and when possible these are tied to a specific timetable in order to avoid uncertainty amongst those who have to carry out the changes.

4 **Commitment planning**. This activity involves identifying key people and groups whose commitment and support is needed for change to occur, and deciding how to gain their support. Designating someone as a key person has less to do with their nominal position or level of authority in an organisation and is more concerned with their ability to block or promote particular changes. This may be because they have power to dispense or withhold specific resources or information, or that others look to them for guidance or leadership, even though they may have no formal role in this respect. It can be seen in the case of Midshires College that the Project Leader appreciated neither the importance of gaining key people's commitment nor the difficulty of achieving it. The Nissan SDT, on the other hand, establishes the support of senior management before beginning and then goes on to win the support of others, in particular by involving them in selecting and planning change. It should be recognised that commitment planning is a fundamental component of the 'backstage' expertise that change agents require.

5 **Audits and post-audits**. It is important to monitor progress and see to what extent objectives are being met. This allows plans to be modified in the light of experience. The more uncertain and unclear the change process, the greater the need for periodic review. After change or when a particular milestone has been passed, a post-audit should be carried out (a) to establish that the objectives have really been met, and (b) to ascertain what lessons can be learned for future projects. Though this sounds straightforward, it rarely is. Large projects, in particular, are collections of a number of relatively smaller sub-projects. These can start at different times and operate at different levels and in different areas of an organisation. Some of these sub-projects will run concurrently, some consecutively and a few may even be largely free-standing. By their nature, they will also be geared to different sub-objectives which may need to be monitored and measured in different ways. Seen in this way, it becomes easier to understand why conducting audits and post-audits, and even day-to-day monitoring of progress, can be exceedingly difficult but is also exceedingly necessary.

6 **Training**. This is a key part of any change project and takes a number of forms. The obvious one is in relation to new skills that might be necessary. However, as the Nissan approach to suppliers shows, training can have a number of other purposes. It may aim to give staff the skills to undertake the change themselves.

It may be the intention to leave them with the ability to pursue continuous improvement, once the change has been substantially achieved, or it may be intended to make them aware of the need for change and to win them over. Also, there is a need to give general awareness training to those in the organisation who might be indirectly affected. Even where the primary objective is to enhance skills, training can also contribute to other objectives, such as culture change, by structuring it in such a way that training promotes teamworking or inter-departmental co-operation. To ensure that the various types of training are targeted at the right people or groups, a training programme – starting before implementation and continuing after completion – should be established, showing who needs training, the form of the training and when it will take place.

Though planning change is in some ways a 'technical' issue, its success is always likely to hinge on an organisation's ability to involve and motivate the people concerned and those whose support is necessary.

### People

As mentioned earlier, organisational change takes many forms. It can be of a structural or technical form which requires little of individuals in terms of behavioural or attitudinal change. On the other hand, as the case studies have shown, increasingly it requires individuals and groups to reconsider radically their attitudes towards how work is performed, and how they behave towards both their colleagues internally and their counterparts externally. However, whatever form it takes, there are three people-related activities that need to be undertaken: creating a willingness to change; involving people; and sustaining the momentum.

**Creating a willingness to change**. Even where change is purely of a technical or structural form, there has to be a willingness amongst those concerned to change; to want to be involved. There are organisations who have put, and are continuing to put, a great deal of effort into creating a climate where change is accepted as the norm (as described in Chapter 9, Oticon and Flair are examples of this). However, perhaps most organisations are still at the stage where they have to convince staff of the need for change. This is especially the case in those organisations where each change project is perceived to be a one-off event.

For many people, organisational change involves moving from the known to the unknown, with the possibility of loss as well as gain. Companies therefore need to create a readiness for change amongst their employees, and adopt an approach which is aware of the possibility and causes of resistance, and deals with these at an early stage. In order to achieve this, there are four steps an organisation can take:

1 **Make people aware of the pressures for change**. The organisation should inform employees on a regular basis of its plans for the future, the competitive/market pressures it faces, customer requirements and the performance of its key

competitors. Obviously, promoting the vision and explaining the strategic plan are vital components in this. Through this approach, members of the organisation come to appreciate that change is not only inevitable, but is being undertaken to safeguard rather than threaten their future. It should also be recognised that in any organisation, department or team there are key individuals who are opinion-formers; people to whom others look for guidance. Therefore, to get the message across successfully, managers must identify who these are and ensure that they not only understand the message being transmitted but will also pass a favourable judgement on it.

2 **Give regular feedback on the performance of individual processes and areas of activity within the organisation**. This allows a company to draw attention to any discrepancy between actual performance and desired present and future performance. It allows those concerned to begin to think about how this situation can be improved, and prepares them for the need for change. In looking at the case study companies, it is noticeable that there was a greater readiness to change in those organisations where management was open about its objectives and the company's or function's current performance than in those organisations where information was guarded. This can clearly be seen by comparing the approach of Nissan's Supplier Development Team with that of the management of Midshires College. In the former, the SDT's openness appeared to encourage change, whilst in the latter, secrecy and uncertainty had the opposite effect.

3 **Publicise successful change**. In order to create a positive attitude towards change, companies should publicise the projects which are seen as models of how to undertake change, and the positive effects change can have for employees. This does not mean that mistakes should be hidden or poor outcomes ignored; these should be examined, explained and lessons learned. However, staff should be encouraged to expect and set credible and positive outcomes for change programmes. Once again, the experience of the case study companies illustrates this point. At Flair, there have now been two decades of successful change, which have produced a positive attitude amongst employees and managers alike. In Midshires, on the other hand, the management and outcome of change led to the demoralisation of both managers and employees.

4 **Understand people's fears and concerns**. One of the major mistakes made by the Project Leader at Midshires was his failure to recognise, and deal with, the real and legitimate fears of the managers and staff in the colleges that were being amalgamated. The fact that the Project failed to address their fears was a key factor in the lack of progress made in amalgamating the colleges. A similar observation could also be made with regard to the PSA's inability to recognise or tackle employee's fears and concerns. Organisations need to recognise that change does create uncertainty and that individuals and groups may resist, or may not fully co-operate with it, if they fear the consequences. In this respect, resistance can be seen as a signal that there is something wrong with the change

process or its objectives rather than with those who are opposing or questioning it. From this perspective, resistance can be viewed as positive: it reminds the organisation that it has not considered all the consequences of its actions, and forces it to review its plans. It follows that those championing change need to pay special attention to the potential for resistance, both in terms of the adverse consequences it can bring and the underlying problems it may indicate.

**Involve people**. Though some change projects can be short-lived and easily achieved, many are not. Achieving a successful change can be and usually is a long and complex task. There will be difficult obstacles to overcome, not all of which can be anticipated in advance. To cope with these, and to develop the momentum necessary to ensure that the project is successful, requires the commitment and support of all concerned, especially those who are most closely affected. In effect, it requires them to take ownership of the process so that it is 'their' project and 'their' success. In most cases this will be difficult to achieve unless they can be involved in its planning and execution. This type of involvement has two main facets:

- **Communication**. One way of avoiding the uncertainty that change can promote is to establish a regular and effective communications process. The purpose of this should be to inform those who will be affected by the change process from the early stages what is happening, how it might or definitely will affect them, and to give them reports on the progress being made. It is important to give both the context for proposed changes, as well as the details and consequences.

  Communication should be a regular rather than a one-off exercise. In some cases, such as the first phase of change at GK Printers where all those affected were involved, this ceases to be an issue. The same can be said of TRW's Frankley assembly operation. However, the small size of the organisations in these instances makes them something of an exception. In most cases, it is impractical to give everyone this level of involvement; therefore, as at Flair and Rover, it is important to communicate proposals from the outset. This involves not only providing information, but also listening to the response and taking it seriously. This has a number of benefits. The change management team will very quickly pick up any worries and concerns and can respond to these; they will also be made aware of aspects that need to be taken into consideration which have been overlooked; and assumptions which have been made will be tested and sometimes challenged.

- **Getting people involved**. Communication does help to overcome fears and does encourage those concerned to assist rather than resist change. However, one of the most vital initiatives an organisation can take with staff is not to treat them as objects of, or obstacles to, change, but to involve them in it and make them responsible for it. Particularly where large-scale projects are concerned, not everyone can be involved in all aspects of planning and execution.

Therefore, it is necessary to have some criteria for selecting who will be involved. Obviously, where it is possible, it is a good idea to ensure that all those most closely affected are involved in some, if not all, aspects. Similarly, again where possible, responsibility for aspects of the change project should be given to those who will be directly affected by the result. However, in many cases the numbers involved will prevent all those affected being involved and, consequently, managers will need to select who to involve. Sometimes, volunteers will be asked for. Sometimes, people who are perceived to have 'the right attitude' will be chosen. On the other hand, Flair found that including sceptics can be useful. This not only ensures that awkward questions are asked but can also, if the sceptic is won over, create a powerful advocate for the change. Likewise, it is useful to consider involving key opinion-formers: people to whom their colleagues look for guidance.

**Sustaining the momentum.** Even in the best-run organisations, it sometimes happens that initial enthusiasm for change wanes and, in the face of the normal day-to-day pressures to meet customer needs, progress becomes slower and can grind to a halt. In organisations which are less well-run, the momentum may not even be present in the beginning. In such situations, people will return to the methods and types of behaviour with which they are familiar. Given that momentum does not arise of itself nor continue without encouragement, organisations need to consider how to build and sustain it. The points already made above regarding planning and implementation, and especially involvement, are clearly part of this. However, in addition, organisations should do as follows:

- **Provide resources for change**. To achieve any change will normally require additional resources, both financial and human. In cases where staff are required to keep up the same level of output during the transition phase, it may require considerable additional resources to achieve this. The 1999 case of the UK's Passport Office, which failed to provide sufficient extra staff during the introduction of a new computer system, is a case in point. Not only did this result in inexcusable delays in issuing passports, but the Passport Office eventually had to provide the extra staff anyway. It is important, therefore, that the need for any extra resources is identified and extra resources allocated, whether for the provision of temporary staff, the training of existing staff, senior management time or whatever. As the example of the Passport Office showed, nothing is guaranteed to be more demoralising than having to make changes without the necessary resources or support.

- **Give support to the change agents**. As Buchanan and Boddy (1992) noted, an enormous responsibility falls upon the change management team. They have not only to plan and oversee the change project, but also to motivate others and deal with difficulties, sometimes very personal problems. However, just as they have to support others, so too must they receive support themselves. Otherwise they may be the ones who become demoralised and lose their ability to motivate others.

- **Develop new competencies and skills.** Change frequently demands new knowledge, skills and competencies. Increasingly, managers are having to learn new leadership styles, staff are having to learn to work as teams, and all are expected to be innovators and improvers. This requires more than just training and re-training. It may also include on-the-job counselling and coaching. Therefore, organisations need to consider what is required, who requires it and – the difficult part – how to deliver it in a way that encourages rather than threatens staff.

- **Reinforce desired behaviour.** In organisations, people generally do those things which bring rewards or avoid criticism. Consequently, one of the most effective ways of sustaining momentum for change is to reinforce the kinds of behaviour required to make it successful. Sometimes this may be monetary, such as increased pay or bonuses to particular types of activity or progress. Sometimes it may be symbolic, such as Oticon's tearing down of walls and elimination of personal desks. Sometimes it may be through recognition, whereby senior managers openly or privately single out individuals or groups for special praise. Such activities are particularly important during the early stages of change, when achieving an identifiable and openly recognised success helps participants develop a positive attitude about the change project.

The actual change process, therefore, is a complex blend of objective-setting, planning and people. With few exceptions, none of these are purely technical exercises. Establishing objectives involves testing assumptions and challenging preconceived ideas. It also involves gathering both fact and opinion, and making judgements about which is the most important. Similarly, planning change often involves an impressive and daunting array of challenges and activities, some of which are amenable to straightforward techniques of analysis and decision, many of which are not. The final element, though, is the most complex: people. People are not just important because they are often the 'object' of change, but also because they are the ones who have to carry it out. In a real sense, they are the glue that holds it together. They can influence the choice of objectives and the way change is planned. In turn, objectives and planning can also affect their willingness to accept or become involved in change.

One final point: even after a change project has been 'completed', the story does not end there. As the Japanese have shown, even when change has resulted in a stable state being achieved, there always remains scope for improvement. However, as is clear from the case studies, many change projects are open-ended. Change will continue to take place. Therefore, both in planning a project and evaluating its outcomes, it is necessary to identify the open-endedness of it, and the degree to which the final outcome will require a continuous improvement approach or a continuing change approach. However, as mentioned earlier, there is a marked difference between organisations where change is seen as an every-day occurrence and those where it is seen as a one-off event. In the latter, it is very difficult to develop the capabilities and commitment necessary to achieve continuous improvement; whereas in the former, continuous improvement and continuous change, and the capabilities, skills and commitment required of both, go hand in hand.

## CONCLUSIONS

This chapter has sought to merge the theory and practice of strategy development and change management as presented in Chapters 5–11. In doing so, it has also drawn on many of the arguments and insights into the behaviour, operation and rationality of organisations presented in Chapters 1–4. Based on these eleven chapters, this chapter introduced and elaborated on the Choice Management–Change Management model for understanding and managing organisational change. This comprised three interrelated organisational processes: the choice process, the trajectory process and the change process (*see* Figure 13.1). It was argued that not only did this model incorporate and go beyond both the Planned and Emergent approaches to strategy and change, but it also demonstrated how managers could attempt to change their organisation's circumstances to fit them to the approach which best suited them and their organisation.

It was asserted that the Choice Management–Change Management model incorporates the full scope of the various approaches to strategy and change, including the Planned and Emergent approaches, and that it also accommodates and explains the use of more directive approaches. However, one of the fundamental differences between this model and many other approaches to strategy and change is that it recognises that managers are active players rather than passive spectators in the development of their own organisations. The model is based on the assumption that not only can managers choose to align their organisation with the external conditions and constraints it faces, but they can also do the reverse and align these external conditions and constraints to their preferred way of structuring and running their organisation. Whether they choose to attempt to influence, alter or align their organisation to the circumstances it faces will depend on a range of issues, not least their own views about whether they or the organisation are better suited by a stable, planned situation or whether more turbulent/emergent conditions are preferable.

Though the Choice Management–Change Management model appears to offer significant theoretical avenues for understanding how organisations and managers operate, it also offers considerable practical benefits as well. In Chapter 3, we examined the Culture–Excellence perspective on organisations. The proponents of this view, especially Tom Peters, argue that organisations have no choice but to change radically if they are to survive. The Culture–Excellence theory is based on a particular view of the environment and other constraints organisations face. Assuming that this view is accurate, the Choice Management–Change Management model indicates that organisations need not radically restructure themselves, but could seek to influence the constraints they face to bring them more in line with their existing organisational arrangements. Even if, in the long term, organisations did have to structure themselves along the lines advocated by Peters, Kanter and Handy, they could still seek to influence the conditions under which they operated to achieve this over a longer timescale than might otherwise be assumed. Indeed, as Chapter 3 revealed, this is just the approach the Japanese take. Between the 1950s and the 1980s, Japan's leading organisations transformed themselves. However, this was achieved by slow and gradual transformation rather than by rapid shock tactics. Japanese companies achieved this gradual transformation by a combination of long-term vision allied to the ability to influence and restructure the constraints under which they operate, especially, as argued by Hamel and Prahalad (1989), their ability to change the rules of competition in their particular industries. In so doing, they provide much support for Kanter *et al*'s (1992) view that a Long March is more effective than a Bold Stroke for building competitive organisations.

Therefore, the Choice Management–Change Management model, in conjunction with the Change Framework presented in Chapter 8, potentially at least, resolves the dispute between proponents of Planned and Emergent approaches to strategy development and change. However, it also raises fundamental questions about what managers *can* do and what they *do* do in terms of running and shaping their organisations. In particular, it raises questions about the way that managers can make sense of their situation for themselves and others and, in so doing, construct alternative scenarios or realities for their organisation's future. Many writers, especially from the Culture–Excellence perspective, have made a case for visionary leadership being the key to an organisation's success. Certainly, the transactional, steady-as-she-goes type of manager is very much out of favour (Kotter, 1996; Peters, 1997a; Senge, 1990). However, the case for transforming managers, as well as organisations, tends to be based on a biased view of what managers need to do and, often, only a shallow understanding of what they actually do. In order to come to grips with the nature of managerial work and the extent to which the Choice Management–Change Management model requires a rethink of how managers operate, the concluding chapter of this book will examine the role of managers.

## TEST YOUR LEARNING

### Short answer questions

1 Briefly describe the choice process.

2 How might a SWOT analysis help an organisation to understand better the context in which it operates?

3 What are the key features of the trajectory process?

4 Describe how an organisation might construct a vision for itself.

5 List the key components of the change process.

6 Discuss the role of the change agent in planning and implementing change.

## Essay questions

1 Critically evaluate the key linkages between the three processes that make up the Choice Management–Change Management model.

2 Use the Choice–Change model to assess one of the ten case studies from Part 3.

# Chapter 14

# MANAGEMENT – ROLES AND RESPONSIBILITIES

**Learning objectives**

After studying this chapter, you should be able to:

1 list the key duties of managers;

2 understand that much of what managers do is reactive and driven by expediency;

3 describe the three main perspectives on leadership;

4 state the strengths and weaknesses of the three perspectives on leadership;

5 identify the primary approaches to managerial development and education;

6 appreciate the need for managers to identify and examine the full range of choices facing them;

7 understand the impact of managers' decisions on society as a whole, and their wider and longer-term responsibilities.

## INTRODUCTION

With the advent of a new millennium, many writers and commentators have felt the urge to provide us with their views on the future. Sometimes these have a postmodern rosy glow about them, whilst often they have painted a gloomy doomsday picture of the future. One thing we do know about attempts to predict the future is that they usually fall very short of the mark. This is no excuse, however, for ignoring the many serious and daunting challenges that organisations and those who manage them, not to mention the world at large, have to face in the decades to come. The globalisation of world trade may open up new markets and create new opportunities, but it also brings with it new competitors and new uncertainties. The same holds true for scientific advance. The beneficial effects of computers are there for all to see, with the range of applications expanding daily. However, advances such as genetically modified crops and even genetically modified human beings are much more controversial and unpredictable. For most of the developed world, the spectre of an increasingly ageing population also looms large. Then there is the reality of global warming, the dwindling of natural resources and the threat to the natural world of indiscriminate industrialisation; we are reminded of these almost daily (Paton *et al*, 1996).

Though we might like to think that the final outcome of many of these developments will be decided by democratically elected governments acting in the best interests of all their peoples, we also know that organisations, driven by market forces, will have a major influence on decisions and decision-makers. As Dunphy and Griffiths (1998: 183) argued in their book *The Sustainable Corporation*:

> There is a widespread view that governments must solve environmental problems. However, the major multinationals outstrip many of the world's national economies in terms of wealth and power, and their global coverage allows them to escape the requirements of particular governments seeking to place severe environmental restrictions on them. They can simply move their operations across national borders. The world's multinationals are in fact more powerful than most national governments.

Nevertheless, nothing is inevitable until it actually happens, and even then it may be reversed. As well as sounding a pessimistic note, Dunphy and Griffiths also sound an optimistic one. They point out that those who run organisations live in the same world as the rest of us, and, to a large extent, experience the consequences of their actions in the same way everyone else does. Therefore, they argue, managers cannot divorce their actions from the wider impact they have on society; nor can they ignore the fact that a sustainable future for their organisations requires a sustainable future for the world. This presents a major challenge for managers, particularly at the senior level. Whilst operating in competitive and hostile markets, they have to marry the desire of their shareholders for increased profit with the need to act in the wider and longer-term interests of society as a whole. They will not achieve this without pressure and support from governments and the force of public opinion. However, as Dunphy and Griffiths (1998) persuasively argue, unless managers accept the challenge and recognise their wider responsibilities, societal pressure alone is unlikely to prove sufficient. To hark back to the discussion of postmodernism in Chapter 4, managers have a choice: they can create a better reality or a worse reality.

This clearly highlights the importance of the manager's role, and of managers' performance. Managers will need to recognise that in the future, as in the past, regardless of the particular issues involved, the environment in which their organisations operate will continue to change. Consequently, managers will continue to have to find ways of ensuring that their organisation and its environment, and the other constraints under which it operates, are, as far as possible, kept aligned. As pointed out in previous chapters, this does not necessarily mean that each and every organisation has to change rapidly and radically, though many will. Instead, managers can seek to influence the constraints under which their organisation operates, and the pace and timing of change, to make them more favourable to their preferred way of working. However, over time, both organisations and their environments will change.

As the case studies in Part 3 have shown, and as most people's everyday experiences confirm, change is neither easy nor necessarily always successful.

However, regardless of this, organisations either by design or default do change, and managers do play a crucial role in determining whether the outcome is success or failure. Managers are the ones who have the responsibility for ensuring that options are identified, choices made and action taken. They are also the ones who have the responsibility for making sense, presenting a coherent picture, of the events and developments that make up an organisation's past, present and potential future. Therefore, in concluding this book, it is only right that we look at how well or not managers are equipped for this task.

The chapter begins by reviewing the literature on what managers are supposed to do and what they really do. This shows that, despite what leading thinkers such as Fayol and Weber believed and advocated, most managers are driven by expediency and operate in a responsive mode. The chapter then moves on to discuss the importance and nature of leadership in organisations. In particular, it seeks to identify the characteristics and contexts that make for effective leadership. Arising from this, the leadership role played by managers in the case studies is explored. This is followed by an examination of the education and development of managers. The chapter and the book conclude by arguing that managers have an important responsibility to identify and exercise choice, when faced with situations which require change. Though choice can be determined on a very narrow basis of short-term financial return, increasingly managers will have to take into account wider organisational and societal factors. Especially important in this respect is that managers should be prepared to question trends and advice which seem designed to increase organisational and societal instability and fragmentation, as the interests of society in general and their own organisations in particular may be better served by seeking stability.

## THE MANAGER'S ROLE

It has never been to easy define the role of managers, though this has not prevented a great number of attempts over the years (*see* Barnard, 1938; Brewer and Tomlinson, 1964; Carlson, 1951; Constable and McCormick, 1987; Handy *et al*, 1987; Horne and Lupton, 1965; Kotter, 1982; Mintzberg, 1973, 1975; Silverman and Jones, 1976; Stewart, 1976). As Hales (1986) found when he reviewed many of these studies, the information available presents the reader with a confusing and conflicting picture of what managers should do and how they should do it.

Definitions of the role of managers have ranged from attempts to list basic tasks:

> [The manager] plans, organises, directs and controls, on proprietors' or own behalf, an industrial, commercial or other undertaking, establishment or organisation, and co-ordinates the work of departmental managers or other immediate subordinates.
> (Quoted in Dakin and Hamilton, 1990: 32)

to more ambitious attempts to define the essence of the manager's role:

> [The manager has the] task of creating a true whole that is larger than the sum of its parts, a productive entity that turns out more than the sum of the resources put into it.
> (Drucker 1985: 53)

Drucker (1985) also likened the manager to the conductor of a symphony orchestra. As conductor, the manager is the one through whose effort, vision and leadership the various instrumental parts, that are so much noise by themselves, become the living whole of music. In this instance, the manager is also the composer as well as the conductor.

Handy (1986), on the other hand, likened the manager to a doctor: the manager is the first recipient of problems. The manager's role is, therefore, to identify the symptoms in any situation; to diagnose the disease or cause of the trouble; to decide how it might be dealt with, through a strategy for health; and to start the treatment.

Such analogies are useful in that they create a concrete picture of the manager's role, but they can also be misleading. Conducting is an art form; is management an art form? Or, as Handy's analogy implies, is it a science in the same way that medicine is a science? As Part 1 of this book showed, the clash between those who see management as a rational, science-based process, and those who believe it to be more intuitive and less rational, is not new.

Duncan (1975) tried to resolve this conflict by taking a holistic view of the job of the manager. He identifies three distinct levels of management activity: *philosophical* (goal formation); *scientific* (goal accomplishment and evaluation); and *art* (implementation of decisions). At the philosophical level in forming goals, the manager – Duncan argues – is mainly concerned with the effects of the actions and reactions of other individuals and groups within the wider economic and social context within which the organisation is set. At this level, managers and their associates formulate clear and precise strategies that will encompass all envisaged effects that can result from the set goals, not only on the various pressure groups within its internal and external environment, but also on competitors and regulatory agencies. It is also at this level that the ethics of managerial behaviour, values and priorities of the organisation are formulated and established. At the scientific level, management develops plans, methods and techniques for achieving set goals, and establishes procedures for monitoring and evaluating progress.

The art level is concerned with the implementation of decisions; this is the level at which tactical and administrative decisions are made to deploy the organisation's resources and attain the optimum degree of operational efficiency. This level is an 'art' because, according to Duncan, there appears to be a particular talent necessary to persuade others that management-generated goals and decisions should be accepted.

Whilst one might not necessarily agree with his definitions, especially in terms of strategy formulation, Duncan's three-level approach is extremely useful in that it shows, as Mullins (1989) argued, that management is both a science and an art. By its very nature, management is forced to deal with both rational, science-based activities, such as the design and operation of manufacturing and administrative systems, and less rational, more intuitive activities, especially those concerning managing and motivating people. The extent to which a manager is involved in any of these activities, however, will depend on the kind of organisation the manager works for, the type of job the manager has, and crucially the manager's level in the organisation's hierarchy (Hales, 1986). Position in the hierarchy, formally at least, is likely to exert the greatest influence on the role given to and expected of a manager. The three main hierarchical levels are as follows:

- *Top management*: the policy-making group responsible for the overall direction of the company.

- *Middle management*: responsible for the execution and interpretation of policies throughout the organisation and for the successful operation of assigned divisions or departments.

- *First level or supervisory management*: directly responsible to the middle management group for ensuring the execution of policies by their subordinates. They are also responsible for the attainment of objectives by the units they control, through practices and procedures approved and issued by top or middle management.

Superficially, at least, these three categories appear to mirror Duncan's three levels. However, on a closer examination, it becomes more difficult to match them because each category can encompass all three levels. This can be seen more clearly by examining what it is that managers actually do, as averse to what academics say they should do.

There have been a number of important studies conducted to determine how managers spend their time (*see* for example Brewer and Tomlinson, 1964; Child and Ellis, 1973; Kotter, 1982). Perhaps the most widely known and replicated work in this area is by Mintzberg (1973, 1975). Synthesising his results and the previous research on the role of managers, he concluded as follows:

- Although much managerial work is unprogrammed, all managers do have regular, ordinary duties to perform.

- Rather than being systematic, reflective thinkers and planners, managers simply respond to the pressures or demands of their jobs.

- Managerial activities are characterised by brevity, variety and discontinuity.

- Managers' jobs are remarkably similar and their work can be described in terms of three very important roles: interpersonal, informational and decision-making.

### Interpersonal roles

One of the most time-consuming and important aspects of most managerial jobs is to work with, direct and represent people. The three key functions in this respect are as follows:

- **figurehead** – as the formal representative of the organisation;

- **liaison** – forming connections with other organisations;
- **leader** – in relation to members of a group within the organisation.

### Informational roles

Those in managerial positions have unique opportunities to obtain and disseminate information. The three key functions involved are given below:

- **monitor** – as monitors, managers seek, receive and store information that can be used to the advantage of the company;
- **disseminator** – the manager must broadcast this useful information to the organisation;
- **spokesperson** – on behalf of the organisation, the manager communicates information to other relevant groups and bodies, both internal and external.

### Decision-making roles

One of the main parts of any manager's job is to take decisions. In this respect, there are four key functions involved:

- **entrepreneur** – looking for ways to improve the operation of the organisation or for new product/market opportunities;
- **disturbance-handler** – managers must handle crises effectively;
- **resource allocator** – responsible for constructing budgets and allocating resources;
- **negotiator** – according to Mintzberg, managers spend a great deal of their time as negotiators, because only they have the necessary information and the authority to carry out this role.

Mintzberg (1975) argued that the lack of uniformity within managerial jobs can be accounted for by hierarchical and functional differentiation. He contended that chief executives, for example, focus considerable attention on external roles, such as liaison, spokesperson and figurehead, which link the organisation to its environment. At lower levels, work is more focused, more short-term in outlook, and the characteristics of brevity and fragmentation are more pronounced. As a result of this, the external managerial roles are less important, and real-time internal roles (disturbance-handler and negotiator) concerned with daily operating problems and maintaining the work flow become relatively more important. Furthermore, he argued that interpersonal roles are more important to sales managers, that staff managers give more attention to informational roles, and production managers focus on decisional roles. Mintzberg's observations have been supported by a number of other studies (Kotter, 1982; Silverman and Jones, 1976; Stewart, 1976).

Hales (1986: 102), in reviewing the research on the manager's role, concluded that:

> Much of what managers do is, of necessity, an unreflective response to circumstances. The manager is less a slow and methodical decision maker, more a 'doer' who has to react rapidly to problems as they arise, 'think on his feet', take decisions in situ and develop a preference for concrete activities. This shows in the pace of managerial work and the short time span of most activities . . .

Therefore, in examining the role of managers, it can be seen that there is a discrepancy between what the literature says managers should do and what the managers actually do. Indeed, as Mintzberg (1975: 49) pointed out, this discrepancy even extends to managers' own observations on their role:

> If you ask a manager what he does, he will most likely tell you he plans, organizes, co-ordinates and controls. Then watch what he does. Don't be surprised if you can't relate what you see to those four words.

Nevertheless, regardless of the difficulty in identifying what managers do or how they should do it, there is a strong tradition in the literature on organisations that it is a manager's leadership ability, especially in situations of change and crisis, which is the crucial attribute (Yukl, 1994). However, as the following shows, leadership is a nebulous concept.

## MANAGEMENT AND LEADERSHIP

It has been a long-held belief that the major factor which distinguishes successful organisations from their less successful counterparts is the presence of dynamic and effective leadership (Yukl, 1994). Though the literature suggests that an organisation's strategy is not always driven by senior managers (*see* Chapter 5), it is certainly the case that they are held responsible for success or failure. They are the people who are formally charged with taking decisions, directing others and creating a framework of rules, systems and expectations within which the organisation operates.

Given the importance of leadership, therefore, it is surprising to find that it is such an elusive concept. Even in the 1950s, when there had been much less research on the subject than now, Bennis (1959: 259) commented, 'Always it seems that the concept of leadership eludes us or turns up in another form to taunt us again with its slipperiness and complexity. So we have invented a proliferation of terms to deal with it . . . and still the concept is not sufficiently defined.' Now, at the beginning of the third millennium, we are faced with a greater proliferation of articles and books on the subject than ever before, yet the topic is more fragmented than ever. However, it is possible to separate leadership theorists into three main groups: those who focus on the personal characteristics and process of leadership; those who concentrate on the leader–follower situation; and those who attempt to relate leadership styles to the overall organisation context and climate.

## The personal characteristics approach to leadership

Early investigations into leadership tended to concentrate on such factors as personal qualities (intelligence, age, experience), or personality traits (extroversion, dominance). Consequently, regardless of the task or situation, if a person did not possess the appropriate personal attributes, then he or she was deemed unlikely to be a good leader. However, the numerous studies of leadership failed to reveal any consistent pattern of traits or characteristics related to leadership (Arnold *et al*, 1998; Gibb, 1969; Yukl, 1994).

In an effort to breathe new life into this approach, attempts were made to view leadership as a process, and the focus moved to examining the interaction between leaders and followers, and how leaders influence individuals and groups to pursue the achievement of a given goal. This view, that leadership behaviour rather than attributes may more effectively predict leadership success, has been advanced in a variety of approaches. Fleishman (1953, 1969) identified two separate classes of behaviour as important in determining effective leadership:

1 *Consideration* – the quality of the interpersonal relationship between the leader and his or her subordinates, and in particular the degree to which a leader shows trust of subordinates, respect for their ideas and consideration for their feelings.

2 *Initiating structure* – the degree to which leaders define and structure their own and their subordinates' roles towards achieving set goals. It also covers the extent to which a leader directs group activities through planning, communication, information, scheduling, trying out new ideas, and praise and criticism.

Another related dimension of leadership behaviour which received much attention in the 1950s and 1960s was participation – whether the leader leans towards an autocratic or democratic style of management. As was noted in Chapters 2 and 7, both the Human Relations school and proponents of Planned change believed that, in the aftermath of the Second World War, participation and democracy would prove to be essential components of organisational effectiveness. Therefore it is not surprising that those studying leadership at the same time should also develop an interest in this topic. According to Gastil (1994), there are three key elements of democratic leadership:

- maximising participation and involvement of group members;
- empowerment;
- facilitating group decision-making.

In the 1950s and 1960s, this stress on leadership characteristics gave rise to a number of 'universal theories' of effective leader behaviour – which is to say, researchers began to argue for a 'one best way' approach to leadership (*see* for example Argyris, 1964; Likert, 1967; McGregor, 1960). These theories postulated that the same style of leadership is optimal in all situations (Yukl, 1994).

Perhaps the best known and most influential of these 'universal theories' is Blake and Mouton's (1969) Managerial Grid. Their grid has two critical dimensions:

*concern for people* – similar to *consideration*; and *concern for production* – similar to *initiating structure*. By examining how these two dimensions interact, in both their strong and weak states, Blake and Mouton identified four different styles of management, which they labelled as follows:

- **Team management**. This arises from a high concern for people and a high concern for production. The objectives are to achieve high levels of both performance and job satisfaction by gaining subordinates' willing commitment to achieving their assigned tasks.

- **Country club management**. This occurs when concern for production is low but concern for people is high. The main concern of this approach is to achieve the harmony and well-being of the group in question by satisfying people's social and relationship needs.

- **Task management**. This can be defined as a high concern for production but a low concern for people. The objective is to achieve high productivity by planning, organising and directing work in such a way that human considerations are kept to a minimum.

- **Impoverished management**. This ensues from a low concern for both production and people. This form of managerial behaviour centres on exacting the minimum effort from subordinates in order to achieve the required result.

Though Blake and Mouton (1969) identify these four forms of management, for them the most effective is team management, where leaders are both task- and people-orientated – the so-called 'high–high' leader. However, despite the wide number of studies seeking to test and elaborate this concept, the evidence in support of it, or for any of the universal theories, is limited (Evans, 1970; Filley *et al*, 1976; Larson *et al*, 1976; Wagner, 1994; Yukl, 1994). Because of the difficulty of relating leadership traits and behaviours to effectiveness, many writers turned to looking at the relationship between leaders and their subordinates.

## The leader–follower situation approach

In response to the inability of researchers to make a convincing case for a 'one best way' approach to leadership, attention began to focus on identifying the situations in which leaders were effective. Kerr *et al* (1974) took the two forms of leadership behaviour identified by Fleishman (1969) – consideration and initiating structure – and applied these to a framework that included three situational variables or contingencies:

1 *Subordinate Considerations* – such as the subordinates' experience and abilities, and their expectations of the leader.

2 *Superior Considerations* – in particular, the amount of influence subordinates have over the behaviour of their superiors.

3 *Task Considerations* – including factors such as time urgency, amount of physical danger, permissible error rate, presence of external stress, degree of autonomy and scope, importance and meaningfulness of work, and degree of ambiguity.

Kerr *et al* (1974) argued that the effectiveness of the two forms of leadership behaviour (consideration and initiating structure) in promoting high levels of performance from subordinates is moderated by the three situational variables. For example, if the task to be performed is characterised by time pressure, subordinates will be more amenable to a higher level of initiating structure (i.e. direction by superiors) and there will be a stronger relationship between job satisfaction, performance and initiating structure. Alternatively, when a task is seen as intrinsically very satisfying to a subordinate, a leadership style with high consideration will not significantly increase satisfaction or performance. Support for the central premises of Kerr *et al*'s (1974) model has been limited. Research by Schriesheim and Murphy (1976) produced mixed results. There was evidence that high levels of initiating structure did increase performance in high-pressure situations and reduce it under low levels of pressure. However, different levels of pressure did not appear to impact on subordinates' satisfaction with their superiors. Nor, where tasks were viewed as having higher clarity, were either consideration-based or initiating structure-based styles significantly related to satisfaction.

The most influential situational theory of leadership has been Fiedler's (1967) Least Preferred Co-worker (LPC) model. Based on a decade of research, Fiedler argued that leaders have relatively stable personal characteristics which, in turn, leave them with a particular set of leadership behaviours which they cannot change. Therefore, there is no point in trying to train or educate managers to adopt different behaviours towards their subordinates. Instead, both they and their subordinates have to learn to live with the leader's behaviour. For Fiedler, the key personal characteristics involved in leadership concern how positively or not the leader views his or her Least Preferred Co-worker. Fiedler developed a questionnaire to determine a leader's LPC measure. The questionnaire is built around a scale of 16 bi-polar adjectives (e.g. pleasant–unpleasant, distant–close, efficient–inefficient) which purports to measure whether a person is 'task' or 'relationship' orientated. As Arnold *et al* (1998) note, there is some dispute about exactly what a leader's LPC score means and how it relates to other leadership dimensions such as consideration and structure. In general, leaders with a high LPC are often seen as being people- or relationship-orientated, whilst those with a low LPC are seen as being task-orientated. From his work, Fiedler concluded that the effectiveness of particular leadership traits or behaviours, as measured by a high or low LPC score, are moderated by the situation in which they are deployed. Therefore, it is important to match the leader to the situation (Fiedler and Chemers, 1984). Fiedler identified three key aspects of a work situation which taken together, he argued, determined the effectiveness or not of particular leadership characteristics. In descending order of importance, these are as follows:

1 *The leader–follower relationship* – friendliness and loyalty from subordinates increases the leader's influence over them.

2 *Task structure* – the greater the degree of standardisation, detailed instructions and objective measures of performance, the more favourable the situation for the leader.

3 *The leader's formal position and power* – the more discretion and authority the leader has regarding the reward and punishment of subordinates, the more influence he or she will be able to exert.

By attributing a high or low score to each of these three aspects, Fielder constructed eight (i.e. $2 \times 2 \times 2$) types of work situation. He maintained that the most favourable situation is where leader–follower relations are good, the task is well-defined and highly structured, and the leader has a high level of formal authority. In contrast, the least favourable situation is where leader–follower relations are poor, the task structure is ill-defined, and the leader has only a low level of formal authority.

Although (or perhaps because) it is the most influential and widely utilised situational theory of leadership, it is also the most widely criticised. The main criticisms are that it lacks empirical support, that it fails to explain how particular leadership behaviour affects subordinates' performance, and that the measures used by Fiedler are arbitrary and lack any explicit rationale (Ashour, 1973; Shiflett, 1973; Vecchio, 1983). Fiedler's model has also been subjected to the same type of criticism as other contingency/situational approaches (*see* Chapter 2). In particular, critics maintain that it ignores a manager's ability to change or influence factors such as task structure to favour their style of leadership. In this respect, a number of writers have pointed out that Fiedler treats structure, an important component of his model, as a given, whereas in many instances, determining and changing organisation and job structures is a major component of a manager's role (O'Brien and Kabanoff, 1981). In any case, as the following shows, there are those who believe that managers can and do change their leadership behaviours (Vroom and Jago, 1988).

## The contextual approach to leadership

One of the weaknesses of the leadership literature is, as the above demonstrates, that it tends to concentrate on the traits of individual managers and their relations with subordinates. The assumption, both explicit and implicit, is that effectiveness is an attribute of the individual manager, moderated by the leader–subordinate situation; a good manager in one organisation will be a good manager in all organisations. Yet, as Burnes (1991) and Hales (1986) argued, a manager's effectiveness may be determined as much by the nature of the organisation in which he or she operates as by the qualities of the individual manager.

It is out of and in response to such observations that the contextual approach to leadership developed. This approach is a variant of the leader–follower approach to leadership; however, instead of concentrating on leadership behaviour, it focuses on leadership style, and instead of the narrow leader–follower situation, it focuses on the overall organisation context and climate. In addition, it is the only one of the three approaches to leadership that incorporates change as a variable. One of the most influential contingency approaches to leadership was developed by Vroom and Yetton (1973). This was later extended by Vroom and Jago (1988). In contrast to Fielder, this approach suggests that leaders can and do change their behaviour from situation to situation. The theory identifies five styles of leader decision-making, ranging from the most autocratic to the most democratic. To complement these, Vroom and Jago (1988) also identified some key features of problem situations which leaders have to take into account, such as the need to resolve conflict or achieve goal congruence. By combining leadership styles with problem situations, Vroom and Jago developed a computer package to help managers to identify how suitable or not their style is for particular situations. Nevertheless, it is a very complex package and Vroom and Jago have expressed the hope that knowledge of its general principles may be sufficient for most situations. To this end, as Arnold *et al* (1998) note, Vroom and Jago's model has been used to provide some general 'rules of thumb' for leaders. However, as the following examples show, these may be too general to be of much use:

- Where subordinates' commitment is important, a more participative style of leadership is better.

- Where subordinates do not share the organisation's goals, group decision-making should be avoided.

Even if they were not so general, these rules of thumb are still subject to being overridden by factors such as time constraints or the development needs of managers and subordinates. This is perhaps why other contextual approaches have also been put forward.

One of the most interesting and influential of these was developed not by a social scientist but by a political scientist, James MacGregor Burns, in his 1978 Pulitzer Prize winning book, *Leadership*. Burns' book combines biography, history and political theory to produce a major study of the nature of leadership. Primarily, he identifies two basic organisation states or contexts, convergent and divergent; and two matching leadership styles, transactional and transformational.

A *convergent* state occurs when an organisation is operating under stable conditions; where there are established and accepted goals and a predictable external and internal environment. The most appropriate style of management in such a situation, it is contended, is *transactional*. Transactional managers concentrate on optimising the performance of the organisation through incremental changes within the confines of existing policy, structures and practices – basically, they seek to work within and maintain the status quo.

A *divergent* state occurs when environmental changes challenge the efficiency and appropriateness of an organisation's established goals, structures and ways of working. The most appropriate style of leadership in this situation, it is argued, is *transformational*. Transformational leaders are seen as being opposed to the status quo; they aim to change their followers' behaviour and beliefs and unite them behind a new vision of the organisation's future.

The compatibility between organisational state and leadership style is seen as essential for successful leadership. Where the organisation is required to face new challenges and develop new ways of adapting to these for the sake of survival, then a purely transactional approach would be counter-productive – the phrase 'fiddling while Rome burns' springs to mind. However, transformational leadership is just as likely to be counter-productive during periods where maintenance of the current operational systems would be most appropriate.

Since its publication, Burns' work has been taken up and cited by a wide range of organisation theorists who subscribe to the view that managers need to, and can, match or adapt their style and approach to the circumstances of the organisation in which they operate (Arnold *et al*, 1998; Beatty and Lee, 1992; Burnes and James, 1995; French and Bell, 1995; Gibbons, 1992; Yukl, 1994). Nevertheless, as can be seen, the contextual approach does not seek to invalidate either the characteristics or situational approaches; rather it tries to incorporate them within and link them to the wider organisational context. It explicitly recognises that a manager's personal characteristics are an important component of leadership style, and consequently, effectiveness. In addition, it acknowledges the crucial importance not just of the relationship between leaders and followers, but also of the overall context within which this takes place (Burns, 1978). In particular, as Gibbons (1992: 5) remarked, 'organizational survival and success are dependent on the ability of leader–follower relations to resolve the problems of internal integration and external adaptation'. However, it should be noted that, despite its attractiveness, as Arnold *et al* (1998) argue, there is little evidence to prove that the contextual approach to leadership is superior to either of the other two approaches.

Despite this criticism, Kanter (1989) developed a similar leadership style categorisation to Burns (1978). She argued that archetypal images of managers tend to derive from two basic models: the 'corpocrat' (i.e. the transactional manager) and the 'cowboy' (i.e. the transformational manager). The former is the corporate bureaucrat, the conservative resource-preserver who lives by, and controls the organisation through, established and detailed rules. The latter, the 'cowboy', is a maverick who challenges the established order, who wants to seize every opportunity, question every rule and who motivates and controls through personal loyalty. However, instead of arguing that there is a need to relate these two approaches to their appropriate organisational setting, Kanter (1989: 361) argues that, in future, organisations will require managers who combine the best of both the corpocrat and cowboy:

> Without the bold impulses of the take-action entrepreneurs and their constant questioning of the rules, we would miss one of the most potent sources of business revitalization and development. But without the discipline and coordination of conventional management, we could find waste instead of growth, unnecessary risk instead of revitalization.

In effect, Kanter is attempting to turn the leadership debate full circle and make the case for a universal – one best way – approach to leadership. Her argument, as mentioned in Chapter 3, is basically that all organisations operate in the same turbulent context, face the same challenges and, consequently, require the same style of management.

Just as a review of the role of managers produced a confusing and conflicting picture, so too appears to be the case when we look at the three approaches to leadership. Nevertheless, the idea of considering context and style together does fit in, partly at least, with the argument developed in the previous parts of this book; namely that there is a need to match the approach to change to the context of the organisation. That argument was developed further to include the possibility that managers could reverse this process and match the organisation's context to their preferred style of working. However, one major factor needs to be remembered: most of the research and writing on leadership is set in Western, and particularly American, organisations, and addresses their concerns. As discussed in Chapter 3, Hofstede's (1980, 1990) work on cultural differences has shown that organisational culture, and the values and behaviours of managers, do vary from country to country. Arnold *et al* (1998) maintain that there is also sufficient evidence to show that leader behaviour is interpreted differently in different cultures. Consequently, managerial behaviour that might be considered supportive in one society may be seen as threatening in another. Therefore, we have to be very wary of taking work on managerial styles and behaviour developed in one setting, and assuming it applies to all organisations and all societies.

Nevertheless, though the style–context approach to leadership is as open to criticism as any of the other approaches – especially regarding a lack of empirical support (*see* Yukl, 1994) – it does offer a useful categorisation for analysing the behaviour of the managers in the ten case studies in Part 3. By establishing whether their approach was transactional or transformational and the context convergent or divergent, it becomes possible to judge not only the appropriateness of their behaviour in the situation in which they were operating, but also the usefulness of the contextual approach to leadership.

## LEADERSHIP IN ACTION

If we examine the case studies in Part 3, we find that managers and the context within which they operated varied enormously. Merely analysing what managers did in each situation, interesting though it would undoubtedly prove, is to produce more heat than light. However, using the transactional–transformational and convergent–divergent categorisation identified above, allows a clearer picture to develop. Taking the case studies in order:

**Oticon**. There is little doubt that the company's Chief Executive exhibited transformational qualities and that it was operating in a divergent environment.

However, it should be noted that, for the first two years of his appointment, the Chief Executive operated within the same industrial and organisational mould as his predecessors. It was only then that he recognised the limitations of continuing to attempt to improve incrementally an organisation that was out of step with its environment and competitors. His response was to change the internal organisation of the company, not to align it with the external environment, but in an attempt to change that as well, by changing the rules of the game in his industry.

**Flair.** At one level this is a similar story to Oticon – a company in decline appoints a new Managing Director who transforms its fortunes. Certainly there is little doubt that the company operated in a divergent environment, and that the Managing Director was in the transformational mould. However, it could be assumed, because he was promoted, that the Managing Director had operated successfully as a transactional manager before seeing the need to change. The process of transformation was slow and emergent; he was not seeking to realign the company with its environment, but instead, he wanted to build a new company in a new environment.

**PSA.** The way in which the privatisation of the PSA was conducted appears to be a classic case of a situation requiring transformational leadership undertaken by managers operating in a transactional mode. The move from the public to the private catapulted the PSA from a convergent to a divergent state, and though there was a recognition of this from both managers and staff, the latter did not want it and the former appeared unable to adjust to it (and probably did not want it either). However, when the PSA was eventually privatised, the new management of the companies, and indeed most of their employees, did appear to recognise the need to manage and operate in a more transformational mode if they were to survive.

**Midshires College.** In many respects, the Midshires story is similar to the PSA's. This was very much a case of an organisation in a divergent state being managed by a transactional manager. The result of this mismatch was that the organisation failed to change and the Project Leader became increasingly ineffective. Even when he had been replaced, what followed seemed very much in the transactional mode and very much brought about by force of circumstances rather than any real vision for the organisation's future.

**Volvo.** Though there have been considerable changes at Volvo, it is not easy to place either the organisation or its leadership on the convergent–divergent, transactional–transformational scale. For example, in the early 1970s, Volvo diverged from the expectations of Swedish society in terms of Job Design, but was very much convergent with the rest of the car industry. Similarly, though Volvo transformed the way it assembled cars and made other significant structural changes, it does not appear to have reinvented itself in the way that, for example,

Honda or Toyota did. However, what is clear is that the way Volvo now assembles cars, and the ethos it has tried to promote in the organisation, is very divergent to that of its new owners, Ford. It will therefore be interesting to see how or whether the Ford and Volvo managements seek to resolve this difference.

**Rover**. This was a company that was in a state of almost terminal divergence in the late 1970s. Through a series of major initiatives, the early phases of which could be classed as transactional, the organisation was to a large extent transformed. In the process, successive waves of new senior managers were brought into the company, each one of whom appeared to be more transformational than the last. However, the continuity of ideas and developments appeared to come to an end with the takeover of Rover by BMW. In particular, the Rover approach, whatever its merits or drawbacks, appeared to be out of step with the beliefs and practices of BMW. Therefore, a period of divergence set in which, because it was not resolved, led to the decision by BMW to break up and sell Rover.

**GK Printers**. Certainly the company can be characterised as one which was out of step with its environment. Though initial changes appeared to be transformational, it was only later, when the organisation came to tackle internal relationships and managerial behaviour, that a more genuinely transformational approach to the company began to emerge.

**Rover–TRW**. This was very much a case of operational transformation which was not matched with significant changes at more senior levels in either organisation. Undoubtedly, the way that the TRW managers at Frankley established and continuously improved the assembly operation, and the way they developed a new working relationship with Rover's assembly line personnel, was transformational. However, the behaviour of senior managers in both companies appeared to be very much fixed in a transactional and antagonistic mode, in part at least because the overall climate was more convergent than divergent.

**Nissan**. This is an instance of a company which, starting from a clean sheet, tried to develop a relationship with its suppliers which broke with past UK traditions. However, Nissan was attempting to transform its suppliers in order to align their practices and values with its own. Therefore, in order to create convergence, Nissan had to adopt a transformational approach towards managing them.

**Speedy Stationers**. In this case, the company was trying to develop a new business area which could not be approached or managed in the same way as its existing business. However, it eventually chose to isolate the new business from its existing activities. This allowed it to pursue a transformational approach to the new business, whilst allowing its existing business, which was operating in a more convergent climate, to be managed as before. It also enabled it to limit the transformation of external relationships to the new business customers.

As can be seen, the case studies show a very diverse range of approaches, situations and outcomes. They also show the limitations of attempting to apply simple definitions to complex situations. The categorisation of leadership types and organisational states are useful in situations where a clear and relatively unambiguous picture of events is possible, such as in the case of Oticon, Midshires College and the PSA. However, in many of the cases – Volvo, GK Printers and Rover–TRW – the picture is less clear. Elements of divergence exist, but these appear to be limited to certain areas of their environment or to change over time. Because of this, managers can be required to exhibit both transactional and transformational qualities either at the same time or in turn. As Midshires College and the PSA showed, not all managers are capable of doing this. In addition, the case studies also show instances where managers attempted to alter their environment to limit the need for internal changes and to bring it into line with their preferred style of management.

Though the evidence from the case studies fits in with the general literature on managers' activities, which sees these as fragmented, lacking in consistency and reactive, it does appear to contradict leadership theory, which tends to value consistency of approach. The picture that emerges from the case studies is one where effective managers are required to possess and utilise a wide range of skills and attributes depending upon the situation and context. Effective managers must be capable, often at the same time, of being both transactional and transformational, given that the environmental pressures and other constraints do not appear to affect all parts of an organisation in the same manner nor at the same time. In particular, as Thompson (1967) remarked in relation to Contingency Theory (*see* Chapter 2), some organisations do at least seem adept at sealing off their productive cores from environmental uncertainty whilst other functions are more directly affected. The result is that managers can be required to adopt distinct approaches towards managing different parts of the same organisation. Despite what the contextual approach to leadership maintains regarding the ability of managers to change their leadership style, this 'Jekyll and Hyde' view of management raises important questions about how managers can be prepared and developed to cope with situations where they might have to maintain some parts of their organisation on a transactional basis, whilst rebuilding other parts in a transformational style and, at the same time, be attempting to influence constraints either to prevent, reduce or even promote the need for transformational change. In order to address this question, the next part of this chapter will discuss management development.

## MANAGERIAL LEARNING AND ADAPTATION

Like the literature on management and leadership, the case studies give some support for the notion that different situations require different approaches from managers. They also show that managers are, sometimes at least, required to move from a transactional to a transformational approach or even exhibit both approaches to different parts of their organisations at the same time. This is consistent with the arguments in Chapters 12 and 13, that managers can and do adopt both the Planned and Emergent approaches to strategy and change management simultaneously. In addition, the case studies show that managers, not necessarily by conscious design, create situations where the context in which their organisations operate is changed to suit their preferred or existing approach to both management and change. As argued in Chapters 12 and 13, changing the situational context can be very important; yet in terms of leadership roles and managerial expectations, the main finding from the case studies is the apparent ability of some managers not only to adapt their style to the particular situation, but also to adopt transactional and transformational approaches at the same time. However, the case studies also show that some managers have great difficulty in changing their leadership approach or influencing their circumstances.

In part at least, the argument that there are managers who can change their style of leadership runs counter to some of the literature on managerial learning discussed in Chapter 8. Miller (1993: 119) argued that as they gain experience, managers 'form quite definite opinions of what works and why'. This view was supported by earlier work from Nystrom and Starbuck (1984) who maintained that managers interpret the world through their own perceptions and expectations, which are built up over time. Yet, as illustrated, some managers do seem capable, under certain conditions – especially when a crisis is looming or imminent – of restructuring their mental models of how the world is and how they should respond. In Chapter 12, the concept of Cognitive Dissonance was used to explain why it was that employees could, in crisis situations, support radical change without involvement. However, this does not help to explain how some managers, in situations necessitating organisational change, can shift their mental model from a transactional to a transformational one or, indeed, become capable of adopting both at the same time.

The work of Mintzberg (1976) offers some clues as to how managers might accomplish this mental juggling act. In studying brain functions and successful managers, he concluded that effective and proficient managers are 'whole thinkers' – they use both the left and the right hemispheres of their brain. That is, they can combine a rational-analytical approach to management with creativity and lateral thinking. However, Mintzberg argued that, in general, Western managers tend to think on the left side of their brain – they tend to adopt a rational-analytical approach. Interestingly, this is compatible not only with a transactional approach to management, but also with the Planned approach to strategy and change.

In contrast, Nonaka (1991) argued that one of the great strengths of Japanese companies is that, whilst Western managers place great emphasis on scientific and quantifiable knowledge, Japanese managers believe that creating new knowledge depends more on tapping the tacit and often subjective insights and intuitions of employees. He maintains that traditional Western management sees organisations as information processing machines with the only useful knowledge being formal, scientific and rational. He contends that such a perspective limits the creation of new knowledge which, in turn, makes it difficult for organisations to respond to changing and new situations. He argues that new knowledge always begins with the individual. One of the main foundations of the success of Japanese companies is, he states, managers' ability to gather and combine the insights and intuitions of individual employees and use them for the benefit of the entire organisation. The tendency of Japanese managers to use softer, more creative approaches and to involve staff in decision-making was also noted in Chapters 5 and 6 when discussing approaches to strategy.

The case studies, and the success of many Western firms, particularly those concerned with creative processes (such as software development) and the performing arts (such as film-making), show that it is not inevitable that Western managers should operate solely in a rational-analytical mode. However, Hofstede's (1980, 1990) work on national cultures does reveal a predisposition in Western societies towards this way of working. Also, as Miller (1993) points out, a manager's view of the world and what works is shaped by his or her previous work experience. If this has been in organisations that have operated on traditional Western principles, which are structured in a Classical way and give credence only to formal and scientific knowledge, then they undoubtedly will tend to operate on the left side of the brain. Nevertheless, this does not mean that such managers cannot develop or access the right side of their brain. Managers can broaden their outlook and develop the creative, inductive and questioning side of their personalities through more formal learning situations, in addition to learning from experience.

In this respect, Kirton's (1989) Adaption–Innovation theory, and subsequent work by Talbot (1993, 1997), provide a useful approach. Kirton contends that not only do people exhibit different degrees of creativity, but that they also express their creativity in different ways, along a spectrum which runs from *adaptors* to *innovators*. Those who tend towards the adaptor end of the spectrum prefer to work within the existing system to improve things. Adaptors are efficient, tend to conform to existing norms and like to deal with only a few ideas at a time. Innovators tend to ignore or challenge the system and to come up with radical proposals for change. Clearly, transactional managers tend towards the adaptor end of the spectrum and transformational managers towards the innovator end. However, there are also many managers who fall at points in between the two ends, who may find it easier than some to operate in either mode. This may be the reason for why some people, as demonstrated by our case studies and the leadership literature, can change their style of leadership or even adopt different styles at the same time. However, the story does not end there. Talbot (1997) demonstrated that, regardless of where an individual is located on the adaptor–innovator spectrum, there are proven structured approaches to increasing his or her individual level of creativity. By increasing their levels of creativity, trans-actional managers may therefore find it easier to operate in or adapt to a more transformational style. Talbot (1993) also points out that such approaches can only overcome barriers to creativity that lie within the individual. He argues that superiors, colleagues and the way the organisation operates can also block individual creativity. Therefore, in leadership, as with so many other aspects of organisational life, we cannot consider the individual in isolation from the rest of the organisation.

Unfortunately, even if there were not these organisational constraints on creativity, a number of studies revealed in the 1980s that the UK was particularly poor at providing the type of formal and structured education necessary for nurturing managerial creativity (Constable and McCormick, 1987). In response to these findings, the 1980s and 1990s saw a growing interest in management education, or management development as it is now usually referred to (OECD, 1996; Sissons and Storey, 1988; Storey, 1989, 1990; Worrall and Cooper, 1997, 1998).

Management development has been defined in a number of ways:

> ...a conscious and systematic decision-action process to control the development of managerial resources in the organisation for the achievement of organisational goals and strategies. (Ashton *et al*, 1975: 5)

> ...that function which from deep understanding of business goals and organisational requirements, undertakes: (a) to forecast needs, skill mixes and profiles for many positions and levels; (b) to design and recommend the professional, career and personal development programmes necessary to ensure competence; (c) to move from the concept of 'management' to the concept of 'managing'. (Beckhard, 1985: 22)

> ...an attempt to improve managerial effectiveness through a planned and deliberate learning process. (Quoted in Mumford, 1987: 29)

The above help to define management development, but they do not indicate what the objectives of such programmes are. To an extent this is understandable, given that individual organisations will initiate such programmes for different reasons. Nevertheless, the 1980s saw more and more companies recognising the benefits that management development can bring for organisational change and renewal (Lippitt, 1982; Marsh, 1986; Morgan, 1988; Pearson, 1987; Storey, 1989).

If management development programmes are to be successful in developing effective managers and improving the performance of organisations, then it is self-evident not only that they will vary from company to company, but also that they will need to vary from individual to individual. This makes it important to determine the training needs of individual managers accurately, in order to ensure that it is these that determine the nature of the management development programme, rather than vice versa. Unfortunately, there is plenty of evidence that this is not the case, and that management development programmes are often standard packages which everyone is sent on, regardless of how appropriate they are in relation to the needs of the individual and the objectives of the organisation that employs them (Mangham Working Party, 1987; Sissons, 1989; Storey, 1989; Thornberry, 1987).

Though there are many reasons why such programmes are inappropriate, ranging from cost to sheer laziness, the main problems appear to be twofold. First, many organisations do not know sufficiently well what their future needs will be and tend to wish to develop managers within their existing patterns and expectations. Therefore, traditional organisations will tend to continue to produce transactional managers, regardless of the presence or not of formal training and education programmes. The second reason relates to the difficulty in assessing the needs of individual managers, and shaping these into a tailor-made programme of development and training. Whilst it is relatively easy to identify a manager's training requirements in terms of technical skills (such as accountancy, engineering, etc.), the difficulty comes in trying to identify the skills, mental attitudes and behaviours necessary to be an effective manager. This chapter has already shown that it is difficult to define the role of a manager and that, in any case, this will vary from organisation to organisation and is likely to change over time.

In order to overcome this second problem, some organisations have moved away from standard packages of off-the-job training, which some see as an expensive waste of time (Newstrom, 1985; Wilkinson and Orth, 1986), to more individually tailored and job-related programmes. These types of personalised programmes have a number of common characteristics:

- The use of assessment and assessment centres to identify potential managers and the developmental needs of existing managers (Long, 1986).

- Regular coaching by a more senior manager, a mentor, to allow the manager to talk over problems and issues and learn from the experience of the senior manager (Willbur, 1987).

- Self-development appears to have come to the fore as a reaction to disappointing results from formal training courses. The purpose of self-development is to allow a manager to identify and develop a programme to meet their own needs. Obviously, managers are more likely to feel that such a programme is better suited to their needs; they may consequently be more committed to it and may get more out of it than a standard programme (Burgoyne and Germaine, 1984).

As with all general developments, this move away from formal, off-the-job training programmes to more personalised and on-the-job programmes needs to be viewed critically. Drawbacks have been identified, particularly the need to avoid isolation if self-development is too heavily relied upon (Stuart, 1986). Also, as Storey (1989) pointed out in a major review of the management development literature, drawing a distinction between on-the-job and off-the-job training may miss the main issue, which is the requirement to assess development and training needs of individual managers accurately and to provide programmes that allow managers to develop a much more critical and intuitive approach to their situation.

However, as Argyris (1991) argues, one of the main barriers to developing more critical and intuitive approaches is that, within the narrow confines of transactional behaviour, many managers do operate effectively, even though, looking at the wider picture, their organisation may be in trouble. This is akin to Peters and Waterman's (1982) concept of 'irrational rationality' – managers applying the 'right' solution even when the situation means that it is no longer appropriate. Argyris believes that managers need to experience failure or recognise the inappropriateness of their approaches before they can begin questioning their assumptions and practices, and develop their ability to be critical and creative. Senge (1990) argued that the most important factor in developing such a questioning approach and achieving organisational success is the ability to comprehend in a critical way the overall organisational context. This takes us back to the point made by Talbot (1993, 1997), cited earlier, that it is insufficient to develop managers if the organisation as a whole – people, values and systems – does not also change, or perceive the need for change. The case studies in Part 3 support this argument. In some of the companies, the combination of a form of crisis, which threatened the organisation's future, triggered the need to search for alternatives to the status quo, which in turn forced or enabled some managers to think critically and creatively about solutions to the problems their organisations faced.

From this examination of managerial learning and adaptation, four factors can be discerned as important in enabling managers successfully to align organisations, contexts and style of leadership. These are as follows:

1 Managers' past experience, and whether this has reinforced their beliefs or, instead, led them to question their appropriateness.

2 The manager's learning style: are they adaptors or innovators?

3 Do they perceive the whole picture? Can they see the organisation in its context? Particularly, do they perceive the choices for change in the organisation itself, its context, and their approach to leadership, strategy and change?

4 Is the organisational context amenable, or can it be made more amenable, to a more critical and creative style of leadership?

As far as the UK is concerned, as surveys by Worrall and Cooper (1997, 1998) found, the 1990s saw a considerable increase in the provision of education and training for managers. This was driven by a number of factors: individuals seeing the need to maintain their marketability; organisations recognising the importance to them of well-trained managers; and successive governments identifying the link between good management and the overall health of the UK economy. Nevertheless, as Worrall and Cooper also found, some 20 per cent of managers still receive no formal training for their role. Furthermore, they found that many managers question the appropriateness of the training they do receive and feel the quantity is insufficient; in addition, the increasing pressure of work, and their longer working hours, are reducing their ability to take advantage of and apply the training and education that is available.

# SUMMARY AND CONCLUSIONS

In reading some of the literature on strategy and change, one might be forgiven for asking whether managers and what they do matter at all. If strategy is Emergent, often unrelated to conscious decisions, does an important role exist for managers? Or if, as the evolutionary perspective on strategy would have it, luck plays a greater part in success than conscious action, does the quality of the manager matter? The answer, of course, is yes. As the case studies show, this is for both negative and positive reasons.

On the negative side, managers can act to hold back organisations, to prevent change and to create a climate of blame and in-fighting. On the positive side, managers can identify opportunities for progress, and can ensure the organisation and its environment remain in harmony. They can create the conditions for growth and prosperity. Effective managers are, therefore, for very positive reasons, important to an organisation. However, they do not operate in isolation or have a totally free rein.

The Chief Executive of Oticon and the Board of the PSA both wanted to transform their organisations. The former gained the support of his colleagues and employees and succeeded, the latter did not and, to a very large extent, failed. This is not to say that successful organisations are based solely on dominant or charismatic leaders. There may be leaders, such as Lee Iacocca when he ran Chrysler, Pehr Gyllenhammar before his departure from Volvo, Richard Branson at Virgin, Bill Gates at Microsoft or Rupert Murdoch at News International, who through sheer force of personality dominated and transformed organisations. Nevertheless, these are a minority. In any case, such people may outstay their welcome, or their organisations are so idiosyncratic that, once the leader leaves, they have to be completely re-shaped in order to survive under new management.

Most managers, even of very large corporations, have to rely far less on their personality than on their business knowledge, skills and experience. They are also called upon to perform a wide range of duties and activities. Though the theories and approaches to strategy and change appear to paint managers as either directing change or facilitating it, and the leadership literature tends to dwell on whether they are transactional or transformational managers, the reality is that they are often required to be all of these things, depending on the circumstances. In bringing about organisational change, there will be occasions when managers will need to devolve responsibility to subordinates; sometimes, though, they will need to encourage and support change projects; and, in other instances, they will have to lead the process themselves. Although the approach adopted will depend to a certain extent upon the size and importance of the change project, the timescale involved and the state of the organisation, in the final analysis it will rely on managerial judgement to make the appropriate choice. Changing organisations is a complex process fraught with more opportunities for failure than success. If managers are to accomplish and keep accomplishing this task, as this book has argued, they have to be aware of the choices and approaches available and be willing themselves to change their beliefs and attitudes.

Despite the views of some writers, there can never be any general recipes or formulas for organisational success. The vast variety of organisations, each with its own differing constraints and pressures, makes that impossible. What there is, however, is a large body of theories and associated advice which organisations can draw upon to assist them. As this book has shown, there is no such thing as an uncontested theory – all have their drawbacks. In particular, most tend to be situation-specific, even if they do not acknowledge this. Managers and organisations need to treat theories with a degree of scepticism. However, they also need to realise that if they can identify the main theories for running and changing organisations, and they do understand the context in which they operate, they are in a position to identify choices and make changes.

Sometimes managers may choose to change their organisations radically and quickly; sometimes they may choose to influence the context. In other cases, change may take place more slowly and over a long period, as both organisation and context are shaped and changed. The key factor in all this is to make conscious decisions rather than rely on untested assumptions. This will require managers to question and challenge their own assumptions. It will also require them to gather and be open to a wide variety of information – as Chapter 3 showed, the experience of more and more successful companies is that learning should be an organisation-wide and continuous process, rather than one limited to a few like-minded individuals at one point in time.

Even where choices are identified, managers should not assume that exercising choice is easy or that the results will be beneficial for all concerned, including themselves. For this reason, managers have a responsibility in making and implementing choices to consider the implications in the widest context. In the West, especially the UK and USA, there is a tendency to think mainly in terms of short-term profitability, and ignore the long-term and social consequences of actions. We can see this in the context of the Classical school, whose concentration on narrow issues of control and efficiency leads to the creation of jobs that are both physically strenuous and mind-numbingly boring. However, the adverse consequences of organisation theory are not limited to the Classical school; in many ways, the policies and approaches advocated by the Culture–Excellence school could be considered even worse. Though both Handy (1997) and, to a lesser extent, Kanter (1997) are concerned about the impact of fragmented organisations and insecure jobs on society at large and family life in particular, neither appears to believe that these can be avoided.

Yet the consequences of this approach in creating instability and unpredictability in the job market are disastrous. As was noted in Chapter 3, the 1990s saw the UK become more socially divided than at any time since the Second World War, with some 60 per cent of the population either marginalised or living in very insecure circumstances (Hutton, 1995; Saul, 1997; White, 1999). The situation is even worse in the USA where, increasingly, the better-off are retreating into walled compounds patrolled by armed guards (Dunphy and Griffiths, 1998; Elliott, 1997; Reich, 1997). If this seems a somewhat apocalyptic vision, then bear in mind that one of the most fashionable American gurus of the late 1990s, William Bridges, advocated the jobless organisation. He believes that there should no longer be any permanent jobs, not even for managers. Instead, he wants to see the labour force form one enormous pool of labour waiting for temporary employment – the just-in-time workforce to complement the just-in-time organisation (Bridges, 1996, 1998; Golzen, 1995). In support of his view that jobless organisations are the future, he points out that General Motors is no longer the largest employer in the USA; instead, it is the temporary employment agency, Manpower.

Some would argue that these developments are only the inevitable consequence of capitalism (Collins, 1998). However, as Crouch and Streeck (1997) and Whitley (1998) demonstrated, capitalism comes in many forms and guises. The fragmentation and insecurity of the labour market that was a growing characteristic of the USA and UK in the 1980s and 1990s was much less pronounced in some other countries. This was especially the case in those nations which, historically, had seen the objectives of individual organisations as subservient to national interests. In the 1990s for example, despite economic problems associated with reunification, Germany still had an enviable record of attempting to prevent job losses and reduce job insecurity, as did the Scandinavian states and Japan.

This, of course, emphasises that national governments as well as individual organisations have a major contribution to make when considering the wider context and implications of managers' decisions. In the West, especially the UK, the last 20 years have seen an increasing move towards deregulation, privatisation and the introduction of market forces into the operation of the public sector. Whatever the merits of these policies in terms of efficiency, and they are debatable (Flynn, 1993; Ferlie et al, 1996), no one can doubt that they acted to increase instability both in the economy at large and in public sector bodies such as the National Health Service. As the case study of Midshires College showed, there are now high levels of unpredictability in what was a very stable system. Whether it leads eventually to better patient care or not is obviously an issue, but so is the effect on the social fabric. Post-1945, all Western governments used their public sectors both to provide services and as a means of creating employment and maintaining economic and social stability. These latter functions have now been abandoned in many countries, and the resulting insecurity is evident for all to see.

The point of mentioning this is not merely to show concern, but to argue that it need not be the case. The Culture–Excellence concept is only one of many approaches to running organisations. All have their down side, but not all result in job cuts and labour market instability. One alternative is for managers to choose to adopt approaches that reduce instability in their environment, rather than to implement policies that increase the use of short-term contracts, part-time and casual working. If followed widely, this would have two effects. First, the result of many organisations seeking stability would be to reduce the overall level of turbulence in the environment. This is because organisations and their

507

environment are not separate entities, but part of the same system. If organisations become more stable, so too does the environment. Similarly, if, as recommended by Tom Peters, organisations adopt internal chaos to cope with external chaos, this merely acts to increase the overall turbulence in the system; in effect, a vicious spiral of increasing chaos is created. The second consequence of organisations seeking stability is that it increases the stability in society – jobs and communities become more stable.

Therefore, as a final note: organisations face many challenges and choices. Some organisations will find that their room for manoeuvre is very limited. Others may find that there is considerable scope for discretion. It is the role of managers to ensure that all available options and choices are identified, and that the choices made take account of both the short- and long-term interests of all their stakeholders – whether these be shareholders, employees, the managers themselves or the community at large. The worst managers may not be those who make poor choices; it may be those who fail to recognise that there are choices to be made.

## TEST YOUR LEARNING

### Short answer questions

1 Describe Duncan's (1975) three levels of management.
2 Briefly discuss Mintzberg's (1973, 1975) description of managerial roles.
3 What is the personal characteristics approach to leadership?
4 State the key features of the leader–follower approach to leadership.
5 Describe the contextual approach to leadership.
6 How does Kirton's (1989) Adaption–Innovation theory help us to understand managerial behaviour?
7 Describe two approaches to managerial development.
8 List three ways in which managers' decisions can have a wider impact on society.

### Essay questions

1 Discuss the following statement: In future, transactional and transformational managers will have to work side by side if organisations are to be successful.
2 How can the concept of managerial choice help managers to reconcile the needs of their organisation with the wider needs of society?

### SUGGESTED FURTHER READING

1 Yukl, G (1994). *Leadership in Organizations* (3rd edition). Prentice Hall: Englewood Cliffs, NJ, USA.
Gary Yukl's book is an excellent guide to the literature and research on management and leadership.

2 Robbins, SP (1997). *Managing Today!* Prentice Hall: Upper Saddle River, New Jersey, USA.
This book provides a well-researched and well-written guide to the role of managers in contemporary organisations.

3 Dunphy, DD and Griffiths, A (1998). *The Sustainable Corporation: Organizational Renewal in Australia*. Allen & Unwin: St Leonards, Australia.
This is a thought-provoking book which highlights the responsibilities of managers, both individually and collectively, for maintaining the global environment.

# Bibliography

Abegglen, J (1958). *The Japanese Factory*. Free Press: Glencoe, IL, USA.

Abegglen, J and Stalk, G (1984). *Kaisha, the Japanese Corporation*. Basic Books: New York, USA.

Abell, DF (1977). *Using PIMS and Portfolio Analysis in Strategic Market Planning: A Comparative Analysis*. Intercollegiate Case Clearing House, Harvard Business School: Boston, MA, USA.

Abell, P (1975). Organisations as technically constrained bargaining and influence systems. In P Abell (ed): *Organisations as Bargaining and Influence Systems*. Heinemann: London.

Abodaher, D (1986). *Iacocca*. Star: London.

Ackroyd, S, Burrell, G, Hughes, M and Whitaker, A (1988). The Japanisation of British industry. *Industrial Relations Journal*, 19(1), 11–23.

Aglietta, M (1979). *A Theory of Capitalist Regulation: The US Experience*. NLB: London.

Aguren, S, Bredbacka, C, Hansson, R, Ihregren, K and Karlsson, KG (1984). *Volvo/Kalmar Revisited: Ten Years of Experience*. The Development Council: Stockholm, Sweden.

Aitken, H (1960). *Taylorism at the Watertown Arsenal: Scientific Management in Action 1908–1915*. Harvard University Press: Cambridge, MA, USA.

Akao, Y (ed) (1991). *Hoshin Kanri: Policy Deployment for Successful TQM*. Productivity Press: Cambridge, MA, USA.

Albrow, M (1970). *Bureaucracy*. Pall Mall Press: London.

Albrow, M (1997). *Do Organizations Have Feelings?* Routledge: London.

Allaire, Y, and Firsirotu, ME (1984). Theories of organizational culture. *Organization Studies*, 5(3), 193–226.

Allaire, Y and Firsirotu, ME (1989). Coping with strategic uncertainty. *Sloan Management Review*, 30(3), 7–16.

Allen, FR and Kraft, C (1982). *The Organizational Unconscious. How to Create the Corporate Culture You Want and Need*. Prentice Hall: Englewood Cliffs, NJ, USA.

Allen, RW, Madison, DL, Porter, LW, Renwick, PA and Mayes, BT (1979). Organizational politics: tactics and characteristics of its actors. *California Management Review*, 22, 77–83.

Allport, GW (1948). Foreword. In GW Lewin and GW Allport (eds): *Resolving Social Conflict*. Harper & Row: London.

Alvesson, M and Deetz, S (1996). Critical theory and postmodern approaches to organizational studies. In SR Clegg, C Hardy and WR Nord (eds): *Handbook of Organization Studies*. Sage: London.

Amin, A and Robins, K (1990). The re-emergence of regional economics? The mythical geography of flexible accumulation. *Environment and Planning D: Society and Space*, 8, 7–34.

Anderson, C and Paine, F (1978). PIMS: a re-examination. *Academy of Management Review*, 3(3), 602–12.

Andrews, KR (1980). *The Concept of Corporate Strategy*. Irwin: Homewood, IL, USA.

Ansoff, HI (1965). *Corporate Strategy*. McGraw-Hill: New York, USA.

Ansoff, HI (1987). *Corporate Strategy* (revised version). McGraw-Hill: New York, USA.

Appignanesi, R and Garratt, C (1995). *Postmodernism for Beginners*. Icon Books: Cambridge.

Argenti, J (1974). *Systematic Corporate Planning*. Nelson: London.

Argyris, C (1960). *Understanding Organizational Behavior*. Dorsey: Homewood, IL, USA.

Argyris, C (1962). *Interpersonal Competence and Organizational Effectiveness*. Irwin: Homewood, IL, USA.

Argyris, C (1964). *Integrating the Individual and the Organization*. Wiley: London.

Argyris, C (1970). *Intervention Theory and Method*. Addison-Wesley: Reading, MA, USA.

Argyris, C (1973). Peter Blau. In G Salaman and K Thompson (eds): *People and Organizations*. Longman: London.

Argyris, C (1977). Double-loop learning in organizations. *Harvard Business Review*, September–October, 115–25.

Argyris, C (1980). *Inner Contradictions of Rigorous Research*. Academic Press: New York, USA.

Argyris, C (1990). *Overcoming Organizational Defenses: Facilitating Organizational Learning*. Allyn & Bacon: Boston, MA, USA.

Argyris, C (1991). Teaching smart people how to learn. *Harvard Business Review*, May–June, 99–109.

Argyris, C (1992). *On Organizational Learning*. Blackwell: Oxford.

Argyris, C and Schon, D (1978). *Organizational Learning: A Theory of Action Perspective*. Addison-Wesley: Reading, MA, USA.

Arnold, J, Cooper, CL and Robertson, IT (1998). *Work Psychology* (3rd edition). Pitman: London.

Aronowitz, S (1989). Postmodernism and politics. In A Ross (ed): *Universal Abandon: the Politics of Postmodernism*. Edinburgh University Press: Edinburgh.

Ashforth, BE and Fried, Y (1988). The mindlessness of organizational behaviours. *Human Relations*, 41(4), 305–29.

Ashour, AS (1973). The contingency model of leadership effectiveness: an evaluation. *Organizational Behavior and Human Performance*, 9, 339–55.

Ashton, D, Easterby-Smith, M, and Irvine C (1975). *Management Development: Theory and Practice*. MCB: Bradford.

Ashton, TS (1948). *The Industrial Revolution 1760–1830*. Oxford University Press: Oxford.

Ashworth, W (1987). *A Short History of the International Economy since 1850*. Longman: London.

AT Kearney (1989). *Computer Integrated Manufacturing: Competitive Advantage or Technological Dead End?* Kearney: London.

AT Kearney (1992). *Total Quality: Time to Take Off the Rose-Tinted Spectacles*. IFS: Kempston.

AT Kearney Ltd (1994). *Partnership or Powerplay?* AT Kearney: London.

Auer, P and Riegler, C (1990). *Post-Taylorism: The Enterprise as a Place of Learning Organizational Change – A Comprehensive Study on Work Organization Changes and its Context at Volvo*. The Swedish Work Environment Fund: Stockholm, Sweden.

Babbage, C (1835). *On the Economy of Machinery and Manufacture*. Knight: London.

Bachman, JG, Bowers, DG and Marcus, PM (1968). Bases of supervisory power: a comparative study in five organizational settings. In AS Tannenbaum (ed): *Control in Organizations*. McGraw-Hill: New York, USA.

Barnard, C (1938). *The Functions of the Executive*. Harvard University Press: Cambridge, MA, USA.

Barratt, ES (1990). Human resource management: organisational culture. *Management Update*, 2(1), 21–32.

Barrie, C (1995). Saatchi loses accounts to new agency. *The Guardian*, 16 February, 15.

Barrie, C (1999). It's a far cry from safe and secure. *The Guardian* – Jobs Section, 2 January, 12–13.

Bateson, G (1972). *Steps to an Ecology of the Mind*. Ballantine: New York, USA.

Batten, JD and Swab, JL (1965). How to crack down on company politics. *Personnel*, 42, 8–20.

Baudrillard, J (1983). *Simulations*. Semiotexte: New York, USA.

Beach, SD (1980). *Personnel*. Macmillan: London.

Beatty, CA and Lee, GL (1992). Leadership among middle managers – an exploration in the context of technological change. *Human Relations*, 45(9), 957–89.

Beckhard, R (1969). *Organization Development: Strategies and Models*. Addison-Wesley: Reading, MA, USA.

Beckhard, R (1985). Whither management development? *Journal of Management Development*, 4(2).

Beer, M and Walton, RE (1987). Organizational change and development. *Annual Review of Psychology*, 38, 339–68.

Beer, M, Eisenstat, RA and Spector, B (1993). Why change programmes don't produce change. In C Mabey and B Mayon-White (eds): *Managing Change* (2nd edition). The Open University/Paul Chapman Publishing: London.

Bell, D (1973). *The Coming of Post-Industrial Society*. Basic Books: New York, USA.

Bell, RM (1973). *The Behaviour of Labour, Technical Change, and the Competitive Weakness of British Manufacturing*. Technical Change Centre: London.

Benjamin, G and Mabey, C (1993). Facilitating radical change. In C Mabey and B Mayon-White (eds): *Managing Change* (2nd edition). The Open University/Paul Chapman Publishing: London.

Bennett, J and Jayes, S (1995). *Trusting the Team: The Best Practice Guide to Partnering in Construction*. Reading University, Centre for Strategic Studies in Construction: Reading.

Bennett, R (1983). *Management Research. Management Development Series, 20*. International Labour Office: Geneva.

Bennis, WG (1959). Leadership theory and administrative behaviour. *Administrative Science Quarterly*, 4, 259–301.

Bennis, WG (1966). The coming death of bureaucracy. *Think*, November–December, 30–5.

Bennis, W and Namus, B (1985). *Leaders: The Strategies for Taking Charge*. Harper & Row: New York, USA.

Berggren, C (1992). *The Volvo Experience*. Macmillan: London.

Bernstein, L (1968). *Management Development*. Business Books: London.

Bessant, J (1983). Management and manufacturing innovation: the case of information technology. In G Winch (ed): *Information Technology in Manufacturing Processes*. Rossendale: London.

Bessant, J and Haywood, B (1985). *The Introduction of Flexible Manufacturing Systems as an Example of Computer Integrated Manufacture*. Brighton Polytechnic: Brighton.

Bhote, KR (1989). *Strategic Supply Management*. American Management Association: New York.

Biberman, J and Whitty, M (1997). A postmodern spiritual future for work. *Journal of Organizational Change*, 10(2), 130–8.

Bigge, LM (1982). *Learning Theories for Teachers*. Gower: Aldershot.

Blackler, FHM and Brown, CA (1978). *Job Redesign and Management Control: Studies in British Leyland and Volvo*. Saxon House: Farnborough.

Blackler, F and Brown, C (1984). Alternative models to guide the design and introduction of new information technologies into work organisations. *Journal of Occupational Psychology*, 59(4), 287–314.

Blake, RR and Mouton, JS (1969). *Building a Dynamic Corporation Through Grid Organisation Development*. Addison-Wesley: Reading, MA, USA.

Blake, RR and Mouton, JS (1976). *Organizational Change by Design*. Scientific Methods: Austin, Texas, USA.

Blanchard, K (1994). Changing role of executives. *Executive Excellence*, 11(4), 7.

Blau, PM (1970). The formal theory of differentiation in organizations. *American Sociological Review*, 35, 201–18.

Blau, PM and Schoenherr, RA (1971). *The Structure of Organizations*. Basic Books: New York, USA.

Block, P (1981). *Flawless Consulting: A Guide to Getting Your Expertise Used*. Learning Concepts: Austin, Texas, USA.

Boddy, D and Buchanan, D (1992). *Take the Lead: Interpersonal Skills for Change Agents*. Prentice Hall: London.

Borchardt, K (1973). Germany 1700–1914. In C Cipolla (ed): *The Fontana Economic History of Europe Vol. 4, The Emergence of Industrial Societies* – Part 1. Fontana: London.

Bower, T (1996). *Maxwell: The Final Verdict*. HarperCollins: London.

Bowers, DG, Franklin, JL and Pecorella, P (1975). Matching problems, precursors and interventions in OD: a systematic approach. *Journal of Applied Behavioural Science*, 11, 391–410.

Bowles, M (1989). Myth, meaning and work organisation. *Organization Studies*, 10(3), 405–23.

Bowman, C and Asch, D (1985). *Strategic Map*. Macmillan: London.

Bracker, J (1980). The historical development of the strategic management concept. *Academy of Management Review*, 5(2), 219–24.

Brandenburger, AM and Nalebuff, BJ (1996). *Co-opetition*. Doubleday: New York, USA.

Bratton, J (1992). *Japanization at Work: Managerial Studies for the 1990s*. Macmillan: London.

Breslin, J and McGann, J (1998). *The Business Knowledge Repository: Consolidating and Accessing Your Ways of Working*. Quorum Books: Westport, CT, USA.

Brewer, E and Tomlinson, JWC (1964). The manager's working day. *Journal of Industrial Economics*, 12, 191–7.

Bridges, W (1996). *Jobshift: How to Prosper in a Workplace Without Jobs*. Nicholas Brealey: London.

Bridges, W (1998). *Creating You & Co: Learn to Think Like the CEO of Your Own Career*. Perseus Books: New York, USA.

Brindle, D (1998a). Gap between rich and poor widens again. *The Guardian*, 16 October, 7.

Brindle, D (1998b). Benefits payments in chaos: computer collapse wipes out records. *The Guardian*, 10 September, 1.

Brindle, D (1999). Pensions computer upgrade hit by 1,900 bugs as deadline looms. *The Guardian*, 26 January, 3.

Brown, A (1995). *Organisational Culture*. Pitman: London.

Brown, DH and Jopling, D (1994). Some experiences of outsourcing: a systemic analysis of strategic and organisational issues. Paper presented to the British Academy of Management Annual Conference, University of Lancaster, September.

Brown, SL and Eisenhardt, KM (1997). The art of continuous change: linking complexity theory and time-paced evolution in relentlessly shifting organizations. *Administrative Science Quarterly*, 42, March, 1–34.

Bruland, K (1989). The transformation of work in European industrialization. In P Mathias and JA Davis (eds): *The First Industrial Revolutions*. Blackwell: Cambridge.

Brummer, A (1999). Weinstock's heirs look for an encore. *The Guardian*, 20 January, 21.

Brummer, A and Cowe, R (1998). *Weinstock*. HarperCollins: London.

Bryant, D (1979). The psychology of resistance to change. *Management Services*, March, 9–10.

Buchanan, DA (1984). The impact of technical implications and managerial aspirations on the organization and control of the labour process. Paper presented to the Second Annual Conference on the Control and Organisation of the Labour Process, UMIST/Aston, 28–30 March.

Buchanan, DA and Boddy, D (1992). *The Expertise of the Change Agent*. Prentice Hall: London.

Buchanan, DA and Storey, J (1997). Role-taking and role-switching in organizational change: the four pluralities. In I McLoughlin and M Harris (eds): *Innovation, Organizational Change and Technology*. International Thompson: London.

Buckingham, L and Finch, J (1999). SmithKline bows to revolt over directors' pay. *The Guardian*, 24 April, 22.

Buckley, PJ and Mirza, H (1985). The wit and wisdom of Japanese management. *Management International Review*, 25, 16–32.

Buckley, W (1968). *Modern Systems and Research for the Behavioral Scientist*. Aldine Publishing: Chicago, USA.

Bullock, RJ and Batten, D (1985). It's just a phase we're going through: a review and synthesis of OD phase analysis. *Group and Organization Studies*, 10, December, 383–412.

Burawoy, M (1979). *Manufacturing Consent: Changes in the Labour Process under Monopoly Capital*. University of Chicago Press: Chicago, USA.

Burgoyne, J (1995). Feeding minds to grow the business. *People Management*, 1(19), 22–6.

Burgoyne, J and Germaine, C (1984). Self development and career planning: an exercise in mutual benefit. *Personnel Management*, 16(4), April, 21–3.

Burgoyne, J, Pedler, M and Boydell, T (1994). *Towards the Learning Company*. McGraw-Hill: London.

Burke, W (1980). *Organisation Development*. Little, Brown and Co: Toronto, Canada.

Burke, W, Michael, RS, Luthems, F, Odiorne, S and Hayden, S (1981). *Techniques of Organisational Change*. McGraw-Hill: London.

Burnes, B (1988). *Strategy for Success: Case Studies in Advanced Manufacturing Technologies*. EITB: Watford.

Burnes, B (1989). *New Technology in Context*. Gower: Aldershot.

Burnes, B (1991). Managerial competence and new technology: don't shoot the piano player – he's doing his best. *Behaviour and Information Technology*, 10(2), 91–109.

Burnes, B (1996). No such thing as ... a 'one best way' to manage organizational change. *Management Decision*, 34(10), 11–18.

Burnes, B (1997) Organisational choice and organisational change. *Management Decision*, 35(10), 753–9.

Burnes, B (1998a) Recipes for organisational effectiveness: mad, bad, or just dangerous to know. *Career Development International*, 3(3), 100–6.

Burnes, B (1998b) The planned approach to change: come back Kurt Lewin – all is forgiven. Paper presented to the Second Maintaining Organizational Effectiveness Conference, Edge Hill University College, Ormskirk, June, 17.

Burnes, B and Coram, R (1999). Barriers to partnership in the public sector: the case of the UK construction industry. *Supply Chain Management*, 4(1), 43–50.

Burnes, B and Dale, B (eds) (1998). *Working in Partnership*. Gower: Aldershot.

Burnes, B and James, H (1995). Culture, cognitive dissonance and the management of change. *International Journal of Operations and Production Management*, 15(8), 14–33.

Burnes, B and New, S (1996). *Strategic Advantage and Supply Chain Collaboration*. AT Kearney: London.

Burnes, B and New, S (1997). Collaboration in customer–supplier relationships: strategy, operations and the function of rhetoric. *International Journal of Purchasing and Materials Management*, 33(4), 10–17.

Burnes, B and Salauroo, M (1995). The impact of the NHS internal market on the merger of colleges of midwifery and nursing: not just a case of putting the cart before the horse. *Journal of Management in Medicine*, 9(2), 14–29.

Burnes, B and Weekes, B (1989). *AMT: A Strategy for Success?* NEDO: London.

Burnes, B and Whittle, P (1995). Supplier development: getting started. *Logistics Focus*, February, 10–14.

Burns, JM (1978). *Leadership*. Harper & Row: New York, USA.

Burns, T and Stalker, GM (1961). *The Management of Innovation*. Tavistock: London.

Burrell, G (1988). Modernism, post modernism and organisational analysis 2: the contribution of Michel Foucault. *Organization Studies*, 9(2), 221–35.

Burrell, G (1997). Organization paradigms. In A Sorge and M Warner (eds): *The IEBM Handbook of Organizational Behaviour*. International Thompson Business Press: London.

Burton, F, Yamin, M and Young, S (eds) (1996). *Europe in Transition*. MacMillan: London.

Butler, R (1997). Decision making. In A Sorge and M Warner (eds): *The IEBM Handbook of Organizational Behaviour*. International Thompson Business Press: London.

Butler, VG (1985). *Organisation and Management*. Prentice Hall: London.

Buzzell, RD and Gale, BT (1987). *The PIMS Principles – Linking Strategy to Performance*. Free Press: New York, USA.

Byars, LL (1984). *Strategic Management: Planning and Implementation*. Harper & Row: London.

Bywater PLC (1997). *Executive Briefings: The Executive Role in Sponsoring Change – Making It Happen*. Bywater PLC: Reading.

Callinicos, A (1989). *Against Postmodernism*. Polity: Cambridge.

Camp, RC (1989). *Benchmarking*. ASQC Quality Press: Milwaukee, USA.

Campbell, A and Warner, M (1988). Organization of new forms of manufacturing operations. In M Wild (ed): *International Handbook of Production and Operations Management*. Cassells: London.

Carew, A (1987). *Labour Under the Marshall Plan: The Politics of Productivity and the Market*. Manchester University Press: Manchester.

Carlson, S (1951). *Executive Behaviour*. Strombergs: Stockholm.

Carnall, CA (1990). *Managing Change in Organizations*. Prentice Hall: London.

Carnall, CA (1995). *Managing Change in Organizations* (2nd edition). Prentice Hall: London.

Carr, C, Tomkins, C and Bayliss, B (1991). Strategic controllership – a case study approach. *Management Accounting Research*, 2, 89–107.

Carr, P and Donaldson, L (1993). Managing healthily: how an NHS region is managing change. *Personnel Management*, October, 48–51.

Carroll, DT (1983). A disappointing search for excellence. *Harvard Business Review*, November–December, 78–88.

Carroll, GR (ed) (1988). *Ecological Models of Organisations*. Ballinger: Cambridge, MA, USA.

Chandler, AD (1962). *Strategy and Structure: Chapters in the History of American Industrial Enterprise*. MIT: Cambridge, USA.

Chapman, L (1978). *Your Disobedient Servant Published*. Chatto & Windus: London.

Chapman, SD and Chassagne, S (1981). *European Textile Printers in the Eighteenth Century. A Study of Peel and Oberkampf*. Heinemann: London.

Chawla, S and Renesch, J (1995). *Learning Organizations: Developing Cultures for Tomorrow's Workplace*. Productivity Press: Portland, OR, USA.

Child, J (1972). Organizational structure, environment and performance: the role of strategic choice. *Sociology*, 6(1), 1–22.

Child, J (1984). *Organization*. Harper & Row: Cambridge.

Child, J and Ellis, T (1973). Predictors of variation in managerial roles. *Human Relations*, 26(2), 227–50.

Child, J and Smith, C (1987). The context and process of organisational transformation – Cadbury Limited in its sector. *Journal of Management Studies*, 24(6), 565–93.

Chin, R and Benne, KD (1976). General strategies for effecting changes in human systems. In WG Bennis, KD Benne, R Chin and KE Corey (eds): *The Planning of Change* (3rd edition). Holt, Rinehart and Winston: New York, USA.

Christopher, M (1998). *Logistics and Supply Chain Management* (2nd edition). Pitman: London.

Cipolla, C (ed) (1973). *The Fontana Economic History of Europe, Vol. 4*. Fontana: London.

Clark, P (1972). *Action Research and Organisational Change*. Harper & Row: London.

Clark, RC (1979). *The Japanese Company*. New Haven, CT, USA.

Clarke, L (1994). *The Essence of Change*. Prentice Hall: London.

Clegg, CW (1984). The derivation of Job Design. *Journal of Occupational Behaviour*, 5, 131–46.

Clegg, CW and Symon, G (1991). Technology-led change: a case study of the implementation of CADCAM. *Journal of Occupational Psychology*, 64(4), 273–90.

Clegg, S (1990). *Modern Organisation: Organisation Studies in the Postmodern World*. Sage: London.

Coghlan, D (1993). In defence of process consultation. In C Mabey and B Mayon-White (eds): *Managing Change* (2nd edition). The Open University/Paul Chapman Publishing: London.

Cohen, MD, March, JG and Olsen, JP (1972). A garbage can model of organizational choice. *Administrative Science Quarterly*, **17**, 1–25.

Cole, RE (1979). *Work, Mobility and Participation: A Comparative Study of Japanese and American Industry*. University of California Press: Los Angeles, USA.

Collins, D (1998). *Organizational Change*. Routledge: London.

Collins, JC and Porras, JI (1991). Organizational vision and visionary organizations. *California Management Review*, Fall, 30–52.

Conner, PE (1977). A critical enquiry into some assumptions and values characterizing OD. *Academy of Management Review*, 2(1), 635–44.

Constable, J and McCormick, R (1987). *The Making of British Managers*. British Institute of Management/Confederation of British Industry: London.

Cook, T (1998). New Labour, New NHS . . . New internal market? *Management Accounting*, 76(3), March, 24–6.

Cool, K and Schendel, D (1988). Performance differences among strategic group members. *Strategic Management Journal*, 9(3), 207–23.

Coombs, R and Hull, R (1994). The best or the worst of both worlds: BPR, cost reduction, and the strategic management of IT. Paper presented to the OASIG Seminar on Organisation Change Through IT and BPR: Beyond the Hype, September, London.

Cooper, CL and Jackson, SE (eds) (1997). *Creating Tomorrow's Organizations*. Wiley: Chichester.

Cooper, J and Fazio, RH (1984). A new look at dissonance theory. In L Berkowitz (ed): *Advances in Experimental Social Psychology*, Vol. 17, 229–67. Academic Press: New York, USA.

Cooper, R and Burrell, G (1988). Modernism, postmodernism and organizational analysis: an introduction. *Organization Studies*, 9, 91–112.

Copley, FB (1923). *Frederick Winslow Taylor: Father of Scientific Management*, Vol. 2. Harper & Row: New York.

Coram, WR (1997). The privatisation of the Property Services Agency, Vols 1 & 2. Unpublished PhD Thesis. UMIST: Manchester.

Coulson-Thomas, C and Coe, T (1991). *The Flat Organization*. British Institute of Management: London.

Covin, JG (1991). Entrepreneurial versus conservative firms: a comparison of strategies and performance. *Journal of Management Studies*, 28, 439–62.

Cowe, R (1995). Compete carefully. *The Guardian*, 25 March, 40.

Crainer, S (ed) (1995). *The Financial Times Handbook of Management*. FT Pitman: London.

Cressey, P (1996). Enriching production: perspectives on Volvo's Uddevalla plant as an alternative to lean production. *Industrial Relations Journal*, 27(1), 77–80.

Cringely, RX (1992). *Accidental Empires: How the Boys of Silicon Valley Make their Millions, Battle Foreign Competition, and Still Can't Get a Date*. Addison-Wesley: Reading, MA, USA.

Crosby, PB (1979). *Quality is Free*. McGraw-Hill: New York, USA.

Crossan, MM and Guatto, T (1996). Organizational learning research profile. *Journal of Organizational Change Management*, 9(1), 107–12.

Crouch, C and Streeck, W (eds) (1997). *Political Economy of Modern Capitalism*. Sage: London.

Crozier, M (1964). *The Bureaucratic Phenomenon*. Tavistock: London.

Cruise O'Brien, R and Voss, C (1992). *In Search of Quality*. Working Paper, London Business School: London.

Cummings, TG and Huse, EF (1989). *Organization Development and Change* (4th edition). West: St Paul, MN, USA.

Cummings, TG and Worley, CG (1997). *Organization Development and Change* (6th edition). South-Western College Publishing: Cincinnati, OH, USA.

Cuthbert, N (1970). Readings from Henri Fayol, General and Industrial Management. In A Tillett, T Kempner and G Willis (eds): *Management Thinkers*. Pelican: Harmondsworth.

Cyert, RM and March, JG (1963). *A Behavioral Theory of the Firm*. Prentice Hall: Englewood Cliffs, NJ, USA.

Daft, RL (1998). *Organizational Theory and Design* (6th edition). Southwestern: Cincinnati, OH, USA.

Dakin, SR and Hamilton, RT (1990). How 'general' are your general managers? *Management Decision*, 28(2), 32–7.

Dale, BG (ed) (1999). *Managing Quality* (3rd edition). Blackwell: Oxford.

Dale, BG and Cooper, CL (1992). *TQM and Human Resources: An Executive Guide*. Blackwell: Oxford.

Dale, PN (1986). *The Myth of Japanese Uniqueness*. Croom Helm: London.

Dastmalchian, A (1984). Environmental dependencies and company structure in Britain. *Organization Studies*, 5(3), 222–41.

Davenport, TH (1993). *Process Innovation: Re-engineering Work Through IT*. Harvard Business School Press: Boston, MA, USA.

Davis, E and Star, J (1993). The world's best performing companies. *Business Strategy Review*, 4(2), 1–16.

Davis, JA (1989). Industrialisation in Britain and Europe before 1850. In P Mathias and JA Davis (eds): *The First Industrial Revolutions*. Blackwell: Cambridge.

Davis, LE (1979). Job Design: historical overview. In LE Davis and JC Taylor (eds): *Design of Work*. Goodyear: Santa Monica, CA, USA.

Davis, LE and Canter, RR (1955). Job Design. *Journal of Industrial Engineering*, 6(1), 3.

Davis, LE, Canter, RR and Hoffman, J (1955). Current job design criteria. *Journal of Industrial Engineering*, 6(2), 5–11.

Davis, R (1928). *The Principles of Factory Organization and Management*. Harper & Row: New York, USA.

Davis, TRV (1985). Managing culture at the bottom. In R Kilmann, M Saxton, R Serpa and Associates (eds): *Gaining Control of the Corporate Culture*. Jossey-Bass: San Francisco, CA, USA.

Dawkins, W (1993). Costly burden of tradition. *Financial Times*, 1 December, 10.

Dawkins, W (1994). Loosening of the corporate web. *Financial Times*, 30 November, 15.

Dawson, P (1994). *Organizational Change: A Processual Approach*. Paul Chapman Publishing: London.

Deal, T and Kennedy, A (1982). Culture: a new look through old lenses. *Journal of Applied Behavioural Science*, 19(4), 497–507.

Deming, WE (1982). *Quality, Productivity and Competitive Position*. MIT Press: Boston, MA, USA.

Derrida, J (1978). *Writing and Difference*. Routledge and Kegan Paul: London.

Dess, GG and Davis, PS (1984). Porter's (1980) generic strategies as determinants of strategic group membership and original performance. *Academy of Management Journal*, 27(3), 467–88.

Dixit, A (1980). The role of investment in entry deterrence. *Economic Journal*, 90, 95–106.

Dobson, P (1988). Changing culture. *Employment Gazette*, December, 647–50.

Dolvik, JE and Stokland, D (1992). Norway: the 'Norwegian Model' in transition. In A Ferner and R Hyman (eds): *Industrial Relations in the New Europe*. Blackwell: Oxford.

Done, K (1994). Up to strength once again: Volvo. *Financial Times*, 2 December.

Donovan, P (1995). Saatchis in row over share deal. *The Guardian*, 15 February, 22.

Drennan, D (1992). *Transforming Company Culture*. McGraw-Hill: London.

Drory, A and Romm, T (1988). Politics in the organization and its perception within the organization. *Organization Studies*, 9(2), 165–79.

Drucker, PF (1974). *Management: Tasks, Responsibilities, Practices*. Harper & Row: London.

Drucker, PF (1985). *Innovation and Entrepreneurship*. Pan: London.

Dukakis, MS and Kanter, RM (1988). *Creating the Future*. Summit Books: New York, USA.

Duncan, WJ (1975). Organisations as political coalitions: a behavioral view of the goal function process. *Journal of Behavioral Economics*, 5, Summer, 25–44.

Dunham, AL (1955). *The Industrial Revolution in France*. Exposition Press: New York, USA.

Dunphy, DD and Griffiths, A (1998). *The Sustainable Corporation: Organisational Renewal in Australia*. Allen & Unwin: St Leonards, Australia.

Dunphy, DD and Stace, DA (1988). Transformational and coercive strategies for planned organizational change: beyond the OD model. *Organization Studies*, 9(3), 317–34.

Dunphy, DD and Stace, DA (1992). *Under New Management: Australian Organizations in Transition*. McGraw-Hill: Roseville, NSW, Australia.

Dunphy, DD and Stace, DA (1993). The strategic management of corporate change. *Human Relations*, 46(8), 905–18.

Easterby-Smith, M (1997). Disciplines of organizational learning: contributions and critiques. *Human Relations*, 50(9), 1085–113.

Economist, The (1998). All fall down. *The Economist*, 28 February.

Economist Intelligence Unit (1992). *Making Quality Work – Lessons from Europe's Leading Companies*. Economist Intelligence Unit: London.

Edwardes, M (1983). *Back from the Brink*. Collins: London.

Egan, G (1994). Cultivate your culture. *Management Today*, April, 39–42.

Elden, M and Chisholm, RF (1993). Emerging varieties of action research: introduction to the special issue. *Human Relations*, 46(20), 121–42.

Eldridge, JET and Crombie, AD (1974). *A Sociology of Organizations*. George Allen and Unwin: London.

Elliot, K and Lawrence, P (1985). *Introducing Management*. Penguin: Harmondsworth.

Elliott, L (1997). The weightless revolution. *The Guardian*, 10 November, 17.

Elliott, L and Brittain, V (1998). The rich and poor grow further apart. *The Guardian*, 9 September, 18.

Etzioni, A (1975). *A Comparative Analysis of Complex Organizations*. Free Press: New York, USA.

Evans, MG (1970). The effects of supervisory behaviour on the path–goal relationship. *Organizational Behavior and Human Performance*, 5, 277–98.

Ezzamel, M, Green, C, Lilley, S and Willmott, H (1994). *Change Management: Appendix 1 – A Review and Analysis of Recent Changes in UK Management Practices*. The Financial Services Research Centre, UMIST: Manchester.

Farrell, D and Petersen, JC (1983). Patterns of political behaviour in organizations. *The Academy of Management Review*, 7, 403–12.

Fawn, J and Cox, B (1985). *Corporate Planning in Practice*. Strategic Planning Society: London.

Fayol, H (1949). *General and Industrial Management* (trans). Pitman: London.

Fazio, RH, Zanna, MP and Cooper, J (1977). Dissonance and self-perception: an integrative view of each theory's proper domain of application. *Journal of Experimental Social Psychology*, 13, 464–79.

Featherstone, M (1988a). In pursuit of postmodernism: an introduction. *Theory, Culture and Society*, 5, 195–215.

Featherstone, M (ed) (1988b). *Postmodernism*. Sage: Newbury Park, CA, USA.

Ferguson, CH (1988). From the people who brought you Voodoo Economics. *Harvard Business Review*, May–June, 55–62.

Ferlie, E, Ashburner, L, Fitzgerald, L and Pettigrew, A (1996). *The New Public Sector in Action*. Oxford University Press: Oxford.

Ferner, A and Hyman, R (eds) (1992). *Industrial Relations in the New Europe*. Blackwell: Oxford.

Festinger, L (1957). *The Theory of Cognitive Dissonance*. Stanford University Press: Stanford, CA, USA.

Fiedler, FE (1967). *A Theory of Leadership Effectiveness*. McGraw-Hill: New York, USA.

Fiedler, FE and Chemers, MM (1984). *Improving Leadership Effectiveness: The Leader Match Concept* (2nd edition). Wiley: New York, USA.

Filby, I and Willmott, H (1988). Ideologies and contradictions in a public relations department. *Organization Studies*, 9(3), 335–51.

Filley, AC, House, RJ and Kerr, S (1976). *Managerial Process and Organization Behavior*. Scott, Foresman and Company: Glenview, IL, USA.

Finstad, N (1998). The rhetoric of organizational change. *Human Relations*, 51(6), 717–40.

Fiol, MC and Lyles, MA (1985). Organizational learning. *Academy of Management Review*, 10(4), 803–13.

Fitton, R and Wadsworth, A (1958). *The Strutts and the Arkwrights 1758–1830*. Manchester University Press: Manchester.

Fleishman, EA (1953). The description of supervisory behaviour. *Personnel Psychology*, 37, 1–6.

Fleishman, EA (1969). *Manual for the Leadership Opinion Questionnaire*. Science Research Associates: USA.

Flynn, J, Dawley, H, Templeman, J and Bernier, L (1995). Suddenly British carmaking is burning rubber. *Business Week*, 3 April, 21.

Flynn, N (1993). *Public Sector Management*. Harvester-Wheatsheaf: London.

Fohlen, C (1973). France 1700–1914. In C Cipolla (ed): *The Fontana Economic History of Europe*, Vol. 4. Fontana: London.

Ford, TM (1981). Strategic planning – myth or reality? A chief executive's view. *Long Range Planning*, 14, December, 9–11.

Fortune (1990). Global 500: the world's biggest industrial corporations. *Fortune*, 30 July.

Foucault, M (1977). *The Archaeology of Knowledge*. Tavistock: London.

Foucault, M (1983). The subject and power. In HL Dreyfus and P Rabinow (eds): *Michel Foucault: Beyond Structuralism and Hermeneutics* (2nd edition). University of Chicago Press: Chicago, USA.

Fox, JM (1975). Strategic planning: a case study. *Managerial Planning*, 23, May/June, 32–8.

Fox, M (1994). *The Reinvention of Work: A New Vision of Livelihood for Our Times*. Harper: San Francisco, USA.

Francks, P (1992). *Japanese Economic Development: Theory and Practice*. Routledge: London.

Franklin, B (1997). *Newszak and News Media*. Arnold: London.

Freeman, C (1988). The factory of the future: the productivity paradox, Japanese just-in-time and information technology. *ESRC PICT Policy Research Paper 3*. ESRC: Swindon.

French, WL and Bell, CH (1973). *Organization Development*. Prentice Hall: Englewood Cliffs, NJ, USA.

French, WL and Bell, CH (1984). *Organization Development* (4th edition). Prentice Hall: Englewood Cliffs, NJ, USA.

French, WL and Bell, CH (1995). *Organization Development* (5th edition). Prentice Hall: Englewood Cliffs, NJ, USA.

Friedman, G (1961). *The Anatomy of Work*. Heinemann: London.

Froebel, F, Heinrichs, J, and Kreye, O (1980). *The New Industrial Division of Labour: Structural Unemployment in Industrialized Countries and Industrialization in Developing Countries*. Cambridge University Press: Cambridge.

Frost, PJ and Hayes, DC (1979). An exploration in two cultures of a model of political behaviour in organizations. In RW Allen and LW Porter (eds): *Organizational Influence Processes*. Scott, Foresman and Co: Glenview, IL, USA.

Fruin, WM (1992). *The Japanese Enterprise System*. OUP: Oxford.

Fullerton, H and Price, C (1991). Culture change in the NHS. *Personnel Management*, March, 50–3.

Fulton, The Lord (1968). *The Civil Service: Report of the Committee Cmnd 3638*. HMSO: London.

Gandz, J and Murray, VV (1980). The experience of workplace politics. *Academy of Management Journal*, 23, 237–51.

Gardner, J (1990). *On Leadership*. Free Press: New York, USA.

Garratt, B (1987). *The Learning Organization*. Fontana: London.

Garvin, DA (1993). Building a learning organization. *Harvard Business Review*, July/August, 78–91.

Gastil, J (1994). A definition and an illustration of Democratic Leadership. *Human Relations*, 47, 953–75.

Gellerman, W, Frankel, MS and Ladenson, RF (1990). *Values and Ethics in Organizational and Human Systems Development: Responding to Dilemmas in Professional Life*. Jossey-Bass: San Francisco, CA, USA.

Genus, A (1998). *The Management of Change: Perspective and Practice*. International Thompson: London.

Gephart, RP, Thatchenkery, TJ and Boye, DM (1996). Reconstructing organizations for future survival. In DM Boye, RP Gephart and TJ Thatchenkery (eds): *Postmodern Management and Organizational Theory*. Sage: Thousand Oaks, CA, USA.

Gergen, KJ (1992). Organization theory in the postmodern era. In M Reed and M Hughes (eds): *Rethinking Organization: New Directions in Organization Theory and Analysis*. Sage: London.

Gersick, CJG (1991). Revolutionary change theories: a multilevel exploration of the punctuated equilibrium paradigm. *Academy of Management Review*, 16(1), 10–36.

Ghemawat, P (1991). *Commitment: The Dynamics of Strategy*. Free Press: New York, USA.

Gibb CA (1969). Leadership. In G Lindzey and E Aronson (eds): *Handbook of Social Psychology*, Vol. 4 (2nd edition). Addison-Wesley: Reading, MA, USA.

Gibbons, PT (1992). Impacts of organisational evolution on leadership roles and behaviors. *Human Relations*, 45(1), 1–18.

Gibson, JL, Ivancevich, JM and Donnelly, JH (1988). *Organizations: Behaviour–Structure–Processes*. Business Publications: Plano, Texas, USA.

Gilbert, RJ and Newbury, DMG (1982). Preemptive patenting and the persistence of monopoly. *American Economic Review*, 72, 514–26.

Gilbert, X and Strebel, P (1992). Developing competitive advantage. In H Mintzberg and JB Quinn (eds): *The Strategy Process: Concepts, Contexts and Cases*. Prentice Hall: London.

Gilbreth, FB and Gilbreth, LM (1914). *Applied Motion Study*. Sturgis and Walton: New York, USA.

Gillespie, R (1991). *Manufacturing Knowledge: A History of the Hawthorne Experiments*. Cambridge University Press: Cambridge.

Gittings, J (1998). Weakest pay the price for recession as African poverty comes to Asia. *The Guardian*, 17 October, 16.

Glueck, WF (1978). *Business Policy and Strategic Management*. McGraw-Hill: New York, USA.

Gold, KA (1982). Managing for success: a comparison of the private and public sectors. *Public Administration Review*, November–December, 568–75.

Golzen, G (1995). Jobbing guru. *Human Resources*, 16, January/February, 42–8.

Goold, M, Campbell, A and Alexander, M (1994). *Corporate-Level Strategy: Creating Value in the Multi-Business Company*. Wiley: Chichester.

Gordon, G (1985). The relationship of corporate culture to industry sector and corporate performance. In R Kilmann, M Saxton, R Serpa and Associates (eds): *Gaining Control of the Corporate Culture*. Jossey-Bass: San Francisco, CA, USA.

Gould, SJ (1989). Punctuated equilibrium in fact and theory. *Journal of Social Biological Structure*, 12, 117–36.

Gow, D (1999a). Vultures still circling Rover plant as BMW remains silent on investment. *The Guardian*, 6 February, 11–12.

Gow, D (1999b). BMW to put £3bn into Rover car plants. *The Guardian*, 24 June, 25.

Gow, D and Traynor, I (1999). BMW split raises fears for Rover plant. *The Guardian*, 2 February, 1.

Grant, A (1983). *Against the Clock*. Pluto: London.

Grant, GM (1991a). *Contemporary Strategy Analysis*. Blackwell: Oxford.

Grant, GM (1991b). The resource-based theory of competitive advantage: implications for strategy formulation. *California Management Review*, 33(3), 114–22.

Greenwald, J (1996). Reinventing Sears. *Time*, 23 December, 53–5.

Grinyer, PH, Mayes, DG and McKiermon, P (1988). *Sharpbenders: The Secrets of Unleashing Corporate Potential*. Blackwell: Oxford.

Grove, G (1998). The automotive industry – the customer's perspective: a study of Rover group. In B Burnes and B Dale (eds) (1998): *Working in Partnership*. Gower: Aldershot.

Grundy, T (1993). *Managing Strategic Change*. Kogan Page: London.

Guest, RH (1957). Job enlargement – revolution in Job Design. *Personnel Administration*, 20, 9–16.

Gyllenhammar, PG (1977). *People at Work*. Addison-Wesley: Reading, MA, USA.

Habakkuk, HJ and Postan, M (eds) (1965). *The Cambridge Economic History of Europe*, Vol. VI. Cambridge University Press: Cambridge.

Hackman, JR and Lawler, EE (1971). Employee relations and job characteristics. *Journal of Applied Psychology*, 55, 259–86.

Hackman, JR and Oldham, GR (1980). *Work Redesign*. Addison-Wesley: Reading, MA, USA.

Hales, CP (1986). What do managers do?: a critical review of the evidence. *Journal of Management Studies*, 22(1), 88–115.

Hall, DT and Nougaim, KE (1968). An examination of Maslow's need hierarchy in an organizational setting. *Organizational Behaviour and Performance*, 3, February, 12–35.

Hambrick, DC (1983). High profit strategies in mature capital goods industries: a contingency approach. *Academy of Management Journal*, 26, 687–707.

Hamel, G and Prahalad, CK (1989). Strategic intent. *Harvard Business Review*, May–June, 63–76.

Handfield, RB and Nichols, EL Jr (1999). *Introduction to Supply Chain Management*. Prentice Hall: Englewood Cliffs, NJ, USA.

Handy, C (1979). *Gods of Management*. Pan: London.

Handy, C (1984). *The Future of Work*. Blackwell: Oxford.

Handy, C (1986). *Understanding Organizations* (3rd edition). Penguin: Harmondsworth.

Handy, C (1989). *The Age of Unreason*. Arrow: London.

Handy, C (1993). *Understanding Organizations* (4th edition). Penguin: Harmondsworth.

Handy, C (1994). *The Empty Raincoat*. Hutchinson: London.

Handy, C (1997). *The Hungry Spirit*. Hutchinson: London.

Handy, C, Gow, I, Gordon, C, Randlesome, C and Moloney, M (1987). *The Making of a Manager*. NEDO: London.

Hannam, R (1993). *Kaizen for Europe*. IFS: Kempston.

Hannan, MT and Freeman, J (1977). The population ecology of organizations. *American Journal of Sociology*, 82, 929–64.

Hannan, MT and Freeman, J (1988). *Organizational Ecology*. Harvard University Press: Cambridge, MA, USA.

Hanson, P (1993). Made in Britain – the true state of manufacturing industry. Paper presented at the Institution of Mechanical Engineers' Conference on Performance Measurement and Benchmarking, Birmingham, June.

Hardy, C (1996). Understanding power: bringing about strategic change. *British Journal of Management*, 7 (Special Issue) March, S3–S16.

Harrigan, RK (1980). *Strategy for Declining Businesses*. Lexington Books: Lexington, MA, USA.

Harris, PR (1985). *Management in Transition*. Jossey-Bass: San Francisco, CA, USA.

Harrison, R (1970). Choosing the depth of an organisational intervention. *Journal of Applied Behavioural Science*, 6, 181–202.

Harrison, R (1972). How to describe your organization. *Harvard Business Review*, 50, September–October.

Hartley, J, Bennington, J and Binns, P (1997). Researching the roles of internal-change agents in the management of organizational change. *British Journal of Managment*, 8(1), 61–73.

Harukiyo, H and Hook, GD (eds) (1998). *Japanese Business Management: Restructuring for Low Growth and Globalization*. Routledge: London.

Hassard, J (1990). An alternative to paradigm incommensurability in organization theory. In J Hassard and D Pym (eds): *The Theory and Philosophy of Organizations*. Routledge: London.

Hassard, J (1993). *Sociology and Organization Theory: Positivism, Paradigms and Post-modernity*. Cambridge University Press: Cambridge.

Hassard, J and Parker, M (eds) (1993). *Postmodernism and Organizations*. Sage: London.

Hassard, J and Sharifi, S (1989). Corporate culture and strategic change. *Journal of General Management*, 15(2), 4–19.

Hatch, MJ (1997). *Organization Theory: Modern, Symbolic and Postmodern Perspectives*. Oxford University Press: Oxford.

Hatvany, N and Pucik, V (1981). An integrated management system: lessons from the Japanese experience. *Academy of Management Review*, 6, 469–80.

Hax, CA and Majluf, NS (1982). Competitive cost dynamics. *Interfaces*, 12, October, 50–61.

Hax, CA and Majluf, NS (1996). *The Strategy Concept and Process* (2nd edition). Prentice Hall: New Jersey, USA.

Hax, CA and Nicholson, SM (1983). The use of the growth share matrix in strategic planning. *Interfaces*, 13, February, 46–60.

Hedberg, B (1981). How organizations learn and unlearn. In PC Nystrom and WH Starbuck (eds): *Handbook of Organizational Design*. Oxford University Press: London.

Hedberg, B, Nystrom, P and Starbuck, W (1976). Camping on seesaws: prescriptions for a self-designing organization. *Administrative Science Quarterly*, 17, 371–81.

Hedlund, G and Nonaka, I (1993). Models of knowledge management in the West and Japan. In P Lorange (ed): *Implementing Strategic Processes*. Blackwell: Oxford.

Heller, F (1970). Group feed-back analysis as a change agent. *Human Relations*, 23(4), 319–33.

Hendry, C (1979). Contingency theory in practice, I. *Personnel Review*, 8(4), 39–44.

Hendry, C (1980). Contingency theory in practice, II. *Personnel Review*, 9(1), 5–11.

Hendry, C (1996). Understanding and creating whole organizational change through learning theory. *Human Relations*, 48(5), 621–41.

Herzberg, F (1968). One more time: how do you motivate employees? *Harvard Business Review*, 46, 53–62.

Herzberg, F, Mausner, B and Snyderman, B (1959). *The Motivation to Work*. Wiley: New York, USA.

Hickson, DJ and Butler, RJ (1982). Power and decision-making in the organisational coalition. Research report presented to the Social Science Research Council.

Hickson, DJ, Pugh, DS and Pheysey, DC (1969). Operations technology and organisation structure: an empirical reappraisal. *Administrative Science Quarterly*, 14, 378–97.

Hines, P (1994). *Creating World Class Suppliers: Unlocking Mutual Competitive Advantage*. Pitman: London.

HMSO (1989). *Working for Patients*, Cmnd 555. HMSO: London.

HMSO (1991). *Competing for Quality*, Cmnd 1730. HMSO: London.

Ho, DYF (1976). On the concept of face. *American Journal of Sociology*, 81(4), 867–84.

Hobsbawm, EJ (1968). *Industry and Empire*. Pelican: Harmondsworth.

Hobsbawm, EJ (1979). *The Age of Revolution*. Abacus: London.

Hofer, CH and Schendel, DE (1978). *Strategy Formulation: Analytical Concepts*. West: St Paul, MN, USA.

Hofstede, G (1980). *Culture's Consequences: International Differences in Work-Related Values*. Sage: London.

Hofstede, G (1990). The cultural relativity of organizational practices and theories. In DC Wilson and RH Rosenfeld (eds): *Managing Organizations: Text, Readings and Cases*. McGraw-Hill: London.

Hofstede, G (1993). Cultural constraints in management theories. *Academy of Management Executive*, 7(1), 81–94.

Holden, N and Burgess, M (1994). *Japanese-Led Companies*. McGraw-Hill: London.

Horne, JH and Lupton, T (1965). The work activities of 'middle managers' – an exploratory study. *Journal of Management Studies*, 2(1), 14–33.

Horsley, W and Buckley, R (1990). *Nippon New Superpower; Japan Since 1945*. BBC Books: London.

Horton, S (1996). The Civil Service. In D Farnham and S Horton (eds): *Managing the New Public Services*, (2nd edition). MacMillan: Basingstoke.

Hoskin, K (1990). Using history to understand theory: a re-consideration of the historical genesis of 'strategy'. Paper prepared for the EIASM Workshop on Strategy, Accounting and Control, Venice.

Howarth, C (1988). Report of the Joint Design of Technology, Organisation and People Growth Conference – Venice, 12–14, October. *Information Services News and Abstracts*, 95 November/December, Work Research Unit: London.

Huber, GP (1991). Organizational learning: the contributing processes and the literatures. *Organization Science*, February, 88–115.

Huczynski, AA (1993). *Management Gurus*. Routledge: London.

Hughes, M (1995). Halifax and Leeds clear the courts. *The Guardian*, 29 March, 15.

Hunter, JE (1989). *The Emergence of Modern Japan*. Longman: London.

Hurley, RF, Church, AH, Burke, WW and Van Eynde, DF (1992). Tension, change and values in OD. *OD Practitioner*, 29, 1–5.

Huse, EF (1980). *Organization Development and Change*. West: St Paul, MN, USA.

Hussey, DE (1978). Portfolio analysis: practical experience with the Directional Policy Matrix. *Long Range Planning*, 11, August, 2–8.

Hutton, W (1995). *The State We're In*. Cape: London.

Inagami, T (1988). *Japanese Workplace Industrial Relations*. Japan Institute of Labour: Tokyo.

Inagami, T (1995). *Enterprise Unions in a Mature Society*. Japan Institute of Labour: Tokyo, Japan.

Industrial Society (1997). *Culture Change. Managing Best Practice 35*. Industrial Society: London.

Institute of Management (1995). *Finding the Time – A Survey of Managers' Attitudes to Using and Managing Time*. Institute of Management: London.

Ishikawa, K (1985). *What is Total Quality Control? The Japanese Way*. Prentice Hall: Englewood Cliffs, NJ, USA.

Ishizuna, Y (1990). The transformation of Nissan – the reform of corporate culture. *Long Range Planning*, 23(3), 9–15.

Ivancevich, J (1970). An analysis of control, bases of control, and satisfaction in an organizational setting. *Academy of Management Journal*, December, 427–32.

Jaques, E (1952). *The Changing Culture of a Factory*. Dryden Press: New York, USA.

Jacques, E (1998). On leaving the Tavistock Institute. *Human Relations*, 51(3), 251–7.

Johnson, G (1987). *Strategic Change and the Management Process*. Blackwell: Oxford.

Johnson, G (1993). Processes of managing strategic change. In C Mabey and B Mayon-White (eds): *Managing Change* (2nd edition). The Open University/Paul Chapman Publishing: London.

Johnson, G and Scholes, K (1993). *Exploring Corporate Strategy*. Prentice Hall: London.

Johnson, R and Ouchi, W (1974). Made in America (under Japanese management). *Harvard Business Review*, 52(5), 61–9.

Jones, EE (1990). *Interpersonal Perception*. Freeman: New York, USA.

Jones, H (1989). Private property. *New Civil Engineer*, 29 June, 23.

Jorberg, L (1973). The Nordic countries 1850–1914. In C Cipolla (ed): *The Fontana Economic History of Europe* Vol. 4. Fontana: London.

Juran, JM (1988). *Quality Control Handbook*. McGraw-Hill: New York, USA.

Kahn, H and Weiner, A (1978). *The Year 2000*. Macmillan: London.

Kamata, S (1982). *Japan in the Passing Lane*. Pantheon: New York, USA.

Kanter, RM (1977). *Men and Women of The Corporation*. Basic Books: New York, USA.

Kanter, RM (1979). Power failure in management circuits. *Harvard Business Review*, 57(4), 65–75.

Kanter, RM (1983). *The Change Masters*. Simon & Schuster: New York, USA.

Kanter, RM (1989). *When Giants Learn to Dance: Mastering the Challenges of Strategy, Management, and Careers in the 1990s.* Unwin: London.

Kanter, RM (1997). *World Class: Thriving Locally in the Global Economy.* Simon & Schuster: New York, USA.

Kanter, RM, Stein, BA and Jick, TD (1992). *The Challenge of Organizational Change.* Free Press: New York, USA.

Kanter, RM, Kao, J and Wiersema, F (eds) (1997). *Innovation: Breakthrough Thinking at 3M, DuPont, GE, Pfizer, and Rubbermaid.* HarperBusiness: New York, USA.

Karlsson, C (1996). Radically new production systems. *International Journal of Operations and Production Management*, 16(11), 8–19.

Karlsson, LE (1973). *Experiences in Employee Participation in Sweden: 1969–1972.* Mimeograph, Cornell University: New York, USA.

Kawakita, T (1997). Corporate strategy and human resource management. In M Sako and H Sato (eds): *Japanese Labour and Management in Transition.* Routledge: London.

Kay, J (1993). *Foundations of Corporate Success.* OUP: Oxford.

Kazunori, O (1998). New trends in Enterprise Unions and the Labour Movement. In H Harukiyo and GD Hook (eds): *Japanese Business Management: Restructuring for Low Growth and Globalization.* Routledge: London.

Kelly, JE (1982a). Economic and structural analysis of Job Design. In JE Kelly and CW Clegg (eds): *Autonomy and Control at the Workplace.* Croom Helm: London.

Kelly, JE (1982b). *Scientific Management, Job Redesign and Work Performance.* Academic Press: London.

Kemp, T (1979). *Industrialization in Nineteenth Century Europe.* Longman: London.

Kempner, T (1970). Frederick Taylor and scientific management. In A Tillett, T Kempner and G Wills (eds): *Management Thinkers.* Pelican: Harmondsworth.

Kennedy, C (1994). *Managing with the Gurus.* Century Business Books: London.

Kerr, C and Fisher, L (1957). Plant sociology: the elite and the Aborigines. In M Komarovsky (ed): *Common Frontiers of the Social Sciences.* Greenwood: Westport, CT, USA.

Kerr, S, Schriesheim, CA, Murphy, CJ and Stogdill, RM (1974). Towards a contingency theory of leadership based upon the consideration and initiating structure literature. *Organizational Behavior and Human Performance*, 12, 62–82.

Keshavan, K and Rakesh, KS (1979). Generating future scenarios – their use in strategic planning. *Long Range Planning*, 12, June, 57–61.

Keys, JB and Miller, TR (1984). The Japanese management theory jungle. *Academy of Management Review*, 9, 342–53.

Kidd, P and Karwowski, W (eds) (1994). *Advances in Agile Manufacture.* IOS: Amsterdam.

Kimberley, J and Miles, R (eds) (1980). *The Organizational Life Cycle.* Jossey Bass: San Francisco, CA, USA.

Kipnis, D, Schmidt, SM and Wilkinson, I (1980). Intraorganizational influence tactics: explorations in getting one's way. *Journal of Applied Psychology*, August, 440–52.

Kipnis, D, Schmidt, SM, Swaffin-Smith, C and Wilkinson, I (1984). Patterns of managerial influence: shotgun managers, tacticians, and bystanders. *Organizational Dynamics*, Winter, 58–67.

Kirton, MJ (1989). *Adaptors and Innovators: Styles of Creativity and Problem Solving.* Routledge: London.

Kjellberg, A (1992). Sweden: can the model survive. In A Ferner and R Hyman (eds): *Industrial Relations in the New Europe.* Blackwell: Oxford.

Koch, R (1995). *The Financial Times Guide to Strategy*. FT Pitman: London.

Koji, O (1998). Small headquarters and the reorganisation of management. In H Harukiyo and GD Hook (eds): *Japanese Business Management: Restructuring for Low Growth and Globalization*. Routledge: London.

Kotler, P (1978). Harvesting strategies for weak products. *Business Horizons*, 21(4), August, 15–22.

Kotter, JP (1982). *The General Manager*. Free Press: New York, USA.

Kotter, JP (1995). Leading change: why transformation efforts fail. *Harvard Business Review*, March–April.

Kotter, JP (1996). *Leading Change*. Harvard Business School Press: Boston, MA, USA.

Kotter, JP and Hesketh, JL (1992). *Corporate Culture and Performance*. Free Press: New York, USA.

Krell, TC (1981). The marketing of organization development: past, present and future. *Journal of Applied Behavioral Science*, 10(2), 485–502.

Kreps, DM and Wilson, R (1982). Reputation and imperfect information. *Journal of Economic Theory*, 27, 253–79.

Kriedt, P, Medick, H and Schlumbohm, J (1981). *Industrialization Before Industrialization*. Cambridge University Press: Cambridge.

Kuhn, TS (1962). *The Structure of Scientific Revolutions*. University of Chicago Press: Chicago, IL, USA.

Laage-Hellman, J (1997). *Business Networks in Japan*. Routledge: London.

Lacey, R (1986). *Ford: The Men and the Machine*. Heinemann: London.

Laird, L (1998). Predators hover over Lonrho's African diamonds. *The Guardian*, 14 November, 28.

Lamming, R (1993). *Beyond Partnership: Strategies for Innovation and Lean Supply*. Prentice Hall: Hemel Hempstead.

Lamming, R (1994). *A Review of the Relationships Between Vehicle Manufacturers and Suppliers*. DTI/SMMT: London.

Landes, DS (1969). *The Unbound Prometheus*. Cambridge University Press: Cambridge.

Landsberger, HA (1958). *Hawthorne Revisited: 'Management and the Worker'. Its Critics and Developments in Human Relations in Industry*. Cornell University Press: New York, USA.

Lanford, HW (1972). *Technological Forecasting Methodologies: A Synthesis*. American Management Association: New York, USA.

Larson, LL, Hunt, JG and Osborne, RN (1976). The great hi-hi leader behavior myth: a lesson from Occam's razor. *Academy of Management Journal*, 19, 628–41.

Laudon, K and Starbuck, WH (1997). Organization information and knowledge. In A Sorge and M Warner (eds): *The IEBM Handbook of Organizational Behaviour*. International Thompson Business Press: London.

Lawler, EE (1985). Challenging traditional research assumptions. In EE Lawler and Associates (eds): *Doing Research That is Useful for Theory and Practice*. Jossey-Bass: San Francisco, USA.

Lawler, EE and Suttle, JL (1972). A causal correlation of the need hierarchy concept in an organizational setting. *Organization Behaviour and Human Performance*, 7, April, 265–87.

Lawrence, PR and Lorsch, JW (1967). *Organization and Environment*. Harvard Business School: Boston, USA.

Lawrence, PR (1973). How to deal with resistance to change. In GW Dalton, PR Lawrence and E Grenier (eds): *Organizational Change and Development*. Dorsey: Homewood, IL, USA.

Lawson, H (1985). *Reflexivity, the Post Modern Predicament*. Hutchinson: London.

Learned, EP, Christensen, CR, Andrews, KR and Guth, WD (1965). *Business Policy: Texts and Cases*. Irwin: Homewood, IL, USA.

Lee, J (1978). Labour in German industrialization. In P Mathias and M Postan (eds): *Cambridge Economic History of Europe*, Vol. VII. Cambridge University Press: Cambridge.

Leemhuis, JP (1990). Using scenario development strategies at Shell. In B Taylor and J Harrison (eds): *The Manager's Casebook of Business Strategy*. Butterworth-Heinemann: Oxford.

Leifer, R and Huber, GP (1977). Relations amongst perceived environmental uncertainty, organisation structure and boundary-spanning behaviour. *Administrative Science Quarterly*, 22, 235–47.

Lenin, VI (1918). The immediate tasks of the Soviet government. Reprinted in: *On the Development of Heavy Industry and Electrification*. Progress Publishers: Moscow, Russia.

Leontiades, M (1986). *Managing the Unmanageable*. Addison-Wesley: Reading, MA, USA.

Lessem, R (1998). *Management Development Through Cultural Diversity*. Routledge: London.

Levine, AL (1967). *Industrial Retardation in Britain 1880–1914*. Basic Books: New York, USA.

Lewin, K (1943). Psychological ecology. In D Cartwright (ed) (1952): *Field Theory in Social Science*. Social Science Paperbacks: London.

Lewin, K (1946). Action research and minority problems. In GW Lewin and GW Allport (eds) (1948): *Resolving Social Conflict*. Harper & Row: London.

Lewin, K (1947a). Frontiers in group dynamics. In D Cartwright (ed) (1952): *Field Theory in Social Science*. Social Science Paperbacks: London.

Lewin, K (1947b). Group decisions and social change. In TM Newcomb and EL Hartley (eds): *Readings in Social Psychology*. Henry Holt: New York, USA.

Lichtenstein, BM (1997). Grace, magic and miracles: a 'chaotic logic' of organizational transformation. *Journal of Organizational Change Management*, 10(5), 393–411.

Likert, R (1961). *New Patterns of Management*. McGraw-Hill: New York, USA.

Likert, R (1967). *The Human Organization: Its Management and Values*. McGraw-Hill: New York, USA.

Lincoln, JR and Kalleberg, AL (1985). Work organisation and workforce commitment: a study of plants and employees in the US and Japan. *American Sociological Review*, 50, 738–60.

Lindblom, CE (1959). The science of muddling through. *Public Administration Review*, 19, Spring, 79–88.

Lindblom, CE (1968). *The Policy-Making Process*. Prentice Hall: Englewood Cliffs, NJ, USA.

Linneman, RE and Klein, HE (1979). The use of multiple scenarios by US industrial companies. *Long Range Planning*, 12, February, 83–90.

Linstead, S (1993). From postmodern anthropology to deconstructive ethnography. *Human Relations*, 46(1), 97–120.

Lippitt, G (1982). Management development as the key to organisational renewal. *Journal of Management Development*, 1(2).

Lippitt, R, Watson, J and Westley, B (1958). *The Dynamics of Planned Change*. Harcourt, Brace and World: New York.

Litschert, R and Nicholson, E (1974). Corporate long range planning groups – some different approaches. *Long Range Planning*, 7, August, 62–6.

Little, R (1984). Conglomerates are doing better than you think. *Fortune*, 28 May, 60.

Littler, CR (1978). Understanding Taylorism. *British Journal of Sociology*, 29(2), 185–202.

Lloyd, AR, Dale, BG and Burnes, B (1994). A study of Nissan Motor Manufacturing (UK) Supplier Development Team Activities. *Proceedings of the Institute of Mechanical Engineers, 208, Part D: Journal of Automobile Engineering*, 63–8.

Locke, EW (1982). The ideas of Frederick W Taylor. *Academy of Management Review*, 7(1), 14–24.

Long, P (1986). *Performance Appraisal Revisited*. IPM: London.

Lorsch, JW (1970). Introduction to the structural design of organizations. In GW Dalton, PR Lawrence and JW Lorsch (eds): *Organization Structure and Design*. Irwin-Dorsey: London.

Lorsch, JW (1986). Managing culture: the invisible barrier to strategic change. *California Management Review*, 28(2), 95–109.

Lovell, R (1980). *Adult Learning*. Croom Helm: London.

Lu, DJ (1987). *Inside Corporate Japan*. Productivity Press: Cambridge, MA, USA.

Luthans, F (1989). Conversation with Edgar H Schein. *Organizational Dynamics*, 17, Spring, 70–5.

Luthans, F, McCaul, HS and Dodd, NG (1985). Organizational commitment: a comparison of American, Japanese and Korean employees. *Academy of Management Journal*, 28, 213–19.

Lynch, R (1997). *Corporate Strategy*. Pitman: London.

Lyotard, J-F (1984). *The Postmodern Condition*. Manchester University Press: Manchester.

Mabey, C and Mayon-White, B (1993). *Managing Change* (2nd edition). The Open University/Paul Chapman Publishing: London.

Maguire, K, Milner, M and Watt, N (2000). The Secret Deal That Left Rover a Museum Piece. *The Guardian*, 18 March, 4–5.

Mahoney, MJ (1974). *Cognition and Behavior Modification*. Ballinger: Cambridge, MA, USA.

Malaska, P, Malmivirta, M, Meristo, T and Hansen, SO (1984). Scenarios in Europe – who uses them and why? *Long Range Planning*, 17, October, 45–9.

Mallory, G (1997). March, James Gardner (1928–) and Cyert, Richard Michael (1921–). In A Sorge and M Warner (eds): *The IEBM Handbook of Organizational Behaviour*. International Thompson Business Press: London.

Mangham Working Party (1987). *The Mangham Working Party Report: A Survey of the In-house Activities of Ten Major Companies*. British Institute of Management/Confederation of British Industry: London.

Mansfield, R (1984). Formal and informal structures. In M Gruneberg and T Wall (eds): *Social Psychology and Organizational Behaviour*. Wiley: Chichester.

Mantoux, P (1964). *The Industrial Revolution in the Eighteenth Century*. Cape: London.

Marczewski, J (1963). The take-off hypothesis and French experience. In WW Rostow: *The Economics of Take-Off into Sustained Growth*. Macmillan: London.

Marglin, SA (1976). What do bosses do? In A Gorz (ed): *The Division of Labour: The Labour Process and Class Struggle in Modern Capitalism*. Harvester: Brighton.

Marrow, AJ (1969). *The Practical Theorist: The Life and Work of Kurt Lewin*. Teachers College Press (1977 edition): New York, USA.

Marsh, N (1986). Management development and strategic management change. *Journal of Management Development*, 5(1).

Marsh, RM and Mannari, H (1976). *Modernization and the Japanese Factory*. Princeton University Press: Princeton, NJ, USA.

Martin, J (1992). *Cultures in Organizations: Three Perspectives*. Oxford University Press: Oxford.

Martin, J, Feldman, MS, Hatch, MJ and Sitkin, SB (1983). The uniqueness paradox in organizational stories. *Administrative Science Quarterly*, 28, 438–53.

Masayoshi, I (1998). Globalisation's impact on the subcontracting system. In H Harukiyo and GD Hook (eds): *Japanese Business Management: Restructuring for Low Growth and Globalization*. Routledge: London.

Masayuki, M (1998). The end of the 'mass production system' and changes in work practices. In H Harukiyo and GD Hook (eds): *Japanese Business Management: Restructuring for Low Growth and Globalization*. Routledge: London.

Maslow, AH (1943). A theory of human motivation. *Psychology Review*, 50, 370–96.

Massie, JL (1965). Management theory. In JG March (ed): *Handbook of Organizations*. Rand McNally: Chicago, USA.

Mathias, P (1969). *The First Industrial Nation*. Methuen: London.

Mathias, P and Davis, JA (eds) (1989). *The First Industrial Revolutions*. Blackwell: Cambridge.

Mayes, BT and Allen, RW (1977). Towards a definition of organizational politics. *Academy of Management Review*, October, 672–8.

Mayo, E (1933). *The Human Problems of Industrial Civilization*. Macmillan: New York, USA.

Mayon-White, B (1993). Problem-solving in small groups: team members as agents of change. In C Mabey and B Mayon-White (eds): *Managing Change* (2nd edition). The Open University/Paul Chapman Publishing: London.

McCalman, J and Paton, RA (1992). *Change Management: A Guide to Effective Implementation*. Paul Chapman Publishing: London.

McGregor, D (1960). *The Human Side of Enterprise*. McGraw-Hill: New York, USA.

McGregor, D (1967). *The Professional Manager*. McGraw-Hill: New York, USA.

McIvor, G (1995). Retuned Volvo rises from the ashes. *The Guardian*, 24 June, 37.

McKenna, S (1988). 'Japanisation' and recent developments in Britain. *Employee Relations*, 10(4).

McKiernan, P (1992). *Strategies for Growth: Maturity, Recovery and Internationalization*. Routledge: London.

McKracken, JK (1986). Exploitation of FMS technology to achieve strategic objectives. Paper to the 5th International Conference on Flexible Manufacturing Systems, Stratford-Upon-Avon.

McLennan, R (1989). *Managing Organizational Change*. Prentice Hall: Englewood Cliffs, NJ, USA.

McMillan, J (1985). *The Japanese Industrial System*. De Gruyter: Berlin.

McNamee, BP (1985). *Tools and Techniques of Strategic Management*. Pergamon: Oxford.

McNulty, CAR (1977). Scenario development for corporate planning. *Futures*, 9(2), 128–38.

Meek, VL (1988). Organizational culture: origins and weaknesses. *Organization Studies*, 9(4), 453–73.

Meyer, MW and Zucker, LG (1989). *Permanently Failing Organizations*. Sage: Beverly Hills, CA, USA.

Meyerson, D and Martin, J (1987). Cultural change: an integration of three different views. *Journal of Management Studies*, 24(6), 623–47.

Miewald, RD (1970). The greatly exaggerated death of bureaucracy. *California Management Review*, Winter, 65–9.

Miles, RE and Snow, CC (1978). *Organisational Strategy, Structure and Process*. McGraw-Hill: New York, USA.

Milgrom, P and Roberts, J (1982). Predation, reputation and entry deterrence. *Journal of Economic Theory*, 27, 280–313.

Mill, J (1994). No pain, no gain. *Computing*, 3 February, 26–7.

Miller, D (1992). The generic strategy trap. *Journal of Business Strategy*, 13(1), 37–41.

Miller, D (1993). The architecture of simplicity. *Academy of Management Review*, 18(1), 116–38.

Miller, D and Friesen, PH (1984). *Organizations: A Quantum View*. Prentice Hall, Englewood Cliffs, NJ, USA.

Miller, E (1967). *Systems of Organisation*. Tavistock: London.

Miller, E (1993). *From Dependency to Autonomy – Studies in Organization and Change*. Free Association Books: London.

Milner, M (1998). Productivity as seen by hamsters. *The Guardian*, 22 October, 27.

Milward, A and Saul, SB (1973). *The Economic Development of Continental Europe 1780–1870*. George Allen & Unwin: London.

Minett, S (1992). *Power, Politics and Participation in the Firm*. Ashgate: Brookfield, VT, USA.

Mink, OG (1992). Creating new organizational paradigms for change. *International Journal of Quality and Reliability Management*, 9(3), 21–35.

Mintzberg, H (1973). *The Nature of Managerial Work*. Harper & Row: New York, USA.

Mintzberg, H (1975). The manager's job: folklore and fact. *Harvard Business Review*, 53(4), 49–61.

Mintzberg, H (1976). Planning on the left side and managing on the right. *Harvard Business Review*, July/August, 49–58.

Mintzberg, H (1978). Patterns in strategy formation. *Management Science*, 24(9), 934–48.

Mintzberg, H (1979). *The Structure of Organizations*. Prentice Hall: Englewood Cliffs, NJ, USA.

Mintzberg, H (1983). *Power in and Around Organizations*. Prentice Hall: Englewood Cliffs, NJ, USA.

Mintzberg, H (1987). Crafting strategy. *Harvard Business Review*, 19(2), 66–75.

Mintzberg, H (1994). *The Rise and Fall of Strategic Planning*. Prentice Hall: London.

Mintzberg, H and Quinn, JB (1991). *The Strategy Process: Concepts, Contexts and Cases*. Prentice Hall: London.

Mintzberg, H, Quinn, JB and James, RM (1988). *The Strategy Process: Concepts, Contexts and Cases*. Prentice Hall: London.

Mintzberg, H, Ahlstrand, B and Lampel, J (1998). *Strategy Safari*. Prentice Hall: Hemel Hempstead.

Mirvis, P (1988). Organizational development: an evolutionary perspective. In W Pasmore and R Woodman (eds): *Research in Organizational Change and Development*, Vol. 2. JAI Press: Greenwich, CT, USA.

Mirvis, PH (1990). Organization development: Part 2 – a revolutionary perspective. *Research in Organizational Change and Development*, 4, 1–66.

Mitroff, II and Mason, RO (1981). *Challenging Strategic Planning Assumptions*. Wiley: New York, USA.

Moore, JI (1992). *Writers on Strategy and Strategic Management*. Penguin: Harmondsworth.

Morgan, G (1986). *Images of Organizations*. Sage: Beverly Hills, CA, USA.

Morgan, G (1988). *Riding the Waves of Change*. Jossey-Bass: San Francisco, USA.

Morgan, G (1990). *Organisations in Society*. Macmillan: London.

Morieux, YUH and Sutherland, E (1988). The interaction between the use of information technology and organization change. *Behaviour and Information Technology*, 7(2), 205–13.

Morris, J and Imrie, R (1992). *Transforming Buyer–Supplier Relationships*. Macmillan: Basingstoke.

Mullins, L (1989). *Management and Organisational Behaviour*. Pitman: London.

Mullins, LJ (1993). *Management and Organisational Behaviour* (3rd edition). Pitman: London.

Mumford, A (1987). Myths and reality in developing directors. *Personnel Management*, 19(2), February, 29–33.

Mumford, E (1979). The design of work: new approaches and new needs. In JE Rijnsdorp (ed): *Case Studies in Automation Related to the Humanisation of Work*. Pergamon: Oxford.

Murray, F (1989). The organizational politics of information technology: studies from the UK financial services industry. *Technology Analysis & Strategic Management*, 1(30), 285–97.

Myers, CS (1934). *An Account of the Work Carried out at the National Institute of Industrial Psychology during the Years 1921–34*. NIIP: London.

Nadler, DA (1988). Concepts for the management of organizational change. In ML Tushman and WL Moore (eds): *Readings in the Management of Innovation*. Ballinger: New York, USA.

Nadler, DA (1993). Concepts for the management of strategic change. In C Mabey and B Mayon-White (eds): *Managing Change* (2nd edition). The Open University/Paul Chapman Publishing: London.

Nadworthy, M (1957). Frederick Taylor and Frank Gilbreth: competition in scientific management. *Business History Review*, 31(1), 23–34.

NAO (1995). *Interim Report: PSA Services, The Sale of PSA Projects. Report by the National Audit Office*. HMSO: London.

NAO (1996). *PSA Service: The Transfer of PSA Building Management to the Private Sector. Report of the National Audit Office*. HMSO: London.

Naoi, A and Schooler, C (1985). Occupational conditions and psychological functioning in Japan. *American Journal of Sociology*, 90, 729–52.

Naylor, TH (1979). *Simulation Models in Corporate Measuring*. Draeger: New York, USA.

Naylor, TH (1981). Strategic planning models. *Managerial Planning*, 30, July/August, 3–11.

NEDC (1991a). *The Experience of Nissan Suppliers: Lessons for the United Kingdom Engineering Industry*. NEDC: London.

NEDC (1991b). *Winning Together: Collaborative Sourcing in Practice*. NEDC: London.

Nelson, RR and Winter, SG (1982). *An Evolutionary Theory of Economic Change*. Harvard University Press: Cambridge, MA, USA.

New, C (1989). The challenge of transformation. In B Burnes and B Weekes (eds): *AMT: A Strategy for Success?* NEDO: London.

New, S and Burnes, B (1998). Developing effective customer–supplier relationships: more than one way to skin a cat. *Journal of Quality and Reliability Management*, 15(4), 377–88.

Newstrom, J (1985). Modern management: does it deliver? *Journal of Management Development*, 4(1).

NHS Executive (1999). *NHS Annual Report*. NHS Executive: London.

Nonaka, I (1988). Creating organizational order out of chaos: self-renewal in Japanese firms. *Harvard Business Review*, November–December, 96–104.

Nonaka, I (1991). The knowledge-creating company. *Harvard Business Review*, November/December, 96–104.

Nord, W (1985). Can organizational culture be managed: a synthesis. In R Kilmann, M Saxton, R Serpa and Associates (eds): *Gaining Control of Corporate Culture*. Jossey-Bass: San Francisco, CA, USA.

Norrie, J (1993). *Winning By Continuous Improvement: Facilitators' Guide*. Norrie: Northampton.

Norse, D (1979). Scenario analysis in interfutures. *Futures*, 11(5), 412–22.

Nystrom, PC and Starbuck, WH (1984). To avoid crises, unlearn. *Organizational Dynamics*, 12(4), 53–65.

O'Brien, GE and Kabanoff, B (1981). The effects of leadership style and group structure upon small group productivity: a test of discrepancy theory of leader effectiveness. *Australian Journal of Psychology*, 33(2), 157–8.

Odaka, K (1975). *Towards Industrial Democracy: Management and Workers in Modern Japan*. Harvard University Press: Cambridge, MA, USA.

OECD (1996). *The OECD Economic Survey: The UK 1996*. OECD: Paris.

Ohmae, K (1986). *The Mind of the Strategist*. Penguin: Harmondsworth.

Ohmae, K (1990). Untitled article in *Special Report 1202, The Management Briefing, The Economist*, London.

Ohmi, N (1997). The public sector and privatisation. In M Sako and H Sato (eds): *Japanese Labour and Management in Transition*. Routledge: London.

O'Reilly, C (1989). Corporations, culture and commitment. *California Management Review*, 31(4), 9–24.

Osborne, D and Gaebler, T (1992). *Reinventing Government: How the Entrepreneurial Spirit is Transforming the Public Sector*. Addison-Wesley: Reading, MA, USA.

Oticon (1994). *Oticon's Fundamental Human Values – Vision and Reality*. Oticon: Copenhagen, Denmark.

Ouchi, W (1981). *Theory Z: How American Business Can Meet the Japanese Challenge*. Addison-Wesley: Reading, MA, USA.

Pang, K and Oliver, N (1988). Personnel strategy in eleven Japanese manufacturing companies. *Personnel Review*, 17(3).

Parsons, T (1947). Introduction. In M Weber (ed): *The Theory of Social and Economic Organization*. Free Press: Glencoe, IL, USA.

Partnership Sourcing Ltd (1991a). *Case Studies in Partnership Sourcing*. Partnership Sourcing Ltd: London.

Partnership Sourcing Ltd (1991b). *Partnership Sourcing*. Partnership Sourcing Ltd: London.

Pascale, RT (1993). The benefit of a clash of opinions. *Personnel Management*, October, 38–41.

Pascale, RT and Athos, AG (1982). *The Art of Japanese Management*. Penguin: Harmondsworth.

Patel, P and Younger, M (1978). A frame of reference for strategy development. *Long Range Planning*, 11, April, 6–12.

Paton, R, Clark, G, Jones, G, Lewis, J and Quintas, P (eds) (1996). *The New Management Reader*. Routledge/Open University: London.

Pavlov, IP (1927). *Conditioned Reflexes* (trans). Oxford University Press: London.

Pearson, AE (1987). Muscle-build the organization. *Harvard Business Review*, 65(4), 49–55.

Pearson, B (1977). How to manage turnarounds. *Management Today*, April, 75.

Pedler, M, Boydell, T and Burgoyne, JG (1989). Towards the learning company. *Management Education and Development*. 20(1), 1–8.

Pelling, H (1960). *American Labor*. Chicago University Press: Chicago, USA.

Perez, C (1983). Structural change and the assimilation of new technologies in the economic and social systems. *Futures*, 15, 357–75.

Perrow, C (1967). A framework for the comparative analysis of organizations. *American Sociological Review*, 32, 194–208.

Perrow, C (1970). *Organizational Analysis: A Sociological View*. Tavistock: London.

Perrow, C (1983). The organizational context of human factors engineering. *Administrative Science Quarterly*, 28, 521–41.

Peters, T (1989). *Thriving on Chaos*. Pan: London.

Peters, T (1993). *Liberation Management*. Pan: London.

Peters, T (1995). *The Pursuit of WOW!* Macmillan: London.

Peters, T (1997a). *The Circle of Innovation: You Can't Shrink Your Way to Greatness*. Alfred A Knopf: New York, USA.

Peters, T (1997b). Foreword. In RM Kanter, J Kao and F Wiersema (eds): *Innovation: Breakthrough Thinking at 3M, DuPont, GE, Pfizer, and Rubbermaid*. HarperBusiness: New York, USA.

Peters, T, and Waterman, RH (1982). *In Search of Excellence: Lessons from America's Best-Run Companies*. Harper & Row: London.

Pettigrew, AM (1973). *The Politics of Decision-Making*. Tavistock: London.

Pettigrew, AM (1980). The politics of organisational change. In NB Anderson (ed): *The Human Side of Information Processing*. North Holland: Amsterdam, Netherlands.

Pettigrew, AM (1985). *The Awakening Giant: Continuity and Change at ICI*. Blackwell: Oxford.

Pettigrew, AM (1987). Context and action in the transformation of the firm. *Journal of Management Sciences*, 24(6), 649–70.

Pettigrew, AM (1990a). Longitudinal field research on change: theory and practice. *Organizational Science*, 3(1), 267–92.

Pettigrew, AM (1990b). Studying strategic choice and strategic change. *Organizational Studies*, 11(1), 6–11.

Pettigrew, AM and Whipp, R (1993). Understanding the environment. In C Mabey and B Mayon-White (eds): *Managing Change* (2nd edition). The Open University/Paul Chapman Publishing: London.

Pettigrew, AM, Ferlie, E and McKee, L (1992). *Shaping Strategic Change*. Sage: London.

Pfeffer, J (1978). *Organizational Design*. AHM Publishing: Arlington Heights, IL, USA.

Pfeffer, J (1981). *Power in Organizations*. Pitman: Cambridge, MA, USA.

Pfeffer, J (1992). *Managing with Power: Politics and Influence in Organizations*. Harvard Business School Press: Boston, MA, USA.

Piore, M and Sabel, C (1984). *The Second Industrial Divide*. Basic Books: New York, USA.

Plowden, The Lord. (1961). *Control of Public Expenditure*, Cmnd 1432. HMSO: London.

Pollard, S (1965). *The Genesis of Modern Management*. Pelican: Harmondsworth.

Pollard, S (1981). *Peaceful Conquest: The Industrialization of Europe, 1760–1970*. Oxford University Press: Oxford.

Pontusson, J (1990). The politics of new technology and job redesign: a comparison of Volvo and British Leyland. *Economic and Industrial Democracy*, 11, 311–36.

Porter, LW (1976). Organizations as political animals. *Presidential Address, Division of Industrial Organizational Psychology, 84th Annual Meeting of the American Psychological Association*, Washington, DC.

Porter, LW, Allen, RW and Angle, HL (1983). The politics of upward influence in organizations. In RW Allen and LW Porter (eds): *Organizational Influence Processes*. Scott, Foresman and Co: Glenview, IL, USA.

Porter, M (1980). *Competitive Strategy*. Free Press: New York, USA.

Porter, M (1985). *Competitive Advantage*. Free Press: New York, USA.

Prahalad, CK and Hamel, G (1990). The core competence of the corporation. *Harvard Business Review*, May/June, 71–91.

Prigogine, I and Stengers, I (1984). *Order out of Chaos: Man's New Dialogue with Nature*. Bantam Books: New York, USA.

Probst, G and Buchel, B (1997). *Organizational Learning*. Prentice Hall: London.

Pruijt, HD (1997). *Job Design and Technology: Taylorism vs Anti-Taylorism*. Routledge: London.

PSA (1988). *PSA Annual Report 1987–88*. HMSO: London.

PSA (1989). *PSA to be Privatised*. PSA Press Release No.96, 27 September. DoE: London.

Pugh, DS (ed) (1984). *Organization Theory*. Penguin: Harmondsworth.

Pugh, DS (1993). Understanding and managing organizational change. In C Mabey and B Mayon-White (eds): *Managing Change* (2nd edition). The Open University/Paul Chapman Publishing: London.

Pugh, DS and Hickson, DJ (1976). *Organizational Structure in its Context: The Aston Programme 1*. Saxon House: Farnborough.

Pugh, DS, Hickson, DJ, Hinings, CR and Turner, C (1969a). The context of organization structures. *Administrative Science Quarterly*, 14, 91–114.

Pugh, DS, Hickson, DJ and Hinings, CR (1969b). An empirical taxonomy of structures of work organisation. *Administrative Science Quarterly*, 14, 115–26.

Quinn, JB (1980a). Managing strategic change. *Sloan Management Review*, 21(4), 3–20.

Quinn, JB (1980b). *Strategies for Change: Logical Incrementalism*. Irwin: Homewood, IL, USA.

Quinn, JB (1982). Managing strategies incrementally. *Omega*, 10(6), 613–27.

Quinn, JB (1993). Managing strategic change. In C Mabey and B Mayon-White (eds): *Managing Change* (2nd edition). The Open University/Paul Chapman Publishing: London.

Quinn, RE (1996). *Deep Change: Discovering the Leader Within*. Jossey-Bass: San Francisco, CA, USA.

Quinn, RE and McGrath, MR (1985). The transformation of organizational cultures: a competing values perspective. In PJ Frost, LF Moore, MR Louis, CC Lundberg and J Martin (eds): *Organizational Culture*. Sage: Newbury Park, CA, USA.

Rafferty, K (1995). Tokyo and Mitsubishi banks to merge to create world's largest bank. *The Guardian*, 25 March, 15.

Reed, M (1992). *The Sociology of Organizations*. Harvester Wheatsheaf: Hemel Hempstead.

Reed, M and Hughes, M (eds) (1992). *Rethinking Organization: New Directions in Organization Theory and Analysis*. Sage: London.

Reich, R (1997). The menace of prosperity: widening inequality poses a threat to US and other societies. *Financial Times*, 3 March, 20.

Robbins, SP (1986). *Organizational Behavior: Concepts, Controversies, and Applications*. Prentice Hall: Englewood Cliffs, NJ, USA.

Robbins, SP (1987). *Organization Theory: Structure, Design, and Applications*. Prentice Hall: Englewood Cliffs, NJ, USA.

Robbins, SP (1997). *Managing Today!* Prentice Hall: Upper Saddle River, NJ, USA.

Roethlisberger, F and Dickson, WJ (1938). *Management and the Worker*. Wiley: New York, USA.

Rogers, R (1997). Handy man. *Training*, November, 19.

Roll, E (1930). An early experiment in industrial organisation: Boulton and Watt, 1775–1805. Reprinted in M Berg (ed) (1979): *Technology and Toil in Nineteenth Century Britain*. CSE Books: London.

Romanelli, E and Tushman, ML (1994). Organizational transformation as punctuated equilibrium: an empirical test. *Academy of Management Journal*, 37(5), 1141–66.

Rose, M (1988). *Industrial Behaviour*. Penguin: Harmondsworth.

Rosenbrock, H (1982). *Unmanned Engineering*. Report 12 to the FMS Steering Committee. UMIST: Manchester.

Rosenzweig, PM (1994). When can management science research be generalized internationally? *Management Science*, 40(1), 28–39.

Rothwell, S (1994). Human resources management. *Manager Update*, 5(3), Spring, 22–35.

Rubin, I (1967). Increasing self-acceptance: a means of reducing prejudice. *Journal of Personality and Social Psychology*, 5, 233–8.

Rumelt, RP (1991). How much does industry matter? *Strategic Management Journal*, 12(3), 167–85.

Sakai, K (1992). The feudal world of Japanese manufacturing. In RM Kanter, BA Stein and TD Jick: *The Challenge of Organizational Change*. Free Press: New York.

Sako, M (1997). Introduction. In M Sako and H Sato (eds): *Japanese Labour and Management in Transition*. Routledge: London.

Sako, M and Sato, H (eds) (1997). *Japanese Labour and Management in Transition*. Routledge: London.

Salaman, G (1979). *Work Organisations*. Longman: London.

Salauroo, M and Burnes, B (1998). The impact of a market system on public sector organisations: a study of organisational change in the NHS. *The International Journal of Public Sector Management*, 11(6), 451–67.

Sathe, V (1983). Some action implications of corporate culture: a manager's guide to action. *Organizational Dynamics*, Autumn, 4–23.

Saul, JR (1997). *The Unconscious Civilization*. Penguin: London.

Saunders, M (1997). *Strategic Purchasing & Supply Chain Management* (2nd edition). Pitman: London.

Sayer, A (1989). Post-Fordism in question. *International Journal of Urban and Regional Research*, 13(4), 666–95.

Schein, EH (1969). *Process Consultation*. Addison-Wesley: Reading, MA, USA.

Schein, EH (1984). Coming to a new awareness of organizational culture. *Sloan Management Review*, 25(2), 3–16.

Schein, EH (1985). *Organizational Culture and Leadership: A Dynamic View*. Jossey-Bass: San Francisco, USA.

Schein, EH (1988). *Organizational Psychology* (3rd edition). Prentice Hall: Englewood Cliffs, NJ, USA.

Schein, EH (1989). Organizational culture: what it is and how to change it. In P Evans, T Doz and A Laurent (eds): *Human Resource Management in International Firms*. Macmillan: London.

Schilit, WK and Locke, EA (1982). A study of upward influence in organizations. *Administrative Science Quarterly*, June, 304–16.

Schmalensee, R (1983). Advertising and entry deterrence: an exploratory model. *Journal of Political Economy*, 91(4), 636–53.

Schoeffler, S (1980). *Nine Basic Findings on Business Strategy*. The Strategic Planning Institute: Cambridge, MA, USA.

Schonberger, RJ (1982). *Japanese Manufacturing Techniques*. Free Press: New York, USA.

Schmuck, R and Miles, M (1971). *Organizational Development in Schools*. National Press: Palo Alto, CA, USA.

Schriesheim, CA and Murphy, CJ (1976). Relationships between leader behavior and subordinate satisfaction and performance: a test of some situational moderators. *Journal of Applied Psychology*, 61, 634–41.

Schumacher, EF (1973). *Small is Beautiful: A Study of Economics as if People Mattered*. Vintage Books: London.

Schuyt, TNM and Schuijt, JJM (1998). Rituals and rules: about magic in consultancy. *Journal of Organizational Change Management*, 11(5), 399–406.

Schwartz, H and Davis, S (1981). Matching corporate culture and business strategy. *Organizational Dynamics*, 10, 30–48.

Scott, WR (1987). *Organizations: Rational, Natural and Open Systems*. Prentice Hall: Englewood Cliffs, NJ, USA.

Seike, A (1997). Ageing workers. In M Sako and H Sato (eds): *Japanese Labour and Management in Transition*. Routledge: London.

Selznick, P (1948). Foundations of the theory of organization. *American Sociological Review*, 13, 25–35.

Senge, PM (1990). *The Fifth Discipline: The Art and Practice of the Learning Organization*. Century Business: London.

Senior, B (1997). *Organisational Change*. Pitman: London.

Shapiro, C (1989). The theory of business strategy. *RAND Journal of Economics*, 20(1), 125–37.

Sheahan, J (1969). *An Introduction to the French Economy*. Merill: Columbus, OH, USA.

Sheldrake, J (1966). *Management Theory: From Taylorism to Japanization*. International Thompson Business Press: London.

Sheridan, K (1993). *Governing the Japanese Economy*. Polity Press: Oxford.

Shiflett, SC (1973). The contingency model of leadership effectiveness: some implications of its statistical and methodological properties. *Behavioral Science*, 18(6), 429–40.

Shirai, T (1997). Foreword. In M Sako and H Sato (eds): *Japanese Labour and Management in Transition*. Routledge: London.

Short, JE and Venkatraman, N (1992). Beyond business process redesign: redefining Baxter's business network. *Sloan Management Review*, Fall, 7–21.

Shortell, S and Zajac, E (1990). Perceptual and archival measures of Miles and Snow's strategic types: a comprehensive assessment of reliability and validity. *Academy of Management Journal*, 33, 817–32.

Silverman, D (1970). *The Theory of Organizations*. Heinemann: London.

Silverman, D and Jones, J (1976). *Organizational Work*. Macmillan: London.

Simon, HA (1957). *Administrative Behaviour: A Study of Decision-making Processes in Administrative Organizations* (2nd edition). Macmillan: New York, USA.

Sissons, K (ed) (1989). *Personnel Management in Britain*. Blackwell: Oxford.

Sissons, K and Storey, J (1988). Developing effective managers: a review of the issues and an agenda for research. *Personnel Review*, 17(4), 3–8.

Skinner, BF (1974). *About Behaviourism*. Cape: London.

Sloan, AP (1986). *My Years with General Motors*. Penguin: Harmondsworth.

Smircich, L and Calás, M (1987). Organizational culture: a critical assessment. In F Jabin, L Putnam, K Roberts and L Porter (eds): *Handbook of Organizational Communication*. Sage: Newbury Park, CA, USA.

Smith, A (1776). *The Wealth of Nations*, Volume 1. Methuen (1950 edition): London.

Smith, JG (1985). *Business Strategy*. Blackwell: Oxford.

Smith, JH (1987). Elton Mayo and the hidden Hawthorne. *Work, Employment and Society*, 1(1), 107–120.

Smith, JH (1998). The enduring legacy of Elton Mayo. *Human Relations*, 51(3), 221–49.

Smith, M, Beck, J, Cooper, CL, Cox, C, Ottaway, D and Talbot, R (1982). *Introducing Organizational Behaviour*. Macmillan: London.

Smith, PB and Misumi, J (1989). Japanese management – a sun rising in the West. In CL Cooper and I Robertson (eds): *The International Review of Industrial and Organizational Psychology*. Wiley: London.

Smith, S and Tranfield, D (1987). The implementation and exploitation of advanced manufacturing technology – an outline methodology. *Change Management Research Unit, Research Paper No 2*, Sheffield Business School.

Smith, T (1994). Flexible production and capital/wage labour relation in manufacturing. *Capital and Class*, 53, Summer, 39–63.

Smithers, R (1995). Power chiefs pay themselves £72m in share options. *The Guardian*, 13 February, 20.

Snow, C, Miles, R and Coleman, H (1993). Managing 21st century network organizations. In C Mabey and B Mayon-White (eds): *Managing Change* (2nd edition). The Open University/Paul Chapman Publishing: London.

Sorge, A (1997). Organization behaviour. In A Sorge and M Warner (eds): *The IEBM Handbook of Organizational Behaviour*. International Thompson Business Press: London.

Stace, DA and Dunphy, DD (1994). *Beyond the Boundaries: Leading and Re-Creating the Successful Enterprise*. McGraw-Hill: Sydney, Australia.

Stacey, R (1990). *Dynamic Strategic Management for the 1990s*. Kogan Page: London.

Stacey, R (1992). *Managing Chaos: Dynamic Business Strategies in an Unpredictable World*. Kogan Page: London.

Stacey, R (1993). *Strategic Management and Organisational Dynamics*. Pitman: London.

Stalk, G, Evans, P and Shulman, LE (1992). Competing on capabilities – the new rules of corporate strategy. *Harvard Business Review*, March–April, 57–69.

Stata, R (1989). Organization learning – the key to management innovation. *Sloan Management Review*, Spring, 63–74.

Steiner, GA (1969). *Top Management Planning*. Macmillan: London.

Stewart, R (1976). *Contrasts in Management*. McGraw-Hill: London.

Stickland, F (1998). *The Dynamics of Change: Insights into Organisational Transition from the Natural World*. Routledge: London.

Storey, J (1989). Management development: a literature review and implications for future research – Part 1: conceptualisations and practices. *Personnel Review*, 18(6), 3–19.

Storey, J (1990). Management development: a literature review and implications for future research – Part 2: profiles and context. *Personnel Review*, 19(1), 3–11.

Storey, J (1992). *Developments in the Management of Human Resources*. Blackwell: Oxford.

Streeck, W (1987). The uncertainties of management and the management of uncertainties: employers, labour relations and industrial adjustments in the 1980s. *Work, Employment and Society*, 1(3), 281–308.

Stuart, R (1986). Social learning. *Management Decision*, 24(6), 32–5.

Student, J (1968). Supervisory influence and work-group performance. *Journal of Applied Psychology*, June, 188–94.

Sugeno, K and Suwa, Y (1997). Labour law issues in a changing labour market: in search of a new support system. In M Sako and H Sato (eds): *Japanese Labour and Management in Transition*. Routledge: London.

Sullivan, J (1983). A critique of Theory Z. *Academy of Management Review*, 8, 132–42.

Sullivan, J and Nonaka, I (1986). The application of organizational learning theory to Japanese and American management. *Journal of International Business Studies*, Fall, 127–47.

Taguchi, G (1986). *Introduction to Quality Engineering*. Asian Production Organization: Dearborn, MI, USA.

Talbot, R (1993). Creativity in the organizational context: implications for training. In SG Isaksen, MC Murdock, RL Firestien and DJ Treffinger (eds): *Nurturing and Developing Creativity*. Ablex: Norwood, NJ, USA.

Talbot, R (1997). Taking style on board. *Creativity and Innovation Management*, 6(3), 177–84.

Taylor, FW (1911a). *Shop Management*. Harper (1947 edition): New York, USA.

Taylor, FW (1911b). *The Principles of Scientific Management*. Harper (1947 edition): New York, USA.

Teece, DJ, Pisano, G and Shuen, A (1997). Dynamic capabilities and strategic management. *Strategic Management Journal*, 18(7), 509–33.

Terry, PT (1976). The contingency theory and the development of organisations. *Paper presented to the British Sociological Association*.

Tett, G (1994). Partnerships in business grow. *Financial Times*, 28 June, 12.

Thickett, M (1970). Gilbreth and the measurement of work. In A Tillett, T Kempner and G Willis (eds): *Management Thinkers*. Pelican: Harmondsworth.

Thomas, AB (1993). *Controversies in Management*. Routledge: London.

Thompkins, JM (1990). Politics – the illegitimate discipline. *Management Decision*, 28(4), 23–8.

Thompson, AA Jnr and Strickland, AJ (1983). *Strategy Formulation and Implementation*. Business Publications Inc: Illinois, USA.

Thompson, J (1967). *Organizations in Action*. McGraw-Hill: New York, USA.

Thompson, JW (1995). The renaissance of learning in business. In S Chawla and J Renesch (eds): *Learning Organizations: Developing Cultures for Tomorrow's Workplace*. Productivity Press: Portland, OR, USA.

Thornberry, NE (1987). Training the engineer as project manager. *Training and Development Journal*, 41(10).

Tillett, A (1970). Industry and Management. In A Tillett, T Kempner and G Willis (eds): *Management Thinkers*. Pelican: Harmondsworth.

Toffler, A (1970). *Future Shock*. Random House: New York, USA.

Tomaney, J (1990). The reality of workplace flexibility. *Capital and Class*, 40, Spring, 29–60.

Trice, HM and Beyer, JM (1984). Studying organizational cultures through rites and ceremonials. *Academy of Management Review*, 9, 653–69.

Trice, HM and Beyer, JM (1990). Using six organizational rites to change culture. In RH Kilmann, MJ Saxton, R Serpa and Associates (eds): *Gaining Control of the Corporate Culture*. Josey Bass: San Francisco, CA, USA.

Trist, EL, Higgin, GW, Murray, H and Pollock, AB (1963). *Organisational Choice*. Tavistock: London.

Tsang, EWK (1997). Organizational learning and the learning organization: a dichotomy between descriptive and prescriptive research. *Human Relations*, 50(1), 73–89.

Turnbull, P (1986). The Japanisation of production and industrial relations at Lucas Electrical. *Industrial Relations Journal*, 17(3), 193–206.

Turner, B (1971). *Exploring the Industrial Subculture*. Macmillan: London.

Turner, B (1986). Sociological aspects of organizational symbolism. *Organization Studies*, 7(2), 101–17.

Turner, I (1990). Strategy and organisation. *Manager Update*, 1(3), 1–10.

Tushman, ML and Romanelli, E (1985). Organizational evolution: a metamorphosis model of convergence and reorientation. In LL Cummings and BM Staw (eds): *Research in Organizational Behavior*. 7, 171–222. JAI Press: Greenwich, CT, USA.

Tushman, M and Virany, B (1986). Changing characteristics of executive teams in an emerging industry. *Journal of Business Venturing*, 37–49.

Udy, SH Jnr (1959). 'Bureaucracy' and 'rationality' in Weber's organization theory. *American Sociological Review*, 24, December, 791–5.

Urabe, K (1986). Innovation and the Japanese management system. Keynote address, First International Symposium on Management, Japan Society for the Study of Business Administration, Kobe University, 11–49.

Ure, A (1835). *The Philosophy of Manufactures*. Frank Cass (1967 edition): London.

Ure, A (1836). *The Cotton Manufacture of Great Britain*, Vol. 1. Johnson (1970 edition): London.

Urwick, L (1949). Introduction. In H Fayol (ed): *General and Industrial Management* (trans). Pitman: London.

Uttal, B (1983). The corporate culture vultures. *Fortune*, 17 October, 66–72.

Van der Wiele, A (1998). *Beyond Fads*. Eburon: Delft, The Netherlands.

Van Maanen, J and Kunda, G (1989). Real feelings: emotional expression and organisational culture. In B Staw and L Cummings (eds): *Research in Organizational Behaviour*, 11, 43–103.

Vecchio, RP (1983). Assessing the validity of Fielder's contingency model of leadership effectiveness: a closer look at Strube and Garcia. *Psychological Bulletin*, 93, 404–8.

Voss, CA (1985). *Success and failure in advanced manufacturing technology*. Warwick University Working Paper.

Vroom, VH and Jago, AG (1988). *The New Leadership: Managing Participation in Organizations*. Prentice Hall: Englewood Cliffs, NJ, USA.

Vroom, VH and Yetton, PW (1973). *Leadership and Decision Making*. Pittsburg Press: Pittsburg, PA, USA.

Wack, P (1985). Scenarios: uncharted waters ahead. *Harvard Business Review*, September/October, 73–89.

Wagner, JA (1994). Participation's effects on performance and satisfaction: a reconsideration of research evidence. *Academy of Management Review*, 19, 312–30.

Wakisata, A (1997). Women at work. In M Sako and H Sato (eds): *Japanese Labour and Management in Transition*. Routledge: London.

Waldersee, R and Sheather, S (1996). The effects of strategy type on strategy implementation actions. *Human Relations*, 49(1), 105–22.

Wall, TD, Burnes, B, Clegg, CW and Kemp, NJ (1984). New technology, old jobs. *Work and People*, 10(2), 15–21.

Waller, DL (1999). *Operations Management: A Supply Chain Approach*. International Thompson: London.

Warner, M (1984). New technology, work organisation and industrial relations. *Omega*, 12(3), 203–10.

Warner, M (1997). The year of the very big deals. *Fortune*, 24, November, 3.

Warr, P (ed) (1987). *Psychology at Work*. Penguin: Harmondsworth.

Warwick, DP and Thompson, JT (1980). Still crazy after all these years. *Training and Development Journal*, 34(2), 16–22.

Wastell, DG, White, P and Kawalek, P (1994). A methodology for business process redesign: experience and issues. *Journal of Strategic Information Systems*, 3(1), 23–40.

Watson, G (1994). The flexible workforce and patterns of working hours in the UK. *Employment Gazette*, July, 239–47.

Watson, T (1982). Group ideologies and organisational change. *Journal of Management Studies*, 19(3), 259–77.

Watson, TJ (1986). *Management Organisation and Employment Strategy: New Directions in Theory and Practice*. Routledge and Kegan Paul: London.

Watson, TJ (1997). *Sociology, Work and Industry* (3rd edition). Routledge: London.

Watts, J (1998). Japanese 'bullied' out of work. *The Guardian*, 29 August, 13.

Weber, M (1928). *General Economic History*. George Allen and Unwin: London.

Weber, M (1947). *The Theory of Social and Economic Organization* (trans). Free Press: Glencoe, IL, USA.

Weber, M (1948). *From Max Weber: Essays in Sociology* (Translated, edited and with an introduction by HH Gerth and C Wright Mills). Routledge and Kegan Paul: London.

Weick, KE (1979). *The Social Psychology of Organizing*. Addison-Wesley: Reading, MA, USA.

Weick, KE (1987). Substitute for Corporate Strategy. In DJ Teece (ed) *The Competitive Challenge: Strategies for Industrial Innovation and Renewal*. Ballinger: Cambridge, MA, USA.

Weick, KE (1995). *Sensemaking in Organizations*. Sage: London.

West, P (1994). The concept of the learning organization. *Journal of European Industrial Training*, 18(1), 15–21.

Wheatley, MJ (1992a). *The Future of Middle Management*. British Institute of Management: London.

Wheatley, MJ (1992b). *Leadership and the New Science*. Berrett-Koehler: San Francisco, CA, USA.

Wheelen, TL and Hunger, DJ (1989). *Strategic Management and Business Policy*. Addison-Wesley: Reading, MA, USA.

Whitaker, A (1992). The transformation in work: post-Fordism revisited. In M Reed and M Hughes (eds): *Rethinking Organization: New Directions in Organization Theory and Analysis*. Sage: London.

White, M (1999). PM's deadline to end child poverty. *The Guardian*, 19 March, 10.

White, RE (1986). Generic business strategies: organisational context and performance. *Strategic Management Journal*, May/June, 217–31.

White, S and Mitchell, T (1976). Organization development: a review of research content and research design. *Academy of Management Review*, 1(2), 57–73.

Whitehill, AM (1991). *Japanese Management: Tradition and Transition*. Routledge: London.

Whitley, R (1998). *Divergent Capitalisms*. Oxford University Press: London.

Whittington, R (1993). *What is Strategy and Does it Matter?* Routledge: London.

Whyte, J and Witcher, B (1992). *The Adoption of Total Quality Management in Northern England*. Durham University Business School: Durham.

Whyte, WH (1960). *The Organization of Man*. Penguin: Harmondsworth.

Wickens, P (1987). *The Road To Nissan*. Macmillan: London.

Wickens, P (1995). *The Ascendent Organization: Combining Commitment and Control for Long Term Sustainable Business Success*. Macmillan: London.

Wilkinson, A (1991). *TQM and HRM*. Working Paper, Manchester School of Management, UMIST.

Wilkinson, HE and Orth, DC (1986). Soft skill training in management development. *Training and Development Journal*, 40(3).

Willbur, J (1987). Does mentoring breed success? *Training and Development Journal*, 41(11).

Willcocks, SG (1994). Organizational analysis: a health service commentary. *Leadership & Organization Development Journal*, 15(1), 29–32.

Williams, K, Cutler, T and Haslan, C (1987). The end of mass production? *Economy and Society*, 1(3), 404–39.

Williams, K, Haslam, C and Williams, J (1991). Management Accounting: the Western Problematic Against the Japanese Application. *9th Annual Conference of the Labour Process*, UMIST, Manchester.

Williamson, O (1991). Strategizing, economizing and economic organization. *Strategic Management Journal*, 12, 75–94.

Willmott, H (1995). Strength is ignorance; slavery is freedom: managing culture in modern organizations. *Journal of Management Studies*, 30(40), 511–12.

Wilson, DC (1992). *A Strategy of Change*. Routledge: London.

Wilson, JF (1995). *British Business History, 1720–1994*. Manchester University Press: Manchester.

Witcher, B (1993). *The Adoption of Total Quality Management in Scotland*. Durham University Business School: Durham.

Womack, JP, Jones, DT and Roos, D (1990). *The Machine That Changed the World*. Rawson Associates: New York, USA.

Wood, S (1979). A reappraisal of the contingency approach to organization. *Journal of Management Studies*, 16, 334–54.

Wood, S (1991). Japanisation and/or Toyotaism? *Work, Employment and Society*, 5(4), 567–600.

Woodward, J (1965). *Industrial Organization: Theory and Practice*. Oxford University Press: London.

Woodward, J (1970). *Industrial Organization: Behaviour and Control*. Oxford University Press: London.

Wooten, KC and White, LP (1999). Linking OD's philosophy with justice theory: postmodern implications. *Journal of Organizational Change Management*, 12(1), 7–20.

Worrall, L and Cooper, CL (1997). *The Quality of Working Life: The 1997 Survey of Managers' Changing Experiences*. Institute of Management: London.

Worrall, L and Cooper, CL (1998). *The Quality of Working Life: The 1998 Survey of Managers' Changing Experiences*. Institute of Management: London.

Wren, D (1994). *The Evolution of Management Thought*. Wiley: Chichester.

Yukl, G (1994). *Leadership in Organizations* (3rd edition). Prentice Hall: Englewood Cliffs, NJ, USA.

Yutaka, N (1998). Japanese-style industrial relations in historical perspective. In H Harukiyo and GD Hook (eds): *Japanese Business Management: Restructuring for Low Growth and Globalization*. Routledge: London.

Zairi, M, Letza, S and Oakland, J (1994). Does TQM impact on bottom line results? *TQM Magazine*, 6(1), 38–43.

Zaleznik, A (1970). Power and politics in organisational life. *Harvard Business Review*, May–June, 47–60.

Zentner, RD (1982). Scenarios, past, present and future. *Long Range Planning*, 15, June, 12–20.

Zimmerman, BJ (1992). *Chaos and Self-Renewing Organizations: Designing Transformation Processes for Co-evolution.* Faculty of Administrative Studies, York University: Ontario, Canada.

Zinn, H (1980). *A People's History of the United States.* Longman: London.

Zwerman, WL (1970). *New Perspectives in Organization Theory.* Greenwood: Westport, CT, USA.

# Index